THE HISTORY OF

The lawyer, politician, and histor
Wiltshire in 1609. While training as a barrister during the 1620s and 1630s, he was associated with Ben Jonson and other figures of literary London; he also formed a close literary and political alliance with Viscount Falkland, the centre of a philosophical circle based around Falkland's house at Great Tew in Oxfordshire. Elected to the Short and Long Parliaments in 1640, he was prominent in the reaction against the abuses of Charles I's government in the 1630s. Concerned by the growing demands for fundamental alterations to the constitution, however, Hyde became a supporter of the King in his confrontation with Parliament in 1642. One of the King's officials and advisers during the ensuing Civil War, he went into exile with the Prince of Wales after his defeat, and began to write an enormous history of the war and its origins. Following the execution of the King in 1649, from 1651 Hyde became the principal adviser to the new King, Charles II, for the remainder of the Interregnum, masterminding the negotiations in 1660 which led to the Restoration. After the Restoration, although he was made Earl of Clarendon, his influence ebbed, and he was eventually forced into a second exile in 1667 following an impeachment and the loss of the King's favour. Living in France until his death in 1674, he completed his *History* and other works. The *History* was eventually published in 1702–4.

PAUL SEAWARD is Director of the History of Parliament Trust, London. He has published *The Cavalier Parliament and the Reconstruction of the Old Regime* (1989); *The Restoration, 1660–1688* (1990); and articles on politics in the seventeenth century, and on Parliament in the twentieth. He has completed an edition of Thomas Hobbes's *Behemoth*, and is General Editor, with Martin Dzelzainis, of an Oxford edition of the works of Clarendon.

OXFORD WORLD'S CLASSICS

*For over 100 years Oxford World's Classics have brought
readers closer to the world's great literature. Now with over 700
titles—from the 4,000-year-old myths of Mesopotamia to the
twentieth century's greatest novels—the series makes available
lesser-known as well as celebrated writing.*

*The pocket-sized hardbacks of the early years contained
introductions by Virginia Woolf, T. S. Eliot, Graham Greene,
and other literary figures which enriched the experience of reading.
Today the series is recognized for its fine scholarship and
reliability in texts that span world literature, drama and poetry,
religion, philosophy, and politics. Each edition includes perceptive
commentary and essential background information to meet the
changing needs of readers.*

OXFORD WORLD'S CLASSICS

===

EDWARD HYDE, EARL OF CLARENDON

The History of the Rebellion

A new selection

===

Selected and Edited with an Introduction and Notes by
PAUL SEAWARD

OXFORD
UNIVERSITY PRESS

OXFORD

UNIVERSITY PRESS

Great Clarendon Street, Oxford OX2 6DP

Oxford University Press is a department of the University of Oxford.
It furthers the University's objective of excellence in research, scholarship,
and education by publishing worldwide in

Oxford New York

Auckland Cape Town Dar es Salaam Hong Kong Karachi
Kuala Lumpur Madrid Melbourne Mexico City Nairobi
New Delhi Shanghai Taipei Toronto

With offices in

Argentina Austria Brazil Chile Czech Republic France Greece
Guatemala Hungary Italy Japan Poland Portugal Singapore
South Korea Switzerland Thailand Turkey Ukraine Vietnam

Oxford is a registered trade mark of Oxford University Press
in the UK and in certain other countries

Published in the United States
by Oxford University Press Inc., New York

British Library Cataloguing in Publication Data

Data available

Library of Congress Cataloging-in-Publication Data

Clarendon, Edward Hyde, Earl of, 1609-1674.
[History of the Rebellion and civil wars in England begun
in the year 1641. Selections. 2009]
The history of the Rebellion : a new selection / Edward Hyde,
Earl of Clarendon ; selected and edited with an introduction and notes by Paul Seaward.
p. cm. — (Oxford World's Classics)
Includes bibliographical references.
Includes passages from The life, Clarendon's autobiography.
ISBN 978-0-19-922817-1
1. Great Britain—History—Puritan Revolution, 1642-1660.
2. Great Britain—History—Civil War, 1642-1649. I. Seaward, Paul.
II. Clarendon, Edward Hyde, Earl of, 1609-1674. Life of Edward,
Earl of Clarendon. III. Title.
DA400.C6 2009
942.06'2—dc22
2008043470

Typeset by Cepha Imaging Private Ltd., Bangalore, India
Printed in Great Britain by
Clays Ltd., St Ives plc

ISBN 978-0-19-922817-1

1 3 5 7 9 10 8 6 4 2

CONTENTS

THE HISTORY OF THE CIVIL WAR
EXTRACTS FROM *THE HISTORY OF THE REBELLION* AND *THE LIFE*

CLARENDON BEFORE THE CIVIL WAR
EXTRACTS FROM *THE LIFE*

INTRODUCTION

EDWARD HYDE restlessly started to write what he called *A True Historicall Narration of the Rebellion and Civil Wars in England* on 18 March 1646, on the Scilly Isles. Just over two weeks before, his hasty departure from Cornwall with the young heir to the throne, Charles, Prince of Wales, had marked the effective end of royalist resistance to the parliamentary forces in the Civil War. For the past four and a half gruelling years, Hyde had been one of Charles I's principal advisers: personally close to the King, who had told his wife in 1643 that 'Ned Hyde must be Secretary [of State], for indeed I can trust no other'; a gifted propagandist, responsible for the great majority of the statements and declarations that went out under the King's name; and a member of the royal council confident and forthright in his own views, and brutally frank in his assessment of those of his colleagues. The shipwreck of the royalist cause—with the King in England, in the hands of his enemies; the Queen in Paris, imperiously trying to orchestrate an alliance with the Scots (much to Hyde's disapproval); and the King's councillors dispersed throughout Britain and the continent—left Hyde for once remote from royal policy-making, with time on his hands, and with no more to contribute to the King's cause than his historical analysis of the reasons for its failure.

More than half a century later, at the beginning of the reign of Queen Anne, *The History of the Rebellion* was finally published by the press at Oxford, a very different work from the one that Hyde had begun as a refugee. Revelatory in its circumstantial accounts of the debates and rows in the royalist camp, merciless in its depiction of the sins of omission and commission of numerous prominent political figures, and ruthlessly promoted as a weapon in the party politics of its time, it immediately attracted controversy. Hostile commentators noticed inaccuracies, condemned Hyde's prejudices, preferred accounts which had different biases. But, more sophisticated than anything of its kind, at least in English, until the late nineteenth century it dominated the historiography of the Civil War, capturing the imagination with its vivid portrayals of people and incidents. Today, critical historical methods have provided much more accurate descriptions of events and very different insights into their causes; yet the *History* still captures the imagination, and remains the indispensable account of the war—not only for a narrative which provides a sense of the constant

struggles and dilemmas of politics, but also as a depiction of an epic
political journey.

The Life of Edward, Earl of Clarendon

Hyde was born at Dinton, close to Salisbury in Wiltshire, in 1609, the
son of a country gentleman whom he regarded as epitomizing the
virtues of country society. Looking back from a later, and, he felt, less
innocent, world, Hyde admired his integrity, his willingness to live
privately and frugally, without travelling to London (for his mother
'never was in London in her life'), and his learning. Henry Hyde had
been a sort of moral compass for his life — 'not only the best father, but
the best friend and the best companion he ever had or could have', and
'the greatest instance of the felicity of a country life that was seen in
that age'. Initially destined for a career in the Church, the young
Edward Hyde was admitted to Magdalen Hall, Oxford — much to his
lasting irritation, for Magdalen Hall was a hotbed of puritanism and
the socially less exclusive neighbour of Magdalen College, where an
apparent administrative bungle compounded by the obstinacy of the
fellows had lost him his place. He turned to a legal career only after the
death of his elder brother left him his father's sole surviving son. It was
a profession in which the Hydes were already prominent. One of his
uncles, Sir Nicholas Hyde, became Lord Chief Justice of the King's
Bench in 1627; another, Laurence, held prominent legal positions at
court. Hyde was enrolled at the Middle Temple — one of the Inns of
Court, where lawyers were trained — and was called to the bar in 1633.

His first wife, Anne Ayliffe, whom he married in 1632, was 'nearly
[closely] allied to many noble families in England': to the St John
family — of great importance within Wiltshire society — but, crucially,
to the Villiers family, the relations of the Duke of Buckingham who had
been so commanding a political figure in the reigns of James I and his
son Charles. Buckingham had been assassinated in 1628 (Hyde could
remember exactly what he had been doing when he heard the news);
but Buckingham had built up a family clan which was to have a wide
reach throughout the social and political life of mid-seventeenth century England. Hyde marked his accession to it by taking its side during
one of the minor scandals of the court of Charles I, the *affaire* of
Eleanor Villiers with Henry Jermyn in 1633, a business which gave
him his first idea of the viciousness of court life. Hyde's marriage,
though, lasted barely six months: the death of his young wife of small-
pox sent Hyde into the profound melancholy which marked all of his

bereavements—though not so profound as to prevent him contracting another, and equally successful, marriage two years later, to Frances Aylesbury, the daughter of Sir Thomas Aylesbury, a legal and financial official of the Crown.

Hyde in the 1630s was leading the life of a successful barrister. Much of his business had local, Wiltshire, connections—the St Johns and others are known to have sought his advice—and he came into contact with the Earl of Pembroke, the King's Lord Chamberlain, a near neighbour of his father's close to Salisbury, probably before Hyde's involvement in the promotion of a masque presented by the Inns of Court for the Queen required him to have direct dealings with him. But his law business quickly brought him more powerful associations still. In the mid-1630s he became known to William Laud, the recently appointed Archbishop of Canterbury, and came to like and admire him. Yet he was also watching the proceedings of the government of which Laud was so prominent a part with some disquiet. Charles I's third Parliament ended in confrontation, uproar, and dissolution in 1629. Vowing to avoid further encounters for the time being, his government dusted off such obsolete money-raising expedients as fining men who refused to accept the honour of knighthood, and pushed the boundaries of legality by extending levies for coastal defence into a national tax, ship money. These were worrying enough; but what angered Hyde most was the failure of the law to provide adequate redress. When ship money had been challenged in a court of law, the judges, meant to act as impartial umpires between the rights of the Crown and of the subject, had been prepared to accept political reasoning as justification for its use, rather than determine the case on the basis of the law. It made Hyde, like many others, into a critic of the government when he was elected to Parliament in 1640. The 'Short' Parliament—the first Parliament for eleven years—was Hyde's first, but he intervened already with remarkable confidence. Called when Charles found himself unable to raise money to overcome the religiously inspired rebellion in his other kingdom, Scotland, the King expected it to provide money as quickly as possible. When it did not, and set about enquiring into the misgovernment of the past eleven years, the King peremptorily dissolved it—a decision which Hyde regarded as an easily avoidable disaster—and tried to find sufficient money to combat the Covenanting movement by other means. His humiliating defeat at the hands of the Scots in the summer forced him to summon another Parliament at the end of the year to help to bring an end to the war, and to raise enough money to pay off both armies.

Elected to the second 1640 Parliament, Hyde was one of its busiest members. In the Short Parliament he had worked with some of the leaders of the reform movement such as John Pym and Oliver St John in tackling the abuses of law perpetrated by the Caroline regime; in its successor he remained associated with them, prominent in their attacks on the ship money judges and the 'prerogative' courts which were seen to be challenging the roles of the ordinary common law courts at Westminster. His attitude at the tensest moment in the first six months of the Long Parliament—the condemnation for high treason of the King's minister, the Earl of Strafford, on highly dubious grounds—is uncertain, but Hyde's reformism was decidedly moderate. He watched with dismay as its leaders reached beyond the removal of abuses towards a fundamental alteration of the civil constitution, and as they became more dependent for support on those who wanted profound change in the ecclesiastical constitution as well. He set himself up as one of the principal opponents of church reform—the abolition of bishops, and their replacement with a Presbyterian form of government—and became, in his own account, marked out as an enemy by the more radical reformers, and as an ally by the King. The threat of violence hung around London as its people rioted to demand the abolition of bishops, and as soldiers loyal to the King plotted to seize the initiative by arresting the parliamentary leaders. Hyde and other moderates became the nucleus of a party of royal supporters in the Commons. Acting on the advice of Lord Digby, a favourite and a friend of Hyde's, the King at the end of 1641 sought to co-opt Hyde, and two of those with whom he worked in the House: another friend, Lucius Cary, Viscount Falkland, and Sir John Culpepper. Falkland and Culpepper accepted formal appointments, as Secretary of State and Chancellor of the Exchequer respectively; Hyde preferred to remain without a position. Not long afterwards, though, he began to act secretly as the King's propagandist, drafting statements and declarations for the King to publish as his own. Hyde's accomplished royal declarations repeatedly identified the King with the law, and condemned the innovations, encroachments, and illegalities perpetrated by a Parliament that was rapidly taking control of the state.

After his bungled effort at a counter-coup in January 1642 when he failed to arrest five principal members of the House of Commons, the King prepared for a military confrontation. Once he had ensured the safety of the Queen by seeing her off to the Netherlands, he moved north, and began to gather money and arms. Many of his parliamentary colleagues strongly suspected that Hyde was working for the King, and in mid to late May he quietly slipped out of London and joined the King at York. As confrontation turned into Civil War, he became an essential cog in the King's war machine: first as an unofficial undersecretary of state, assisting Falkland, and then, from early 1643, as a member of the Privy Council and as Chancellor of the Exchequer. Closely involved in the principal attempts to negotiate a peaceful settlement at Oxford in early 1643 and the Treaty of Uxbridge in early 1645, he also tried to secure the defection of leading members of the parliamentary side, especially the earls of Northumberland and Holland, in 1643. In March 1645, however, as the war reached its climax, Charles dispatched him, Culpepper, and other senior members of the Council as advisers, with his eldest son Prince Charles, to oversee the royalist war effort in the south-west—and to take the Prince out of England if he should be threatened with capture by Parliament. Although the battle of Naseby in early July inflicted a blow on the King from which he could not hope to recover, it was not until April the following year that the situation in the west was sufficiently dire to make the Prince's Council comply with the King's increasingly urgent orders to leave England.

The Council was still reluctant to take the Prince abroad, fearing to put him into the hands of a foreign power—and perhaps also to trust him to the Queen, whose influence on royal policy Hyde certainly saw as pernicious. So at first they sailed to the Scillies, where Hyde began to compose the *History*. Threatened by Parliament's navy a few weeks later, they moved on to Jersey. There, under intense pressure from the Queen, the Prince finally agreed to move to Paris. Dissenting from the decision, Hyde and other councillors elected to remain in Jersey. Although the others dispersed a little while after, Hyde remained, lodged in Queen Elizabeth Castle, reading, writing the *History*, and keeping up a stream of correspondence commenting on and arguing about royalist policy. The King, meanwhile, within the custody successively of the Scottish army, Parliament, and the English army, tried to play off his enemies against one another. In 1648 he succeeded in securing Scottish intervention in England. Royalists planned uprisings to coincide with their invasion. In this hopeful turn of events, Hyde was asked to return to advise the Prince—though, he thought, it was only with the Queen's reluctant consent. As it happened, by the time he managed to reach the royal court, the Scots invasion had been beaten and the uprisings crushed. Hyde, Prince Charles, and the court based at The Hague could do nothing more than look on as the King played his remaining negotiating hand badly, making concessions, especially on the Church, that Hyde thought fundamentally mistaken;

was put on trial by a Parliament largely under the army's control; and, in January 1649, was executed.

The regicide propelled the Prince into kingship, but exiled him permanently from his kingdom. Charles II's prospects were bleak: hopes of gaining a foothold in Ireland from which to launch a Restoration in England were dashed by Cromwell's defeat of the royalists there in 1650; another alliance with the Scots was only available at the cost of compromises on religious policy which Hyde continued resolutely to oppose. Depressed by the vicious life of an under-employed court, Hyde agreed to accompany his old friend and fellow councillor, Lord Cottington, on an embassy to Spain in June that year. Although Hyde was rather taken with aspects of Spanish life, the mission—aimed at securing financial or other help—was a failure. In his absence, the King had embarked upon his Scottish adventure, which exposed him to misery and humiliation at the hands of his hosts and ended in the complete annihilation of his army at Worcester in September 1651. Escaping by the skin of his teeth, the King summoned Hyde to join him in Paris. In spite of the resentment of the Queen, the envy and scheming of much of the rest of the court, and his own disregard for the arts of the courtier, Hyde established himself, and survived as the King's chief adviser over the remainder of the exile. Impoverished and dependent on the goodwill of foreign kings and petty princes to house and feed them, there was little the King and his advisers could do to bring about a Restoration until almost 1660. The chances of a royalist uprising in England overcoming a firmly united English army were negligible, while the military success of the republic and even more of Lord Protector Cromwell after his seizure of power in 1653 made foreign princes reluctant to offer their support.

Cromwell's death in 1658 began to unravel the Protectorate's combination of a fragile political legitimacy and military power. When one of the military commanders, General George Monck, responded to popular pressure by forcing a free Parliament in early 1660, it was virtually inevitable that Charles II would be recalled, though still surprising that he was recalled without any of the conditions demanded in all of the negotiations with his father. Hyde, now Lord Chancellor, returned with the King and his court. Advancement to the peerage, as Earl of Clarendon, reflected his prominence within government and the marriage of his bright young daughter Anne to the King's brother James, Duke of York. Disgusted rivals believed he had masterminded the liaison, although it was without his approval and caused him great alarm. For the next two or three years, Clarendon was the unrivalled architect of a project to re-establish the pre-Civil War monarchy. But he accumulated enemies: his old ally George Digby, now Earl of Bristol, whose conversion to Catholicism had ended their friendship; the ambitious former servant of the Duke of York, Henry Bennet; the King's mistress, the Countess of Castlemaine, whom he regarded with unconcealed distaste; and the King's unstable friend George Villiers, Duke of Buckingham. There were battles and rows which left permanent scars: over religious policy, where Clarendon's efforts to find some middle course between the advocates of a strict uniformity to the practices of the Church of England and the many arguments for a more liberal settlement cost him the goodwill of some friends and failed to lose any enemies; over foreign policy, where France and Spain carried out a diplomatic proxy war in vying for an alliance with England; and over Clarendon's disapproval of the King's dissolute life, which resulted in at least one major confrontation between servant and master. The calamitous effort to emulate Cromwell's and the republic's success on the international stage by provoking war with the Dutch in 1664—a war which Clarendon opposed—brought naval humiliation three years later when the Dutch navy triumphantly sailed up the Medway and burned or captured many of the greatest vessels of an English fleet laid up in the Medway for want of money. Clarendon, already a marked man, was dismissed in its wake; when Parliament met in October that year, the King, turning on his old servant, encouraged it to impeach him for treason. The King hinted that he should leave the country—which he eventually did, in December, when almost directly ordered to do so.

The remainder of his life Clarendon spent in a second exile, in France. In the meantime he read, and he wrote—a memoir, *The Life*; a vindication of himself against the impeachment charges; essays; meditations; critiques of Thomas Hobbes's *Leviathan*, and of Serenus Cressy's Roman Catholic apologia; a lengthy account of the steps by which popes had encroached on temporal power. He also returned, eventually, to his manuscript of the 1640s, creating out of it and his *Life* what is now known as the *History of the Rebellion*. He cherished hopes of a return to England. With his daughter married to the heir to the throne, he had been regarded as a threat to powerful interests at court. But over six years, the fear of Clarendon's own influence had faded, while his sons' growing political careers helped to counteract the influence of his enemies. In 1674 he was allowed to move closer to home, to Rouen; but on 9 December, he died there. His body was brought back to England and buried at Westminster Abbey.

History, Religion, and Politics

Clever, well-read, and formidably industrious, Hyde before the Civil War was a man of considerable literary interests and pretensions, with a wide acquaintance among the intellectual and political elite of Jacobean and Caroline England. The law was part of his intellectual life, for he formed friendships with many of the rising stars of the pre-Civil War bar—Bulstrode Whitelocke, John Maynard, Geoffrey Palmer, John Vaughan—as well as one of its established luminaries—John Selden, a man whose mind he regarded with something approaching awe. But the law did not attract him intellectually: he admitted to a lack of interest in the minutiae of legal learning, preferring 'polite learning and history' (p. 429), particularly Roman history. The circle he moved in during his early twenties was dominated by poets, above all Ben Jonson, but was also imbued with Latin learning and obsessed with the history of the end of the Roman Republic and the beginning of the Empire. Jonson—the author of plays dealing with the politics of the reign of the Emperor Tiberius—was his mentor, until, Clarendon wrote, his young protégé 'betook himself to business, which he believed ought never to be preferred before his company' (p. 436). Thomas May was a friend, whose translation of Lucan's poem on the Roman Civil War—despite its taint of republicanism, confirmed by May's subsequent allegiance in the Civil War—Clarendon praised as 'one of the best dramatic poems in the English language'.

The greatest intellectual influence on Hyde, though, was, famously, his friend Lucius Cary, Viscount Falkland, and the collection of intellectuals Falkland brought together in the early 1630s at his house at Great Tew in Oxfordshire. Hyde's well-known account of the 'Great Tew Circle' makes this the best-known example of a type of salon that was becoming more common in the early seventeenth century, although his enchanted description of it and its host makes it seem the most attractive. Hyde called it 'one continued *convivium philosophicum*, or *convivium theologicum*, enlivened and refreshed with all the facetiousness of wit, and good humour, and pleasantness of discourse' (p. 444), and compared it to its great advantage with the University of Oxford, twenty miles away, of which his experience had not been particularly happy. Its interests were literary, reflecting the stoical moralism of Jonson, to whom Falkland, as well as Hyde, had been close. But with opponents of dogmatic theology (both Roman Catholic and Calvinist) such as John Hales and William Chillingworth, as well as the Platonist Falkland, at its centre, the group's natural theme was the place of reason and authority in religion, discussed in an atmosphere of mildly sceptical theological enquiry. With the involvement of Gilbert Sheldon, Warden of All Souls' College and the University's Vice Chancellor, it also reflected a concern to establish the distinctive identity of the Church of England, a concern that emerged in the enthusiasm of a number of its members for the works of Richard Hooker, the Church's polemicist of the late sixteenth century.

These encounters helped to establish Hyde's interests and attitudes, and helped to stimulate his wide reading. Hyde was notorious for his book-buying habits: even during the Interregnum, when hard put to finance his ordinary living expenses, he was purchasing volumes, tormenting his correspondents throughout Europe with his requests for books. As he read, like many others of his time, he extracted, filling sheets of paper with notes of passages of particular relevance. There must have been many more, but two volumes of these commonplace books still exist in the Bodleian Library: apart from the jurist Hugo Grotius' *De Jure Belli ac Pacis*, the bulk of the two surviving volumes deals with histories—of antiquity (Josephus, Plutarch, Livy, Thucydides); of Britain (Camden's *Britannia*, Speed's *History of Great Britain*, Harpsfield's *Historia Ecclesiastica Anglicana*); and of the relatively recent European past (de Commynes's *History*, Sarpi's *Council of Trent*). Some of these notes were compiled in the 1630s, some on Jersey in the 1640s, and some late in his life, in France in 1668–74. As he read he thought and commented: among the notes there are a number of pages of what Clarendon referred to as 'Extravagancies', 'Cursory and occasionall considerations', 'Fragments to be used upon occasion', many of which have been carefully numbered and indexed for reuse in his own writings.

Works like Paolo Sarpi's sceptical history of the machinations of the papacy in the mid-sixteenth century and Philippe de Commynes's authoritative account of the weaknesses of policy-making at the court of Louis XI of France in the late fifteenth had a profound influence on Hyde's approach to and understanding of politics. On Jersey in the 1640s he was rereading his notes on Commynes and drawing from them precepts relating to the practice of princes and particularly the giving of counsel, noting that princes were poor judges of character, as they could never see men act on equal terms; and—perhaps wryly—that princes 'abhor being compelled to anything their own inclinations do not lead them, though never so profitable and advantageous to them'. Such works plugged into the fashionable contemporary enthusiasm for the Roman historian Tacitus and his coolly cynical eye on princely politics.

Probably most important, though, in Hyde's understanding of the writing of history was a relatively new—and equally Tacitist—work, Enrico Caterino Davila's history of the French wars of religion, published in Venice in 1630. Very popular in France and Italy, it came as a revelation to the royalists holed up in Oxford during the Civil War. One of them, Sir Philip Warwick, wrote of John Hampden that 'He was very well read in history; and I remember the first time I ever saw that of D'Avila of the Civil Warrs of France, it was lent me under the title of Mr Hampden's *Vade Mecum*; and I believe no copy was liker an originall, than that rebellion was like ours'. Clarendon himself remarked in a letter in early 1647 that Davila had written the history of the French wars 'as our's should be written', and that it was from Davila that 'no question our gamesters learnt much of their play'. Translating it was a project very close to Hyde himself (who, at the time, read no Italian or French): the translators of the version published in 1647 were his brother-in-law William Aylesbury and a friend, Sir Charles Cotterell. In the preface to the second, 1678, edition of the English translation the publisher remarked that Charles I, in Oxford during the war, had read it eagerly,

wishing he had had it some years sooner, out of a Beliefe, that being forewarned thereby, He might have prevented many of those Mischiefs we then groaned under; and which the grand Contrivers of them, had drawn from this Original, as spiders do poison from the most wholesome plants. The Truth is, their Swords had already transcribed it in English Blood, before this pen had done it in English Ink.

Clarendon later, probably in his second exile, came to read, and admire, other continental historians, particularly the accounts by Famiano Strada, Grotius, and Guido Bentivoglio of the Dutch revolt in the late sixteenth century and the Spanish attempts to suppress it, although nothing else seems to have had quite the impact on his writing that his encounters with the classical historians, and with Commynes, Sarpi, and Davila, had done.

These encounters were with friends and with books; but also important in shaping Hyde's thought and his prose were his encounters with his enemies. During 1642 Hyde became the most accomplished polemicist the royalists had, whose responses to the Grand Remonstrance of late 1641, and to the major parliamentary Declarations of May 1642 were masterpieces of controlled invective, capturing a tone of just outrage and indignation that helped to efface the impression of undeliberated ire left by the King's disastrous attempt to arrest the five members in January. Persistently and trenchantly challenging Parliament's challenge to the legality of the King's actions, Hyde's closely argued pamphlets created not only an ideology of moderate royalism, but also a highly effective polemical style.

The life of the History

Hyde's friend Edward Nicholas accused him of 'an itch of writing'. Hyde was an indefatigable talker — he wrote of his delight in conversation — but when friends were unavailable to talk to, he wrote to them instead, long letters full of his opinions and requests for news; and he wrote the *History*. On the Scillies and Jersey in 1646–8 Hyde completed seven books and began an eighth, taking the story from the accession of Charles I to roughly the beginning of 1644. Progress at the beginning was rapid, while he wrote out of general knowledge about the politics of the 1620s and 1630s, and as he described the proceedings of the Long Parliament in which he was intimately involved. Initially he was encouraged by the King's support for the project, and the interest of his friends, to whom he wrote volubly and enthusiastically about it. But Hyde could not rely on his own knowledge for the whole history of the war. He sought information from others: some complied willingly, especially his friend Lord Hopton, and, eventually, the King himself sent him some material compiled by Sir Edward Walker. But not all were so enthusiastic. He grumbled that 'I find most men so unconcerned to contribute towards it, and some who are very able to satisfy me in what I have desired, so positive against the doing of it'; and, more bitterly, 'I often wish I had never begun, having found less assistance from it, than I thought I should have done, as if all men had a desire, the ill should be remembered and the good forgotten'. Progress slowed, and Hyde was diverted to other tasks, including a pamphlet condemning the Vote of No More Addresses to the King in 1648. Progress was halted completely when Hyde received the summons in June 1648 to the royal court.

The *History* was then left untouched for twenty years, until after Clarendon's sudden flight from England in December 1667. As ever, when at leisure, Clarendon began writing. It seems unlikely that he originally intended to return to the *History*, the draft of which had been left behind. In July 1668 he began writing a more personal memoir, and although he broke off almost immediately to write instead a vindication of himself from the impeachment charges which had been levelled against him the previous year, he resumed shortly afterwards and had finished the work up to the Restoration within two years, by August 1670. The *Life* covered some of the same ground as the *History*, with Clarendon himself at its centre. With little thought (to start with, certainly) of an audience beyond his family it was more personal, less guarded in its judgements, more direct in its criticism. As he went on, however, it quickly became more ambitious, and more literary: the pen portraits, or 'characters', so signal a feature of the published work to its eighteenth-century audience, were vastly expanded. In 1671, when his second son Laurence Hyde (later the Earl of Rochester) was allowed to leave England to visit him, he brought with him the original *History*, and other papers. After he left Clarendon set about putting together the two works, splicing into the *History* his recently composed memoir. For the period not covered by the original *History*, he enhanced the memoir so that it provided a more complete narrative of the period, rather than simply an account of his own part in it. By June 1672 he must have completed the task, finishing what is now *The History of the Rebellion*, providing a full account of the war and Interregnum up to the Restoration of 1660. Clarendon then returned to his own memoir, and provided a 'Continuation' up to the present, which took the story into the Restoration and up to his own exile in 1667.

After Clarendon's death, two years later, the *History* lay dormant for nearly thirty more, although a few friends and political allies of the Hyde family were allowed to read it. Its eventual publication in 1702–4 was a response to a new, ideologically charged, phase of interest in the Civil War. The histories of the events of 1640–60 published before the late 1690s were mainly dull affairs, compiled from newsbooks. But when the regicide Edmund Ludlow's heavily edited memoirs were published in 1698, as a sort of historical manifesto of the Whigs—the heirs to the Civil War parliamentary tradition—it sparked a publishing war. The publication of the *History* was masterminded by its custodian, Clarendon's son Laurence, now Earl of Rochester. He, and a knot of supporters based in Oxford, spun it to support the principles maintained by the Tories—the heirs to the royalists. While the preface to the first volume laid claims to impartiality, those to the second and third, dedicated to Clarendon's granddaughter Queen Anne, advanced clearly Tory arguments about the relationship between the security of the state and the security of the established Church: 'next to treason against your sacred person', it argued, 'an invasion upon the church ought to be watched and prevented by those who have the honour to be trusted in the public administration, with the strictest care and diligence, as the best way to preserve your person and government in their just dignity and authority'. Whigs were irritated, as they were intended to be. In the 1720s John Oldmixon, a minor literary figure and Whig journalist, began a partisan crusade against Clarendon's *History* and its Tory promoters, comparing the *History* with Whitelocke's *Annals*, and accusing the Oxford establishment figures responsible for the editing of Clarendon's text—Francis Atterbury, Henry Aldrich, and George Smalridge—of tampering with it (a charge comprehensively refuted by John Burton in 1744). The leftovers from the *History of the Rebellion*—the remaining fragments of the *Life*—emerged only in 1759.

Its complex genesis makes *The History of the Rebellion* a far from straightforward work. It was made more complicated still by Hyde's decision to incorporate into the early books of the *History* the text of many of the declarations and other official statements which he had written on behalf of the King in the early 1640s. The early twentieth-century historian Sir Charles Firth regarded that part of the *History* containing them as 'a sort of Serbonian bog in which many readers of the *History of the Rebellion* flounder and sink'. Many have also regretted the conflation of the 1640s *History* with the 1660s *Life*. Firth called it a 'literary crime'. The *History* was a political work, written in heat, though at least written at a time when memory had not mangled the sequence of events; the *Life* was a literary one, whose slips in chronology and detail, though more glaring, are more forgivable. Not all of the editing was done very efficiently: there remain overlaps and contradictions in the final text, and those who edited it for publication had much to do to make sense of many an over-extended clause. Although Clarendon wrote fluently, his barely revised writing is a copy-editor's despair: his style, sometimes called Ciceronian, is more often conversational, his nouns tripping over one another as he loses track of the subject of the sentence and omits a necessary pronoun or has to begin again. Even the striking and portentous phrase which begins the *History*—based on the opening of Hooker's *Laws of Ecclesiastical Polity*—he found he had to alter in a typically Clarendonian syntactical muddle. But despite these defects it is easy to appreciate the impact that Clarendon's voice and his mind had on his contemporaries and near contemporaries and to recognize the enthusiasm with which the young Samuel Pepys came home from a meeting in 1666 and scribbled in his diary, 'I am mad in love with my Lord Chancellor, for he do comprehend, and speak out well, and with the greatest ease and authority that ever I saw man in my life.' Clarendon's utterly distinctive prose can be mesmerizingly effective even at its most serpentine; and in its best moments, the *History* strikes magnificence out of a mixture of neoclassical elegance and home-grown bluntness; draws pathos from its eloquent and elegiac laments for young lives lost and the other miseries of Civil War; and squeezes mordant wit out of the follies of allies and opponents alike.

The History *as politics*

What was the *History* for? The question is a complex one, for different parts of it were written at different times and with different purposes in mind. In all of it Clarendon had high literary ambitions: he wrote jokingly to friends of his ambition to emulate the great Roman historians, and he worried over questions of style and content—particularly over the inclusion of the royal declarations of 1642. The *Life* of 1668–70 was at least in part intended also as an explanation and vindication of his own actions. But the core of the *History* composed in 1646–8 was meant to convey a set of political messages closely related to the changing fortunes of the King's cause. His preface disclaimed imminent formal publication, and he told one colleague that 'it will make mad work among friends and foes if it were published'. He assumed that it would never be published in complete form, but that it might be the raw material out of which 'somewhat' could eventually be printed. He did, however, expect it to be widely circulated in manuscript among his friends (although its increasing bulk must have made that ambition every day a less practical one), 'to inform myself and some others what we are to do, as well as to comfort us in what we have done' (p. 4).

Hyde's analysis of the causes of the war and the defeat of the King subtly advanced his own views about the direction of royalist strategy in the present. While he was writing it, in 1646–8, the King, in the custody of his enemies, was conducting a series of tortuous negotiations with the Scots, with Parliament, and with the army leadership. Charles was under intense pressure to agree a settlement which would compromise some of his most cherished principles: the government of the Church by bishops; the authority of the monarch over his government; the protection of those who had loyally fought for him during the war. Hyde fully supported his stand: but in this he was in marked contrast to many of the King's former advisers, particularly those who congregated around the Queen in Paris, who was, for the moment, the effective head of the royalist cause. For them, it was worth compromising at least over the Church in order to secure the support of the Scots against the English Parliament. Hyde's vigorous opposition to alterations in the Church was partly to do with his own churchmanship, rooted in the religious conservatism of his father's Wiltshire, deepened in the rarefied conversations of Great Tew, and developed through his admiration for William Laud, a brooding presence in the early pages of the *History*. Yet Hyde's position was as much to do with politics as with religion. The Church with its bishops was one of the fundamentals — 'landmarks' — of a constitution which effectively and harmoniously delivered stability through protecting the rights of the monarch and the liberties of the subject; by negotiating those landmarks away in the pursuit of a chancy military alliance, his advisers risked destroying precisely what they were fighting for. Hyde's history echoed his politics: it suited his argument to belittle the reasons for accepting religious and political compromise, to deny that there was widespread discontent with the English Church before 1640, and to attribute the movement for ecclesiastical reform to the machinations of a malignant faction. Davila's description of how a small number of conspirators could drag a country into a Civil War had helped Hyde (and other royalists) to understand how the war could be explained as the product of an element intent on the seizure of power. Watching what he called 'the violent party', men such as Oliver St John, Sir Henry Vane, John Hampden, and Oliver Cromwell, at work, Hyde interpreted them in Machiavellian terms as politicians merely interested in taking, and retaining, power; yet he also recognized how their success reflected the myriad failures of others: how some were too craven, others too lazy, vain, or passive to resist. The *History* implied the moral: by agreeing to their terms, the King would abandon the essentials of the constitution, and by lending them his legitimacy would help them to achieve their objective.

In this sense, Hyde was among the most rigid and uncompromising of royalists. In another, he was among the most moderate. Hyde began his political career as one of the parliamentary reformers of 1640–1. During the 1630s the government's willingness to push law to its limits, and the judges' willingness to aid and abet it, had genuinely appalled him, offering a nightmare vision of a country in which the law was no longer a reliable 'landmark'. Writing the *History* in 1646–8, his feeling of outrage at the ship money judgement was still palpable: when people saw, he wrote,

in a court of law, (that law that gave them title and possession of all that they had) apophthegms of state urged as elements of law; judges as sharp-sighted as Secretaries of State and in the mysteries of state; judgment of law grounded upon matter of fact of which there was neither inquiry or proof; and no reason given for the payment of the thirty shillings in question but what concluded the estates of all the standers-by; they had no reason to hope that that doctrine or the preachers of it would be contained within any bounds (p. 13).

The certainty and integrity of the law would be central to his political and constitutional thinking—'all governments subsist and are established by firmness and constancy,' he wrote in his examination of Hobbes's *Leviathan* in 1673, 'by every man's knowing what is his right to enjoy, and what is his duty to do'—and it became his fundamental case against the parliamentary leaders. In his most effective piece of polemic against Parliament, the answer he wrote on behalf of the King to its Remonstrance of 26 May 1642, Hyde provided a sententious summary of its doctrine:

That they [the Parliament] have an absolute power of declaring the law, and that whatsoever they declare to be so ought not to be questioned by his majesty or any subject; . . . that no precedents can be limits to bound their proceedings. So they may do what they please; That the Parliament may dispose of any thing wherein the King or subject hath a right, for the public good; that they, without the King, are this Parliament, and judge of this public good; and that his majesty's consent is not necessary. So the life and liberty of the subject, and all the good laws made for the security of them, may be disposed of, and repealed, by the major part of both Houses, at any time present and by any ways and means procured so to be; and his majesty had no power to protect them.

How the King employed his power may have seemed beside the point by 1646, when the King no longer had any power to exercise. But to Hyde it remained *the* point: he wrote to his colleague Lord Digby in 1648 that 'whilst we keep ourselves upon the old foundation of the established government, and the good known laws, how weak soever we are in power, we shall be strong in reputation'—and, he might have added, expose the fact that their opponents remained a revolutionary regime kept in being by military force, whose only legitimacy was the legitimacy of victory. Revulsion at 'parliamentary tyranny' would help to provoke the insurgency of what became known as the Second Civil War in 1648; converting the right of conquest to a political stability based on real legitimacy would continue to be, as Hyde knew it would, the central difficulty of all of the Interregnum regimes.

Presenting these arguments on behalf of the King in 1642 Hyde hoped to win back his more moderate parliamentary opponents—those men with whom he had until recently worked on reforming the abuses of the government of the 1630s—and to peel them away from those he saw as pushing the reform movement in a dangerously radical direction.

In a series of negotiations—the Treaty at Oxford at the beginning of 1643; the attempt to make contact with the Earl of Essex, through the Oxford Parliament he organized in 1644; and the Uxbridge Treaty of early 1645—he pursued the aim of creating a moderate alliance. In part, he attributed his failure to the inability of the parliamentary moderates, the Westminster 'peace party', many of them old friends such as Bulstrode Whitelocke, to break away from the clutches of the radicals. But the fate of the negotiations with the Earl of Northumberland at Oxford in 1643 (stifled, Hyde wrote, by the King's lack of enthusiasm) and even more of the brief defection of the earls of Holland, Bedford, and Clare in the summer of the same year (who were given little encouragement by the King and the court) showed that others in the King's party had seen little virtue in the plan. To Hyde, it was another missed opportunity. He protested in the *History* that 'a body that is not formed by policy, with any avowed and fixed principles of government, but by the discontent of particular persons, who rather agree against a common adversary than are united to one just interest, cannot so easily be dissolved as by tampering with particular persons, and rending those branches from the trunk, whose beauty and advantage consists only in the spreading' (p. 200).

The failure to 'tamper' with the parliamentarian earls was one of many symptoms of what the *History* exposed as the central problem of royalist strategy. Throughout it, Hyde carefully laid bare the unattractive, incoherent, and faction-ridden processes of royalist decision-making: the King listened too much to his wife; his military and civilian advisers were constantly at loggerheads; decisions arrived at formally were routinely unpicked later as the King was lobbied by those unhappy with the result. It was inconceivable that he would have explicitly drawn the obvious conclusion when writing the *History* in 1646–8, while the King was still alive, but he hinted at it in his sketch of Charles I, written twenty years later: 'if he was not the best King, if he was without some parts and qualities which have made some kings great and happy, no other prince was ever unhappy who was possessed of half his virtues and endowments, and so much without any kind of vice' (p. 336). In 1646–8 he merely insisted on the formalities of policy-making, most notably in an essay on the operation of the Privy Council (pp. 67–8), but throughout the work he underlined the value of counsel disinterestedly given. The point is a conventional one, common in political and historical literature of the sixteenth and seventeenth centuries. But in an age obsessed with the Tacitist values of secrecy and dissimulation it might appear a little old-fashioned, almost quaint; Hyde nevertheless elevated it into a principle related to his celebration of law and the constitution. The giving of counsel is the proper function of both Parliament and the King's advisers; by frustrating or corrupting the process—through the dissolutions of Parliament in the 1620s and in May 1640, through the regular procedural irregularities of the parliamentary leadership in the 1640s, or through the acceptance of other channels of influence and advice—government itself may begin to break down.

When he originally sketched out the *History* Hyde meant to include a treatise on the constitution. He never did so. It may have been because he could not obtain the books he needed; it may have been because he was daunted by the depth and erudition of the arguments advanced over the authority to govern the militia by John Selden, writing for the other side. But it might have been because he recognized that the law of the constitution—however much it could contribute to the learned but arid debates over the commission of array or the appointments of the King's senior officials—was of little help in explaining what had happened, or recommending what might happen next. Hyde was not a 'constitutional royalist' if that meant accepting that the power of the King could be formally limited through changed structures of law or government; but he recognized that it was the way in which power was exercised that created or jeopardized legitimacy and stability. For Hyde, the conservative but moderate royalist, the complexities of constitutional law could in 1646–8 provide little insight into the causes of the breakdown of royal authority in 1642, nor into the way out of the King's current predicament; but a close examination of the recent past might, by helping royalists to a sufficient grasp of the fundamental political realities, give them some greater understanding of how they might rescue what was left of their cause.

Writing for posterity

Full of political messages as it was, the *History* also had a commemorative purpose. The *History* would ensure that posterity was not deceived; it would 'tell posterity that the whole nation was not so bad as it will be then thought to have been'; he told the King that he was 'preparing the story of your sufferings, that posterity may tremble at the reading of what the present age blushes not to execute'. He excused his long encomium of Falkland because 'if the celebrating the memory of eminent and extraordinary persons, and transmitting their great virtues for the imitation of posterity, be one of the principal ends and duties of history, it will not be thought impertinent in this place to remember a loss which no time will suffer to be forgotten, and no success or good fortune could repair' (p. 182). With its lists of the dead and its sketches of their characters, the *History* is a royalist war memorial as well as a political essay.

Posterity was important to Clarendon. How important has Clarendon been to posterity? When it appeared, the *History* was seized on with delight and astonishment by Whigs and Tories alike, despite its High Tory pedigree. Its author was dubbed 'the noble historian', because of both his title and the stateliness of the work. Its reputation was international: Jean Le Clerc, a French popularizer of scholarship, compiled the first abridged version in 1710; in Hanover, the philosopher Leibniz and the Electress herself (the mother of George I) read it with pleasure. Clarendon's grand style was widely admired, and his willingness to criticize both friends and enemies seen as the mark of a truly impartial historian—even though (according to its most determined critic, John Oldmixon) 'the Vogue it got for its unhistorical Qualities, study'd Periods, and florid Narrations, at once insensibly took in unwary and unskilful Readers to like the Facts as well as the Stile. It had such a Torrent of Currency at first, that it bore all down before it.' But Clarendon's actual influence on the writing of history was more limited. Although Gilbert Burnet substantially recast his *History of my Own Time* as a result of reading the *History*, it had no other direct imitators, perhaps because its epic manner seemed no longer so appropriate for the less violent domestic politics of the eighteenth century; more probably because the detachment so widely praised in Clarendon was much more difficult to achieve in the open party conflict of Whigs and Tories. In the nineteenth century interest waned: elbowed out of the way by Cromwell among those, like Thomas Carlyle, who preferred the rough-hewn in seventeenth-century history, sidelined in a progressive age as the work of a conservative opponent of change, and (partly thanks to the publication of W. D. Macray's fine edition of 1888) shown up for his errors of fact by a new generation of scientific historians, Clarendon and his *History* started to slip out of the national consciousness. Only in Oxford did they live on, where the printing house was built from the publication profits of the *History*, and Clarendon's name was given to the academic imprint of the university press. Even in 1909, when Sir Charles Firth delivered a tercentenary lecture at Oxford, he noticed that Clarendon was 'to-day but a vague and indistinct personality, and his works are amongst those English classics which educated people put into their shelves, and leave there'.

Yet Clarendon never slipped altogether. Images and judgements from the *History* — the raising of the royal standard, Viscount Falkland 'ingeminating peace', and the 'brave bad man' Oliver Cromwell — formed a stratum of general knowledge about the Civil War even when it was only tenuously connected to Clarendon. And if nineteenth-century historians like Firth and Samuel Rawson Gardiner found that Clarendon's account was limited in some of its insights and partial in many of its judgements, they also rescued it from the dull bellelettrism of excerpts or abridged versions by beginning to provide a more complex understanding of the events it covered. Clarendon and his *History* started to emerge in sharper focus. Since then, by discovering more about the literary and political contexts of the *History*, scholars have started to remove it and its author from the Augustan, Tory, world into which it was published, and set them back in time: into the rumbustious London of Ben Jonson; the exhilarating intellectual milieu of Falkland and his friends; the febrile Oxford of the Civil War; and the fascinating but frustrating Madrid of his exile. As they have done so, the 'noble historian' has become a more real, more substantial figure; not a historian of Olympian detachment, but a vigorous participant in events, constantly engaged with things and people: the warmest of friends and most constant of correspondents; the most acute observer, whether of his contemporaries or of a Spanish bull-fight; passionately committed to his cause and determined in his stances; and throughout it all, incessantly writing.

NOTE ON THE TEXT

INCLUDED here is around a sixth of Clarendon's *History of the Rebellion* as published in 1702–4 (incorporating passages written in 1646–8 and in 1668–70) plus some key passages from the *Life* as published in 1759. It has not been possible to include material from the so-called *Continuation* of the *Life* (also published in 1759), covering the period after 1660. No attempt to compress Clarendon's long and complex text into a small compass can hope to catch all of its best elements. The aim has been to produce a text that is capable of being read as a continuous narrative, while retaining some of the most characteristic digressions— the sketch of Falkland and the discussions of the proper arrangement of the business of the Privy Council, for example. A few liberties have been taken with the text as arranged by Clarendon and published in 1702–4, by introducing some of the passages from the *Life* which Clarendon left out of the final *History*, particularly those covering Hyde's activities in the Long Parliament and his encounters with the King: these give a more personal perspective on some of the events recounted in the *History* itself. At the end of each segment of the text, the origin of the passage is stated.

The text of the *History of the Rebellion* is essentially that of W. D. Macray's 1888 Clarendon Press edition. The text of the *Life* is that of the most recent, 1857, edition, also published by the Clarendon Press. Macray corrected, where he could, Clarendon's grammar, changing for example singular to plural verbs or vice versa where necessary; the editor of the 1857 edition of the *Life* did the same, although silently. In most cases, these corrections have been made silently in this edition, although Macray's square brackets have been retained for more significant alterations. Macray modernized much of Clarendon's spelling, but not all of it, and did not standardize the spelling of proper names. In this edition proper names have usually been modernized and standardized.

SELECT BIBLIOGRAPHY

Clarendon's life and thought

Dzelzainis, Martin, '"Undouted realities": Clarendon on sacrilege', *Historical Journal*, 33 (1990), 515–40.

Firth, C. H., 'Hyde, Edward, earl of Clarendon', in *Dictionary of National Biography* (1891).

Ollard, Richard, *Clarendon and his Friends* (1980).

Scott, David, 'Counsel and cabal in the king's party, 1642–46', in Jason McElligott and David L. Smith (eds.), *Royalists and Royalism during the English Civil Wars* (2007).

Seaward, Paul, 'Hyde, Edward, earl of Clarendon', in *Oxford Dictionary of National Biography* (2004).

——, 'Constitutional and unconstitutional royalism', *Historical Journal*, 47 (1997), 227–39.

Smith, David, *Constitutional Royalism and the Search for a Settlement* (1994).

Wormald, B. H. G., *Clarendon: History, Politics, Religion* (1951).

The context

Adamson, John, *The Noble Revolt* (2007). The most detailed reconstruction available of the events of 1640–2.

Cust, Richard, *Charles I: A Political Life* (2005).

Gentles, Ian, *The English Revolution and the Wars of the Three Kingdoms, 1638–1652* (2007).

Hayward, J. C., 'New directions in studies of the Falkland circle', *Seventeenth Century* (Jan. 1987), 19–48.

Hutton, Ronald, *The Royalist War Effort, 1642–46* (2003).

Smith, Geoffrey, *The Cavaliers in Exile, 1640–60* (2003).

Trevor-Roper, Hugh, 'The Great Tew Circle', in *Catholics, Anglicans and Puritans* (1987).

Underdown, David, *Royalist Conspiracy in England* (1960).

Woolrych, Austin, *Britain in Revolution* (2002).

Clarendon's writings and the histories of the Civil War

Brownley, Martine Watson, *Clarendon and the Rhetoric of Historical Form* (1985).

Firth, C. H., 'Clarendon's *History of the Rebellion*', *English Historical Review*, 19 (1904), 26–54, 246–62, 464–83.

Green, Ian, 'The publication of Clarendon's autobiography and the acquisition of his papers by the Bodleian Library', *Bodleian Library Record*, 10 (1982), 349–67.

Hicks, Philip, *Neoclassical History and English Culture, Clarendon to Hume* (1996).

Hutton, Ronald, 'Clarendon's History of the Rebellion', *English Historical Review*, 97 (1982), 70–88.

Macgillivray, Royce, *Restoration Historians and the English Civil War* (1974).

Ricks, Christopher, 'The wit and weight of Clarendon', in Douglas Patey and Timothy Keegan (eds.), *Augustan Studies* (1985).

Roebuck, Graham, *Clarendon and Cultural Continuity* (1981). An annotated bibliography of Clarendon's works.

Seaward, Paul, 'Davila, Clarendon, and the Civil Wars of France and England', in Paulina Kewes (ed.), *The Uses of History in Early Modern England* (*Huntingdon Library Quarterly*, 68/1 and 2 (2005)).

Watson, George, 'The reader in Clarendon's *History of the Rebellion*', *Review of English Studies*, NS 25 (1974), 369–409.

A CHRONOLOGY OF EDWARD HYDE

1609 (18 Feb.) Hyde born at Dinton, Wilts. (p. 427).

1623 Matriculated at Magdalen Hall, Oxford (p. 427).

1625 First Parliament of Charles I.

1626 Second Parliament of Charles I (dissolved in June); Hyde enters the
Middle Temple to study for the bar (p. 428).

1628–9 Third Parliament of Charles I (dissolved in March 1629).

1628 (23 Aug.) Assassination of the Duke of Buckingham (p. 430).

1632 (4 Feb.) Hyde marries Anne Ayliffe. She dies in July (p. 430).

1633 (Nov.) Hyde called to the bar (p. 433).

1634 (10 July) Marries Frances Aylesbury (p. 433); (Sept.) Death of his father
(p. 434).

1638 Judgement given in the ship money case (p. 11); (Feb.) National
Covenant signed in Edinburgh (p. 32).

1639 Charles I's attempt to suppress the Scottish Covenanting movement (the
'First Bishops' War') ends in failure and a treaty in June (p. 35).

1640 (Apr.) Opening of Short Parliament, in which Hyde sat for Wootton
Bassett. The Parliament was dissolved in May (p. 47); (Aug.) Charles I's
second attempt to suppress the Covenanters ends in defeat at Newburn
(p. 49); (3 Nov.) opening of the Long Parliament, in which Hyde sat for
Saltash (p. 50).

1641 (21 Apr.) Vote in House of Commons on attainder of the Earl of Strafford
(p. 74); (May) execution of the Earl of Strafford (p. 86); 'root and
branch' bill introduced in the Commons (p. 88); (June) first bill to
remove the bishops from the Lords rejected in the Lords; (Aug.) the
King leaves London for Scotland (p. 90); (Oct.) news arrives in London
of the Irish rebellion (p. 90); second bill to remove the bishops from the
Lords; (8 Nov.) Grand Remonstrance presented (p. 93); (25 Nov.) the
King arrives back in London; (Dec.) Grand Remonstrance printed.
Hyde prepares a response to it on behalf of the King (pp. 98, 111–13).

1642 (Jan.) Appointments of Hyde's parliamentary allies Viscount Falkland
and Sir John Culpepper as Secretary of State and Chancellor of the
Exchequer (p. 110); Charles I attempts to arrest five members of the
House of Commons (p. 116); (5 Feb.) bill excluding bishops from the
Lords passed by the House of Lords; (Mar.) the King leaves the south-
east for York; (23 Apr.) the King attempts to seize Hull and is rebuffed
(p. 130); (May) Hyde leaves London for York; (22 Aug.) raising of the

Royal Standard at Nottingham (p. 141); (23 Oct.) battle of Edgehill (p. 151).

1643 Hyde appointed to Privy Council (22 Feb.) and made Chancellor of the Exchequer (3 Mar.) (p. 161); (Mar./Apr.) negotiations at Oxford with parliamentarian commissioners (p. 162); (July) Prince Rupert captures Bristol; (20 Sept.) Falkland killed at Newbury (p. 182).

1644 (Jan.) Scottish army marches into northern England to support Parliament (p. 204); (2 July) battle of Marston Moor (p. 209); (2 Sept.) surrender of Essex's army in Cornwall (p. 229); (25 Nov.) Cromwell attacks the army leadership in the House of Commons (p. 233).

1645 (31 Jan.) Treaty negotiations opened at Uxbridge; continue until 23 Feb. (pp. 240–57); (4 Mar.) Hyde leaves Oxford with the Prince's council for the south-west (p. 257); (Apr.) self-denying ordinance passed by Parliament to remove members of either House of Parliament from commands in the army (p. 239); (1 July) battle of Naseby (p. 262); (Sept.) Prince Rupert surrenders Bristol to Parliament; Montrose defeated in Scotland.

1646 (Mar.) the Prince of Wales and his council leave Cornwall and sail to the Scilly Isles; (18 Mar.) Hyde begins the *History*; (Apr.) the Prince of Wales, with Hyde and the Council, move to Jersey; (5 May) the King places himself in the hands of the Scots army (p. 277); (25 June) the Prince of Wales and other councillors leave for France; Hyde remains in Jersey (p. 282).

1647 (Feb.) The King is transferred into the custody of the English Parliament; (4 June) the King is taken from Parliament's custody at Holmby by the army and moved to Hampton Court (p. 288); (6 July) the army presents impeachment charges against Presbyterian members of the House of Commons. Presbyterians leave the House; followed by rioting in the City (p. 292); (6 Aug.) the Army occupies the City (p. 292); (Nov.) the King attempts to escape from Hampton Court; is held in Carisbrooke Castle; (Dec.) Parliament presents the Four Bills to the King, which he rejects; the King makes a secret agreement, the Engagement, with the Scots (p. 297).

1648 (3 Jan.) Vote of no more addresses to the King (p. 298); (May) rising in Kent and mutiny of the fleet (p. 312); (June) Hyde is summoned to Paris (p. 308); (July) Scottish army enters England (p. 317); (Aug.) Scottish army defeated at the Battle of Preston (17th); surrender of Colchester (28th) (p. 320); (Sept.) Hyde arrives at The Hague; (Sept./Oct.) the King negotiates with parliamentary commissioners at the Treaty of Newport; (6 Dec.) Pride's Purge: members supporting an agreement with the King are excluded from the House of Commons, leaving the 'Rump'.

1649 (Jan.) Trial and execution (on 30th) of the King (pp. 330–3), followed by the abolition of the House of Lords and the declaration of a republic;

(June) Hyde and Cottington leave the Netherlands for Spain (p. 340); (Nov.) Hyde and Cottington arrive in Madrid.

1650 (Jan.) Privy Council reopens negotiations with the Scots; (June) Charles II arrives in Scotland.

1651 (Mar.) Hyde leaves Madrid; (3 Sept.) Scottish army defeated at Worcester (p. 348).

1653 (Apr.) Cromwell dismisses the Rump Parliament; (Dec.) Cromwell becomes Lord Protector under the Instrument of Government.

1654 (June) Royal court leaves Paris for Germany, and settles in Sept. at Cologne (p. 368).

1655 (Mar.) Penruddock's rising (p. 377).

1656 (Apr.) Treaty agreed by royalists with Spain (p. 385).

1658 (Jan.) Hyde appointed Lord Chancellor; (3 Sept.) death of Cromwell; accession of Richard Cromwell (p. 388).

1659 (June) Richard Cromwell deposed; the Army brings back the Rump Parliament; (Aug.) Booth's rising (p. 398); (Oct.) the army assumes power again: General Monck, commander of the army in Scotland, declares his opposition to the coup; (26 Dec.) the army readmits the Rump to the House of Commons.

1660 (Jan.) Monck begins to march south from Scotland; (May) restoration of the King (p. 424); (Nov.) Hyde is made a peer as Baron Hyde of Hindon.

1661 (Apr.) Hyde is given additional titles of Viscount Cornbury and Earl of Clarendon.

1664–7 Second Dutch War.

1667 (Aug.) dismissal of Clarendon from chancellorship; (Oct.) impeachment of Clarendon; (Nov.) Clarendon leaves for France.

1668 (July) Begins writing the *Life*.

1671 Clarendon's son visits him, bringing the manuscript of the *History*. Clarendon works on putting the two together.

1674 (Dec.) Clarendon dies at Rouen.

1702–4 Publication of the *History* in three volumes.

1759 Publication of the *Life*.

THE
HISTORY OF THE CIVIL WAR

Extracts from
The History of the Rebellion and *The Life*

1. The Misgovernment of Caroline England

The opening of the History *is dated 'Scilly. March 18, 1645' (i.e. 1646).*
Hyde began this preface two weeks after he had arrived in the Scilly Isles with
Prince Charles, and a few days after the final surrender of the royal army in
the west of England. He completed Book I of the History, *from which all of*
the following passage is taken, in June the same year, on Jersey.

THAT posterity may not be deceived, by the prosperous wickedness of
these times, into an opinion that less than a general combination, and
universal apostasy in the whole nation from their religion and allegiance, could, in so short a time, have produced such a total and prodigious alteration and confusion over the whole kingdom; and so the
memory of those few who, out of duty and conscience, have opposed
and resisted that torrent which hath overwhelmed them may lose the
recompense due to their virtue, and, having undergone the injuries
and reproaches of this, may not find a vindication in a better, age; it
will not be unuseful, (at least to the curiosity if not the conscience of
men,) to present to the world a full and clear narration of the grounds,
circumstances, and artifices of this Rebellion, not only from the time
since the flame hath been visible in a civil war, but, looking farther
back, from those former passages, accidents, and actions, by which the
seed-plots were made and framed from whence these mischiefs have
successively grown to the height they are now at.

And then, though the hand and judgment of God will be very visible,
in the infatuating a people (as ripe and prepared for destruction) into
all the perverse actions of folly and madness, making the weak to
contribute to the designs of the wicked, and suffering even those by
degrees, out of the conscience of their guilt, to grow more wicked than
they intended to be; letting the wise to be imposed upon by men of no
understanding, and possessing the innocent with laziness and sleep in
the most visible article of danger; uniting the ill, though of the most
different opinions, divided interests, and distant affections, in a firm
and constant league of mischief; and dividing those whose opinions
and interests are the same into faction and emulation, more pernicious
to the public than the treason of the others: whilst the poor people,
under pretence of zeal to Religion, Law, Liberty, and Parliaments,
(words of precious esteem in their just signification,) are furiously hur-
ried into actions introducing Atheism, and dissolving all the elements

of Christian Religion, cancelling all obligations, and destroying all foundations of Law and Liberty, and rendering not only the privileges but very being of Parliaments desperate and impossible: I say, though the immediate finger and wrath of God must be acknowledged in these perplexities and distractions, yet he who shall diligently observe the distempers and conjunctures of time, the ambition, pride, and folly of persons, and the sudden growth of wickedness, from want of care and circumspection in the first impressions, will find all this bulk of misery to have proceeded, and to have been brought upon us, from the same natural causes and means which have usually attended kingdoms swollen with long plenty, pride, and excess, towards some signal mortification, and castigation of Heaven. And it may be, upon the view of the impossibility of foreseeing many things that have happened, and of the necessity of overseeing many other things, [we] may not yet find the cure so desperate, but that, by God's mercy, the wounds may be again bound up, though no question many must first bleed to death; and then this prospect may not make the future peace less pleasant and durable.

And I have the more willingly induced myself to this unequal task out of the hope of contributing somewhat to that end: and though a piece of this nature (wherein the infirmities of some, and the malice of others, both things and persons, must be boldly looked upon and mentioned) is not likely to be published, (at least in the age in which it is writ,) yet it may serve to inform myself and some others what we are to do, as well as to comfort us in what we have done; and then possibly it may not be very difficult to collect somewhat out of that store more proper, and not unuseful, for the public view. And as I may not be thought altogether an incompetent person for this communication, having been present as a member of Parliament in those councils before and till the breaking out of the Rebellion, and having since had the honour to be near two great kings in some trust, so I shall perform the same with all faithfulness and ingenuity, with an equal observation of the faults and infirmities of both sides, with their defects and oversights in pursuing their own ends; and shall no otherwise mention small and light occurrences than as they have been introductions to matters of the greatest moment; nor speak of persons otherwise than as the mention of their virtues or vices is essential to the work in hand: in which as I shall have the fate to be suspected rather for malice to many than of flattery to any, so I shall, in truth, preserve myself from the least sharpness that may proceed from private provocation or a more public indignation; in the whole observing the rules that a man should, who deserves to be believed.

I shall not then lead any man farther back in this journey, for the discovery of the entrance into these dark ways, than the beginning of this King's reign. For I am not so sharp-sighted as those who have discerned this rebellion contriving from, if not before, the death of Queen Elizabeth, and fomented by several Princes and great ministers of state in Christendom to the time that it brake out. Neither do I look so far back as believing the design to be so long since formed; (they who have observed the several accidents, not capable of being contrived, which have contributed to the several successes, and do know the persons who have been the grand instruments towards this change, of whom there have not been any four of familiarity and trust with each other, will easily absolve them from so much industry and foresight in their mischief;) but that, by viewing the temper, disposition, and habit, of that time, of the court and of the country, we may discern the minds of men prepared, of some to do, and of others to suffer, all that hath since happened: the pride of this man, and the popularity of that; the levity of one, and the morosity of another; the excess of the court in the greatest want, and the parsimony and retention of the country in the greatest plenty; the spirit of craft and subtlety in some, and the rude and unpolished integrity of others, too much despising craft or art; like so many atoms contributing jointly to this mass of confusion now before us.

King James in the end of March 1625 died, leaving his majesty that now is* engaged in a war with Spain, but unprovided with money to manage it, though it was undertaken by the consent and advice of Parliament: the people being naturally enough inclined to the war (having surfeited with the uninterrupted pleasures and plenty of twenty-two years peace) and sufficiently inflamed against the Spaniard, but quickly weary of the charge of it. And therefore, after an unprosperous and chargeable attempt in a voyage by sea upon Cadiz, and as unsuccessful and more unfortunate a one upon France, at the Isle of Rhé,* (for some difference had likewise at the same time begotten a war with that prince,) a general peace was shortly concluded* with both kingdoms; the exchequer being so exhausted with the debts of King James, the bounty of his majesty that now is, (who, upon his first access to the crown, gave many costly instances of his favour to persons near him,) and the charge of the war upon Spain and France, that, both the known and casual revenue being anticipated, the necessary subsistence of the household was unprovided for; and the King on the sudden driven to those straits for his own support that many ways were resorted to, and inconveniences submitted to, for supply; as, selling the crown-lands, creating peers for money, and many other particulars, which no access of power or plenty since could repair.

Parliaments were summoned, and again dissolved:* and in the fourth year that (after the dissolution of two former) was determined with a profession and declaration that there should be no more assemblies of that nature expected,* and all men inhibited upon the penalty of censure so much as to speak of a Parliament. And here I cannot but let myself loose to say, that no man can shew me a source from whence these waters of bitterness we now taste have more probably flowed, than from this unseasonable, unskilful, and precipitate dissolution of Parliaments; in which, by an unjust survey of the passion, insolence, and ambition of particular persons, the Court measured the temper and affection of the country; and by the same standard the people considered the honour, justice, and piety of the Court; and so usually parted, at those sad seasons, with no other respect and charity one toward the other than accompanies persons who never meant to meet but in their own defence. In which always the King had the disadvantage to harbour persons about him who with their utmost industry, information, and malice, improved the faults and infirmities of the Court to the people; and again, as much as in them lay, rendered the people suspected if not odious to the King.

I am not altogether a stranger to the passages of those Parliaments, (though I was not a member of them,) having carefully perused the Journals of both Houses, and familiarly conversed with many who had principal parts in them; and I cannot but wonder at those counsels which persuaded the courses then taken; the habit and temper of men's minds being, no question, very applicable to the public ends, and those ends being only discredited by the jealousies the people entertained, from the manner of the prosecution, that they were other, and worse, than in truth they were. It is not to be denied that there were in all those Parliaments, especially in that of the fourth year, several passages, and distempered speeches of particular persons, not fit for the dignity and honour of those places, and unsuitable to the reverence due to his majesty and his councils. But I do not know any formed Act of either House (for neither the Remonstrance or votes of the last day* were such) that was not agreeable to the wisdom and justice of great courts upon those extraordinary occasions. And whoever considers the acts of power and injustice in the intervals of Parliaments, will not be much scandalized at the warmth and vivacity of those meetings.

In the second Parliament there was a mention, and intention declared, of granting five subsidies, a proportion (how contemptible soever in respect of the pressures now every day imposed) never before heard of in Parliament.* And that meeting being, upon very unpopular and unplausible reasons, immediately dissolved, those five subsidies were exacted throughout the whole kingdom* with the same rigour, as if, in truth, an Act had passed to that purpose. And very many gentlemen of prime quality, in all the several counties of England, were, for refusing to pay the same, committed to prison, with great rigour and extraordinary circumstances. And could it be imagined, that these men would meet again in a free convention of Parliament without a sharp and severe expostulation, and inquisition into their own right, and the power that had imposed upon that right? And yet all these provocations, and many other, almost of as large an extent, produced no other resentment than the Petition of Right,* (of no prejudice to the Crown,) which was likewise purchased at the price of five more subsidies, and, in a very short time after that supply granted, that Parliament was likewise, with strange circumstances of passion on all sides, dissolved.

The abrupt and ungracious breaking of the two first Parliaments was wholly imputed to the duke of Buckingham, and of the third principally to the lord Weston, then Lord High Treasurer of England; both in respect of the great power and interest they then had in the affections of his majesty, and for that the time of the dissolutions happened to be when some charges and accusations* were preparing and ready to be preferred against those two great persons. And therefore the envy and hatred that attended them thereupon was insupportable, and was visibly the cause of the murder of the first,* (stabbed to the heart by the hand of an obscure villain, upon the mere impious pretence of his being odious to the Parliament,) and made, no doubt, so great an impression upon the understanding and nature of the other, that by degrees he lost that temper and serenity of mind he had been before master of, and which was most fit to have accompanied him in his weighty employments; insomuch as, out of indignation to find himself worse used than he deserved, he cared less to deserve well than he had done, and insensibly grew into that public hatred that rendered him less useful to the service that he only intended.

I wonder less at the errors of this nature in the duke of Buckingham; who, having had a most generous education in courts, was utterly ignorant of the ebbs and floods of popular councils, and of the winds that move those waters; and could not, without the spirit of indignation, find himself in the space of a few weeks, without any visible cause intervening, from the greatest height of popular estimation that any person hath ascended to, (insomuch as sir Edward Coke blasphemously called him our Saviour,) by the same breath thrown down to the depth of calumny and reproach. I say, it is no marvel, (besides that he was naturally [inclined] to follow such counsel as was given him,) that he could think of no better way to be freed of the inconveniences and troubles the passions of those meetings gave him, than to dissolve them, and prevent their coming together: and, that when they seemed to neglect the public peace out of animosity to him, that he intended his own ease and security in the first place, and easily believed the public might be otherwise provided for by more intent and dispassionate councils. But that the other, the lord Weston, who had been very much and very popularly conversant in those conventions, who exactly knew the frame and constitution of the kingdom, the temper of the people, the extent of the courts of law, and the jurisdiction of parliaments, which at that time had never committed any excess of jurisdiction, (—modesty and moderation in words never was, nor ever will be, observed in popular councils, whose foundation is liberty of speech—) should believe that the union, peace, and plenty of the kingdom could be preserved without parliaments, or that the passion and distemper gotten and received into parliaments could be removed and reformed by the more passionate breaking and dissolving them; or that that course would not inevitably prove the most pernicious to himself; is as much my wonder as any thing that hath since happened.

There is a protection very gracious and just which princes owe to their servants, when, in obedience to their just commands, upon extraordinary and necessary occasions in the execution of their trusts, they swerve from the strict rule of the law, which, without that mercy, would be penal to them. In any case, it is as legal (the law presuming it will be always done upon great reason) for the king to pardon, as for the party to accuse, and the judge to condemn. But for the supreme power to interpose, and shelter an accused servant from answering, does not only seem an obstruction of justice, and lay an imputation upon the prince of being privy to the offence, but leaves so great a scandal upon the party himself that he is generally concluded guilty of whatsoever he is charged; which is commonly more than the worst man ever deserved. And it is worthy the observation, that, as no innocent man who made his defence ever suffered in those times by judgment of Parliament, so, many guilty persons, and against whom the spirit of the time went as high, by the wise managing their defence have been freed from their accusers, not only without censure but without reproach; as the bishop of Lincoln, then Lord Keeper, sir H. Marten, and sir H. Spiller;* men in their several degrees as little beholding to the charity of that time as any men since. Whereas scarce a man who, with industry and skill, laboured to keep himself from being accused, or by power to stop or divert the course of proceeding, escaped without some signal mark of infamy or prejudice. And the reason is clear; for—besides that after the first storm there is some compassion naturally attends men like to be in misery, and besides the latitude of judging in those places, whereby there is room for kindness and affection and collateral considerations to interpose—the truth is, those accusations (to which this man contributes his malice, that his wit, all men what they please, and most upon hearsay, with a kind of uncharitable delight of making the charge as heavy as may be) are commonly stuffed with many odious generals, that the proofs seldom make good: and then a man is no sooner found less guilty than he is expected but he is concluded more innocent than he is; and it is thought but a just reparation for the reproach that he deserved not, to free him from the censure he deserved. So that, very probably, those two noble persons had been happy if they had stoutly submitted to the proceedings were designed against them; and, without question, it had been of sovereign use to the King if, in those peaceable times, parliaments had been taught to know their own bounds by being suffered to proceed as far as they could go; by which the extent of their power would quickly have been manifested. From whence no inconvenience of moment could have proceeded; the House of Commons never then pretending to the least part of judicature, or exceeding the known verge of their own privileges; the House of Peers observing the rules of law and equity in their judgments, and proceeding deliberately upon clear testimony and evidence of matter of fact; and the King retaining the sole power of pardoning, and receiving the whole profit of all penalties and judgments, and indeed having so great an influence upon the body of the peerage, that it was never known that any person of honour was severely censured in that House, (before this present Parliament,)* who was not either immediately prosecuted by the Court or in evident disfavour there; in which, it may be, (as it usually falls out) some doors were opened at which inconveniences to the Crown have got in, that were not then enough weighed and considered.

But the course of exempting men from prosecution by dissolving of parliaments made the power of parliaments much more formidable, as conceived to be without limit; since the sovereign power seemed to be compelled (as unable otherwise to set bounds to their proceedings) to that rough cure, and to determine their being because it could not determine their jurisdiction. Whereas, if they had been frequently summoned, and seasonably dissolved after their wisdom in applying medicines and cures, as well as their industry in discovering diseases, had been discerned, they would easily have been applied to the uses for which they were first instituted, and been of no less esteem with the Crown than of veneration with the people. And so I shall conclude this digression, which I conceived not unseasonable for this place nor upon this occasion, and return to the time when that brisk resolution was taken of totally declining those conventions; all men being inhibited (as I said before) by proclamation, at the dissolution of the Parliament in the fourth year, so much as to mention or speak as if a Parliament should be called. [*HR*, I, 1–12]

That proclamation, mentioned before, at the breach of the last Parliament, and which inhibited all men to speak of another Parliament, produced two very ill effects of different natures. It afflicted many good men (who otherwise were enough scandalized at those distempers which had incensed the King) to that degree that it made them capable of receiving some impressions from those who were diligent in whispering and infusing an opinion into men that there was really an intention to alter the form of government, both in Church and State; 'of which,' said they, 'a greater instance cannot be given than this public declaring that we shall have no more Parliaments.' Then, this freedom from the danger of such an inquisition did not only encourage ill men to all boldness and license, but wrought so far upon men less inclined to ill (though not built for examples) that they kept not those strict guards upon themselves they used to do; especially, if they found themselves above the reach of ordinary justice, and feared not extraordinary, they by degrees thought that no fault which was like to find no punishment. Supplemental acts of state were made to supply defect of laws; and so tonnage and poundage,* and other duties upon merchandises, were collected by order of the Board,* which had been perversely refused to be settled by Act of Parliament, and new and greater impositions laid upon trade. Obsolete laws were revived and rigorously executed, wherein the subject might be taught how unthrifty a thing it was by too strict a detaining of what was his to put the King as strictly to inquire what was his own. And by this ill husbandry the King received a vast sum of money from all persons of quality, or indeed of any reasonable condition throughout the kingdom, upon the law of knighthood,* which, though it had a foundation in right, yet, in the circumstances of proceeding, was very grievous, and no less unjust.

Projects of all kinds, many ridiculous, many scandalous, all very grievous, were set on foot; the envy and reproach of which came to the King, the profit to other men, insomuch as, of two hundred thousand pound drawn from the subject by these ways in a year, scarce fifteen hundred came to the King's use or account. To recompense the damage the Crown sustained by the sale of the old lands, and by the grant of new pensions,* the old laws of the forest* are revived, by which not only great fines are imposed, but great annual rents intended and like to be settled by way of contract; which burden lighted most upon persons of quality and honour, who thought themselves above ordinary oppressions, and therefore like to remember it with more sharpness. Lastly, for a spring and magazine that should have no bottom, and for an everlasting supply of all occasions, a writ is framed in a form of law, and directed to the sheriff of every county of England, to provide a ship of war for the King's service, and to send it, amply provided and fitted, by such a day to such a place; and with that writ were sent to each sheriff instructions that, instead of a ship, he should levy upon his county such a sum of money, and return the same to the Treasurer of the Navy for his majesty's use, with direction in what manner he should proceed against such as refused: and from hence that tax had the denomination of *Ship-Money*,* a word of a lasting sound in the memory of this kingdom; by which for some years really accrued the yearly sum of two hundred thousand pounds to the King's coffers, and was in truth the only project that was accounted to his own service. And, after the continued receipt of it for four years together, was at last (upon the refusal of a private gentleman to pay thirty shillings as his share) with great solemnity publicly argued before all the judges of England* in the Exchequer-chamber, and by the major part of them the King's right to impose asserted, and the tax adjudged lawful; which judgment proved of more advantage and credit to the gentleman condemned, Mr Hampden, than to the King's service.

For the better support of these extraordinary ways, and to protect the agents and instruments who must be employed in them, and to discountenance and suppress all bold inquirers and opposers, the Council-table and Star-chamber* enlarge their jurisdictions to a vast extent, 'holding' (as Thucydides said of the Athenians)* 'for honourable that which pleased, and for just that which profited;' and, being the same persons in several rooms, grew both courts of law to determine right and courts of revenue to bring money into the treasury; the Council-table by proclamations enjoining this to the people that was not enjoined by the law, and prohibiting that which was not prohibited; and the Star-chamber

censuring the breach and disobedience to those proclamations by very
great fines and imprisonment; so that any disrespect to acts of state
or to the persons of statesmen was in no time more penal, and those
foundations of right by which men valued their security, to the apprehension and understanding of wise men, never more in danger to be
destroyed.

And here I cannot but again take the liberty to say, that the circumstances and proceedings in these new extraordinary cases, stratagems,
and impositions, were very unpolitic, and even destructive to the services intended. As, if the business of ship-money, being an imposition
by the State under the notion of necessity, upon a prospect of danger,
which private persons could not modestly think themselves qualified
to discern, had been managed in the same extraordinary way as the
royal loan (which was the imposing the five subsidies after the second
Parliament spoken of before) was, men would much easier have submitted to it; as it is notoriously known that pressure was borne with
much more cheerfulness before the judgment for the King than ever it
was after; men before pleasing themselves with doing somewhat for
the King's service, as a testimony of their affection, which they were
not bound to do; many really believing the necessity, and therefore
thinking the burden reasonable; others observing that the access to the
King was of importance, when the damage to them was not considerable; and all assuring themselves that when they should be weary, or
unwilling to continue the payment, they might resort to the law for
relief and find it. But when they heard this demanded in a court of law
as a right, and found it by sworn judges of the law adjudged so, upon
such grounds and reasons as every stander-by was able to swear was
not law, and so had lost the pleasure and delight of being kind and
dutiful to the King; and instead of giving were required to pay, and by
a logic that left no man any thing which he might call his own; they
no more looked upon it as the case of one man but the case of the kingdom, nor as an imposition laid upon them by the King but by the
judges; which they thought themselves bound in conscience to the
public justice not to submit to. It was an observation long ago by
Thucydides,* that 'men are much more passionate for injustice than
for violence; because,' says he, 'the one, coming as from an equal,
seems rapine; when the other, proceeding from one stronger, is but
the effect of necessity.' So, when ship-money was transacted at the
Council-board, they looked upon it as a work of that power they
were always obliged to trust, and an effect of that foresight they were
naturally to rely upon. Imminent necessity and public safety were

convincing persuasions; and it might not seem of apparent ill consequence to them that upon an emergent occasion the regal power
should fill up an hiatus, or supply an impotency in the law. But when
they saw in a court of law, (that law that gave them title and possession
of all that they had) apophthegms of state urged as elements of law;
judges as sharp-sighted as Secretaries of State and in the mysteries of
state; judgment of law grounded upon matter of fact of which there
was neither inquiry or proof; and no reason given for the payment of
the thirty shillings in question but what concluded the estates of all
the standers-by; they had no reason to hope that that doctrine or the
preachers of it would be contained within any bounds. And it was no
wonder that they who had so little reason to be pleased with their
own condition, were not less solicitous for, or apprehensive of, the
inconveniences that might attend any alteration.

And here the damage and mischief cannot be expressed, that the
Crown and State sustained by the deserved reproach and infamy that
attended the judges, by being made use of in this and the like acts of
power; there being no possibility to preserve the dignity, reverence, and
estimation of the laws themselves but by the integrity and innocency
of the judges. And no question, as the exorbitancy of the House of
Commons this Parliament hath proceeded principally from their contempt of the laws, and that contempt from the scandal of that judgment,
so the concurrence of the House of Peers in that fury can be imputed to
no one thing more than to the irreverence and scorn the judges were
justly in; who had been always before looked upon there as the oracles of
the law, and the best guides and directors of their opinions and actions:
and they now thought themselves excused for swerving from the rules
and customs of their predecessors (who in altering and making of laws,
in judging of things and persons, had always observed the advice and
judgment of those sages) in not asking questions of those whom they
knew nobody would believe; and thinking it a just reproach upon them,
(who out of their gentilesses had submitted the difficulties and mysteries
of the law to be measured by the standard of general reason and
explained by the wisdom of state,) to see those men make use of the
license they had taught, and determine that to be law which they thought
reasonable or found to be convenient. If these men had preserved the
simplicity of their ancestors in severely and strictly defending the laws,
other men had observed the modesty of theirs in humbly and dutifully
obeying them.

And upon this consideration it is very observable that, in the wisdom
of former times, when the prerogative went highest, (as very often it

hath been swollen above any pitch we have seen it at in our times,)
never any court of law, very seldom any judge, or lawyer of reputation,
was called upon to assist in an act of power; the Crown well knowing
the moment of keeping those the objects of reverence and veneration
with the people, and that though it might sometimes make sallies upon
them by the prerogative, yet the law would keep the people from
any invasion of it, and that the King could never suffer whilst the law
and the judges were looked upon by the subject as the asyla for their
liberties and security. And therefore you shall find the policy of many
princes hath endured as sharp animadversions and reprehensions from
the judges of the law, as their piety hath from the bishops of the
church; imposing no less upon the people under the reputation of
justice by the one, than of conscience and religion by the other.

To extend this consideration of the form and circumstance of proceeding in cases of an unusual nature a little farther:—As it may be most
behoveful for princes in matters of grace and honour, and in conferring
of favours upon their people, to transact the same as publicly as may be,
and by themselves, or their ministers, to dilate upon it, and improve the
lustre by any addition, or eloquence of speech; (where, it may be, every
kind word, especially from the prince himself, is looked upon as a new
bounty;) so it is as requisite in matters of judgment, punishment, and
censure, upon things or persons, (especially when the case, in the nature
of it, is unusual, and the rules in judging as extraordinary,) that the same
be transacted as privately, and with as little noise and pomp of words,
as may be. For (as damage is much easier borne and submitted to by
generous minds than disgrace) in the business of the ship-money, and in
many other cases in the Star-chamber and at Council-board, there were
many impertinencies, incongruities, and insolencies, in the speeches and
orations of the judges, much more offensive and much more scandalous
than the judgments and sentences themselves; besides that men's minds
and understandings were more instructed to discern the consequence
of things, which before they considered not. As, undoubtedly, my lord
Finch's speech* in the Exchequer-chamber made ship-money much
more abhorred and formidable than all the commitments by the
Council-table and all the distresses* taken by the sheriffs in England; the
major part of men (besides the common unconcernedness in other men's
sufferings) looking upon those proceedings as a kind of applause to
themselves, to see other men punished for not doing as they had done;
which delight was quickly determined when they found their own interest by the unnecessary logic of that argument no less concluded than
Mr Hampden's.

And he hath been but an ill observer of the passages of those times we speak of who hath not seen many sober men, who have been clearly satisfied with the conveniency, necessity, and justice of many sentences, depart notwithstanding extremely offended and scandalized with the grounds, reasons, and expressions of those who inflicted those censures, when they found themselves, thinking to be only spectators of other men's sufferings, by some unnecessary influence or declaration in probable danger to become the next delinquent.

They who look back upon the Council-books of Queen Elizabeth, and the acts of the Star-chamber then, shall find as high instances of power and sovereignty upon the liberty and property of the subject as can be since given. But the art, order, and gravity of those proceedings (where short, severe, constant rules were set and smartly pursued, and the party only felt the weight of the judgment, not the passion of his judges) made them less taken notice of, and so less grievous to the public, though as intolerable to the person. Whereas, since those excellent rules of the Council-board were less observed, and debates (which ought to be in private, and in the absence of the party concerned, and thereupon the judgment of the Table to be pronounced by one, without the interposition of others or reply of the party,) suffered to be public, questions to be asked, passions discovered, and opinions to be promiscuously delivered; all advice, directions, reprehensions, and censures of those places grew to be in less reverence and esteem; so that, (besides the delay and interruption in despatch,) the justice and prudence of the counsels did not many times weigh down the infirmity and passion of the counsellors, and both suitors and offenders returned into their country with such exceptions and arguments against persons as brought and prepared much prejudice to whatsoever should proceed from thence. And whatever excuses shall be made, or arguments given, that upon such extraordinary occasions there was a necessity of some pains and care to convince the understandings of men with the reasons and grounds of their proceeding, (which, if what was done had been only *ad informandam conscientiam,** without reproach or penalty, might have been reasonable,) it is certain the inconvenience and prejudice that grew thereby was greater than the benefit: and the reasons of the judges being many times not the reasons of the judgment, that might more satisfactorily and more shortly [have] been put in the sentence itself than spread in the discourses of the censurers. . . .

Now after all this (and I hope I cannot be accused of much flattery in this inquisition) I must be so just as to say, that, during the whole time that these pressures were exercised, and those new and extraordinary ways were run, that is, from the dissolution of the Parliament in the fourth year to the beginning of this Parliament,* which was above twelve years, this kingdom, and all his majesty's dominions, (—of the interruption in Scotland somewhat shall be said in its due time and place—) enjoyed the greatest calm and the fullest measure of felicity that any people in any age for so long time together have been blessed with; to the wonder and envy of all the parts of Christendom.

And in this comparison I am neither unmindful of, nor ungrateful for, the happy times of Queen Elizabeth, or for those more happy under King James. But, for the former, the doubts, hazards, and perplexities upon a total change and alteration of religion, and some confident attempts upon a farther alteration by those who thought not the reformation enough; the charge, trouble, and anxiety of a long continued war (how prosperous and successful soever) even during that Queen's whole reign; and (besides some domestic ruptures into rebellion, frequently into treason, and besides the blemish of an unparalleled act of blood upon the life of a crowned neighbour, queen, and ally) the fear and apprehension of what was to come (which is one of the most unpleasant kinds of melancholy) from an unknown, at least an unacknowledged, successor to the crown; clouded much of that prosperity then which now shines with so much splendour before our eyes in chronicle.

And, for the other, under King James, (which indeed were excellent times *bona si sua norint,*)* the mingling with a stranger nation,* (formerly not very gracious with this,) which was like to have more interest of favour: the subjection to a stranger prince, whose nature and disposition they knew not: the noise of treason* (the most prodigious that had ever been attempted) upon his first entrance into the kingdom: the wants of the Crown, not inferior to what it hath since felt, (I mean whilst it sat right on the head of the King,) and the pressures upon the subject of the same nature, and no less complained of: the absence of the Prince in Spain,* and the solicitude that his highness might not be disposed in marriage to the daughter of that kingdom; rendered the calm and tranquillity of that time less equal and pleasant. To which may be added the prosperity and happiness of the neighbour kingdoms, not much inferior to that of this; which, according to the pulse of states, is a great diminution of their health; at least, their prosperity is much improved and more visible by the misery and misfortunes of their neighbours.

The happiness of the times I mentioned was enviously set off by this, that every other kingdom, every other province, were engaged, many entangled, and some almost destroyed, by the rage and fury of

arms; those which were ambitiously in contention with their neighbours having the view and apprehensions of the miseries and desolation which they saw other states suffer by a civil war; whilst alone the
kingdoms we now lament were looked upon as the garden of the world;
Scotland (which was but the wilderness of that garden) in a full, entire,
undisturbed peace, which they had never seen; the rage and barbarism
(that is, the blood, for of charity we speak not) of their private feuds
being composed to the reverence or to the awe of public justice; in
a competency, if not in an excess, of plenty, which they had never hope
to see, and in a temper (which was the utmost we desired and hoped to
see) free from rebellion: Ireland, which had been a sponge to draw, and
a gulph to swallow, all that could be spared and all that could be got
from England, merely to keep the reputation of a kingdom, reduced
to that good degree of husbandry and government that it not only
subsisted of itself and gave this kingdom all that it might have expected
from it, but really increased the revenue of the Crown forty or fifty
thousand pounds a year, besides much more to the people in the
traffick and trade from thence; arts and sciences fruitfully planted
there; and the whole nation beginning to be so civilized that it was a
jewel of great lustre in the most royal diadem.

When these outworks were thus fortified and adorned, it was no
wonder if England was generally thought secure, with the advantages of
its own climate; the Court in great plenty, or rather (which is the
discredit of plenty) excess and luxury; the country rich, and, which is
more, fully enjoying the pleasure of its own wealth, and so the easier
corrupted with the pride and wantonness of it; the Church flourishing
with learned and extraordinary men, and (which other good times
wanted) supplied with oil to feed those lamps; and the Protestant
religion more advanced against the Church of Rome by writing, especially (without prejudice to other useful and godly labours) by those
two books of the late lord archbishop of Canterbury his grace, and of
Mr Chillingworth,* than it had been from the Reformation; trade
increased to that degree, that we were the Exchange of Christendom,
(the revenue thereof to the Crown being almost double to what it had
been in the best times,) and the bullion of all other kingdoms was
brought to receive a stamp from the Mint of England; all foreign
merchants looking upon nothing as their own but what they laid up
in the warehouses of this kingdom; the royal navy, in number and equipage much above former times, very formidable at sea, and the reputation of the greatness and power of the King much more with foreign
princes than any of his progenitors; for those rough courses which

made him haply less loved at home made him more feared abroad, by how much the power of kingdoms is more reverenced than their justice by their neighbours: and it may be this consideration might not be the least motive, and may not be the worst excuse, for those counsels. Lastly, for a complement of all these blessings, they were enjoyed by and under the protection of a King of the most harmless disposition and the most exemplar piety, the greatest example of sobriety, chastity, and mercy, that any prince hath been endued with, (and God forgive those that have not been sensible of, and thankful for, those endowments,) and who might have said that which Pericles was proud of upon his deathbed,* 'that no Englishman had ever worn black gown through his occasion.' In a word, many wise men thought it a time wherein those two unsociable adjuncts which Nerva was deified for uniting,* *imperium et libertas*, were as well reconciled as is possible.

But all these blessings could but enable, not compel, us to be happy: we wanted that sense, acknowledgment, and value of our own happiness which all but we had, and took pains to make, when we could not find, ourselves miserable. There was in truth a strange absence of understanding in most, and a strange perverseness of understanding in the rest: the Court full of excess, idleness and luxury, and the country full of pride, mutiny and discontent; every man more troubled and perplexed at that they called the violation of one law, than delighted or pleased with the observation of all the rest of the charter: never imputing the increase of their receipts, revenue and plenty to the wisdom, virtue and merit of the Crown, but objecting every little trivial imposition to the exorbitancy and tyranny of the government; the growth of knowledge and learning being disrelished for the infirmities of some learned men, and the increase of grace and favour upon the Church more repined and murmured at than the increase of piety and devotion in the Church, which was as visible, acknowledged or taken notice of; whilst the indiscretion and folly of one sermon at Whitehall was more bruited abroad, and commented upon, than the wisdom, sobriety and devotion of a hundred.

It cannot be denied but there was sometimes preached there matter very unfit for the place, and very scandalous for the persons, who presumed often to determine things out of the verge of their own profession, and, *in ordine ad spiritualia*,* gave unto Caesar what Caesar refused to receive as not belonging to him. But it is as true (as was once said by a man fitter to be believed in that point than I, and one not suspected for flattering of the clergy) that 'if the sermons of those times preached in Court were collected together and published, the

world would receive the best bulk of orthodox divinity, profound learning, convincing reason, natural powerful eloquence, and admirable
devotion, that hath been communicated in any age since the Apostles'
time.' And I cannot but say, for the honour of the King and of those
who were trusted by him in his ecclesiastical collations (who have
received but sad rewards for their uprightness) in those reproached,
condemned times, there was not one churchman in any degree of
favour or acceptance, (and this the inquisition that hath been since
made upon them—a stricter never was in any age—must confess,) of
a scandalous insufficiency in learning, or of a more scandalous condition in life; but, on the contrary, most of them of confessed eminent
parts in knowledge, and of virtuous or unblemished lives. And therefore wise men knew that that which looked like pride in some and like
petulance in others would, by experience in affairs and conversation
amongst men, both of which most of them wanted, be in time wrought
off or in a new succession reformed, and so thought the vast advantage
from their learning and integrity an ample recompense for any inconvenience from their passion; and yet by the prodigious impiety of those
times the latter was only looked on with malice and revenge, without
any reverence or gratitude for the former. That which in the consequence was worse than all this, that is, which made the consequence of
all the rest the worse, was, that by all the access of those vast receipts
and disbursements by the people, the King's coffers were not at all,
or not considerably, replenished. Whether by the excess of the Court,
(which had not been enough contracted;) the unaptness of ministers,
or the intentness of ministers upon their own, more than the public,
profit; the maintaining great fleets at sea, more for the glory than
benefit of the King, in a time of entire peace, and when his jurisdiction
in the deep was not questioned, at least not contested; or, which was
a greater, and at that time thought a more unnecessary, charge, the
building of many great ships; or, whether the popular axiom of Queen
Elizabeth, that as her greatest treasure was in the hearts of her people,
so she had rather her money should be in their purses than in her own
Exchequer, (which she never said but at the closing of some Parliament,
when she had gotten all she could from them,) was grown current
policy; or whether all these together contributed thereunto, I know
not; but I am sure the oversight or the misfortune proved very fatal.
For as the Crown never advanced itself by any remarkable attempt that
depended wholly upon the bounty of the people, so it never suffered
from abroad or at home when the Exchequer was plentifully supplied,
what circumstances soever had accompanied or attended that plenty.

And without doubt, if such provision had been made, the disjointed affections and dispositions of that time had not been so apt to lay hold [of] and countenance the first interruption: and the first possible opportunity of interruption they did lay hold of. [*HR*, I, 147–65]

In 1633, Charles I visited Scotland for his coronation in his northern kingdom. He also planned to promote a set of ecclesiastical reforms designed to draw the liturgy and ceremonial of the Scottish Church closer to those of the Church of England. The clergy and laity of the Scottish Church, more Calvinist and Presbyterian than the Church of England, had already, in the reign of James I, strongly resisted the strengthening of the authority of bishops, and changes to the liturgy. Charles was persuaded to delay the reforms, but he nevertheless established a committee to draw up a new liturgy. Accompanying the King on his journey, and closely involved in the reforms, had been the Bishop of London, William Laud. Soon after his return, Laud's already powerful influence over the English Church was extended further.

It was about the end of August in the year 1633 when the King returned from Scotland to Greenwich, where the Queen kept her Court; and the first accident of moment that happened after his coming thither was the death of Abbot, archbishop of Canterbury;* who had sat too many years in that see, and had too great a jurisdiction over the Church, though he was without any credit in the Court from the death of King James, and had not much in many years before. He had been head or master of one of the poorest colleges in Oxford, and had learning sufficient for that province. He was a man of very morose manners and a very sour aspect, which in that time was called gravity; and under the opinion of that virtue, and by the recommendation of the earl of Dunbar, (the King's first Scotch favourite,) he was preferred by King James to the bishopric of Coventry and Litchfield, and presently after to London, before he had ever been parson, vicar, or curate of any parish-church in England, or dean or prebend of any cathedral church, and was in truth totally ignorant of the true constitution of the Church of England, and the state and interest of the clergy; as sufficiently appeared throughout the whole course of his life afterward.

He had scarce performed any part of the office of a bishop in the diocese of London when he was snatched from thence and promoted to Canterbury, upon the never enough lamented death of Dr Bancroft,* that metropolitan who understood the Church excellently, and had almost rescued it out of the hands of the Calvinian party, and very much subdued the unruly spirit of the Non-conformists, by and after the conference at Hampton Court;* countenanced men of the greatest parts in learning, and disposed the clergy to a more solid course of study than they had been accustomed to; and if he had lived would quickly have extinguished all that fire in England which had been kindled at Geneva;* or if he had been succeeded by bishop Andrewes, bishop Overall,* or any man who understood and loved the Church, that infection would easily have been kept out which could not afterwards be so easily expelled.

But Abbot brought none of this antidote with him, and considered Christian religion no otherwise than as it abhorred and reviled Popery, and valued those men most who did that most furiously. For the strict observation of the discipline of the Church, or the conformity to the Articles or Canons established, he made little inquiry and took less care; and having himself made a very little progress in the ancient and solid study of divinity, he adhered wholly to the doctrine of Calvin, and, for his sake, did not think so ill of the discipline as he ought to have done, but if men prudently forbore a public reviling and railing at the hierarchy and ecclesiastical government, let their opinions and private practice be what it would, they were not only secure from any inquisition of his but acceptable to him, and at least equally preferred by him. And though many other bishops plainly discerned the mischiefs which daily brake in to the prejudice of religion by his defects and remissness, and prevented it in their own dioceses as much as they could, and gave all their countenance to men of other parts and other principles; and though the bishop of London (Dr Laud) from the time of his authority and credit with the King had applied all the remedies he could to those defections, and from the time of his being Chancellor of Oxford had much discountenanced and almost suppressed that spirit by encouraging another kind of learning and practice in that university, which was indeed according to the doctrine of the Church of England; yet that temper in the archbishop, whose house was a sanctuary to the most eminent of that factious party, and who licensed their most pernicious writings, left his successor a very difficult work to do, to reform and reduce a Church into order that had been so long neglected, and that was so ill inhabited by many weak and more wilful churchmen.

It was within one week after the King's return from Scotland that Abbot died at his house at Lambeth. And the King took very little time to consider who should be his successor, but the very next time the bishop of London (who was longer upon his way home than the King had been) came to him, his majesty entertained him very cheerfully with this compellation, 'My lord's grace of Canterbury, you are very welcome,' and gave order the same day for the despatch of all the necessary forms for the translation: so that within a month or thereabouts after the death of the other archbishop he was completely invested in that high dignity, and settled in his palace at Lambeth. This great prelate had been before in great favour with the duke of Buckingham, whose great confidant he was, and by him recommended to the King as fittest to be trusted in the conferring all ecclesiastical preferments, when he was but bishop of St David's or newly preferred to Bath and Wells, and from that time he entirely governed that province without a rival; so that his promotion to Canterbury was long foreseen and expected, nor was it attended with any increase of envy or dislike.

He was a man of great parts, and very exemplar virtues, allayed and discredited by some unpopular natural infirmities; the greatest of which was (besides a hasty, sharp way of expressing himself,) that he believed innocence of heart and integrity of manners was a guard strong enough to secure any man in his voyage through this world, in what company soever he travelled and through what ways soever he was to pass: and sure never any man was better supplied with that provision. He was born of honest parents, who were well able to provide for his education in the schools of learning, from whence they sent him to St John's college in Oxford, the worst endowed at that time of any in that famous university. From a scholar he became a fellow, and then the president of that college, after he had received all the graces and degrees, the proctorship and the doctorship, could be obtained there. He was always maligned and persecuted by those who were of the Calvinian faction, which was then very powerful, and who, according to their useful maxim and practice, call every man they do not love, Papist; and under this senseless appellation they created him many troubles and vexations, and so far suppressed him that, though he was the King's chaplain and taken notice of for an excellent preacher and a scholar of the most sublime parts, he had not any preferment to invite him to leave his poor college, which only gave him bread, till the vigour of his age was past: and when he was promoted by King James, it was but to a poor bishopric in Wales, which was not so good a support for a bishop as his college was for a private scholar, though a doctor.

Parliaments in that time were frequent, and grew very busy; and the party under which he had suffered a continual persecution appeared very powerful and full of design, and they who had the courage to oppose them began to be taken notice of with approbation and countenance: and under this style he came to be first cherished by the duke of Buckingham, after he had made some experiments of the temper and spirit of the other people, nothing to his satisfaction. From this time he prospered at the rate of his own wishes, and being transplanted out of his cold barren diocese of St David's into a warmer climate, he was left, as was said before, by that omnipotent favourite in that great trust with the King, who was sufficiently indisposed towards the persons or the principles of Mr Calvin's disciples.

When he came into great authority, it may be he retained too keen a memory of those who had so unjustly and uncharitably persecuted him before, and, I doubt, was so far transported with the same passions he had reason to complain of in his adversaries, that, as they accused him of Popery because he had some doctrinal opinions which they liked not, though they were nothing allied to Popery, so he entertained too much prejudice to some persons as if they were enemies to the discipline of the Church, because they concurred with Calvin in some doctrinal points, when they abhorred his discipline, and reverenced the government of the Church, and prayed for the peace of it with as much zeal and fervency as any in the kingdom; as they made manifest in their lives, and in their sufferings with it and for it. He had, from his first entrance into the world, without any disguise or dissimulation, declared his own opinion of that *classis* of men; and as soon as it was in his power he did all he could to hinder the growth and increase of that faction, and to restrain those who were inclined to it from doing the mischief they desired to do. But his power at Court could not enough qualify him to go through with that difficult reformation whilst he had a superior in the Church, who, having the reins in his hand, could slacken them according to his own humour and indiscretion, and was thought to be the more remiss to irritate his choleric disposition. But when he had now the primacy in his own hand, the King being inspired with the same zeal, he thought he should be to blame, and have much to answer, if he did not make haste to apply remedies to those diseases which he saw would grow apace. . . .

Though the nation generally, as was said before, was without any ill talent to the Church, either in the point of the doctrine or the discipline, yet they were not without a jealousy that Popery was not enough discountenanced, and were very averse from admitting any thing they had not been used to, which they called *innovation*, and were easily persuaded that any thing of that kind was but to please the Papists. Some doctrinal points in controversy had been in the late years agitated in the pulpits with more warmth and reflections than had used to be; and thence the heat and animosity increased in books *pro* and *con* upon the same arguments: most of the popular preachers, who had not looked into the ancient learning, took Calvin's word for it, and did all they could to propagate his opinions in those points: they who had studied more, and were better versed in the antiquities of the Church, the Fathers, the Councils and the ecclesiastical histories, with the same heat and passion in preaching and writing, defended the contrary.

But because, in the late dispute in the Dutch churches, those opinions were supported by Jacobus Arminius,* the divinity professor in the university of Leyden in Holland, the latter men we mentioned were called Arminians, though many of them had never read word written by Arminius. Either side defended and maintained their different opinions as the doctrine of the Church of England, as the two great orders in the Church of Rome, the Dominicans and Franciscans, did at the same time, and had many hundred years before, with more vehemence and unchar-itableness, maintained the same opinions one against the other; either party professing to adhere to the doctrine of the Catholic Church, which had been ever wiser than to determine the controversy. And yet that party here which could least support themselves with reason were very solicitous, according to the ingenuity they always practise to advance any of their pretences, to have the people believe that they who held with Arminius did intend to introduce Popery; and truly the other side was no less willing to have it thought that all who adhered to Calvin in those controversies did in their hearts adhere likewise to him with reference to the discipline, and desired to change the government of the Church, destroy the bishops, and so set up the discipline that he had established at Geneva. And so both sides found such reception generally with the people as they were inclined to the persons; whereas, in truth, none of the one side were at all inclined to Popery, and very many of the other were most affectionate to the peace and prosperity of the Church, and very pious and learned men.

The archbishop had all his life eminently opposed Calvin's doctrine in those controversies, before the name of Arminius was taken notice of or his opinions heard of; and thereupon, for want of another name, they had called him a Papist, which nobody believed him to be, and he had more manifested the contrary in his disputations and writings than most men had done; and it may be the other found the more severe and rigor-ous usage from him for their propagating that calumny against him. He was a man of great courage and resolution, and being most assured within himself that he proposed no end in all his actions or designs than what was pious and just, (as sure no man had ever a heart more entire to the King, the Church, or his country,) he never studied the best ways to those ends; he thought, it may be, that any art or industry that way would discredit, at least make the integrity of the end suspected. Let the cause be what it will, he did court persons too little; nor cared to make his designs and purposes appear as candid as they were by shewing them in any other dress than their own natural beauty and roughness; and did not consider enough what men said or were like to say of him. If the faults and vices were fit to be looked into and discovered, let the persons be who they would that were guilty of them, they were sure to find no connivance of favour from him. He intended the discipline of the Church should be felt, as well as spoken of, and that it should be applied to the greatest and most splendid transgressors, as well as to the punishment of smaller offences and meaner offenders; and thereupon called for or cherished the discovery of those who were not careful to cover their own iniquities, thinking they were above the reach of other men, or their power and will to chastise. Persons of honour and great quality, of the Court and of the country, were every day cited into the High Commission court,* upon the fame of their incontinence, or other scandal in their lives, and were there prosecuted to their shame and punishment: and as the shame (which they called an insolent triumph upon their degree and quality, and levelling them with the common people) was never forgotten, but watched for revenge, so the fines imposed there were the more questioned and repined against because they were assigned to the rebuilding and repairing St Paul's church,* and thought therefore to be the more severely imposed, and the less compassionately reduced and excused; which likewise made the jurisdiction and rigour of the Star Chamber more felt and murmured against, which sharpened many men's humours against the bishops before they had any ill intention towards the Church.

There were three persons most notorious for their declared malice against the government of the Church by bishops in their several books and writings, which they had published to corrupt the people, with circumstances very scandalous and in language very scurrilous and impudent, which all men thought deserved very exemplary punishment. They were of three several professions which had the most influence upon the people, a divine, a common lawyer, and a doctor of physic;* neither of them of interest or any esteem with the worthy part of their several professions, having been formerly all looked upon under characters of reproach: yet when they were all sentenced, and for the execution of that sentence brought out to be punished as common and signal rogues, exposed upon scaffolds to have their ears cut off and their faces and foreheads branded with hot irons, as the poorest and most mechanic malefactors used to be when they were not able to redeem themselves by any fine for their trespasses or to satisfy any damages for the scandals they had raised against the good name and reputation of others, men began no more to consider their manners, but the men; and every profession, with anger and indignation enough, thought their education and degrees and quality would have secured them from such infamous judgments, and treasured up wrath for the time to come.

The remissness of Abbot, and of other bishops by his example, had introduced, or at least connived at, a negligence that gave great scandal to the Church, and no doubt offended very many pious men. The people took so little care of the churches, and the parsons as little of the chancels, that, instead of beautifying or adorning them in any degree, they rarely provided for their stability and against the very falling of very many of their churches; and suffered them, at least, to be kept so indecently and slovenly that they would not have endured it in the ordinary offices of their own houses; the rain and the wind to infest them, and the Sacraments themselves to be administered where the people had most mind to receive them. This profane liberty and uncleanliness the archbishop resolved to reform with all expedition, requiring the other bishops to concur with him in so pious a work; and the work sure was very grateful to all men of devotion; yet, I know not how, the prosecution of it, with too much affectation of expense, it may be, or with too much passion between the minister and the parishioners, raised an evil spirit towards the Church, which the enemies of it took much advantage of as soon as they had opportunity to make the worst use of it.

The removing the Communion table out of the body of the church, where it had used to stand and used to be applied to all uses, and fixing it to one place in the upper end of the chancel, which frequently made the buying a new table to be necessary; the inclosing it with a rail of joiner's work, and thereby fencing it from the approach of dogs, and all servile uses; the obliging all persons to come up to those rails to receive the Sacrament; how acceptable soever to grave and intelligent persons who loved order and decency, (for acceptable it was to such,) yet introduced, first, murmurings amongst the people, upon the very charge and expense of it, and, if the minister were not a man of discretion and reputation to compose and reconcile those indispositions, (as too frequently he was not, and rather inflamed and increased the distemper,) it begat suits and appeals at law. The opinion that there was no necessity of doing any thing, and the complaint that there was too much done, brought the power and jurisdiction to impose the doing of it to be called in question, contradicted, and opposed. Then the manner and gesture and posture in the celebration of it brought in new disputes, and administered new subjects of offence, according to the custom of the place and humour of the people; and those disputes brought in new words and terms (*altar*, and *adoration*, and *genuflexion*, and other expressions) for the more perspicuous carrying on those disputations; new books were written for and against this new practice, with the same earnestness and contention for victory as if the life of Christianity had been at stake. There was not an equal concurrence in the prosecution of this matter amongst the bishops themselves; some of them proceeding more remissly in it, and some not only neglecting to direct any thing to be done towards it, but restraining those who had a mind to it from meddling in it. And this again produced as inconvenient disputes, when the subordinate clergy would take upon them not only without the direction of, but expressly against, the diocesan's injunctions, to make those alterations and reformations themselves, and by their own authority.

The archbishop, guided purely by his zeal and reverence for the place of God's service, and by the canons and injunctions of the Church, with the custom observed in the King's chapel and in most cathedral churches, without considering the long intermission and discontinuance in many other places, prosecuted this affair more passionately than was fit for the season, and had prejudice against those who, out of fear or foresight or not understanding the thing, had not the same warmth to promote it. The bishops who had been preferred by his favour, or hoped to be so, were at least as solicitous to bring it to pass in their several dioceses, and some of them with more passion and less circumspection than they had his example for or than he approved; prosecuting those who opposed them very fiercely, and sometimes unwarrantably, which was kept in remembrance. Whilst other bishops, not so many in number or so valuable in weight, who had not been beholding to [him] nor had hope of being so, were enough contented to give perfunctory orders for the doing it and to see the execution of those orders not intended, and not the less pleased to find that the prejudice of that whole transaction reflected solely upon the archbishop.

The bishop of Lincoln (Williams) who had been heretofore Lord Keeper of the Great Seal of England, and the most generally abominated whilst he had been so, was, since his disgrace at Court and prosecution from thence, become very popular; and having faults enough to be ashamed of, the punishment whereof threatened him every day, he was very willing to change the scene, and to be brought upon the stage for opposing these *innovations* (as he called them) in religion. It was an unlucky word, and cozened very many honest men into apprehensions very prejudicial to the King and to the Church. He published a discourse and treatise* against the matter and manner of the prosecution of that matter; a book so full of good learning, and that learning so close and solidly applied, (though it abounded with too many light expressions,) that it gained him reputation enough to be able to do hurt, and shewed that in his retirement he had spent his time with his books very profitably. He used all the wit and all the malice he could to awaken the people to a jealousy of these agitations and innovations in the exercise of religion; not without insinuations that it aimed at greater alterations, for which he knew the people would quickly find a name; and he was ambitious to have it believed that the archbishop was his greatest enemy for his having constantly opposed his rising to any government in the Church, as a man whose hot and hasty spirit he had long known.

Though there were other books written with good learning, and which sufficiently answered the bishop's book, and to men of equal and dispassionate inclinations fully vindicated the proceedings which had been and were still very fervently carried on, yet it was done by men whose names were not much reverenced by many men, and who were taken notice of with great insolence and asperity to undertake the defence of all things which the people generally were displeased with, and who did not affect to be much cared for by those of their own order. So that from this unhappy subject, not in itself of that important value to be either entered upon with that resolution or to be carried on with that passion, proceeded upon the matter a schism among the bishops themselves, and a world of uncharitableness in the learned and moderate clergy towards one another: which, though it could not increase the malice, added very much to the ability and power of the enemies of the Church to do it hurt, and added to the number of them. For, without doubt, many who loved the established government of the Church and the exercise of religion as it was used, and desired not a change in either, nor did dislike the order and decency which they saw mended, yet they liked not any novelties, and so were liable to entertain jealousies that more was intended than was hitherto proposed; especially when those infusions proceeded from men unsuspected to have any inclinations to change, and from known assertors of the government both in Church and State. They did observe the inferior clergy took more upon them than they had used to do, and did not live towards their neighbours of quality or their patrons themselves with that civility and condescension they had used to do; which disposed them likewise to a withdrawing their good countenance and good neighbourhood from them. [*HR*, I, 185–202]

2. The Scottish Covenant and the Short Parliament

Following his return from Scotland in 1633, Charles I continued to press for reforms in the Scottish Church. The Canons (or orders for the government of the Church) and Liturgy drafted by the Scottish bishops were amended by Laud and two other bishops in England, and then promulgated in Scotland. Clarendon's account of the reaction in Scotland, and the Short Parliament in 1640, was written as part of his Life *in 1668–9. It was later incorporated into the* History of the Rebellion.

IT was about the month of July in the year 1637 that the Liturgy (after it had been sent out of Scotland, and perused by the three bishops in England, and then approved and confirmed by the King) was published, and appointed to be read in all the churches. And in this particular there was the same affected and premeditated omission as had been in the preparation and publication of the Canons; the clergy not at all consulted in it, and, which was more strange, not all the bishops acquainted with it, which was less censured afterwards when some of them renounced their function and became ordinary presbyters, as soon as they saw the current of the time. The Privy Council had no other notice of it than all the kingdom had, the Sunday before,* when it was declared that the next Sunday the Liturgy should be read; by which they were the less concerned to foresee or prevent any obstructions which might happen.

The proclamation had appointed it to be read the Easter before,* but the earl of Traquair, High Treasurer of Scotland, (who was the only counsellor or layman relied upon by the archbishop of Canterbury in that business) persuaded the King to defer it till July, that some good preparation might be made for the more cheerful reception of it. And as this pause gave the discontented party more heart and more time for their seditious negociations, so the ill consequences of it, or the actions which were subsequent to it, made him suspected to be privy to all the conspiracy, and in truth to be an enemy to the Church; though, in truth, there neither appeared then, nor in all the very unfortunate part of his life afterwards, any just ground for that accusation and suspicion: but as he was exceedingly obliged to the archbishop, so he was a man of great parts, and well affected to the work in hand in his own judgment; and if he had been as much depended upon to have advised the bishops in the prosecution and for the conduct of it, as he was to assist them in the carrying on whatsoever they proposed, it is very probable that either so much would not have been undertaken together, or that it would have succeeded better; for he was without doubt not inferior to any man of that nation in wisdom and dexterity. And though he was often provoked by the insolence and petulance of some of the bishops to a dislike of their overmuch fervour and too little discretion, his integrity to the King was without blemish, and his affection to the Church so notorious that he never deserted it till both it and he were overrun and trod under foot; and they who were the most notorious persecutors of it never left persecuting him to the death.

Nor was any thing done which he had proposed for the better adjusting things in that time of that suspension, but every thing left in the same state of unconcernedness as it had been hitherto, not so much as the Council being better informed of it; as if they had been sure that all men would have submitted to it for conscience sake.

On the Sunday morning appointed for the work,* the Chancellor of Scotland and others of the Council being present in the cathedral church, the dean began to read the Liturgy, which he had no sooner entered upon but a noise and clamour was raised throughout the church that no voice could be heard distinctly, and then a shower of stones and sticks and cudgels were thrown at the dean's head. The bishop went up into the pulpit, and from thence put them in mind of the sacredness of the place, of their duty to God and the King: but he found no more reverence, nor was the clamour or disorder less than before. The Chancellor, from his seat, commanded the provost and magistrates of the city to descend from the gallery in which they sat and by their authority to suppress the riot; which at last with great difficulty they did, by driving out the rudest of those who made the disturbance out of the church and shutting the doors, which gave the dean occasion to proceed in the reading of the Liturgy, which was not at all intended or hearkened to by those who remained within the church; and if it had, they who were turned out continued their barbarous noise, brake the windows, and endeavoured to break down the doors; so that it was not possible for any to follow their devotion.

When all was done that at that time could be done there, and the Council and magistrates went out of the church to their houses, the rabble followed the bishops with all the opprobrious language they could invent, of bringing in superstition and Popery into the kingdom, and making the people slaves; and were not content to use their tongues, but employed their hands too in throwing dirt and stones at them, and treated the bishop of Edinburgh, (whom they looked upon as most active that way,) so rudely that with great difficulty he got into a house after they had torn his habit, and was from thence removed to his own with great hazard of his life. As this was the reception it had in the cathedral, so it fared not better in the other churches in the city, but was entertained with the same hollowing and outcries, and threatening the men whose office it was to read it, with the same bitter execrations against bishops and Popery.

Hitherto no person of condition or name appeared, or seemed to countenance this seditious confusion; it was the rabble, of which nobody was named, and, which is more strange, not one apprehended: and it seems the bishops thought it not of moment enough to desire or require any help or protection from the Council, but, without conferring with them or applying themselves to them, they despatched away an express to the King with a full and particular information of all that had passed, and a desire that he would take that course he thought best for the carrying on his service.

Until this advertisement arrived from Scotland there were very few in England who had heard of any disorders there, or of any thing done there which might produce any. The King himself had been always so jealous of the privileges of that his native kingdom, (as hath been touched before,) and that it might not be dishonoured by a suspicion of having any dependence upon England, that he never suffered any thing relating to that to be debated or so much as communicated to his Privy Council in this, (though many of that nation were, without distinction, Councillors of England,) but handled all those affairs himself with two or three Scotchmen who always attended in the Court for the business of that kingdom, which was upon the matter still despatched by the sole advice and direction of the marquis of Hamilton.

And the truth is, there was so little curiosity either in the Court or the country to know any thing of Scotland, or what was done there, that when the whole nation was solicitous to know what passed weekly in Germany and Poland and all other parts of Europe, no man ever inquired what was doing in Scotland, nor had that kingdom a place or mention in one page of any gazette, so little the world heard or thought of that people; and even after the advertisement of this preamble to rebellion, no mention was made of it at the Council-board, but such a despatch made into Scotland upon it as expressed the King's dislike and displeasure and obliged the lords of the Council there to appear more vigorously in the vindication of his authority and suppression of those tumults. But all was too little. That people, after they had once begun, pursued the business vigorously, and with all imaginable contempt of the government; and though in the hubbub of the first day there appeared nobody of name or reckoning, but the actors were really of the dregs of the people, yet they discovered by the countenance of that day that few men of rank were forward to engage themselves in the quarrel on the behalf of the bishops; whereupon more considerable persons every day appeared against them, and, as heretofore in the case of St Paul, (Acts xiii. 50,) *the Jews stirred up the devout and honourable women*, the women and ladies of the best quality declared themselves of the party, and with all the reproaches imaginable made war upon the bishops as introducers of Popery and superstition, against which they avowed themselves to be irreconcilable enemies: and their husbands did not long defer the owning the same spirit; insomuch as within few days the bishops durst not appear in the streets nor in any courts or houses, but were in danger of their lives; and such of the lords as durst be in their company, or seemed to desire to rescue them from violence, had their coaches torn in pieces and their persons assaulted, insomuch as they were glad to send for some of those great men who did indeed govern the rabble though they appeared not in it, who readily came and redeemed them out of their hands. So that by the time new orders came from England, there was scarce a bishop left in Edinburgh, and not a minister who durst read the Liturgy in any church.

All the kingdom flocked to Edinburgh, as in a general cause that concerned their salvation, and resolved themselves into a method of government, erected several Tables,* in which deputies sat for the nobility, the gentlemen, the clergy, and the burgesses; out of either of which Tables a council was elected to conduct their affairs, and a petition drawn up in the names of the nobility, lairds, clergy, and burgesses, to the King, complaining of the introduction of Popery, and many other grievances. And if the Lords of the Council issued out any order against them, or if the King himself sent a proclamation for their repair to their houses and for the preservation of peace, presently some nobleman deputed by the Tables published a protestation against those orders and proclamations, with the same confidence and with as much formality as if the government were regularly in their hands.

They called a General Assembly,* whither they summoned the bishops to appear before them, and for not appearing excommunicated them; and then they united themselves by subscribing a Covenant,* which they pretended, with their usual confidence, to be no other than had been subscribed in the reign of King James, and that his majesty himself had subscribed it; by which imposition people of all degrees, supposing it might be a means to extinguish the present fire, with all alacrity engaged themselves in it; whereas, in truth, they had inserted a clause never heard of, and quite contrary to the end of that Covenant, whereby they obliged themselves to pursue the extirpation of bishops,* and had the impudence to demand the same in express terms of the King, in answer to a very gracious message the King had sent to them. They published bitter invectives against the bishops and the whole government of the Church, which they were not contented to send only into England to kindle the same fire there, but, with their letters, sent them to all the Reformed Churches, by which they raised so great a prejudice to the King that too many of them believed that the King had a real design to change religion and to introduce Popery.

It is very true there were very many of the nobility and persons of principal quality of that nation, and in Edinburgh at that time, who did not appear yet, and concur in this seditious behaviour, or own their being yet of their party, but on the contrary seemed very much to dislike their proceedings: but it is as true that very few had the courage to do any thing in opposition of them, or to concur in the prosecution of any regal act against them; and did in some respects more advance their designs than if they had manifestly joined with them. For these men, many of whom were of the Council, by all their letters into England exceedingly undervalued the disorder, as being very easy to be suppressed in a short time when the people's eyes should be opened, and that the removing the courts to some other place, and a gracious condescension in the King in offering pardon for what was past, would suddenly subdue them, and every body would return to his duty. And the city of Edinburgh itself writ an humble letter to the archbishop of Canterbury himself, excusing the disorders which had been raised by the ignorance and rudeness of the meanest of the people, besought him to intercede with his majesty for the suspension of his prejudice to them, till they should manifest their duty to him by taking exemplary punishment upon the chief offenders, and causing the Liturgy to be received and submitted to in all their churches, which they professed they would in a short time bring to pass. So that by this means, and the interposition of all those of that nation who attended upon his majesty in his bed-chamber and in several offices at Court, who all undertook to know by their intelligences that all was quiet or would speedily be so, his majesty (who well knew that they who appeared most active in this confederacy were much inferior to those who did not appear, and who professed great zeal for his service) hardly prevailed with himself to believe that he could receive any disturbance from thence till he found all his condescensions had raised their insolence, all his offers rejected, and his proclamation of pardon slighted and contemned; and that they were listing men towards the raising an army under the obligation of their Covenant, and had already chosen colonel Leslie, a soldier of that nation of long experience and eminent command under the king of Sweden in Germany, to be their general; who, being lately disobliged (as they called it) by the King, that is, denied somewhat he had a mind to have, which to that people was always the highest injury, had accepted of the command. Then the King thought it time to resort to other counsels, and to provide force to chastise them who had so much despised all the gentler remedies.

He could now no longer defer the acquainting his Council-board and the whole kingdom of England with the indignities he had sustained in Scotland, which he did by Proclamations and Declarations at large,* setting out the whole proceedings which had been; and in the end of the year 1638 declared his resolution to raise an army to suppress their rebellion, for which he gave present order.

And this was the first alarm England received towards any trouble, after it had enjoyed for so many years the most uninterrupted prosperity, in a full and plentiful peace, that any nation could be blessed with: and as there was no apprehension of trouble from within, so it was secured from without by a stronger fleet at sea than the nation had ever been acquainted with, which drew reverence from all the neighbour princes. The revenue had been so well improved and so warily managed that there was money in the exchequer proportionable for the undertaking any noble enterprise: nor did this first noise of war and approach towards action seem to make any impression upon the minds of men, the Scots being in no degree either loved or feared by the people; and most men hoped that this would free the Court from being henceforth troubled with those vermin, and so seemed to embrace the occasion with notable alacrity. And there is no doubt but if that whole nation had been entirely united in the rebellion, and all who stayed in the Court had marched in their army and publicly owned the Covenant which in their hearts they adored, neither King nor kingdom could have sustained any damage by them, but the monument of their presumption and their shame would have been raised together, and no other memory preserved of their rebellion but in their memorable overthrow and infamous defeat.

God Almighty would not suffer this discerning spirit of wisdom to govern at this time. The King thought it unjust to condemn a nation for the transgression of a part of it, and still hoped to redeem it from the infamy of a general defection by the exemplar fidelity of a superior party, and therefore withdrew not his confidence from any of those who attended his person, and who, in truth, lay leiger* for the Covenant, and kept up the spirits of their countrymen by their intelligence. [*HR*, II, 11–24]

The King marched north with his army in March 1639, and set up camp outside Berwick, at the Birks, at the end of May. The Marquess of Hamilton's half-hearted attempt to land troops by sea to combat the Covenanters failed dismally, and the hastily gathered and poorly paid English army seemed unlikely to withstand the Covenanting army. The Scots, recognizing the lack of enthusiasm for the war in England, approached the commanders of the English army—the earls of Arundel, Essex, and Holland—to offer talks. Charles agreed in early June, and a treaty was signed at Berwick on the 18th.

Whosoever will take upon him to relate all that passed in that treaty, must be beholding to his own invention; the most material matters having passed in discourse, and very little was committed in writing. Nor did any two who were present agree in the same relation of what was said and done, and, which was worse, not in the same interpretation of the meaning of what was comprehended in writing. An agreement was made, if that can he called an agreement in which nobody meant what others believed he did: the armies were to be disbanded; an Act of Oblivion passed; the King's forts and castles to be restored; and an Assembly and Parliament to be called for a full settlement; no persons reserved for justice, because no fault had been committed. The King's army, by the very words of the agreement, was not to be disbanded until all should be executed on their part, and the King himself at that time resolved to be present in the Assembly at least, if not the Parliament. But the impatience of all was such for peace that the King's army was presently disbanded; his majesty making all possible haste himself to London, and sending the earl of Traquair to Edinburgh, to prepare all things for the Assembly; whilst the Scots made all the caresses to many of the English, and breathed out in mutual confidence their resentments to each other.

The marquis of Hamilton (whether upon the fame of the treaty, or sent for by the King, few knew) left his fleet before Leith in a very peaceable posture, and came to the Birks some hours after the treaty was signed; which was very convenient to him, for thereby he was free from the reproach that attended it, and at liberty to find fault with it, which he did freely to the King and to some others, whereby he preserved himself in credit to do more mischief. Many were then of opinion, and still are,

that the marquis at that time was very odious to his countrymen; and it is
certain that the chief managers at the treaty did persuade the English in
whom they most confided that their principal aim was to remove him
from the Court, which was a design willingly heard and universally grateful. But whatever state of grace he stood in when he came thither, he did
himself so good offices before he parted that he was no more in their
disfavour. The King's army was presently disbanded, and the Scots
returned to Edinburgh with all they desired, having gotten many more
friends in England than they had before, kept all their officers and as
many of their men as they thought fit in pay, and prosecuted all those
who had not shewed the same zeal in their Covenant as themselves with
great rigour, as men whose affections they doubted; and, instead of remit-
ting any thing of their rage against the bishops, they entered a public
protestation that they did not intend by any thing contained in the treaty
to vacate any of the proceedings which had been in the late General
Assembly at Glasgow, by which all the bishops stood excommunicated,
and renewed all their menaces against them by proclamation, and
imposed grievous penalties upon all who should presume to harbour any
of them in their houses. So that by the time the King came to London, it
appeared plainly that the army was disbanded without any peace made,
and the Scots in more reputation and equal inclination to affront his
majesty than ever. Upon which a paper published by them, and avowed
to contain the matter of the treaty, was burned by the common hangman;*
every body disavowing the contents of it, but nobody taking upon him to
publish a copy that they owned to be true.

The mischief that befell the King from this wonderful atonement
cannot be expressed, nor was it ever discovered what prevailed over his
majesty to bring it so wofully to pass: all men were ashamed who had
contributed to it; nor had he dismissed his army with so obliging
circumstances as was like to incline them to come so willingly together
if there were occasion to use their service. The earl of Essex, who had
merited very well throughout the whole affair, and had never made
a false step in action or in council, was discharged in the crowd, without
ordinary ceremony; and an accident happening at the same time, or
very soon after, by the death of the lord Aston,* whereby the command
of the forest of Needwood fell into the King's disposal, which lay at the
very door of his estate and would infinitely have gratified him, [it] was
denied to him and bestowed upon another: all which wrought very
much upon his rough proud nature, and made him susceptible of some
impressions afterwards which otherwise would not have found such
easy admission.

The factions and animosities at Court were either greater or more visible than they had been before. The earl of Newcastle (who was governor to the Prince,* and one of the most valuable men in the kingdom, in his fortune, in his dependences, and in his qualifications) had at his own charge drawn together a goodly troop of horse of two hundred; which for the most part consisted of the best gentlemen of the north, who were either allied to the earl or of immediate dependence upon him, and came together purely upon his account; and called this troop the Prince of Wales his troop; whereof the earl himself was captain. When the earl of Holland marched with that party into Scotland, the earl of Newcastle accompanied him with that troop, and, upon occasion of some orders, desired that troop, since it belonged to the Prince of Wales, might have some precedence; which the general of the horse refused to grant him, but required him to march in the rank he had prescribed; and the other obeyed it accordingly, but with resentment, imputing it to the little kindness that was between them. But as soon as the army was disbanded, he sent a challenge to the earl of Holland by a gentleman very punctual and well acquainted with those errands, who took a proper season to mention it to him, without a possibility of suspicion. The earl of Holland was never suspected to want courage, yet in this occasion he shewed not that alacrity but that the delay exposed it to notice; and so by the King's authority the matter was composed, though discoursed of with liberty enough to give the whole Court occasion to express their affections to either party.

The King himself was very melancholic, and quickly discerned that he had lost reputation at home and abroad; and those counsellors who had been most faulty, either through want of courage or wisdom, (for at that time few of them wanted fidelity,) never afterwards recovered spirit enough to do their duty, but gave themselves up to those who had so much overwitted them; every man shifting the fault from himself, and finding some friend to excuse him. And it being yet necessary that so infamous a matter should not be covered with absolute oblivion, it fell to secretary Coke's* turn, (for whom nobody cared,) who was then near fourscore years of age, to be made the sacrifice; and, upon pretence that he had omitted the writing what he ought to have done, and inserted somewhat he ought not to have done, he was put out of his office, and within a short time after sir Henry Vane (who was Treasurer of the house) by the dark contrivance of the marquis [of] Hamilton, and by the open and visible power of the Queen, made Secretary of State; which was the only thing that could make the removal of the other old man censured and murmured at. And this was attended again with a declared and unseasonable dislike and displeasure in the Queen against the Lieutenant of Ireland, newly made earl of Strafford, who out of some kindness to the old man, who had been much trusted by him and of use to him, and out of contempt and detestation of Vane, but principally out of a desire to have had that miscarriage expiated by a greater sacrifice, opposed the removal of Secretary Coke with all the interest he could, got it suspended for some time, and put the Queen to the exercise of her full power to perfect her work; which afterwards produced many sad disasters. So that this unhappy Pacification kindled many fires of contention in Court and country, though the flame broke out first again in Scotland.

On the other side, the Scots got so much benefit and advantage by it that they brought all their other mischievous devices to pass with ease, and a prosperous gale in all they went about. They had before no credit abroad in any foreign parts, and so could neither procure arms or ammunition; and though they could lead the people at home, out of the hatred and jealousy of Popery, into unruly tumults, yet they had not authority enough over them to engage them in a firm resolution of rebellion: the opinion of their unquestionable duty and loyalty to the King was that which had given them reputation to affront him: nor durst they yet attempt to lay any tax or imposition upon the people, or to put them to any charge. But after this Pacification they appeared much more considerable abroad and at home; abroad, (where they were without a name and considered by nobody, now that they had brought an army into the field against the King, [and had] gained all they pretended to desire without reproach or blemish,) France, their old ally, looked upon them as good instruments to disturb their neighbours, and Cardinal Richelieu (who had never looked upon the defeat and overthrow at the Isle of Rhé* as any reparation for the attempt and dishonour of the invasion) was very glad of the opportunity of disturbing a rest and quiet which had not been favourable to his designs, and sent an agent privately to Edinburgh, to cherish and foment their unpeaceable inclinations, and received another from thence, who solicited supplies and communicated counsels: he sent them arms and ammunition, and promised them encouragement and assistance proportionable to any enterprise they should frankly engage themselves in. Holland entered into a closer correspondence with them; and they found credit there for a great stock of arms and ammunition, upon security of payment within a year, which security they easily found a way to give. And thus countenanced and supplied, they quickly got credit and power over the people at home; and as soon as they had formed some troops of those who had been listed by them under good officers, (whereof store resorted to them of that nation out of Germany and Sweden,) and assigned pay to them, they made no longer scruple to impose what money they thought fit upon the people, and to levy it with all rigour upon them who refused or expressed any unwillingness to submit to the imposition; and made the residence of any amongst them very uneasy and very insecure who were but suspected by them not to wish well to their proceedings: and so they renewed all those forms for the administration of the government which they had begun in the beginning of the disorders, and which they disclaimed upon making the Pacification; and refused to suffer the King's governor of the castle of Edinburgh (which was put into his hands about the same time) either to repair some works which were newly fallen down, or so much as to buy provision in the town for the food of the garrison.

But that which was the greatest benefit and advantage that accrued unto them from that agreement, and which was worth all the rest, was the conversation they had with the English, with so much reputation that they had persuaded very many to believe that they had all manner of fidelity to the King, and had too much cause to complain of the hard proceedings against them by the power of some of their own countrymen; and the acquaintance they made with some particular lords, to that degree that they did upon the matter agree what was to be done for the future, and how to obstruct any opposition or proceedings by those who were looked upon as enemies by both sides: for none in Scotland more disliked all that was done in Court and the chief actors there than those lords of England did, though they were not so well prepared for an expedient for the cure.

The people of Scotland being now reduced to a more implicit obedience, and nobody daring to oppose the most violent proceedings of the most violent persons in authority, they lost no time, (as hath been said,) to make all preparations for a war they meant to pursue. Most of the King's Privy Council and great ministers, who (though they had not vigorously performed their duty in support of the regal power) till now had been so reserved that they seemed not to approve the disorderly proceeding, now as frankly wedded that interest as any of the leaders, and quickly became the chief of the leaders. [*HR*, II, 50–7]

The Scottish General Assembly formally abolished episcopacy in August 1639. In October, however, the King refused to assent to a consequential Act of the Scottish Parliament, and required the Parliament to be prorogued. A renewal of the war was inevitable. The only practical solution to Charles's

search for finance to resume the war was the summoning of a new English
Parliament, the first to be held since 1629. Elections were held in March
1640. Edward Hyde, a first-time MP, was elected at Wootton Bassett, in
Wiltshire.

When Parliament opened on 13 April, the King and the Lord Keeper set
out the events of the last two years, and asked for sufficient money to raise
an army; once he had that, they said, they would be given the opportunity
to bring forward the grievances of the people. After the election of a
Speaker, the Commons set to work.

The House met always at eight of the clock, and rose at twelve; which
were the old Parliament hours, that the committees, upon whom the
greatest burden of business lay, might have the afternoons for their
preparation and despatch. It was not the custom to enter upon any
important business in the first fortnight, both because many members
used to be absent so long, and because that time was usually thought
necessary for the appointment and nomination of committees, and for
other ceremonies and preparations that were usual: but there was no
regard now to that custom; and the appearance of the members was
very great, there having been a large time between the issuing out of the
writs and the meeting of the Parliament, so that all elections were made
and returned, and every body was willing to fall to the work.

Whilst men gazed upon each other, looking who should begin, (much
the greatest part having never before sat in Parliament), Mr Pym, a man
of good reputation, but much better known afterward, who had been as
long in those assemblies as any man then living, brake the ice;* and, in a
set discourse of above two hours, after mention of the King with the
most profound reverence and commendation of his wisdom and justice,
he observed that by the long intermission of Parliaments many unwarrantable things had been practised, notwithstanding the great virtue of
his majesty: and then enumerated all the projects which had been set on
foot, all the illegal proclamations which had been published and the
proceedings which had been upon those proclamations, the judgment
upon ship-money, and many grievances which related to the ecclesiastical jurisdiction; summing up shortly and sharply all that most reflected
upon the prudence and the justice of the government; concluding,
that he had only laid that scheme before them that they might see how
much work they had to do to satisfy their country, the method and manner of the doing whereof he left to their wisdoms. Mr Grimston*
insisted only on the business of ship-money; the irregular and preposter-
ous engaging the judges to deliver their opinion to the King, and their

being afterwards divided in their judgment; and said he was persuaded
that they who gave their opinions for the legality of it did it against the
dictamen of their own conscience. Peard, a bold lawyer,* of little note,
inveighed more passionately against it, calling it 'an abomination'; upon
which, Herbert the King's Solicitor, with all imaginable address, in
which he then excelled, put them in mind with what candour his majesty
had proceeded in that and all other things which related to the administration of justice to all his people; that, how persuaded soever he was
within himself of the justice as well as necessity of levying ship-money,
he would not send out a writ for the doing thereof till he received the
affirmative advice of all the judges of England; and when the payment
was opposed by a gentleman, (and then he took occasion to stroke and
commend Mr Hampden, who sat under him, for his great temper and
modesty in the prosecution of that suit,) the King was very well contented that all the judges of England should determine the right; that
never any cause had been debated and argued more solemnly before the
judges; who, after long deliberation between themselves, and being
attended with the records, which had been cited on both sides, delivered
each man his opinion and judgment publicly in the court, and so largely
that but two judges argued in a day; and after all this, and a judgment
with that solemnity pronounced for the King, by which the King was
as legally possessed of that right as of any thing else he had, that any
particular man should presume to speak against it with that bitterness,
and to call it *an abomination*, was very offensive and unwarrantable;
and desired that 'that gentleman who had used that expression might
explain himself, and then withdraw.' Very many called him to the bar;
and the Solicitor's discourse was thought to have so much weight in
it that Mr Peard very hardly escaped a severe reprehension: which is
mentioned only that the temper and sobriety of that House may be taken
notice of, and their dissolution, which shortly after fell out, the more
lamented.

Though the Parliament had not sat above six or seven days, and had
managed all their debates and their whole behaviour with wonderful
order and sobriety, the Court was impatient that no advance was yet
made towards a supply; which was foreseen would take up much time
whensoever they went about it, though never so cordially; and therefore they prevailed with the House of Peers, which was more entirely
at the King's disposal, that it would demand a conference with the
House of Commons, and then propose to them, by way of advice,
'That they would begin with giving the King a supply, in regard of the
urgency and even necessity of his affairs, and afterwards proceed upon

their grievances, or any thing else, as they thought fit.' And the House of Peers accordingly did give their advice to this purpose at a conference.* This conference was no sooner reported in the House of Commons than their whole temper seemed to be shaken. It was the undoubted fundamental privilege of the Commons in Parliament that all supplies should have their rise and beginning from them; this had never been infringed or violated, or so much as questioned in the worst times; and that now, after so long intermission of Parliaments that all privileges might be forgotten, the House of Peers should begin with an action their ancestors never attempted, administered too much cause of jealousy of somewhat else that was intended; and so with an unanimous consent they declared it to be 'so high a breach of privilege that they could not proceed upon any other matter until they first received satisfaction and reparation from the House of Peers;' and which the next day they demanded at a conference. The Lords were sensible of their error, which had been foreseen and dissuaded by many of them. They acknowledged the privilege of the Commons as fully as they demanded it, and hoped they had not broken it by offering their advice to them without mentioning the nature of the supply, the proportion, or the manner of raising it, which they confessed belonged entirely to them: in fine, they desired them, 'that this might be no occasion of wasting their time, but that they would proceed their own way, and in their own method, upon the affairs of the kingdom.' This gave no satisfaction; was no reparation; and served their turn who had no mind to give any supply, without discovering any such disaffection which would have got them no credit, the House generally being exceedingly disposed to please the King and to do him service. But this breach of privilege, which was craftily enlarged upon as if it swallowed up all their other privileges and made them wholly subservient to the Peers, was universally resented. A committee was appointed to examine precedents of former times in the case of violation of their privileges by the Lords, though not of that magnitude, and thereupon to prepare a protestation to be sent up to the House of Peers, and to be entered in their own Journal; and in the mean time no proceedings to be in the House upon any public [business], except upon some report from a committee.

After some days had been passed in this manner, and it not being in view when this debate would be at an end, the King thought of another expedient, and sent a message in writing to the Commons by sir Harry Vane, who was now both Secretary of State and Treasurer of the Household, and at that time of good credit there; wherein his majesty took notice, that there was some difference between the two Houses, which retarded the transaction of the great affairs of the kingdom, at a time when a foreign army was ready to invade it: that he heard the payment of ship-money, notwithstanding that it was adjudged his right, was not willingly submitted to by the people; to manifest therefore his good affection to his subjects in general, he made this proposition, that, if the Parliament would grant him twelve subsidies, to be paid in three years in the manner proposed, (that was, five subsidies to be paid the first year, four the second, and three to be paid in the last year,) his majesty would then release all his title or pretence to ship-money for the future, in such a manner as his Parliament should advise.

Though exceptions might have been taken again in point of privilege, because his majesty took notice of the difference between the two Houses, yet that spirit had not then taken so deep root: so that they resolved to enter, the next day after the delivery of it, upon a full debate of his majesty's message; they who desired to obstruct the giving any supply believing they should easily prevail to reject this proposition upon the greatness of the sum demanded, without appearing not to favour the cause in which it was to be employed, which they could not have done with any advantage to themselves, the number of that *classis* of men being then not considerable in the House. It was about the first day of May that the message was delivered, and the next day it was resumed* about nine of the clock in the morning, and the debate continued till four of the clock in the afternoon; which had been seldom used before, but afterwards grew into custom. Many observed, 'that they were to purchase a release of an imposition very unjustly laid upon the kingdom, and by purchasing it they should upon the matter confess it had been just, which no man in his heart acknowledged;' and therefore wished that the judgment might be first examined, and being once declared void, what they should present the King with would appear a gift and not a recompense. But this was rather modestly insinuated than insisted upon, and the greater number reflected more of the proportion demanded, which some of those who were thought very well to understand the state of the kingdom confidently affirmed to be more than the whole stock in money of the kingdom amounted to; which appeared shortly after to be a very gross miscomputation. There were very few, except those of the Court, (who were ready to give all that the King would ask, and indeed had little to give of their own,) who did not believe the sum demanded to be too great, and wished that a less might be accepted, and therefore were willing, when the day was so far spent, that the debate might be adjourned till the next morning; which was willingly consented to by all, and so the House rose. All this agitation had been in a Committee of the whole House, the Speaker having left the chair, to which Mr Lenthall, a lawyer of no eminent account, was called. But there was not in the whole day, in all the variety of contradictions, an offensive or angry word spoken: except only that one private country gentleman, little known, said, he observed that the supply was to be employed in the supporting *bellum episcopale*, which he thought the bishops were fittest to do themselves: but as there was no reply, or notice taken of it, so there was nobody who seconded that envious reflection, nor any other expression of that kind.

The next day as soon as the House met and prayers were read, it resolved again into a Grand Committee, the same person being again called to the chair. It was expected and hoped that there would have been some new message from the King that might have facilitated the debate; but nothing appearing of that kind, the proposition was again read, and men of all sides discoursed much of what had been said before, and many spake with more reflection upon the judgment of ship-money than they had done the day past, and seemed to wish that whatsoever we should give the King should be a free testimony of our affection and duty, without any release of ship-money, which deserved no consideration, but in a short time would appear void and null. And this seemed to agree with the sense of so great a part of the House that Mr Hampden, the most popular man in the House, and the same who had defended the suit against the King in his own name upon the illegality of ship-money, thought the matter ripe for the question, and desired that the question might be put, 'Whether the House would consent to the proposition made by the King as it was contained in the message?' which would have been sure to have found a negative from all who thought the sum too great, or were not pleased that it should be given in recompense of ship-money.

When many called to have this question, sergeant Glanvill, the Speaker, (who sat by amongst the other members whilst the House was in a committee, and hath rarely used to speak in such seasons,) rose up, and in a most pathetical speech, in which he excelled, endeavoured to persuade the House to comply with the King's desire for the good of the nation, and to reconcile him to Parliaments for ever, which this seasonable testimony of their affections would infallibly do. He made it manifest to them how very inconsiderable a sum twelve subsidies amounted to, by telling them that he had computed what he was to pay for those twelve subsidies, and when he named the sum, and he being known to be possessed of a great estate, it seemed not worth any further deliberation. And in the warmth of his discourse, which he plainly discerned made a wonderful impression upon the House, he let fall some sharp expressions against the imposition of ship-money, and the judgment in the point, which he said plainly 'was against law, if he understood what law was,' (who was known to be very learned,) which expression, how necessary and artificial soever to reconcile the affections of the House to the matter in question, very much irreconciled him at Court and to those upon whom he had the greatest dependence.

There was scarce ever a speech that more gathered up and united the inclinations of a popular council to the speaker; and if the question had been presently put it was believed the number of the dissenters would not have appeared great. But, after a short silence, some men who wished well to the main expressed a dislike of the way, so that other men recovered new courage, and called again with some earnestness, 'That the question formerly proposed by Mr Hampden should be put:' which seemed to meet with a concurrence. Mr Hyde then stood up, and desired 'that question might not be put;' said, 'it was a captious question, to which only one sort of men could clearly give their vote, which were they who were for a rejection of the King's proposition and no more resuming the debate upon that subject: but that they who desired to give the King a supply, as he believed most did, though not in such a proportion nor, it may be, in that manner, could receive no satisfaction by that question;' and therefore he proposed, to the end that every man might frankly give his yea or his no, that the question might be put only upon the giving the King a supply: which being carried in the affirmative, another question might be upon the proportion and the manner; and if the first were carried in the negative, it would produce the same effect as the other question proposed by Mr Hampden would do.

This method was received with great approbation, but opposed by others with more than ordinary passion, and diverted by other propositions, which being seconded took much time without pointing to any conclusion. In the end sergeant Glanvill said, 'That there had been a question proposed by his countryman that agreed very well with his sense,' and moved that the gentleman might be called upon to propose it again. Whereupon Mr Hyde stated the case again as he had done, answered somewhat that had been said against it, and moved 'that question might be put.' Whereupon for a long time there was nothing said but a confused clamour and call, 'Mr Hampden's question,' 'Mr Hyde's question,' the call appearing much stronger for the last than the former; and it was generally believed that the question had been put and carried in the affirmative, though it was positively opposed by Herbert the Solicitor General, for what reason no man could imagine if sir H. Vane, the Secretary, had not stood up and said, 'That, as it had been always his custom to deal plainly and clearly with that House in all things, so he could not but now assure them that the putting and carrying that question could be of no use; for that he was most sure, and had authority to tell them so, that if they should pass a vote for the giving the King a supply, if it were not in the proportion and manner proposed in his majesty's message it would not be accepted by him,' and therefore desired that question might be laid aside; which being again urged by the Solicitor General upon the authority of what the other had declared, and the other Privy Councillors saying nothing, though they were much displeased with the Secretary's averment, the business was no more pressed; but it being near five of the clock in the afternoon, and every body weary, it was willingly consented to that the House should be adjourned till the next morning.

Both sir H. Vane and the Solicitor General Herbert, (whose opinion was of more weight with the King than the other's,) had made a worse representation of the humour and affection of the House than it deserved, and undertook to know that if they came together again they would pass such a vote against ship-money as would blast that revenue and other branches of the receipt; which others believed they would not have had the confidence to have attempted, and very few that they would have had the credit to have compassed. What followed in the next Parliament, within less than a year, made it believed that sir H. Vane acted that part maliciously and to bring all into confusion; he being known to have an implacable hatred against the earl of Strafford, Lieutenant of Ireland, whose destruction was then upon the anvil. But what transported the Solicitor, who had none of the ends of the other, could not be imagined, except it was his pride and peevishness when he found that he was like to be of less authority there than he looked to be; and yet he was heard with great attention, though his parts were most prevalent in puzzling and perplexing that discourse he meant to cross. Let their motives be what they would, they two, and they only, wrought so far with the King that, without so much deliberation as the affair was worthy of, his majesty the next morning, which was on the fourth or fifth of May,* not three weeks from their first meeting, sent for the Speaker to attend him, and took care that he should go directly to the House of Peers, upon some apprehension that if he had gone to the House of Commons that House would have entered upon some ingrateful discourse (which they were not inclined to do); and then sending for that House to attend him, the Keeper by his majesty's command dissolved the Parliament.

There could not a greater damp have seized upon the spirits of the whole nation than this dissolution caused, and men had much of the misery in view which shortly after fell out. It could never be hoped that more sober and dispassioned men would ever meet together in that place, or fewer who brought ill purposes with them; nor could any man imagine what offence they had given which put the King to that resolution. But it was observed that in the countenances of those who had most opposed all that was desired by his majesty there was a marvellous serenity, nor could they conceal the joy of their hearts: for they knew enough of what was to come to conclude that the King would be shortly compelled to call another Parliament, and they were as sure that so many grave and unbiassed men would never be elected again.

Within an hour after the dissolving, Mr Hyde met Mr St John, who had naturally a great cloud in his face and very seldom was known to smile, but then had a most cheerful aspect, and seeing the other melancholic, as in truth he was from his heart, asked him, 'What troubled him?' who answered, 'That the same which troubled him, he believed troubled most good men; that in such a time of confusion, so wise a Parliament, which could only have found remedy for it, was so unseasonably dismissed.' The other answered with a little warmth, 'That all was well: and that it must be worse before it could be better; and that this Parliament would never have done what was necessary to be done;' as indeed it would not what he and his friends thought necessary. [*HR*, II, 67–78]

At the fateful meeting of the Privy Council at which the decision was taken to dissolve the Short Parliament, it was also determined on the advice of the Earl of Strafford, but against the will of the Earl of Northumberland, the man the King had appointed as commander of his army, to try once more to suppress the Covenanters. Northumberland fell ill shortly afterwards. Facing widespread discontent over the dissolution, the King found it extremely difficult to obtain money and soldiers for the attempt. Nevertheless, in August he marched north with his poorly equipped and mutinous forces against a threatened pre-emptive invasion of England by the Covenanters. Hyde's account of the 'Second Bishops' War' was written in the Scillies and Jersey in 1646.

The progress in the King's advance for Scotland was exceedingly hindered by the great and dangerous sickness of the earl of Northumberland the general, whose recovery was either totally despaired of by the physician, or pronounced to be expected very slowly, so that there would be no possibility for him to perform the service of the north: whereupon he sent to the King, that he would make choice of another general. And though the lord Conway* in all his letters sent advertisement that the Scots had not advanced their preparations to that degree that they would be able to march that year, yet the King had much better intelligence that they were in readiness to move, and so concluded that it was necessary to send another general; and designed the earl of Strafford for that command, and to leave the forces in Ireland which were raised to make a diversion in Scotland to be governed by the earl of Ormond. The earl of Strafford was scarce recovered from a great sickness, yet was willing to undertake the charge out of pure indignation to see how few men were forward to serve the King with that vigour of mind they ought to do, and knowing well the malicious designs which were contrived against himself, but he would rather serve as lieutenant-general under the earl of Northumberland than that he should resign his commission: and so, with and under that qualification, he made all possible haste towards the north, before he had strength enough for the journey.

And before he could arrive with the army, that infamous, irreparable rout at Newburn* was fallen out; where the enemy marched at a time and place when and where they were expected, through a river deep though fordable, and up a hill where our army was ranged to receive them. Through those difficulties and disadvantages, without giving or taking any blows, (for the five or six men of ours who were killed fell by their cannon before the passing of the river,) they put our whole army to the most shameful and confounding flight that was ever heard of, our foot making no less haste from Newcastle than our horse from Newburn; both leaving the honour and the coal of the kingdom to those who had not confidence enough (notwithstanding the evidence they had seen of our fear) to possess that town in two days after, not believing it possible that such a place, which was able to have waged war with their nation, could be so kindly quit to them: the lord Conway never after turning his face towards the enemy, or doing any thing like a commander, though his troops were quickly brought together again without the loss of a dozen men, and were so ashamed of their flight that they were very willing as well as able to have taken what revenge they would upon the enemy, who were possessed with all the fears imaginable, and could hardly believe their own success till they were assured that the lord Conway with all his army rested quietly in Durham, and then they presumed to enter into Newcastle.

But it seemed afterwards to be a full vindication to the honour of the nation, that, from this infamous defeat at Newburn to the last

entire conquest of Scotland by Cromwell, the Scots' army never performed one signal action against the English, but were always beaten
by great inequality of numbers as oft as they approached towards any
encounter, if they were not supported by English troops.

In this posture the earl of Strafford found the army about Durham,
bringing with him a body much broken with his late sickness, which
was not clearly shaken off, and a mind and temper confessing the dregs
of it, which being marvellously provoked and inflamed with indignation at the late dishonour, rendered him less gracious, that is, less
inclined to make himself so, to the officers upon his entrance into his
first charge; it may be, in that mass of disorder and unsoldierliness not
quickly discerning to whom kindness and respect was justly due. But
those who by this time, no doubt, were retained for that purpose, took
that opportunity to incense the army against him, and so far prevailed
in it that in a short time it was more inflamed against him than against
the enemy, and was willing to have their want of courage imputed to
excess of conscience, and that their being not satisfied in the grounds
of the quarrel was the only cause that they fought no better. And in
this indisposition on all parts, the earl found it necessary to retire with
the army to the skirts of Yorkshire, and himself to York, whither the
King was come, leaving Northumberland and the bishopric of Durham
to be possessed by the victors; who, being abundantly satisfied with
what they never hoped to possess, made no haste to advance their new
conquests. [*HR*, II, 88–91]

*Following the rout at Newburn, the Scots occupied Newcastle and Durham
and demanded that the King summon the English Parliament and that they
should receive a contribution towards the costs of their army. Charles
initially summoned not a full Parliament, but all of the members of the
House of Lords—a 'Great Council'—to meet at York. By the time it
met on 24 September, however, he had accepted that a Parliament was
unavoidable, and he summoned one to meet at Westminster in November.
In the meantime, commissioners from both Scotland and England negotiated at Ripon. A ceasefire was agreed, but the Scots were to remain in the
two northern counties until a final treaty was signed.*

3. The Opening of the Long Parliament

Edward Hyde was returned to the new Parliament for Saltash in Cornwall. It opened on 3 November 1640.

THERE was observed a marvellous elated countenance in most of the members of Parliament before they met together in the house; the same men who six months before were observed to be of very moderate tempers, and to wish that gentle remedies might be applied without opening the wound too wide and exposing it to the air, and rather to cure what was amiss than too strictly to make inquisition into the causes and original of the malady, talked now in another dialect both of things and persons. Mr Hyde, who was returned to serve for a borough in Cornwall, met Mr Pym in Westminster Hall some few days before the Parliament, and conferring together upon the state of affairs, the other told him, [Hyde,] and said, 'that they must now be of another temper than they were the last Parliament; that they must not only sweep the house clean below, but must pull down all the cobwebs which hung in the top and corners, that they might not breed dust and so make a foul house hereafter; that they had now an opportunity to make their country happy, by removing all grievances and pulling up the causes of them by the roots, if all men would do their duties;' and used much other sharp discourse to him to the same purpose: by which it was discerned that the warmest and boldest counsels and overtures would find a much better reception than those of a more temperate allay; which fell out accordingly. And the very first day they met together* in which they could enter upon business, Mr Pym, in a long, formed discourse, lamented the miserable state and condition of the kingdom, aggravated all the particulars which had been done amiss in the government as done and contrived maliciously, and upon deliberation, to change the whole frame, and to deprive the nation of all the liberty and property which was their birthright by the laws of the land, which were now no more considered, but subjected to the arbitrary power of the Privy-Council, which governed the kingdom according to their will and pleasure; these calamities falling upon us in the reign of a pious and virtuous King, who loved his people and was a great lover of justice. And thereupon enlarging in some specious commendation of the nature and goodness of the King, that he might wound him with less suspicion, he said, 'We must inquire from what fountain these waters of bitterness flowed; what persons they were who had so far insinuated themselves into his royal affections as to be able to pervert his excellent judgment, to abuse his name, and wickedly apply his authority to countenance and support their own corrupt designs. Though he doubted there would be many found of this *classis*, who had contributed their joint endeavours to bring this misery upon the nation, yet he believed there was one more signal in that administration than the rest, being a man of great parts and contrivance, and of great industry to bring what he designed to pass; a man who in the memory of many present had sat in that house an earnest vindicator of the laws, and a most zealous assertor and champion for the liberties of the people; but that it was long since he turned apostate from those good affections, and, according to the custom and nature of apostates, was become the greatest enemy to the liberties of his country, and the greatest promoter of tyranny, that any age had produced;' and then named 'the earl of Strafford, Lord Lieutenant of Ireland, and Lord President of the Council established in York for the northern parts of the kingdom: who,' he said, 'had in both places, and in all other provinces wherein his service had been used by the King, raised ample monuments of his tyrannical nature: and that he believed, if they took a short survey of his actions and behaviour, they would find him the principal author and promoter of all those counsels which had exposed the kingdom to so much ruin;' and so instanced some high and imperious actions done by him in England and in Ireland, some proud and over-confident expressions in discourse, and some passionate advices he had given in the most secret councils and debates of the affairs of state; adding some lighter passages of his vanity and amours, that they who were not inflamed with anger and detestation against him for the former might have less esteem and reverence for his prudence and discretion: and so concluded, 'that they would well consider how to provide a remedy proportionable to the disease, and to prevent the farther mischiefs which they were to expect from the continuance of this great man's power and credit with the King and his influence upon his councils.'

From the time that the earl of Strafford was named most men believed that there would be some committee named to receive information of all his miscarriages, and that upon report thereof they would farther consider what course to take in the examination and prosecution thereof: but they had already prepared and digested their business to a riper period.

Mr Pym had no sooner finished his discourse, than sir John Clotworthy* (a gentleman of Ireland, and utterly unknown in England, who was by the contrivance and recommendation of some powerful persons returned to serve for a borough in Devon, that so he might be enabled to act this part against the Lord Lieutenant) made a long and confused relation of his tyrannical carriage in that kingdom; of the army he had raised there to invade Scotland; how he had threatened the Parliament if they granted not such supplies as he required; of an oath he had framed to be administered to all the Scots' nation which inhabited that kingdom, and his severe proceeding against some persons of quality who refused to take that oath; and that he had with great pride and passion publicly declared at his leaving that kingdom, 'If ever he should return to that sword he would not leave a Scotchman to inhabit in Ireland:' with a multitude of very exalted expressions, and some very high actions, in his administration of that government, in which the lives as well as the fortunes of men had been disposed of out of the common road of justice: all which made him to be looked upon as a man very terrible, and under whose authority men would not choose to put themselves.

Several other persons appearing ready to continue the discourse, and the morning being spent, so that, according to the observation of parliament hours, the time of rising being come, an order was suddenly made that the door should be shut, and nobody suffered to go out of the house; which had been rarely practised: care having been first taken to give such advertisement to some of the Lords that that House might likewise be kept from rising; which would very much have broken their measures.

Then sir John Hotham, and some other Yorkshire men who had received some disobligation from the earl in the country, continued the invective, mentioning many particulars of his imperious carriage, and that he had, in the face of the country, upon the execution of some illegal commission, declared, 'that they should find the little finger of the King's prerogative heavier upon them than the loins of the law;' which expression, though upon after-examination it was found to have a quite contrary sense, marvellously increased the passion and prejudice towards him.

In conclusion, after many hours of bitter inveighing, and ripping up the course of his life before his coming to Court and his actions after, it was moved, according to the secret resolution taken before, 'that he might be forthwith impeached of high treason;' which was no sooner mentioned than it found an universal approbation and consent from the whole: nor was there in the whole debate one person who offered to stop the torrent by any favourable testimony concerning the earl's carriage, save only that the lord Falkland, who was very well known to be far from having any kindness for him, when the proposition was made for the present accusing him of high treason, modestly desired the House to consider, 'Whether it would not suit better with the gravity of their proceedings first to digest many of those particulars which had been mentioned, by a committee?' declaring himself to be abundantly satisfied that there was enough to charge him before they sent up to accuse him: which was very ingenuously and frankly answered by Mr Pym, 'That such a delay might probably blast all their hopes, and put it out of their power to proceed farther than they had done already; that the earl's power and credit with the King, and with all those who had most credit with King or Queen, was so great, that when he should come to know that so much of his wickedness was discovered his own conscience would tell him what he was to expect, and therefore he would undoubtedly procure the Parliament to be dissolved rather than undergo the justice of it, or take some other desperate course to preserve himself, though with the hazard of the kingdom's ruin: whereas, if they presently sent up to impeach him of high treason before the House of Peers, in the name and on the behalf of all the Commons of England, who were represented by them, the Lords would be obliged in justice to commit him into safe custody, and so sequester him from resorting to Council or having access to his majesty: and then they should proceed against him in the usual form with all necessary expedition.'

To those who were known to have no kindness for him, and seemed to doubt whether all the particulars alleged, being proved, would amount to high treason, it was alleged that the House of Commons were not judges but only accusers, and that the Lords were the proper judges whether such a complication of enormous crimes in one person did not amount to the highest offence the law took notice of, and therefore that it was fit to present it to them. These reasons of the haste they made, so clearly delivered, gave that universal satisfaction, that, without farther considering the injustice and unreasonableness of it, they voted unanimously,* (for aught appeared to the contrary by any avowed contradiction,) 'That they would forthwith send up to the Lords and accuse the earl of Strafford of high treason and several other crimes and misdemeanours, and desire that he might be presently sequestered from Council, and committed to safe custody;' and Mr Pym was made choice of for the messenger to perform that office. And this being determined, the doors were opened, and most of the House accompanied him on the errand. . . .

When this work was so prosperously over they began to consider that, notwithstanding all the industry that had been used to procure such members to be chosen, or returned though not chosen, who had been most refractory to the government of the Church and State, yet that the House was so constituted that when the first heat (which almost all men brought with them) should be a little allayed, violent counsels would not be long hearkened to: and therefore, as they took great care by their committee of elections to remove as many of those members as they suspected not to be inclinable to their passions upon pretence that they were not regularly chosen, that so they might bring in others more compliable in their places; (in which no rule of justice was so much as pretended to be observed by them, insomuch as it was often said by leading men amongst them, 'That they ought in those cases of elections to be guided by the fitness and worthiness of the person, whatever the desire of those was in whom the right of election remained;' and therefore one man hath been admitted upon the same rule by which another hath been rejected:) so they declared,* that no person, how lawfully and regularly soever chosen and returned, should be and sit as a member with them who had been a party or a favourer of any project, or who had been employed in any illegal commission.

And by this means (contrary to the custom and rights of Parliament) many gentlemen of good quality were removed, in whose places commonly others were chosen of more agreeable dispositions: but in this likewise there was no rule observed; for no person was hereby removed of whom there was any hope that he might be applied to the violent courses which were intended. Upon which occasion the King charged them in one of his Declarations* that when under that notion of projectors they expelled many, they yet never questioned sir H. Mildmay, or Mr Laurence Whitaker, who had been most scandalously engaged in those pressures, though since more scandalously in all enterprises against his majesty; to which never any answer or reply was made.

The next art was to make the severity and rigour of the House as formidable as was possible, and to make as many men apprehend themselves obnoxious to the House as had been in any trust or employment in the kingdom. Thus they passed many general votes concerning ship-money, in which all who had been high sheriffs, and so collected it, were highly concerned; the like sharp conclusions upon all lords lieutenants and their deputies, which were the prime gentlemen of quality in all the counties of England. Then upon some disquisition of the proceedings in the Star-Chamber and at the Council-table, all who concurred in such a sentence, and consented to such an order, were declared criminous and to be proceeded against. So that, in a moment, all the lords of the Council, all who had been deputy lieutenants or high sheriffs during the late years, found themselves within the mercy of these grand inquisitors: and hearing new terms of art, that a complication of several misdemeanours might grow up to treason, and the like, it was no wonder if men desired by all means to get their favour and protection.

When they had sufficiently startled men by these proceedings, and upon half an hour's debate sent up an accusation against the lord archbishop of Canterbury* of high treason, and so removed him likewise from the King's Council, they rested satisfied with their general rules, votes, and orders, without making haste to proceed either against things or persons; being willing rather to keep men in suspense and to have the advantage of their fears, than, by letting them see the worst that could befall them, lose the benefit of their application. For this reason they used their utmost skill to keep off any debate of ship-money, that that whole business might hang like a meteor over the heads of those that were in any degree faulty in it; and it was observable, when, notwithstanding all their diversions, that business was brought into debate, and upon that (which could not be avoided) the lord Finch named as an avowed factor and procurer of that odious judgment, (who, if their rule were true that an endeavour to alter the government by law and to introduce an arbitrary power were treason, was the most notoriously and unexcusably guilty of that crime of any man that could be named) before they would endure the mention of an accusation of high treason, they appointed a committee, with great deliberation and solemnity, to bring in a charge formally prepared, which had not been done in the case of the lord archbishop or the earl of Strafford and then gave him a day to be heard for himself at the House of Commons' bar, and so, against all order, to take notice of what was handled in the House concerning him; and then, finding that by their own rules he would be likewise accused of high treason, they continued the debate so long that the Lords' house was risen, so that the accusation was not carried up till the next morning. And before that time the Lord Keeper (being well informed of all that had passed) had withdrawn himself, and shortly after went into Holland; the lord Littleton, then Chief Justice of the court of Common Pleas, being made Keeper of the Great Seal of England in his place.

About the same time, sir Francis Windebank, one of the principal Secretaries of State, and then a member of the House of Commons, was accused of many transactions on the behalf of the Papists of several natures, (whose extraordinary patron indeed he was,) and, he being then present in the House, several warrants under his own hand were produced for the discharge of prosecutions against priests and for the release of priests out of prison; whereupon, whilst the matter should be debated, according to custom he was ordered to withdraw, and so went into the usual place, the committee-chamber; immediately whereupon, the House of Commons went to a conference with the Lords upon some other occasion, and returning from that conference, no more resumed the debate of the Secretary, but, having considered some other business, rose at their usual hour. And so the Secretary had liberty to go to his own house, from whence, observing the disposition of the House, and well knowing what they were able to say against him, he had no more mind to trust himself in that company, but the same night withdrew himself* from any place where inquiry might be made for him, and was no more heard of till the news came of his being landed in France.

So that within less than six weeks, for no more time was yet elapsed, these terrible reformers had caused the two greatest counsellors of the kingdom, and whom they most feared and so hated, to be removed from the King and imprisoned under an accusation of high treason, and frighted away the Lord Keeper of the Great Seal of England and one of the principal Secretaries of State into foreign kingdoms, for fear of the like; besides the preparing all the lords of the Council, and very many of the principal gentlemen throughout England, who (as was said before) had been high sheriffs and deputy lieutenants, to expect such measure of punishment from their general votes and resolutions as their future demeanour should draw upon them for their past offences; by which means, they were like to find no very vigorous resistance or opposition in their farther designs. [*HR*, III, 3–17]

It will not be impertinent nor unnatural to this present discourse, to set down in this place the present temper and constitution of both Houses of Parliament, that it may be the less wondered at that so prodigious an alteration should be made in so short a time, and the Crown fallen so low that it could neither support itself and its own majesty nor them who would appear faithful to it.

Of the House of Peers, the great contrivers and designers were:— The earl of Bedford, a wise man, and of too great and plentiful a fortune to wish a subversion of the government; and it quickly appeared, that he only intended to make himself and his friends great at Court, not at all to lessen the Court itself:—

The lord viscount Saye, a man of a close and reserved nature, of a mean and a narrow fortune, of great parts and of the highest ambition, but whose ambition would not be satisfied with offices and preferment without some condescensions and alterations in ecclesiastical matters. He had for many years been the oracle of those who were called Puritans in the worst sense, and steered all their counsels and designs. He was a notorious enemy to the Church and to most of the eminent churchmen, with some of whom he had particular contests. He had always opposed and contradicted all acts of state and all taxes and impositions which were not exactly legal, and so had as eminently and as obstinately refused the payment of ship-money as Mr Hampden had done; though the latter by the choice of the King's Council had brought his cause to be first heard and argued, with which judgment, that was intended to conclude the whole right in that matter and to overrule all other cases, the lord Saye would not acquiesce, but pressed to have his own case argued, and was so solicitous in person with all the judges, both privately at their chambers and publicly in the courts at Westminster, that he was very grievous to them. His commitment at York the year before,* because he refused to take an oath, or rather subscribe a protestation, against holding intelligence with the Scots when the King first marched against them, had given him much credit. In a word, he had very great authority with all the discontented party throughout the kingdom, and a good reputation with many who were not, who believed him to be a wise man, and of a very useful temper in an age of license, and one who would still adhere to the law:—

The lord Mandeville, eldest son to the Lord Privy Seal, was a person of great civility and very well bred, and had been early in the Court under the favour of the duke of Buckingham, a lady of whose family he had married: he had attended upon the Prince when he was in Spain, and had been called to the House of Peers in the lifetime of his father, which was a very extraordinary favour. Upon the death of the duke of Buckingham, his wife being likewise dead, he married the daughter of the earl of Warwick; a man in no grace at Court, and looked upon as the greatest patron of the Puritans because of much the greatest estate of all who favoured them, and so was esteemed by them with great application and veneration, though he was of a life very licentious and unconformable to their professed rigour, which they rather dispensed with than to withdraw from a house where they received so eminent a protection and such notable bounty. From this latter marriage the lord Mandeville totally estranged himself from the Court, and upon all occasions appeared enough to dislike what was done there, and engaged himself wholly in the conversation of those who were most notoriously of that party, whereof there was a kind of fraternity of many persons of good condition, who chose to live together in one family at a gentle-man's house of a fair fortune, near the place where the lord Mandeville lived; whither others of that *classis* likewise resorted, and maintained a joint and mutual correspondence and conversation together with much familiarity and friendship: that lord, to support and the better to improve that popularity, living at a much higher rate than the narrow exhibition* allowed to him by his wary father could justify, malting up the rest by contracting a great debt, which long lay heavy upon him; by which generous way of living, and by his natural civility, good manners, and good nature, which flowed towards all men, he was universally acceptable and beloved; and no man more in the confidence of the discontented and factious party than he, and [none] to whom the whole mass of their designs, as well what remained in chaos as what was formed, was more entirely communicated and consulted with. And therefore these three lords are nominated as the principal agents in the House of Peers, (though there were many there of quality and interest much superior to either of them,) because they were princi-pally and absolutely trusted by those who were to manage all in the House of Commons, and to raise that spirit which was upon all occa-sions to inflame the Lords, [it] being enough known and understood that, how indisposed and angry soever many of them at present appeared to be, there would still be a major part there who would, if they were not overreached, adhere to the King and the established government. And therefore these three persons were trusted without reserve, and relied upon so to steer as might increase their party by all the arts imaginable; and they had dexterity enough to appear to depend upon those lords who were looked upon as greater and as popular men, and to be subservient to their purposes, whom in truth they governed and disposed of.

And by these artifices, and application to his vanity, and magnifying the general reputation and credit he had with the people, and sharpen-ing the sense he had of his late ill treatment at Court, they fully prevailed [upon] and possessed themselves of the earl of Essex; who, though he was no good speaker in public, yet having sat long in Parliament, and so acquainted with the order of it in very active times, was a better speaker there than any where else, and, being always heard with atten-tion and respect, had much authority in the debates. Nor did he need any incitement (which made all approaches to him the more easy) to do any thing against the persons of the lord archbishop of Canterbury and the lord lieutenant of Ireland, towards whom he professed a full dislike; who were the only persons against whom there was any declared design, and the Scots having in their manifesto demanded justice against those two great men as the cause of the war between the nations. And in this prosecution there was too great a concurrence: Warwick, Brooke, Wharton, Paget, Howard,* and some others, implicitly followed and observed the dictates of the lords mentioned before, and started or seconded what they were directed.

In the House of Commons were many persons of wisdom and gravity, who, being possessed of great and plentiful fortunes, though they were undevoted enough to the Court, had all imaginable duty for the King, and affection to the government established by law or ancient custom; and, without doubt, the major part of that body consisted of men who had no mind to break the peace of the kingdom, or to make any considerable alteration in the government of Church or State: and therefore all inventions were set on foot from the beginning to work upon them and corrupt them by suggestions of the dangers which threatened all that was precious to the subject in their liberty and their property, by overthrowing or overmastering the law and subjecting it to an arbitrary power, and by countenancing Popery to the subversion of the Protestant religion; and then by infusing terrible apprehensions into some, and so working upon their fears, of being called in question for somewhat they had done, by which they would stand in need of their protection, and raising the hopes of others that by concurring with them they should be sure to obtain offices and honours and any kind of preferment. Though there were too many corrupted and misled by these several temptations, and others who needed no other temptations than from the fierceness and barbarity of their own natures and the malice they had contracted against the Church and against the Court, yet the number was not great of those in whom the government of the rest was vested, nor were there many who had the absolute authority to lead, though there were a multitude that was disposed to follow.

Mr Pym was looked upon as the man of greatest experience in Parliaments, where he had served very long, and was always a man of business, being an officer in the Exchequer, and of a good reputation generally, though known to be inclined to the Puritan party; yet not of those furious resolutions against the Church as the other leading men were, and wholly devoted to the earl of Bedford, who had nothing of that spirit.

Mr Hampden was a man of much greater cunning, and it may be of the most discerning spirit and of the greatest address and insinuation to bring any thing to pass which he desired of any man of that time, and who laid the design deepest. He was a gentleman of good extraction and a fair fortune, who from a life of great pleasure and license had on a sudden retired to extraordinary sobriety and strictness, and yet retained his usual cheerfulness and affability; which, together with the opinion of his wisdom and justice and the courage he had shewed in opposing the ship-money, raised his reputation to a very great height, not only in Buckinghamshire where he lived but generally throughout the kingdom. He was not a man of many words, and rarely began the discourse, or made the first entrance upon any business that was assumed; but a very weighty speaker, and, after he had heard a full debate and observed how the House was like to be inclined, took up the argument, and shortly and clearly and craftily so stated it that he commonly conducted it to the conclusion he desired; and if he found he could not do that, he never was without the dexterity to divert the debate to another time, and to prevent the determining any thing in the negative which might prove inconvenient in the future. He made so great a show of civility and modesty and humility, and always of mistrusting his own judgment and of esteeming his with whom he conferred for the present, that he seemed to have no opinions or resolutions but such as he contracted from the information and instruction he received upon the discourses of others, whom he had a wonderful art of governing and leading into his principles and inclinations whilst they believed that he wholly depended upon their counsel and advice. No man had ever a greater power over himself or was less the man that he seemed to be, which shortly after appeared to every body when he cared less to keep on the mask.

Mr St John, who was in a firm and entire conjunction with the other two, was a lawyer of Lincoln's Inn, known to be of parts and industry, but untaken notice of for practice in Westminster Hall* till he argued at the Exchequer-chamber the case of ship-money on the behalf of Mr Hampden, which gave him much reputation, and called him into all courts and to all causes where the King's prerogative was most contested. He was a man reserved, and of a dark and clouded countenance, very proud, and conversing with very few, and those, men of his own humour and inclinations. He had been questioned, committed, and brought into the Star-chamber many years before, with other persons of great name and reputation, (which first brought his name upon the stage,) for communicating some paper among themselves which some men had a mind at that time to have extended to a design of sedition:* but, it being quickly evident that the prosecution would not be attended with success, they were all shortly after discharged; but he never forgave the Court the first assault, and contracted an implacable displeasure against the Church purely from the company he kept. He was of intimate trust with the earl of Bedford, to whom he was allied, (being a natural son of the house of Bullingbrook,) and by him brought into all matters where himself was to be concerned. It was generally believed that these three persons, with the other three lords mentioned before, were of the most intimate and entire trust with each other, and made the engine which moved all the rest; yet it was visible, that Nathaniel Fiennes, the second son of the lord Saye, and sir Harry Vane, eldest son to the Secretary and Treasurer of the House, were received by them with full confidence and without reserve.

The former, being a man of good parts of learning, after some years spent in New college in Oxford, of which his father had been formerly fellow, (that family pretending and enjoying many privileges there, as of kin to the founder,) had spent his time abroad, in Geneva and amongst the cantons of Switzerland, where he improved his disinclination to the Church with which milk he had been nursed. From his travels he returned through Scotland (which few travellers took in their way home) at the time when that rebellion was in the bud, and was very little known, except amongst that people which conversed wholly amongst themselves, until he was now found in Parliament, when it was quickly discovered, that as he was the darling of his father so he was like to make good whatsoever he had for many years promised.

The other, sir H. Vane, was a man of great natural parts and of very profound dissimulation, of a quick conception and very ready, sharp, and weighty expression. He had an unusual aspect, which, though it might naturally proceed both from his father and mother, neither of which were beautiful persons, yet made men think there was somewhat in him of extraordinary; and his whole life made good that imagination. Within a very short time after he returned from his studies in Magdalen College in Oxford, where, though he was under the care of a very worthy tutor, he lived not with great exactness, he spent some little time in France and more in Geneva, and after his return into England contracted a full prejudice and bitterness against the Church, both against the form of the government and the liturgy, which was generally in great reverence, even with many of those who were not friends to the other. In this giddiness, which then much displeased, or seemed to displease, his father, who still appeared highly conformable and exceedingly sharp against those who were not, he transported himself into New England, a colony within few years before planted by a mixture of all religions which disposed the professors to dislike the government of the Church; who were qualified by the King's charter to choose their own government and governors, under the obligation that every man should take the oaths of allegiance and supremacy; which all the first planters did when they received their charter, before they transported themselves from hence, nor was there in many years after the least scruple amongst them of complying with those obligations; so far men were, in the infancy of their schism, from refusing to take lawful oaths. He was no sooner landed there but his parts made him quickly taken notice of, and very probably his quality, being the eldest son of a Privy Councillor, might give him some advantage; insomuch that, when the next season came for the election of their magistrates, he was chosen their governor, in which place he had so ill fortune (his working and unquiet fancy raising and infusing a thousand scruples of conscience which they had not brought over with them nor heard of before) that, he unsatisfied with them and they with him, he re-transported himself into England; having sowed such seed of dissension there as grew up too prosperously, and miserably divided the poor colony into several factions and divisions, and persecutions of each other, which still continue to the great prejudice of that plantation: insomuch as some of them, upon the ground of their first expedition, Liberty of Conscience, have withdrawn themselves from their jurisdiction, and obtained other charters from the King, by which, in other forms of government, they have enlarged their plantations, within new limits adjacent to the other. He was no sooner returned into England than he seemed to be much reformed in those extravagancies, and, with his father's approbation and direction, married a lady of a good family, and by his father's credit with the earl of Northumberland, who was High Admiral of England, was joined presently and jointly with sir William Russell in the office of Treasurer of the Navy, (a place of great trust and profit,) which he equally shared with the other, and seemed a man well satisfied and composed to the government. When his father received the disobligation from the lord Strafford by his being created baron of Raby,* the house and land of Vane, (and which title he had promised himself,) which was unluckily cast upon him, purely out of contempt, they sucked in all the thoughts of revenge imaginable; and from thence he betook himself to the friendship of Mr Pym and all other discontented or seditious persons, and contributed all that intelligence which will be hereafter mentioned, as he himself will often be, that designed the ruin of the earl, and which grafted him in the entire confidence of those who promoted the same; so that nothing was concealed from him, though it is believed that he communicated his own thoughts to very few.

Denzil Holles, the younger son and younger brother of the earl of Clare, was as much valued and esteemed by the whole party as any man, as he deserved to be, being a man of more accomplished parts than any of them, and of great reputation by the part he acted against the Court and the duke of Buckingham in the Parliament of the fourth year of the King, (the last Parliament that had been before the short one in April,) and his long imprisonment and sharp prosecution afterwards* upon that account; of which he retained the memory with acrimony enough. But he would in no degree intermeddle in the counsel or prosecution of the earl of Strafford, (which he could not prevent,) who had married his sister (by whom all his children were,) which made him a stranger to all those consultations, though it did not otherwise interrupt the friendship he had with the most violent of those prosecutors. In all other contrivances he was in the most secret councils with those who most governed, and respected by them with very submiss applications as a man of authority. Sir Gilbert Gerard, the lord Digby, Strode, Haselrig,* and the northern gentlemen who were most angry with the earl, or apprehensive of their own being in the mercy of the House, as Hotham, Cholmeley and Stapleton,* with some popular lawyers of the House, who did not suspect any wickedness in design and so became involved by degrees in the worst, observed and pursued the dictates and directions of the other, according to the parts which were assigned to them, upon emergent occasions; whilst the whole House looked on with wonder and amazement, without one man's interposing to allay the passion and the fury with which so many were transported.

This temper and constitution of both Houses of Parliament was very different from the last; and upon their first coming together, (as Tacitus says of the Jews that 'they exercised the highest offices of kindness and friendship towards each other, *et adversus omnes alios hostile odium'**) they watched all those who they knew were not of their opinions, nor like to be, with all possible jealousy, and if any of their elections could be brought into question they were sure to be voted out of the House, and then all the artifices were used to bring in more sanctified members; so that every week increased the number of their party, both by new elections and the proselytes they gained upon the old. Nor was it to be wondered at; for they pretended all public thoughts, and only the reformation of disapproved and odious enormities, and dissembled all purposes of removing foundations, which, though it was in the hearts of some, they had not the courage and confidence to communicate it.
[*HR*, III, 24–36]

Writing the Life *in 1668–9, Clarendon described his own activity in the*
Long Parliament.

He was very much in the business of the house; the greatest chairman
in the committees of the greatest moment; and very diligent in attending the service both in the house and at committees: for he had
from the beginning of the parliament laid aside his gown and practice,*
and wholly given himself up to the public business; which he saw so
much concerned the peace and very being of the kingdom. He was
in the chair in that committee which considered of the illegality of
the court of York:* and the other, that examined the miscarriages of
the judges, in the case of ship-money, and in other cases of judicatory,
in their several courts; and prepared charges thereupon against them.
He was in the chair against the marshal's court:* in that committee
which was against the court of York, which was prosecuted with great
passion, and took up many weeks debate: in that which concerned
the jurisdiction of the lord president and council of the marches of
Wales; which likewise held a long time, and was prosecuted with great
bitterness and animosity: in which the inhabitants of the four neighbour counties of Salop, Worcester, Hereford, and Gloucester, and
consequently the knights and burgesses which served for the same,
were passionately concerned to absolve themselves from the burden
of that jurisdiction; and all the officers of that court and council,
whereof some were very great men, and held offices of great value,
laboured with equal passion and concernment to support and maintain
what was in practice and possession; and their friends appeared
accordingly.

　　He was in the chair in many committees made upon private complaints; insomuch as he was seldom in the afternoon free from that
service in the committees, as he was never absent in mornings from the
house: and he was often heard to mention one private committee, in
which he was put accidentally into the chair, upon an enclosure which
had been made of great wastes, belonging to some [of] the queen's
manors, without the consent of the tenants, the benefit whereof had
been given by the queen to a servant of near trust; who forthwith
sold the lands enclosed to the earl of Manchester, lord privy seal; who,
together with his son Mandeville, were now most concerned to maintain the enclosure; against which, as well the inhabitants of other
manors, who claimed common in those wastes, as the queen's tenants
of the same, made loud complaints, as a great oppression, carried upon
them with a very high hand, and supported by power.

The committee sat in the queen's court, and Oliver Cromwell, being one of them, appeared much concerned to countenance the petitioners, who were numerous, together with their witnesses; the lord Mandeville being likewise present as a party, and, by the direction of the committee, sitting covered.* Cromwell (who had never before been heard to speak in the house of commons) ordered the witnesses and petitioners in the method of the proceeding, and seconded and enlarged upon what they said with great passion; and the witnesses and persons concerned, who were a very rude kind of people, interrupted the council and witnesses on the other side with great clamour, when they said any thing that did not please them; so that Mr Hyde (whose office it was to oblige men of all sorts to keep order) was compelled to use some sharp reproofs and some threats to reduce them to such a temper, that the business might be quietly heard. Cromwell in great fury reproached the chairman for being partial, and that he discountenanced the witnesses by threatening them: the other appealed to the committee, which justified him, and declared that he behaved himself as he ought to do; which more inflamed him, who was already too much angry. When upon any mention of matter of fact, or the proceeding before and at the enclosure, the lord Mandeville desired to be heard, and with great modesty related what had been done, or explained what had been said, Mr Cromwell did answer and reply upon him with so much indecency and rudeness, and in language so contrary and offensive, that every man would have thought, that as their natures and their manners were as opposite as it is possible, so their interest could never have been the same. In the end, his whole carriage was so tempestuous, and his behaviour so insolent, that the chairman found himself obliged to reprehend him; and to tell him, if he proceeded in the same manner, he would presently adjourn the committee, and the next morning complain to the house of him; which he never forgave; and took all occasions afterwards to pursue him with the utmost malice and revenge, to his death. [*Life*, I, 86–8]

4. Strafford

The processes of parliamentary inquiry and reform dominated the first few months of the Long Parliament. At the end of January 1641, the Commons sent to the House of Lords their articles of impeachment against Strafford. In February the reformers gained a major concession when Charles I agreed to a Triennial Act, which required the holding of Parliament at least every three years. Calls were made for the abolition of episcopacy. The King made some effort to draw the reformers into his government. At the end of January Oliver St John was appointed Solicitor General. The biggest concessions came in February. Writing the History in 1646, Hyde reflected on the King's policy and the strategy of the reformers.

IT was now time to intend themselves as well as the public, and to repair as well as to pull down; and therefore, as the principal reason (as was said before) for the accusing those two great persons* of high treason (that is, of the general consent to it before any evidence was required) was, that they might be removed from the King's presence and his counsels, without which they conceived theirs would have no power with him; so, that being compassed, care was taken to infuse into the King by marquis Hamilton, (who you heard before was licensed to take care of himself,* and was now of great intimacy with the governing and undertaking party,) that, his majesty having declared to his people that he really intended a reformation of all those extravagancies which former necessities, or occasions, or mistakes, had brought into the government of Church or State, he could not give a more lively and demonstrable evidence, and a more gracious instance, of such his intention, than by calling such persons to his Council whom the people generally thought most inclined to, and intent upon, such reformation: besides, that this would be a good means to preserve the dignity and just power of that board, which might otherwise for the late excess be more subject to violation, at least to some inconvenient attempts.

Hereupon in one day* were sworn Privy Councillors, much to the public joy, the earl of Hertford, (whom the King shortly after made marquis,) the earl of Bedford, the earl of Essex, the earl of Bristol, the lord Saye, the lord Saville, and the lord Kimbolton, and within two or three days after the earl of Warwick: being all persons at that time very gracious to the people, or to the Scots, by whose election and discretion the people chose; and had been all in some umbrage at Court, and most of them in visible disfavour there. This act the King did very cheerfully, heartily inclined to some of them, as he had reason, and not apprehending any inconvenience by that act from the other, whom he thought this light of his grace would reform, or at least restrain.

But the calling and admitting men to that board is not a work that can be indifferent, the reputation, if not the government, of the State so much depending on it. And though, it may be, there hath been too much curiosity heretofore used to discover men's particular opinions in particular points before they have received that honour, (whereas possibly such differences were rather to have been desired than avoided,) yet there are certain opinions, certain propositions, and general principles, that whosoever does not hold, does not believe, is not without great danger to be accepted for a Privy Councillor. As, whosoever is not fixed to monarchic grounds, the preservation and upholding whereof is the chief end of such a Council; whosoever does not believe that, in order to that great end, there is a dignity, a freedom, a jurisdiction, most essential to be preserved in and to that place, and takes not the preservation thereof to heart, ought never to be received there. What in prudence is to be done towards that end admits a latitude that honest and wise men may safely and profitably differ [in]; and those differences (which I said before there was too much unskilful care to prevent) usually produce great advantages in knowledge and wisdom: but the end itself, that which the logicians call the *terminus ad quem*, ought always to be a *postulatum*,* which whosoever doubts destroys. And princes cannot be too strict, too tender, in this consideration, in the constituting the body of their Privy Council; upon the prudent doing whereof much of their safety, more of their honour and reputation (which is the life itself of princes) both at home and abroad, necessarily depends; and the inadvertencies in this point have been, mediately or immediately, the root and the spring of all the calamities that have ensued.

Two reasons have been frequently given by princes for oversights, or for wilful breaches, in this important dispensation of their favours. The first, 'that such a man can do no harm;' when, God knows, few men have done more harm than those who have been thought to be able to do least; and there cannot be a greater error than to believe a man whom we see qualified with too mean parts to do good to be therefore incapable of doing hurt: there is a supply of malice, of pride, of industry, and even of folly, in the weakest, when he sets his heart upon it, that makes a strange progress in mischief. The second, when persons of ordinary faculties, either upon importunity or other collateral respects, have been introduced thither, 'that it is but a place of honour, and a general testimony of the king's affection;' and so it hath been as it were reserved as a preferment for those who were fit for no other preferment; as amongst the Jesuits they have a rule that they who are unapt for greater studies shall study cases of conscience. By this means the number hath been increased, which in itself breeds great inconveniences, since a less number are fitter both for counsel and despatch in matters of the greatest moment that depend upon a quick execution, than a greater number of men equally honest and wise: and for that, and other reasons of unaptness and incompetency, committees of dexterous men have been appointed out of the table to do the business of the table. And so men have been no sooner exalted with the reverent title, and pleased with the obligation of being made Privy Councillors, than they have checked that delight with discerning that they were not fully trusted; and so been more incensed with the reproachful distinction at, than obliged with the honourable admission to, that board, where they do not find all persons equally members. And by this kind of resentment many sad inconveniences have befallen to the King, and to those men who have had the honour and misfortune of those secret trusts.

The truth is, the sinking and near desperate condition of monarchy in this kingdom can never be buoyed up but by a prudent and steady Council attending upon the virtue and vivacity of the king; nor be preserved and improved when it is up but by cherishing and preserving the wisdom, integrity, dignity, and reputation of that Council: the lustre whereof always reflects upon the king himself, who is not thought a great monarch when he follows the reins of his own reason and appetite, but when, for the informing his reason and guiding his actions, he uses the service, industry, and faculties of the wisest men. And though it hath been, and will be, always necessary to admit to those Councils some men of great power who will not take the pains to have great parts, yet the number of the whole should not be too great, and the capacities and qualities of the most [should be] fit for business; that is, either for judgment and despatch, or for one of them at least; and integrity above all. . . .

That it might appear that what was done within the Houses was agreeable to those who were without, and that the same spirit reigned in Parliament and people, all possible license was exercised in preaching, and printing any old scandalous pamphlets and adding new to them, against the Church: petitions presented by many parishioners against their pastors, with articles of their misdemeanours and behaviours; most whereof consisted, in their bowing at the name of Jesus, and obliging the communicants to come up to the altar, (as they enviously called it,) that is, to the rails which enclosed the communion-table, to receive the Sacrament. All which petitions were read with great delight, and presently referred to the committee for religion, where Mr White,* a grave lawyer, but notoriously disaffected to the Church, sat in the chair; and then both petition and articles were suffered to be printed and published (a license never practised before,) that the people might be inflamed against the clergy; who were quickly taught to call all those against whom such petitions and articles were exhibited (which were frequently done by a few of the rabble and meanest of the people against the sense and judgment of the parish) *the scandalous clergy*; which appellation was frequently applied to men of great gravity and learning and the most unblemished lives.

There cannot be a better instance of the unruly and mutinous spirit of the city of London, which was the sink of all the ill humour of the kingdom, than the triumphant entry which some persons at that time made into London who had been before seen upon pillories and stigmatized as libellous and infamous offenders: of which *classis* of men scarce any age can afford three such.

There had been three persons of several professions some years before censured in [the] Star Chamber; William Prynne, a barrister of Lincoln's Inn, John Bastwick, a doctor of physic, and Henry Burton,* a minister and lecturer in London.

The first, not unlearned in the profession of the law, as far as learning is acquired by the mere reading of books; but, being a person of great industry, had spent more time in reading divinity, and, which marred that divinity, in the conversation of factious and hotheaded divines: and so, by a mixture of all three with the rudeness and arrogancy of his own nature, had contracted a proud and venomous dislike against the discipline of the Church of England, and so by degrees (as the progress is very natural) an equal irreverence to the government of the State too; both which he vented in several absurd, petulant, and supercilious discourses in print.

The second, a half-witted, crack-brained fellow, unknown to either University, or the College of Physicians; but one that had spent his time abroad, between the schools and the camp, (for he had been in or passed through armies,) and had gotten a doctorship, and Latin; with which, in a very flowing style, with some wit and much malice, he inveighed against the prelates of the Church in a book which he printed in Holland, and industriously dispersed in London and throughout the Kingdom; having presumed (as their modesty is always equal to their obedience) to dedicate it '*to the sacred majesty of the King.*'

The third had formerly a kind of relation by service to the King; having, before he took orders, waited as closet-keeper,* and so attended at canonical hours, with the books of devotion, upon his majesty when he was prince of Wales; and a little before the death of King James took orders: and so his highness coming shortly to be King, the vapours of ambition fuming into his head that he was still to keep his place, he would not think of less than being clerk of the closet to the new King, which place his majesty conferred upon, or rather continued in, the bishop of Durham, doctor Neile, who had long served King James there. Mr Burton thus disappointed, and, as he called it, despoiled of his rights, would not, in the greatness of his heart, sit down by the affront; but committed two or three such weak, saucy indiscretions, as caused an inhibition to be sent him that he should not presume to come any more to Court: and from that time [he] resolved to revenge himself of the bishop of Durham upon the whole order, and so turned lecturer, and preached against them; being endued with malice and boldness, instead of learning and any tolerable parts.

These three persons having been for several follies and libelling humours first gently reprehended, and after for their incorrigibleness more severely censured and imprisoned, found some means in prison of correspondence, which was not before known to be between them, and to combine themselves in a more pestilent and seditious libel than they had ever before vented;* in which the honour of the King, Queen, counsellors, and bishops, was with equal license blasted and traduced; which was faithfully dispersed by their proselytes in the city. The authors were quickly and easily known, and had indeed too much ingenuity to deny it; and were thereupon brought together to the Star-Chamber-bar *ore tenus;** where they behaved themselves with marvellous insolence, with full confidence demanding that the bishops who sat in the court (being only the archbishop of Canterbury, and the bishop of London) might not be present, because they were their enemies, and so parties: which, how scandalous and ridiculous soever it seemed then there, was good logic and good law two years after in Scotland, and served to banish the bishops of that kingdom both from the Council-table and the Assembly. Upon a very patient and solemn hearing, in as full a court as I ever saw, without any difference in opinion or dissenting voice, they were all three censured as scandalous, seditious, and infamous persons, to lose their ears in the pillory, and to be imprisoned in several gaols during the King's pleasure: all which was executed with rigour and severity enough. But yet their itch of libelling still brake out; and their friends of the city found a line of communication. Hereupon the wisdom of the State thought fit that those infectious sores should breathe out their corruption in some air more remote from that catching city and less liable to the contagion: and so, by an order of the Lords of the Council, Mr Prynne was sent to a castle in the island of Jersey, Dr Bastwick to Scilly, and Mr Burton to Guernsey; where they remained unconsidered, and truly I think unpitied (for they were men of no virtue or merit,) for the space of two years, till the beginning of this present Parliament.

Shortly upon that, petitions were presented* by their wives or friends to the House of Commons, expressing their heavy censures and long sufferings; and desiring, by way of appeal, that the justice and rigour of that sentence might be reviewed and considered; and that their persons might be brought from those remote and desolate places to London, that so they might be able to solicit or attend their own business. The sending for them out of prison (which was the main) took up much consideration: for, though very many who had no kindness had yet compassion towards them, as thinking they had suffered enough, and that, though they were scurvy fellows, they had been scurvily used; and others had not only affection to their persons, as having suffered for a common cause, but were concerned to revive and improve their useful faculties of libelling and reviling authority, and to make those ebullitions not thought noisome to the State; yet a sentence of a supreme court, the Star Chamber, (of which they had not yet spoke with irreverence,) was not lightly to be blown off: but when they were informed, and had considered, that by that sentence the petitioners were condemned to some prisons in London, and were afterward removed thence by an order of the lords of the Council, they looked upon that order as a violation of the sentence; and so made no scruple to order that the prisoners should be removed from those foreign prisons to the places to which they were regularly first committed. And to that purpose warrants were signed by the Speaker to the governors and captains of the several castles to bring them in safe custody to London: which were sent with all possible expedition.

Prynne and Burton being neighbours (though in distinct islands) landed at the same time at Southampton; where they were received and entertained with extraordinary demonstration of affection and esteem, attended by a marvellous conflux of company, and their charges not only borne with great magnificence, but liberal presents given to them. And this method and ceremony kept them company all their journey, great herds of people meeting them at their entrance into all towns, and waiting upon them out with wonderful acclamations of joy. When they

came near London multitudes of people of several conditions, some on
horseback, others on foot, met them some miles from the town, very
many having been a day's journey; and so they were brought,* about
two of the clock in the afternoon, in at Charing Cross, and carried into
the city by above ten thousand persons with boughs and flowers in their
hands, the common people strewing flowers and herbs in the ways
as they passed, making great noise and expressions of joy for their deliverance and return, and in those acclamations mingling loud and virulent exclamations against the bishops, 'who had so cruelly prosecuted
such godly men.' In the same manner, within five or six days after, and
in like triumph, Dr Bastwick returned from Scilly, landing at Dover;
and from thence, bringing the same testimonies of the affections and
zeal of Kent as the others had done from Hampshire and Surrey, was
met before he came to Southwark by the good people of London, and
so conducted to his lodging likewise in the city.

I should not have wasted this much time and paper in a discourse of
this nature, but that it is and was then evident, that this insurrection
(for it was no better) and frenzy of the people was an effect of great
industry and policy, to try and publish the temper of the people; and
to satisfy themselves in the activity and interest of their tribunes, to
whom that province of shewing the people was committed. And from
this time the license of preaching and printing increased to that degree
that all pulpits were freely delivered to the schismatical and silenced
preachers, who till then had lurked in corners or lived in New England;
and the presses were at liberty for the publishing the most invective,
seditious, and scurrilous pamphlets that their wit and malice could
invent. Whilst the ministers of the State, and judges of the law, like
men in an ecstasy, surprised and amazed with several apparitions,
had no speech or motion; as if, having committed such an excess of
jurisdiction, as men upon great surfeits are enjoined for a time to eat
nothing, they had been prescribed to exercise no jurisdiction at all.
Whereas, without doubt, if either the Privy Council, or the judges and
the King's learned counsel, had assumed the courage to have questioned the preaching, or the printing, or the seditious riots upon the
triumph of these three scandalous men, before the uninterruption
and security had confirmed the people in all three, it had been no
hard matter to have destroyed those seeds and pulled up those plants,
which, neglected, grew up and prospered to a full harvest of rebellion
and treason. But this was yet but a rudeness and rankness abroad,
without any visible countenance or approbation from the Parliament:
all was chaste within those walls.

The first malignity that was apparent there (for the accusation of the
archbishop and the earl of Strafford were looked upon as acts of passion, directed against particular persons, who were thought to have
deserved some extraordinary measure and proceeding) was against the
Church: not only in their committee for religion, (which had been
assumed ever since the latter times of King James, but no such thing
had been before heard of in parliaments,) where, under pretence of
receiving petitions against clergymen, they often debated points
beyond the verge of their understanding; but by their cheerful reception of a declaration* of many sheets of paper against the whole government of the Church, presented by ten or a dozen ministers at the
bar, and pretended to be signed by seven hundred ministers of London
and the counties adjacent: and a petition,* presented by alderman
Pennington, and alleged to be subscribed by twenty thousand men,
inhabitants within the city of London, who required, in plain terms,
the total extirpation of episcopacy. But the House was then so far from
being possessed with that spirit that the utmost that could be obtained,
upon a long debate upon that petition, was that it should not be
rejected; against which the number of the petitioners was urged as
a powerful argument; only it was suffered to remain in the hands of the
clerk of the House, with direction that no copy of it should be given.
And for the ministers' declaration, one part only of it was insisted on
by them and read in the House; which concerned the exercise of their
jurisdiction, and the excess of ecclesiastical courts: the other parts were
declined by many of them, and especially ordered to be sealed up by
the clerk, that it might be perused by no man. So that all that envy and
animosity against the Church seemed to be resolved into a desire that
a bill might be framed to remove the bishops from their votes in the
Lords' House and from any office in secular affairs; which was the
utmost men pretended to wish: and to such a purpose a bill was shortly
after prepared, and brought into the House; of which more shall be
said in its proper place.

It was a strange uningenuity and mountebankry that was practised
in the procuring those petitions, which continued ever after in the like
addresses. The course was, first, to prepare a petition, very modest and
dutiful for the form, and for the matter not very unreasonable; and to
communicate it at some public meeting, where care was taken it should
be received with approbation: the subscription of very few hands filled
the paper itself where the petition was written, and therefore many
more sheets were annexed, for the reception of the number which gave
all the credit and procured all the countenance to the undertaking.

When a multitude of hands was procured, the petition itself was cut off and a new one framed suitable to the design in hand, and annexed to the long list of names which were subscribed to the former. And by this means many men found their names subscribed to petitions of which they before had never heard. As several ministers, whose hands were to the petition and declaration of the London ministers before mentioned, have professed to many persons that they never saw that petition or declaration before it was presented to the House, but had signed another, the substance of which was, not to be compelled to take the oath enjoined by the new Canons:* and when they found, instead of that, their names set to a desire of an alteration of the government of the Church, they with much trouble went to Mr Marshall* with whom they had intrusted their petition and their hands, who gave them no other answer but that it was thought fit by those who understood business better than they that the latter petition should rather be preferred than the former. And when he found they intended by some public act to vindicate themselves from that calumny, such persons upon whom they had their greatest dependence were engaged, by threats and promises, to prevail with them to sit still, and to pass by that indirect proceeding. [*HR*, III, 49–67]

Strafford's impeachment trial opened on 22 March before the House of Lords sitting in Westminster Hall. The principal evidence against him was words he was alleged to have said at the meeting of the Privy Council at which the dissolution of the Short Parliament was decided. His effective defence seemed to make a conviction unlikely. The reformers proceeded by a bill of attainder instead, which could declare him guilty of treason, without requiring the same standards of proof. The bill was read a third time on 21 April and sent up to the Lords. This account of the proceedings, published in the History of the Rebellion, *comes from the* History *written in 1646. The following material concerning the debates on episcopacy and the Church was written as part of the* Life *in 1668–9, and published in the* History *of the Rebellion.*

The bill of attainder in few days passed the House of Commons; though some lawyers of great and known learning declared that there was no ground or colour in law to judge him guilty of high treason; and the lord Digby (who had been, from the beginning, of that committee for the prosecution, and had much more prejudice than kindness to the earl) in a very pathetical speech declared that he could not give his consent to the bill, not only for that he was unsatisfied in the matter of law, but for that he was more unsatisfied in the matter of fact; those words upon which the impeachment was principally grounded being so far from being proved by two witnesses that he could not acknowledge it to be by one; since he could not admit sir Harry Vane to be a competent witness, who being first examined denied that the earl spake those words, and upon his second examination remembered some, and at his third the rest of the words: and thereupon related* many circumstances, and made many sharp observations upon what had passed, which none but one of the committee could have done: for which he was presently after questioned in the House, but made his defence so well, and so much to the disadvantage of those who were concerned, that from that time they prosecuted him with an implacable rage and uncharitableness upon all occasions. The bill passed with only fifty-nine dissenting voices, there being near 200 in the House;* and was immediately sent up to the Lords, with this addition, 'that the Commons would be ready the next day in Westminster Hall, to give their lordships satisfaction in the matter of law, upon what had passed at the trial.'

The earl was then again brought to the bar;* the Lords sitting as before, in their robes, and the Commons as they had done; amongst them, Mr St John (whom his majesty had made his Solicitor-general since the beginning of the Parliament,) from his place argued for the space of near an hour the matter of law. Of the argument itself I shall say little, it being in print and in many hands; I shall only remember two notable propositions, which are sufficient characters of the person and the time. Lest what had been said on the earl's behalf in point of law and upon the want of proof should have made any impression in their lordships, he averred that 'in that way of bill private satisfaction to each man's conscience was sufficient, although no evidence had been given in at all:' and as to the pressing the law, he said, 'It was true we give law to hares and deer, because they be beasts of chase; but it was never accounted either cruelty, or foul play, to knock foxes and wolves on the head as they can be found, because they be beasts of prey.' In a word, the law and the humanity were alike; the one being more fallacious, and the other more barbarous, than in any age had been vented in such an auditory.

The same day, as a better argument to the Lords speedily to pass the bill, the nine and fifty members of the House of Commons, who (as is said before) had dissented from that act, had their names written in pieces of parchment or paper, under this superscription, *Straffordians, or enemies to their country*,' and those papers fixed upon posts and other the most visible places about the city; which was as great and destructive a violation of the privileges and freedom of Parliament as can be imagined: yet, being complained of in the House, not the least countenance was given to the complaint, or the least care taken for the discovery.

The persons who had still the conduct of the designs began to find that their friends abroad (of whose help they had still great need, for the getting petitions to be brought to the House, and for all tumultuous appearances in the city, and negotiations with the Common Council)* were not at all satisfied with them for their want of zeal in the matter of religion; and, though they had branded as many of the bishops and others of the prelatical party as had come in their way, and received all petitions against the Church with encouragement, yet that there was nothing done, or visibly in projection to be done, towards lessening their jurisdiction, or indulging any of that liberty to their weak brethren which they had from the beginning expected from them. And then the discourse of their ambition, and hopes of preferment at Court, was grown public, and raised much jealousy of them.

But the truth is, they who had made in their hearts the most destructive vows against the Church never durst communicate their bloody wishes to their best friends, whose authority gave them their greatest credit. For, besides that their own clergy, (whose hands they produced in great numbers to complaints against the innovations, which had, as they said, been introduced, and against the ceremonies, which had been in constant practice since the Reformation as well as before,) were far from being of one mind in the matter or manner of what they wished should be altered, (as appeared whenever they appeared before the House or a committee, when any of them were asked questions they did not expect,) there was less consent amongst their lay friends in ecclesiastical affairs than amongst the other.

The earl of Bedford had no desire that there should be any alteration in the government of the Church, and had always lived towards my lord of Canterbury himself with all respect and reverence, and frequently visited and dined with him, subscribed liberally to the repair of St Paul's church, and seconded all pious undertakings: though it is true he did not discountenance notoriously those of the clergy who were unconformable.

The earl of Essex was rather displeased with the person of the archbishop and some other bishops than indevoted to the function; and towards some of them he had great reverence and kindness, as bishop Morton, bishop Hall,* and some other of the less formal and more popular prelates: and he was as much devoted as any man to the Book of Common Prayer, and obliged all his servants to be constantly present with him at it, his household chaplain being always a most conformable man and a good scholar.

In truth, in the House of Peers there were only at that time taken notice of the lords Saye and Brooke, and they believed to be positive enemies to the whole fabric of the Church, and to desire a dissolution of that government; the earl of Warwick himself having never discovered any aversion to episcopacy, and much professed the contrary.

In the House of Commons, though, of the chief leaders, Nathaniel Fiennes and young sir H. Vane, and shortly after Mr Hampden (who had not before owned it), were believed to be for 'root and branch,' (which grew shortly after a common expression, and discovery of the several tempers,) yet Mr Pym was not of that mind, nor Mr Holles, nor any of the Northern men, or those lawyers who drove on most furiously with them: all who were pleased with the government itself of the Church.

The first design that was entertained against the Church, and which was received in the House of Commons with a visible countenance and approbation of many who were neither of the same principles or purposes, was a short bill that was brought in* to take away the bishops' votes in Parliament and to leave them out in all commissions of the peace and with relation to any temporal affairs. This was contrived with great deliberation and preparation to dispose men to consent to it, and to this many of the House of Peers were much disposed, and amongst them none more than the earl of Essex and all the popular lords; who observed that they seldom carry any thing which directly opposed the King's interest by [reason of] the number of the bishops, who for the most part unanimously concurred against it, and opposed many of their other designs: and they believed that it could do the Church no harm by the bishops' having fewer diversions from their spiritual charges.

In the House of Commons they used that and other arguments to remove the prejudice from it; and, as there were many who were persuaded that the passing that bill would be no prejudice and were as unwilling that the bishops should be justices of peace and in any other secular commissions as the lords were that they should sit with them, so they prevailed with others, who heartily desired that there might be no such diminution of their honour and authority, by persuading them that there was so great concurrence towards the passing this bill, and so great a combination throughout the nation against the whole government of the Church and a resolution to destroy it absolutely: in which the Scots were so resolutely engaged that they discoursed in all companies that it was impossible for a firm peace to be preserved between the nations if bishops were not taken away, and that the army would never march out of the kingdom till that were brought to pass: but that if this bill were once passed, a greater number in both Houses would be so well satisfied that the violenter party would be never able to prosecute their desires. And this reason did prevail over many men of excellent judgments and unquestionable affections, who did in truth at that time believe that the passing this Act was the only expedient to preserve the Church: insomuch as when it was brought into the House it found a better reception than was expected, and some men, who others thought would have opposed it, spake on its behalf, expressing their desire that it might pass.

There was a difference in opinion in this debate between two persons who had been never known to differ in the House, and the entire friendship they had for each other was very remarkable; which administered much pleasure to very many who loved neither of them. When the bill was put to the question, Mr Hyde (who was from the beginning known to be an enemy to it) spake very earnestly for the throwing it out; said, 'It was changing the whole frame and constitution of the kingdom, and of the Parliament itself: that from the time that Parliaments began there had never been one Parliament when the bishops were not part of it: that if they were taken out of the House, there would be but two estates left: for that they as the clergy were the third estate, and being taken away, there was nobody left to represent the clergy: which would introduce another piece of injustice, which no other part of the kingdom could complain of, who were all represented in Parliament, and were therefore bound to submit to all that was enacted because it was upon the matter with their own consent: whereas, if the bishops were taken from sitting in the House of Peers, there was nobody who could pretend to [re]present the clergy; and yet they must be bound by their determinations.'

When he had done, the lord Falkland, who always sat next to him, (which was so much taken notice of, that if they came not into the House together, as usually they did, every body left the place for him that was absent,) suddenly stood up, and declared himself to be of another opinion; and that, 'as he thought the thing itself to be absolutely necessary for the benefit of the Church, which was in so great danger, so he had never heard that the constitution of the kingdom would be violated by the passing that Act; and that he had heard many of the clergy protest that they could not acknowledge that they were [re]presented by the bishops. However, we might presume that if they could make that appear, that they were a third estate, that the House of

Peers (amongst whom they sat and had yet their votes) would reject it.'
And so, with some facetiousness answering some other particulars,
concluded for the passing the Act.

The House was so marvellously delighted to see the two inseparable
friends divided in so important a point, that they could not contain
from a kind of rejoicing, and the more because they saw Mr Hyde was
much surprised with the contradiction; as in truth he was, having
never discovered the least inclination in the other towards such a compliance: and therefore they entertained an imagination and hope that
they might work the lord Falkland to a farther concurrence with them.
But they quickly found themselves disappointed, and that, as there
was not the least interruption of the close friendship between the other
two, so, when the same argument came again into debate about six
months after,* the lord Falkland changed his opinion, and gave them
all the opposition he could: nor was he reserved in acknowledging that
he had been deceived, and by whom, and confessed to his friends, with
whom he would deal freely, that Mr Hampden had assured him that if
that bill might pass there would be nothing more attempted to the
prejudice of the Church: which he thought, as the world then went,
would be no ill composition. [*HR*, III, 139–52]

*Following the passage of the attainder bill, frantic negotiations were mounted
to try to find a compromise which would save Strafford's life — and what
the King saw as his own honour. Hyde was drawn into them.*

In the afternoon of the same day when the conference had been* in the
Painted Chamber upon the Court of York, Mr Hyde going to a place
called Piccadilly,* (which was a fair house for entertainment and gaming, and handsome gravel walks with shade, and where were an upper
and a lower bowling-green, whither very many of the nobility and
gentry of the best quality resorted, both for exercise and conversation,)
as soon as ever he came into the ground the earl of Bedford came to
him; and after some short compliments upon what had passed in the
morning, he told him he was glad he was come thither, for there was a
friend of his in the lower ground who needed his counsel. He then
lamented the misery the kingdom was like to fall into, by their own
violence and want of temper in the prosecution of their own happiness.
He said 'this business concerning the earl of Strafford was a rock upon
which we should all split, and that the passion of the Parliament would
destroy the kingdom: that the King was ready to do all they could
desire if the life of the earl of Strafford might be spared: that he was
satisfied that he had proceeded with more passion in many things than

he ought to have done, by which he had rendered himself useless to his service for the future, and therefore he was well contented that he might be made incapable of any employment for the time to come, and that he should be banished, or imprisoned for his life, as they should choose: that if they would take his death upon them by their own judicatory, he would not interpose any act of his own conscience: but since they had declined that way, and meant to proceed by an Act of Parliament to which he himself must be a party, that it could not consist with his conscience ever to give his royal assent to that Act; because, having been present at the whole trial,' (as he had been, in a box provided on purpose, *incognito,* though conspicuous enough,) 'and heard all the testimony they had given against him, he had heard nothing proved by which he could believe that he was a traitor either in fact or in intention: and therefore his majesty did most earnestly desire that the two Houses would not bring him a bill to pass [to] which in conscience he could not, and therefore would not, consent.'

The earl said, 'though he yet was satisfied so well in his own conscience that he believed he should have no scruple in giving his own vote for the passing it,' (for it yet depended in the Lords' House,) 'he knew not how the King could be pressed to do an act so contrary to his own conscience; and that, for his part, he took all the pains he could to persuade his friends to decline their violent prosecution, and to be contented with the remedy proposed by the King, which he thought might be rendered so secure that there need remain no fears of that man's ever appearing again in business: and that how difficult a work soever he found it to be, he should not despair of it if he could persuade the earl of Essex to comply, but that he found him so obstinate that he could not in the least degree prevail with him; that he had left his brother, the earl of Hertford,' (who was that day made a marquis,) 'in the lower ground, walking with him, who he knew would do all he could;' and he desired Mr Hyde to walk down into that place, and take his turn to persuade him to what was reasonable; which he was very willing to do.

He found the marquis and the earl walking there together, and no other persons there; and as soon as they saw him they both came to him, and the marquis, after a short salutation, departed, and left the other two together; which he did purposely. The earl began merrily, in telling him that 'he had that morning performed a service which he knew he did not intend to do; that by what he had said against the Court of York, he had revived their indignation against the earl of Strafford; so that he now hoped they should proceed in their bill against him with vigour, (whereas they had slept so long upon it,) which,' he said, 'was the effect of which he was sure he had no mind to be the cause.' Mr Hyde confessed he had indeed no such purpose; and hoped that somewhat he had said might put other thoughts into them, to proceed in another manner upon his crimes: that he knew well that the cause of their having slept so long upon the bill was their disagreement upon the point of treason, which the longer they thought of would administer the more difficulties: but that if they declined that, they would all agree that there were crimes and misdemeanours evidently enough proved to deserve so severe a censure as would determine all the activity hereafter of the earl of Strafford that might prove dangerous to the kingdom, or mischievous to any particular person to whom he was not a friend.

He shook his head, and answered, 'Stone-dead hath no fellow: that if he were judged guilty in a *praemunire*,* according to the precedents cited by him, or fined in any other way, and sentenced to be imprisoned during his life, the King would presently grant him his pardon and his estate, release all fines, and would likewise give him his liberty as soon as he had a mind to receive his service; which would be as soon as the Parliament should be ended.' And when he was ready to reply to him, the earl told him familiarly, that he had been tired that afternoon upon that argument, and therefore desired him to continue the discourse no longer then; assuring him he would be ready to confer with him upon it at any other time.

And shortly after Mr Hyde took another opportunity to speak freely with him again concerning it, but found him upon his guard; and though he heard all the other would say with great patience, yet he did not at all enlarge in his answers, but seemed fixed in his resolution; and when he was pressed, how unjustifiable a thing it was for any man to do any thing which his conscience informed him was sinful; that he knew him so well that if he were not satisfied in his own conscience of the guilt of the earl of Strafford the King would never be able to oblige him to give his vote for that bill; and therefore he wondered how he could urge the King to do an act which he declared to be so much against his conscience that he neither could nor would ever give his royal assent to that bill; he answered more at large, and with some commotion, (as if he were in truth possessed with that opinion himself,) 'that the King was obliged in conscience to conform himself and his own understanding to the advice and conscience of his Parliament:' which was a doctrine newly resolved by their divines, and of great use to them for the pursuing their future counsels. [*HR*, III, 161–5]

The moderate parliamentary leader, the Earl of Bedford, fell ill with small-
pox on 30 April, the day after the second reading of the bill of attainder,
while an air of violence hung over London as the King struggled to save
Strafford from execution.

The earl of Bedford secretly undertook to his majesty that the earl of
Strafford's life should be preserved; and to procure his revenue to be
settled as amply as any of his progenitors, the which he intended so
really that, to my knowledge, he had it in design to endeavour the setting
up the excise in England as the only natural means to advance the King's
profit. He fell sick within a week after the bill of attainder was sent up to
the Lords' House, and died shortly after,* much afflicted with the
passion and fury which he perceived his party inclined to: insomuch as
he declared to some of near trust with him that he feared the rage and
madness of this Parliament would bring more prejudice and mischief
to the kingdom than it had ever sustained by the long intermission of
parliaments. He was a wise man, and would have proposed and advised
moderate courses; but was not incapable, for want of resolution, of being
carried into violent ones, if his advice would not have been submitted to:
and therefore many who knew him well thought his death not unseasonable as well to his fame as his fortune, and that it rescued him as well
from some possible guilt as from those visible misfortunes which men of
all conditions have since undergone.

As soon as the earl of Bedford was dead the lord Saye (hoping to
receive the reward of the Treasurership) succeeded him in his undertaking, and faithfully promised the King that he should not be pressed in
the matter of the earl of Strafford's life: and under that promise got
credit enough to persuade his majesty to whatsoever he told was necessary to that business. And thereupon, when the bill was depending with
the Lords, and when there was little suspicion that it would pass, though
the House of Commons every day by messages endeavoured to quicken
them, he persuaded the King to go to the House of Peers, and, according
to custom, to send for the House of Commons, and then to declare himself that he could not with the safety of a good conscience ever give his
consent to the bill that was then depending before them concerning the
earl of Strafford, if it should be brought to him, because he was not
satisfied in the point of treason: but he was so fully satisfied that the earl
was unfit ever to serve him more, in any condition of employment, that
he would join with them in any Act to make him utterly incapable of ever
bearing office, or having any other employment in any of his majesty's
dominions; which he hoped would satisfy them.

This advice, upon the confidence of the giver, the King resolved to follow: but when his resolution was imparted to the earl, he immediately sent his brother to him, beseeching his majesty by no means to take that way, for that he was most assured it would prove very pernicious to him, and therefore desired he might depend upon the honour and conscience of the Peers, without his majesty's interposition. The King told his brother that he had taken that resolution by the advice of his best friends; but since he liked [it] not, he would decline it. The next morning the lord Saye came again to him, and finding his majesty altered in his intention, told him, if he took that course he had advised him, he was sure it would prevail; but if he declined it, he could not promise his majesty what would be the issue, and should hold himself absolutely disengaged from any undertaking. The King observing his positiveness, and conceiving his intentions to be very sincere, suffered himself to be guided by him, and immediately went to the House* and said as the other had advised. Whether that lord did in truth believe the discovery of his majesty's conscience in that manner would produce the effect he foretold, or whether he advised it treacherously, to bring on those inconveniences which afterwards happened, I know not: but many, who believed his will to be much worse than his understanding, had the uncharitableness to believe that he intended to betray his master, and to put the ruin of the earl out of question.

The event proved very fatal; for the King no sooner returned from the House than the House of Commons, in great passion and fury, declared this last act of his majesty's to be 'the most unpar[all]eled breach of privilege that had ever happened; that if his majesty might take notice what bills were passing in either House and declare his own opinion, it was to prejudge their counsels, and they should not be able to supply the commonwealth with wholesome laws suitable to the diseases it laboured under; that this was the greatest obstruction of justice that could be imagined; that they, and whosoever had taken the late Protestation,* were bound to maintain the privileges of Parliament, which were now so grossly invaded and violated:' with many other sharp discourses to that purpose.

The next day great multitudes of people came down to Westminster, and crowded about the House of Peers, exclaiming, with great outcries, that 'they would have justice;' and publicly reading the names of those who had dissented from that bill in the House of Commons as enemies to their country; and as any lord passed by, called, *Justice, justice!* with great rudeness and insolence pressing upon and thrusting those lords whom they suspected not to favour that bill; professing aloud that 'they would be governed and disposed by the honourable House of Commons, and would defend their privileges according to their late Protestation.' This unheard-of act of insolence and sedition continued so many days, till many lords grew so really apprehensive of having their brains beaten out that they absented themselves from the House, and others, finding what seconds the House of Commons was like to have to compass whatever they desired, changed their minds; and so in an afternoon, when of the fourscore who had been present at the trial there were only six and forty lords in the House, (the good people still crying at the doors for *Justice*,) they put the bill to the question, and, eleven lords only dissenting, it passed that House* and was ready for the King's assent.

The King continued as resolved never to give his consent. The same oratory then attended him at Whitehall which had prevailed at Westminster, and a rabble of many thousand people besieged that place, crying out, *Justice, justice; that they would have justice*; not without great and insolent threats and expressions what they would do if it were not speedily granted. The Privy Council was called together, to advise what course was to be taken to suppress these traitorous riots. Instead of considering how to rescue their master's honour and his conscience from this infamous violence and constraint, they press the King to pass the bill of attainder, saying there was no other way to preserve himself and his posterity than by so doing; and therefore that he ought to be more tender of the safety of the kingdom than of any one person, how innocent soever: not one councillor interposing his opinion to support his master's magnanimity and innocence: they who were of that mind either suppressing their thoughts through fear, upon the new doctrine established then by the new councillors, 'that no man ought to presume to advise any thing in that place contrary to the sense of both Houses,' others sadly believing the force and violence offered to the King would be, before God and man, a just excuse for whatsoever he should do.

His majesty told them that 'what was proposed to him to do was in a diameter contrary to his conscience, and that being so, he was sure they would not persuade him to it though themselves were never so well satisfied.' To that point they desire him to confer with his bishops, who, they made no question, would better inform his conscience. The archbishop of York* was at hand; who, to his argument of conscience, told him that 'there was a private and a public conscience; that his public conscience as a king might not only dispense with, but oblige him to do, that which was against his private conscience as a man: and that the question was not, whether he should save the earl of Strafford, but, whether he should perish with him: that the conscience of a king to preserve his kingdom, the conscience of a husband to preserve his wife, the conscience of a father to preserve his children, (all which were now in danger,) weighed down abundantly all the considerations the conscience of a master or a friend could suggest to him for the preservation of a friend or servant.' And by such unprelatical, ignominious arguments, in plain terms advised him, 'even for conscience sake, to pass that Act.'

Though this bishop acted his part with more prodigious boldness and impiety, the other of the same function (of whose learning and sincerity the King and the world had greater reverence) did not what might have been expected from their calling or their trust, but at least forbore to fortify and confirm a conscience upon the courage and piety of which themselves and their order did absolutely depend.

During these perplexities, the earl of Strafford, taking notice of the straits the King was in, the rage of the people still increasing, (from whence he might expect a certain outrage and ruin, how constant soever the King continued to him;) and, it may be, knowing of an undertaking (for such an undertaking there was) by a great person* who then had a command in the Tower, that, if the King refused to pass the bill, to free the kingdom from the hazard it seemed to be in he would cause his head to be strucken off in the Tower, writ a most pathetical letter to the King, full of acknowledgment of his favours, but lively presenting the dangers, 'which threatened himself and his posterity by his obstinacy in those favours; and therefore by many arguments conjuring him no longer to defer his assent to the bill, that so his death might free the kingdom from the many troubles it apprehended.

The delivery of this letter being quickly known, new arguments were applied, that this free consent of his own clearly absolved the King from any scruple that could remain with him; and so in the end they extorted from him to sign a commission to some lords to pass the bill, which was as valid as if he had signed it himself; though they comforted him even with that circumstance, that his own hand was not in it.

It may easily be said that, the freedom of the Parliament and his own negative voice being thus barbarously invaded, if his majesty had, instead of passing that Act, come to the House and dissolved the Parliament, or if he had withdrawn himself from that seditious city and put himself in the head of his own army, much of the mischief which hath since happened would have been prevented. But whoever truly considers the state of affairs at that time; the prevalency of that faction

in both Houses; the rage and fury of the people; the use that was made
by the schismatical preachers (by whom all the orthodox were silenced)
of the late Protestation in their pulpits; the fears and jealousies they
had infused into the minds of many sober men upon the discourse of
the late plot; the constitution of the Council-table, that there was not
an honest man durst speak his conscience to the King, for fear of his
ruin; and that those whom he thought most true to him betrayed him
every hour, insomuch as his whispers in his bedchamber were instantly
conveyed to those against whom those whispers were; so that he had
very few men to whom he could breathe his conscience and complaint
that were not suborned against him or averse to his opinions: that, on
the other side, if some expedient were not speedily found out to allay
that frantic rage and combination in the people, there was reason
enough to believe their impious hands would be lifted up against his
own person, and (which he much more apprehended) against the person of his royal consort; and lastly, that (besides the difficulty of getting thither, except he would have gone alone) he had no ground to be
very confident of his own army: I say, whoever sadly contemplates this
will find cause to confess, the part which the King had to act was not
only harder than any prince but than any private gentleman had been
incumbent to; and that it is much easier upon the accidents and occurrences which have since happened to determine what was not to have
been done, than at that time to have foreseen by what means to have
freed himself from the labyrinth in which he was involved.

All things being thus transacted, to conclude the fate of this great
person, he was on the twelfth day of May brought from the Tower of
London (where he had been a prisoner near six months) to the scaffold
on Tower Hill; where, with a composed undaunted courage, he told the
people 'he was come thither to satisfy them with his head; but that he
much feared the reformation which was begun in blood would not
prove so fortunate to the kingdom as they expected and he wished:' and
after great expressions of his devotion to the Church of England, and
the Protestant religion established by law and professed in that Church,
of his loyalty to the King and affection to the peace and welfare of the
kingdom, with marvellous tranquillity of mind, he delivered his head to
the block, where it was severed from his body at a blow: many of the
standers by, who had not been over charitable to him in his life, being
much affected with the courage and Christianity of his death.

Thus fell the greatest subject in power, and little inferior to any in
fortune, that was at that time in either of the three kingdoms; who
could well remember the time when he led those people who then

pursued him to his grave. He was a man of great parts and extraordinary endowments of nature, not unadorned with some addition of art and learning, though that again was more improved and illustrated by the other; for he had a readiness of conception and sharpness of expression which made his learning thought more than in truth it was. His first inclinations and addresses to the Court were only to establish his greatness in the country, where he apprehended some acts of power from the old lord Saville, who had been his rival always there, and of late had strengthened himself by being made a Privy Councillor and officer at Court: but his first attempts were so prosperous that he contented not himself with being secure from his power in the country, but rested not till he had bereaved him of all power and place in Court, and so sent him down, a most abject disconsolate old man, to his country, where he was to have the superintendency over him too, by getting himself at that time made Lord President of the North. These successes, applied to a nature too elate and arrogant of itself, and a quicker progress into the greatest employments and trust, made him more transported with disdain of other men, and more contemning the forms of business, than happily he would have been if he had met with some interruptions in the beginning, and had passed in a more leisurely gradation to the office of a statesman.

He was, no doubt, of great observation, and a piercing judgment, both into things and persons; but his too good skill in persons made him judge the worse of things: for it was his misfortune to be of a time wherein very few wise men were equally employed with him, and scarce any (but the lord Coventry, whose trust was more confined) whose faculties and abilities were equal to his: so that upon the matter he wholly relied upon himself, and, discerning many defects in most men, he too much neglected what they said or did. Of all his passions his pride was most predominant, which a moderate exercise of ill fortune might have corrected and reformed, and which was by the hand of Heaven strangely punished, by bringing his destruction upon him by two things that he most despised, the people and sir Harry Vane. In a word, the epitaph which Plutarch records* that Silla wrote for himself may not be unfitly applied to him; that 'no man did ever pass him either in doing good to his friends or in doing mischief to his enemies;' for his acts of both kinds were most exemplar and notorious. [*HR*, III, 192–205]

5. The Grand Remonstrance and the Making of a Royalist Party

At the same time as he accepted Strafford's attainder, the King agreed to a bill preventing the dissolution of Parliament without its own consent. More radical measures against the Church were being planned: both Houses were debating a bill removing the clergy from all civil jurisdiction—which included their membership of the House of Lords—and at the end of May the 'root and branch' bill, abolishing episcopacy entirely, was introduced. Hyde, a vigorous opponent of the attacks on the Church, was put into the chair of the committee of the whole House that discussed the bill in detail in June 1641.

WHEN Mr Hyde sat in the chair, in the grand committee of the house for the extirpation of episcopacy, all that party made great court to him; and the house keeping those disorderly hours, and seldom rising till after four of the clock in the afternoon, they frequently importuned him to dine with them at Mr Pym's lodging, which was at sir Richard Manly's house, in a little court behind Westminster hall; where he, and Mr Hampden, sir Arthur Haselrig, and two or three more, upon a stock kept a table, where they transacted much business, and invited thither those of whose conversion they had any hope.

One day after dinner, Nathaniel Fiennes, who that day likewise dined there, asked Mr Hyde whether he would ride into the fields, and take a little air, it being a fine evening: which the other consenting to, they sent for their horses, and riding together in the fields between Westminster and Chelsea, Mr Fiennes asked him what it was that inclined him to adhere so passionately to the church, which could not possibly be supported. He answered, that he could have no other obligation than that of his conscience, and his reason, that could move with him; for he had no relation or dependence upon any churchmen that could dispose him to it; that he could not conceive how religion could be preserved without bishops, nor how the government of the state could well subsist, if the government of the church were altered; and asked him what government they meant to introduce in its place. To which he answered, that there would be time enough to think of that; but assured him, and wished him to remember what he said, that if the king resolved to defend the bishops, it would cost the kingdom much blood, and would be the occasion of as sharp a war as had ever been in England; for that there was so great a number of good men who resolved to lose their lives before they would ever submit to that government. Which was the first positive declaration he had ever heard from any particular man of that party, very few of them having at that time that resolution, much less avowing it; and if they had, the kingdom was in no degree at that time infected with that poison, how much soever it was spread afterwards.

Within two days after this discourse from Mr Fiennes, Mr Hyde, walking between the parliament house and Westminster, in the churchyard, met with Harry Marten, with whom he lived very familiarly; and speaking together about the proceedings of the houses, Marten told him, that he would undo himself by his adhering to the court; to which he replied, that he had no relation to the court, and was only concerned to maintain the government and preserve the law: and then told him, he could not conceive what he proposed to himself, for he did not think him to be of the opinion or nature with those men who governed the house; and asked him, what he thought of such and such men: and he very frankly answered, that he thought them knaves; and that when they had done as much as they intended to do, they should be used as they had used others. The other pressed him then to say what he desired; to which, after a little pause, he very roundly answered, 'I do not think one man wise enough to govern us all:' which was the first word he had ever heard any man speak to that purpose; and would without doubt, if it had been then communicated or attempted, been the most abhorred by the whole nation, of any design that could be mentioned; and yet it appears it had even so early entered into the hearts of some desperate persons, that gentleman being at that time possessed of a very great fortune, and having great credit in his country.

Whilst things were thus depending, one morning, when there was a conference with the lords, and so the house adjourned, Mr Hyde being walking in the house, Mr Percy, brother to the earl of Northumberland, being a member of the house, came to him, and told him that the king would speak with him, and would have him that afternoon to come to him. He answered, he believed it was some mistake, for that he had not the honour to be known to the king; and that there was another of the same name, of the house. Mr Percy assured him he was the man; and so it was agreed, that at such an hour in the evening he should call on him at his chamber; which he did, and was by him conducted into the gallery, and so into the square room, where he stayed till the other went to the king; who in a very short time came thither, attended only by Mr Percy, who, as soon as Mr Hyde had kissed his majesty's hand, withdrew.

The king told him, 'that he heard from all hands how much he was beholden to him; and that when all his servants in the house of commons either neglected his service, or could not appear usefully in it, he took all occasions to do him service; for which be thought fit to give him his own thanks, and to assure him that he would remember it to his advantage.' He took notice of his affection to the church, for which, he said, 'he thanked him more than for all the rest;' which the other acknowledged with the duty that became him, and said, he was very happy that his majesty was pleased with what he did; but if he had commanded him to have withdrawn his affection and reverence for the church, he would not have obeyed him' which his majesty said made him love him the better. Then he discoursed of the passion of the house, and of the bill then brought in against episcopacy; and asked him, 'whether he thought they would be able to carry it;' to which he answered, 'he believed they could not, at least that it would be very long first.' 'Nay, (replied the king,) if you will look to it, that they do not carry it before I go for Scotland, which will be at such a time, when the armies shall be disbanded, I will undertake for the church after that time:' 'Why then, (said the other,) by the grace of God, it will not be in much danger:' with which the king was well pleased; and dismissed him with very gracious expressions. And this was the first introduction of him to the king's taking notice of him. [*Life*, I, 86–93]

On 11 August, despite efforts by Parliament to prevent it, the King left to visit Scotland, formally to signal the final agreement of a peace treaty ending the Scottish war, but mainly in the hope of opening cracks in the Covenanting movement and in the alliance between the Covenanters and the English parliamentary reformers. His failure to do so, and the ratification by the Scots of the treaty of peace, gave the parliamentary leaders sufficient assurance to allow Parliament to adjourn on 9 September until 20 October. As it was reconvening, news arrived in London that a plan to seize or assassinate the Covenanting leaders had been discovered in Scotland. A few days later came yet more alarming news. Clarendon's account of the impact of the latter was written in 1668–9 as part of the Life.

There was a worse accident than all these which fell out in the time of the King's stay in Scotland, and about the time of the two Houses re-convening, which made a wonderful impression upon the minds of men, and proved of infinite disadvantage to the King's affairs which were then recovering new life; and that was the rebellion in Ireland, which brake out about the middle of October in all parts of the kingdom. Their design upon Dublin was miraculously discovered the night before it was to be executed,* and so the surprisal of that castle prevented, and the principal conspirators who had the charge of it apprehended. In the other parts of the kingdom they observed the time appointed, not hearing of the misfortunes of their friends at Dublin. A general insurrection of the Irish spread itself over the whole country, in such an inhuman and barbarous manner that there were forty or fifty thousand of the English Protestants murdered before they suspected themselves to be in any danger, or could provide for their defence by drawing together into towns or strong houses.

From Dublin the Lords Justices and Council despatched their letters by an express (the same man who had made the discovery, one O'Conelly, who had formerly been a servant to sir John Clotworthy)* to London, to the earl of Leicester, the Lord Lieutenant of Ireland. From the parts of the north and Ulster an express was sent to the King himself at Edinburgh; and the King's letters from thence to the two Houses arrived within less than two days after the messenger from Dublin.

It was upon a Sunday night that the letters from Dublin came to the earl of Leicester,* who immediately caused the Council to be summoned, and as soon as it was met informed them of the condition of Ireland, that is, so much as those letters contained, which were written when little more was known than the discovery at Dublin, and what the conspirators had confessed upon their examinations. The House of Peers had then adjourned itself to the Wednesday following, but the House of Commons were to meet on the next day, Monday morning; and the Council resolved that they would in a body go to the House of Commons as soon as it sat, and inform them of it; which they did, notice being first given to the House that the lords of the Council had some matters of importance to impart to them, and were above in the Painted Chamber ready to come to them: whereupon chairs were set in the House for them to repose themselves, and the sergeant sent to conduct them. As soon as they entered the House the Speaker desired them to sit down; and then, being covered,* Littleton, Lord Keeper, told the Speaker that 'the Lord Lieutenant of Ireland having received letters from the Lords Justices and Council there, had communicated them to the Council, and, since the House of Peers was not then sitting, they had thought fit, for the importance of the letters, to impart them to that House;' and so referred the business to the Lord Lieutenant, who, without any enlargement, only read the letters he had received, and so the lords departed from the House.

There was a deep silence in the House, and a kind of consternation, most men's heads having been intoxicated, from their first meeting in

Parliament, with imaginations of plots and treasonable designs through the three kingdoms. The affair itself seemed to be out of their conusance;* and the communication of it only served to prepare their thoughts what to do when more should be known, and when they should hear what the King thought fit to be done. And when the King's letters arrived, they were glad the news had come to him when he had so good council about him to advise him what to do.

The King was not then informed of what had been discovered at Dublin, but the letters out of Ulster (which he sent to the Parliament) gave him notice of the general insurrection in the north, and of the inhuman murders committed there upon a multitude of the Protestants, and that sir Phelim O'Neale appeared as the general and commander in chief.

Upon which his majesty writ to the two Houses that he was satisfied that it was no rash insurrection but a formed rebellion, which must be prosecuted with a sharp war; the conducting and prosecuting whereof he wholly committed to their care and wisdom, and depended upon them for the carrying it on; and that for the present he had caused a strong regiment of fifteen hundred foot, under good officers, to be transported out of Scotland into Ulster, for the relief of those parts; which were upon the matter wholly inhabited by Scots and Irish, there being fewer English than in any part of Ireland.

This fell out to their wish; and thereupon they made a committee of both Houses for the consideration of the affairs of Ireland, and providing for the supply of men, arms, and money, for the suppressing that rebellion, the Lord Lieutenant of Ireland being one of the committee, which sat every morning in the Painted Chamber. And the Lord Lieutenant first communicated all the letters he received to them, to be consulted upon, and to be thence reported to the two Houses, which were hereby possessed of a huge power and dependence, all men applying themselves to them, that is, to the chief leaders, for their preferments in that war: the mischief whereof, though in the beginning little taken notice of, was afterwards felt by the King very sensibly.

These concurrent circumstances much altered and suppressed that good humour and spirit the Houses were well disposed to meet with, and the angry men, who were disappointed of the preferments they expected and had promised themselves, took all occasions by their emissaries to insinuate into the minds of the people that this rebellion in Ireland was contrived or fomented by the King, or at least by the Queen, for the advancement of Popery, and that the rebels published and declared that they had the King's authority for all they did; which calumny, though without the least shadow or colour of truth, made more impression upon the minds of sober and moderate men (and who till then had much more disliked the passionate proceedings of the Parliament) than could be then imagined or can yet be believed, so great a prejudice, or want of reverence, was universally contracted against the Court, especially toward the Queen, whose power and activity was thought too great. [*HR*, IV, 24–31]

The Irish rebellion created a new opportunity for the parliamentary leaders to force further concessions. It was made plain that the House of Commons would agree to finance the suppression of the rebellion only if the King accepted some parliamentary control over his ministers. The demand was resisted in the House of Lords. The Remonstrance had originally been pro-posed in the House of Commons months before, and a Committee charged with its preparation. It was finally presented on 8 November, as part of a campaign to put pressure on the Lords, which depended not just on agree-ment of the text, but also on publishing it to mobilize the people of London. Clarendon's account of the ensuing proceedings, published in the History of the Rebellion, *was written in 1668–9 as part of the* Life.

About the time the news came of the King's being to begin his journey from Scotland upon a day appointed, and that he had settled all things in that kingdom to the general satisfaction, the committee for prepar-ing the Remonstrance offered their report to the House, which caused the draught they offered to be read. It contained a very bitter represen-tation of all the illegal things which had been done from the first hour of the King's coming to the crown to that minute, with all those sharp reflections which could be made upon the King himself, the Queen, and Council; and published all the unreasonable jealousies of the present government, of the introducing Popery, and all other particu-lars which might disturb the minds of the people, which were enough discomposed.

The House seemed generally to dislike it; many saying, 'that it was very unnecessary and unseasonable: unnecessary, all those grievances being already fully redressed, and the liberty and property of the sub-ject being as well secured for the future as can possibly be done: and then, that it was very unseasonable, after the King had gratified them with granting every thing which they had desired of him, and after so long absence in the settling the disorders in another kingdom, which he had happily composed, to be now welcomed home with such a volume of reproaches for what others had done amiss and which he himself had reformed.' Notwithstanding all which, all the other party appeared passionately concerned that it might not be rejected, and enlarged themselves with as high expressions against the government as at first; with many insinuations 'that we were in danger of being deprived of all the good Acts which we had gained if great care and vigilance was not used to disappoint some counsels which were still entertained;' making doubtful glances and reflections upon the rebellion in Ireland, (with which they perceived many good men were easily amused,) and in the end prevailed 'that a day should be appointed when the House should be resolved into a grand committee, and the Remonstrance to be then retaken into consideration:' and in the mean time they employed all their credit and interest with particular men, to persuade them that the passing that Remonstrance was most necessary for the preservation and maintenance of all those good laws which they had already made; giving several reasons to several persons, according to their natures and inclinations; assuring many that they intended it only for the mortification of the Court, and manifestation that that malignant party which appeared to be growing up in the House could not prevail, and then, that it should remain still in the clerk's hands and never be published.

And by these and the like arts they promised themselves that they should easily carry it: so that the day it was to be resumed, they entertained the House all the morning with other debates, and towards noon called for the Remonstrance: and it being urged by some that it was too late to enter upon it, with much difficulty they consented that it should be entered upon the next morning at nine of the clock, and every clause should be debated, the Speaker in the chair; for they would not have the House resolved into a committee, which they believed would spend too much time. Oliver Cromwell (who at that time was little taken notice of) asked the lord Falkland, 'Why he would have it put off, for that day would quickly have determined it?' He answered, 'There would not have been time enough, for sure it would take some debate.' The other replied, 'A very sorry one:' they supposing, by the computation they had made, that very few would oppose it.

But he quickly found he was mistaken: for, the next morning,* the debate being entered upon about nine of the clock in the morning, it continued all that day; and candles being called for when it grew dark, (neither side being very desirous to adjourn it till the next day; though it was evident very many withdrew themselves out of pure faintness, and disability to attend the conclusion,) the debate continued till after it was twelve of the clock, with much passion; and the House being then divided upon the passing or not passing it, it was carried for the affirmative by nine voices and no more: and as soon as it was declared, Mr Hampden moved 'that there might be an order entered for the present printing it;' which produced a sharper debate than the former. It appeared then, that they did not intend to send it up to the House of Peers for their concurrence, but that it was upon the matter an appeal to the people, and to infuse jealousies into their minds. It had never been the custom to publish any debates or determinations of the House which were not regularly first transmitted to the House of Peers, nor was it thought, in truth, that the House had authority to give warrant for the printing of any thing; all which was offered by Mr Hyde with some warmth, as soon as the motion was made for the printing it; and he said 'he did believe the printing it in that manner was not lawful, and he feared it would produce mischievous effects; and therefore desired the leave of the House that, if the question should be put and carried in the affirmative, he might have liberty to enter his protestation.' Which he no sooner said than Geoffrey Palmer (a man of great reputation, and much esteemed in the House) stood up and made the same motion for himself, that he might likewise protest, when immediately together many afterwards, without distinction and in some disorder, cried out, 'They did protest:' so that there was after scarce any quiet and regular debate. But the House by degrees being quieted, they all consented, about two of the clock in the morning, to adjourn till two of the clock the next afternoon. And as they went out of the House the lord Falkland asked Oliver Cromwell, 'Whether there had been a debate?' to which he answered. 'that he would take his word another time,' and whispered him in the ear, with some asseveration,* 'that if the Remonstrance had been rejected he would have sold all he had the next morning, and never have seen England more; and he knew there were many other honest men of the same resolution.' So near was the poor kingdom at that time to its deliverance!

And, however they got this victory, they did not in a long time recover the spirits they lost, and the agony they had sustained, whilst it was in suspense; and they discerned well enough that the House had not at that time half its members, though they had provided that not a man of their party was absent, and that they had even then carried it by the hour of the night, which drove away a greater number of old and infirm opposers than would have made those of the negative superior in number: so that they had little hope in a fuller House to prevail in any of their unjust designs, except they found some other expedient, by hopes or fears, to work upon the affections of the several members.

In order to which, they spent most part of the next day in their private consultations how to chastise some of those who had most offended them the day before, and resolved, in the first place, not to suffer that precedent to be introduced into the House, 'that men should protest against the sense of the House:' which it is true had not been used in the House of Commons. And this subject was the more grateful to them because they should hereby take revenge upon Mr Hyde, whom they perfectly hated above any man, and to whose activity they imputed the trouble they had sustained the day before; and he was the first who made the protestation, that is, asked leave to do it, which produced the other subsequent clamour, that was indeed in some disorder. But here they differed amongst themselves; all the leading violent men, who bore the greatest sway, were most glad of the occasion, as it gave them opportunity to be rid of Mr Hyde, which they passionately desired: but sir John Hotham, Cholmeley, and Stapleton,* who never severed, and had a numerous train which attended their motions, remembered the service Mr Hyde had done against the court of York,* (the overthrowing whereof was their peculiar glory,) and would not consent that they should question him, but were ready to concur with them in the prosecution of any other of the protesters, whereof there was number enough. This made so great difference amongst them that for the present they agreed no further than that they would that afternoon only provide that the next morning they would fall upon the matter; and so they might consult together at night what person they would sacrifice.

And so, about three of the clock, when the House met, Mr Pym lamented the disorder of the night before, which, he said, might probably have engaged the House in blood, and proceeded principally by the offering a protestation, which had been never before offered in that House, and was a transgression that ought to be severely examined, that mischief hereafter might not result from that precedent: and therefore proposed that the House would the next morning enter upon that examination, and in the meantime men might recollect themselves, and they who used to take notes might peruse their memorials, that the persons who were the chief causers of the disorder might be named, and defend themselves as best they could. And with this resolution the House rose; the vexation of the night before being very visible in the looks and countenance of many. And that night's deliberation, nor all the artifice or importunity that could be used, could not remove the obstinate Northern men from their resolution: and they declared positively that if they prosecuted Mr Hyde, they and all their friends would engage in his defence: but the others would not incur the danger or inconvenience of such a schism; and so they unanimously agreed upon a third person whom they would accuse.

The next morning they first enlarged upon the offence itself; of 'the mischief it had liked to have produced, and of the mischief it would unavoidably produce if the custom or liberty of it was ever introduced; that it was the first time it had ever been offered in that House; and that care ought to be taken that it should be the last, by the severe judgment of the House upon those persons who had begun the presumption.'

Mr Hyde, who had then known nothing of the private consultation, and had many reasons to believe himself to be designed, stood up (notwithstanding some signs made to him at a distance by his Northern friends, which he understood not) and said 'it concerned him to justify what he had done, being the first man who mentioned the protest-ation:' upon which there was a general noise and clamour 'to withdraw,' and as great 'to speak:' upon which he proceeded, and said 'he was not old enough to know the ancient customs of that House; but that he well knew it was a very ancient custom in the House of Peers, and leave was never denied to any man who asked that he might protest, and enter his dissent, against any judgment of the House to which he would not be understood to have given his consent: that he did not understand any reason why a commoner should not have the same liberty, if he desired not to be involved in any vote which he thought might possibly be inconvenient to him. That he had not offered his protestation against the Remonstrance, though he had opposed [it] all he could, because it remained still within those walls; that he had only desired leave to protest against the printing it, which he thought was not in many respects lawful for them to do, and might prove very pernicious to the public peace.'

They were very much offended with all he said and his confidence in speaking; and Mr Strode could not contain himself from saying, 'that that gentleman had confessed that he had first proposed the prot-estation,' and therefore desired he might withdraw, which many others likewise called for: till sir John Hotham appeared with some warmth against it; and young Hotham, his son, accused Geoffrey Palmer of giving the cause of disorder, by saying '*I do protest*,' without asking the leave of the House, and encouraging men to cry out every man, '*I do protest*,' whereupon they all fell into that noise and confusion; and so, without much more discourse, Mr Palmer was called upon 'to explain.' Which as he was about to do, Mr Hyde (who loved him much, and had rather have suffered himself than that he should) spake to the orders of the House, and said that 'it was against the orders and practice of the House that any man should be called upon to explain for any thing he said in the House two days before, when it could not be presumed that his own memory could recollect all the words he had used, or that any body else could charge him with them;' and appealed to the House whether there was any precedent of the like. And there is no doubt there never had been; and it was very irregular. But they were too positively resolved not to be diverted; and, after two hours' debate, Mr Palmer himself desiring that, to save the House further trouble, he might answer, and withdraw, which he did, and when it drew towards night, after many hours' debate it was ordered that he should be committed to the Tower; the angry men pressing with all their power that he might be expelled the House, having borne him a long grudge for the civility he shewed in the prosecution of the earl of Strafford, that is, that he had not used the same reproachful language which the others had done: but they were at last glad to compound for his bare commitment to the Tower, from whence he was within few days enlarged, and returned again to the House. And in the close of that day and the rising of the House, without much opposition, they obtained an order* for the printing their Remonstrance. . . .

I know not how those men have already answered it to their own consciences, or how they will answer it to Him who can discern their consciences, who, having assumed their country's trust, and, it may be, with great earnestness laboured to procure that trust, by their supine laziness, negligence and absence were the first inlets to these inundations, and so contributed to those licenses which have overwhelmed us. For by this means, a handful of men, much inferior in the beginning in number and interest, came to give laws to the major part; and, to shew that three diligent persons are a greater number in arithmetic, as well as a more significant number in logic, than ten unconcerned, they, by plurality of voices, in the end converted or reduced the whole body to their opinions. It is true, men of activity and faction, in any design, have many advantages that a composed and settled council, though industrious enough, usually have not, and some that gallant men cannot give themselves leave to entertain; for, besides their through considering and forming their counsels before they begin to execute, they contract a habit of ill nature and uningenuity, necessary to their affairs and the temper of those upon whom they are to work, that liberal-minded men would not persuade themselves to entertain, even for the prevention of all the mischief the others intend. And whoever observed the ill arts these men used, to prevail upon the people in general; their absurd, ridiculous lying, to win the affections and corrupt the understandings of the weak, and the bold scandals to confirm the wilful; the boundless promises they presented to the ambitious, and their gross, abject flatteries and applications to the vulgar-spirited; would hardly give himself leave to use those weapons for the preservation of the three kingdoms. [*HR*, IV, 49–74]

The King arrived back in London on 25 November, the same day as the vote against Geoffrey Palmer. Although the parliamentary leaders had won that and the vote on the Remonstrance, their initial failure to secure its printing showed that a King's party was beginning to coalesce in the House of Commons, while the Lords — including, in the bishops, the King's most reliable supporters — remained an insuperable obstacle to further reform. The King and the parliamentary leaders were locked in stalemate. In the last week of December, Charles, hoping to capitalize on the growth in his support, was planning to secure his control of London by replacing the commander of the Tower, and to put his opponents on trial. Clarendon's account of the militia bill was written in 1668–9 as part of the Life; *the subsequent description of the bill excluding the bishops from the Lords comes from the* History, *written in 1646–7.*

However for all this, and the better, it may be, for all this, the King upon his arrival at Whitehall found both his Houses of Parliament of a much better temper than they had been; many having great indignation to see his majesty so ill treated by his own servants and those who were most obliged to his bounty and magnificence, and likewise to discern how much ambition and private interest was covered under public pretences. They who were in truth zealous for the preservation of the law, the religion, and true interest of the nation, were solicitous to preserve the King's honour from any indignity and his regal power from violation; and so always opposed those who trenched upon either, and who could compass their ends by no other means than by trampling upon both. So that, in truth, that which was called the King's party in both Houses was made up of persons who were strangers, or without any obligation, to the Court, of the best fortunes and the best reputation in their several countries, where they were known as having always appeared very zealous in the maintenance of their just rights, and opposed, as much as in them lay, all illegal and grievous impositions: whilst his own Privy Council, (two or three only excepted,) and much the greater number of all his own servants, either publicly opposed or privately betrayed him, and so much the more virulently abhorred all those who now appeared to carry on his service, because they presumed to undertake, at least to endeavour, (for they undertook nothing nor looked for any thanks for their labour,) to do that which they ought to have done. And so they were upon this disadvantage, that, whenever they pressed any thing in the House which seemed immediately to advance the King's power and authority, some of the King's Council or his servants most opposed it, under the notion of being 'prejudicial to the King's interest': whilst they who had used to govern and impose upon the House made show of being more modest, and were more silent, and endeavoured by setting new counsels on foot to entangle and engage, and indeed to overreach, the House, by cozening them into opinions which might hereafter be applicable to their ends, rather than to pursue their old designs, in hope to obtain in the end a success by their authority. The night of the Remonstrance had humbled them in that point: and from that time they rather contrived ways to silence those who opposed them by traducing them abroad, and taking any advantage against them in the House for any expressions they used in debate which might be misinterpreted, and so calling them to the bar, or committing them to the Tower: which did in truth strike such a terror into the minds of many that they forbore to come to the House, rather than expose themselves to so many uneasinesses there.

There was at this time, or thereabout, a debate started in the House, as if by mere chance, which produced many inconveniences after, and, if there had not been too many concurrent causes, might be thought the sole cause and ground of all the mischiefs which ensued. Upon some report or discourse of some accident which had happened upon or in the disbanding the late army, an obscure member moved, 'That the House would enter upon the consideration whether the militia of the kingdom was so settled by law that a sudden force or army could be drawn together, for the defence of the kingdom if it should be invaded, or to suppress an insurrection or rebellion if it should be attempted.'

The House kept a long silence after the motion, the newness of it amazing most men, and few in truth understanding the meaning of it; until one and another of the members who were least taken notice of, seeming to be moved by the weight of what had been said, enlarged upon the same argument: and in the end it was proposed, 'That a committee might be appointed to consider of the present state of the militia and the power of it; and to prepare such a bill for the settling it as might provide for the public peace, and for the suppressing any foreign enemy or domestic insurrection.'

And hereupon they were inclined to nominate a committee to prepare such a bill as should be thought necessary: upon which Mr Hyde spake against the making any such committee, [and] said, 'There could be no doubt that the power of the militia resided in the King, in whom the right of making war and peace was invested; that there had never yet appeared any defect of power by which the kingdom had been in danger, and we might reasonably expect the same security for the future.' With which the House seemed well satisfied and composed, and inclined to resume some other debate, until St John, who was then the King's Solicitor, and the only man in the House of his learned counsel, stood up, and said, 'He could not suffer that debate, in which there had been so many weighty particularities mentioned, to be discontinued without some resolution: that he would be very glad there were that power in the King, (whose rights he was bound to defend) as the gentleman who spake last seemed to imagine; which, for his part, he knew there was not; that the question was not about taking any power from the King which was vested in him, (which was his duty always to oppose,) but to inquire, whether there be such a power in him, or any where else, as is necessary for the preservation of the King and the people in many cases that may fall out; and if there be not, then to supply him with that power and authority;' and he said, 'he did take upon him with confidence to say that there was a defect of such power and authority.' He put them in mind, 'how that power had been executed in the age in which we live; that the Crown had granted commissions to great men to be lord lieutenants of counties, and they to gentlemen of quality to be their deputy lieutenants, and to colonels and other officers to conduct and list soldiers;' and then he wished them to consider what votes they had passed of the illegality of all those commissions, and the unjustifiableness of all the proceedings which had [been] by virtue of those commissions; so that, let the occasion or necessity be what it would, he did presume no man would hereafter execute any such commission, and if there were any men so hardy, that nobody would obey them; and therefore desired them to consider 'whether there be not a defect of power, and whether it ought not to be supplied.'

It was now evident enough that the debate had not begun by chance, but had been fully deliberated; and what use they would make, upon occasions, of those volumes of votes they had often poured out upon all accidental debates; and no man durst take upon him to answer all that had been alleged by saying all those votes were of no validity, and that the King's right was, and would be judged, the same it had been before, notwithstanding those votes; which is very true: but this being urged by the King's own Solicitor, they appointed him to bring in and prepare such a bill as he thought necessary; few men imagining that such a sworn officer would not be very careful and tender of all his master's prerogatives, which he was expressly sworn to defend.

Within few days after, he brought in a very short bill,* in which was mentioned by way of preface, 'That the power over the militia of the kingdom was not settled in any such manner that the security of the kingdom was provided for in case of invasion, or insurrection, or such like accidents;' and then an enacting clause, 'That henceforward the militia, and all the power thereof, should be vested in, &c.——,' and then a large blank left for inserting names; and afterwards, the 'absolute authority to execute, &c.' The ill meaning whereof was easily understood, and with some warmth pressed, 'that by this bill all the power would be taken out of the Crown, and put into the hands of commissioners.' To which the Solicitor made answer, 'That the bill took no power from any body who had it, but was provided to give power where it was not; nor was there mention of any commissioners; but a blank was therefore left that the House might fill it up as they thought fit, and put the power into such hands as they thought proper; which, for ought he knew, might be the King's, and he hoped it would be so.'

And with this answer the bill was received, notwithstanding all opposition, and read; all those persons who had formerly been deputy lieutenants,* and lay under the terror of that vote, presuming that this settlement would provide for the indemnity of all that had passed before; and the rest, who might still be exposed to the same hazards if they should be required to act upon the like occasions, concurring in the desire that somewhat might be done for a general security. And they who had contrived it were well enough contented that it was once read, not desiring to prosecute it till some more favourable conjuncture should be offered: and so it rested. . . .

All this time the bill depended in the Lords' House for the taking away the votes of bishops and removing them from the House of Peers, which was not like to make a more prosperous progress there than it had six months before;* it being evident that the jurisdiction of the peerage was invaded by the Commons, and therefore that it was not reasonable to part with any of their supporters. But the virulence against them still increased; and no churches frequented but where they were preached against as antichristian; the presses swelled with the most virulent invectives against them; and a sermon was preached at Westminster, and afterwards printed under the title of *The Protestation Protested*, by the infamous Burton,* whereby he declared that all men were obliged by their late protestation, by what means soever, to remove both bishops and the Common Prayer Book out of the Church of England as impious and papistical: whilst all the learned and orthodox divines of England were looked upon under the notion of *scandalous ministers*, and if the meanest and most vicious parishioner they had could be brought to prefer a petition against either of them to the House of Commons, (how false soever,) he was sure to be prosecuted as such.

In the end, a petition was published in the name of 'the apprentices and those whose apprenticeships were lately expired, in and about the city of London;' and directed 'To the King's most excellent majesty in the Parliament now assembled;' shewing, 'That they found by experience, both by their own and masters' tradings, the beginning of great mischiefs coming upon them, to nip them in the bud when they were first entering into the world; the cause of which they could attribute to no others but the Papists and the prelates and that malignant party which adhered to them: that they stood solemnly engaged, with their utmost of their lives and fortunes, to defend his sacred majesty and royal issue, together with the rights and liberties of Parliaments, against Papists, and popish innovators, such as archbishops, bishops, and their dependents, appear to be. They desired his majesty in Parliament to take notice that notwithstanding the much unwearied pains and industry of the House of Commons to subdue Popery and popish innovators, neither is Popery yet subdued, nor prelates are yet removed; whereby many had taken encouragements desperately to plot against the peace and safety of his dominions: witness the most barbarous and inhuman cruelties perpetrated by the Papists in Ireland; from whence,' they said, 'a new spring of fears and jealousies arose in them: and therefore they desired that the popish lords and other eminent and dangerous Papists in all parts of the kingdom might be looked unto and secured, the laws against priests and Jesuits fully executed, and the prelacy rooted up: that so the work of reformation might be prosperously carried on, their distracting fears removed, that the freedom of commerce and trade might pass on more cheerfully, for the encouragement of the petitioners,' &c.

This and such stuff being printed and scattered amongst the people, multitudes of mean people flocked to Westminster Hall, and about the Lords' House, crying, as they went up and down, '*No bishops, no bishops*,' that so they might carry on the reformation.

I said before, that upon the King's return from Scotland he discharged the guards that attended upon the Houses.* Whereupon the House of Commons (for the Lords refused to join with them) petitioned the King, 'in regard of the fears they had of some design from the Papists, that they might continue such a guard about them as they thought fit.'

To which his majesty answered,* 'That he was confident they had no just cause of fear, and that they were as safe as himself and his children: but, since they did avow such an apprehension of danger, that he would appoint a sufficient guard for them.' And thereupon directed the train-bands* of Westminster and Middlesex (which consisted of the most substantial householders, and were under known officers) in fit numbers to attend.

This security was not liked, and it was asked, *Quis custodiet ipsos custodes?* And when the disorderly rabble I spake of now first came down they resisted them, and would not suffer them to disturb the Houses; and some of them with great rudeness pressing to the door of the House of Peers, their lordships appointed the guard to be called up to remove them; and the earl of Dorset, being then lord lieutenant of Middlesex, the crowd oppressing him and refusing to leave the room, in some passion called upon the guard 'to give fire upon them;' whereupon the rabble, frighted, left the place, and hasted away.

The House of Commons, much incensed that their friends should be so used, much inveighed against the earl of Dorset, and talked of accusing him of high treason, at least of drawing up some impeachment against him, for some judgment he had been party to in the Star-Chamber or Council-table: and so, giving these hints of their displeasure that he might have the more care hereafter to carry himself, they concluded that, since they could not have such a guard as pleased them, they would have none at all: and so sent to the Lords for the discharge of the train-bands that attended, who willingly consented to it; which was done accordingly, the House of Commons declaring, 'That it should be lawful for every member to bring his own servants to attend at the door, armed with such weapons as they thought fit.'

It was quickly understood abroad that the Commons liked well the visitation of their neighbours: so that the people assembled in greater numbers than before about the House of Peers, calling still out with one voice, '*No bishops, no popish lords*,' crowded and affronted such lords as came near them, and whom they knew affected not their ends, calling them '*rotten-hearted lords*.'

Hereupon the House of Peers desired a conference with the Commons, at which they complained of these tumults, and told them 'that such disorders would be an imputation upon the Parliament, and make it be doubted whether they had freedom, and so might happily become a blemish to those many good laws they had already passed, as well as prevent the making more:' and therefore desired them, that they would, for the 'dignity of parliaments,' join with them in a declaration for the suppressing such tumults. This was reported to the Commons; and as soon laid aside, for the handling of other matters of more importance.

The tumults continued, and their insolencies increased; insomuch as many dissolute and profane people went into the abbey at Westminster, and would have pulled down the organs and some ornaments of the church; but being resisted, and by force driven out, they threatened they would come with greater numbers, and pull down the church.

Hereupon the Lords again send to the House of Commons to join with them in their declaration; and many members of that House complained that they could not come with safety to the House, and that some of them had been assaulted, and very ill entreated, by those people that crowded about that door. But this could not be procured; the debate being still put off to some other time, after several speeches had been made in justification of them and commendation of their affections: some saying 'they must not discourage their friends, this being a time they must make use of all friends;' Mr Pym himself saying, 'God forbid the House of Commons should proceed, in any way, to dishearten people to obtain their just desires in such a way.'

In the end, the Lords required the advice of the judges what course was legally to be taken to suppress and prevent those disorders: and thereupon directed the Lord Keeper of the Great Seal to issue out a writ, upon the statute of Northampton, to the sheriff and justices, to appoint strong watches in such places as they judged most convenient, to hinder that unlawful conflux of people to Westminster, to the disturbance of their consultations. Which writ issuing accordingly, the justices of peace, in obedience thereunto, appointed the constables to attend at the water-side and places near about Westminster, with good watches, to hinder that tumultuous resort.

This was no sooner done than the constables were sent for, and, after the view of their warrants, required to discharge their watches; and then the justices convened, and examined; and, albeit it appeared that what they had done was in pursuance of a legal writ, directed to them under the Great Seal of England, by the advice of the Lords in Parliament, without so much as conferring with the Lords upon that act of theirs, the setting such a watch was voted to be a breach of privilege, and one of the justices of the peace, who according to his oath had executed that writ, was committed to the Tower for that offence.

Upon this encouragement all the factious and schismatical people about the city and suburbs assembled themselves together with great license, and would frequently, as well in the night as the day, convene themselves, by the sound of a bell or other token, in the fields, or some convenient place, to consult, and receive orders from those by whom they were to be disposed. A meeting of this kind being about the time we speak of in Southwark, in a place where their arms and magazine for that borough was kept, the constable, being a sober man, and known to be an enemy to those acts of sedition, went amongst them to observe what they did: he was no sooner espied but he was reproached with disdainful words, beaten, and dragged in so barbarous a manner that he hardly escaped with his life. Complaint was made to the next justices, and oath of the truth of the complaint: whereupon a writ was directed to the sheriff to impanel a jury, according to the law, for the inquisition and examination of that riot.

This was complained of in the House of Commons as an act that concerned their privileges: for that it was pretended 'that meeting in Southwark had been by godly and well affected men, only to draw up and prepare a petition against bishops, and that the constable, being a friend to bishops, came amongst them to cross them, and to hinder men from subscribing that wholesome petition.' And upon this discourse, without any further examination, an order was made by that House, 'that the under-sheriff of Surrey should be enjoined not to suffer any proceedings to be made upon any inquisition that might concern any persons who met together to subscribe a petition to be preferred to that House.'

By this, and other means, all obstacles of the law being removed, and the people taught a way to assemble lawfully together, in how tumultuous a manner soever, and the Christmas holidays giving more leave and license to all kinds of people, the concourse grew more numerous about Westminster; the people sometimes, in their passage between the city and Westminster, making a stand before Whitehall, and crying out, '*No bishops, no bishops, no popish lords*,' would say aloud 'that they would have no more porter's lodge, but would speak with the King when they pleased:' and, where they came near the two Houses, took out papers from their pockets, and, getting upon some place higher than the rest, would read the names of several persons under the title of '*disaffected members of the House of Commons*;' and called many lords '*false, evil, and rotten-hearted lords*.' But their rage and fury against the bishops grew so high that they threatened to pull down the lodgings where they lay, offered to force the doors of the abbey at Westminster, which were kept locked many days and defended by a continual guard within, and assaulted the persons of some of the bishops in their coaches; and laid hands on the archbishop of York* in that manner that, if he had not been seasonably rescued, it was believed they would have murdered him: so that all the bishops, and many other members of both Houses, withdrew themselves from attending in the Houses, out of a real apprehension of endangering their lives.

These insurrections by this means were so countenanced that no industry or dexterity of the lord mayor of London, sir Richard Gurney, could give any check to them; but, instead thereof, himself with great and very notable courage opposing all their fanatic humours both in the Court of Aldermen and at the Common Council,* grew to be reckoned in the first form of the *Malignants*, (which was the term they imposed upon all those they meant to render odious to the people,) insomuch as his house was no less threatened and disquieted by the tumults than the House of Lords: and when he apprehended some of those who were most notorious in the riot, and committed them to the custody of both the sheriffs of London in person, to be carried to Newgate,* they were by the power and strength of their companions rescued from them in Cheapside, and the two sheriffs compelled to shift for their own safety. And when it was offered to be proved by a member in the House of Commons that the wife of captain Venn,* (having received a letter from her husband to that purpose, who was one of the burgesses for London, and was known himself to lead those men that came tumultuously down to Westminster and Whitehall at the time of the passing the bill of attainder of the earl of Strafford,) had with great industry solicited many people to go down with their arms to Westminster upon a day that was named, when, she said, her husband had sent her word that in the House of Commons they were together by the ears, and that the worser party was like to get the better of the good party, and therefore her husband desired his friends to come with their arms to Westminster to help the good party, and that thereupon very many in a short time went thither, they who offered to make proof of the same were appointed to attend many days, but, notwithstanding all the importunity that could be used, were never admitted to be heard. [*HR*, IV, 104–20]

In the week between Christmas and New Year 1641, the atmosphere of confrontation and danger in the capital grew even greater than it had been in May. The King's replacement of the commander of the Tower of London on 22 December implied preparations for a military coup. In response, the rioting in London, and hostility to the bishops, intensified. By 28 December the bishops were unable to attend the House of Lords; their absence removed the obstacle preventing the passage of further reform legislation. The bishops' protests only served to inflame the situation further, and provided an excuse for the presentation of charges of high treason against all of them, and their imprisonment in the Tower. Charles attempted to retrieve the situation. He replaced his new commander at the Tower with someone more acceptable to the reformers; and he made approaches to some of the more moderate of them.

He was rebuffed, however, and thrown back on trying to consolidate his own party within the Commons. The description of the appointments of well-known moderates to lead the King's party comes from the Life, *written in 1669, and was included in the* History of the Rebellion.

All this time the King (who had been with great solemnity invited [by] the city of London, and desired to make his residence nearer to them than Hampton Court) was at Whitehall, where, besides his ordinary retinue and menial servants, many officers of the late disbanded army, who solicited their remainder of pay from the two Houses which was secured to them by Act of Parliament, and expected some farther employment in the war with Ireland, upon observation and view of the insolence of the tumults and the danger that they might possibly bring to the Court, offered themselves for a guard to his majesty's person, and were with more formality and ceremony entertained by him than, upon a just computation of all distempers, was by many conceived season-able. And from these officers, warm with indignation at the insolencies of that vile rabble which every day passed by the Court, first words of great contempt, and then (those words commonly finding a return of equal scorn) blows, were fastened upon some of the most pragmatical of the crew. This was looked upon by the House of Commons like a levying war by the King, and much pity expressed by them that the poor people should be so used who came to them with petitions, (for some few of them had received some cuts and slashes that had drawn blood,) and that made a great argument for reinforcing their numbers. And from those contestations the two terms of '*Roundhead*' and '*Cavalier*' grew to be received in discourse, and were afterwards continued, for the most succinct distinction of affections throughout the quarrel: they who were looked upon as servants to the King being then called '*Cavaliers*,' and the other of the rabble contemned and despised under the names of '*Roundheads*.'

The House of Commons being at this time without any member who, having relation to the King's service, would express any zeal for it, and could take upon him to say to others whom he would trust what the King desired, or to whom they who wished well could resort for advice and direction; so that whilst there was a strong conjunction and combination to disturb the government by depraving it, whatever was said or done to support it was as if it were done by chance, and by the private dictates of the reason of private men; the King resolved to call the lord Falkland, and sir John Culpepper, who was knight of the shire for Kent, to his Council, and to make the former Secretary of State in the place of Vane that had been kept vacant, and the latter Chancellor of the Exchequer, which office the lord Cottington had resigned that Mr Pym might be put into that office when the lord Bedford should have been Treasurer, as is mentioned before. They were both of great authority in the House; neither of them of any relation to the Court, and therefore what they said made the more impression; and they were frequent speakers. The lord Falkland was wonderfully beloved by all who knew him, as a man of excellent parts, of a wit so sharp and a nature so sincere that nothing could be more lovely. The other was generally esteemed as a good speaker, being a man of an universal understanding, a quick comprehension, a wonderful memory, who commonly spake at the end of the debate, when he would recollect all that had been said of weight on all sides with great exactness, and express his own sense with much clearness, and such an application to the House that no man more gathered a general concurrence to his opinion than he; which was the more notable because his person and manner of speaking were ungracious enough; so that he prevailed only by the strength of his reason, which was enforced with confidence enough. His infirmities were known only to his nearest friends, or those who were admitted into his most intimate conversation.

The King knew them to be of good esteem in the House, and good affections to his service and the quiet of the kingdom, and was more easily persuaded to bestow those preferments upon them than the lord Falkland was to accept that which was designed to him. No man could be more surprised than he was when the first insinuation was made to him of the King's purpose: he had never proposed any such thing to himself, nor had any veneration for the Court, but only such a loyalty to the person of the King as the law required from him. And he had naturally a wonderful reverence for parliaments, as believing them most solicitous for justice, the violation whereof, in the least degree, he could not forgive any mortal power: and it was only his observation of the uningenuity and want of integrity in this [Parliament], which lessened that reverence to it, and which had disposed him to cross and oppose their designs. He was so totally unacquainted with business, and the forms of it, that he did believe really he could not execute the office with any sufficiency. But there were two considerations that made most impression upon him; the one, lest the world should believe that his own ambition had procured this promotion, and that he had therefore appeared signally in the House to oppose those proceedings that he might thereby render himself gracious to the Court: the other, lest the King should expect such a submission and resignation of himself and his own reason and judgment to his commands, as he should never give or pretend to give; for he was so severe an adorer of truth that he could as easily have given himself leave to steal as to dissemble, or to suffer any man to think that he would do any thing which he resolved not to do; which he thought a more mischievous kind of lying than a positive averring what could be most easily contradicted.

It was a very difficult task to Mr Hyde, who had most credit with him, to persuade him to submit to this purpose of the King cheerfully, and with a just sense of the obligation, by promising that in those parts of the office which required most drudgery he would help him the best he could, and would quickly inform him of all the necessary forms. But, above all, he prevailed with him by enforcing the ill consequence of his refusal to take the office, which would be interpreted to his dislike of the Court and his opinion that more would be required from him than he could honestly comply with, which would bring great prejudice to the King: on the other hand, the great benefit that probably would redound to the King and the kingdom by his accepting such a trust in such a general defection, by which he would have opportunity to give the King a truer information of his own condition and the state of the kingdom than it might be presumed had been given to him, and to prevent any counsels or practice which might more alienate the affections of the people from the government; and then, that by this relation he would be more able to do the King service in the House, where he was too well known to have it believed that he attained to it by any unworthy means or application. And, in the end, he was persuaded to submit to the King's good pleasure, though he could not prevail upon himself to do it with so good a grace as might raise in the King any notable expectation of his departing from the severity of his own nature.

And so they were both invested in those offices,* to the no small displeasure of the governing party, which could not dissemble their indignation that any of their members should presume to receive those preferments which they had designed otherwise to have disposed of. They took all opportunities to express their dislike of them, and to oppose any thing they proposed to them. And within few days there came a letter out in print, pretended to be intercepted, as written from a Roman Catholic to another of the same profession, in which he gives an account that 'they had at last, by the interest of their friends, procured those two noble persons' (who are mentioned before) 'to be preferred to those offices, and that they were well assured that they would be ready to do them and all their friends all good offices.' Sir John Culpepper thought fit to take notice of it in the House, and to make those professions of his religion which he thought necessary. But the lord Falkland chose rather to contemn it, without taking any notice of the libel, well knowing that he was superior to those calumnies; as indeed he was, all of that profession knowing that he was most irreconcilable to their doctrine, though he was always civil to their persons. However grievous this preferment was to the angry part of the House, it was very grateful to all those both within and without the House who wished well to the King and to the kingdom. [*HR*, IV, 121–5]

Hyde was also in line for an appointment, particularly as he had already started to act as the King's propagandist. In this passage from the Life, *Clarendon described how his answer to the Grand Remonstrance was adopted as the King's official response.*

As soon as the remonstrance, so much mentioned before, was printed, Mr Hyde, only to give vent to his own indignation, and without the least purpose of communicating it, or that any use should be made of it, had drawn such a full answer to it, as the subject would have enabled any man to have done who had thought of it: and the lord Digby, who had much conversation and friendship with him, coming accidentally and suddenly into the room, where he was alone amongst his books and papers; conferring together of the extravagant proceedings of the parliament, he, upon the familiarity that was between them, and upon the argument that was then between them, read the answer to him which he had prepared to the remonstrance; with which he seemed much pleased, and desired him, that he would permit it to be made use of by the king, and that he might shew it to his majesty; who found it absolutely necessary to publish some answer in his own name to that remonstrance, which had so much poisoned the hearts of the people; and that his majesty was endeavouring to procure such an answer to be drawn. The other expressly and positively refused to give it him, or that any use should be made of it; and reproached him for proposing a thing to him which might prove ruinous to him, if the house should have the least imagination that he exercised himself in such offices; with which answer he seemed satisfied, and departed: no other person having seen it but the lord Falkland, from whom nothing was ever concealed.

Within few days after, the lord Digby, with whom the king advised in the business of the parliament without reserve, came again to him; and, after some apologies, told him freely, that very many had been with the king, desiring him that he would take care that some answer might be published to that remonstrance, which had already done much harm, and would do much more if it were not answered; and that the king had spoken to him; upon which he had confessed that he had seen an answer that pleased him very well, but could not prevail with the author of it to suffer it to be made use of; and told him who it was: whereupon the king seemed to wonder very much, that a person, who had appeared so publicly in defence of his service, should be so wary of assisting him in private: and after many expressions of grace towards that gentleman, his majesty had commanded him to come in his name to him; and to conjure him to send that paper to him; and to give him his royal word, that no person living should know that he had the least hand in it; so that no danger should accrue to him thereby.

Mr Hyde, though he was very unsatisfied with what the lord Digby had done, (whose affection to him he did not in any degree make question of, but did not like his over activity, to which his restless fancy always disposed him; and as he doubted not that himself had given the occasion to the king to send those commands, so he had likewise enlarged those commands, as he believed, in such a manner as he thought might most oblige him,) yet, upon the real consideration that it might do the king much service, he did, without delay, deliver the papers; insisting upon the promise of secrecy, and, likewise, that his majesty would not publish without first communicating it to his council, and as done with their advice. And to that purpose he affixed that title to it, before he delivered the papers out of his hands; believing, that as it would be more for the king's service to carry such an authority in the front of it, as 'The king's answer with the advice of his council;' so it could not be refused by them, and yet might engage them in some displeasure with the house of commons, which probably might be offended at it. The king was very punctual in doing what was desired, and caused it to be read at a full council, where many of the lords commended it very much, and none spake against it; and so it was published and printed;* and it was very apparent to all men, that the king's service was very much advanced by it; and it was not more evident to any than to the house of commons, who knew not how to make any expostulation upon it, it being in the king's own name, and published with the advice of his privy-council: so that all they could do was, to endeavour to discover who was the penner of it; to which discovery they were most intent by all their secret friends in court, who found means to discover most other secrets to them, but in this could do them no service.

As soon as the lord Falkland and sir John Culpepper were called to the privy council, the king sent for Mr Hyde to him, who had not seen his majesty from the time he had been presented by Mr Percy.* He commanded the lord Digby to bring him when it was night to the queen's back stairs; and as soon as he was there, both king and queen came into the room; and when he had kissed their hands, and the lord Digby was withdrawn, the king told him, 'he was much beholden to him for many good services, and that now he had preferred two of his friends, it was time to give him some testimony of his favour; and therefore he had sent to him to tell him that he intended to make him his solicitor general, in the place of him who had served him so ill.'* Mr Hyde suddenly answered, 'God forbid!' With which the king seeming surprised, said, 'Why God forbid?' The other replied, 'It was in no degree fit at this time that he should remove the other; and if he were removed, himself was in no degree fit for it.' The queen said 'he ought not to suffer for his modesty: she had heard men, who could judge well, say, that he was as fit for it as the other.' Mr Hyde said, 'that was an argument that gentleman thought the other not fit for it, not that he believed *him* fit; which in truth, he said, he was not. That it might be, that when the place was actually void, the king might have filled it better with another man than with Mr St John, whose parts were not above many others, and his affections were below most men's: but now that he was invested in that office, it was not a good conjuncture to remove him; and when it should be, he did humbly advise his majesty to make choice of the ablest man of the profession, whose affections were clear, by whom he might indeed have great benefit; whereas himself was young, and without any of that learning or experience which might make him capable of that great trust.' The queen saying again this was his modesty, he replied, 'Madam, when you know me better, you will not find me so modest a man, but that I hope by your majesty's favour, in due time, to be made a better man than I am at present: but, if you believe that I know any thing of the disposition of the present time, or of what may conduce to the king's service, I pray believe, that though the solicitor will never do much service, he will be able to do much more mischief if he be removed.' The king at the same time resolved to remove another officer, who did disserve him notoriously, and to prefer Mr Hyde to that place; with which their gracious intention both their majesties acquainted him: but he positively refused it; and assured both their majesties, that he should be able to do much more service in the condition he was in. [*Life*, II, 1–6]

6. The Five Members

Lord Digby, the son of one of Charles's oldest advisers, the Earl of Bristol, and one of the reformers associated earlier with the Earl of Bedford, had been behind the studied moderation of the King's new appointments. He was also closely involved in the King's decision to attempt to arrest some of the parliamentary leaders, which went spectacularly wrong in the first week of 1642. Clarendon's sketch of Digby, and his relationship to Hyde, Falkland, and Culpepper, comes from the Life, *written in 1669, and published in the* History of the Rebellion. *The following passage on the events of 3 January 1642, comes from the original* History, *and its sequel from the* Life, *though both were published in the* History of the Rebellion.

BY what hath been said before it appears that the lord Digby was much trusted by the King, and he was of great familiarity and friendship with the other three, at least with two of them; for he was not a man of that exactness as to be in the entire confidence of the lord Falkland, who looked upon his infirmities with more severity than the other two did, and he lived with more frankness towards those two than he did towards the other: yet between them two there was a free conversation and kindness to each other. He was a man of very extraordinary parts by nature and art, and had surely as good and excellent an education as any man of that age in any country: a graceful and beautiful person; of great eloquence and becomingness in his discourse, (save that sometimes he seemed a little affected,) and of so universal a knowledge that he never wanted subject for a discourse: he was equal to a very good part in the greatest affair, but the unfittest man alive to conduct it, having an ambition and vanity superior to all his other parts, and a confidence peculiar to himself, which sometimes intoxicated and transported and exposed him. He had from his youth, by the disobligations his family had undergone from the duke of Buckingham and the great men who succeeded him, and some sharp reprehension himself had met with* which obliged him to a country life, contracted a prejudice and ill-will to the Court; and so had in the beginning of the Parliament engaged himself with that party which discovered most aversion from it, with a passion and animosity equal to their own, and therefore very acceptable to them. But when he was weary of their violent counsels, and withdrew himself from them with some circumstances which enough provoked them, and made a reconciliation and mutual confidence in each other for the future manifestly impossible, he made private and secret offers of his service to the King, to whom, in so general a defection of his servants, it could not but be very agreeable: and so his majesty, being satisfied both in the discoveries he made of what had passed and in his professions for the future, removed him from the House of Commons, where he had rendered himself marvellously ungracious, and called him by writ to the House of Peers,* where he did visibly advance the King's service, and quickly rendered himself grateful to all those who had not thought too well of him before, when he deserved less; and men were not only pleased with the assistance he gave upon all debates by his judgment and vivacity, but looked upon him as one who could derive the King's pleasure to them, and make a lively representation of their good demeanour to the King, which he was very luxuriant in promising to do, and officious enough in doing as much as was just.

He had been instrumental in promoting the three persons abovementioned to the King's favour, and had himself, in truth, so great an esteem of them that he did very frequently, upon conference together, depart from his own inclinations and opinions and concurred in theirs; and very few men of so great parts are, upon all occasions, more counsellable than he; so that he would seldom be in danger of running into great errors if he would communicate and expose all his own thoughts and inclinations to such a disquisition; nor is he uninclinable in his nature to such an entire communication in all things which he conceives to be difficult. But his fatal infirmity is, that he too often thinks difficult things very easy; and doth not consider possible consequences when the proposition administers somewhat that is delightful to his fancy, and by pursuing whereof he imagines he shall reap some glory to himself, of which he is immoderately ambitious; so that, if the consultation be upon any action to be done, no man more implicitly enters into that debate, or more cheerfully resigns his own conceptions to a joint determination: but when it is once affirmatively resolved, (besides that he may possibly reserve some impertinent circumstance, as he thinks, the imparting whereof would change the nature of the thing,) if his fancy suggests to him any particular which himself might perform in that action, upon the imagination that every body would approve it if it were proposed to them he chooses rather to do it than to communicate, that he may have some signal part to himself in the transaction in which no other person can claim a share. And by this unhappy temper he did often involve himself in very unprosperous attempts.

The King himself was the unfittest person alive to be served by such a counsellor, being too easily inclined to sudden enterprises, and as easily amazed when they were entered upon. And from this unhappy composition in the one and the other, a very unhappy counsel was entered upon, and resolution taken, without the least communication with either of the three which had been so lately admitted to an entire trust. [*HR*, IV, 127–9]

In the afternoon of a day when the two Houses sat,* Herbert, the King's Attorney, informed the House of Peers that he had somewhat to say to them from the King; and thereupon, having a paper in his hand, he said that the King commanded him to accuse the lord Kimbolton, a member of that House, and five gentlemen who were all members of the House of Commons, of high treason, and that his majesty had himself delivered him in writing several articles upon which he accused them; and thereupon he read in a paper the ensuing articles,* by which the lord Mandeville, Denzil Holles, sir Arthur Haselrig, Mr Pym, Mr Hampden, and Mr Strode, stood accused of high treason for conspiring against the King and the Parliament. . . .

The House of Peers was somewhat appalled at this alarum, but took time to consider of it till the next day, that they might see how their masters the Commons would behave themselves; the lord Kimbolton being present in the House and making great professions of his innocence, and no lord being so hardy [as] to press for his commitment on the behalf of the King.

At the same time, a sergeant at arms demanded to be heard at the House of Commons from the King, and, being sent for to the bar, demanded the persons of the five members to be delivered to him in his majesty's name, his majesty having accused them of high treason. But the Commons were not so much surprised with the accident; for, besides that they quickly knew what had passed with the Lords, some servants of the King's, by special warrant, had visited the lodgings of some of the accused members, and sealed up their studies and trunks; upon information whereof, before the sergeant came to the House, or public notice was taken of the accusation, an order was made by the Commons, 'That if any person whatsoever should come to the lodgings of any member of that House, and there offer to seal the doors, trunks, or papers, of such member, or to seize upon their persons, that then such member should require the aid of the next constable, to keep such persons in safe custody till the House should give further order: that if any person whatsoever should offer to arrest or detain any member of that House, without first acquainting that House therewith and receiving further order from thence, that it should be lawful for such member to stand upon his guard and make resistance, and [for] any person to assist him, according to the protestation taken to defend the privileges of Parliament.' And so, when the sergeant had delivered his message, he was no more called in, but a message sent to the King 'that the members should be forthcoming as soon as a legal charge should be preferred against them;' and so the House adjourned till the next day, every one of the accused persons taking a copy of that order which was made for their security.

The next day in the afternoon, the King, attended only by his own guard, and some few gentlemen who put themselves into their company in the way, came to the House of Commons, and, commanding all his attendants to wait at the door and to give offence to no man, himself, with his nephew, the Prince Elector,* went into the House, to the great amazement of all; and the Speaker leaving the chair, the King went into it, and told the House, 'He was sorry for that occasion of coming to them; that yesterday he had sent a sergeant at arms to apprehend some that by his command were accused of high treason, whereunto he expected obedience, but instead thereof he had received a message.' He declared to them that 'no King of England had been ever, or should be, more careful to maintain their privileges than he would be; but that in cases of treason no man had privilege; and therefore he came to see if any of those persons whom he had accused were there; for he was resolved to have them, wheresoever he should find them.' And looking then about, and asking the Speaker whether they were in the House, and he making no answer, he said, 'he perceived the birds were all flown, but expected they should be sent to him as soon as they returned thither;' and assured them, in the word of a king, that he never intended any force but would proceed against them in a fair and a legal way; and so returned to Whitehall; the accused persons, upon information and intelligence what his majesty intended to do, how secretly soever it was carried at Court, having withdrawn from the House about half an hour before the King came thither.

The House, in great disorder, as soon as the King was gone adjourned till the next day in the afternoon; the Lords being in so great apprehension upon notice of the King's being at the House of Commons that the earl of Essex expressed a tender sense he had of the inconveniences which were like to ensue those divisions, and moved, 'that the House of Peers, as a work very proper for them, would interpose between the King and his people, and mediate to his majesty on the behalf of the persons accused;' for which he was reprehended by his friends, and afterwards laughed at himself when he found how much a stronger defence they had than the best mediation could prove on their behalf. . . .

That night the persons accused removed themselves into their strong hold, the city: not that they durst not venture themselves at their old lodgings, for no man would have presumed to trouble them, but that the city might see that they relied upon that place for a sanctuary of their privileges against violence and oppression, and so might put on an early concernment for them. And they were not disappointed; for, in spite of all the lord mayor could do to compose their distempers, (who like a very wise and stout magistrate bestirred himself,) the city was that whole night in arms; some people, designed to that purpose, running from one gate to another, and crying out that 'the *Cavaliers* were coming to fire the city;' and some saying that 'the King himself was in the head of them.'

The next morning, the King, being informed of much that had passed that night, according to the advice he had received, sent to the lord mayor to call a Common Council immediately; and about ten of the clock, himself, attended only by three or four lords, went to the Guildhall, and in the room where the people were assembled told them, 'he was very sorry to hear of the apprehensions they had entertained of danger; that he was come to them to shew how much he relied upon their affections for his security and guard, having brought no other with him; that he had accused certain men of high treason, against whom he would proceed in a legal way, and therefore he presumed they would not shelter them in the city.' And using many other very gracious expressions of his value of them, and telling one of the sheriffs, (who was of the two thought less inclined to his service,) that he would dine with him, he departed, without that applause and cheerfulness which he might have expected from the extraordinary grace he vouchsafed to them, and, in his passage through the city, the rude people flocking together, and crying out, '*Privilege of parliament, privilege of parliament*,' some of them pressing very near his own coach, and amongst the rest one calling out with a very loud voice, '*To your tents, O Israel*.'* However, the King, though much mortified, continued his resolution, taking little notice of the distempers; and, having dined at the sheriff's, returned in the afternoon to Whitehall; and published, the next day, a proclamation for the apprehension of all those whom he accused of high treason, forbidding any person to harbour them; the articles of their charge being likewise printed and dispersed. . . . [*HR*, IV, 148–57]

The truth is, it cannot be expressed how great a change there appeared to be in the countenance and minds of all sorts of people, in town and country, upon these late proceedings of the King. They who had before even lost their spirits, having lost their credit and reputation, except amongst the meanest people who could never have been made use of by them when the greater should forsake them, and so, despairing of ever being able to compass their designs of malice or ambition, some of them were resuming their old resolutions of leaving the kingdom, now again recovered greater courage than ever, and quickly found that their credit and reputation was as great as ever it had been; the Court being reduced to a lower condition, and to more disesteem and neglect, than ever it had undergone. All that they had formerly said of plots and conspiracies against the Parliament, which had before been laughed at, [was] now thought true and real, and all their fears and jealousies looked upon as the effects of their great wisdom and foresight. All that had been whispered of Ireland was now talked aloud and printed, as all other seditious pamphlets and libels were. The shops of the city generally shut up, as if an enemy were at their gates ready to enter and to plunder them; and the people in all places at a gaze, as if they looked only for directions, and were then disposed to any undertaking.

On the other side, they who had, with the greatest courage and alacrity, opposed all their seditious practices, between grief and anger were confounded with the consideration of what had been done and what was like to follow. They were far from thinking that the accused members had received much wrong, yet they thought it an unseasonable time to call them to account for it; that if any thing had been to be done of that kind, there should have been a better choice of the persons, there being many of the House of more mischievous inclinations and designs against the King's person and the government, and were more exposed to the public prejudice, than the lord Kimbolton was, who was a civil and well natured man, and had rather kept ill company than drank deep of that infection and poison that had wrought upon many others. Then sir Arthur Haselrig and Strode were persons of too low an account and esteem; and though their virulence and malice was as conspicuous and transcendent as any men's, yet their reputation and interest to do any mischief, otherwise than in concurring in it, was so small that they gained credit and authority by being joined with the rest, who had indeed a great influence. However, if there was a resolution to proceed against those men, it would have been much better to have caused them to have been all severally arrested and sent to the Tower or to other prisons, which might have been very easily done before suspected, than to send in that manner to the Houses with that formality which would be liable to so many exceptions. At least, they ought so far to have imparted it to members in both Houses who might have been trusted, that, in the instant of the accusation, when both Houses were in that consternation, (as in a great consternation they were) somewhat might have been pressed confidently towards the King's satisfaction; which would have produced some opposition and contradiction, which would have prevented that universal concurrence and dejection of spirit which seized upon and possessed both Houses.

But, above all, the anger and indignation was very great and general that to all the other oversights and presumptions [was added] the exposing the dignity and majesty and safety of the King, in his coming in person in that manner to the House of Commons, and in going the next day, as he did, to the Guildhall and to the lord mayor's, which drew such reproaches upon him to his face. All which was justly imputed to the lord Digby, who had before fewer true friends than he deserved, and had now almost the whole nation his enemies, being the most universally odious of any man in it. [*HR*, from the *Life*, IV, 191–3]

Digby left the country shortly after the debacle; the King himself left Whitehall on 10 January, determined to ensure the safety of his wife, Queen Henrietta Maria, by sending her out of England. Both sides began to prepare for war. In a series of exchanges, the King responded to the Commons' demand that the militia and military bases be put under the command of those acceptable to Parliament. The bill excluding the bishops from the House of Lords formally passed the Upper House on 5 February, and was presented for the King's assent. In the History, *written in 1646–7 but published in the* History of the Rebellion, *Hyde made clear his own opposition to the King's acceptance of the bill.*

The bill for the taking away the votes of bishops out of the House of Peers, which was called, *A bill for taking away all temporal jurisdiction from those in holy orders*, was no sooner passed the House of Peers* than the King was earnestly desired to give his royal assent to it. The King returned, 'that it was a matter of great concernment, and therefore he would take time to advise, and would return an answer in convenient time.' But this delay pleased not their appetite; they could not attempt their perfect reformation in Church and State till those votes were utterly abolished. Therefore they sent the same day again to the King, who was yet at Windsor, and gave him reasons to persuade him immediately to consent to it; one of which was, 'the grievances the subjects suffered by their exercising of temporal jurisdiction, and their making a party in the Lords' House:' a second, 'the great content of all sorts by the happy conjunction of both Houses in their absence:' and a third, 'that the passing of that bill would be a comfortable pledge of his majesty's gracious assent to the future remedies of those evils which were to be presented to him, this once being passed.'

Reasons sufficient to have converted him, if he had the least inclination or propensity to have concurred with them; for it was, upon the matter, to persuade him to join with them in this, because, that being done, he should be able to deny them nothing.

However those of greatest trust* about the King, and who were very faithful to his service, (though in this particular exceedingly deceived in their judgments, and not sufficiently acquainted with the constitution of the kingdom,) persuaded him that the passing this bill was the only way to preserve the Church, there being so united a combination in this particular that he would not be able to withstand it; whereas by the passing this bill so many persons in both Houses would be fully satisfied, that they would join in no further alteration: but, on the other hand, if they were crossed in this, they would violently endeavour an extirpation of bishops and a demolition of the whole fabric of the Church.

They alleged that he was, upon the matter, deprived of their votes already, they being not suffered to come to the House, and the major part in prison under an accusation of high treason, of which there was not like to be any reformation till these present distempers were composed; and then that by his power, and the memory of the indirect means that had been used against them, it would be easier to bring them in again than to keep them in now. They told him, there were two matters of great importance pressed upon him for his royal assent, but they were not of equal consequence and concernment to his sovereign power; the first, that bill for the bishops' votes; the other, the whole militia of the kingdom, the granting of which would absolutely divest him of all regal power; that he would not be able to deny both, but by the granting the former, in which he parted with no matter of moment, he would, it may be, not be pressed in the second; or if he were, that as he could not have a more popular quarrel to take up arms than to defend himself, and preserve that power in his hands which the law had vested in him, and without which he could not be a king, so he could not have a more unpopular argument for that contention than the preservation of the bishops in the House of Peers, which few men thought essential, and most men believed prejudicial, to the peace and happiness of the kingdom.

These arguments, though used by men whom he most trusted, and whom he knew to have opposed that bill in its passage and to be cordially friends to the Church of England in discipline and doctrine, prevailed not so much with his majesty as the persuasions of the Queen; who was not only persuaded to think those reasons valid, and that indeed the Church could be only that way preserved, (and there are that believe that infusion to have been made in her by her own priests, by instructions from France, and for reasons in state of that kingdom,) but that her own safety very much depended upon the King's consent to that bill, and that if he should refuse it her journey into Holland would be crossed by the Parliament, and possibly her person in danger, either by the tumults which might easily be brought to Windsor from Westminster, or by the insurrection of the counties in her passage from thence to Dover, where she intended to take shipping. Whereas by her intercession with the King to do it, she would lay a most seasonable and popular obligation upon the whole nation, and leave a pleasant odour of her grace and favour to the people behind her, which would prove much to her advantage in her absence; and she should have the thanks for that act as acquired by her goodness, which otherwise would be extorted from the King when she was gone.

These insinuations and discourses so far satisfied the Queen, and she the King, that, contrary to his most positive resolution, the King consented, and sent a commission for the enacting both that bill and the other for pressing;* which was done accordingly, to the great triumph of the *boutefeus*,* the King sending the same day that he passed those bills, which was the fourteenth of February, a message to both Houses, 'That he was assured his having passed those two bills, being of so great importance, so suddenly, would serve to assure his Parliament that he desired nothing more than the satisfaction of his kingdom.' For Ireland, he said, 'as he had concurred in all propositions made for that service by his Parliament, so he was resolved to leave nothing undone for their relief which should fall within his possible power, nor would refuse to venture his own person in that war, if the Parliament should think it convenient, for the reduction of that miserable kingdom.'

The passing that bill for the taking away the bishops' votes exceedingly weakened the King's party, not only as it perpetually swept away so considerable a number out of the House of Peers which were constantly devoted to him, but as it made impression on others, whose minds were in suspense and shaken, as when foundations are dissolved. Besides, they that were best acquainted with the King's nature, opinions, and resolutions, had reason to believe that no exigents could have wrought upon him to have consented to so anti-monarchical an act, and therefore never after retained any confidence that he would deny what was importunately asked; and so, either absolutely withdrew themselves from those consultations, thereby avoiding the envy and the danger of opposing them, or quietly suffered themselves to be carried by the stream, and consent to any thing that was boldly and lustily attempted.

And then it was so far from dividing the other party, that I do not remember one man who furiously insisted on, or indeed heartily wished, the passing of that bill that ever deserted them, till the kingdom was in a flame: but, on the contrary, very many who cordially and constantly opposed that act, as friends rather to monarchy than religion, after that bill never considered or resisted any attempt or further alteration in the Church, looking upon the bishops as useless to sovereignty, and so not of importance enough to defend by the sword. And I have heard the same men who urged before, 'that their places in that House had no relation to the discipline of the Church and their spiritual jurisdiction, and therefore ought to be sacrificed to the preservation of the other, upon which the peace and unity of religion so much depended,' since argue, 'that since their power in that House, which was a good outwork to defend the King's from invasion, was taken away, any other form of government would be equally advantageous to his majesty; and therefore that he ought not to insist on it with the least inconvenience to his condition.' [*HR*, IV, 297–304]

Hyde, Culpepper, Falkland, and others continued to attempt to rebuild royalist support in Parliament, despite threats of arrest and impeachment, and the steady departure of the King's sympathizers. The King saw the Queen off at Dover, bound for France, on 23 February, and then turned his mind to securing his son, Prince Charles, from the clutches of Parliament. Clarendon's narrative of his meetings with the King at Greenwich is taken from the Life, *written in 1669, but not included in the published* History.

When the king accompanied the queen to Dover, where they expected a wind many days, he sent the prince, under his new governor,* the marquis of Hertford, to Richmond; that there might be no room for the jealousy that the prince should be transported beyond the seas; which had been infused into the minds of many; and would have made a great noise, if he had waited upon his mother to Dover: but as soon as the wind appeared hopeful for her majesty's embarkation, the king sent an express to Richmond, that the prince should attend his majesty at Greenwich the Saturday following: the marquis being at that time very much indisposed by a defluxion upon his eyes, and a catarrh.

The parliament, being presently informed, as they had spies in all places, of this direction, and there being yet no certainty of the queen's being embarked, was much troubled; and resolved to send to his majesty,* by members of both houses, to desire that the prince might not remove from Richmond, at least till the marquis recovered health enough to be able to attend him; and at the same time sent an express order to the marquis, that he should not suffer the prince to go from thence, till he himself should be able to go with him.

They appointed one lord and two commoners to carry the message to the king, whom they believed to be still at Dover; and Mr Hyde coming accidentally into the house, when the matter was in debate, they appointed him to be one of the messengers; which no excuses could free him from, for they did not intend it as a favour to him; so that they were obliged presently to begin their journey; and that night they went to Gravesend. The next day they were fully informed of the queen's being gone to sea, and that the king would be that night at Canterbury; whither the messengers made what haste they could, and found his majesty there, with a very little court, most of his servants having leave to go before to London, the better to provide themselves for a further journey. When they read their message to the king, in the hearing whereof he shewed no satisfaction, he appointed them to attend him after he had supped, and they should receive their answer: and accordingly, about nine of the clock, he caused it to be read, and delivered it to them; taking no notice of Mr Hyde, as if he had been known to him. That messenger, who was a member of the house of peers, received it from his majesty, as of right he ought to do, that it might be first reported to that house.

Mr Hyde was very much troubled when he heard the answer read; for it had much sharpness in it, which at that time could only provoke them: so without taking any notice of it to his companions, he pretended to them only to be very weary, and desirous to go to bed, and bade them good night; having the conveniency offered him by the lord Grandison (his familiar friend) to lodge with him in a house next the court: and so the other two messengers making haste to find some lodging in an inn, he sent the lord Grandison to the duke of Richmond, to desire the king that he might speak with him before he went into his bed. The king was half undressed, yet said he would stay for him, and bade that he should make haste to the back stairs; and as soon as he came thither, the duke went in to the king, who immediately came out in his nightdress; and the duke having before sent all other servants from thence, retired likewise himself.

He told the king, that 'he was sorry that his majesty had expressed so much displeasure in his answer; which could produce no good, and might do hurt; and therefore he desired he would call for it, and alter some expressions;' which his majesty was not inclined to do; enlarging himself with much sharpness upon the insolence of the message, and of the order they had sent to the marquis of Hertford; and seemed to apprehend that the prince would not be suffered to attend him at Greenwich; the thought whereof had caused that warmth in him. It was now Friday night, and his majesty resolved the next night to be at Greenwich, and to stay there all Sunday; and then to pursue his former resolutions: upon which, Mr Hyde told him, 'that he hoped the prince would be at Greenwich as soon as he, and then that point would be cleared; that they could not report his message to the parliament till Monday morning; and that they might well attend upon his majesty again on Sunday, and receive his pleasure; and at that time the lord Falkland and sir John Culpepper would be likewise present; when his majesty might take what resolution he pleased in that matter; and therefore he besought his majesty that he would presently send a servant to the other two messengers, at such an inn, for the answer he had delivered to them, of which he would further consider when he came to Greenwich; where he commanded them to attend him on Sunday, and that he would despatch them soon enough for them to be at London that night,' All which his majesty was pleased to consent to, and immediately sent a gentleman to them for the paper, with that injunction; and then sent it by the lord Grandison the same night to Mr Hyde, whom he had commanded to attend him on Sunday morning, saying he had very much to say to him.

When his majesty came to Greenwich, he found the prince there with his governor, who, though indisposed in his health, without returning any answer to the parliament, brought the prince very early from Richmond to Greenwich; with which the king was very much pleased, and in very good humour. And the next morning, when Mr Hyde came to court, (to whom his companions had told that the king had sent for his answer to them again, and appointed them to attend him for it at Greenwich* that afternoon; which they had agreed together to do,) the king being come into the privy chamber, and seeing him there, asked him aloud, where the others who came in the message with him were; and said, he would expect them in the afternoon; and so discoursing somewhat of the weather, that all men heard, he came near him, and, as it were passing by, (which nobody took notice of, the room not being full,) he bade him dine with Porter,* at the back stairs, that he might be in the privy chamber when he rose from dinner; and after he had dined he found him there; and at that hour most people looking after their own dinner, his majesty did, without any body's taking notice of it, bid him follow him into the privy gallery; where he was no sooner entered, than the king locked the door with his own key, saying, 'We will not now be disturbed, for there is no man in the house now who hath a key to this door.' Then he said, 'I will say nothing of the answer, for I am sure Falkland and Culpepper will be here anon; and then prepare one, and I will not differ with you; for now I have gotten Charles, I care not what answer I send to them.'

Then he spake of many particulars of the parliament with warmth enough; and lamented his having consented to the bill concerning the bishops, which he said he was prevailed upon to do for his wife's security; but he should now be without any fear to displease them. He said, he would lay the next night at Theobalds;* where he would stay a day or two, that his servants might provide themselves to attend him northward: that he should not see him any more before he took that journey, and therefore he required him upon all occasions to write to him, and advertise him of such matters as were fit for him to know; and to prepare and send him answers to such declarations or messages as the parliament should send to him. He said, he knew well the danger he underwent, if it were discovered; but his majesty assured him, and bade him be confident of it, that no person alive, but himself and his two friends, should know that he corresponded with his majesty; and that he would himself transcribe every paper in his own hand before he would shew it to any man, and before his secretary should write it out. Mr Hyde told him, that he writ a very ill hand, which would give his majesty too much trouble to transcribe himself; and that he had so much friendship with secretary Nicholas, that he was well contented he should be trusted: to which the king said, Nicholas was a very honest man, and he would trust him in any thing that concerned himself; but in this particular, which would be so penal to the other, if it should be known, it was not necessary; for he would quickly learn to read the hand, if it were writ at first with a little the more care; and nobody should see it but himself. And his majesty continued so firm to this resolution, that though the declarations from the houses shortly after grew so voluminous, that the answers frequently contained five or six sheets of paper very closely writ, his majesty always transcribed them with his own hand; which sometimes took him up two or three days, and a good part of the night, before he produced them to the council, where they were first read; and then he burned the originals. And he gave himself no ease in this particular, till Mr Hyde left the parliament, and by his majesty's command attended upon him at York; which will be mentioned in its time.

Whilst the king held this discourse with him in the privy gallery, many of the lords were come from London: and not finding him, the earls of Essex and Holland, who by their offices had keys to the gallery, opened that door, and went in; and seeing nobody there, walked to the further end; where in a turning walk the king and Mr Hyde were: and though they presently drew back, the king himself, as well as Mr Hyde, was a little discomposed; and said, 'I am very sorry for this accident; I meant to have said somewhat to you of those gentlemen, but we must not stay longer together: forget not what I have said; and send me presently the answer for your message, and then attend with your companions in the privy chamber, and I will come out and deliver it to them:' and so he withdrew; the two earls smiling, and saluting Mr Hyde civilly. He quickly found the lord Falkland and Culpepper, and they as quickly agreed upon the answer, which the lord Falkland carried to the king: and his majesty approving and signing it, he came out and delivered it, after he had caused it to be read, to the messengers who attended to receive it; and who went that night to London; and the next morning,* at the first sitting of the houses, reported and delivered it. [*Life*, II, 23–9]

At the beginning of March, Charles began a slow journey to York, punctuated by voluminous exchange of Declarations with Parliament. Many of the King's were written by Hyde.

This new spirit in the king's actions, and steadiness in his proceedings, and his new dialect in his words and answers to them, so contrary to the softness they expected, infinitely discomposed them, and raised the spirits of others, who had sunk under their insolence. In the house of peers they found more opposition than of late they had done, and many in the house of commons recovered new mettle. Alderman Gurney, who was lord mayor of London, was a man of courage and discretion, very well affected to the king, and to the government in church and state, and perfectly abhorred the proceedings of the parliament; gave not that obedience to the orders they expected; did all he could to discountenance and suppress the riotous assemblies in the city, and especially the insolencies committed in churches; and expressly refused to call common-halls,* and sometimes common-councils, when the house of commons desired it, which was the only way they had to scatter their fire about the city; and the refractoriness of this lord mayor discouraged them much by making it evident, that it was only the rabble and inferior sort of the city which was in truth devoted to them. But they were now gone too far to retire with their honour, or indeed with their safety; and they easily discerned, that if their spirits seemed to sink, their friends would leave them as fast as they had resorted to them; and if they now appeared more moderate in their demands from the king, they should but censure and condemn their own former fervour and importunity, and therefore they made all haste to make it appear that they had no such temper and inclination. They made committees to prepare new messages to the king, and to prepare new declarations; and sent their agents into the country to stir up the people in those counties and places through which the king was to pass; so that, wherever he made any stay, he was sure to be encountered with a petition from the county, that is, in the name of it, or of some eminent town in it where he lodged, that he would return to his parliament; but at the very time appeared to be the work of a few factious people, by the repair of the best persons of quality and interest to his majesty with all professions of affections and duty to him. . . .

The king in his journey sent an answer from Huntingdon* to some propositions they had sent to him, which contained not only a positive refusal of what they had desired, but making some sharp reflections upon somewhat they had said or done, put them into wonderful passion. They would not believe that it came from the king, but that it was forged in the town, for that it took notice of what had been done the night before, which could not be communicated to the king before the date of that despatch; and therefore they would make inquiry how it came to the speaker, to whom it had been delivered under the king's signet. The lord Falkland owning the having received it that morning from the king, and that he sent it by a messenger to the speaker, and putting them in mind that the matter they reflected upon as done the night before, had likewise been done three or four days before that, which, being manifest, they suppressed their choler as to the forgery, and took revenge upon the message itself, and voted, 'that whosoever had advised the king to send that message, was a disaffected person, an enemy to the peace of the kingdom, and a promoter of the rebellion in Ireland;' which was a new style they took up upon that occasion, and continued afterwards in their most angry votes, to make those they liked not odious, and to make their punishment to pass with the more ease when they should be discovered. And now they tried all ways imaginable to find what new counsellors and secretary the king had found, who supplied him with so much resolution and bitterness; and though they made no doubt of the two new counsellors' concurrence in all, yet they did not impute the framing and forming the writing itself to either of them.

They had long detested and suspected Mr Hyde, from the time of their first remonstrance, for framing the king's messages and answers, which they now every day received, to their intolerable vexation; yet knew not how to accuse him. But now that the earls of Essex and Holland had discovered his being shut up with the king at Greenwich, and the marquis of Hamilton had once before found him very early in private with the king at Windsor, at a time when the king thought all passages had been stopped; together with his being of late more absent from the house than he had used to be; and the resort of the other two every night to his lodging, as is mentioned before, satisfied them that he was the person; and they resolved to disenable him to manage that office long. Sir John Culpepper had as many eyes upon them as they had upon the other, and an equal animosity against them; and had familiarity and friendship with some persons, who from the second or third hand came to know many of the greatest designs before they were brought upon the stage. For though they managed those councils with the greatest secrecy, and by few persons, which amounted to no more than pure designs in speculation; yet when any thing was to be transacted in public by the house, they were obliged, not only to prepare those of whom they were themselves confident, but to allow those confidents to communicate it to others in whom they confided: and so men, who did not concur with them, came to know sometimes their intentions time enough to prevent the success they proposed to themselves.

And by this means, sir John Culpepper, meeting at night with the lord Falkland and Mr Hyde, assured them, that it had been resolved that day to have seized upon all three, and sent them to the Tower: of which he having received notice as he was going to the house, returned to his lodging, not being able to give the same information to the other two; but that his own being absent prevented the mischief. For he knew it was resolved the night before, that, when the three were together in the house, somebody should move the house, 'that they would apply themselves to make some strict inquiry after the persons who were most like to give the king the evil counsel he had lately followed, and who prepared those answers and messages they received from his majesty:' upon which, by one and another, those three persons should be named, and particular reasons given for their suspicion; and that they did not doubt, but, if their friends were well prepared beforehand, they should be able to cause them to be all sent to the Tower; and then they doubted not they should be able to keep them there. But it was then likewise agreed, that they would not make the attempt but at a time when they were all three in the house; upon hearing whereof, and finding that they two were there, he went back to his lodging; knowing that thereupon there would be nothing done.

Upon this communication, though they were all of opinion that the design was so extravagant, and exceeding all the rules of common justice, that they would not be able to procure the consent of the major part of the house in it, if there were any considerable number present; yet because very many usually absented themselves, and they were not governed by any rules which had been formerly observed, they thought fit to resolve, that one of them would be always present in the house, that they might know all that was done; but that they would never be there all together, and seldom two of them; and when they were, they would only hear, and speak no more than was of absolute necessity. For it was now grown a very difficult thing for a man who was in their disfavour to speak against what they proposed, but that they would find some exception to some word or expression; upon which, after he had been called upon to explain, he was obliged to withdraw; and then they had commonly a major part to send him to the Tower, or to expel him the house; or at least oblige him to receive a reprehension at the bar upon his knees. And so they had used sir Ralph Hopton* at that time; who excepting to some expression that was used in a declaration prepared by a committee, and presented to the house, which he said was dishonourable to the king, they said, it was a tax upon the committee;* caused him to withdraw, and committed him to the Tower; which terrified many from speaking at all, and caused more to absent themselves from the house; where too small numbers appeared any day. These three gentlemen kept the resolution agreed upon, till they all found it necessary to forbear any further attendance upon the house. [*Life*, II, 37–40]

The King's attempt to obtain control of the magazine at Hull on 23 April and his efforts to raise money and soldiers precipitated the events that led up to war over the next few weeks. On 20 May Parliament voted that the King 'intended to make war against the Parliament'. Very shortly afterwards Hyde secretly left London and made his way to York. Hyde's reflections on the strategy of the parliamentary leaders were written in Jersey in 1647 as part of the History, *and published in the* History of the Rebellion.

It will be wondered at hereafter, that, in a judging and discerning state, where men had, or seemed to have, their faculties of reason and understanding at the height, in a kingdom then unapt and generally uninclined to war, (how wantonly soever it hath since seemed to throw away its peace,) those men who had the skill and cunning out of froward and peevish humours and indispositions to compound fears and jealousies, and to animate and inflame those fears and jealousies into the most prodigious and the boldest rebellion that any age or country ever brought forth; who very well saw and felt that the King had not only to a degree wound himself out of that labyrinth in which four months before they had involved him with their privileges, fears, and jealousies, but had even so well informed the people that they began to question both their logic and their law, and to suspect and censure the improvement and gradation of their fears, and the extent and latitude of their privileges: and that they were not only denied by the King what they required, but that the King's reasons of his denial made very many conclude the unreasonableness of their demands: I say, it may seem strange that these men could entertain the hope and confidence to obtrude such a declaration and vote upon the people, 'that the King did intend to make war against the Parliament,' when they were so far from apprehending that he would be able to get an army to disturb them, that they were most assured he would not be able to get bread to sustain himself three months without submitting all his counsels to their conduct and control; and that the offering to impose it did not awaken the people to an indignation which might have confounded them. For, besides their presumption in endeavouring to search what the Scripture itself told them was unsearchable, the heart of the King,* the very law of the land, whose defence they pretended, makes no conclusion of the intention of the meanest subject, in a matter of the highest and tenderest consideration, even treason itself against the life of the King, without some overt, unlawful act, from whence, and other circumstances, the ill intention may be reasonably made appear; and therefore, to declare that the King intended to make war against his Parliament, when he had neither ship, harbour, arms, or money, and knew not how to get either, and when he offered to grant any thing to them which they could pretend a justifiable reason for asking, was an undertaking of that nature that even the almightiness of a Parliament might have despaired to succeed in.

But, notwithstanding all this, they very well knew what they did, and understood what infinite advantage that vote would (as it did) bring to them, and that a natural way would never bring them to their unnatural end. The power and reputation of Parliament, they believed, would implicitly prevail over many, and amaze and terrify others from disputing or censuring what they did and upon what grounds they did it. The difficulty was, to procure the judgment of Parliament, and to incline those different constitutions and different affections to such a concurrence as the judgment might not be discredited by the number of the dissenters, nor wounded or prejudged by the reasons and arguments given against it: and then, their judgments of the cure being to be grounded upon the nature and information of the disease, it was necessary to confine and contract their fancies and opinions within some bounds and limits: the mystery of rebellion challenging the same encouragement with other sciences, to grow by; that there may be certain *postulata*, some principles and foundations, upon which the main building may subsist. So, in the case of the militia, an imminent danger must be first supposed, by which the kingdom is in an apparent danger, and then the King's refusal to apply any remedy against that danger, before the two Houses would pretend to the power of disposing that militia; it being too ridiculous to have pretended the natural and ordinary jurisdiction over it: but, in case of danger, and danger so imminent that the usual recourse would not serve the turn, and for the saving of a kingdom which must otherwise be lost, many good men thought it was reasonable to apply a very extraordinary prevention, without imagining such a supposition might possibly engage them in any action contrary to their own inclinations; and, without doubt, very many who frankly voted that imminent necessity, were induced to it as an argument that the King should be therefore importuned to consent to the settlement; which would not have appeared so necessary a request if the occasion had not been important; never suspecting that it would have proved an argument to them to adventure the doing it without the King's consent. And it is not here unseasonable, (how merry soever it may seem to be,) as an instance of the incogitancy* and inadvertency of those kind of votes and transactions, to remember, that, the first resolution of the power of the militia being grounded upon a supposition of an imminent necessity, the ordinance first sent up from the Commons to the Lords for the execution of the militia* expressed an *eminent* necessity; whereupon some lords, who understood the difference of the words, and that an *eminent* necessity might be supplied by the ordinary provision which possibly an *imminent* necessity might not safely attend, desired a conference with the Commons for the amendment; which, I remember, was at last with great difficulty consented to, many (who, I presume, are not yet grown up to conceive the difference) supposing it an unnecessary contention for a word, and so yielding to them for saving of time rather than for the moment of the thing.

They who contrived this scheme never doubted that, after a resolution what was to be done upon a suppositious necessity, they would easily (when they found it convenient) make that necessity real. It was no hard matter to make the fearful apprehensive of dangers, and the jealous of designs; and they wanted not evidence of all kinds, letters from abroad and discoveries at home, to make those apprehensions formidable enough; and then, though before the resolution there was a great latitude in law and reason what was lawfully to be done, they had now forejudged themselves, and resolved of the proper remedy, except they would argue against the evidence; which usually would have been to discountenance or undervalue some person of notable reputation or his correspondence, and always to have opposed that that was of such an allay as, in truth, did operate upon the major part. So, in the case upon which we now discourse, if they had in the most advantageous article of their fury professed the raising an army against the King, there was yet that reverence to majesty, and that spirit of subjection and allegiance in most men, that they would have looked upon it with opposition and horror: but defensive arms were more plausible divinity; and if the King should commit such an outrage as to levy war against his Parliament, to destroy the religion, laws, and liberty of the kingdom, good men were persuaded that such a resistance might be made as might preserve the whole; and he that would have argued against this thesis, besides the impertinency of arguing against a supposition that was not like to be real, and in which the corrupt consideration of safety seemed to bribe most men, could never escape the censure of promoting tyranny and lawless dominion. Then to incline men to concur in the declaration of the 'King's intention to make war against the Parliament,' they were persuaded it might have a good, could have no ill, effect: the remedies that were to be applied upon an actual levying of war were not justifiable upon the intention; and the declaring this intention, and the dangers it carried with it to the King himself and to all those who should assist him, would be a probable means of reforming such intention and preventing the execution: inconvenience it could produce none, (for the disquieting or displeasing the King was not thought inconvenient,) if there were no progress in the supposed intention; if there were, it were fit the whole kingdom should stand upon its guard, and not be surprised to its confusion.

By these false and fallacious mediums the clearness of men's understandings was dazzled, and, upon the matter, all their opinions and judgments for the future captivated and pre-engaged by their own votes and determinations. For, how easy a matter was it to make it appear to that man who consented that the King intended to make war against the Parliament, that when he should do it he had broken his oath and dissolved his government, and that whosoever should assist him were traitors; I say, how easy was it to persuade that man, that he was obliged to defend the Parliament, to endeavour to uphold that government, and to resist those traitors. And whosoever considers that the nature of men, especially of men in authority, is inclined rather to commit two errors than to retract one, will not marvel that from this root of unadvisedness so many and tall branches of mischief have proceeded. And therefore it were to be wished that those who have the honour to be trusted in public consultations were endued with so much natural logic as to discern the consequences of every public act and conclusion, and with so much conscience and courage as to watch the first impressions upon their understanding and compliance: and, neither out of the impertinency of the thing, which men are too apt to conclude, out of impatiency of despatch, or out of stratagem to make men odious, (as in this Parliament many forbore to oppose unreasonable resolutions out of an opinion that they would make the contrivers odious,) or upon any other (though seeming never so politic) considerations, consent to any propositions by which truth or justice are invaded. And I am confident, with very good warrant, that many men have from their souls abhorred every article of this rebellion, and heartily deprecated the miseries and desolation we have suffered by it, who have themselves with great alacrity and some industry contributed to, if not contrived, those very votes and conclusions from whence the evils they abhor have most naturally and regularly flowed and been deduced, and which they could not reasonably, upon their own concessions, contradict and oppose.

But to conclude, a man shall not unprofitably spend his contemplation that, upon this occasion, considers the method of God's justice, (a method terribly remarkable in many passages, and upon many persons, which we shall be compelled to remember in this discourse); that the same principles, and the same application of those principles, should be used to the wresting all sovereign power from the Crown, which the Crown had a little before made use of* for the extending its authority and power beyond its bounds, to the prejudice of the just rights of the subject. A supposed necessity was then thought ground enough to create a power, and a bare averment of that necessity to beget a practice, to impose what tax they thought convenient upon the subject by writs of ship-money never before known; and a supposed necessity now, and a bare averment of that necessity, is as confidently and more fatally concluded a good ground to exclude the Crown from the use of any power by an ordinance never before heard of; and the same maxim of *Salus populi suprema lex*,* which had been used to the infringing the liberties of the one, made use of for the destroying the rights of the other: only that of the Psalmist is yet inverted;* for many of those who were the principal makers of the first pit are so far from falling into it that they have been the chiefest diggers of the second ditch in which so many have been confounded. [*HR*, V, 150–4]

7. Edgehill

In the History, *Hyde described Parliament's preparations for war as rapid and effective, with access to money set aside for suppressing the Irish rebellion, and financial support from the City of London. In May it ordered that its Militia Ordinance, placing the militia in the hands of their appointees, be put into execution. In early July it secured control of the fleet, voted to raise an army, and appointed the Earl of Essex as its general. On behalf of the King, Queen Henrietta Maria raised some money abroad, and some more was obtained from individual supporters. In June, the King forbade the execution of the Militia Ordinance, and began to issue commissions of array, in which he asserted his rights to levy soldiers on the basis of medieval legislation. In July he appointed the Earl of Lindsey as the general of his army. Here, from the* History, *Hyde discusses the strategic dilemmas which hampered royal efforts.*

ON the other side, preparations were not made with equal expedition and success by the King towards a war: for, though he well understood and discerned that he had nothing else to trust to, he was to encounter strange difficulties to do that. He was so far from having money to levy or pay soldiers that he was at this very time compelled, for very real want, to let fall all the tables kept by his officers of state* in Court, by which so many of all qualities subsisted; and the prince and duke of York* eat with his majesty; which only table was kept. And whoever knows the constitution of a Court, well knows what indispositions naturally flow from those declensions, and how ill those tempers bear any diminutions of their own interest, and, being once indisposed themselves, how easily they infect others. And that which made the present want of money the more intolerable, there was no visible hope from whence supply could come in any reasonable time: and that which was a greater want than money, which men rather feared than found, there were no arms; for, notwithstanding the fame of the great store of ammunition brought in by that ship,* it consisted only in truth of cannon, powder, and bullet, with eight hundred muskets, which was all the King's magazine. So that the hastening of levies, which at that time was believed would not prove difficult, would be to little purpose, when they should continue unarmed. But that which troubled the King more than all these real incapacities of making war, was the temper and constitution of his own party; which was compounded, for the most part, in

Court, Council, and country, of men drawn to him by the impulsion of conscience, and abhorring the unjust and irregular proceedings of Parliament; otherwise, unexperienced in action, and unacquainted with the mysteries and necessary policy of government, severe observers of the law, and as scrupulous in all matters of relation as the other pretended to be: all his majesty's ancient counsellors and servants, (except some few of lasting honour, whom we shall have occasion often to mention,) being, to redeem former oversights, or for other unworthy designs, either publicly against him in London, or privately discrediting his interests and actions in his own Court. These men still urged the execution of the law; that what extravagances soever the Parliament practised, the King's observation of the law would, in the end, suppress them all: and, indeed, believed the raising a war to be so wicked a thing that they thought it impossible the Parliament should intend it, even when they knew what they were doing; however, concluded that he that was forwardest in the preparing an army would be first odious to the people; by the affections of whom the other would be easily suppressed.

This was the general, received doctrine; and though it appeared plainly to others, (of equal affection to the public peace,) how fatal those conclusions, in that sense in which they were urged, must prove to the whole kingdom, and how soon the King must be irrecoverably lost if he proceeded not more vigorously in his defence, yet even those men durst not in any formed and public debate declare themselves, or speak that plain English the state of affairs required, but satisfied themselves with speaking what they thought necessary to the King in private; so that by this means the King wanted those firm and solid foundations of counsel and foresight as were most necessary for his condition: so that he could neither impart the true motives and grounds of any important action, nor discover the atmost of his designs. And so he still pretended, (notwithstanding the greatest and avowed preparations of the enemy) to intend nothing of hostility but in order to the reducing of Hull; the benefit of which he hoped would engage the train-bands of that great county, (which was the sole strength he yet drew thither,) till he could bring other forces thither which might be fit for that or any other design. [*HR*, V, 430–2]

By July, both parties were manoeuvring for military advantage, trying to secure the two great fortified towns that contained arsenals: Hull and Portsmouth. The King tried a second time to obtain the surrender of Hull. At Portsmouth, the governor, George Goring, declared at the beginning of August for the King. Parliamentary forces were sent to lay siege to the town.

In this passage, written for the Life *in the late 1660s, but published in the* History of the Rebellion, *Clarendon described the events that led up to the raising of the King's standard.*

It gave no small reputation to his majesty's affairs, when there was so great a damp upon the spirits of men upon the misadventures at Beverley, that so notable a place as Portsmouth had declared for him in the very beginning of the war, and that so good an officer as Goring was returned to his duty, and in the possession of the town: and the King, who was not surprised with the matter, knowing well the resolution of the colonel, made no doubt but that he was very well supplied with all things, as he might well have been, to have given the rebels work for three or four months at the least. However, he forthwith published a Declaration, that had been long ready, in which he recapitulated all the insolent and rebellious actions which the two Houses had committed against him, and declared them to be guilty, and forbad all his subjects to yield any obedience to them: and at the same time published his proclamation by which he required all men who could bear arms to repair to him at Nottingham by the 25th day of August following; on which day he would set up his royal standard there, which all good subjects were obliged to attend. And at the same time he sent the marquis of Hertford to raise forces in the west, or at least to restrain those parts, where his interest and reputation was greater than any man's, within the limits of their duty to the King, and from being corrupted or perverted by the Parliament; and with him went the lord Seymour, his brother, the lord Poulett, Hopton, Stowell, Coventry, Berkeley, Wyndham, and some other gentlemen of the prime quality and interest in the western parts, and who were like to give as good examples in their persons, and to be followed by as many men, as any such number of gentlemen in England could be. And from this party, enlivened by the power and reputation of the marquis, the King was in hope that Portsmouth would be shortly relieved, and made the head-quarter to a good army. And when all this was done, he did all that was possible to be done without money to hasten his levies of horse and foot, and to prepare a light train of artillery, that he might appear at Nottingham, at the day when the standard was to be set up, with such a body of men as might be at the least a competent guard to his person.

Many were then of opinion that it had been more for his majesty's benefit and service if the standard had been appointed to be set up at York; and so that the King had stayed there, without moving further south, until he could have marched in the head of an army, and not to depend upon gathering an army up in his march. All the northern counties were at present most at his devotion, and so it would be most easy to raise men there: Newcastle was the only port in his obedience, and whither he had appointed his supplies of arms and ammunition to be sent; of which he had so present need, that all his magazine which was brought in the *Providence* was already distributed to those few gentlemen who had received commissions, and were most like speedily to raise their regiments; and it would be a very long, and might prove a very dangerous, passage to get the supplies, which were daily expected, to be brought with security from Newcastle, when the King should be advanced so many days' journey beyond York. All which were very important considerations, and ought to have prevailed; but the King's inclination to be nearer London, and the expectation he had of great effects from Portsmouth and the west, disposed him to a willingness to prefer Nottingham; but that which determined the point was an apparent and manifest aversion in the Yorkshire gentlemen whose affections were least suspected that his majesty should continue and remain at York; which, they said, the people apprehended would inevitably make that country the seat of the war, unskilfully imagining that the war would be nowhere but where the King's army was; and therefore they facilitated all things which might contribute to his remove from thence; undertook to provide convoys for any arms and ammunition from Newcastle, to hasten the levies in their own country, and to borrow of the arms of some of the train-bands, which was the best expedient that could be found out to arm the King's troops, and had its reverse in the murmurs it produced, and in leaving the best affected men, by being disarmed, at the mercy of their enemies, who carefully kept their weapons, that they might be ready to fight against the King. This caused the resolution to be taken for Nottingham, without enough weighing the objections, which upon the entrance into great actions cannot be too much deliberated, though in the execution they shall be best shut out. And it quickly appeared in those very men who prevailed most in that counsel; for, when the time drew on in which his majesty was to depart and leave the country, then they remembered that the garrison of Hull would be left as a thorn in their sides, where there were well formed and active troops, which might march over the country without control, and come into York itself without resistance; that there were many disaffected persons of quality and interest in the country, who as soon as the King should be gone would appear amongst their neighbours, and find a concurrence from them in their worst designs; and that there were some places, some whole corporations, so notoriously disaffected, especially in matters relating to the Church, that they wanted only conductors to carry them into rebellion.

These and the like reflections made too late impressions upon them; and now, too much they magnified this man's power whom before they contemned, and doubted that man's affection of which they were before secure; and made a thousand propositions to the King this day, whereof they rejected the greatest part to-morrow; and as the day approached nearer for the King's departure, their apprehensions and irresolutions increased. In the end, they were united in two requests to the King; that he would commit the supreme command of the country, with reference to all military affairs, to the earl of Cumberland, and qualify him with an ample commission to that purpose: the other, that his majesty would command sir Thomas Glemham to remain with them, to govern and command such forces as the earl of Cumberland should find necessary for their defence: and this provision being made by the King, they obliged themselves to concur in making any preparations and forming any forces the earl should require. And his majesty as willingly gratified them in both their desires. The earl of Cumberland was a man of great honour and integrity, who had all his estate in that country, and had lived most amongst them, with very much acceptation and affection from the gentlemen and the common people: but he was not in any degree active, or of a martial temper, and rather a man more like not to have many enemies than to oblige any to be firmly and resolutely his friends or to pursue his interests: the great fortune of the family was divided, and the greater part of it carried away by an heir female; and his father had so wasted the remainder that the earl could not live with that lustre, nor draw so great a dependence upon him, as his ancestors had done. In a word, he was a man of honour, and popular enough in peace, but not endued with those parts which were necessary for such a season. Sir Thomas Glemham was a gentleman of a noble extraction and a fair fortune, though he had much impaired it; he had spent many years in armies beyond the seas, and he had been an officer of very good esteem in the King's armies, and of courage and integrity unquestionable; but he was not of so stirring and active a nature as to be able to infuse fire enough into the phlegmatic constitutions of that people, who did rather wish to be spectators of the war than parties in it, and believed if they did not provoke the other party they might all live quietly together; until sir John Hotham by his excursions and depredations out of Hull, and their seditious neighbours by their insurrections, awakened them out of that pleasant dream; and then the greatest part of the gentry of that populous country, and very many of the common people, did behave themselves with signal fidelity and courage in the King's service: of all which particulars, which deserve well to be remembered and transmitted to posterity, there will be occasion to make mention in the following discourse. . . .

The King came to Nottingham two or three days before the day he had appointed to set up the standard; having taken Lincoln in his way, and drawn some arms from the train-bands of that country with him to Nottingham; from whence the next day he went to take a view of his horse, whereof there were several troops well armed, and under good officers, to the number of seven or eight hundred men; with which, being informed that there were some regiments of foot marching towards Coventry, by the earl of Essex his orders, he made haste thither; making little doubt but that he should be able to get thither before them, and so to possess himself of that city; and he did get thither the day before they came, but found not only the gates shut against him, but some of his servants shot and wounded from the walls: nor could all his messages and summons prevail with the mayor and magistrates, (before there was any garrison there,) to suffer the King to enter into the city. So great an interest and reputation the Parliament had gotten over the affections of the people, whose hearts were alienated from any reverence to the government.

The King could not remedy the affront, but went that night to Stoneleigh, the house then of sir Thomas Lee, where he was well received; and the next day, his body of horse, having a clear view upon an open *campania** for five or six miles together of the [enemy's] small body of foot, which consisted not of above 1200 men, with one troop of horse which marched with them over that plain, retired before them, without giving them one charge; which was imputed to the lashty* of Wilmot, who commanded, and had a colder courage than many who were under him, and who were of opinion that they might have easily defeated that body of foot: which would have been a very seasonable victory, would have put Coventry unquestionably into the King's hands, and sent him with a good omen to the setting up of his standard. Whereas, that unhappy retreat, which looked like a defeat, and the rebellious behaviour of Coventry, made his majesty's return to Nottingham very melancholic; and he returned thither the very day the standard was appointed to be set up.

According to the proclamation, upon the twenty-fifth day of August* the standard was erected, about six of the clock in the evening of a very stormy and tempestuous day. The King himself, with a small train, rode to the top of the castle-hill, Verney the knight-marshal, who was standard-bearer, carrying the standard, which was then erected in that place, with little other ceremony than the sound of drums and trumpets. Melancholic men observed many ill presages about that time. There was not one regiment of foot yet levied and brought thither; so that the train-bands, which the sheriff had drawn thither, was all the strength the King had for his person and the guard of the standard. There appeared no conflux of men in obedience to the proclamation; the arms and ammunition were not yet come from York, and a general sadness covered the whole town, and the King himself appeared more melancholic than he used to be. The standard itself was blown down the same night it had been set up, by a very strong and unruly wind, and could not be fixed again in a day or two till the tempest was allayed. [*HR*, V, 443–9]

This anecdote about Hyde's conversation with Sir Edmund Verney comes from the Life, *and was left out of the published* History.

Mr Hyde was wont often to relate a passage in that melancholic time, when the standard was set up at Nottingham, with which he was much affected. Sir Edmund Verney, knight-marshal, who was mentioned before as standard-bearer, with whom he had great familiarity, who was a man of great courage, and generally beloved, came one day to him, and told him, 'he was very glad to see him, in so universal a damp, under which the spirits of most men were oppressed, retain still his natural vivacity and cheerfulness; that he knew that the condition of the king, and the power of the parliament, was not better known to any man than to him; and therefore he hoped that he was able to administer some comfort to his friends, that might raise their spirits, as well as it supported his own.' He answered, 'that he was, in truth, beholden to his constitution, which did not incline him to despair; otherwise, that he had no pleasant prospect before him, but thought as ill of affairs as most men did; that the other was as far from being melancholic as he, and was known to be a man of great courage, (as indeed he was of a very cheerful and a generous nature, and confessedly valiant,) and that they could not do the king better service, than by making it their business to raise the dejected minds of men, and root out those apprehensions which disturbed them, of fear and despair, which could do no good, and did really much mischief.'

He replied smiling, 'I will willingly join with you the best I can, but I shall act it very scurvily. My condition,' said he, 'is much worse than yours, and different, I believe, from any other man's; and will very well justify the melancholic that, I confess to you, possesses me. You have satisfaction in your conscience that you are in the right; that the king ought not to grant what is required of him; and so you do your duty and your business together: but for my part, I do not like the quarrel, and do heartily wish that the king would yield and consent to what they desire; so that my conscience is only concerned in honour and in gratitude to follow my master. I have eaten his bread, and served him near thirty years, and will not do so base a thing as to forsake him; and choose rather to lose my life (which I am sure I shall do) to preserve and defend those things which are against my conscience to preserve and defend: for I will deal freely with you, I have no reverence for the bishops, for whom this quarrel [subsists.]' It was not a time to dispute; and his affection to the church had never been suspected. He was as good as his word; and was killed, in the battle of Edgehill, within two months after this discourse. And if those who had the same and greater obligations, had observed the same rules of gratitude and generosity, whatever their other affections had been, that battle had never been fought, nor any of that mischief been brought to pass that succeeded it. [*Life*, II, 66–7]

Writing the History *in 1647, Hyde condemned what he saw as Parliament's ruthless attitude to those it felt to be its enemies, and the efforts of the London clergy to whip up enthusiasm for its cause.*

For wherever they found any person of quality inclined to the King, or but disinclined to them, they immediately seized upon his person, and sent him in great triumph to the Parliament, who committed him to prison, with all circumstances of cruelty and inhumanity.

Thus they took prisoner the lord Montagu of Boughton, at his house in Northamptonshire, a person of great reverence, being above fourscore years of age, and of unblemished reputation, for declaring himself unsatisfied with their disobedient and undutiful proceedings against the King, and more expressly against their ordinance for the militia; and notwithstanding that he had a brother of the House of Peers, the Lord Privy Seal, and a nephew, the lord Mandeville, who had as full a power in that council as any man, and a son in the House of Commons very unlike his father, his lordship was committed to the Tower a close prisoner; and, though he was afterwards remitted to more air, he continued a prisoner to his death.

Thus they took prisoner in Oxfordshire the earl of Berkshire, and three or four principal gentlemen of that county, and committed them to the Tower, for no other reason but wishing well to the King; for they never appeared in the least action in his service. And thus they took prisoner the earl of Bath in Devonshire, who neither had or ever meant to do the King the least service, but only, out of the morosity of his own nature, had before in the House expressed himself not of their mind; and carried him, with many other gentlemen of Devon and Somerset, with a strong guard of horse to London; where, after they had been exposed to the rudeness and reproach of the common people, who called them 'traitors and rebels to the Parliament,' and pursued them with such usage as they use to the most infamous malefactors, they were, without ever being examined or charged with any particular crime, committed to several prisons. So that not only all the prisons about London were quickly filled with persons of honour, and great reputation for sobriety and integrity to their counties, but new prisons were made for their reception; and, (which was a new and barbarous invention,) very many persons of very good quality, both of the clergy and laity, were committed to prison on board the ships in the river of Thames, where they were kept under decks, and no friend suffered to come to them; by which many lost their lives. And that the loss of their liberty might not be all their punishment, it was the usual course, (and very few scaped it,) after any man was committed as a *notorious malignant*, (which was the brand,) that his estate and goods were seized or plundered, by an order from the House of Commons or some committee, or [by] the soldiers, (who in their march took the goods of all Catholics and eminent malignants as lawful prize), or by the fury and license of the common people, who were in all places grown to that barbarity and rage against the nobility and gentry, (under the style of *cavaliers*,) that it was not safe for any to live at their houses who were taken notice of as no votaries to the Parliament. . . .

I must not forget, though it cannot be remembered without much horror, that this strange wild-fire among the people was not so much and so furiously kindled by the breath of the Parliament as of the clergy, who both administered fuel and blowed the coals in the Houses too. These men having creeped into, and at last driven all learned and orthodox men from, the pulpits, had, (as is before remembered,) from the beginning of this Parliament, under the notion of reformation and extirpating of Popery, infused seditious inclinations into the hearts of men against the present government of the Church, with many libellous invectives against the State too. But since the raising an army and rejecting the King's last overture of a treaty, they contained themselves within no bounds, and as freely and without control inveighed against the person of the King as they had before against the worst malignant; profanely and blasphemously applying whatsoever had been spoken and declared by God Himself or the prophets against the most wicked and impious kings, to incense and stir up the people against their most gracious sovereign.

There are monuments enough in the seditious sermons at that time printed, and in the memories of men of others not printed, of such wresting and perverting of Scripture to the odious purposes of the preacher, that pious men will not look over without trembling. One takes his text out of Moses' words in the 32d chapter of Exodus and the 29th verse, *Consecrate yourselves to-day to the Lord, even every man upon his son and upon his brother, that he may bestow upon you a blessing this day*: and from thence incites his auditory to the utmost prosecution of those, under what relation soever of blood, neighbourhood, dependence, who concurred not in the reformation proposed by the Parliament. Another makes as bold with David's words, in the 1 Chron., 22 ch., and the 16th verse, *Arise therefore, and be doing*: and from thence assures them it was not enough to wish well to the Parliament; if they brought not their purse as well as their prayers, and their hands as well as their hearts, to the assistance of it, the duty in the text was not performed. There was more than Mr Marshall, who, from the 23rd verse of the 5th chapter of Judges, *Curse ye Meroz, said the angel of the Lord; curse ye bitterly the inhabitants thereof, because they came not to the help of the Lord, to the help of the Lord against the mighty*, presumed to inveigh against, and in plain terms to pronounce God's own curse against, all those who came not with their utmost power and strength to destroy and root out all the malignants who in any degree opposed the Parliament.

There was one who from the 48th [chapter] of the prophet Jeremy, and the 10th verse, *Cursed be he that keepeth back his sword from blood*, reproved those who gave any quarter to the King's soldiers. And another out of the 5th verse of the 25th chapter of Proverbs, *Take away the wicked from before the king, and his throne shall be established in righteousness*, made it no less a case of conscience by force to remove the evil counsellors from the King, (with bold intimation what might be done to the King himself if he would not suffer them to be removed,) than to perform any Christian duty that is enjoined. It would fill a volume to insert all the impious madness of this kind, so that the complaint of the prophet Ezechiel might most truly and seasonably have been applied, *There is a conspiracy of her prophets in the middest thereof, like a roaring lion ravening the prey; they have devoured souls; they have taken the treasure and precious things; they have made her many widows in the midst thereof*.* . . .

And indeed no good Christian can without horror think of those ministers of the church, who, by their function being messengers of peace, are the only trumpets of war and incendiaries towards rebellion. How much more Christian was that Athenian nun in Plutarch,* and how shall she rise up in judgment against those men, who, when Alcibiades was condemned by the public justice of the State, and a decree made that all the religious priests and women should ban and curse him, stoutly refused to perform that office; answering, 'that she was professed religious to pray and to bless, not to curse and to ban.' And if the person and the place can improve and aggravate the offence, (as without doubt it doth, both before God and man,) methinks the preaching treason and rebellion out of the pulpit should be worse than the advancing it in the market, as much as poisoning a man at the Communion would be worse than murdering him at a tavern. And it may be, in that catalogue of sins which the zeal of some men [hath] thought to be the sin against the Holy Ghost, there may not be any one more reasonably thought to be such than a minister of Christ's turning rebel against his prince, (which is a most notorious apostasy against his order,) and his preaching rebellion to the people as the doctrine of Christ; which, adding blasphemy and pertinacy to his apostasy, hath all the marks by which good men are taught to avoid that sin against the Holy Ghost. [*HR*, VI, 34–42]

As the Earl of Essex marched northwards to confront him, Charles left Nottingham and marched to Shrewsbury, gradually attracting support and money from the nobility and gentry. Out of Wales, Shropshire, and Cheshire he finally recruited a respectable army, albeit one that was smaller and less well equipped than Parliament's. The account printed in The History of the Rebellion *of the events leading up to the first set-piece battle of the war, at Edgehill, was put together from passages in both the* History *and the* Life.

In this equipage the King marched from Shrewsbury on the 12th of October to Bridgnorth, never less baggage attending a royal army, there being not one tent and very few waggons belonging to the whole train; having in his whole army not one officer of the field who was a Papist, except sir Arthur Aston,* if he were one; and very few common soldiers of that religion. However, the Parliament in all their declarations, and their clergy much more in their sermons, assured the people that the King's army consisted only of Papists, whilst themselves entertained all of that religion that they could get; and very many, both officers and soldiers, of that religion engaged with them; whether it was that they really believe that that army did desire liberty of conscience for all religions, as some of the chief of them pretended, or that they desired to divide themselves for communication of intelligence and interest. And here it is not fit to forget one particular, that, when the committee of Parliament appointed to advance the service, upon the propositions for plate and horses,* in the county of Suffolk, sent word to the House of Commons that some Papists offered to lend money upon those propositions, and desired advice whether they should accept of it, it was answered that if they offered any considerable sum, whereby it might be conceived to proceed from a real affection to the Parliament, and not out of policy to bring themselves within their protection and so to excuse their delinquency, it should be accepted of.

When the King was ready for his march, there was some difference of opinion which way he should take; many were of opinion that he should march towards Worcester, where the earl of Essex still remained; those countries were thought well-affected to the King, where his army would be supplied with provisions and increased in numbers; and that no time should be lost in coming to a battle, because the longer it was deferred the stronger the earl would grow by the supplies which were every day sent to him from London; and he had store of arms with him to supply all defects of that kind. However, it was thought more counsellable to march directly towards London, it being morally sure that the earl of Essex would put himself in their way. The King had much confidence in his horse, (his nephew, prince Rupert, being in the head of them,) which were fleshed by their success at Worcester;* and if he had made his march that way, he would have been entangled in the enclosures, where his horse would have been less useful; whereas there were many great *campanias* near the other way, much fitter for an engagement. And so, about the middle of October, the King marched from Shrewsbury, and quartered that night at Bridgnorth, ten miles from the other place, where there was a rendezvous of the whole army, which appeared very cheerful; and so to Wolverhampton, Birmingham, and Kenilworth, a house of the King's, and a very noble seat, where the King rested one day; where the lord chief justice Heath,* who was made Chief Justice for that purpose, (Bramston, a man of great learning and integrity, being, without any purpose of disfavour, removed from that office, because he stood bound by recognizance to attend the Parliament upon an accusation depending there against him,) began to sit upon a commission of oyer and terminer,* to attaint the earl of Essex, and many other persons who were in rebellion, of high treason.

Some days had passed without any notice of that army; some reporting that it remained still at Worcester; others, that they were marched the direct way from thence towards London. But intelligence came from London that very many officers of name and command in the Parliament army [had] undergone that service with a full resolution to come to the King as soon as they were within any distance; and it was wished that the King would send a proclamation into the army itself, to offer pardon to all who would return to their obedience. And a proclamation was prepared accordingly, and all circumstances resolved upon, that a herald should be sent to proclaim it in the head of the earl's army, when it should be drawn up in battle. But that, and many other particulars prepared and resolved upon, were forgotten, or omitted, at the time appointed, which would not admit any of those formalities.

When the whole army marched together, there was quickly discovered an unhappy jealousy and division between the principal officers, which grew quickly into a perfect faction between the foot and the horse. The earl of Lindsey was general of the whole army by his commission, and thought very equal to it. But when prince Rupert came to the King, which was after the standard was set up, and received a commission to be general of the horse, which all men knew was designed for him, there was a clause inserted into it which exempted him from receiving orders from any body but from the King himself; which, upon the matter, separated all the horse from any dependence upon the general, and had other ill consequences in it: for when the King at midnight, being in his bed, and receiving intelligence of the enemy's motion, commanded the lord Falkland, his principal Secretary of State, to direct prince Rupert what he should do, he took it very ill, and expostulated with the lord Falkland for giving him orders. But he could not have directed his passion against any man who would feel or regard it less. And he told him that 'it was his office to signify what the King bad him; which he should always do; and that he in neglecting it neglected the King;' who did neither the prince nor his own service any good by complying in the beginning with his rough nature, which rendered him very ungracious to all men. But the King was so indulgent to him that he took his advice in all things relating to the army, and so upon consideration of their march, and the figure of the battle they resolved to fight in with the enemy, he concurred entirely with prince Rupert's advice, and rejected the opinion of the general, who preferred the order he had learned under prince Maurice and prince Harry,* with whom he had served at the same time when the earl of Essex and he had both regiments. The uneasiness of the prince's nature, and the little education he had in courts, made him unapt to make acquaintance with any of the lords, who were likewise thereby discouraged from applying themselves to him; whilst some officers of the horse were well pleased to observe that strangeness, and fomented it, believing their credit would be the greater with the prince, and desired that no other person should have any credit with the King. So the war was scarce begun when there appeared such faction and designs in the army, which wise men looked upon as a very evil presage; and the inconveniences which flowed from thence gave the King great trouble in a short time after.

Within two days after the King marched from Shrewsbury, the earl of Essex moved from Worcester to attend him, with an army superior in number far to the King's; the horse and foot being completely armed, and the men very well exercised, and the whole equipage (being supplied out of the King's magazines) suitable to an army set forth at the charge of a kingdom. The earl of Bedford* had the name of general of the horse, though that command principally depended upon sir William Balfour. Of the nobility he had with him the lords Kimbolton, St John's, Wharton, Robartes, Rochford, and Feilding,* (whose fathers, the earls of Dover and Denbigh, charged as volunteers in the King's guards of horse,) and many gentlemen of quality; but his train was so very great that he could move but in slow marches. So that the two armies, though they were but twenty miles asunder when they first set forth, and both marched the same way, they gave not the least disquiet in ten days' march to each other; and in truth, as it appeared afterwards, neither army knew where the other was.

The King by quick marches, (having seldom rested a day in any place,) came on Saturday the 22nd of October to Edgecott, a village in Northamptonshire, within four miles of Banbury in which the rebels had a garrison. As soon as he came thither he called a council of war, and having no intelligence that the earl of Essex was within any distance, it was resolved the King and the army should rest in those quarters the next day, only that sir Nicholas Byron should march with his brigade and attempt the taking in of Banbury. And with this resolution the council brake up, and all men went to their quarters, which were at a great distance, without any apprehension of an enemy. But that night, about 12 of the clock, prince Rupert sent the King word that the body of the rebels' army was within seven or eight miles, and that the head quarter was at a village called Keinton on the edge of Warwickshire, and that it would be in his majesty's power, if he thought fit, to fight a battle the next day; which his majesty liked well, and therefore immediately despatched orders to cross the design for Banbury, and that the whole army should draw to a rendezvous on the top of Edgehill, which was a very high hill, about two miles from

Keinton where the head-quarters of the earl was, and which had a clear prospect of all that valley.

In the morning, (being Sunday the 23rd of October,) when the rebels were beginning their march, (for they suspected not the King's forces to be near,) they perceived a fair body of horse on the top of that hill, and easily concluded their march was not then to be far. It is certain they were exceedingly surprised, having never had any other confidence of their men than by the disparity they concluded would be still between their numbers and the King's; the which they found themselves now deceived in, for two of their strongest and best regiments of foot, and one regiment of horse, was a day's march behind with their ammunition. So that though they were still superior in number, yet that difference was not so great as they promised themselves. However, it cannot be denied that the earl with great dexterity performed whatsoever could be expected from a wise general. He chose that ground which best liked him. There was between the hill and the town a fair *campania*, save that near the town it was narrower, and on the right hand some hedges and inclosures: so that there he placed musketeers, and not above two regiments of horse, where the ground was narrowest; but on his left wing he placed a body of 1000 horse, commanded by one Ramsey a Scotchman; the reserve of horse (which was a good one) was commanded by the earl of Bedford, general of their horse, and sir William Balfour with him. The general himself was with the foot, which were ordered as much to advantage as might be. And in this posture they stood from 8 of the clock in the morning.

On the other side, though prince Rupert was early in the morning with the greatest part of the horse on the top of the hill, which gave the first alarum of the necessity of fighting to the other party, yet the foot were quartered at so great a distance that many regiments marched seven or eight miles to the rendezvous: so that it was past one of the clock before the King's forces marched down the hill. The general himself alighted at the head of his own regiment of foot, his son the lord Willoughby being next to him with the King's regiment of guards, in which was the King's standard, carried by sir Edmund Verney, knight marshal. The King's right wing of horse was commanded by prince Rupert, the left wing by Mr Wilmot, commissary general of the horse, who was assisted by sir Arthur Aston with most of the dragoons, because that left wing was opposed to the enemy's right which had the shelter of some hedges lined with musketeers: and the reserve was committed to sir John Byron, and consisted indeed only of his own regiment. At the entrance into the field, the King's troop of guards, either provoked by some unseasonable scoffs amongst the soldiery, or out of their desire of glory, or both, besought the King that he would give them leave to be absent that day from his person, and to charge in the front amongst the horse; the which his majesty consented to. They desired prince Rupert 'to give them that honour which belonged to them,' who accordingly assigned them the first place; which, (though they performed their parts with admirable courage,) may well be reckoned amongst the oversights of that day.

It was near three of the clock in the afternoon before the battle began; which, at that time of the year, was so late, that some were of opinion that the business should be deferred till the next day. But against that there were many objections; the King's numbers could not increase, the enemy's might; for they had not only their garrisons, Warwick, Coventry, and Banbury, within distance, but all that county so devoted to them that they had all provisions brought to them without the least trouble; whereas, on the other side, the people were so disaffected to the King's party that they had carried away or hid all their provisions, insomuch as there was neither meat for man or horse; and the very smiths hid themselves, that they might not be compelled to shoe the horses, of which in those stony ways there was great need. This proceeded not from any radical malice, or disaffection to the King's cause or his person, (though it is true that circuit in which this battle was fought, being between the dominions of the lord Saye and the lord Brooke, was the most eminently corrupted of any county in England,) but by the reports and infusions which the other very diligent party had wrought into the people's belief, that the cavaliers were of a fierce, bloody, and licentious disposition, and that they committed all manner of cruelty upon the inhabitants of those places where they came, of which robbery was the least; so that the poor people thought there was no other way to preserve their goods than by hiding them out of the way; which was confessed by them when they found how much that information had wronged them, by making them so injurious to their friends. And therefore where the army rested a day they found much better entertainment at parting than when they came; for it will not be denied that there was no person of honour or quality who paid not punctually and exactly for what they had; and there was not the least violence or disorder amongst the common soldiers in their march which scaped exemplary punishment; so that at Birmingham, a town so generally wicked that it had risen upon small parties of the King's, and killed or taken them prisoners and sent them to Coventry, declaring a more peremptory malice to his majesty than any other place, two soldiers were executed for having taken some small trifle of no value out of a house whose owner was at that time in the rebels' army. So strict was the discipline in this army, when the other without control practised all the dissoluteness imaginable. But the march was so fast, that the leaving a good reputation behind them was no harbinger to provide for their better reception in their next quarters. So that their wants were so great at the time when they came to Edgehill, that there were very many companies of the common soldiers who had scarce eaten bread in eight and forty hours before. The only way to cure this was a victory; and therefore the King gave the word, though it was late, the enemy keeping their ground to receive him without advancing at all.

In this hurry, there was an omission of somewhat which the King intended to have executed before the beginning of the battle. He had caused many proclamations to be printed of pardon to all those soldiers who would lay down their arms, which he resolved, as is said before to have sent by a herald to the earl of Essex, and to have found ways to have scattered and dispersed them in that army, as soon as he understood they were within any distance of him. But all men were now so much otherwise busied that it was not soon enough remembered; and when it was, the proclamations were not at hand; which, by that which follows, might probably have produced a good effect. For as the right wing of the King's horse advanced to charge the left wing, which was the gross of the enemy's horse, sir Faithful Fortescue, (whose fortune and interest being in Ireland, he had come out of that kingdom to hasten supplies thither, and had a troop of horse raised for him for that service; but as many other of those forces were, so his troop was likewise disposed into that army, and he was now major to sir William Waller; he) with his whole troop advanced from the gross of their horse, and discharging all their pistols on the ground, within little more than carabine* shot of his own body, presented himself and his troop to prince Rupert; and immediately with his highness charged the enemy. Whether this sudden accident, (as it might very well,) and [the] not knowing how many more were of the same mind, each man looking upon his companion with the same apprehension as upon the enemy, or whether the terror of prince Rupert and the King's horse, or all together, with their own evil consciences, wrought upon them, I know not, but that whole wing, having unskilfully discharged their carabines and pistols into the air, wheeled about, our horse charging them in flank and rear, and having thus absolutely routed them, pursued them flying, and had the execution of them above two miles.

The left wing, commanded by Mr Wilmot, had as good success, though they were to charge in worse ground, amongst hedges, and through gaps and ditches, which were lined with musketeers. But sir Arthur Aston, with great courage and dexterity, beat off those musketeers with his dragoons; and then the right wing of their horse was as easily routed and dispersed as their left, and those followed the chase as furiously as the other. The reserve, seeing none of the enemy's horse left, thought there was nothing more to be done but to pursue those that fled, and could not be contained by their commanders, but with spurs and loose reins followed the chase which their left wing had led them. And by this means, whilst most men thought the victory unquestionable, the King was in danger of the same fate which his predecessor Harry the Third felt at the battle of Lewes* against his barons, when his son the prince, having routed their horse, followed the chase so far that before his return to the field his father was taken prisoner; and so his victory served only to make the misfortune of that day the more intolerable. For all the King's horse having thus left the field, many of them only following the execution, others intending the spoil in the town of Keinton, where all the baggage was, and the earl of Essex's own coach, which was taken and brought away; their reserve, commanded by sir William Balfour, moved up and down the field in good order, and marching towards the King's foot pretended to be friends, till, observing no horse to be in readiness to charge them, [they] brake in upon the foot, and did great execution. Then was the general the earl of Lindsey, in the head of his regiment, being on foot, shot in the thigh, with which he fell, and was presently encompassed by the enemy, and his son, the lord Willoughby, piously endeavouring the rescue of his father, taken prisoner with him. Then was the standard taken, (sir Edmund Verney, who bore it, being killed,) but rescued again by captain John Smith, an officer of the lord Grandison's regiment of horse, and by him brought off. And if those horse had bestirred themselves, they might with little difficulty [have] destroyed or taken prisoner the King himself, and his two sons, the prince and the duke of York, being with fewer than one hundred horse and those without officer or command, within half musket shot of that body before he suspected them to be enemies.

When prince Rupert returned from the chase, he found this great alteration in the field, and his majesty himself with few noblemen and a small retinue about him, and the hope of so glorious a day quite vanished. For though most of the officers of horse were returned, and that part of the field covered again with the loose troops, yet they could not be persuaded or drawn to charge either the enemy's reserve of horse, which alone kept the field, or the body of their foot, which only kept their ground; the officers pretending that their soldiers were so dispersed that there were not ten of any troop together, and the soldiers, that their horses were so tired that they could not charge. But the truth is, where many soldiers of one troop or regiment were rallied together, there the officers were wanting; and where the officers were ready, there the soldiers were not together; and neither officers or soldiers desired to move without those who properly belonged to them. Things had now so ill an aspect that many were of opinion that the King should leave the field, though it was not easy to advise whither he should have gone; which if he had done, he had left an absolute victory to those who even at this time thought themselves overcome. But the King was positive against that advice, well knowing that as that army was raised by his person and presence only, so it could by no other means be kept together; and he thought it unprincely to forsake them who had forsaken all they had to serve him: besides, he observed the other side looked not as if they thought themselves conquerors; for that reserve which did so much mischief before, since the return of his horse betook themselves to a fixed station between their foot, which at best could but be thought to stand their ground; which two brigades of the King's did with equal courage, and gave equal volleys; and therefore he tried all possible ways to get the horse to charge again; easily discerning by some little attempts which were made what a notable impression a brisk one would have made upon the enemy. And when he saw it was not to be done, he was content with their only standing still. Without doubt, if either party had known the constitution of the other, they had not parted so fairly; and, very probably, which soever had made a bold offer had compassed his end upon his enemy. This made many believe, (though the horse vaunted themselves aloud to have done their part,) that the good fortune of the first part of the day, which well managed would have secured the rest, was to be imputed rather to their enemy's want of courage than to their own virtue, (which, after so great a victory, could not so soon have forsaken them,) and to the sudden and unexpected revolt of sir Faithful Fortescue with a whole troop, no doubt much to the consternation of those he left; which had not so good fortune as they deserved; for by the negligence of not throwing away their orange-tawny scarfs, (which they all wore as the earl of Essex's colours,) and being immediately engaged in the charge, many of them, not fewer than seventeen or eighteen, were suddenly killed by those to whom they joined themselves.

In this doubt of all sides, the night, (the common friend to wearied and dismayed armies,) parted them; and then the King caused his cannon which were nearest the enemy to be drawn off; and with his whole forces himself spent the night in the field, by such a fire as could be made of the little wood and bushes which grew thereabouts, unresolved what to do the next morning, many reporting that the enemy was gone: but when the day appeared, the contrary was discovered, for then they were seen standing in the same posture and place in which they fought, from whence the earl of Essex wisely never suffered them to stir all that night; presuming reasonably that if they were drawn off never so little from that place, their numbers would lessen, and that many would run away; and therefore he caused all manner of provisions, of which the country supplied him plentifully, to be brought thither to them for their repast, and reposed himself with them in the place. Besides, that night he received a great addition of strength, not only by rallying those horse and foot which had run out of the field in the battle, but by the arrival of colonel Hampden and colonel Grantham with two thousand fresh foot, (which were reckoned amongst the best of the army,) and five hundred horse, which marched a day behind the army for the guard of their ammunition, and a great part of their train, not supposing there would have been any action that would have required their presence. All the advantage this seasonable recruit brought them was to give their old men so much courage as to keep the field, which it was otherwise believed they would hardly have been persuaded to have done. After a very cold night spent in the field, without any refreshment of victual or provision for the soldiers, (for the country was so disaffected, that it not only not sent in provisions but many soldiers who straggled into the villages for relief were knocked in the head by the common people,) the King found his troops very thin; for though by conference with the officers he might reasonably conclude that there were not many slain in the battle, yet a third part of his foot were not upon the place, and of the horse many missing; and they that were in the field were so tired with duty, and weakened with want of meat, and shrunk up with the cruel cold of the night, (for it was a terrible frost, and there was not shelter of either tree or hedge,) that though they had reason to believe, by the standing still of the enemy whilst a small party of the King's horse in the morning took away four pieces of their cannon very near them, that any offer towards a charge, or but marching towards them, would have made a very notable impression in them, yet there was so visible an averseness from it in most officers as well as soldiers that the King thought not fit to make the attempt, but contented himself to keep his men in order, the body of horse facing the enemy upon the field where they had fought.

Towards noon the King resolved to try that expedient which was prepared for the day before, and sent sir William Le Neve, Clarencieux king at arms, with his proclamation of pardon to such as would lay down arms, to the enemy; believing, (though he expected then little benefit by the proclamation,) that he should by that means receive some advertisement of the condition of the army, and what prisoners they had taken, for many persons of command and quality were wanting; giving him order likewise to desire to speak with the earl of Lindsey, who was known to be in their hands. Before sir William came to the army he was received by the out-guards, and conducted with strictness, that he might say or publish nothing amongst the soldiers, to the earl of Essex; who, when he offered to read the proclamation aloud, and to deliver the effect of it, that he might be heard by those who were present, rebuked him with some roughness, and charged him as he loved his life not to presume to speak a word to the soldiers; and, after some few questions, sent him presently back, well guarded through the army, without any answer at all. At his return he had so great and feeling a sense of the danger he had passed that he made little observation of the posture or numbers of the enemy. Only he seemed to have seen or apprehended so much trouble and disorder in the faces of the earl of Essex and the principal officers about him, and so much dejection in the common soldiers, that they looked like men who had no farther ambition than to keep what they had left. He brought word of the death of the earl of Lindsey.

The number of the slain, by the testimony of the minister and others of the next parish, who took care for the burying of the dead, and which was the only computation that could be made, amounted to above five thousand; whereof two parts were conceived to be of those of the Parliament party, and not above a third of the King's. Indeed the loss of both sides was so great, and so little of triumph appeared in either, that the victory could scarce be imputed to the one or the other. Yet the King's keeping the field and having the spoil of it, by which many persons of quality who had lain wounded in the field were preserved, his pursuing afterwards the same design he had when he was diverted to the battle and succeeding in it, (as shall be touched anon,) were greater ensigns of victory on that side, than the taking the general prisoner, and the taking the standard, which was likewise recovered, were on the other. Of the King's, the principal persons who were lost were, the earl of Lindsey, general of the army, the lord George Stewart, lord Aubigny, son to the duke of Lenox and brother to the then duke of Richmond and Lenox, sir Edmund Verney, knight marshal of the King's horse and standard bearer, and some others of less name, though of great virtue and good quality.

The earl of Lindsey was a man of a very noble extraction, and inherited a great fortune from his ancestors; which though he did not manage with so great care as if he desired much to improve, yet he left it in a very fair condition to his family, which more intended the increase of it. He was a man of great honour, and spent his youth and vigour of his age in military actions and commands abroad; and albeit he indulged to himself great liberties of life, yet he still preserved a very good reputation with all men, and a very great interest in his country, as appeared by the supplies he and his son brought to the King's army; the several companies of his own regiment of foot being commanded by the principal knights and gentlemen of Lincolnshire, who engaged themselves in the service principally out of their personal affection to him. He was of a very generous nature, and punctual in what he undertook and in exacting what was due to him; which made him bear that restriction so heavily which was put upon him by the commission granted to prince Rupert, and by the King's preferring the prince's opinion in all matters relating to the war before his. Nor did he conceal his resentment: the day before the battle he said to some friends, with whom he used freedom, that 'he did not look upon himself as general; and therefore he was resolved when the day of battle should come that he would be in the head of his regiment as a private colonel, where he would die.' He was carried out of the field to the next village; and if he could then have procured surgeons, it was thought his wound would not have proved mortal. And it was imputed to the earl of Essex's too well remembering former grudges that he neither sent any surgeon to him nor performed any other offices of respect towards him; but it is most certain that the disorder the earl of Essex himself was in at that time, by the running away of the horse, and the confusion he saw the army in, and the plundering the carriages in the town where the surgeons were to attend, was the cause of all the omissions of that kind. And as soon as the other army was composed by the coming on of the night, the earl of Essex about midnight sent sir William Balfour and some other officers to see him, and to offer him all offices, and meant himself to have visited him. They found him upon a little straw in a poor house, where they had laid him in his blood, which had run from him in great abundance, no surgeon having been yet with him; only he had great vivacity in his looks, and told them he was sorry to see so many gentlemen, some whereof were his old friends, engaged in so foul a rebellion: and principally directed his discourse to sir William Balfour, whom he put in mind of the great obligations he had to the King; how much his majesty had disobliged the whole English nation by putting him into the command of the Tower; and that it was the most odious ingratitude in him to make him that return. He wished them to tell my lord of Essex, 'that he ought to cast himself at the King's feet to beg his pardon; which if he did not speedily do, his memory would be odious to the nation;' and continued this kind of discourse with so much vehemence that the officers by degrees withdrew themselves, and prevented the visit the earl of Essex intended him, who only sent the best surgeons to him; who in the very opening of his wounds died before the morning, only upon the loss of blood. He had very many friends and very few enemies, and died generally lamented. [*HR*, VI, 75–90]

8. The Death of Falkland

The King replaced Lindsey at the head of his army with the Scot Patrick Ruthven, Earl of Forth. A few days after the battle he entered Oxford, his base for the rest of the war, while Essex returned to London. In early November he marched towards London. On the 12th, he briefly secured possession of the town of Brentford, within ten miles of the capital, but was forced to withdraw. Both sides continued to discuss peace terms, and under pressure from advocates of peace within both Houses and outside them, Parliament agreed to a formal negotiation with the King on 26 December. During the treaty preliminaries, as discussions went on about the arrangements and basis for the negotiation, Hyde finally accepted a position in the royal administration, as he explained in his Life.

AND at this time there was a change in Mr Hyde's fortune, by a preferment the king conferred upon him. Every body knew that he was trusted by the king in his most secret transactions; but he was under no character in his service. When the commissioners who were sent for the safe-conduct came to Oxford, some who came in their company, amongst other matters of intelligence, brought the king a letter of his own to the queen,* printed, that had been intercepted, and printed by the license, if not order, of the parliament. In this letter, of the safe conveyance whereof his majesty had no apprehension, the king had lamented the uneasiness of his own condition, in respect of the daily importunity which was made to him by the lords and others, for honours, offices, and preferments; and named several lords, who were solicitous by themselves, or their friends, for this and that place; in all which he desired to receive the queen's advice, being resolved to do nothing with reference to those pretences till he should receive it. But he said there were some places which he must dispose of without staying for her answer, the necessity of his service requiring it; which were the mastership of the wards; applications being still made to the lord Saye in those affairs, and so that revenue was diverted from him: and therefore, as he had revoked his patent, so he was resolved to make secretary Nicholas master of the wards; 'and then,' (these were his majesty's own words,) 'I must make Ned Hyde secretary of state, for the truth is, I can trust nobody else.' Which was a very envious expression, and extended, by the ill interpretation of some men, to a more general comprehension than could be intended. This was quickly made public, for there were several prints of it in many hands; and some men had reason to be troubled to find their names mentioned in that manner, and others were glad that theirs were there, as having the pretence to pursue their importunities the more vehemently, being, as the phrase was, brought upon the stage, and should suffer much in their honour, if they should be now rejected; which kind of argumentation was very unagreeable and grievous to the king.

One morning, when the king was walking in the garden, as he used to do, Mr Hyde being then in his view, his majesty called him, and discoursed of the trouble he was in at the intercepting that letter; and finding by his countenance that he understood not the meaning, he asked him, 'whether he had not heard a letter of his, which he writ to the queen, had been intercepted and printed.' And he answering, 'that he had not heard of it,' as in truth he had not, the king gave him the printed letter to read, and then said, that 'he wished it were as much in his power to make every body else amends as he could him; for,' he said, 'he was resolved that afternoon to swear him secretary of state, in the place of Nicholas, whom he would likewise then make master of the wards.'* Mr Hyde told him, 'he was indeed much surprised with the sight of the letter; which he wished had not been communicated in that manner: but that he was much more surprised to find his own name in it, and his majesty's resolution upon it, which he besought him to change; for as he never had the ambition to hope or wish for that place, so he knew he was very unfit for it, and unable to discharge it.' To which the king with a little anger replied, that 'he did the greatest part of the business now:' and he answered, that 'what he did now would be no part of the business, if the rebellion were ended; and that his unskillfulness in languages, and his not understanding foreign affairs, rendered him very incapable of that trust.' The king said, 'he would learn as much as was necessary of that kind very quickly.' He continued his desire, that his majesty would lay aside that thought; and said, 'that he had great friendship for secretary Nicholas, who would be undone by the change; for he would find that his majesty would receive very little, and he nothing, by that office, till the troubles were composed.' The king said, 'Nicholas was an honest man, and that his change was by his desire;' and bade him speak with him of it; which he went presently to do, leaving his majesty unsatisfied with the scruples he had made.

When he came to the secretary's lodging, he found him with a cheerful countenance, and embracing him, called him his son. Mr Hyde answered him, that 'it was not the part of a good son to undo his father, or to become his son that he might undo him:' and so they entered upon the discourse; the one telling him what the king had resolved, and how grateful the resolution was to him; and the other informing him of the conference he had then had with the king, and that for his sake, as well as his own, he would not submit to the king's pleasure in it. And so he debated the whole matter with him, and made it evident to him, that he would be disappointed in any expectation he should entertain of profit from the wards, as the state of affairs then stood: so that he should relinquish an honourable employment, which he was well acquainted with, for an empty title, with which he would have nothing to do: and so advised him to consider well of it, and of all the consequences of it, before he exposed himself to such an inconvenience.

Whilst this was in suspense, sir Charles Caesar, who, with great prejudice to the king, and more reproach to the archbishop of Canterbury, Laud, had been made master of the rolls, died:* and sir John Culpepper had long had a promise from the king of that place, when it should become void, and now pressed the performance of it: which was violently opposed by many, partly out of ill-will to him, (for he had not the faculty of getting himself much loved,) and as much out of good husbandry, and to supply the king's necessities with a good sum of money, which Dr Duck was ready to lay down for the office. And the king was so far wrought upon, that he paid down three thousand pounds in part of what he was to give; but his majesty caused the money to be repaid, and resolved to make good his promise to sir John Culpepper, who would by no means release him. This was no sooner declared, than the lord Falkland (who was much more solicitous to have Mr Hyde of the council, than he was himself for the honour) took an opportunity to tell the king, that he had now a good opportunity to prefer Mr Hyde, by making him chancellor of the exchequer, in the place of sir John Culpepper; which the king said he had resolved to do, and bid him take no notice of it, until he had told him so himself: and shortly after sent for him, and said, 'that he had now found an office for him, which he hoped he would not refuse: that the chancellorship of the exchequer was void by the promotion of Culpepper, and that he resolved to confer it upon him;' with many gracious expressions of the satisfaction he had in his service. The other answered, 'that though it was an office much above his merit, yet he did not despair of enabling himself by industry to execute it, which he would do with all fidelity.' [*Life*, II, 73–6]

Hyde's appointment as Chancellor was dated 3 March 1643. He had already become a Privy Councillor on 22 February.

*The formal negotiations opened at Oxford on 1 March, when the parlia-
mentary commissioners met the King. This account comes from Clarendon's
Life, left out of the published History.*

The persons were the earl of Northumberland, (the rest appointed by
the house of peers were dispensed with,) and of the commons the lord
Wenman, Mr Pierrepoint, Mr Whitelocke,* and the king intended to
have appointed some of his council to have treated with them; but they
discovered at their first audience, that they had authority only to treat
with his majesty himself, and not with any other persons; whereupon
his majesty gave them admission whenever they desired it, and
received what they had to propose in writing, and then consulted and
debated it at his council, and delivered his answer again in writing, the
chancellor of the exchequer being always appointed to prepare those
answers. The commissioners had very sincere desires to have made
a peace, none of them having ever had inclination to alter the government, and the short experience they had, made it manifest to them that
others were possessed with contrary resolutions; but their instructions
were very strict, and nothing left to their own discretions; they who
sent them well knowing how their affections stood, and though they
had not power to hinder a treaty, which all the kingdom called for, and
to refuse it had been to declare that they would continue the war that
was universally abominated; yet they knew well how to elude it, which
they were the less suspected to incline to, because they were still willing that such persons should be employed to treat who were known to
be most solicitous for peace. When the propositions were formed in
the house, upon the debate of them, when objections were made of
their unreasonableness: that the king had already refused those very
overtures when his condition was much lower, and therefore that it
was not probable he would yield to the same when he was in the head
of a good army: it was answered by those who resolved it should come
to nothing, that it was the course and rule in all treaties *iniquum petere
ut aequum feras;** that they did not expect that the king would yield
to all they desired, or indeed that a peace would ever be made upon
what they did or could propose; but that thereupon the king would
be wrought upon to make his propositions; which must be the ground
of the peace; and that they must first know what the king would grant
before they abated any thing of their demands; and hereby (which
seemed to have somewhat of reason) they still prevailed to keep up their
propositions to the utmost they had insisted upon, in their proudest
and most insolent conjuncture, but still implied that they would be

glad to depart from any thing of it, when they should see any approach made towards peace by any concessions from the king that would make it safe and valid: yet they bound up their commissioners to the strictest letter of their propositions; nor did their instructions at this time (which they presented to the king) admit the least latitude to them, to interpret a word or expression, that admitted a doubtful interpretation. Insomuch as the king told them, 'that he was sorry that they had no more trust reposed in them; and that the parliament might as well have sent their demands to him by the common carrier, as by commissioners so restrained.' They had only twenty days allowed them to finish the whole treaty: whereof they might employ six days in adjusting a cessation,* if they found it probable to effect it in that time; otherwise they were to decline the cessation, and enter upon the conditions of the peace; which, if not concluded before the end of the twenty days, they were to give it over, and to return to the parliament.

These propositions and restrictions much abated the hopes of a good issue of the treaty. Yet every body believed, and the commissioners themselves did not doubt, that if such a progress should be made in the treaty, that a peace was like to ensue, there would be no difficulty in the enlargement of the time; and therefore the articles for a cessation were the sooner declined, that they might proceed in the main business. For though what was proposed by them in order to it was agreeable enough to the nature of such an affair; yet the time allowed for it was so short, that it was impossible to make it practicable: nor could notice be timely given to all the quarters on either side to observe it.

Besides that, there were many particulars in it, which the officers on the king's side (who had no mind to a cessation) formalized much upon; and (I know not from what unhappy root, but) there was sprung up a wonderful aversion in the town against a cessation. Insomuch as many persons of quality of several counties, whereof the town was full, applied themselves in a body to the king, not to consent to a cessation till a peace might be concluded; alleging, that they had several agitations in their countries, for his majesty's and their own conveniences, which would be interrupted by the cessation; and if a peace should not afterwards ensue, would be very mischievous. Which suggestion, if it had been well weighed, would not have been found to be of importance. But the truth is, the king himself had no mind to the cessation, for a reason which shall be mentioned anon, though it was never owned: and so they waved all further mention of the cessation, and betook themselves to the treaty; it being reasonable enough to believe, that if both sides were heartily disposed to it, a peace might as soon have been agreed upon as a cessation could be. All the transactions of that treaty having been long since published, and being fit only to be digested into the history of that time, are to be omitted here. Only what passed in secret, and was never communicated, nor can otherwise be known, since at this time no man else is living who was privy to that negotiation but the chancellor of the exchequer, will have a proper place in this discourse.

The commissioners, who had all good fortunes and estates, had all a great desire of peace, but knew well that there must be a receding mutually on both sides from what they demanded; for if the king insisted on justice, and on the satisfaction and reparation the law would give him, the lives and the fortunes of all who had opposed him would be at his mercy; and there were too many concerned to submit to that, and that guilt was in truth the foundation of their union. On the other side, if the parliament insisted on all that they had demanded, all the power of the crown and monarchy itself would be thrown off the hinges, which as they could never imagine the king would ever consent to, so they saw well enough their own concernment in it, and that themselves should be as much involved in the confusion as those they called their enemies.

The propositions brought by the commissioners in the treaty were so unreasonable, that they well knew that the king would never consent to them: but some persons amongst them, who were known to wish well to the king, endeavoured underhand to bring it to pass. And they did therefore, whilst they publicly pursued their instructions, and delivered and received papers upon their propositions, privately use all the means they could, especially in conferences with the lord Falkland and the chancellor of the exchequer, that the king might be prevailed with in some degree to comply with their unreasonable demands.

In all matters which related to the church, they did not only despair of the king's concurrence, but did not in their own judgments wish it; and believed, that the strength of the party which desired the continuance of the war, was made up of those who were very indifferent in that point; and that, if they might return with satisfaction in other particulars, they should have power enough in the two houses to oblige the more violent people to accept or submit to the conditions. They wished therefore that the king would make some condescensions in the point of the militia; which they looked upon as the only substantial security they could have, not to be called in question for what they had done amiss. And when they saw nothing could be digested of that kind, which would not reflect both upon the king's authority and his honour, they gave over insisting upon the general; and then Mr Pierrepoint (who was of the best parts, and most intimate with the earl of Northumberland) rather desired than proposed, that the king would offer to grant his commission to the earl of Northumberland, to be lord high admiral of England. By which condescension he would be restored to his office, which he had lost for their sakes; and so their honour would be likewise repaired, without any signal prejudice to the king; since he should hold it only by his majesty's commission, and not by any ordinance of parliament: and he said, if the king would be induced to gratify them in this particular, he could not be confident that they should be able to prevail with both houses to be satisfied therewith, so that a peace might suddenly be concluded; but, as he did not despair even of that, he did believe, that so many would be satisfied with it, that they would from thence take the occasion to separate themselves from them, as men who would rather destroy their country than restore it to peace.

And the earl of Northumberland himself took so much notice of this discourse to secretary Nicholas, (with whom he had as much freedom as his reserved nature was capable of,) as to protest to him, that he desired only to receive that honour and trust from the king, that he might be able to do him service; and thereby to recover the credit he had unhappily lost with him. In which he used very decent expressions towards his majesty; not without such reflections upon his own behaviour, as implied that he was not proud of it: and concluded that if his majesty would do him that honour, as to make that offer to the houses, upon the proposition of the militia, he would do all he could that it might be effectual towards a peace; and if it had not success, he would pass his word and honour to the king, that as soon, or whensoever his majesty would please to require it, he would deliver up his commission again into his hands; he having no other ambition or desire, than by this means to redeliver up the royal navy to his majesty's as absolute disposal, as it was when his majesty first put it into his hands; and which he doubted would hardly be done by any other expedient, at least not so soon.

When this proposition (which, from the interest and persons who proposed it, seemed to carry with it some probability of success, if it should be accepted) was communicated with those who were like with most secrecy to consult it; secretary Nicholas having already made some approach towards the king upon the subject, and found his majesty without inclination to hear more of it; it was agreed and resolved by them, that the chancellor of the exchequer should presume to make the proposition plainly to the king, and to persuade his majesty to hear it debated in his presence; at least, if that might not be, to enlarge upon it himself as much as the argument required: and he was not unwilling to embark himself in the affair.

When he found a fit opportunity for the representation, and his majesty at good leisure, in his morning's walk, when he was always most willing to be entertained; the chancellor related ingenuously to him the whole discourse, which had been made by Mr Pierrepoint, and to whom; and what the earl himself had said to secretary Nicholas; and what conference they, to whom his majesty gave leave to consult together upon his affairs, had between themselves upon the argument, and what occurred to them upon it: in which he mentioned the earl's demerit towards his majesty with severity enough, and what reason he had not to be willing to restore a man to his favour, who had forfeited it so unworthily. Yet he desired him to consider his own ill condition; and how unlike it was that it should be improved by the continuance of the war; and whether he could ever imagine a possibility of getting out of it upon more easy conditions than what was now proposed; the offer of which to the parliament could do him no signal prejudice, and could not but bring him very notable advantages: for if the peace did not ensue upon it, such a rupture infallibly would, as might in a little time facilitate the other. And then he said as much to lessen the malignity of the earl as he could, by remembering, how dutifully he had resigned his commission of admiral upon his majesty's demand, and his refusal to accept the commission the parliament would have given him;* and observed some vices in his nature, which would stand in the place of virtues, towards the support of his fidelity to his majesty, and his animosity against the parliament, if he were once reingratiated to his majesty's trust.

The king heard him very quietly without the least interruption, which he used not to do upon subjects which were not grateful to him; for he knew well that he was not swayed by any affection to the man, to whom he was more a stranger than he was to most of that condition; and he, upon occasions, had often made sharp reflections upon his ingratitude to the king. His majesty seemed at the first to insist upon the improbability that any such concession by him would be attended with any success; that not only the earl had not interest in the houses to lead them into a resolution that was only for his particular benefit, but that the parliament itself was not able to make a peace, without such conditions as the army would require; and then he should suffer exceedingly in his honour, for having shewn an inclination to a person who had requited his former graces so unworthily: and this led him into more warmth than he used to be affected with. He said, 'indeed he had been very unfortunate in conferring his favours upon many very ungrateful persons; but no man was so inexcusable as the earl of Northumberland.' He said, 'he knew that the earl of Holland was generally looked upon as the man of the greatest ingratitude; but,' he said, 'he could better excuse him than the other: that it was true, he owed all he had to his father's and his bounties, and that himself had conferred great favours upon him; but that it was as true, he had frequently given him many mortifications, which, though he had deserved, he knew had troubled him very much; that he had oftener denied him, than any other man of his condition; and that he had but lately refused to gratify him in a suit he had made to him, of which he had been very confident; and so might have some excuse (how ill soever) for being out of humour, which led him from one ill to another: but that he had lived always without intermission with the earl of Northumberland as his friend, and courted him as his mistress; that he had never denied any thing he had ever asked; and therefore his carriage to him was never to be forgotten.'

And this discourse he continued with more commotion, and in a more pathetical style than ever he used upon any other argument. And though at that time it was not fit to press the matter further, it was afterwards resumed by the same person more than once; but without any other effect, than that his majesty was contented that the earl should not despair of being restored to that office, when the peace should be made; or upon any eminent service performed by him, when the peace should be despaired of. The king was very willing and desirous that the treaty should be drawn out in length; to which purpose a proposition was made to the commissioners for an addition of ten days, which they sent to the parliament, without the least apprehension that it would be denied. But they were deceived; and for answer, received an order upon the last day but one of the time before limited, by which they were expressly required to leave Oxford the next day.* From that time all intercourse and commerce between Oxford and London, which had been permitted before, was absolutely interdicted under the highest penalties by the parliament.

If this secret underhand proposition had succeeded, and received that encouragement from the king that was desired, and more application of the same remedies had been then made to other persons, (for alone it could never have proved effectual,) it is probable, that those violent and abominable counsels, which were but then in projection between very few men of any interest, and which were afterwards miserably put in practice, had been prevented. And it was exceedingly wondered at, by those who were then privy to this overture, and by all who afterwards came to hear of it, that the king should in that conjuncture decline so advantageous a proposition; since he did already discern many ill humours and factions, growing and nourished, both in his court and army, which would every day be uneasy to him; and did with all his soul desire an end of the war. And there was nothing more suitable and agreeable to his magnanimous nature, than to forgive those, who had in the highest degree offended him: which temper was notorious throughout his whole life. It will not be therefore amiss, in this discourse, which is never to see light, and so can reflect upon nobody's character with prejudice, to enlarge upon this fatal rejection, and the true cause and ground thereof.

The king's affection to the queen was of a very extraordinary alloy; a composition of conscience, and love, and generosity, and gratitude, and all those noble affections which raise the passion to the greatest height; insomuch as he saw with her eyes, and determined by her judgment; and did not only pay her this adoration, but desired that all men should know that he was swayed by her: which was not good for either of them. The queen was a lady of great beauty, excellent wit and humour, and made him a just return of noblest affections; so that they were the true idea of conjugal affection, in the age in which they lived. When she was admitted to the knowledge and participation of the most secret affairs, (from which she had been carefully restrained by the duke of Buckingham whilst he lived,) she took delight in the examining and discussing them, and from thence in making judgment of them; in which her passions were always strong.

She had felt so much pain in knowing nothing, and meddling with nothing, during the time of that great favourite,* that now she took pleasure in nothing but knowing all things, and disposing all things; and thought it but just, that she should dispose of all favours and preferments, as he had done; at least, that nothing of that kind might be done without her privity: not considering that the universal prejudice that great man had undergone, was not with reference to his person, but his power; and that the same power would be equally obnoxious to murmur and complaint, if it resided in any other person than the king himself. And she so far concurred with the king's inclination, that she did not more desire to be possessed of this unlimited power, than that all the world should take notice that she was the entire mistress of it: which in truth (what other unhappy circumstance soever concurred in the mischief) was the foundation upon which the first and the utmost prejudices to the king and his government were raised and prosecuted. And it was her majesty's and the kingdom's misfortune, that she had not any person about her, who had either ability or affection, to inform and advise her of the temper of the kingdom or humour of the people, or who thought either worth the caring for.

When the disturbances grew so rude as to interrupt this harmony, and the queen's fears, and indisposition, which proceeded from those fears, disposed her to leave the kingdom, which the king, to comply with her, consented to; (and if that fear had not been predominant in her, her jealousy and apprehension, that the king would at some time be prevailed with to yield to some unreasonable conditions, would have dissuaded her from that voyage;) to make all things therefore as sure as might be, that her absence should not be attended with any such inconvenience, his majesty made a solemn promise to her at parting, that he would receive no person into any favour or trust, who had disserved him, without her privity and consent; and that, as she had undergone so many reproaches and calumnies at the entrance into the war, so he would never make any peace, but by her interposition and mediation, that the kingdom might receive that blessing only from her.

This promise (of which his majesty was too religious an observer) was the cause of his majesty's rejection, or not entertaining this last overture; and this was the reason that he had that aversion to the cessation, which he thought would inevitably oblige him to consent to the peace, as it should be proposed; and therefore he had countenanced an address, that had been made to him against it, by the gentlemen of several counties attending the court: and in truth they were put upon that address by the king's own private direction. Upon which the chancellor of the exchequer told him, when the business was over, that he had raised a spirit he would not be able to conjure down; and that those petitioners had now appeared in a business that pleased him, but would be as ready to appear, at another time, to cross what he desired; which proved true. For he was afterwards more troubled with application and importunity of that kind, and the murmurs that arose from that liberty, when all men would be counsellors, and censure all that the council did, than with the power of the enemy.

About the time that the treaty began, the queen landed in the north,* having been chased by the parliament ships into Burlington bay, their ships discharging all their cannon upon a small village where she lodged after her landing, that she was glad to resort for shelter to some banks in the field, where she spent most part of the night, and was the next day received by the earl of Newcastle, with some troops of his army, and was by him conveyed to York. Her majesty had brought with her a good supply of arms and ammunition, which was exceedingly wanted in the king's quarters; and she resolved, with a good quantity of ammunition and arms, to make what haste she could to the king; having at her first landing expressed, by a letter to his majesty, her apprehension of an ill peace by that treaty; and declared, that she would never live in England, if she might not have a guard for the security of her person: which letter came accidentally afterwards into the hands of the parliament; of which they made use to the queen's disadvantage. And the expectation of her majesty's arrival at Oxford was the reason that the king so much desired the prolongation of the treaty. And if it had pleased God that she had come thither time enough, as she did shortly after, she would have probably conde-scended to many propositions for the gratifying particular persons, as appeared afterwards, if thereby a reasonable peace might have been obtained. [*Life*, III, 2–18]

Fighting had continued during the negotiations, but immediately after their conclusion the Earl of Essex moved towards Oxford with his army, capturing Reading on the way on 26 April. He was slow to carry his attack further, waiting for further supplies of money from Oxford, and not until 10 June did he cautiously move forward to Thame. While he was there, the King's nephew Prince Rupert organized a daring attack with a small force on units of Essex's now scattered army, and after a violent skirmish at Chalgrove Field, retreated in good order as Essex's men gathered to repel them.

The prince his success in this last march was very seasonable, and raised the spirits at Oxford very much, and for some time allayed the jealousies and animosities which too often broke out in several factions to the disquiet of the King. It was visibly great in the number of the prisoners, whereof many were of condition; and the names of many officers were known who were left dead upon the field, as colonel Gunter, who was looked upon as the best officer of horse they had, and a man of known malice to the government of the Church; which had drawn some severe censure upon him before the troubles, and for which he had still meditated revenge. And one of the prisoners who had been taken in the action said that he was confident Mr Hampden was hurt, for he saw him ride off the field before the action was done, which he never used to do, and with his head hanging down, and rest-ing his hands upon the neck of his horse; by which he concluded he was hurt. But the news the next day made the victory much more

important than it was thought to have been. There was full information brought of the great loss the enemy had sustained in their quarters, by which three or four regiments were utterly broken and lost: the
names of many officers, of the best account, were known, who were
either killed upon the place, or so hurt as there remained little hope of
their recovery.

Among the prisoners, there were taken colonel Sheffeild, a younger
son of the earl of Mulgrave, and one colonel Berkely, a Scotchman;
who, being both visibly wounded, acted their hurts so well, and pretended to be so ready to expire, that, upon their paroles neither to
endeavour or endure a rescue, they were suffered to rest at a private
house in the way, within a mile of the field, till their wounds should be
dressed, and they recover so much strength as to be able to render
themselves prisoners at Oxford. But the King's forces were no sooner
gone, than they found means to send to their comrades, and were the
next day strong enough to suffer themselves to be removed to Thame,
by a strong party sent from the earl of Essex; and, between denying
that they had promised and saying that they would perform it, they
never submitted themselves to be prisoners, as much against the law of
arms as their taking arms was against their allegiance. But that which
would have been looked upon as a considerable recompense for a
defeat, could not but be thought a glorious crown of a victory, which
was the death of Mr Hampden; who, being shot into the shoulder with
a brace of bullets, which brake the bone, within three weeks after died
with extraordinary pain; to as great a consternation of all that party as
if their whole army had been defeated or cut off.

Many men observed (as upon signal turns of great affairs, as this
was, such observations are frequently made) that the field in which the
late skirmish was, and upon which Mr Hampden received his death's
wound, Chalgrove field, was the same place in which he had first executed the ordinance of the militia, and engaged that county, in which
his reputation was very great, in this rebellion: and it was confessed by
the prisoners that were taken that day, and acknowledged by all, that
upon the alarm that morning, after their quarters were beaten up, he
was exceedingly solicitous to draw forces together to pursue the
enemy, and, being himself a colonel of foot, put himself amongst those
horse, as a volunteer, who were first ready; and that when the prince
made a stand, all the officers were of opinion to stay till their body
came up, and he alone being second to none but the general himself in
the observance and application of all men) persuaded and prevailed
with them to advance; so violently did his fate carry him to pay the

mulct in the place where he had committed the transgression about a year before.

He was a gentleman of a good family in Buckinghamshire, and born to a fair fortune, and of a most civil and affable deportment. In his entrance into the world he indulged to himself all the license in sports and exercises and company which was used by men of the most jolly conversation. Afterwards he retired to a more reserved and melancholic society, yet preserving his own natural cheerfulness and vivacity, and, above all, a flowing courtesy to all men. Though they who conversed nearly with him found him growing into a dislike of the ecclesiastical government of the Church, yet most believed it rather a dislike of some churchmen, and of some introducements of theirs which he apprehended might disquiet the public peace. He was rather of reputation in his own country than of public discourse or fame in the kingdom before the business of ship-money: but then he grew the argument of all tongues, every man inquiring who and what he was that durst at his own charge support the liberty and property of the kingdom, and rescue his country from being made a prey to the Court. His carriage throughout that agitation was with that rare temper and modesty that they who watched him narrowly to find some advantage against his person, to make him less resolute in his cause, were compelled to give him a just testimony. And the judgment that was given against him infinitely more advanced him than the service for which it was given. When this Parliament began, (being returned knight of the shire for the county where he lived,) the eyes of all men were fixed on him as their *Patriae pater*, and the pilot that must steer their vessel through the tempests and rocks which threatened it. And I am persuaded his power and interest at that time was greater to do good or hurt than any man's in the kingdom, or than any man of his rank hath had in any time: for his reputation of honesty was universal, and his affections seemed so publicly guided that no corrupt or private ends could bias them.

He was of that rare affability and temper in debate, and of that seeming humility and submission of judgment, as if he brought no opinions with him, but a desire of information and instruction; yet he had so subtle a way of interrogating, and under the notion of doubts insinuating his objections, that he left his opinions with those from whom he pretended to learn and receive them. And even with them who were able to preserve themselves from his infusions, and discerned those opinions to be fixed in him with which they could not comply, he always left the character of an ingenious and conscientious person. He was indeed a very wise man, and of great parts, and possessed with the most absolute spirit of popularity, that is, the most absolute faculties to govern the people, of any man I ever knew. For the first year of the Parliament he seemed rather to moderate and soften the violent and distempered humours than to inflame them. But wise and dispassioned men plainly discerned that that moderation proceeded rather from prudence, and observation that the season was not ripe, than that he approved of the moderation; and that he begat many opinions and motions, the education whereof he committed to other men, so far disguising his own designs that he seemed seldom to wish more than was concluded; and in many gross conclusions, which would hereafter contribute to designs not yet set on foot, when he found them sufficiently backed by majority of voices, he would withdraw himself before the question, that he might seem not to consent to so much visible unreasonableness; which produced as great a doubt in some as it did approbation in others of his integrity. What combination soever had been originally with the Scots for the invasion of England, and what farther was entered into afterwards in favour of them, and to advance any alteration in Parliament, no man doubts was at least with the privity of this gentleman.

After he was amongst those members accused by the King of high treason, he was much altered, his nature and carriage seeming much fiercer than it did before. And without question, when he first drew his sword he threw away the scabbard; for he passionately opposed the overture made by the King for a treaty from Nottingham, and, as eminently, any expedients that might have produced an accommodation in this that was at Oxford; and was principally relied on to prevent any infusions which might be made into the earl of Essex towards peace, or to render them ineffectual if they were made; and was indeed much more relied on by that party than the general himself. In the first entrance into the troubles, he undertook the command of a regiment of foot, and performed the duty of a colonel on all occasions most punctually. He was very temperate in diet, and a supreme governor over all his passions and affections, and had thereby a great power over other men's. He was of an industry and vigilance not to be tired out or wearied by the most laborious, and of parts not to be imposed upon by the most subtle or sharp; and of a personal courage equal to his best parts; so that he was an enemy not to be wished wherever he might have been made a friend, and as much to be apprehended where he was so as any man could deserve to be. And therefore his death was no less congratulated on the one party than it was condoled on the other. In a word, what was said of Cinna might well be applied to him; *Erat illi*

*consilium ad facinus aptum; consilio autem neque lingua neque manu[s]
deerat;** he had a head to contrive, and a tongue to persuade, and a
hand to execute, any mischief. His death therefore seemed to be a great
deliverance to the nation. [*HR, VII*, 79–84]

*Following the fight at Chalgrove Essex withdrew to Aylesbury. Over the next
few weeks there was a string of royalist successes. At the end of June a parliamentarian army led by Lord Fairfax and his son Sir Thomas was defeated
by the Earl of Newcastle near Bradford. Another, under Sir William Waller,
was destroyed at Roundway Down, near Devizes, on 13 July, by forces led
by Prince Maurice, the Marquess of Hertford, and Sir Ralph Hopton. On
26 July Bristol surrendered to Prince Rupert. In the aftermath of these
defeats, the parliamentary commanders Essex and Waller quarrelled over
their responsibility for them. But after Bristol, the royalist momentum began
to be lost. There was a dispute between Prince Rupert and the Marquess of
Hertford over the command in the West; Newcastle became bogged down
before Hull; and then the decision at the beginning of August that the King's
main forces should besiege Gloucester, ably defended by Colonel Massey,
began to appear a costly mistake.*

At Gloucester the business proceeded very slowly: for though the
army increased wonderfully there by the access of forces from all
quarters, yet the King had neither money nor materials requisite for
a siege, and they in the town behaved themselves with great courage
and resolution, and made many sharp and bold sallies upon the King's
forces, and did more hurt commonly than they received, and many
officers of name, besides common soldiers, were slain in the trenches
and approaches; the governor leaving nothing unperformed that
became a vigilant commander. Sometimes, upon the sallies, the horse
got between the town and them, so that many prisoners were taken,
who were always drunk; and after they were recovered, they confessed
that the governor always gave the party that made the sally as much
wine and strong water as they desired to drink: so that it seems their
mettle was not purely natural; yet it is very observable, that in all the
time the King lay there with a very glorious army, and after the taking
of a city of a much greater name, there was no one officer ran from the
town to him, nor above three common soldiers, which is a great argument the discipline within was very good. Besides the loss of men
before the town, both from the walls and by sickness, (which was
not greater than was to be reasonably expected,) a very great license
broke into the army, both amongst officers and soldiers; the malignity
of those parts being thought excuse for the exercise of any rapine or

severity amongst the inhabitants; insomuch as it is hardly to be credited how many thousand sheep were in a few days destroyed, besides
what were brought in by the commissaries for a regular provision; and
many countrymen imprisoned by officers without warrant, or the least
knowledge of the King's, till they had paid good sums of money for
their delinquency; all which brought great clamour upon the discipline
of the army and justice of the officers, and made them likewise less
prepared for the service they were to expect.

In the mean time nothing was left at London unattempted that
might advance the preparations for relief of Gloucester. . . .

The earl of Essex now declared that he would himself undertake the
relief of Gloucester whereas before sir William Waller was designed to
it; and, whencesoever it proceeded, was returned to his old full alacrity
against the King, and recovered those officers and soldiers again to him
who had absented by his connivance or upon an opinion that he would
march no more; yet his numbers increased not so fast as the occasion
required: for colonel Massey found means to send many messengers
out of the town to advertise the straits he was in, and the time that
he should be able to hold out. Their ordinance of pressing,* though
executed with unusual rigour, insomuch as persons of good fortunes
who had retired to London that they might be the less taken notice of
were seized on, and detained in custody till they paid so much money,
or procured an able man to go in their places, brought not in such
a supply as they expected; and such as were brought in and delivered
to the officers, declared such an averseness to the work to which they
were designed, and such a peremptory resolution not to fight, that they
only increased their numbers, not their strength, and ran away upon
the first opportunity. In the end, they had no other resort for men
but to those who had so constantly supplied them with money, and
prevailed with their true friends, the city, which they still alarumed
with the King's irreconcilableness to them, to send three or four of
their train-band regiments, or auxiliaries, to fight with the enemy at
that distance, rather than to expect him at their own walls, where they
must be assured to see him as soon as Gloucester should be reduced;
and then they would be as much perplexed with the malignants within
as with the enemy without their city.

Upon such arguments, and the power of the earl of Essex, so many
regiments of horse and foot as he desired were assigned to march with
him; and so, towards the end of August, he marched out of London;
and having appointed a rendezvous near Aylesbury, where he was met
by the lord Grey and other forces of the associated counties,* from

thence he marched by easy journeys towards Gloucester, with an army of about eight thousand foot and four thousand horse. It would not at first be credited at the leaguer* that the earl of Essex could be in a condition to attempt such a work; and therefore they were too negligent upon the intelligence, and suspected rather that he would give some alarum to Oxford, where the Queen was, and thereby hope to draw the army from Gloucester, than that in truth he would venture upon so tedious a march, where he must march over a *campania* near thirty miles in length, where half the King's body of horse would distress, if not destroy, his whole army, and through a country eaten bare, where he could find neither provision for man or horse; and if he should without interruption be suffered to go into Gloucester, he could neither stay there, nor possibly retire to London, without being destroyed in the rear by the King's army, which should nevertheless not engage itself in the hazard of a battle. Upon these conclusions they proceeded in their works before Gloucester, their galleries being near finished, and visibly a great want of ammunition in the town; yet the lord Wilmot was appointed with a good party of horse to wait about Banbury, and to retire before the enemy, if he should advance, towards Gloucester, and to give such impediments to their march as in such a country might be easy to do; prince Rupert himself staying with the body of horse upon the hills above Gloucester, to join, if the earl of Essex should be so hardy as to venture.

The earl came to Brackley, and having there taken in from Leicester and Bedford the last recruits upon which he depended, he marched steadily over all that *campania*, which they thought he feared, towards Gloucester; and though the King's horse were often within view, and entertained him with light skirmishes, he pursued his direct way; the King's horse still retiring before them, till the foot was compelled to raise their siege, in more disorder and distraction than might have been expected; and so, with less loss and easier skirmishes than can be imagined, the earl with his army and train marched to Gloucester; where he found them reduced to one single barrel of powder; and all other provisions answerable. And it must be confessed, that governor gave a stop to the career of the King's good success, and from his pertinacious defence of that place the Parliament had time to recover their broken forces and more broken spirits, and may acknowledge to this rise the greatness to which they afterwards aspired.

The earl of Essex stayed in that joyful town (where he was received with all possible demonstrations of honour) three days; and in that time, (which was as wonderful as any part of the story,) caused all necessary provisions to be brought in to them out of those very quarters in which the King's army had been sustained, and which they conceived to be entirely spent: so solicitous were the people to conceal what they had, and to reserve it for them; which without a connivance from the King's commissaries could not have been done. All this time the King lay at Sudeley castle, the house of the lord Chandos, within eight miles of Gloucester, watching when that army would return, which they conceived stayed rather out of despair than election in those eaten quarters; and to open them a way for their retreat, his majesty removed to Evesham, hoping the earl would choose to go back the same way he came; which for many reasons was to be desired; and thereupon the earl marched to Tewkesbury, as if he had no other purpose. The King's horse, though bold and vigorous upon action and execution, were always less patient of duty and ill accommodation than they should be, and at this time, partly with weariness and partly with the indisposition that possessed the whole army upon this relief of the town, were less vigilant towards the motion of the enemy: so that the earl of Essex was marched with his whole army and train from Tewkesbury four and twenty hours before the King heard which way he was gone: for he took the advantage of a dark night, and, having sure guides, reached Cirencester before the breaking of the day, where he found two regiments of the King's horse quartered securely; all which, by the negligence of the officers, (a common and fatal crime throughout the war on the King's part,) he surprised, to the number of above three hundred; and, which was of much greater value, he found there a great quantity of provisions, prepared by the King's commissaries for the army before Gloucester, and which they neglected to remove after the siege was raised, and so most sottishly left it for the relief of the enemy, far more apprehensive of hunger than of the sword. And indeed this wonderful supply strangely exalted their spirits, as sent by the special care and extraordinary hand of Providence, even when they were ready to faint.

From hence the earl, having no farther apprehension of the King's horse, which he had no mind to encounter upon the open *campania*, and being at the least twenty miles before him, by easy marches, that his sick and wearied soldiers might overtake him, moved through that deep and enclosed country of North Wiltshire, his direct way to London. As soon as the King had sure notice which way the enemy was gone, he endeavoured by expedition and diligence to recover the advantage which the supine negligence of those he trusted had robbed him of; and himself with matchless industry taking care to lead up the foot, prince

Rupert with near five thousand horse marched day and night over the hills to get between London and the enemy, before they should be able to get out of those enclosed deep countries, in which they were engaged between narrow lanes, and to entertain them with skirmishes till the whole army should come up. This design, pursued and executed with indefatigable pains, succeeded to his wish; for when the van of the enemy's army had almost marched over Aldbourne Chase, intending that night to have reached Newbury, prince Rupert, besides their fear or expectation, appeared with a strong body of horse so near them, that before they could put themselves in order to receive him he charged their rear, and routed them with good execution; and though the enemy performed the parts of good men, and applied themselves more dexterously to the relief of each other than on so sudden and unlooked for an occasion was expected, yet, with some difficulty and the loss of many men, they were glad to shorten their journey, and, the night coming on, took up their quarters at Hungerford.

In this conflict, which was very sharp for an hour or two, many fell of the enemy, and of the King's party none of name but the marquis of Vieuville, a gallant gentleman of the French nation, who had attended the Queen out of Holland, and put himself as a volunteer upon this action into the lord Jermyn's regiment. There were hurt many officers, and amongst those the lord Jermyn received a shot in his arm with a pistol, owing the preservation of his life from other shots to the excellent temper of his arms; and the lord Digby a strange hurt in the face, a pistol being discharged at so near a distance upon him that the powder fetched much blood from his face, and for the present blinded him, without farther mischief, by which it was concluded that the bullet had dropped out before the pistol was discharged; and may be reckoned amongst one of those escapes of which that gallant person hath passed a greater number in the course of his life than any man I know.

By this expedition of prince Rupert the enemy was forced to such delay that the King came up with his foot and train, though his numbers, by his exceeding long and quick marches, and the license which many officers and soldiers took whilst the King lay at Evesham, were much lessened, being above two thousand fewer than when he raised his siege from Gloucester. And when the earl the next day advanced from Hungerford, hoping to recover Newbury, which prince Rupert with his horse would not be able to hinder him from, when he came within two miles of the town he found the King possessed of it, for his majesty with his whole army was come thither two hours before. This put him to

a necessity of staying upon the field that night; it being now the seventeenth day of September.

It was now thought by many that the King had recovered whatsoever had been lost by former oversights, omissions, or neglects, and
that by the destroying the army which had relieved Gloucester, he
should be fully recompensed for being disappointed of that purchase.
He seemed to be possessed of all advantages to be desired, a good town
to refresh his men in, whilst the enemy lodged in the field, his own
quarters to friend, and his garrison of Wallingford at hand, and Oxford
itself within distance for supply of whatsoever should be wanting;
when the enemy was equally tired with long marches, and from the
time that the prince had attacked them the day before had stood in
their arms, in a country where they could not find victual. So that it
was conceived that it was in the King's power whether he would fight
or no, and therefore that he might compel them to notable disadvantages who must make their way through or starve; and this was so fully
understood, that it was resolved over night not to engage in battle but
upon such grounds as should give an assurance of victory. But contrary to this resolution, when the earl of Essex had with excellent
conduct drawn out his army in battalia* upon a hill called Bigg's Hill,
within less than a mile of the town, and ordered his men in all places
to the best advantage, by the precipitate courage of some young officers, who had good commands, and who unhappily always undervalued the courage of the enemy, strong parties became successively so
far engaged that the King was compelled to put the whole to the hazard of a battle, and to give the enemy at least an equal game to play.

It was disputed on all parts with great fierceness and courage; the
enemy preserving good order, and standing rather to keep the ground
they were upon than to get more, by which they did not expose themselves to those advantages which any motion would have offered to the
assailants. The King's horse, with a kind of contempt of the enemy,
charged with wonderful boldness upon all grounds of inequality, and
were so far too hard for the troops of the other side that they routed
them in most places, till they had left the greatest part of their foot
without any guard at all of horse. But then the foot behaved themselves
admirably on the enemy's part, and gave their scattered horse time
to rally, and were ready to assist and secure them upon all occasions.
The London train-bands, and auxiliary regiments, (of whose inexperi-
ence of danger, or any kind of service beyond the easy practice of
their postures in the Artillery Garden,* men had till then too cheap an
estimation,) behaved themselves to wonder, and were in truth the

preservation of that army that day; for they stood as a bulwark and rampire* to defend the rest, and, when their wings of horse were scattered and dispersed, kept their ground so steadily that, though prince Rupert himself led up the choice horse to charge them, and endured their storm of small shot, he could make no impression upon their stand of pikes, but was forced to wheel about. Of so sovereign benefit and use is that readiness, order, and dexterity in the use of their arms, which hath been so much neglected.

It was fought all that day without any such notable turn as that either party could think they had much the better. For though the King's horse made the enemy's often give ground, yet the foot were so immoveable that little was gotten by the other; and the first entrance into the battle was so sudden, and without order, that during the whole day no use was made of the King's cannon, though that of the enemy was placed so unhappily that it did very great execution upon the King's party, both horse and foot. The night parted them when nothing else could; and each party had then time to revolve the oversights of the day. The enemy had fared at least as well as they hoped for; and therefore in the morning, early, they put themselves in order of marching, having an obligation in necessity to gain some place in which they might eat and sleep. On the King's side there was that caution which should have been the day before; and though the number of their slain was not so great as in so hot a day might have been looked for, yet very many officers and gentlemen were hurt, so that they rather chose to take advantage of the enemy's motion, than to charge them again upon the old ground; from whence they had been by order called off the night before, when they had recovered a post the keeping of which would much have prejudiced the adversary. The earl of Essex, finding his way open, pursued his main design of returning to London, and took that way by Newbury which led towards Reading; which prince Rupert observing, suffered him, without interruption or disturbance, to pass, till his whole army was entered into the narrow lanes, and then with a strong party of horse and one thousand musketeers followed his rear, with so good effect that he put them into great disorder, and killed many, and took many prisoners. However, the earl with the gross of his army and all his cannon got safe into Reading, and, after a night or two spent there to refresh and rest his men, he moved in a slow and orderly march to London, leaving Reading to the King's forces; which was presently possessed by sir Jacob Astley, with three thousand foot and five hundred horse, and made again a garrison for the King: his majesty and prince Rupert, with the remainder of the army, retiring to Oxford, and leaving a garrison under the command of colonel Boys in Donnington castle (a house of John Packer's, but more famous for having been the seat of Geoffrey Chaucer,) within a mile of Newbury, to command the great road through which the western trade was driven to London.

At this time sir William Waller was at Windsor with above two thousand horse and as many foot, as unconcerned for what might befall the earl of Essex as he had formerly been on his behalf at Roundway hill;* otherwise, if he had advanced upon the King to Newbury (which was not above twenty miles) when the earl was on the other side, the King had been in great danger of an utter defeat; and the apprehension of this was the reason, or was afterwards pretended to be, for the hasty engagement in battle.

The earl of Essex was received at London with all imaginable demonstrations of affection and reverence; public and solemn thanksgiving was appointed for his victory, for such they made no scruple to declare it. Without doubt, the action was performed by him with incomparable conduct and courage, in every part whereof very much was to be imputed to his own personal virtue, and it may be well reckoned amongst the most soldierly actions of this unhappy war. For he did the business he undertook, and after the relief of Gloucester his next care was to retire with his army to London; which, considering the length of the way and the difficulties he was to contend with, he did with less loss than could be expected. On the other side, the King was not without some signs of a victory. He had followed, and compelled the enemy to fight, by overtaking him, when he desired to avoid it; he had the spoil of the field, and pursued the enemy the next day after the battle, and had a good execution upon them without receiving any loss; and, (which seemed to crown the work,) fixed a garrison again at Reading,* and thereby straitened their quarters as much as they were in the beginning of the year, his own being enlarged by the almost entire conquest of the west, and his army much stronger in horse and foot than when he first took the field. On which side soever the marks and public ensigns of victory appeared most conspicuous, certain it is, that, according to the unequal fate that attended all skirmishes and conflicts with such an adversary, the loss on the King's side was in weight much more considerable and penetrating; for whilst some obscure, unheard of, colonel or officer was missing on the enemy's side, as some citizen's wife bewailed the loss of her husband, there were above twenty officers of the field and persons of honour and public name slain upon the place, and more of the same quality hurt. . . .

But I must here take leave a little longer to discontinue this narration; and if the celebrating the memory of eminent and extraordinary
persons, and transmitting their great virtues for the imitation of posterity, be one of the principal ends and duties of history, it will not be
thought impertinent in this place to remember a loss which no time
will suffer to be forgotten, and no success or good fortune could repair.
In this unhappy battle was slain the lord viscount Falkland: a person
of such prodigious parts of learning and knowledge, of that inimitable
sweetness and delight in conversation, of so flowing and obliging a
humanity and goodness to mankind, and of that primitive simplicity
and integrity of life, that if there were no other brand upon this
odious and accursed civil war than that single loss, it must be most
infamous and execrable to all posterity.

> *Turpe mori, post te, solo non posse dolore.**

Before this Parliament his condition of life was so happy that it was
hardly capable of improvement. Before he came to twenty years of age
he was master of a noble fortune, which descended to him by the gift
of a grandfather, without passing through his father or mother, who
were then both alive, and not well enough contented to find themselves
passed by in the descent. His education for some years had been in
Ireland, where his father was Lord Deputy; so that when he returned
into England to the possession of his fortune, he was unentangled with
any acquaintance or friends, which usually grow up by the custom of
conversation, and therefore was to make a pure election of his company, which he chose by other rules than were prescribed to the young
nobility of that time. And it cannot be denied, though he admitted
some few to his friendship for the agreeableness of their natures and
their undoubted affection to him, that his familiarity and friendship for
the most part was with men of the most eminent and sublime parts,
and of untouched reputation in point of integrity; and such men had a
title to his bosom.

He was a great cherisher of wit and fancy and good parts in any man,
and, if he found them clouded with poverty or want, a most liberal and
bountiful patron towards them, even above his fortune; of which in
those administrations he was such a dispenser as if he had been trusted
with it to such uses, and if there had been the least of vice in his
expense he might have been thought too prodigal. He was constant and
pertinacious in whatsoever he resolved to do, and not to be wearied by
any pains that were necessary to that end. And therefore, having once
resolved not to see London (which he loved above all places) till he had

perfectly learned the Greek tongue, he went to his own house in the country, and pursued it with that indefatigable industry that it will not be believed in how short a time he was master of it, and accurately read all the Greek historians.

In this time, his house* being within ten miles of Oxford, he contracted familiarity and friendship with the most polite and accurate men of that university; who found such an immenseness of wit and such a solidity of judgment in him, so infinite a fancy bound in by a most logical ratiocination, such a vast knowledge that he was not ignorant in any thing, yet such an excessive humility as if he had known nothing, that they frequently resorted and dwelt with him, as in a college situated in a purer air; so that his house was a university bound in a lesser volume, whither they came not so much for repose as study, and to examine and refine those grosser propositions which laziness and consent made current in vulgar conversation.

Many attempts were made upon him by the instigation of his mother (who was a lady of another persuasion in religion, and of a most masculine understanding, allayed with the passion and infirmities of her own sex) to pervert him in his piety to the Church of England, and to reconcile him to that of Rome; which they prosecuted with the more confidence, because he declined no opportunity or occasion of conference with those of that religion, whether priests or laics, having diligently studied the controversies, and exactly read all or the choicest of the Greek and Latin Fathers, and having a memory so stupendous that he remembered on all occasions whatsoever he read. And he was so great an enemy to that passion and uncharitableness which he saw produced by difference of opinion in matters of religion, that in all those disputations with priests and others of the Roman Church he affected to manifest all possible civility to their persons, and estimation of their parts; which made them retain still some hope of his reduction, even when they had given over offering farther reasons to him to that purpose. But this charity towards them was much lessened, and any correspondence with them quite declined, when by sinister arts they had corrupted his two younger brothers, being both children, and stolen them from his house and transported them beyond seas, and perverted his sisters:* upon which occasion he writ two large discourses against the principal positions of that religion, with that sharpness of style and full weight of reason that the Church is deprived of great jewels in the concealment of them, and that they are not published to the world.

He was superior to all those passions and affections which attend vulgar minds, and was guilty of no other ambition than of knowledge, and to be reputed a lover of all good men; and that made him too much a contemner of those arts, which must be indulged in the transactions of human affairs. In the last short Parliament he was a burgess in the House of Commons; and from the debates, which were then managed with all imaginable gravity and sobriety, he contracted such a reverence to parliaments that he thought it really impossible that they could ever produce mischief or inconvenience to the kingdom, or that the kingdom could be tolerably happy in the intermission of them. And from the unhappy and unseasonable dissolution of that convention, he harboured, it may be, some jealousy and prejudice of the Court, towards which he was not before immoderately inclined; his father having wasted a full fortune there in those offices and employments by which other men use to obtain a greater. He was chosen again this Parliament to serve in the same place, and in the beginning of it declared himself very sharply and severely against those exorbitancies which had been most grievous to the State; for he was so rigid an observer of established laws and rules that he could not endure the least breach or deviation from them, and thought no mischief so intolerable as the presumption of ministers of state to break positive rules for reason of state, or judges to transgress known laws upon the title of conveniency or necessity; which made him so severe against the earl of Strafford and the lord Finch, contrary to his natural gentleness and temper: insomuch as they who did not know his composition to be as free from revenge as it was from pride, thought that the sharpness to the former might proceed from the memory of some unkindnesses, not without a mixture of injustice, from him towards his father. But without doubt he was free from those temptations, and was only misled by the authority of those who he believed understood the laws perfectly, of which himself was utterly ignorant; and if the assumption, which was scarce controverted, had been true, that an endeavour to overthrow the fundamental laws of the kingdom had been treason, a strict understanding might make reasonable conclusions, to satisfy his own judgment, from the exorbitant parts of their several charges.

The great opinion he had of the uprightness and integrity of those persons who appeared most active, especially of Mr Hampden, kept him longer from suspecting any design against the peace of the kingdom; and though he differed commonly from them in conclusions, he believed long their purposes were honest. When he grew better informed what was law, and discerned a desire to control that law by a vote of one or both Houses, no man more opposed those attempts, and gave the adverse party more trouble, by reason and argumentation; insomuch as he was, by degrees, looked upon as an advocate for the Court, to which he contributed so little, that he declined those addresses, and even those invitations, which he was obliged almost by civility to entertain. And he was so jealous of the least imagination that he should incline to prefer-ment, that he affected even a morosity to the Court and to the courtiers; and left nothing undone which might prevent and divert the King's or Queen's favour towards him, but the deserving it. For when the King sent for him once or twice to speak with him, and to give him thanks for his excellent comportment in those councils, which his majesty gra-ciously termed doing him service, his answers were more negligent and less satisfactory than might be expected; as if he cared only that his actions should be just, not that they should be acceptable, and that his majesty should think that they proceeded only from the impulsion of conscience, without any sympathy in his affections; which from a stoical and sullen nature might not have been misinterpreted, yet from a person of so perfect a habit of generous and obsequious compliance with all good men might very well have been interpreted by the King as more than an ordinary averseness to his service: so that he took more pains, and more forced his nature to actions unagreeable and unpleasant to it, that he might not be thought to incline to the Court, than any man hath done to procure an office there. And if anything but not doing his duty could have kept him from receiving a testimony of the King's grace and trust at that time, he had not been called to his Council; not that he was in truth averse to the Court or from receiving public employment; for he had a great devotion to the King's person, and had before used some small endeavour to be recommended to him for a foreign negotiation, and had once a desire to be sent ambassador into France; but he abhorred an imagination or doubt should sink into the thoughts of any man that, in the discharge of his trust and duty in Parliament, he had any bias to the Court, or that the King himself should apprehend that he looked for a reward for being honest.

For this reason, when he heard it first whispered that the King had a purpose to make him a councillor, for which in the beginning there was no other ground but because he was known sufficient, (*haud semper errat fama, aliquando et elegit*)* he resolved to decline it, and at last suffered himself only to be overruled by the advice and persuasions of his friends to submit to it. Afterwards, when he found that the King intended to make him his Secretary of State, he was positive to refuse it; declaring to his friends that he was most unfit for it, and that he must either do that which would be great disquiet to his own nature, or leave that undone which was most necessary to be done by one that was honoured with that place, for that the most just and honest men did every day that which he could not give himself leave to do. And indeed he was so exact and strict an observer of justice and truth, *ad amussim*,* that he believed those necessary condescensions and applications to the weakness of other men, and those arts and insinuations which are necessary for discoveries and prevention of ill, would be in him a declension from the rule which he acknowledged fit and absolutely necessary to be practised in those employments; and was so precise in the practick principles he prescribed to himself, (to all others he was as indulgent,) as if he had lived *in republica Platonis, non in faece Romuli*.*

Two reasons prevailed with him to receive the seals, and but for those he had resolutely avoided them. The first, the consideration that it [his avoiding them] might bring some blemish upon the King's affairs, and that men would have believed that he had refused so great an honour and trust because he must have been with it obliged to do somewhat else not justifiable. And this he made matter of conscience, since he knew the King made choice of him before other men especially because he thought him more honest than other men. The other was, lest he might be thought to avoid it out of fear to do an ungracious thing to the House of Commons, who were sorely troubled at the displacing sir Harry Vane, whom they looked upon as removed for having done them those offices they stood in need of; and the disdain of so popular an incumbrance wrought upon him next to the other. For as he had a full appetite of fame by just and generous actions, so he had an equal contempt of it by any servile expedients: and he so much the more consented to and approved the justice upon sir Harry Vane, in his own private judgment, by how much he surpassed most men in the religious observation of a trust, the violation whereof he would not admit of any excuse for.

For these reasons, he submitted to the King's command, and became his Secretary, with as humble and devout an acknowledgment of the greatness of the obligation as could be expressed, and as true a sense of it in his heart. Yet two things he could never bring himself to whilst he continued in that office, that was, to his death; for which he was contented to be reproached, as for omissions in a most necessary part of his place. The one, employing of spies, or giving any countenance or entertainment to them; I do not mean such emissaries as with danger would venture to view the enemy's camp, and bring intelligence of their number or quartering, or such generals as such an observation can comprehend, but those who by communication of guilt or dissimulation of manners wound themselves into such trusts and secrets as enabled them to make discoveries for the benefit of the State. The other, the liberty of opening letters upon a suspicion that they might contain matter of dangerous consequence. For the first, he would say, such instruments must be void of all ingenuity and common honesty before they could be of use, and afterwards they could never be fit to be credited; and that no single preservation could be worth so general a wound and corruption of human society as the cherishing such persons would carry with it. The last, he thought such a violation of the law of nature that no qualification by office could justify a single person in the trespass; and though he was convinced by the necessity and iniquity of the time that those advantages of information were not to be declined, and were necessarily to be practised, he found means to shift it from himself, when he confessed he needed excuse and pardon for the omission: so unwilling he was to resign any thing in his nature to an obligation in his office. In all other particulars he filled his place plentifully, being sufficiently versed in languages to understand any that is used in business and to make himself again understood. To speak of his integrity, and his high disdain of any bait that might seem to look towards corruption, *in tanto viro injuria virtutum fuerit.**

Some sharp expressions he used against the archbishop of Canterbury, and his concurring in the first bill to take away the votes of bishops* in the House of Peers, gave occasion to some to believe, and opportunity to others to conclude and publish, that he was no friend to the Church and the established government of it, and troubled his very friends much, who were more confident of the contrary than prepared to answer the allegations.

The truth is, he had unhappily contracted some prejudice to the archbishop; and having only known him enough to observe his passion, when it may be multiplicity of business or other indisposition had possessed him, did wish him less entangled and engaged in the business of the Court or State, though, (I speak it knowingly,) he had a singular estimation and reverence of his great learning and confessed integrity, and really thought his letting himself to those expressions which implied a disesteem of him, or at least an acknowledgment of his infirmities, would enable him to shelter him from part of the storm he saw raised for his destruction; which he abominated with his soul.

The giving his consent to the first bill for the displacing the bishops did proceed from two grounds: the first, his not understanding the original of their right and suffrage there: the other, an opinion that the combination against the whole government of the Church by bishops was so violent and furious, that a less composition than the dispensing with their intermeddling in secular affairs would not preserve the order.

And he was persuaded to this by the profession of many persons of honour, who declared they did desire the one and would then not press the other; which in that particular misled many men. But when his observation and experience made him discern more of their intentions than he before suspected, with great frankness he opposed the second bill that was preferred for that purpose; and had, without scruple, the order itself in perfect reverence, and thought too great encouragement could not possibly be given to learning, nor too great rewards to learned men; and was never in the least degree swayed or moved by the objections which were made against that government, holding them most ridiculous, or affected to the other which those men fancied to themselves.

He had a courage of the most clear and keen temper, and so far from fear that he was not without appetite of danger; and therefore upon any occasion of action he always engaged his person in those troops which he thought, by the forwardness of the commanders, to be most like to be farthest engaged; and in all such encounters he had about him a strange cheerfulness and companiableness, without at all affecting the execution that was then principally to be attended, in which he took no delight, but took pains to prevent it where it was not, by resistance, necessary: insomuch that at Edgehill, when the enemy was routed, he was like to have incurred great peril by interposing to save those who had thrown away their arms, and against whom it may be others were more fierce for their having thrown them away: insomuch as a man might think he came into the field only out of curiosity to see the face of danger, and charity to prevent the shedding of blood. Yet in his natural inclination he acknowledged he was addicted to the profession of a soldier; and shortly after he came to his fortune, and before he came to age, he went into the Low Countries with a resolution of procuring command and to give himself up to it, from which he was converted by the complete inactivity of that summer: and so he returned into England, and shortly after entered upon that vehement course of study we mentioned before, till the first alarum from the north; and then again he made ready for the field, and though he received some repulse in the command of a troop of horse, of which he had a promise, he went a volunteer with the earl of Essex.

From the entrance into this unnatural war, his natural cheerfulness and vivacity grew clouded, and a kind of sadness and dejection of spirit stole upon him which he had never been used to; yet being one of those who believed that one battle would end all differences, and that there would be so great a victory on one side that the other would be

compelled to submit to any conditions from the victor, (which supposition and conclusion, generally sunk into the minds of most men, prevented the looking after many advantages which might then have
been laid hold of,) he resisted those indispositions, *et in luctu bellum inter
remedia erat*.* But after the King's return from Brentford, and the
furious resolution of the two Houses not to admit any treaty for peace,
those indispositions which had before touched him grew into a perfect
habit of uncheerfulness; and he, who had been so exactly unreserved and
affable to all men that his face and countenance was always present and
vacant to his company, and held any cloudiness and less pleasantness
of the visage a kind of rudeness or incivility, became on a sudden less
communicable, and thence very sad, pale, and exceedingly affected with
the spleen. In his clothes and habit, which he had intended before always
with more neatness and industry and expense than is usual to so great
a mind, he was not now only incurious but too negligent; and in his
reception of suitors, and the necessary or casual addresses to his place,
so quick and sharp and severe, that there wanted not some men (who
were strangers to his nature and disposition) who believed him proud
and imperious, from which no mortal man was ever more free.

The truth is, as he was of a most incomparable gentleness, application, and even a demissness and submission to good and worthy and
entire men, so he was naturally (which could not but be more evident in
his place, which objected him to another conversation and intermixture
than his own election had done) *adversus malos injucundus*,* and was so
ill a dissembler of his dislike and disinclination to ill men that it was not
possible for such not to discern it. There was once in the House of
Commons such a declared acceptation of the good service an eminent
member had done to them, and, as they said, to the whole kingdom, that
it was moved, he being present, that the Speaker might in the name of
the whole House give him thanks, and then that every member might,
as a testimony of his particular acknowledgment, stir or move his hat
towards him; the which (though not ordered) when very many did, the
lord Falkland, (who believed the service itself not to be of that moment,
and that an honourable and generous person could not have stooped
to it for any recompense,) instead of moving his hat, stretched both
his arms out and clasped his hands together upon the crown of his hat,
and held it close down to his head; that all men might see how odious
that flattery was to him, and the very approbation of the person, though
at that time most popular.

When there was any overture or hope of peace he would be more
erect and vigorous, and exceedingly solicitous to press any thing which

he thought might promote it; and sitting amongst his friends, often, after a deep silence and frequent sighs, would, with a shrill and sad accent, ingeminate the word *Peace, Peace,** and would passionately profess that the very agony of the war, and the view of the calamities and desolation the kingdom did and must endure, took his sleep from him, and would shortly break his heart. This made some think, or pretend to think, that he was so much enamoured on peace that he would have been glad the King should have bought it at any price; which was a most unreasonable calumny; as if a man that was himself the most punctual and precise in every circumstance that might reflect upon conscience or honour could have wished the King to have committed a trespass against either. And yet this senseless scandal made some impression upon him, or at least he used it for an excuse of the daringness of his spirit; for at the leaguer* before Gloucester, when his friends passionately reprehended him for exposing his person unnecessarily to danger, (as he delighted to visit the trenches and nearest approaches, and to discover what the enemy did,) as being so much beside the duty of his place that it might be understood against it, he would say merrily, that his office could not take away the privileges of his age, and that a Secretary in war might be present at the greatest secret of danger; but withal alleged seriously that it concerned him to be more active in enterprises of hazard than other men, that all might see that his impatiency for peace proceeded not from pusillanimity or fear to adventure his own person.

In the morning before the battle, as always upon action, he was very cheerful, and put himself into the first rank of the lord Byron's regiment, who was then advancing upon the enemy, who had lined the hedges on both sides with musketeers; from whence he was shot with a musket on the lower part of the belly, and in the instant falling from his horse, his body was not found till the next morning, till when there was some hope he might have been a prisoner; though his nearest friends, who knew his temper, received small comfort from that imagination. Thus fell that incomparable young man, in the four and thirtieth year of his age, having so much despatched the business of life that the oldest rarely attain to that immense knowledge, and the youngest enter not into the world with more innocence: and whosoever leads such a life need not care upon how short warning it be taken from him. [*HR*, VII, 201–34]

9. Marston Moor

During the summer of 1643, a truce was agreed between the rebels in Ireland and the King's army there led by the Marquess of Ormond. Alarmed by the possibility of Catholic Irish troops now intervening in England to support the King, Parliament turned to the Scots. Their agreement, registered in the Solemn League and Covenant, committed the Scots to provide military support, paid for by Parliament. It also contained a commitment to reform the English Church, although Parliament—already engaged in discussions in the Westminster Assembly on a new ecclesiastical order, and increasingly divided between supporters of Presbyterianism on Scottish lines and Independents, who opposed a formal national Church—avoided specifying exactly how. The royalist camp, however, had its own divisions, which Hyde described in the History.

THE discomposures, jealousies, and disgusts, which reigned at Oxford, produced great inconveniences; and as, many times, men in a scuffle lose their weapons, and light upon those which belonged to their adversaries, who again arm themselves with those which belonged to the others, such, one would have thought, had been the fortune of the King's armies in the encounters with the enemy: for those under the King's commanders grew insensibly into all the license, disorder, and impiety, with which they had reproached the rebels; and they, again, into great discipline, diligence, and sobriety, which begat courage and resolution in them, and notable dexterity in achievements and enterprises. Insomuch as one side seemed to fight for monarchy with the weapons of confusion, and the other to destroy the King and government with all the principles and regularity of monarchy.

In the beginning of the troubles, the King had very prudently resolved with himself to confer no honours, or bestow any offices or preferments upon any, till the end and conclusion of the service; and if that resolution had continued he would have found much ease by it, and his service great advantage. The necessity and exigents of the war shortly after made some breach into this seasonable resolution, and, for ready money to carry on the war, his majesty was compelled, against his nature, to dispense some favours, which he would not willingly have suffered to be purchased but by virtue and high merit. Then all men thought money and money-worth to be all one, and that whosoever by his service had deserved a reward of money had deserved any thing that might be had for money. And when it was apparent that the war was like to prove a business of time, it was thought unreasonable that the King would not confer rewards on some, which he was able to do, because he could not do it on all, which was confessedly out of his power. And so, by importunity, and upon the title of old promises, and some conveniences of his service, he bestowed honours upon some principal officers of his army, and offices upon others; [to] which though in the particulars no just exceptions could be taken, yet many were angry to see some preferred; and, not so much extolling their own merit and services as making it equal to those whom they saw advanced, every man thought himself neglected and slighted in that another was better esteemed.

And this poison of envy wrought upon many natures which had skill enough not to confess it. The soldiers, albeit they were emulous amongst themselves, and very unsatisfied with one another, (there being unhappy animosities amongst the principal officers,) yet they were too well united and reconciled against any other body of men; and, thinking the King's crown depended wholly on the fortune of their swords, believed no other persons to be considerable, and no councils fit to be consulted with but the martial; and thence proceeded a fatal disrespect and irreverence to the Council of State, to which, by the wholesome constitution of the kingdom, the militia, garrisons, and all martial power, is purely and naturally subordinate, and by the authority and prudence whereof provision could be only reasonably expected for the countenance and support of the army.

The general* and prince Rupert were both strangers to the government and manners of the kingdom, and utterly unacquainted with the nobility, and public ministers, or with their rights: and the prince's heart was so wholly set upon actions of war, that he not only neglected but too much contemned the peaceable and civil arts which were most necessary even to the carrying on of the other. And, certainly, somewhat like that which Plutarch says of soothsaying,* that Octavius lost his life by trusting to it and that Marius prospered the better because he did not altogether despise it, may be said of popularity: though he that too immoderately and importunately affects it (which was the case of the earl of Essex) will hardly continue innocent, yet he who too affectedly despises or neglects what is said of him, or what is generally thought of persons or things, and too stoically contemns the affections of men, even of the vulgar, (be his other abilities and virtues what can be imagined,) will in some conjuncture of time find himself very unfortunate. And it may be, a better reason cannot be assigned for the misfortunes that hopeful young prince (who had great parts of mind as well as vigour of body, and incomparable personal courage) underwent, and the kingdom by it, than that roughness and unpolishedness of his nature which rendered him less patient to hear, and consequently less skilful to judge of those things which should have guided him in the discharge of his important trust: and thence making an unskilful judgment of the unusefulness of the Councils by his observation of the infirmities and weakness of the particular councillors, he grew to a full disesteem of the acts of that board, which must be accounted venerable as long as the regal power is exercised in England.

And I cannot but on this occasion continue this digression thus much farther, to observe, that they who avoid public debates in Council, or think them of less moment, upon the undervaluing the persons of the councillors, and from the particular infirmities of men, the heaviness of this man, the levity of that, the weakness and simplicity of a third, conclude that their advice and opinions are not requisite to any great design, are exceedingly deceived, and will perniciously deceive others who are misled by those conclusions. For it is in wisdom as it is in beauty. A face that, being taken in pieces, affords scarce one exact feature, an eye, or a nose, or a tooth, or a brow, or a mouth, against which a visible just exception cannot be taken, yet altogether; by a gracefulness and vivacity in the whole, may constitute an excellent beauty, and be more catching than another whose symmetry is more faultless. So there are many men, who in this particular argument may be unskilful, in that affected, who may seem to have levity, or vanity, or formality, in ordinary and cursory conversation, (a very crooked rule to measure any man's abilities, and gives a better evidence of the nature than of the understanding,) and yet in formed counsels, deliberations, and transactions, are men of great insight and wisdom, and from whom excellent assistance is contributed.

And, no question, all great enterprises and designs that are to be executed have many parts, even in the projection, fit for the survey and disquisition of several faculties and abilities, and equally for the decision of sharper and more phlegmatic understandings. And we often hear in debates of great moment animadversions of more weight and consequence from those whose ordinary conversation is not so delightful, than from men of more sublime parts. Certainly Solomon very well understood himself when he said, *In the multitude of counsellors there is safety*.* And though it were confessed that reason would be better stated and discovered, and conclusions easier made, by a few than a greater number, yet when the execution depends on many, and the general interpretation so much depends upon the success, and the success upon the interpretation, we see those counsels most prosperous whereof the considerations and deliberations have been measured by that standard which is most publicly received and acknowledged. And he hath had but small experience in the managing affairs, who is not able experimentally to name to himself some very good and useful conclusions which have therefore only succeeded amiss because not communicated to those who had reason to believe themselves competent parties to any secret. For there was never yet that public-heartedness sunk into the breasts of men, that they were long willing to be left out in those transactions to the privacy whereof they had a right; and therefore they have been willing enough any single advice should miscarry, (of what general concernment soever,) rather than to contribute to the fame of one man who hath thought their approbation not worth the providing for. And though the objection of secrecy and despatch seems to favour a small number and a reservation of communicating, yet (except in those few cases which in their nature are to be consulted and acted together, and the full execution whereof may be by a few) I am not sure that the inconvenience will be greater by a necessary delay, or even such a discovery as can be supposed to proceed from the levity of a counsellor, (—futile and malicious natures ought not to be supposed to be admitted into that rank of men,—) than by wanting the approbation and concurrence of those (admitting there could be no benefit from their information) who will unavoidably know it soon enough to add to or take from the success, at least the reputation. And from this root much of the negligence and disrespect towards the civil councils proceeded. For as all corporations, tribes, and fraternities suffer most by the malignity of some of their own members, so the jealousy and indisposition of some councillors contributed much to the disregard which fell upon the order, and, in them, upon the King.

Amongst those who were nearest the King's trust, and to whom he communicated the greatest secrets in his affairs, there were some who from private (though very good) conditions of life, without such an application to Court as usually ushered those promotions, were ascended to that preferment, and believed to have an equal interest with any in their master's estimation. And these were sure to find no more charity from the Court than from the army; and, having had lately so many equals, it was thought no presumption freely to censure all that they did or spake, what effect soever such freedom had upon the public policy and transactions. It were to be wished that persons of the greatest birth, honour, and fortune would take that care of themselves by education, industry, literature, and a love of virtue, to surpass all other men in knowledge and all other qualifications necessary for great actions, as far as they do in quality and titles, that princes out of them might always choose men fit for all employments and high trusts; which would exceedingly advance their service, when the reputation and respect of the person carries somewhat with it that facilitates the business. And it cannot easily be expressed, nor comprehended by any who have not felt the weight and burden of the envy which naturally attends upon those promotions which seem to be *per saltum*,* how great straits and difficulties such ministers are forced to wrestle with, and by which the charges with which they are intrusted must proportionably suffer, let the integrity and wisdom of the men be what it can be supposed to be. Neither is the patience, temper, and dexterity, to carry a man through those straits, easily attained; it being very hard in the morning of preferment to keep an even temper of mind, between the care to preserve the dignity of the place [which] is committed to him, (without which he shall expose himself to a thousand unchaste attempts, and dishonour the judgment that promoted him, by appearing too vile for such a trust,) and the caution that his nature be not really exalted to an overweening pride and folly upon the privilege of his place; which will expose him to much more contempt than the former, and therefore to be, with a more exact guard upon a man's self, avoided: the errors of gentleness and civility being much more easily reformed, as well as endured, than the other of arrogance and ostentation.

The best provision that such men can make for their voyage, besides a stock of innocence that cannot be impaired, and a firm confidence in God Almighty that he will never suffer that innocence to be utterly oppressed or notoriously infamed, is, an expectation of those gusts and storms of rumour, detraction, and envy; and a resolution not to be over sensible of all calumnies, unkindness, or injustice, but to believe that, by being preferred before other men, they have an obligation upon them to suffer more than other men would do, and that the best way to convince scandals and misreports is, by neglecting them, to appear not to have deserved them. And there is not a more troublesome inconvenient passion, or that often draws more inconveniences with it, than that which proceeds from the indignation of being unjustly calumniated, and from the pride of an upright conscience, when men cannot endure to be spoken ill of when they have not deserved it: in which distemper, though they free themselves from the errors or infirmities with which they were traduced, they commonly discover others of which they had been never suspected. In a word, let no man think, that is once entered into this list, that he can by any skill or comportment prevent these conflicts and assaults, or by any stubborn or impetuous humour that he can suppress and prevail over them: but let him look upon it as a purgatory he is unavoidably to pass through, and depend upon Providence and time for a vindication; and by performing all the duties of his place to the end, with justice, integrity, and uprightness, give all men cause to believe that he was worthy of it the first hour; which is a triumph very lawful to be affected.

As these distempers and indispositions and infirmities of particular men had a great influence upon the public affairs, and disturbed and weakened the whole frame and fabric of the King's designs, so no particular man was more disquieted by them than the King himself, who, in his person as well as in his business, suffered all the vexation of the rude and petulant and discontented humours of Court and army. His majesty now paid interest for all the benefit and advantage he had received in the beginning of the war by his gentleness and princely affability to all men, and by descending somewhat from the forms of majesty, which he had in his life before observed with all punctuality. He vouchsafed then himself to receive any addresses and overtures for his service, and to hold discourse with all men who brought devotion to him; and he must be now troubled with the complaints and murmurs and humours of all, and, how frivolous and unreasonable soever the cause was, his majesty was put both to inform and temper their understandings. No man would receive an answer but from himself, and expected a better from him than he must have been contented to have received from any body else. Every man magnified the services he had done, and his ability and interest to do greater, and proposed honour and reward equal to both in his own sense; and if he received not an answer to his mind, he grew sullen, complained he was neglected, and resolved, (or pretended so,) to quit the service, and to travel into some foreign kingdom. He is deceived that believes the ordinary carriage and state of a king to be matters of indifferency, and of no relation to his greatness. They are the outworks, which preserve majesty itself from approaches and surprisal. We find that the queen of Sheba was amazed at the meat of Solomon's table, and the sitting of his servants, and the attendance of his ministers, and their apparel, and his cup-bearers, &c. as so great instances of Solomon's wisdom that *there was no more spirit in her*.* And, no doubt, whosoever inconsiderately departs from those forms and trappings, and ornaments of his dignity and pre-eminence, will hardly at some time be able to preserve the body itself of majesty from intrusion, invasion, and violation.

And let no man think that the King had now no hard task to master these troubles, and that a short and sharp blast of royal severity would easily have dispersed these clouds. The disease was too violent and catching, and the contagion too universal, to be cured by that remedy; neither were the symptoms or effects the same in all constitutions. It cannot be imagined into how many several shapes men's indispositions were put, and the many artifices which were used to get honours, offices, preferments, and the waywardness and perverseness which attended the being disappointed of their own hopes. One man had been named for such a place, that is, himself and his friends had given it out that he should have it, when, it may be, he was too modest to pretend to it; and upon this vogue he had a title; and if it should be conferred upon another it would be a mark of the King's disfavour to him, and thereby he should lose the ability and credit without which he could do no farther service. Another suggested that his friends and companions in consort had all received some obligation, and if he alone should remain without some testimony of favour it would be a brand upon him of some signal unworthiness. No man was so hard-hearted to himself as not to be able to give a reason for any thing he desired; and he commonly had best success who prosecuted his own wishes with most boldness and importunity, neither was there a better or another reason for some men's preferment than that they had set their hearts upon it, and would have it. And it was a great temptation to modest natures to find forward men had so good fortune that the want of success began to be imputed to want of wit.

I remember, once, a person of good quality, and of a good name in action, came to me very pensive, and told me how conscientiously he had served the King, without any private designs, or other thoughts than the discharge of his own duty and rendering the performance of that duty acceptable to his majesty; yet that, to his unspeakable discomfort, he found that he had been misrepresented to the King, and that his majesty had entertained a sinister opinion of him; and desired me to learn what the ground of the prejudice was, and by my good testimony to endeavour to remove it. I had a very good opinion of the person, and believed the King had so, and therefore persuaded him that the jealousy was groundless, and pressed to know from whence he received those impressions; he excused himself in the particular, and assured me that he had his advertisements from a sure hand, which was to be concealed, not doubted; and that upon my inquiry I would find it true, though he could not imagine the cause. I promised him I would press the King very heartily in it, and if there were anything that stuck with him, I presumed his majesty would be so gracious [as] to let me know it. And accordingly, having shortly after an opportunity to wait on his majesty, I told him the true narrative of what had passed, with my observation of the general comportment of that gentleman, and besought his majesty, if any ill offices had been done to him, or that any prejudice towards him was lodged in his royal breast, that he would graciously vouchsafe to tell me what it was, and that he would allow him an access to clear himself from any imputations. The King very cheerfully assured me that he had not only a very good opinion of that gentleman, but that he was most assured he had no real suspicion to the contrary; and therefore bad me proceed to the other part of my business. I told him I had no more, and that I was sure I should make a very happy man by satisfying him of what I found. 'Then,' said the King, 'you are not throughly instructed, for the other half of this business must be a suit.' I replied, if that were so I was yet more ignorant than I suspected myself. The gentleman shortly after came to me, in pain, as I thought, with the jealousy of being in umbrage; and when I gave him pregnant assurance to the contrary, with the mention of some expressions the King had used, which were indeed very gracious, he seemed to receive it with such a countenance and gusto that I verily believed he had had his heart's desire. But the next morning he came to me again, and told me that I had made him abundantly happy, and that he doubted not there was no just ground for the other reports, but only the malice of those who wished them true; yet that they had lessened his credit abroad, even with his friends, and that he found there was no way to keep up his reputation and interest in the world, whereby he might be able to do the King service, which was all he looked after, but the receiving some testimony of the King's good opinion, which would be a public evidence that the other discourses were false. I was surprised, and as much out of countenance as he should have been, and advised him to patience, and to expect the King's own time and method, rather than to quicken him by any importunity, which would give an ill relish to any obligation. He would not understand that philosophy, but shortly after found some other means to press the King very roundly for a place, upon the title of that good opinion he had declared to me to hold of him, not without some implication that without some such earnest of his majesty's goodness he should not be able to continue in his service; which probably was one of the modestest addresses which were made to him at that time. And it cannot be denied this way the King's trouble was so great, that he many times suffered more vexation and trouble from the indisposition and humours of his own people than from the enemy, or the apprehension of their counsels: which hath made me enlarge this digression so much; conceiving it to be no less a part of history, and more useful to posterity, to leave a character of the times than of the persons, or the narrative of matters of fact, which cannot be so well understood as by knowing the genius that prevailed when they were transacted. [*HR*, VII, 276–86]

Meanwhile, at Westminster the growing strength of what Hyde called 'the violent party' led to a series of defections from the House of Lords. Three peers—the Earl of Bedford, the Earl of Holland, and the Earl of Clare—migrated to the King's camp in August 1643, occasioning a fierce debate in royalist ranks over how to treat them. But, quickly disillusioned either by the political complexion of the royalist court, or by their own reception, they soon returned to the parliamentary fold.

The return of the three earls to London in the winter, who so solemnly applied themselves to the King in the spring, contributed exceedingly to the union of the two Houses at Westminster. The other two stayed longer, and retired with much more decency, if not with a tacit permission; but the earl of Holland, when he saw his place in the bedchamber conferred upon the marquis of Hertford,* in much discontent found an opportunity, (which was not difficult,) to remove out of the King's quarters; and before he was missed at Oxford, intelligence was brought that he had rendered himself to the Parliament at London.* And to make his return the more conscientious, he declared that the ground of his deserting them formerly, and going to the King, was a hope to incline his majesty to a treaty of peace; but that he found he was mistaken in the temper of the Oxford counsels, and that the King had still about him some counsellors who would never consent to a safe and well-grounded peace; and that he heard they had persuaded the King to make a cessation with the rebels in Ireland, which affected his conscience so much, that, though he had been sure to have lost his life by it, he would return to the Parliament, professing exemplary fidelity to them if they would again receive him into their favour.

It may be his discourse of Ireland or the King's averseness to peace wrought upon very few; but the evidence of the King's aversion so far to forgive and forget former trespasses as to receive them into favour and trust again, made a deep impression upon many. For it is undoubtedly true that many of the principal and governing members of both

Houses, that is, of them who had governed and done as much mischief as any, either out of apprehension that the King would prevail, or that they should not prevail soon enough, or the animosity against those who had outgrown their government and followed new leaders of their own, and to other ends than had been originally proposed, or out of some motions of conscience, were quite weary of the Parliament, and desirous to obtain a fair admission to the King, and looked only upon the footing which those doves who went first out of the ark should find. And surely, if that expedient had been dexterously managed, it had been the most probable way to have drawn the Parliament into such contempt that it must have fallen of itself: and it is a way that in no civil war, which is arrived to any vigour and power of contending, ought to be declined. For a body that is not formed by policy, with any avowed and fixed principles of government, but by the distempered affections, ambition, and discontent of particular persons, who rather agree against a common adversary than are united to one just interest, cannot so easily be dissolved as by tampering with particular persons, and rending those branches from the trunk, whose beauty and advantage consists only in the spreading.

And the reasons were unanswerable which the old consul Fabius in Livy, (lib. 24,)* gave in the case of Cassius Altinius, who, after the defeat of Cannae, deserted the Romans, and fled to Hannibal, by which he got the city of Arpos; and when the condition of the Romans was again recovered and flourishing, came again to the Roman army, and offered to betray that city into their hands. Many were of opinion that he should be looked upon as a common enemy; and bound, and sent to Hannibal, as a perfidious person, who knew neither how to be a friend or an enemy. Fabius reprehended the unseasonable severity of those who considered and judged *in medio ardore belli tanquam in pace libera*,* and told them that their principal care must be, that none of their friends and allies might forsake them; the next, that they who had forsaken them might return again into their obedience and protection: for, *si abire a Romanis liceat, redire ad eos non liceat*,* it could not be but the state of Rome, from whom in the late misfortunes many had revolted, must become very desperate.

Such was the King's condition; the number of the guilty being so much superior to the innocent, that the latter could reasonably expect only to be preserved by the conversion and reduction of the former. Neither did the King not foresee, or abhor this expedient; but the temper and spirit of the time was so averse from the stratagem, that it was evident his present loss would be as great by practising it as his future advantage was like to prove by it. And whatever damage his majesty sustained, that unfortunate earl received no acknowledgment or encouragement from the other party who had a benefit by his return; but as his estate was sequestered as soon as he left them, so he was now committed to prison, and that sequestration continued; neither was it in a long time after taken off, nor himself ever admitted to his place in their council, notwithstanding all the intercession of very powerful friends, or to any reputation of doing farther good or hurt.

And verily there may be thought to be some dislike in the very primary law of nature of such tergiversation and inconstancy; since we scarce find, in any story, a deserter of a trust or party he once adhered to, to be prosperous, or in any eminent estimation with those to whom he resorts, though in the change there may appear evident arguments of reason and justice; neither hath it been in the power or prerogative of any authority to preserve such men from the reproach and jealousy and scandal that naturally attend upon any defection. *I have not found evil in thee, since the day of thy coming unto me unto this day; nevertheless, the lords favour thee not,* 1 Sam. xxix., was the profession of king Achish, when he dismissed David himself from marching with the army of the Philistines; and that expostulation of those lords, *Wherewith should he reconcile himself unto his master? should it not be with the heads of these men?* will be always an argumentation to raise a distrust of those who have eminently quitted their party. And the judgment of Fabius himself, which we touched before, of Cassius Altinius, was not much in their favour; for though he reprehended the proposition of sending him to Hannibal, yet he concluded that he would have no trust reposed in him, but that he should be kept in safe custody, with liberty to do any thing but go away, till the war was ended, and *tum consultandum, utrum defectio prior plus merita sit poenae an hic reditus veniae.** And as it fares in civil affairs, and the breach of moral obligations, so it happens in spiritual defections and alterations in religion. For, as among the Jews the proselytes were civilly and charitably treated, without upbraidings or reproaches, yet it was provided that no proselyte should be eligible into the court of their Sanhedrim, and in their very conversation they had a caution of them, (*Vel ad decimam usque generationem a proselytis cave,** was an aphorism against them), so our observation and experience can give us few examples of men who have changed their religion, and not fallen into some jealousy and distrust, or disreputation, even with those [with] whom they side, that have made their future life less pleasant and delightsome; which, it may be, is only because we have rare instances of men of extraordinary parts, or great minds, who have entertained those conversions. [*HR*, VII, 308–12]

About this time the councils at Westminster lost a principal supporter by the death of John Pym, who died, with great torment and agony, of a disease unusual, and therefore the more spoken of, *morbus pediculosus*,* which rendered him an object very loathsome to those who had been most delighted with him. No man had more to answer for the miseries of the kingdom, or had his hand or head deeper in their contrivance; and yet I believe they grew much higher even in his life than he designed. He was a man of a private quality and condition of life; his education in the office of the Exchequer, where he had been a clerk; and his parts rather acquired by industry than supplied by nature or adorned by art. He had been well known in former Parliaments, and was one of those few who had sat in many, the long intermission of Parliaments having worn out most of those who had been acquainted with the rules and orders observed in those conventions; and this gave him some reputation and reverence amongst those who were but now introduced.

He had been most taken notice of for being concerned and passionate in the jealousies of religion, and much troubled with the countenance which had been given to those opinions which had been imputed to Arminius;* and this give him great authority and interest with those who were not pleased with the government of the Church or the growing power of the clergy; yet himself industriously took care to be believed, and he professed to be, very entire to the doctrine and discipline of the Church of England. In the short Parliament before this he spake much, and appeared to be the most leading man; for, besides the exact knowledge of the forms and orders of that council, which few men had, he had a very comely and grave way of expressing himself, with great volubility of words, natural and proper; and understood the temper and affections of the kingdom as well as any man, and had observed the errors and mistakes in government, and knew well how to make them appear greater than they were. After the unhappy dissolution of that Parliament he continued for the most part about London, in conversation and great repute amongst those lords who were most strangers, and believed most averse, from the Court, in whom he improved all imaginable jealousies and discontents towards the State; and as soon as this Parliament was resolved to be summoned, he was as diligent to procure such persons to be elected as he knew to be most inclined to the way he meant to take.

At the first opening of this Parliament he appeared passionate and prepared against the earl of Strafford; and though in private designing he was much governed by Mr Hampden and Mr St John, yet he seemed to all men to have the greatest influence upon the House of Commons of any man; and, in truth, I think he was at that time, and for some months after, the most popular man, and the most able to do hurt, that hath lived in any time. Upon the first design of softening and obliging the powerful persons in both Houses, when it was resolved to make the earl of Bedford Lord High Treasurer of England, the King likewise intended to make Mr Pym, Chancellor of the Exchequer; for which he received his majesty's promise, and made a return of a suitable profession of his service and devotion; and thereupon, the other being no secret, somewhat declined from that sharpness in the House which was more popular than any man's person, and made some overtures to provide for the glory and splendour of the Crown; in which he had so ill success that his interest and reputation there visibly abated, and he found that he was much better able to do hurt than good; which wrought very much upon him to melancholique, and complaint of the violence and discomposure of the people's affections and inclinations. In the end, whether upon the death of the earl of Bedford he despaired of that preferment, or whether he was guilty of any thing which upon his conversion to the Court he thought might be discovered to his damage, or for pure want of courage, he suffered himself to be carried by those who would not follow him, and so continued in the head of those who made the most desperate propositions.

In the prosecution of the earl of Strafford his carriage and language was such that expressed much personal animosity, and he was accused of having practised some arts in it not worthy a good man; as an Irishman of very mean and low condition afterwards acknowledged that, being brought to him as an evidence of one part of the charge against the Lord Lieutenant, in a particular of which a person of so vile quality would not be reasonably thought a competent informer, Mr Pym gave him money to buy him a satin suit and cloak, in which equipage he appeared at the trial, and gave his evidence; which, if true, may make many other things which were confidently reported afterwards of him to be believed. As, that he received a great sum of money from the French ambassador, to hinder the transportation of those regiments of Ireland into Flanders, upon the disbanding that army there, which had been prepared by the earl of Strafford for the business of Scotland; in which if his majesty's directions and commands had not been diverted and contradicted by the Houses, many do believe the rebellion in Ireland had not happened.

Certain it is, that his power of doing shrewd turns was extraordinary, and no less in doing good offices for particular persons, and that he did preserve many from censure who were under the severe displeasure of the Houses, and looked upon as eminent delinquents; and the quality of many of them made it believed that he had sold that protection for valuable consideration. From the time of his being accused of high treason by the King, with the lord Kimbolton and the other members, he never entertained thoughts of moderation, but always opposed all overtures of peace and accommodation; and when the earl of Essex was disposed the last summer* by those lords to an inclination towards a treaty, as is before remembered, Mr Pym's power and dexterity wholly changed him, and wrought him to that temper which he afterwards swerved not from. He was wonderfully solicitous for the Scots coming in to their assistance, though his indisposition of body was so great that it might well have made another impression upon his mind. During his sickness he was a very sad spectacle; but none being admitted to him who had not concurred with him, it is not known what his last thoughts and considerations were. He died towards the end of December, before the Scots entered, and was buried with wonderful pomp and magnificence in that place where the bones of our English kings and princes are committed to their rest.* [*HR*, VII, 409–13]

As the year turned, royalist prospects seemed to worsen. In mid-January, the Scottish army marched into northern England, threatening the Marquess of Newcastle's army, already under pressure from Lord Fairfax, with the danger of being encircled in York. In February Prince Rupert left Oxford to strengthen it. A royalist force in Cheshire reinforced out of the King's army in Ireland was defeated at Nantwich at the end of January. A risky royalist attempt to advance into the south-east ended in failure in late December 1643 and early January 1644, and left the royalist-held south-west vulnerable to attack by Sir William Waller's army. Instead of pursuing his advantage, however, Waller was forced to draw back because his London regiments demanded to return to the City, while Essex was militarily inactive as he wrangled with Parliament over the size of his own army and the nature of his relationship with the other parliamentary commanders. But as the King tried to determine his own strategy, he was similarly beset by indecision, infighting, and a shortage of troops.

There had been several deliberations in the council of war, and always very different opinions, what should be done with the garrisons when the King should take the field; and the King himself was irresolute upon those debates what to do. He communicated the several reasons to prince Rupert by letters, requiring his advice; who, after he had returned answers and received replies, made a hasty journey to Oxford from Chester, to wait upon his majesty. And it was then positively resolved that the garrisons of Oxford, Wallingford, Abingdon, Reading, and Banbury, should be reinforced and strengthened with all the foot; that a good body of horse should remain about Oxford, and the rest should be sent into the west to prince Maurice.* If this counsel had been pursued steadily and resolutely, it might probably have been attended with good success. Both armies of the enemy would have been puzzled what to have done, and either of them would have been unwilling to have engaged in a siege against any place so well provided and resolved; and it would have been equally uncounsellable to have marched to any distance, and have left such an enemy at their backs, that could so easily and quickly have united, and incommoded any march they could have made.

But as it was even impossible to have administered such advice to the King, in the strait he was in, which being pursued might not have proved inconvenient, so it was the unhappy temper of those who were called to those councils that resolutions taken upon full debate were seldom prosecuted with equal resolution and steadiness, but changed upon new shorter debates, and upon objections which had been answered before: some men being in their natures irresolute and inconstant, and full of objections, even after all was determined according to their own proposals; others being positive, and not to be altered from what they had once declared, how unreasonable soever, or what alterations soever there were in the affairs. And the King himself frequently considered more the person who spoke, as he was in his grace or his prejudice, than the counsel itself that was given; and always suspected, at least trusted less to, his own judgment, than he ought to have done; which rarely deceived him so much as that of other men.

The persons with whom he only consulted in his martial affairs, and how to carry on the war, were (besides prince Rupert, who was at this time absent) the general, who was made earl of Brentford; the lord Wilmot, who was general of the horse; the lord Hopton, who usually commanded an army apart, and was not often with the King's army, but now present; sir Jacob Astley, who was major-general of the army; the lord Digby, who was Secretary of State; and sir John Culpepper, Master of the Rolls; for none of the Privy Council, those two only excepted, were called to those consultations; though some of them were still advised with, for the better execution or prosecution of what was then and there resolved.

The general, though he had been without doubt a very good officer, and had great experience, and was still a man of unquestionable courage and integrity, yet he was now much decayed in his parts, and, with the long continued custom of immoderate drinking, dozed in his understanding, which had been never quick and vigorous; he having been always illiterate to the greatest degree that can be imagined. He was now become very deaf, yet often pretended not to have heard what he did not then contradict, and thought fit afterwards to disclaim. He was a man of few words, and of great compliance, and usually delivered that as his opinion which he foresaw would be grateful to the King.

Wilmot was a man of a haughty and ambitious nature, of a pleasant wit, and an ill understanding, as never considering above one thing at once; but he considered that one thing so impatiently that he would not admit any thing else to be worth any consideration. He had from the beginning of the war been very averse to any advice of the Privy Council, and thought fit that the King's affairs (which depended upon the success of the war) should entirely be governed and conducted by the soldiers and men of war, and that no other counsellors should have any credit with his majesty. Whilst prince Rupert was present, his exceeding great prejudice, or rather personal animosity, against him, made any thing that Wilmot said or proposed enough slighted and contradicted: and the King himself, upon some former account and observation, was far from any indulgence to his person or esteem of his parts. But now, by the prince's absence, and his being the second man in the army, and the contempt he had of the old general, who was there the only officer above him, he grew marvellously elated, and looked upon himself as one whose advice ought to be followed and submitted to in all things. He had by his excessive good fellowship (in every part whereof he excelled, and was grateful to all the company,) made himself so popular with all the officers of the army, especially of the horse, that he had in truth a very great interest; which he desired might appear to the King, that he might have the more interest in him. He was positive in all his advices in council, and bore contradiction very impatiently; and because he was most contradicted by the two privy-councillors, the Secretary and the Master of the Rolls, who he saw had the greatest influence upon the King, he used all the artifices he could to render them unacceptable and suspected to the officers of the army, by telling them what they had said in council, which he thought would render them the more ungrateful; and, in the times of jollity, persuaded the old general to believe that they invaded his prerogative, and meddled more in the business of the war than they ought to do, and thereby made him the less disposed to concur with them in advice, how rational and seasonable soever it was; which often put the King to the trouble of converting him.

The lord Hopton was a man superior to any temptation, and abhorred enough the license and the levities with which he saw too many corrupted. He had a good understanding, a clear courage, an industry not to be tired, and a generosity that was not to be exhausted, (a virtue that none of the rest had): but in the debates concerning the war was longer in resolving, and more apt to change his mind after he had resolved, than is agreeable to the office of a commander in chief; which rendered him rather fit for the second than for the supreme command in an army.

Sir Jacob Astley was an honest, brave, plain man, and as fit for the office he exercised of major general of the foot as Christendom yielded, and was so generally esteemed; very discerning and prompt in giving orders, as the occasions required, and most cheerful and present in any action. In council he used few but very pertinent words, and was not at all pleased with the long speeches usually made there, and which rather confounded than informed his understanding: so that he rather collected the ends of the debates, and what he was himself to do, than enlarged them by his own discourses; though he forbore not to deliver his own mind.

The two privy-councillors, though they were of the most different natures and constitutions that can be imagined, always agreed in their opinions; and, being in their parts much superior to the other, usually prevailed upon the King's judgment to like what they approved: yet one of them,* who had in those cases the ascendant over the other, had that excess of fancy that he too often, upon his own recollecting and revolving the grounds of the resolutions which had been taken, or upon the suggestions of other men, changed his own mind; and thereupon caused orders to be altered, which produced, or were thought to produce, many inconveniences.

This unsteadiness in counsels, and in matters resolved upon, made the former determination concerning the garrisons to be little considered. The King's army had lain above three weeks at and about Newbury; in which time their numbers were nothing improved beyond what they had been upon their muster near Marlborough, when the King was present. When it was known that both the Parliament armies were marched out of London, that under Essex to Windsor, and that of Waller to the parts between Hertfordbridge and Basing, without any purpose of going farther west, the King's army marched to Reading; and in three days, his majesty being present, they slighted and demolished all the works of that garrison: and then, which was about the middle of May, with the addition of those soldiers, which increased the army five and twenty hundred old soldiers more, very well officered, the army retired to the quarters about Oxford, with an opinion that it would be in their power to fight with one of the enemy's armies; which they longed exceedingly to do.

The King returned to Oxford, and resolved to stay there till he could have better information what the enemy intended; which was not now so easy as it had formerly been. For since the conjunction with the Scottish commissioners in one council* for the carrying on the war, little business was brought to be consulted in either of the Houses; and there was much greater secrecy than before, none being admitted into any kind of trust but they whose affections were known to concur to the most desperate counsels. So that the designs were still entirely formed before any part of them were communicated to the earl of Essex, nor was more communicated at a time than was necessary for the present execution; of which he was sensible enough, but could not help it. The intention was that the two armies, which marched out together, should always be distinct, and should only not sever till it appeared what course the King meant to take; and if he stayed in Oxford, it would be fit for both to be in the siege; the circumvallation being very great, and to be divided in many places by the river, which would keep both armies still asunder under their several officers. But if the King marched out, which they might reasonably presume he would, then the purpose was that the earl of Essex should follow the King, whither ever he went, which they imagined would be northward; and that Waller should march into the west, and subdue that. So that, having so substantially provided for the north by the Scots and the earl of Manchester, and having an army under the earl of Essex much superior in number to any the King could be attended with, and the third under Waller at liberty for the west, they promised themselves, and too reasonably, that they should make an end of the war that summer. [*HR*, VIII, 26–35]

When the armies of Essex and Waller finally moved on Oxford at the beginning of June, the King left it, to avoid being caught in a siege. Essex diverted to Dorset to relieve Lyme Regis, besieged by Prince Maurice, and then pushed on into the south-west, and the King had the better of Waller in the fight at Cropredy Bridge, in Oxfordshire, on 25 June. Waller's army, relying heavily on London regiments, was mutinous and began to melt away. At the beginning of July, the King determined to follow Essex into the south-west.

The King had scarce marched two days westward when he was surprised with terrible news from the north; for after he had by an express
from Oxford received intelligence that prince Rupert had not only
relieved York but totally defeated the Scots, with many particulars to
confirm it, (all which was so much believed there that they had made
public fires of joy for the victory,) he now received quite contrary information, and was too surely convinced that his whole army was defeated.
It was very true that, after many great and noble actions performed by
[prince Rupert] in the relief of Latham, and the reduction of Bolton,*
and all other places in that large county, (Manchester only excepted,)
in which the rebels lost very many, much blood having been shed in
taking places by assault which were too obstinately defended, the prince
had marched out of Lancashire with so good reputation, and had given
his orders so effectually to Goring, who lay in Lincolnshire with that
body of horse that belonged to the marquis of Newcastle's army, that
they happily joined the prince, and marched together towards York
with that expedition that the enemy was so surprised that they found it
necessary to raise the siege in confusion enough, and, leaving one whole
side of the town free, drew to the other side in great disorder and
consternation; there being irreconcilable differences and jealousies
between the officers, and indeed between the nations: the English
resolving to join no more with the Scots, and they, on the other side, as
weary of their company and discipline; so that the prince had done his
work, and if he had sat still the other great army would have mouldered
to nothing, and been exposed to any advantage his highness would take
of them.

But the dismal fate of the kingdom would not permit so much sobriety of counsel. One side of the town was no sooner free, by which there
was an entire communication with those in the town, and all provision
out of the country brought in abundantly, but the prince, without
consulting with the marquis of Newcastle or any of the officers within
the town, sent for all the soldiers to draw out, and put the whole army
in battalia on that side where the enemy was drawn up; who had no
other hope to preserve them but a present battle, to prevent the
reproaches and mutinies which distracted them.* And though that
party of the King's horse which charged the Scots so totally defeated
and routed their whole army, that they fled all ways for many miles
together, and were knocked on the head and taken prisoners by the
country, and Leslie their general fled ten miles, and was taken prisoner
by a constable, (from whence the news of the victory was speedily
brought to Newark, and thence sent by an express to Oxford, and so

received and spread as aforesaid,) yet the English horse, commanded by Fairfax and Cromwell, charged those on that side so well, and in such excellent order, being no sooner broken than they rallied again and charged as briskly, that, though both Fairfax and Cromwell were hurt, and both above the shoulders, and many good officers killed, they prevailed over that body of horse which opposed them, and totally routed and beat them off the field, so that almost the whole body of the marquis of Newcastle's foot were cut off.

The marquis himself, and his brave brother, sir Charles Cavendish, (who was a man of the noblest and largest mind, though the least, and most inconvenient body that lived,) charged in the head of a troop of gentlemen who came out of the town with him, with as much gallantry and courage as men could do. But it was so late in the evening before the battle began that the night quickly fell upon them, and the generals returned into the town, not enough knowing their own loss, and performing very few compliments each to other. They who most exactly describe that unfortunate battle, and more unfortunate abandoning that whole country, (when there might have been means found to have drawn a good army together,) by prince Rupert's hasty departure with all his troops, and the marquis of Newcastle's as hasty departure to the sea-side, and taking ship and transporting himself out of the kingdom, and all the ill consequences thereupon, give so ill an account of any conduct, courage, or discretion, in the managery of that affair, that, as I can take no pleasure in the draught of it, so posterity would receive little pleasure or benefit in the most particular relation of it.

This may be said of it, that the like was never done or heard or read of before; that two great generals, whereof one had still a good army left, his horse, by their not having performed their duty, remaining, upon the matter, entire, and much the greater part of his foot having retired into the town, the great execution having fallen upon the northern foot; and the other, having the absolute commission over the northern counties, and very many considerable places in them still remaining under his obedience, should both agree in nothing else but in leaving that good city and the whole country as a prey to the enemy; who had not yet the courage to believe that they had the victory, the Scots having been so totally routed, (as hath been said before,) their general made prisoner by a constable and detained in custody, till most part of the next day was passed; and most of the officers and army having marched or run above ten miles northward, before they had news that they might securely return. And though the horse under Fairfax and Cromwell had won the day, yet they were both much wounded, and many others of the best officers killed, or so maimed that they could not in any short time have done more hurt: so that if there had been any agreement to have concealed their loss, which might have been done to a good degree, (for the enemy was not possessed of the field, but was drawn off at a distance, not knowing what the horse, which had done so little, might do the next day,) there might probably many advantages have appeared which were not at the instant in view; however, they might both have done that as securely afterwards, as they did then unseasonably.

But neither of them were friends to such deliberation; but, as soon as they were refreshed with a little sleep, they both sent a messenger to each other, almost at the same time; the one, that he was resolved that morning to march away with his horse, and as many foot as he had left; and the other, that he would in that instant repair to the seaside, and transport himself beyond the seas; both which they immediately performed; the marquis making haste to Scarborough, there embarked in a poor vessel, and arrived at Hamburg: the prince, with his army, begun his march the same morning towards Chester. And so York was left to the discretion of sir Thomas Glemham, the governor thereof, to do with it as he thought fit: being in a condition only to deliver it up with more decency, not to defend it against an enemy that would require it.

Whereas, if prince Rupert had stayed with the army he marched away with, at any reasonable distance, it would have been long before the jealousies and breaches which were between the English and Scotch armies would have been enough composed to have agreed upon the renewing the siege; such great quantities of provision being already brought into the town: and the Scots talked of nothing but returning into their own country, where the marquis of Montrose had kindled already a fire* which the parliament of Edinburgh could not quench. But the certain intelligence that the prince was marched away without thought of returning, and that the marquis had embarked himself, reconciled them so far, (and nothing else could,) that after two days they returned to the posts they had before had in the siege; and so straitened the town that the governor, when he had no hope of relief, within a fortnight was compelled to deliver it up, upon as good articles for the town, and the gentry that were in it, and for himself and the few soldiers he had left, as he could propose: and so he marched with all his troops to Carlisle; which he afterwards defended with very remarkable circumstances of courage, industry, and patience.

The times afterwards grew so bad, and the King's affairs succeeded so ill, that there was no opportunity to call either of those two great persons to account for what they had done or what they had left undone. Nor did either of them ever think fit to make any particular relation of the grounds of their proceeding, or the causes of their mis-adventures, by way of excuse to the King, or for their own vindication. Prince Rupert only, to his friends, and after the murder of the King, produced a letter in the King's own hand, which he received when he was upon his march from Lancashire towards York; in which his majesty said, that his affairs were in so very ill a state, that it would not be enough, though his highness raised the siege from York, if he had not likewise beaten the Scotch army; which he understood to amount to no less than a peremptory order to fight, upon what disadvantage soever: and added, that the disadvantage was so great, the enemy being so much superior in number, that it was no wonder that he lost the day. But as the King's letter would not bear that sense, so the greatest cause of the misfortune was the precipitate entering upon the battle as soon as the enemy drew off, and without consulting at all with the marquis of Newcastle and his officers, who must needs know more of the enemy, and consequently how they were best to be dealt with, than his highness could do. For he saw not the marquis till, upon his summons, he came into the field, in the head of a troop of gentlemen, as a private captain, when the battle was ranged, and which, after a very short salutation, immediately begun; those of the marquis's army who came out of the town being placed upon the ground left by the prince, and assigned to them; which much indisposed both officers and soldiers to the work in hand, and towards those with whom they were to join in it.

Then it was too late in the day to begin the fight, if all the other ill circumstances had been away; for it was past three in the afternoon: whereas, if it had been deferred till next morning, in which time a full consultation might have been had, and the officers and soldiers grown a little acquainted with each other, better success might have been reasonably expected; nor would the confusion and consternation the other armies were then in, which was the only excuse for the present engagement, have been the less, but, on the contrary, very much improved by the delay; for the bitterness and animosity between the chief commanders was such, that a great part of the army was marched six miles, when it appeared by the prince's manner of drawing his army together to that ground that his resolution was to fight: the speedy intelligence whereof prevailed, (and nothing else could,) with those who were gone so far, to return, and with the rest to unite and concur in an action that, in human reason, could only preserve them; and if that opportunity had not then been so unhappily offered, it was

generally believed that the Scots would the next morning have continued their march northward, and the earl of Manchester would have
been necessitated to have made his retreat, as well as he could, into his
associated counties; and it would have been in the prince's power to
have chosen which of them he would have destroyed.

But then, of all the rest, his going away the next morning with all his
troops, in that manner, was most unexcusable, because most prejudicial and most ruinous to the King's affairs in those parts. Nor did those
troops ever after bring any considerable advantage to the King's service, but mouldered away by degrees, and the officers, (whereof many
were gentlemen of quality and great merit,) were killed upon beating
up of quarters, and little actions not worth their presence. The truth
is, the prince had some secret intimation of the marquis's purpose of
immediately leaving the town, and embarking himself for the parts
beyond the seas, before the marquis himself sent him word of it; upon
which, in great passion and rage, he sent him notice of his resolution
presently to be gone, that he who had the command of all those parts,
and thereby an obligation not to desert his charge, might be without
any imagination that the prince would take such a distracted government upon him, and leave him any excuse for his departure: and if in
this joint distemper with which they were both transported any persons of discretion and honour had interposed, they might in all probability have prevailed with both for a good understanding between
them, or at least for the suspension of their present resolutions, and
considering what might best be done. But they both resolved so soon,
and so soon executed what they resolved, that very few had the least
suspicion of their intentions, till they were both out of distance to have
their conversion attempted.

All that can be said for the marquis is, that he was so utterly tired
with a condition and employment so contrary to his humour, nature,
and education, that he did not at all consider the means or the way that
would let him out of it, and free him for ever from having more to do
with it. And it was a greater wonder that he sustained the vexation and
fatigue of it so long, than that he broke from it with so little circumspection. He was a very fine gentleman, active and full of courage, and most
accomplished in those qualities of horsemanship, dancing, and fencing,
which accompany a good breeding; in which his delight was. Besides
that, he was amorous in poetry and music, to which he indulged the
greatest part of his time; and nothing could have tempted him out of
those paths of pleasure which he enjoyed in a full and ample fortune,
but honour, and ambition to serve the King when he saw him in distress,

and abandoned by most of those who were in the highest degree obliged to him and by him. He loved monarchy, as it was the foundation and support of his own greatness; and the Church, as it was well constituted for the splendour and security of the Crown; and religion, as it cherished and maintained that order and obedience that was necessary to both; without any other passion for the particular opinions which were grown up in it and distinguished it into parties, than as he detested whatsoever was like to disturb the public peace.

He had a particular reverence for the person of the King, and the more extraordinary devotion for that of the Prince as he had had the honour to be trusted with his education as his governor; for which office, as he excelled in some, so he wanted other, qualifications. Though he had retired from his great trust, and from the Court, to decline the insupportable envy which the powerful faction had contracted against him, yet the King was no sooner necessitated to possess himself of some place of strength, and to raise some force for his defence, but the earl of Newcastle (for he was made marquis afterwards) obeyed his first call, and with great expedition and dexterity seized upon that town, when till then there was not one port town in England that avowed their obedience to the King: and he then presently raised such regiments of horse and foot as were necessary for the present state of affairs; all which was done purely by his own interest, and the concurrence of his numerous allies in those northern parts, who with all alacrity obeyed his commands, without any charge to the King, which he was not able to supply.

And after the battle of Edgehill, when the rebels grew so strong in Yorkshire, by the influence their garrison of Hull had upon both the East and West Riding there, that it behoved the King presently to make a general who might unite all those northern counties in his service, he could not choose any man so fit for it as the earl of Newcastle, who was not only possessed of a present force and of that important town, but had a greater reputation and interest in Yorkshire itself than at that present any other man had: the earl of Cumberland being at that time (though of entire affection to the King) much decayed in the vigour of his body and his mind, and unfit for that activity which the season required. And it cannot be denied that the earl of Newcastle, by his quick march with his troops as soon as he had received his commission to be general, and in the depth of winter, redeemed or rescued the city of York from the rebels, when they looked upon it as their own, and had it even within their grasp: and as soon as he was master of it, he raised men apace, and drew an army together with which he fought many battles, in which he had always (this last only excepted), success and victory.

He liked the pomp and absolute authority of a general well, and preserved the dignity of it to the full; and for the discharge of the outward state and circumstances of it, in acts of courtesy, affability, bounty, and generosity, he abounded; which in the infancy of a war became him, and made him for some time very acceptable to men of all conditions. But the substantial part, and fatigue of a general, he did not in any degree understand, (being utterly unacquainted with war,) nor could submit to, but referred all matters of that nature to the discretion of his lieutenant general King, who, no doubt, was an officer of great experience and ability, yet, being a Scotsman, was in that conjuncture upon more disadvantage than he would have been if the general himself had been more intent upon his command. In all actions of the field he was still present, and never absent in any battle; in all which he gave instances of an invincible courage and fearlessness in danger; in which the exposing himself notoriously did sometimes change the fortune of the day when his troops begun to give ground. Such articles of action were no sooner over than he retired to his delightful company, music, or his softer pleasures, to all which he was so indulgent, and to his ease, that he would not be interrupted upon what occasion soever; insomuch as he sometimes denied admission to the chiefest officers of the army, even to general King himself, for two days together; from whence many inconveniences fell out.

From the beginning, he was without any reverence or regard for the Privy Council, with few of whom he had any acquaintance; but was of the other soldiers' mind, that all the business ought to be done by councils of war, and was always angry when there were any overtures of a treaty; and therefore, (especially after the Queen had landed in Yorkshire and stayed so long there,) he considered any orders he received from Oxford, though from the King himself, more negligently than he ought to have done; and when he thought himself sure of Hull, and was sure that he should be then master entirely of all the north, he had no mind to march nearer the King, (as he had then orders to march into the associated counties, when, upon the taking of Bristol, his majesty had a purpose to have marched towards London on the other side,) out of apprehension that he should be eclipsed by the Court, and his authority overshadowed by the superiority of prince Rupert, from whom he desired to be at distance. Yet when he found himself in distress, and necessitated to draw his army within the walls of York, and saw no way to be relieved but by prince Rupert, who had then done great feats of arms in the relief of Newark, and afterwards in his expedition into Lancashire, where he was at that time, he writ to the King to Oxford, either upon the knowledge that the absoluteness and illimitedness of his commission was generally much spoken of, or out of the conscience of some discourse of his own to that purpose, which might have been reported, that he 'hoped his majesty did believe that he would never make the least scruple to obey the grandchild of King James:' and assuredly, if the prince had cultivated the good inclinations the marquis had towards him, with any civil and gracious condescensions, he would have found him full of duty and regard to his service and interest.

But the strange manner of the prince's coming, and undeliberated throwing himself, and all the King's hopes, into that sudden and unnecessary engagement, by which all the force the marquis had raised and with so many difficulties preserved was in a moment cast away and destroyed, so transported him with passion and despair, that he could not compose himself to think of beginning the work again, and involving himself in the same undelightful condition of life, from which he might now be free. He hoped his past meritorious actions might outweigh his present abandoning the thought of future action; and so, without farther consideration, as hath been said, he transported himself out of the kingdom, and took with him general King; upon whom they who were content to spare the marquis poured out all the reproaches of infidelity, treason, and conjunction with his countrymen, which, without doubt, was the effect of the universal discontent, and the miserable condition to which the people of those northern parts were on the sudden reduced, without the least foundation or ground for any such reproach: and as he had throughout the whole course of his life been generally reputed a man of honour, and had exercised the highest commands under the King of Sweden with extraordinary ability and success, so he had been prosecuted by some of his countrymen with the highest malice from his very coming into the King's service; and the same malice pursued him after he had left the kingdom, even to his death.

The loss of England came so soon to be lamented, that the loss of York or the too soon deserting the northern parts were comparatively no more spoken of; and the constant and noble behaviour of the marquis in the change of his fortune, and his cheerful submission to all the straits, necessities, and discomforts, which are inseparable from banishment, without the least application to the usurpers, who were possessed of his whole estate, and upon which they committed all imaginable and irreparable waste, in destroying all his woods of very great value, and who were still equally abhorred and despised by him, with his readiness and alacrity again to have embarked himself in the King's quarrel upon the first reasonable occasion, so perfectly reconciled all good men to him, that they rather observed what he had done and suffered for the King and for his country, without farther inquiring what he had omitted to do or been overseen in doing. [*HR*, VIII, 73–88]

10. The Defeat of Essex and the Rise of Cromwell

Despite the news from the North, Charles maintained his plan to pursue Essex, who was advancing into Cornwall. He reached Exeter on 26 July, which the Queen, sick following the birth of her last child, had left a few weeks before to return to France.

AFTER the King had made a small stay at Exeter, where he found his young daughter,* of whom the Queen had been so lately delivered, under the care and government of the lady Dalkeith,* (shortly after countess of Morton, by the death of her husband's father,) who had been long before designed by both their majesties to that charge, and having a little refreshed and accommodated his troops, he marched directly to Cornwall; where he found the earl of Essex in such a part of the country on the sea-side, that he quickly, by the general conflux and concurrence of the whole people, upon which the earl had been persuaded so much to depend, found means, with very little fighting, so to straiten his quarters that there seemed little appearance that he could possibly march away with his army, or compel the King to fight. He was, upon the matter, enclosed in and about Fowey, whilst the King lay encamped about Liskeard; and no day passed without some skirmishes, in which the earl was more distressed, and many of his considerable officers taken prisoners. And here there happened an accident that might very well have turned the King's fortune, and deprived him of all the advantages which were in view. The King being always in the army himself, all matters were still debated before him in the presence of those councillors who were about him; who, being men of better understandings and better expressions than the officers commonly disposed his majesty to their opinions, at least kept him from concurring in every thing which was proposed by the officers. The councillors, as hath been said before, were the lord Digby, Secretary of State, and sir John Culpepper, Master of the Rolls, of whose judgment the King had more esteem, even with reference to the war, than of most of the officers of the army; which raised an implacable animosity in the whole army against them.

General Ruthven, who by this time was created earl of Brentford, was general of the army; but, as hath been said, both by reason of his age and his extreme deafness, was not a man of counsel or of words; hardly conceived what was proposed, and as confusedly and obscurely delivered his opinion, and could indeed better judge by his eye than his ear, and in the field well knew what was to be done. Wilmot was lieutenant general of the horse, and at this time the second officer of the army, and had much more credit and authority in it than any man, which he had not employed to the King's advantage, as his majesty believed. He was a man proud and ambitious, and incapable of being contented; an orderly officer in marches and governing his troops. He drank hard, and had a great power over all who did so, which was a great people. He had a more companionable wit even than his rival Goring, and swayed more among the good fellows and could by no means endure that the lord Digby and sir John Culpepper should have so much credit with the King in councils of war.

The King had no kindness for him upon an old account, as remembering the part he had acted against the earl of Strafford: however, he had been induced, upon the accidents which happened afterwards, to repose trust in him; and this he knew well enough, and foresaw that he should be quickly overshadowed in the war, and therefore desired to get out of it by a seasonable peace; and so in all his discourses urged the necessity of it, as he had begun at Buckingham,* and that the King ought to send propositions to the Parliament in order to obtaining it; and in this march had prosecuted his former design by several cabals among the officers, and disposed them, to petition the King to send to the Parliament again an offer of peace, and that the lord Digby and sir John Culpepper might not be permitted to be present in councils of war; implying that if this might not be granted, they would think of some other way. Which petition, though by the wisdom of some officers [it] was kept from being delivered, yet so provoked the King that he resolved to take the first opportunity to free himself from his impetuous humour; in which good disposition the lord Digby ceased not to confirm his majesty, and as soon as the news came of the northern defeat, and that the marquis of Newcastle had left the kingdom, he prevailed that Goring might be sent for to attend his majesty; who then proposed to himself to make his nephew prince Rupert general of the army, and Goring general of the horse; which Wilmot could not avowedly have excepted against, the other having been always superior to him in command, and yet would be such a mortification to him as he would never have been able to digest.

Whether his apprehension of this, as his jealous nature had much of sagacity in it, or his restless and mutinous humour, transported him, but he gave not the King time to prosecute that gracious method, but even forced him to a quicker and a rougher remedy: for during the whole march he discoursed in all places that the King must send to the earl of Essex to invite him to a conjunction with him, that so the Parliament might be obliged to consent to a peace; and pretended that he had so good intelligence in that army, as to know that such an invitation would prove effectual, and be acceptable to the earl, who, he knew, was unsatisfied with the Parliament's behaviour towards him: and was so indiscreet as to desire a gentleman, with whom he had no intimacy, and who had a pass to go beyond the seas and must go through the earl's quarters, that he would remember his service to the earl of Essex, and assure him that the army so much desired peace that it should not be in the power of any of those persons about the King to hinder it, if his lordship would treat upon any reasonable propositions. All which kind of carriage and discourses were quickly represented in the full magnitude to the King by the lord Digby; and his majesty's own aversion kindled any spark into a formed distrust. So that after the King came into Cornwall, and had his whole army drawn up on the top of the hill, in view of the earl of Essex, who was in the bottom, and a battle expected every day, upon some new discourse Wilmot made, out of pride and vanity (for there was not in all the former the least formed act of sedition in his heart,) the knight marshal, with the assistance of Tom Eliot, who acted the part, arrested him in the King's name of high treason,* and dismounted him from his horse in the head of all the troops, and, putting a guard upon him, he was presently sent prisoner to Exeter; without any other ill effect, which might very reasonably have been apprehended in such a conjuncture, when he was indeed generally well beloved, and none of them for whose sakes he was thought to be sacrificed were at all esteemed, yet, I say, there were no other ill effects of it than a little murmur, which vapoured away.

The same day that Wilmot was arrested, the King removed another general officer of his army, the lord Percy, who had been made general of the ordnance upon very partial and not enough deliberated considerations, and put into that office the lord Hopton, whose promotion was universally approved; the one having no friend, and the other being universally beloved. Besides, the lord Percy (who was the first that had been created a baron at Oxford upon the Queen's intercession; which obliged the King to bestow the same honour on more men) had been as much inclined to mutiny as the lord Wilmot and was a bolder speaker, and had none of those faculties, which the other had, of reconciling men to him. Yet even his removal added to the ill humour of the army, too much disposed to discontent and censuring all that was done: for though he was generally unloved, as a proud and supercilious person, yet he had always three or four persons of good credit and reputation, who were esteemed by him, with whom he lived very well; and though he did not draw the good fellows to him by drinking, yet he eat well; which, in the general scarcity of that time, drew many votaries to him, who bore very ill the want of his table, and so were not without some inclination to murmur even on his behalf.

The very next day after these removals colonel Goring appeared; who had waited upon the King the night before at his quarters with letters from prince Rupert; and then, the army being drawn up, his majesty, attended by the principal officers of the army, rode to every division of the horse, and there declared, that, at the request of his nephew prince Rupert, and upon his resignation, he made Mr Goring general of the horse, and commanded them all to obey him; and for the lord Wilmot, although he had, for very good reasons, justly restrained him for the present, yet he had not taken away from him his command in the army; which declaration visibly raised the countenance of the body of horse more than the King was pleased to observe. And the very next day the greatest part of the officers delivered a petition that 'his majesty would give them so much light of the lord Wilmot's crimes, that they might see that themselves were not suspected, who had so long obeyed and executed his orders;' which is manifestation enough of the ill disposition the army was in, when they were even in view of the enemy, and of which the King had so much apprehension, in respect of the present posture he was in, that he was too easily persuaded to give them a draught of the articles by which he was charged: which though they contained so many indiscretions, vanities, and insolencies, that wise and dispassionate men thought he had been proceeded with very justly, yet generally they seemed not to make him so very black as he had been represented to be: and when the articles were sent to him, he returned so specious an answer to them, that made many men think he had been prosecuted with severity enough. Yet Wilmot himself, when he saw his old mortal enemy Goring put in the command over him, thought himself incapable of reparation, or a full vindication, and therefore desired leave to retire into France; and had presently a pass sent to him to that purpose, of which he made use as soon as he received it, and so transported himself out of the kingdom; which opened the mouths of many, and made it believed that he had been sacrificed to some faction and intrigue of the Court, without any such misdemeanour as deserved it.

The King had some days before this found an opportunity to make a trial whether the earl of Essex, from the notorious indignities which he received from the Parliament, and which were visible to all the world, or from the present ill condition which he and his army were reduced to, might be induced to make a conjunction with his majesty. The lord Beauchamp, eldest son to the marquis of Hertford, desired, for the recovery of his health, not then good, to transport himself into France; and to that purpose had a pass from his uncle, the earl of Essex, for himself, monsieur Richaute, a Frenchman who had been his governor, and two servants, to embark at Plymouth; and being now with the King, it was necessary to pass through the earl's quarters.

By him the King vouchsafed to write a letter with his own hand to the earl, in which he told him 'how much it was in his power to restore that peace to the kingdom which he had professed always to desire, and upon such conditions as did fully comply with all those ends for which the Parliament had first taken up arms; for his majesty was still ready to satisfy all those ends; but that since the invasion of the kingdom by the Scots all his overtures of peace had been rejected; which must prove the destruction of the kingdom, if he did not, with his authority and power, dispose those at Westminster to accept of a peace that might preserve it;' with all those arguments that might most reasonably persuade to a conjunction with his majesty, and such gracious expressions of the sense he would always retain of the service and merit as were most likely to invite him to it. The King desired that a pass might be procured for Mr Harding, one of the grooms of the bedchamber to the Prince, a gentleman who had been before of much conversation with the earl, and much loved by him; and the procuring this pass was recommended to monsieur Richaute.

The earl received his nephew very kindly; who delivered the King's letter to him, which he received and read; and being then told by the lord Beauchamp that monsieur Richaute, who was very well known to him, had somewhat to say to him from the King, the earl called him to his chamber, in the presence only of the lord Beauchamp, and asked him if he had anything to say to him. Richaute told him that his principal business was to desire his permission and pass that Mr Harding might come to him, who had many things to offer, which, he presumed, would not be unacceptable to him. The earl answered in short, that he would not permit Mr Harding to come to him, nor would he have any treaty with the King, having received no warrant for it from the Parliament; upon which, Richaute enlarged himself upon some particulars which Mr Harding was to have urged, of the King's desire of peace, of the concurrence of all the lords, as well those at Oxford as in the army, in the same desire of preserving the kingdom from a conquest by the Scots, and other discourse to that purpose, and of the King's readiness to give him any security for the performance of all he had promised. To all which the earl answered sullenly, that, 'according to the commission he had received, he would defend the King's person and posterity, and that the best counsel he could give him was to go to his Parliament.'

As soon as the King received this account of his letter, and saw there was nothing to be expected by those addresses, he resolved to push it on the other way, and to fight with the enemy as soon as was possible; and so the next day drew up all his army in sight of the enemy, and had many skirmishes between the horse of both armies, till the enemy quitted that part of a large heath upon which they stood, and retired to a hill near the park of the lord Mohun at Boconnock; they having the possession of his house, where they quartered conveniently. That night both armies, after they had well viewed each other, lay in the field; and many are of opinion, that if the King had that day vigorously advanced upon the enemy, to which his army was well inclined, though upon some disadvantage of ground, they would have been easily defeated: for the King's army was in good heart, and willing to engage; on the contrary, the earl's seemed much surprised, and in confusion, to see the other army so near them. But such censures always attend such conjunctures, and find fault for what is not done as well as with that which is done.

The next morning the King called a council, to consider whether they should that day compel the enemy to fight; which was concluded not to be reasonable, and that it was better to expect the arrival of sir Richard Grenville, who was yet in the west of Cornwall, and had a body of eight thousand horse and foot, as was reported, though they were not near that number. It was hereupon ordered, that all the foot should be presently drawn into the enclosures between Boconnock and the heath; all the fences to the grounds of that country being very good breastworks against the enemy. The King's head-quarter was made at the lord Mohun's house, which the earl of Essex had kindly quitted when the King's army advanced the day before. The horse were quartered for the most part between Liskeard and the sea; and every day compelled the earl's forces to retire, and to lodge close together; and in this posture both armies lay within view of each other for three or four days. In this time that inconvenient spirit that had possessed so many of the horse officers appeared again; and some of them, who had conferred with the prisoners who were every day taken, and some of them officers of as good quality as any they had, were persuaded by them, that all the obstinacy in Essex in refusing to treat with the King proceeded only from his jealousy that when the King had got him into his hands he would take revenge upon him for all the mischief he had sustained by him; and that if he had any assurance that what was promised would be complied with, he would be quickly induced to treat.

Upon this excellent evidence, these politic contrivers presumed to prepare a letter, that should be subscribed by the general and all the superior officers of the army; the beginning of which letter was, that 'they had obtained leave of the King to send that letter to him.' There they proposed, that he, with six officers whom he should choose, would the next morning meet with their general, and six other officers, as should be appointed to attend him; and if he would not himself be present, that then six officers of the King's army should meet with six such as he should appoint, at any place that should be thought fit; and that they, and every of them who subscribed the letter, would, upon the honour and reputation of gentlemen and soldiers, with their lives maintain that whatsoever his majesty should promise should be performed, and that it should not be in the power of any private person whatsoever to interrupt or hinder the execution thereof. When they had framed this letter between themselves, and shewed it to many others, whose approbation they received, they resolved to present it to the King, and humbly to desire his permission that it might be sent to the earl of Essex.

How unpardonable soever the presumption and insolence in contriving and framing this letter was, and how penal soever it might justly have been to them, yet, when it was presented to his majesty, many who liked not the manner of it were persuaded, by what they were told, that it might do good; and in the end they prevailed with the King to consent that the officers should sign it, and that the general should send a trumpet with it; his majesty at the same time concluding that it would find no better reception than his own letter had done, and likewise believing that the rejecting of it would purge that unruly spirit out of his army, and that he should never more be troubled with those vexatious addresses, and that it might add some spirit and animosity to the officers and soldiers when they should see with how much neglect and contempt the earl received their application. And so prince Maurice, general Goring, and all the superior officers of the army, signed the letter, which a trumpet delivered to the earl of Essex; who the next day returned his answer to them in these words:

'My lords, in the beginning of your letter you express by what authority you send it; I having no authority from the Parliament, who have employed me, to treat, cannot give way to it without breach of trust. My lords, I am your humble servant, Essex. Lostwithiel, Aug. 10, 1644.'

This short surly answer produced the effect the King wished and expected; they who had been so over active in contriving the address were most ashamed of their folly, and the whole army seemed well composed to obtain that by their swords which they could not by their pen.

Sir Richard Grenville was now come up to the post where he should be, and, at Bodmin, in his march, had fallen upon a party of the earl's horse, and killed many, and taken others prisoners; and presented himself to the King at Boconnock, giving his majesty an account of his proceedings, and a particular of his forces; which, after all the high discourses, amounted really but to eighteen hundred foot, and six hundred horse, above one hundred of which were of the Queen's troop, (left behind when her majesty embarked for France,) under the command of captain Edward Brett; who had done very good service in the western parts of that county from the time of the Queen's departure, and much confirmed the train-bands of those parts. This troop was presently added to the King's guards under the lord Bernard Stewart, and captain Brett was made major of that regiment.

Though the earl of Essex had but strait and narrow room for his quarters for so great an army of horse and foot, yet he had the good town of Fowey and the sea to friend; by which he might reasonably assure himself of store of provisions, the Parliament ships having all the jurisdiction there; and so, if he preserved his post, which was so situated that he could not be compelled to fight without giving him great advantage, he might well conclude that Waller, or some other force sent from the Parliament, would be shortly upon the King's back, as his majesty was upon his: and no question this rational confidence was a great motive to him to neglect all overtures made to him by the King; besides the punctuality and stubbornness of his own nature, which whosoever was well acquainted with might easily have foreseen what effect all those applications would have produced. It was therefore now resolved to make his quarters yet straiter, and to cut off even his provisions by sea, or a good part thereof. To which purpose sir Richard Grenville drew his men from Bodmin, and possessed himself of Lanhydrock, a strong house of the lord Robartes, two miles west of Boconnock, and over the river that runs to Lostwithiel and thence to Fowey, and likewise to Reprin Bridge; by which the enemy was not only deprived of that useful outlet, but a safe communication made between him and the King's army, which was before interrupted. And on the other side, which was of more importance, sir Jacob Astley, with a good party of horse and foot, made himself master of View Hall,* another house of the lord Mohun's, over against Fowey, and of Pernon Fort, a mile below it, at the mouth of the haven; both which places he found so tenable, that he put captain Page into one and captain Garraway into the other, with two hundred commanded men, and two or three pieces of ordnance; which these two captains made good, and defended so well, that they made Fowey utterly useless to Essex, save for the quartering his men; not suffering any provisions to be brought in to him from the sea that way. And it was exceedingly wondered at by all men, that he, being so long possessed of Fowey, did not put strong guards into those places; by which he might have prevented his army's being brought into those extreme necessities they shortly after fell into, which might easily be foreseen, and as easily, that way, have been prevented.

Now the King had leisure to sit still, and warily to expect what invention or stratagem the earl would make use of, to make some attempt upon his army or to make his own escape. In this posture both armies lay still, without any notable action, for the space of eight or ten days; when the King, seeing no better fruit from all that was hitherto done, resolved to draw his whole army together, and to make his own quarters yet much nearer, and either to force Essex to fight or to be uneasy even in his quarters. And it was high time to do so; for it was now certain that either Waller himself or some other forces were already upon their march towards the west. With this resolution the whole army advanced in such a manner that the enemy was compelled still to retire before them, and to quit their quarters, and, among the rest, a rising ground called Beacon Hill; which they no sooner quitted than the King possessed, and immediately caused a square work to be there raised, and a battery made, upon which some pieces of cannon were planted, that shot into their quarters and did them great hurt; when their cannon, though they returned twenty shot for one, did very little or no harm.

And now the King's forces had a full prospect over all the others' quarters; saw how all their foot and horse were disposed, and from whence they received all their forage and provisions: which when clearly viewed and observed, Goring was sent, with the greatest part of the horse and fifteen hundred foot, a little westward to St Blazey, to drive the enemy yet closer together, and to cut off the provisions they received from thence; which was so well executed, that they did not only possess themselves of St Austell, and the westerly part of St Blazey, (so that the enemy's horse was reduced to that small extent of earth that is between the river of Fowey and that at Blazey, which is not above two miles in breadth, and little more in length; in which they had for the most part fed since they came to Lostwithiel, and therefore it could not now long supply them,) but likewise were masters, of the Parr, near St Blazey; whereby they deprived them of the chief place of landing the provisions which came by sea. And now the earl began to be very sensible of the ill condition he was in, and discerned that he should not be able long to remain in that posture; besides, he had received advertisement that the party which was sent for his relief from London had received some brush in Somersetshire, which would much retard their march; and therefore it behoved him to enter upon new counsels, and to take new resolutions. . . .

When the earl found himself in this condition, and that within very few days he must be without any provisions for his army, he resolved that sir William Balfour should use his utmost endeavour to break through with his whole body of horse, and to save them the best he could; and then that he himself would embark his foot at Fowey, and with them escape by sea. And two foot soldiers of the army, whereof one was a Frenchman, came over from them, and assured the King that they intended that night to break through with their horse, which were all then drawn on that side the river and town of Lostwithiel, and that the foot were to march to Fowey, where they should be embarked. This intelligence agreed with what they otherwise received, and was believed as it ought to be; and thereupon order was given that both armies (for that under prince Maurice was looked upon as distinct, and always so quartered) should stand to their arms all that night, and if the horse attempted an escape, fall on them from both quarters; the passage between them, through which they must go, being but a musket-shot over; and they could not avoid going very near a very little cottage that was well fortified, in which fifty musketeers were placed. Advertisement was sent to Goring and all the horse; and the orders renewed, which had formerly been given, for the breaking down the bridges, and cutting down the trees near the highway, to obstruct their passage.

The effect of all this providence was not such as was reasonably to be expected. The night* grew dark and misty, as the enemy could wish; and about three in the morning the whole body of the horse passed with great silence between the armies, and within pistol-shot of the cottage, without so much as one musket discharged at them. At the break of day the horse were discovered marching over the heath, beyond the reach of the foot; and there was only at hand the earl of

Cleveland's brigade, the body of the King's horse being at a greater distance. That brigade, to which some other troops which had taken the alarm joined, followed them in the rear, and killed some, and took more prisoners: but strong parties of the enemy frequently turning upon them, and the whole body often making a stand, they were often compelled to retire; yet followed in that manner that they killed and took about a hundred, which was the greatest damage they sustained in their whole march. The notice and orders came to Goring when he was in one of his jovial exercises; which he received with mirth, and slighting those who sent them, as men who took alarms too warmly; and he continued his delights till all the enemy's horse were passed through his quarters, nor did then pursue them in any time. So that, excepting such who by the tiring of their horses became prisoners, Balfour continued his march even to London, with less loss or trouble than can be imagined, to the infinite reproach of the King's army and of all his garrisons in the way. Nor was any man called in question for this supine neglect; it being not thought fit to make severe inquisition into the behaviour of the rest, when it was so notoriously known how the superior officer had failed in his duty.

The next morning, after the horse were gone, the earl drew all his foot together, and quitted Lostwithiel, and marched towards Fowey, having left order for the breaking down that bridge. And his majesty himself from his new fort discerned it, and sent a company of musketeers, who quickly beat those that were left, and thereby preserved the bridge; over which the King presently marched to overtake the rear of the army, which marched so fast, yet in good order, that they left two demi-culverins and two other very good guns, and some ammunition, to be disposed of by the King. That day was spent in smart skirmishes, in which many fell; and if the King's horse had been more, (whereof he had only two troops of his guards, which did good service,) it would have proved a bloody day to the enemy. The night coming on, the King lay in the field, his own quarters being so near the enemy that they discharged many cannon-shot, which fell within few yards of him when he was at supper. Sunday being the next day, and the first day of September, in the morning, Butler, lieutenant colonel to the earl of Essex, who had been taken prisoner at Boconnock, and was exchanged for an officer of the King's, came from the earl to desire a parley. As soon as he was sent away, the earl embarked himself, with the lord Robartes, and such other officers as he had most kindness for, in a vessel at Fowey, and so escaped into Plymouth; leaving all his army of foot, cannon, and ammunition, to the care of major general

Skippon, who was to make as good conditions for them as he could; and after a very short stay in Plymouth, he went on board a ship of the royal navy that attended there, and was within few days delivered at London; where he was received without any abatement of the respect they had constantly paid him, nor was it less than they could have shewed to him, if he had not only brought back his own army but the King himself likewise with him.

The King consented to the parley; upon which a cessation was concluded, and hostages interchangeably delivered; and then the enemy sent propositions, such as upon delivery of a strong fortified town, after a handsome defence, are usually granted. But they quickly found they were not looked upon as men in that condition; and so, in the end, they were contented to deliver up all their cannon, (which, with the four taken two or three days before, were eight and thirty pieces of cannon,) a hundred barrels of powder, with match and bullets proportionable, and about six thousand arms; which being done, the officers were to have liberty to wear their swords, and to pass with their own money and proper goods; and, to secure them from plunder, they were to have a convoy to Poole or Southampton; all their sick and wounded might stay in Fowey till they were recovered, and then have passes to Plymouth.

This agreement was executed accordingly, on Monday the second of September; and though it was near the evening before all was finished, they would march away that night; and though all care was taken to preserve them from violence, yet first at Lostwithiel, where they had been long quartered, and in other towns through which they had formerly passed, the inhabitants, especially the women, who pretended to see their own clothes and goods about them which they had been plundered of, treated them very rudely, even to stripping of some of the soldiers, and more of their wives, who had before behaved themselves with great insolence in the march. That night there came about one hundred of them to the King's army, and of the six thousand, for so many marched out of Fowey, there did not a third part come to Southampton, where the King's convoy left them; to which Skippon gave a large testimony under his hand, that they had carried themselves with great civility towards them, and fully complied with their obligation. [*HR*, VIII, 93–119]

After the surrender of Essex, Charles began to march back towards Oxford. His attempt to relieve the royalist garrison at Donnington Castle (Newbury) was blocked by the combined forces of the Earl of Essex, the Earl of

*Manchester, and Sir William Waller, on 26–9 October. By 1 November
he was back in Oxford.*

Though the King's condition was now much better than in the beginning of the summer he had reason to expect, [since] he had absolutely
broken and defeated two armies of the Parliament, and returned into
his winter quarter with triumph, and rather with an increase than
diminution of his forces, yet his necessities were still the same, and the
fountains dried up from whence he might expect relief, his quarters
shortened and lessened, by the loss of the whole North: for after the
battle of York* the Scots returned to reduce Newcastle, which they
had already done, and all other garrisons which had held out for the
King; and when that work should be throughly and sufficiently done,
it must be expected that army should again move southward, and take
such other places as the Parliament should not be at leisure to look
after themselves.

The army was less united than ever; the old general was set aside,
and prince Rupert put into the command, which was no popular
change: for the other was known to be an officer of great experience,
and had committed no oversights in his conduct; was willing to hear
every thing debated, and always concurred with the most reasonable
opinion; and though he was not of many words, and was not quick in
hearing, yet upon any action he was sprightly, and commanded well.
The prince was rough and passionate, and loved not debate; liked what
was proposed as he liked the persons who proposed it; and was so great
an enemy to Digby and Culpepper, who were only present in debates
of the war with the officers, that he crossed all they proposed. The
truth is, all the army had been disposed from the first raising it to a
neglect and contempt of the Council, and the King himself had not
been solicitous enough to preserve the respect due to it, in which he
lost of his own dignity.

Goring, who was now general of the horse, was no more gracious to
prince Rupert than Wilmot had been; and had all the other's faults,
and wanted his regularity and preserving his respect with the officers.
Wilmot loved debauchery, but shut it out from his business; and never
neglected that, and rarely miscarried in it. Goring had much a better
understanding and a sharper wit, (except in the very exercise of
debauchery, and then the other was inspired,) a much keener courage,
and presentness of mind in danger: Wilmot discerned it farther off,
and because he could not behave himself so well in it, commonly prevented or warily declined it, and never drank when he was within

distance of an enemy: Goring was not able to resist the temptation when he was in the middle of them, nor would decline it to obtain a victory, and in one of those fits had suffered the horse to escape out of Cornwall; and the most signal misfortunes of his life in war had their rise from that uncontrollable license. Neither of them valued their promises, professions, or friendships, according to any rules of honour or integrity; but Wilmot violated them the less willingly, and never but for some great benefit or convenience to himself: Goring without scruple, out of humour, or for wit sake, and loved no man so well but that he would cozen him, and then expose him to public mirth for having been cozened; and therefore he had always fewer friends than the other, but more company, for no man had a wit that pleased the company better. The ambitions of both were unlimited, and so equally incapable of being contented; and both unrestrained by any respect to good-nature or justice from pursuing the satisfaction thereof: yet Wilmot had more scruples from religion to startle him, and would not have attained his end by any gross or foul act of wickedness: Goring could have passed through those pleasantly, and would without hesitation have broken any trust or done any act of treachery, to have satisfied an ordinary passion or appetite; and, in truth, wanted nothing but industry (for he had wit and courage and understanding and ambition, uncontrolled by any fear of God or man) to have been as eminent and successful in the highest attempt in wickedness of any man in the age he lived in or before. And of all his qualifications dissimulation was his master-piece; in which he so much excelled, that men were not ordinarily ashamed, or out of countenance, with being deceived but twice by him.

The Court was not much better disposed than the army: they who had no preferment were angry with those who had, and thought they had not deserved so well as themselves; and they who were envied found no satisfaction or delight in what they were envied for, being poor and necessitous, and the more sensible of their being so by the titles they had received upon their violent importunity. So that the King was without any joy in the favours he had conferred, and yet was not the less solicited to grant more to others of the same kind, who he foresaw would be no better pleased than the rest: and the pleasing one man this way displeased one hundred; as his creating the lord Culpepper at this time, and making him a baron, (who, in truth, had served him with great abilities, and, though he did imprudently in desiring it, did deserve it,) did much dissatisfy both the Court and the army, to neither of which he was in any degree gracious, by his having no ornament of education to make men the more propitious to his parts of nature; and disposed many others to be very importunate to receive the same obligation. [*HR*, VIII, 167–70]

Parliament suffered just as serious clashes of personality and policy. During the conjunction of its armies at Newbury, differences between its commanders over the conduct of the campaign, and of the war, came out into the open. They were most acute in the confrontation between the Earl of Manchester and Oliver Cromwell, the commander and the lieutenant general of the army formed by the Eastern Association, the organization which coordinated the war effort in East Anglia.

When the King was in this melancholic posture, it was a great refreshment and some advantage to him to hear that the disorder the Parliament was in was superior to his. The cause of all the distractions in his Court or army proceeded from the extreme poverty and necessity his majesty was in, and a very moderate supply of money would in a moment have extinguished all those distempers. But all the wealth of the kingdom, (for they were possessed of all,) could not prevent the same, and greater, distractions and emulations from breaking into the whole government of the Parliament: and all the personal animosities imaginable brake out in their councils and in their armies; and the House of Peers found themselves, upon the matter, excluded from all power or credit when they did not concur in all the demands which were made by the Commons.

That violent party, which had first cozened the rest into the war, and afterwards obstructed all the approaches towards peace, found now that they had finished as much of their work as the tools which they had wrought with could be applied to, and what remained to be done must be despatched by new workmen. They had been long unsatisfied with the earl of Essex, and he as much with them; both being more solicitous to suppress the other than to destroy the King. And they bore the loss and dishonour he had sustained in Cornwall very well, and would have been glad that both he and his army had been quite cut off, instead of being dissolved; for all his officers and soldiers were corrupted in their affections towards them, and desired nothing but peace: so that they resolved never more to trust or employ any of them. But that which troubled more, was, that their beloved earl of Manchester, upon whom they depended as a fast friend, by whom they might insensibly have divested the earl of Essex of all inconvenient authority in the army, appeared now as unapplicable to their purposes as the other, and there was a breach fallen out between him and Oliver

Cromwell which was irreconcilable, and which had brought some counsels upon the stage before they were ripe.

Cromwell accused the earl of Manchester* of having betrayed the Parliament out of cowardice, for that he might at the King's last being at Newbury, when he drew off his cannon, very easily have defeated his whole army, if he would have permitted it to have been engaged: that he went to him, and shewed him evidently how it might be done, and desired him that he would give him leave with his own brigade of horse to charge the King's army in their retreat; and the earl, with the rest of his army, might look on, and do as he should think fit: but that the earl had, notwithstanding all importunity used by him and other officers, positively and obstinately refused to permit him, giving no other reason but that, he said, if they did engage and overthrow the King's army, the King would always have another army to keep up the war; but if that army which he commanded should be overthrown before the other under the earl of Essex should be reinforced, there would be an end of their pretences, and they should be all rebels and traitors, and executed and forfeited by the law.

This pronunciation what the *law* would do against them was very heavily taken by the Parliament, as if the earl believed the law to be against them, after so many declarations made by them that the law was on their side, and that the King's arms were taken up against the law. The earl confessed he had used words to that effect, that they should be treated as traitors if their army was defeated, when he did not approve the advice that was given by the lieutenant general, which would have exposed the army to greater hazard than he thought seasonable in that conjuncture, in the middle of the winter, to expose it to. He then recriminated Cromwell, that at another time Cromwell discoursing freely with him of the state of the kingdom, and proposing somewhat to be done, the earl had answered that the Parliament would never approve it: to which Cromwell presently replied, 'My lord, if you will stick firm to honest men, you shall find yourself in the head of an army that shall give the law to King and Parliament:' which discourse he said made great impression in him, for he knew the lieutenant general to be a man of very deep designs; and therefore he was the more careful to preserve an army which he yet thought was very faithful to the Parliament.

This discourse startled those who had always an aversion to Cromwell, and had observed the fierceness of his nature, and the language he commonly used when there was any mention of peace; so that they desired that this matter might be throughly examined and brought to judgment. But the other side put all obstructions in the way, and rather chose to lose the advantage they had against the earl of Manchester than to have the other matter examined, which would unavoidably have made some discoveries which they were not yet ready to produce. However, the animosities increased, and the parties appeared barefaced against each other, which increased the distractions, and divided the city as well as the Parliament; and new opinions started up in religion, which made more subdivisions, and new terms and distinctions were brought into discourse, and *fanatics* were now first brought into appellation; which kind of confusion exceedingly disposed men of any sober understanding to wish for peace, though none knew how to bring the mention of it into the Parliament.

The Scots' commissioners were as jealous and as unsatisfied as any other party, and found since the battle of York neither their army nor themselves so much considered as before, nor any conditions performed towards them with any punctuality. They had long had jealousy of Cromwell and sir H. Vane and all that party; which they saw increased every day, and grew powerful in the Parliament, in the council, and in the city. Their sacred vow and covenant was mentioned with less reverence and respect, and the Independents, which comprehended many sects in religion, spake publicly against it, of which party Cromwell and Vane were the leaders, with very many clergymen, who were the most popular preachers, and who in the Assembly of Divines had great authority. So that the Scots plainly perceived that, though they had gone as far towards the destruction of the Church of England as they desired, they should never be able to establish their Presbyterian government; without which they should lose all their credit in their own country and all their interest in England. They discerned likewise that there was a purpose, if that party prevailed, to change the whole frame of the government, as well civil as ecclesiastical, and to reduce the monarchy to a republic; which was as far from the end and purpose of that nation as to restore episcopacy. So that they saw no way to prevent the mischief and confusion that would fall out but by a peace; which they began heartily to wish, and to conspire with those of that party which most desired to bring it to pass; but how to set a treaty on foot they knew not.

The House of Peers, three or four men excepted, wished it, but had no power to compass it. In the House of Commons there were enough who would have been very glad of it, but had not the courage to propose it. They who had an inward aversion from it, and were resolved to prevent it by all possible means, wrought upon many of the other to believe that they would accept of a proposition for a treaty if the King desired it, but that it would be dishonourable, and of very pernicious consequence to the nation if the Parliament first proposed it. So that it seemed evident, that if any of the party which did in truth desire peace should propose it to the Parliament, it would be rejected, and rejected upon the point of honour by many of those who in their hearts prayed for it.

They tried their old friends of the city, who had served their turns so often, and set some of them to get hands to a petition by which the Parliament should be moved to send to the King to treat of peace. But that design was no sooner known but others of an opposite party were appointed to set a counter petition on foot, by which they should disclaim any consent [to], or approbation of, the other petition; not that they did not desire peace as much as their neighbours, (nobody was yet arrived at the impudence to profess against peace,) but that they would not presume to move the Parliament in it, because they knew their wisdom knew best the way to obtain it, and would do what was necessary and fit towards it; to which they wholly left it. And this petition found more countenance amongst the magistrates, the mayor, and aldermen; sir Henry Vane having diligently provided that men of his own principles and inclinations should be brought into the government of the city, of which he saw they should always have great need, even in order to keep the Parliament well disposed.

So that they who did in truth desire any reasonable peace found the way to it so difficult, and that it was impossible to prevail with the two Houses to propose it to the King, that they resolved it could only rise from his majesty, and to that purpose they should all labour with their several friends at Oxford to incline the King to send a message to the Parliament, to offer a treaty of peace in any place where they should appoint; and then they would all run the utmost hazard before it should be rejected.

The Independent party, (for under that style and appellation they now acted, and owned themselves,) which feared and abhorred all motions towards peace, were in as great straits as the other how to carry on their designs. They were resolved to have no more to do with either of their generals but how to lay them aside; especially the earl of Essex, who had been so entirely their founder that they owed not more to the power and reputation of Parliament than to his sole name and credit: the being able to raise an army, and conducting it to fight against the King, was purely due to him, and the effect of his power. And now to put such an affront upon him, and to think of another general, must appear the highest ingratitude, and might provoke the army itself, where he was still exceedingly beloved; and to continue him in that trust was to betray their own designs, and to render them unpracticable. Therefore, till they could find some expedient to explicate and disentangle themselves out of this labyrinth, they made no advance towards the recruiting or supplying their armies, nor to provide for any winter expedition; only they sent Waller out with such troops towards the west as they cared not for, and resolved to use their service no more.

They knew not how to propose the great alterations they intended to the Parliament; and of all men, the Scots' commissioners were not to be trusted. In the end, they resolved to pursue the method in which they had been hitherto so successful, and to prepare and ripen things in the Church, that they might afterwards in due time grow to maturity in the Parliament. They agreed therefore in the Houses, (and in those combinations they were always unanimous,) that they would have a solemn fast-day, in which they would *seek God*, (which was the new phrase they brought from Scotland with their Covenant,) and desire his assistance, to lead them out of the perplexities they were in: and they did as readily agree in the nomination of the preachers who were to perform that exercise, and who were more trusted in the deepest designs than most of those who named them were: for there was now a schism among their clergy as well as the laity, and the Independents were the bolder and more political men.

When the fast-day came, which was observed for eight or ten hours together in the churches, the preachers prayed the Parliament might be inspired with those thoughts as might contribute to their honour and reputation, and that they might preserve that opinion the nation had of their honesty and integrity, and be without any selfish ends, or seeking their own benefit and advantage. And after this preparation by their prayers, the preachers, let their texts be what they would, told them very plainly, that it was no wonder that there was such division amongst them in their counsels when there was no union in their hearts: that the Parliament lay under many reproaches, not only amongst their enemies but with their best friends, who were the more out of countenance because they found that the aspersions and imputations which their enemies had laid upon them were so well grounded that they could not wipe them off: that there was as great pride, as great ambition, as many private ends, and as little zeal and affection for the public, as they had ever imputed to the Court: that whilst they pretended, at the public cost and out of the purses of the poor people, to make a general reformation, they took great care to grow great and rich themselves; and that both the city and kingdom took notice, with great anxiety of mind, that all the offices of the army, and all the profitable offices of the kingdom, were in the hands of the members of the two Houses of Parliament, who, whilst the nation grew poor, as it must needs do under such insupportable taxes, grew very rich, and would in a short time get all the money of the kingdom into their hands; and that it could not reasonably be expected that such men, who got so much and enriched themselves to that degree by the continuance of the war, would heartily pursue those ways which would put an end to it, the end whereof must put an end to their exorbitant profit. And when they had exaggerated these reproaches as pathetically as they could, and the sense the people generally had of the corruption of it, even to a despair of ever seeing an end of the calamities they sustained, or having any prospect of that reformation in Church and State which they had so often and so solemnly promised to effect, they fell again to their prayers that God would take his own work into his hand, and if the instruments he had already employed were not worthy to bring so glorious a design to a conclusion, that he would inspire others more fit, who might perfect what was begun, and bring the troubles of the nation to a godly period.

When the two Houses met together the next day after these devout animadversions, there was another spirit appeared in the looks of many of them. Sir H. Vane told them, if ever God had appeared to them it was in the exercise of yesterday; and that it appeared it proceeded from God, because (as he was credibly informed by many who had been auditors in other congregations) the same lamentations and discourses had been made in all other churches as the godly preachers had made before them; which could therefore proceed only from the immediate Spirit of God. He repeated some things which had been said, upon which he was best prepared to enlarge, and besought them to remember their obligations to God and to their country, and that they would free themselves from those just reproaches, which they could do no otherwise than by divesting themselves of all offices and charges which might bring in the least advantage and profit to themselves; and by which they could only make it appear that they were public-hearted men, and as they paid all taxes and impositions with the rest of the nation, so they gave up all their time to their country's service without any reward or gratuity.

He told them, that the reflections of yesterday, none of which had ever entered upon his spirit before, had raised another reflection in him than had been mentioned; which was, that it had been often taken notice of, and objected by the King himself, that the numbers of the members of Parliament who sat in either House were too few to give reputation to acts of so great moment as were transacted in their councils; which, though it was no fault of theirs, who kept their proper stations, but of those who had deserted their places and their trusts by being absent from the Parliament, yet that in truth there were too many absent, though in the service of the House and by their appointment; and if all the members were obliged to attend the service of the Parliament in the Parliament, it would bring great reputation to their numbers, and the people would pay more reverence and yield a fuller obedience to their commands: and then concluded, that he was ready to accuse himself for one of those who gained by an office he had, and though he was possessed of it before the beginning of the troubles, and owed it not to the favour of the Parliament, (for he had been joined with sir William Russell in the treasurership of the navy by the King's grant,) yet he was ready to lay it down, to be disposed of by the Parliament; and wished that the profits thereof might be applied towards the support of the war.

When the ice was thus broke, Oliver Cromwell, who had not yet arrived at the faculty of speaking with decency and temper, commended the preachers for having dealt plainly and impartially, and told them of their faults, which they had been so unwilling to hear of: that there were many things upon which he had never reflected before, yet, upon revolving what had been said, he could not but confess that all was very true, and till there were a perfect reformation in those particulars which had been recommended to them, nothing would prosper that they took in hand: that the Parliament had done very wisely in the entrance into this war to engage many members of their own in the most dangerous parts of it, that the nation might see that they did not intend to embark them in perils of war whilst themselves sat securely at home out of gunshot, but would march with them where the danger most threatened; and those honourable persons who had exposed themselves this way had merited so much of their country that their memories should be held in perpetual veneration, and whatsoever should be well done after them should be always imputed to their example: but that God had so blessed their armies, that there had grown up with it and under it very many excellent officers, who were fit for much greater charges than they were now possessed of; and desired them not to be terrified with an imagination that if the highest offices were vacant they would not be able to put as fit men into them;

for, besides that it was not good to put so much trust in any arm of flesh as to think such a cause as theirs depended upon any one man, he did take upon him to assure them, that they had officers in their armies who were fit to be generals in any enterprise in Christendom.

He said, he thought nothing so necessary as to purge and vindicate the Parliament from the partiality towards their own members; and made a proffer to lay down his commission of command in the army; and desired that an ordinance might be prepared, by which it might be made unlawful for any member of either House of Parliament to hold any office or command in the army, or any place or employment of profit in the State; and so concluded, with an enlargement upon the vices and corruptions which were gotten into the army, the profaneness and impiety and absence of all religion, the drinking and gaming, and all manner of license and laziness; and said plainly, that, till the whole army were new modelled and governed under a stricter discipline, they must not expect any notable success in any thing they went about.

And this debate ended in appointing a committee* to prepare an ordinance for the exclusion of all members from the trust aforesaid; which took up much debate, and depended very long before it was brought to a conclusion, and in the end was called the *Self-denying Ordinance*; the driving on of which exceedingly increased the inclination of the other party to peace, which they did now foresee would only prevent their own ruins in that of the kingdom. [*HR, VIII*, 181–97]

Before the second version of the self-denying ordinance was finally passed, on 3 April 1645, Essex, Manchester, and Waller laid down their commands. Cromwell, though, remained in the army, with his commission renewed on a temporary basis. Parliament had also been working on plans for a reorganization of the army: the new model ordinance was passed on 15 February, giving the command to Sir Thomas Fairfax, and setting out a new system for ensuring that the troops were regularly paid. It was to be the foundation of Parliament's military success.

11. The Failure of Peace and the End of the War: Uxbridge and Naseby

The revival of an attempt to secure a negotiated peace at the end of 1644 was largely the effect of the entry of the Scots into the war. Parliament's propositions for peace, delivered to the King on 24 November 1644, were heavily influenced by the Scots, particularly in demanding a Presbyterian settlement of the Church. The negotiations began at the end of January at Uxbridge, mid-way between the King at Oxford and Parliament in London. Many, though, were confident that they would fail, given the King's adamant refusal to contemplate the removal of episcopacy from the Church of England. Both sides seem to have used the negotiations for propaganda advantage, and perhaps to secure defections from the other camp. Hyde was heavily involved in the treaty.

ABOUT the end of January, or the beginning of February, the commissioners on both sides met at Uxbridge;* which being within the enemy's quarters, the King's commissioners were to have such accommodations as the other thought fit to leave to them; who had been very civil in the distribution, and left one entire side of the town to the King's commissioners, one house only excepted, which was given to the lord of Pembroke; so that they had no cause to complain of their accommodation, which was as good as the town would yield, and as good as the others had. There was a fair house at the end of the town which was provided for the treaty, where was a fair room in the middle of the house, which was handsomely dressed up for the commissioners to sit in; a large square table being placed in the middle, with handsome seats for the commissioners to sit, one side being sufficient for those of either party, and a rail for others who should be thought necessary to be present, which went round. And there were many other rooms on either side of this great room, for the commissioners on either side to retire to, when they thought fit to consult together, and to return again to the public debate; and there being good stairs at either end of the house, they never went through each other's quarters, nor met but in the great room.

As soon as the King's commissioners came to the town, all those of the Parliament came to visit and to welcome them, and within an hour those of the King returned their visits with ordinary civilities; each professing great desire and hope that the treaty would produce a good peace. The visits were all together, and in one room, the Scots being in the same room with the English; either party eating always together, there being two great inns which served very well to that purpose, and the duke of Richmond, being Steward of his majesty's house, kept his table there for all the commissioners. Nor was there any restraint from giving and receiving visits apart, as their acquaintance and inclinations disposed them; in which those of the King's party used their accustomed freedom as heretofore; but on the other side there was great wariness and reservation, and so great a jealousy of each other that they had no mind to give or receive visits from their old friends whom they loved better than their new, nor would any of them be seen alone with any of the King's commissioners, but had always one of their companions with them, and sometimes one whom they least trusted. And it was observed by the town and the people that flocked thither that the King's commissioners looked as if they were at home and governed the town, and the other as if they were not in their own quarters: and the truth is, they had not that alacrity and serenity of mind as men use to have who do not believe themselves to be in a fault.

The King's commissioners would willingly have performed their devotions in the church, nor was there any restraint upon them from doing so, that is, by inhibition from the Parliament, otherwise than that by the Parliament's ordinance (as they called it) the Book of Common Prayer was not permitted to be read,* nor the vestures nor ceremonies of the Church to be used. So that the days of devotion were observed in their great room of the inn; whither many of the country, and of the train of the commissioners, and other persons who came every day from London, usually resorted.

When the commissioners on both sides met first together in the room appointed for the treaty, and had taken their seats, it being left to the King's commissioners which side of the table they would take, the earl of Northumberland, who always delivered any thing that was agreed between them, and read all the papers, after the powers of both sides were examined and perused, proposed some rules to be observed in the treaty; of having nothing binding except all were agreed upon, and such like; to which there was no objection; [and] proposed, as a direction they had received from the Parliament, that they should first enter upon the matter of religion, and treat four entire days upon that subject, without entering upon any other; and if all differences in that particular were not adjusted within those days, they should then proceed to the next point, which was the militia, and observe the same method in that; and from thence pass to the business of Ireland; which three points being well settled, they believed the other differences would be with more ease composed: and after those twelve days were passed, they were to go round again upon the several subjects as long as the time limited would continue; his majesty being left at liberty to propose what he thought fit at his own time, and to break the method proposed. And it was declared that the twenty days limited for the treaty were to be reckoned of the days which should be spent in the treaty, and not the days of coming or returning, or the days spent in devotion; there falling out three Sundays and one fast-day in those first twenty days. The method was willingly consented to; the King's commissioners conceiving that it would be to no purpose to propose any thing on the King's behalf till they discerned what agreement was like to be made in any one particular, by which they might take their measures; and they could propose any thing of moment under one of the three heads which are mentioned before.

There happened a very odd accident the very first morning they met at the house to agree upon their method to be observed in the treaty. It was a market-day, when they used always to have a sermon, and many of the persons who came from Oxford in the commissioners' train went to the church to observe the new forms. There was one Love,* a young man that came from London with the commissioners, who preached, and told his auditory, which consisted of all the people of the town and of those who came to the market, the church being very full, that they were not to expect any good from that treaty; for that they were men of blood who were employed in it from Oxford, who intended only to amuse the people with the expectation of peace till they were able to do some notable mischief to them; and inveighed so seditiously against all cavaliers, that is, against all who followed the King, and against the persons of the commissioners, that he could be understood to intend nothing else but to stir up the people to mutiny, and in it to do some act of violence upon the commissioners; who were no sooner advertised of it by several persons who had been present in the church, and who gave very particular information of the very words which had been spoken, than they informed the other commissioners of it, gave them a charge in writing against the preacher, and demanded public justice. They seemed troubled at it, and promised to examine it, and cause some severe punishment to be inflicted upon the man; but afterwards confessed that they had no authority to punish him, but that they had caused him to be sharply reprehended and to be sent out of the town: and this was all that could be obtained; so unwilling they were to discountenance any man who was willing to serve them. And this is the same Love who some years after, by Cromwell's particular prosecution, had his head cut off upon Tower Hill for being against the army.

It is not the purpose of this discourse to set down the particular transactions of this treaty, which were published by the King's order shortly after the conclusion of it, and all the papers which had been delivered by the commissioners on either side exposed to the view of the kingdom, in the method and manner in which they were delivered. Only such particulars as fell out in that time and were never communicated, and many of them known to very few, shall be shortly mentioned, that they who hereafter may have the perusal of this may know how impossible it was that this treaty could produce such a peace as both sides would have been glad of, and that they who governed the Parliament then had at that time the resolution to act those monstrous things which they brought afterwards to pass.

The first business to be entered upon being that of religion, the divines of both sides were admitted to be present, in places appointed for them, opposite to each other; and Dr Stewart, Clerk of the closet to the King, was a commissioner, as Mr Henderson* was on the other side; and they both sat covered without the bar, at the backs of the commissioners. On the Parliament part it was proposed that all the bishops, deans, and chapters, might be immediately taken away and abolished, and, in the room thereof, that there might be such another government erected as should be most agreeable to God's word and the practice of the best churches: that the Book of Common Prayer might be taken away and totally suppressed, and that, instead thereof, a Directory might be used, in which there was likewise set down as much of the government which they meant to erect for the future as was necessary to be provided for the present, and which supplied all the use of Articles or Canons which they had likewise abolished; and that the King himself would take the Covenant, and consent to an act of Parliament whereby all persons of the kingdom should be likewise obliged to take it. And the copies of the Covenant and the Directory were delivered at the same time to the King's commissioners; which were very long, and necessary to be read over before they could make any answer. And so they took that afternoon to peruse them together, and adjourned their treaty till the next morning; and though they entered upon the reading them before dinner, the Directory was so very long that they spent all that afternoon and some part of the night before they had finished the reading of them. And then, there being many new terms in the Directory, as *congregational, classical, provincial,* and *synodical,* which were not known in practice, and some expressions in the Covenant which were ambiguous, and, they well knew, were left so because the persons who framed them were not all of one mind, nor had the same intentions in some of the other terms mentioned before, the commissioners caused many questions to be prepared in writing, to be offered at the next meeting, wherein they desired to be informed what their meaning was in such and such expressions, in which they knew well they had several meanings and would hardly concur in one and the same answer: the preparing which papers was, throughout the treaty, always committed to the Chancellor.

Within a day or two after the beginning of the treaty, or rather the day before it did begin, the earl of Loudon, Chancellor of Scotland, visited the duke of Richmond privately in his chamber, and either proposed, or was very willing, to have private conference there with the Chancellor of the Exchequer; upon which the duke, who knew well the other would not decline it, sent to him, and he presently went to the duke's chamber, where he found them both; and, after some short compliments, the earl told him how stoutly he had defended his knighthood,* which the Parliament had resolved to have denied if he had not convinced them. From thence he discoursed of the great prejudice the Parliament had against him, as a man who more industriously opposed peace than any other of the King's Council: that he had now a good opportunity to wipe off all those jealousies by being a good instrument in making this peace, and by persuading his majesty to comply with the desires and supplications of his Parliament, which he hoped he would be.

The Chancellor told him, that the King did so much desire a peace that no man need advise him, or could divert him, if fair and honourable conditions of peace were offered to him; but if a peace could not be had but upon such conditions as his majesty judged inconsistent with his honour or his conscience, no man would have credit enough to persuade him to accept it; and that for his own part, without reflecting upon the good or ill opinion the Parliament might have of him, he would dissuade him from consenting to it. The other seemed disappointed in his so positive answer: yet with great freedom entered upon discourse of the whole matter, and, after some kind of apology that Scotland was so far engaged in the quarrel, contrary to their former intentions and professions, he did as good as conclude that if the King would satisfy them in the business of the Church, they would not concern themselves in any of the other demands. In which proposition finding no kind of compliance from the Chancellor of the Exchequer, but sharp protestations against the demand, as inconsistent with conscience, justice, or religion, the conference brake off, without inclination in either of them to renew it. But from that time there was more contradiction and quick repartees between them two throughout the treaty, than between any other of the body of the commissioners. And it was manifest enough, by the private conferences with other of the commissioners, that the Parliament took none of the points in controversy less to heart, or were less united in, than in what concerned the Church.

When upon the next meeting of the commissioners the questions which are mentioned before were read and delivered by the duke of Richmond, who always performed that part on the behalf of the King's as the earl of Northumberland did on the Parliament's, there was a visible disorder in their countenances; some of them, smiling, said we 'looked into their game'; but without offering at any answer, they rose, and went to their room of consultation, where they remained in great passion and wrangling many hours; so that the other commissioners, finding that they were not like suddenly to agree, adjourned till the afternoon, and departed to dinner. As soon as they came together in the afternoon, and were sat, the earl of Northumberland said that they wondered there should appear any difficulty in any expressions upon which those questions had been administered in the morning, which to them seemed very clear and plain; however, to give their lordships satisfaction, that they had appointed another noble lord there present, who was well acquainted with the signification of all those words, to explain what the common sense and meaning of them was. Thereupon the earl of Lauderdale made a discourse upon the several questions, and what acceptation those expressions and words had; and, being a young man, not accustomed to an orderly and decent way of speaking, and having no gracious pronunciation, and full of passion, he made everything much more difficult than it was before: so that the commissioners desired that they might receive an answer in writing; since it was declared upon the entrance of the treaty, that though in debate any man might say what he thought necessary, yet nothing should be understood to be the sense of either side but what was delivered in writing; and therefore they desired that what that noble lord had said, which they presumed was the sense of all the rest, because they had referred to him, and seemed satisfied with what he had delivered, might be given to them in writing; without which they knew not how to proceed, or give an answer to what was proposed to them. This demand, founded upon a rule of their own, which they knew not how to decline, put the Scots' commissioners into great passion: for all the English sat still without speaking word, as if they were not concerned. The lord Lauderdale repeated what he had said before, a little more distinctly; and the Chancellor of Scotland said that the things were so plain that every man could not choose but understand and remember what was spoken, and that the pressing to put it in writing was only to spend time, which would be quickly out, half the four days assigned for the business of religion being already to expire that night; and therefore passionately desired them that they would rest satisfied with what had been spoken, and proceed upon the matter.

It was replied, that they could not trust their memories so far as to prepare an answer to their demand concerning the Covenant or the Directory, except they were sure that they understood the full and declared meaning of their demand; which they had less reason now to believe they did than before, since there was so much difficulty made to satisfy them in writing; and therefore they must insist upon receiving an answer to the papers they had given. And two or three of the King's commissioners withdrew, and prepared another paper, in which they set down the reasons which obliged them not to be satisfied with the discourse which had been made, and why they must insist upon the having it in writing; which being communicated to the rest as they sat, was likewise delivered to them, who could not refuse to receive it, though it was plain enough they never intended to give any answer in writing, nor the others to desist from demanding it. But they declared that as they presumed they should in the end receive their answer in writing, which they should not depart from, so it was their resolution not to defer their further proceeding upon the matter, but they were ready to prosecute that in the method they would desire; and so it was resolved the next morning to hear the divines, who were of either party, what they would say against or for episcopacy, and the government and lands of the Church, which were equally concerned in the debate. . . .

When the last of the four first days was past, for it was near twelve of the clock at night, and the Scots' commissioners observed that nothing was consented to which they looked for, the Chancellor of Scotland entered into a long discourse with much passion against bishops, of the mischief they had done in all ages, and of their being the sole causes of the late troubles in Scotland and of the present troubles in England: remembered that the archbishop of Canterbury had pursued the introduction of the Liturgy and the Canons into Scotland with so great vehemence, that, when it was desired that the publishing them might be suspended for one month that the people might be the better prepared to submit to what they had not been before acquainted with, he would by no means consent to that delay, but caused it to be entered upon the next Sunday, against the advice of many of the bishops themselves, which put the people into such a fury that they could not be appeased. He lamented and complained that four days had been now spent in fruitless debates, and that though their divines had learnedly made it appear that episcopacy had no foundation in Scripture, and that it might lawfully be taken away, and that notwithstanding it was evident that it had been the cause of great mischief, and the wisdom of Parliament had thought the utter taking it away to be absolutely necessary for the preservation of the kingdom, their lordships were still unmoved, and had yielded in no one particular of importance to give them satisfaction; from which they could not but conclude, that they did not bring that hearty inclination to peace which they hoped they would have done; and so concluded with some expressions more rude and insolent than were expected.

Whereupon the Chancellor of the Exchequer, not without some commotion, said, that he did not wonder that their lordships who had for some years been accustomed to such discourses, and the more inclined to suppose all that was confidently said to be reasonably proved, and so having not been used to converse with any persons of a contrary opinion, had been brought to consent and approve those alterations which they had proposed; but that it seemed very admirable to him, that their lordships could expect, or imagine it possible, that they who never had heard such things said before, nor could understand in so little time what had been now said, should depart from a faith and a form of worship in which they had been educated from their cradle, and which, upon so long observation and experience, they looked upon with all possible approbation and reverence, upon only hearing it inveighed against four days; which would have been much too little time to have warranted a conversion from much less important opinions which they had so long entertained, though their arguments had had as much weight as they wanted. He said, they were of opinion that all those mischiefs and inconveniences which they had mentioned had in truth proceeded from an over vehement desire to overthrow episcopacy, not from the zeal to support it: that if the archbishop of Canterbury had been too precipitate in pressing the reception of that which he thought a reformation, he paid dearly for it; which made him the more wonder, that they should blame them for not submitting to much greater alterations than were at that time proposed, in four days, when they reproached him for not having given them a whole month to consider of. He said, he might assure their lordships, with great sincerity, that they were come thither with all imaginable passion and desire that the treaty might conclude in a happy and blessed peace; as he still hoped it would: but if it should be otherwise, that they would still believe that their lordships brought with them the same honourable and pious inclinations, though the instructions and commands from those who trusted them restrained them from consenting to what in their own judgments seemed reasonable. And so, without any manner of reply, both sides rose and departed, it being near midnight.

There happened a pleasant accident on one of those days which were assigned for the matter of religion. The commissioners of both sides, either before their sitting or after their rising, entertaining themselves together by the fire-side, as they sometimes did, it being extremely cold, in general and casual discourses, one of the King's commissioners asking one of the other, with whom he had familiarity, in a low voice, why there was not in their whole Directory any mention of the Lord's Prayer, the Creed, or the Ten Commandments, (as indeed there is not,) the earl of Pembroke, overhearing the discourse, answered aloud, and with his usual passion, that he and many others were very sorry that they had been left out; that the putting them in had taken up many hours' debate in the House of Commons, and that at last the leaving them out had been carried by eight or nine voices, and so they did not think fit to insist upon the addition of them in the House of Peers; but many were afterwards troubled at it, and he verily believed, if it were to do again, they should carry it for the inserting all three. Which made many smile, to hear that the Lord's Prayer, the Creed, and the Ten Commandments, had been put to the question, and rejected: and many of the other were troubled and out of countenance with the reason the good lord had given for the exclusion.

The next subject of the treaty was the business of the militia; which the commissioners positively required to be entirely vested in the Parliament, and in such persons as they thought fit to be confided in. And this they said was more necessary than ever, for the securing the people from their fears and jealousies, which were now much increased, and were capable of being assuaged by no other means: and delivered a large paper to that purpose, which contained no more than had been often said in their declarations, and as often answered in those which had been published by the King. And when the commissioners of the

King, whereof there were four very eminent in the knowledge of the law, Lane, Gardiner, Bridgeman, and Palmer,* made the demand appear to be without any pretence of law or justice, and asserted it to be vested in the King by the law, they never offered to allege any other argument than the determination of the Parliament, which had declared the right of the militia to be in them, from which they could not recede. So that the conferences were very short upon those days, but the papers very long which were mutually delivered, the preparing whereof took up the time; they of that side (even they who most desired the peace) both publicly and privately insisting upon having the whole command of the militia by sea and land, and all the forts and ships of the kingdom at their disposal; without which they looked upon themselves as lost and at the King's mercy, without considering that he must be at theirs if such a jurisdiction was committed to them. But in this particular, he who was most reasonable amongst them thought it very unreasonable to deny them that necessary security; and believed it could proceed from nothing else but a resolution to take the highest vengeance upon their rebellion. [*HR*, VIII, 215–33]

Having failed to come to any resolution on the first two heads of the treaty, the commissioners could not agree on the third either: how to deal with the rebellion in Ireland. Despite twelve fruitless days, the royalist commissioners were excited by intercepted parliamentary correspondence which showed the hostility of the Independents in Parliament to the treaty, to the Earl of Essex, and to the Scots.

The conversation that this letter occasioned between some of the commissioners of both sides, who in private used their old freedom, made a great discovery of the faction that was in the Parliament: that there were many who desired to have peace, without any alteration in the government, so they might be sure of indemnity and security for what was past; that the Scots would insist upon the whole government of the Church, and in all other matters would defer to the King; but that there was another party that would have no peace upon what conditions soever, who did resolve to change the whole frame of the government in State as well as Church, which made a great party in the army: and all those of the Parliament who desired to remove the earl of Essex from being general of the army, and to make another general, were of that party. There was likewise amongst the commissioners themselves very little trust and communication, sir Harry Vane, St John, and Prideaux,* being, upon the matter, but spies upon the rest; and though most of the rest did heartily desire a peace, even upon any terms, yet none of them had the courage to avow the receding from the most extravagant demand. And there was reason enough to believe that if the King had yielded to all that was then proposed, they would likewise have insisted upon all which they had formerly demanded, and upon the delivery up of all those persons who had faithfully served the King, and who had been by them always excepted as persons never to be pardoned.

For though they had assigned those three general heads, of the Church, of the militia, and of Ireland, to be first treated upon, which were all popular and plausible arguments, and in which they who most desired peace would insist at least upon many condescensions, yet they had not in the least degree declined any other of their propositions; as, the exemption of many of the greatest quality, or of the most declared affections to the King, in the three nations of England, Scotland, and Ireland, from pardon, and the making the estates of the rest, under the name of *delinquents*, liable to pay the charges of the war; in which, or any of the other very unreasonable demands, they had not in their instructions given their commissioners authority in the least particle to recede: they who desired peace being satisfied that they had prevailed to have a treaty, which they imagined would do all the rest, and that these lesser demands would fall off of themselves when satisfaction should be given in those important particulars which more concerned the public; and, on the other side, they who resolved the treaty should be ineffectual were well content that their commissioners should be instructed only to insist upon those three generals, without power to depart from any one expression in the propositions concerning those particulars; being satisfied that in the particular which concerned the Church the Scots would never depart from a tittle, and as sure that the King would never yield to it; and that in the militia they who most desired peace would adhere to that which most concerned their own security; and in the business of Ireland, besides the opportunity to asperse the King upon an argument in which the people generally concurred with them, they were safe enough, except the King should absolutely retract and recant all that he had done, and by declaring the cessation void* expose all those who had a hand in it to their censure and judgment, and so dissolve all the authority he had in that kingdom for the future; which they knew he would never do. So that they were safe enough in those three heads for their treaty, without bringing any of their other demands into debate; which would have spent much time, and raised great difference in opinion amongst them; yet they had those still in reserve, and might reasonably conclude that if the

King satisfied them in the terms of those three propositions, he would never insist upon any of the rest, which could not relate so much to his conscience or his honour as the other. Besides, they knew well that, if by the King's condescensions they had full satisfaction in the former three, they who had most passion for peace would, for their own shares in the particular revenge upon those men with whom they were angry enough, and in the preferments which would be then in their disposal, never divide from them in any thing that remained to be demanded.

One night, late, the earl of Pembroke came to the Chancellor of the Exchequer's lodging to return him a visit, and sat with him some hours; all his discourse being to persuade him to think it reasonable to consent to all that the Parliament had demanded. He told him that there was never such a pack of knaves and villains as they who now governed in the Parliament, who would so far prevail if this treaty were broke as to remove the earl of Essex, and then they would constitute such an army as should force the Parliament, as well as the King, to consent to whatsoever they demanded; which would end in the change of the government into that of a commonwealth. The Chancellor told him, if he believed that, it was high time for the Lords to look about them, who would be then no less concerned than the King. He confessed it, and that they were now sensible that they had brought this mischief upon themselves, and did heartily repent it, though too late, and when they were in no degree able to prevent the general destruction which they foresaw: but if the King would be so gracious to them, as to preserve them by consenting to those unreasonable propositions which were made by the Parliament, the other wicked persons would be disappointed by such his concessions; the earl of Essex would still keep his power; and they should be able, in a short time after the peace concluded, by adhering to the King, whom they would never forsake hereafter, to recover all for him that he now parted with, and to drive those wicked men who would destroy monarchy out of the kingdom, and then his majesty would be greater than ever. How extravagant soever this discourse seems to be, the matter of it was the same which the wisest of the rest (and there were men of very good parts amongst them) did seriously urge to other of the King's commissioners, with whom they had the same confidence: so broken they were in their spirits, and so corrupted in their understanding, even when they had their own ruin in their view.

The earl of Northumberland, who was the proudest man alive, could not look upon the destruction of monarchy, and the contempt the nobility was already reduced to, and [which] must be then improved, with any pleasure: yet the repulse he had formerly received at Oxford* upon his addresses thither, and the fair escape he had made afterwards from the jealousy of the Parliament, had wrought so far upon him, that he resolved no more to depend upon the one or to provoke the other, and was willing to see the King's power and authority so much restrained that he might not be able to do him any harm.

The earls of Pembroke and Salisbury were so totally without credit or interest in the Parliament or country, that it was no matter which way their inclinations or affections disposed them; and their fear of the faction that prevailed was so much greater than their hatred towards them, that, though they wished they might rather be destroyed than the King, they had rather the King and his posterity should be destroyed than that Wilton should be taken from the one of them or Hatfield* from the other; the preservation of both which from any danger they both believed to be the highest point of prudence and politic circumspection.

The earl of Denbigh had much greater parts, and saw further before him into the desperate designs of that party that had then the power, than either of the other three, and detested those designs as much as any of them; yet the pride of his nature, not inferior to the proudest, and the conscience of his ingratitude to the King, in some respects superior to theirs who had been most obliged, kept him from being willing to quit their company with whom he had conversed too long, though he had received from them most signal affronts and indignities, and well knew he should never more be employed by them; yet he thought the King's condition to be utterly desperate, and that he would be at last compelled to yield to worse conditions than were now offered to him. He conferred with so much freedom with one of the King's commissioners, and spent so much time with him in the vacant hours, there having been formerly a great friendship between them, that he drew some jealousy upon himself from some of his companions. With him he lamented his own condition, and acknowledged his disloyalty to the King with expressions of great compunction, and protested that he would most willingly redeem his transgressions by any attempt that might serve the King signally, though he were sure to lose his life in it; but that to lose himself without any benefit to the King would expose him to all misery, which he would decline by not separating from his party. He informed him more fully of the wicked purposes of those who then governed the Parliament than others apprehended or imagined, and had a full prospect of the vile condition himself and all the nobility should be reduced to; yet thought it impossible to prevent it by any activity of their own; and concluded, that if any conjuncture fell out in which by losing his life he might preserve the King, he would embrace the occasion; otherwise, he would shift the best he could for himself.

Of the commissioners of the House of Commons, though, the three named before being excepted, the rest did in their hearts desire a peace, and upon much honester conditions than they durst own, yet there were not two of them who had entire confidence in each other, or who durst communicate their thoughts together: so that, though they would speak their minds freely enough, severally, to those commissioners of the King's side with whom they had former friendship, they would not in the presence of any of their own companions use that freedom. The debate that had been in the House upon the self-denying Ordinance had raised so many jealousies, and discomposed the confidence that had formerly been between many of them, that they knew not what any man intended to do; many who had from the beginning of the troubles professed to have most devotion for the earl of Essex, and to abhor all his enemies, had lately seemed to concur in that ordinance, which was contrived principally for his dishonour and destruction; and others who seemed still to adhere to him, did it with so many cautions that there could be no confidence of their perseverance.

Holles, who was the frankest amongst them in owning his animosity and indignation against all the Independent party, and was no otherwise affected to the Presbyterians than as they constituted a party upon which he depended to oppose the other, did foresee that many of those who appear[ed] most resolute to concur with him would by degrees fall from him purely for want of courage, in which he abounded. Whitelocke, who from the beginning had concurred with them without any inclination to their persons or principles, had the same reason still not to separate from them: all his estate was in their quarters, and he had a nature that could not bear or submit to be undone: yet to his friends who were commissioners for the King he used his old openness, and professed his detestation of all their proceedings, yet could not leave them. Pierrepoint and Crew,* who were both men of great fortunes, and had always been of the greatest moderation in their counsels, and most solicitous upon all opportunities for peace, appeared now to have contracted more bitterness and sourness than formerly, and were more reserved towards the King's commissioners than was expected, and in all conferences insisted peremptorily that the King must yield to whatsoever was demanded in the three demands which had been debated. They all valued themselves upon having induced the Parliament, against all opposition, to consent to a treaty; which producing no effect, they should hereafter have no more credit; and it plainly appeared, that they had persuaded themselves that in the treaty they should be able to persuade the King's commissioners to concur with them, and that the King would yield upon the very same argument and expectation that the earl of Pembroke had offered to the Chancellor.

Some of them, who knew how impossible it was to prevail with the commissioners, or, if they could be corrupted so far in their judgments, how much more impossible it would be to persuade the King to consent to what was so diametrically against his conscience and his honour, and, in truth, against his security, did wish that in order to get the time of the treaty prolonged some concessions might be made in the point of the militia, in order to their security; which being provided for might probably take off many persons who, out of that consideration principally, adhered to those who they thought were most jealous of it and most solicitous for it. And this seemed such an expedient to those to whom they proposed it, that they thought fit to make a debate amongst all the commissioners; and if it did produce no other effect than the getting more days to the treaty, and [making] more divisions in the Parliament, both which they might naturally expect from it, the benefit was not small that would attend it; for as long as the treaty lasted there could be no advance made towards new modelling the army, the delay whereof would give the King likewise more time to make his preparations for the field, towards which he was in no forwardness. And this consideration prevailed with the commissioners to send their opinion to the King that he should give them leave to propose, when the next day came for the debate of the point of the militia, that the whole militia of the kingdom should be settled in such a number of persons, for seven or eight years, who should be all sworn to the observation of all the articles which should be agreed upon in the treaty; after the expiration of which time, which would be sufficient to extinguish all jealousies, it should be restored to the King. And they sent the King a list of such names as they wished might be inserted in the proposition, of persons in credit with the Parliament, to which his majesty might add the like number of such of whose fidelity he was most assured.

The earls of Essex, Northumberland, Warwick, and Manchester, with Fairfax and Cromwell, were amongst those they recommended to be named by the King. And with this message they sent two of their own body, who added other reasons, which they conceived might prevail with him; and his majesty was with great difficulty prevailed with to consent that such an overture should be made; and, being unwilling to dissent from his commissioners' judgment, and especially in confidence that it would be rejected, and in hope that it would gain time by lengthening the treaty, his majesty was contented that the commissioners should make such an offer as is mentioned, and name the persons they had proposed of the Parliament party. But then he sent a list of such persons as himself thought fit to trust in that affair, and in whom, together with the other, he would have the power of the militia to be vested. But by this time, the term assigned for the treaty drawing towards an end, they who had first advised this expedient had not the same opinion of the success, and had plainly discovered that the Parliament would not consent to add one day more to the treaty; [and so] the farther prosecution of the overture in that manner was laid aside. For the King's commissioners concluded, that at this time to offer any particular names from the King to be trusted with the militia were but to expose those persons to reproach, as some of them were very ungracious and unpopular, and to give the other side an excuse for rejecting the offer upon exception to their persons. However, that they might see a greater condescension from the King in that point than he had ever yet been induced to, they offered that the militia should be so settled for the space of seven years as they had desired, in such a number of persons as should be agreed upon, a moiety of which persons should be nominated by the King, and the other moiety by the Parliament: which was rejected by them with their usual neglect.

From this time the commissioners on both sides grew more reserved and colder towards each other; insomuch as in the last conferences the answers and replies upon one another were more sharp and reflecting than they had formerly been: and in their conference upon the last day, which held most part of the night, it was evident either side laboured most to make the other seem to be most in fault. And the King's commissioners delivered a paper which contained a sum of all that had been done in the treaty, and observed that, after a war of so many years, entered into, as was pretended, for the defence and vindication of the laws of the land and the liberty of the subject, in a treaty of twenty days they had not demanded any one thing that by the law of the land they had the least title to demand, but insisted only on such particulars as were against law and the established government of the kingdom; and that much more had been offered to them for the obtaining of peace than they could with justice or reason require: with which they were so offended that they for some time refused to receive the paper, upon pretence that the time for the treaty was expired, because it was then after twelve of the clock of the night of the twentieth day: but at last they were contented to receive it, finding that it would not be less public, and would more reflect upon them, if they rejected it: and so they parted a little before the break of day.*

And the next day, being Sunday, they rested in the town, that they might in the afternoon decently take their leave of each other; though Monday, according to the letter of their pass, was the last day of their freedom, and at that season of the year their journey to Oxford might require two days, and they had spent two days in coming thither; and the commissioners for the Parliament had given them a paper in which they declared that they might safely make use of another day for their return, of which no advantage should be taken. But they having on Sunday performed their mutual visits to each other they parted with such a dryness towards each other as if they scarce hoped to meet again; and the King's commissioners were so unwilling to run any hazard, or to depend upon their words, that they were on the Monday morning so early in their coaches that they came to Oxford that night, and kissed the King's hand; who received them very graciously, and thanked them for the pains they had taken. And surely the pains they had taken, with how little success soever, was very great; and they who had been most inured to business had not in their lives ever undergone so great fatigue for twenty days together as at that treaty; the commissioners seldom parting during that whole time till one or two of the clock in the morning, and they being obliged to sit up long after who were to prepare such papers as were directed for the next day, and to write letters to Oxford; so that if the treaty had continued longer it is very probable many of the commissioners would have fallen sick for want of sleep; which some of them were not satisfied with in three or four days after their return to Oxford. And thus ended the treaty of Uxbridge, the particulars whereof were by the King's command shortly after published in print, and never contradicted by the Parliament.

After the treaty of Uxbridge the King spake to those he trusted most at that time with much more melancholique of his own condition and the state of his affairs than he had used to do. The loss of Shrewsbury* was attended with many ill consequences; and that which had seemed to bring some kind of recompense for it, which was the surprise of Weymouth, proved but a dream; for the enemy had lost but one part of the town, which they in a short time after recovered again,* by the usual negligence of the King's governors. So that his majesty told them he found it absolutely necessary to pursue his former resolution of separating the Prince his son from himself, that the enemy might not, upon any success, find them together, which, he said, would be ruin to them both; whereas, though he should fall into their hands, whilst his son was at liberty they would not dare to do him harm. He seemed to have very reasonable apprehensions that upon the loss of a battle he might become a prisoner; but he never imagined that it could enter into their thoughts to take away his life; not that he believed they could be restrained from that impious act by any remorse of conscience, or that they had not wickedness enough to design and execute it, but he believed it against their interest; and would often in discourse say, of what moment the preservation of his life was to the rebels, and how much they were concerned to preserve it, in regard that if his majesty were dead the Parliament stood dissolved, so that there would be an end of their government: which, though it were true in law, would have little shaken their government, of which they were too long possessed to part with easily. [*HR*, VIII, 241–53]

Despite the remarkable successes of the Earl of Montrose and his Highland insurgency against the Covenanting leadership in Scotland, the King's assessment of his situation in early 1645 was not unrealistic. Short of money, soldiers, and supplies, he dabbled in schemes to obtain Irish or foreign troops with funding from the Pope, the French, or other Catholic princes. In an attempt to revive the royalist effort in the south-west, at the beginning of March he sent his son, Charles, Prince of Wales, to take nominal charge, supported by a Council which included the moderates Hopton, Capel, Culpepper, and Hyde. But the Prince's dispatch was also motivated by the need to prevent the heir to the throne from falling into enemy hands. Although Parliament still had problems of its own, the chances had now become stacked heavily against the King. To Hyde, though, writing here when putting together his final version of the text in 1671, the impending disaster of the royal cause was due as much to the failures of leadership on his own side.

We are now entering upon a time, the representation and description whereof must be the most unpleasant and ingrateful to the reader, in respect of the subject matter of it; which must consist of no less weakness and folly on the one side than of malice and wickedness on the other; and as unagreeable and difficult to the writer, in regard that he shall please very few who acted then upon the stage of business, but that he must give as severe characters of the persons, and as severely censure the actions of many who wished very well, and had not the least thought of disloyalty or infidelity, as of those who, with the most deliberate impiety, prosecuted their design to ruin and destroy the Crown: a time in which the whole stock of affection, loyalty, and courage, which at first alone engaged men in the quarrel, seemed to be quite spent, and to be succeeded by negligence, laziness, inadvertency and dejection of spirit, contrary to the natural temper, vivacity, and constancy of the nation, and in which they who pretended most public-heartedness, and did really wish the King all the greatness he desired to preserve for himself, did sacrifice the public peace and the security of their master to their own passions and appetites, to their ambition and animosities against each other, without the least design of treachery or damage towards his majesty: a time in which want of discretion and mere folly produced as much mischief as the most barefaced villainy could have done, and in which the King suffered as much by the irresolution and unsteadiness of his own counsels, and by the ill humour and faction of his counsellors, by their not foreseeing what was evident to most other men, and by their jealousies of what was not like to fall out, sometimes by deliberating too long without resolving, and as often resolving without any deliberation, and, most of all, not executing vigorously what was well deliberated and resolved, as by the indefatigable industry and the irresistible power and strength of his enemies.

All these things must be very particularly enlarged upon, and exposed to the naked view, in the relation of what fell out in this year (1645) in which we are engaged, except we will swerve from that precise rule of ingenuity and integrity which we profess to observe, and thereby leave the reader more perplexed to see the most prodigious accidents fall out without discerning the no less prodigious causes which produced them; which would lead him into as wrong an estimate of things, and persuade him to believe that a universal corruption of the hearts of the whole nation had brought forth those lamentable effects; which proceeded only from the folly and the frowardness, from the weakness and the wilfulness, the pride and the passion, of particular persons, whose memories ought to be charged with their own evil actions, rather than they should be preserved as the infamous charge of the age in which they lived; which did produce as many men eminent for their loyalty and incorrupted fidelity to the Crown as any that had preceded it. Nor is it possible to discourse all these particulars with that clearness that must subject them to common understandings, without opening a door for such reflections upon the King himself as shall seem to call both his wisdom and his courage into question, as if he had wanted the one to apprehend and discover, and the other to prevent, the mischiefs which threatened him. All which considerations might very well discourage, and even terrify, me from prosecuting this part of the work with that freedom and openness as must call many things to memory which are forgotten, or were never understood, and rather persuade me to satisfy myself with a bare relation of what was done, and with the known event of that miserable year, (which in truth produced all that followed in the next,) without prying too strictly into the causes of those effects, which might seem rather to be the production of Providence, and the instances of divine displeasure, than to proceed from the weakness and inadvertency of any men, not totally abandoned by God Almighty to the most unruly lusts of their own appetite and inventions.

But I am too far embarked in this sea already, and have proceeded with too much simplicity and sincerity with reference to things and persons, and in the examination of the grounds and oversights of counsels, to be now frighted with the prospect of those materials which must be comprehended within the relation of this year's transactions. I know myself to be very free from any of those passions which naturally transport men with prejudice towards the persons whom they are obliged to mention, and whose actions they are at liberty to censure. There is not a man who acted the worst part in this ensuing year with whom I had ever the least difference or personal unkindness, or towards whom I had not much inclination of kindness, or from whom I did not receive all invitations of farther endearments. There were many who were not free from very great faults and oversights in the counsels of this year with whom I had great friendship, and which I did not discontinue upon those unhappy oversights, nor did flatter them, when they were past, by excusing what they had done. I knew most of the things myself which I mention, and therefore can answer for the truth of them; and the most important particulars which were transacted in places very distant from me were transmitted to me by the King's immediate direction and order, even after he was in the hands and power of the enemy, and out of his own short memorials and journal. And as he was always severe to himself in censuring his own oversights, so he could not but well foresee that many of the misfortunes of this ensuing year would reflect upon some want of resolution in himself, as well as upon the gross errors and oversights, (to call them no worse) of those who were trusted by him. And therefore as I first undertook this difficult work with his approbation and by his encouragement, and for his vindication, so I enter upon this part of it principally that the world may see (at least if there be ever a fit season for such a communication, which is not like to be in this present age) how difficult it was for a prince, so unworthily reduced to those straits his majesty was in, to find ministers and instruments equal to the great work that was to be done; and how impossible it was for him to have better success under their conduct whom it was very natural for him to trust with it; and then, without being over solicitous to absolve him from those mistakes and weaknesses to which he was in truth liable, he will be found not only a prince of admirable virtue and piety, but of great parts, of knowledge, wisdom, and judgment; and that the most signal parts of his misfortunes proceeded most from the modesty of his nature, which kept him from trusting himself enough, and made him believe that others discerned better who were much inferior to him in those faculties, and so to depart often from his own reason, to follow the opinions of more unskilful men, whose affections he believed to be unquestionable to his service. And so we proceed in our relation of matter of fact. [*HR*, IX, 1–3]

In the south-west of England, with the Prince, Hyde's own war became a different one from the King's war, fought in the Midlands. Hyde, as a member of the Prince's council, became exasperated by what he saw as the capricious, insubordinate, and uncooperative behaviour of the royalist generals in the west — Sir George Goring, Sir Richard Grenville, and Sir John Berkeley. The main focus of military operations in the spring of 1645, however, was the King's own army, led by Prince Rupert. In early May it left Oxford, with plans to secure the Midlands and move north against the Scots. Parliament's army, under Fairfax, besieged Oxford. The King's success in seizing Leicester by storm at the end of May gave hope to the royalists. Charles turned back to relieve Oxford, while Fairfax and Cromwell turned to confront him. The two armies found each other close to the village of Naseby, in Leicestershire.

Upon the 13th of June the King received intelligence that Fairfax was advanced to Northampton with a strong army, much superior to the numbers he had formerly been advertised of. Whereupon he retired the next day to Harborough, and meant to have gone back to Leicester, that he might draw more foot out of Newark, and stand upon his defence till the other forces, which he expected, could come up to him. But that very night an alarum was brought to Harborough that Fairfax himself was quartered within six miles. A council was presently called, and the former resolution of retiring presently laid aside, and a new one as quickly taken to fight; to which there was always an immoderate appetite when the enemy was within any distance. They would not stay to expect his coming, but would go back to meet him. And so, in the morning early, being Saturday the 14th of June, all the army was drawn up, upon a rising ground of very great advantage, about a mile south from Harborough, (which was left at their back,) and there put in order to give or receive the charge. The main body of the foot was led by the lord Astley (whom the King had lately made a baron,) consisting of about two thousand and five hundred foot; the right wing of horse, being about two thousand, was led by prince Rupert; the left wing of horse, consisting of all the northern horse, with those from Newark, which did not amount to above sixteen hundred, was commanded by sir Marmaduke Langdale. In the reserve were the King's lifeguard, commanded by the earl of Lindsey, and prince Rupert's regiment of foot, both which did make very little above eight hundred; with the King's horse-guards, commanded by the lord Bernard Stuart, (newly made earl of Lichfield,) which made that day about five hundred horse.

The army thus disposed, in good order, made a stand on that ground to expect the enemy. About eight of the clock in the morning it began to be doubted whether the intelligence they had received of the enemy was true. Upon which the scoutmaster was sent to make farther discovery, who, it seems, went not far enough, but returned and averred, that he had been three or four miles forward, and could neither discover nor hear any thing of them: and presently a report was raised in the army that the enemy was retired. Prince Rupert thereupon drew out a party of horse and musketeers, both to discover and engage them, the army remaining still in the same place and posture they had been in. And his highness had not marched above a mile, when he received certain intelligence of their advance, and in a short time after he saw the van of their army, but it seems not so distinctly but that he conceived they were retiring. Whereupon he advanced nearer with his horse, and sent back that the army should march up to him; and the messenger who brought the order said, that the prince desired they should make haste. Hereupon the advantage ground was quitted, and the excellent order they were in, and an advance made towards the enemy as well as might be. By that time they had marched about a mile and an half, the horse of the enemy were discerned to stand upon a high ground about Naseby; and from thence seeing the manner of the King's march in a full *campania*, they had leisure and opportunity to place themselves with all the advantages they could desire. The prince his natural heat and impatience could never endure an enemy long in his view, nor believe that they had the courage to endure his charge. And so the army was engaged before the cannon was turned, or the ground made choice of upon which they were to fight: so that courage was only to be relied upon, where all conduct failed so much.

It was about ten of the clock when the battle began: and the first charge was given by prince Rupert, who, with his own and his brother prince Maurice his troop, performed it with his usual vigour, and was so well seconded that he bore down all before him, and was master of six pieces of the rebels' best cannon. The lord Astley, with his foot, though against the hill, advanced upon their foot, who discharged their cannon at them, but overshot them, and so did their musketeers too. For the foot on either side hardly saw each other until they were within carabine-shot, and so only gave one volley; the King's foot, according to their usual custom, falling in with their swords and the but-ends of their muskets, with which they did very notable execution, and put the enemy into great disorder and confusion. The right wing of horse and foot being thus fortunately engaged and advanced, the left wing, under sir Marmaduke Langdale, in five bodies, advanced with equal resolution; and was encountered by Cromwell, who commanded the right wing of the enemy's horse, with seven bodies greater and more numerous than either of the other, and had, besides the odds in number, the advantage of the ground; for the King's horse were obliged to march up the hill before they could charge them: yet they did their duty as well as the place and great inequality of numbers would enable them to do. But being flanked on both sides by the enemy's horse, and pressed hard before they could get to the top of the hill, they gave back, and fled farther and faster than became them. Four of the enemy's bodies, close and in good order, followed them, that they might not rally again; which they never thought of doing; and the rest charged the King's foot, who had so much the advantage over theirs; whilst prince Rupert, with the right wing, pursued those horse which he had broken and defeated.

The King's reserve of horse, which was his own guards, with himself in the head of them, were even ready to charge those horse who followed those of the left wing, when, on a sudden, such a panic fear seized upon them that they all ran near a quarter of a mile without stopping; which happened upon an extraordinary accident, which hath seldom fallen out, and might well disturb and disorder very resolute troops, as these were the best horse in the army. The King, as was said before, was even upon the point of charging the enemy, in the head of his guards, when the earl of Carnwath*, who rode next to him, (a man never suspected for infidelity, nor one from whom the King would have received counsel in such a case,) on a sudden laid his hand on the bridle of the King's horse, and swearing two or three full-mouthed Scots' oaths, (for of that nation he was,) said, 'Will you go upon your death in an instant?' and, before his majesty understood what he would have, turned his horse round; upon which a word ran through the troops that they should march to the right hand; which was both from charging the enemy, or assisting their own men. And upon this they all turned their horse[s] and rode upon the spur, as if they were every man to shift for himself.

It is very true that, upon the more soldierly word *Stand*, which was sent to run after them, many of them returned to the King; though the former unlucky word carried more from him. And by this time prince Rupert was returned with a good body of those horse which had attended him in his prosperous charge on the right wing; but they having, as they thought, acted their parts, they could never be brought to rally themselves again in order, or to charge the enemy. And that difference was observed shortly from the beginning of the war, in the discipline of the King's troops and of those which marched under the command of Cromwell, (for it was only under him, and had never been notorious under Essex or Waller,) that though the King's troops prevailed in the charge, and routed those they charged, they never rallied themselves again in order, nor could be brought to make a second charge again the same day: which was the reason that they had not an entire victory at Edgehill: whereas Cromwell's troops, if they prevailed, or though they were beaten and routed, presently rallied again, and stood in good order till they received new orders. All that the King and prince could do could not rally their broken troops, which stood in sufficient numbers upon the field, though they often endeavoured it with the manifest hazard of their own persons. So that in the end the King was compelled to quit the field, and to leave Fairfax master of all his foot, cannon, and baggage; amongst which was his own cabinet, where his most secret papers were, and letters between the Queen and him; of which they shortly after made that barbarous use as was agreeable to their natures, and published them in print, that is, so much of them as they thought would asperse either of their majesties and improve the prejudice they had raised against them, and concealed other parts which would have vindicated them from many particulars with which they had aspersed them.

It will not be seasonable in this place to mention the names of those noble persons who were lost in this battle, when the King and the kingdom were lost in it; though there were above one hundred and fifty officers, and gentlemen of prime quality, whose memories ought to be preserved, who were dead upon the spot. The enemy left no manner of barbarous cruelty unexercised that day, and in the pursuit killed above one hundred women, whereof some were officers' wives of quality. The King and prince Rupert, with the broken troops, marched by Leicester that night to Ashby de la Zouch; and the next day to Lichfield; and continued two days' march more, till he came to Bewdley in Worcestershire, where he rested one day; and then went to Hereford, with some disjointed imagination that he might, with those forces under Gerard, (who was general of South Wales,) who was indeed upon his march with a body of two thousand horse and foot, be able to have raised a new army. At Hereford prince Rupert, before any formed counsel was agreed upon what the King should do next, left the King, and made haste to Bristol, that he might put that place into a condition to resist a powerful and victorious enemy, which he had reason to believe would in a short time appear before it. And nothing can be here more wondered at, than that the King should amuse himself about forming a new army in counties which had been vexed and worn out with the oppressions of his own troops and the license of those governors whom he had put over them, and not have immediately repaired into the west, where he had an army already formed, and a people generally well devoted to his service, and whither general Gerard, and all his broken troops, might have transported themselves before Fairfax could have given them any interruption, who had somewhat to do before he could bend his course that way: of which unhappy omission we shall have too much occasion to take more notice of, after we have again visited the west. [*HR*, IX, 37–42]

12. The King's Surrender and the Royalist Diaspora

Following the crushing defeat at Naseby, the King retreated to Wales in an attempt to recruit another army: in the following months he moved between the Midlands and Wales, continuing to hope for assistance from Ireland, or the possibility of joining Montrose in Scotland. Fairfax turned to attack the royal army in the west, now led by Goring, and routed it at Langport on 10 July. Prince Rupert surrendered Bristol on 11 September. Montrose was decisively defeated at Philiphaugh, near Selkirk, two days later. Charles returned to Oxford on 5 November, following Rupert's decision to leave the country.

WE left the King in Oxford, free from the trouble and uneasiness of those perpetual and wandering marches in which he had been so many months exercised, and quiet from all rude and insolent provocations. He was now amongst his true and faithful councillors and servants, whose affection and loyalty had first engaged them in his service, and which stuck to him to the end; and who, if they were not able to give him assistance to stem that mighty torrent that overbore both him and them, paid him still the duty that was due to him, and gave him no vexation when they could not give him comfort. There were yet some garrisons which remained in his obedience, and which were like, during the winter season, to be preserved from any attempt of the enemy; but upon the approach of the spring, if the King should be without an army in the field, the fate of those few places was easy to be discerned. And which way an army could possibly be brought together, or where it should be raised, was not within the compass of the wisest man's comprehension. However, the more difficult it was, the more vigour was to be applied in the attempt. Worcester, as it was neighbouring to Wales, had the greatest outlet and elbow-room; and the Parliament party that had gotten any footing there behaved themselves with that insolence and tyranny, that even they who had called them thither were weary of them, and ready to enter into any combination to destroy them. Upon this prospect, and some invitation, the King sent the lord Astley (whom he had before, at his being at Cardiff, constituted governor of those parts, in the place of the lord Gerard) to Worcester, with order to proceed, as he should find himself able, towards the gathering a body of horse together against the spring from those garrisons which were left and from Wales: and what progress he made towards it will be part of the sad account which belongs to the next year.

When a full prospect, upon the most mature deliberation, was taken of all the hopes which might with any colour of reason be entertained, all that occurred appeared so hopeless and desperate [that] it was thought fit to resort to an old expedient that had been found as desperate as any; which was, a new overture for a treaty of peace: for which they who advised it had no other reason but that they could [not] tell what else to do. Cromwell had left Fairfax about Exeter, and with a party selected had sat down before Basing, and his imperious summons having been rejected, he stormed the place and took it, and put most of the garrison to the sword: which so terrified other places, that Winchester shortly after rendered upon easy conditions.* The lesser garrisons in the north, which had stood out till now, were rendered every day; and the Scots' army, which had marched as far as their own borders, was called back, and required to besiege Newark. So that whoever thought the sending to the Parliament (puffed up and swollen with so many successes) for a peace would prove to no purpose, was not yet able to tell what was like to prove to better purpose. And this reflection alone prevailed with the King, who had enough experimented those inclinations, to refer entirely to the Council, to choose any expedient they thought most probable to succeed, and to prepare any message they would advise his majesty to send to the Parliament. And when they had considered it, the overtures he had already made by two several messages, to which he had received no answer, were so ample, that they knew not what addition to make to them, but concluded that this message should contain nothing but a resentment, and demand of an answer to the messages his majesty had formerly sent for a treaty of peace.*

And this message had the same entertainment which the former had received. It was received, read, and then laid aside without any debate, which they who wished well to it had not credit or courage to advance, yet still found means to convey their advice to Oxford that the King should not give over that importunity: and they who had little hope of better effects from it, were yet of opinion that the neglecting those gracious invitations made by his majesty for peace would shortly make the Parliament so odious, that they would not dare long to continue in the same obstinacy. The Scots were grieved and enraged to see their idol Presbytery so undervalued and slighted that, beside the Independents' power in the city, their very Assembly of Divines lost credit and authority every day to support it, and desired nothing more than a treaty for peace: and many others who had contributed most to the suppression of the King's power, were now much more afraid of their own army than ever they had been of his authority, and believed that if a treaty were once set on foot it would not be in the power of the most violent to render it uneffectual: and whatever they believed themselves they conveyed to some about the King, as the concurrent advice of all who pretended to wish well: and some men took upon them to send the subject of what message the King should send, and clothed in such expressions [as] they conceived were like to gain ground; which his majesty could not but graciously accept, though he very seldom imitated their style. . . .

And though the [King] was not willing to acquiesce with this stubborn rejection, but sent message upon message still to them for a better answer, and at last offered* to dismantle all his garrisons, and to come to and reside with his Parliament if all they who had adhered to him might be at liberty to live in their own houses, and to enjoy their own estates, without being obliged to take any oaths but what were enjoined by the law, he could never procure any other answer from them. And lest all this should not appear affront enough, they published an ordinance,* as they called it, That if the King should, contrary to the advice of the Parliament already given to him, come or attempt to come within the lines of communication, that then the committee of the militia should raise such forces as they should think fit, to prevent any tumult that might arise by his coming, and to suppress any that should happen, and to apprehend any who should come with him or resort to him, and to secure his person from danger; which was an expression they were not ashamed always to use, when there was no danger that threatened him but what themselves contrived and designed against him. To this their ordinance they added another injunction, that all who had ever borne arms for his majesty (whereof very many upon the surrender of garrisons, and liberty granted to them by their articles upon those surrenders, were come thither) should immediately depart, and go out of London, upon penalty of being proceeded against as spies. So that all doors being in this obstinate manner shut against a treaty, all thoughts of that, at least with reference to the Parliament, were laid aside, and all endeavours used to gather such a power together as might make them see that his majesty was not out of all possibility of being yet able to defend himself.

Though all hopes, (as I said,) were desperate of any treaty with the Parliament, and consequently many hazards were to be run in the contriving a peace any other way, yet the sustaining the war with any probability of success was the next desirable thing to a peace, and preferable before any such peace as was reasonably to be hoped for from the party that governed the army, which governed the Parliament. The King therefore used all the means which occurred to him, or which were proposed and advised by others, to divide the Independent party, and to prevail with some principal persons of them to find their content and satisfaction in advancing the King's interest.* That party comprehended many who were neither enemies to the State or to the Church, but desired heartily that a peace might be established upon the foundations of both, so their own particular ambitions might be complied with. And to them the King thought he might be able to propose very valuable compensation for any service they could do him: and the power of the Presbyterians, as they were in conjunction with the Scots, seemed no unnatural argument to work upon those who professed to be swayed by matter of conscience in religion: since it was out of all question that they should never find the least satisfaction to their scruples and their principles in church government, from those who pretended to erect the kingdom of Jesus Christ. And it was thought to be no ill presage towards the repairing the fabric of the Church of England, that its two mortal enemies, who had exposed it to so much persecution and oppression, hated each other as mortally, and laboured each other's destruction with the same fury and zeal they had both proscribed her. And this reasonable imagination very much disposed the King, who was well acquainted with the unruly spirit and malice of the Presbytery, to think it possible that he might receive some benefit from the Independents, who were a faction newly grown up, and with which he was utterly unacquainted; and his majesty's extraordinary affection for the Church made him less weigh and con-sider the incompatibility and irreconcilableness of that faction with the government of the State; of which it may be he was the less sensible, because he thought nothing more impossible than that the English nation should submit to any other than monarchic government. Then there were an over-active and busy kind of men, who still undertook to make overtures, as agreeable to the wish of some principal leaders of that party and as with their authority, and so prevailed with the King to suffer some persons of credit near him to make some propositions in his name to particular persons. And it is very probable, that the same men who made the expectations of those people appear to the King much more reasonable and moderate than in truth they were, so they persuaded the others to believe that his majesty would yield to many more important concessions than he would ever be induced to grant. And so either side had in a short time a clear view into each other's intentions, and quickly gave over any expectation of benefit that way; save that the Independents were willing that the King should cherish the hopes of their compliance, and the King as willing that they should believe that his majesty might be prevailed with to grant more than at first he appeared resolved to do.

The truth is, though that party was most prevalent in the Parliament, and comprehended all the superior officers of the army, (the general only excepted, who thought himself a Presbyterian,) yet there were only three men, Vane, Cromwell, and Ireton, who governed and disposed all the rest according to their sentiments; and without doubt they had not yet published their dark designs to many of their own party, nor would their party at that time have been so numerous and considerable, if they had known, or but imagined, that they had entertained those thoughts of heart which they grew every day less tender to conceal and forward enough to discover.

But there was another intrigue now set on foot, with much more probability of success, both in respect of the thing itself, and the circumstances with which it came accompanied; and that was a treaty with the Scots by the interposition and mediation of the Crown of France; which, to that purpose, at this time sent an envoy, one Montreuil, to London,* with some formal address to the Parliament, but intentionally to negotiate between the King and the Scots; whose agent at Paris had given encouragement to the Queen of England, who was then there, to hope that that nation would return to their duty. And the Queen Regent, in the great generosity of her heart, did really desire to contribute all that was in her power to the King's recovery, and to that purpose sent Montreuil at this time with credentials to the King as well as to the Parliament; by which the Queen had opportunity to communicate her advice to the King her husband; and the envoy had authority to engage the faith of France for the performance of whatsoever the King should promise to the Scots.

This was the first instance, and it will appear a very sorry one, that any sovereign prince gave of wishing any reconciliation, or to put a period to the civil war in his majesty's dominions; towards the contrivance whereof, and the frequent fomenting it, too many of them contributed too much. The old mistaken and unhappy maxim, that the Crown of England could balance the differences which fell out between the princes of Europe by its inclining to either party, had made the ministers of that State too negligent in cultivating the affections of their neighbours by any real obligations; as if they were to be arbiters only in the differences which fell out between them, without being themselves liable to any impressions of adverse fortune. This made the unexpected calamity that befell that kingdom not ingrateful to its neighbours on all sides, who were willing to see it weakened and chastised by its own strokes.

Cardinal Richelieu, out of the natural haughtiness of his own nature, and immoderate appetite to do mischief, under the disguise of being jealous of the honour of his master, had discovered an implacable hatred against the English, from that unhappy provocation by the invasion of the Isle of Rhé* and the declared protection of Rochelle; and took the first opportunity from the indisposition and murmurs of Scotland to warm that people into rebellion, and saw the poison thereof prosper and spread to his own wish; which he fomented by the French ambassador in the Parliament with all the venom of his heart, as hath been mentioned before. As he had not unwisely driven the Queen mother out of France, or rather kept her from returning when she had unadvisedly withdrawn herself from thence,* so he was as vigilant to keep her daughter, the Queen of England, from coming thither; which she resolved to have done when she carried the princess royal into Holland,* in hope to work upon the King her brother, to make such a seasonable declaration against the rebels of England and Scotland as might terrify them from the farther prosecution of their wicked purposes. But it was made known to her that her presence would not be acceptable in France; and so for the present that enterprise was declined.

But that great cardinal being now dead, and the King himself within a short time after, the administration of the affairs of that kingdom, in the infancy of the King and under his mother the Queen Regent, was committed to cardinal Mazarin, an Italian by birth, and subject to the King of Spain, raised by Richelieu to the degree of a cardinal for his great dexterity in putting Casal into the hands of France,* when the Spaniard had given it up to him as the nuncio of the Pope, and in trust that it should remain in the possession of his holiness till the title of the duke of Mantua should be determined. This cardinal was a man rather of different than contrary parts from his predecessor, and fitter to build upon the foundations which he had laid than to have laid those foundations, and to cultivate by artifice, dexterity, and dissimulation, (in which his nature and parts excelled,) what the other had begun with great resolution and vigour, and even gone through with invincible constancy and courage. So that the one having broken the heart of all opposition and contradiction of the Crown by the cutting off the head of the duke of Montmorency, and reducing monsieur, the brother of the King, to the most tame submission and incapacity of fomenting another rebellion,* it was very easy for the other to find a compliance from all men, who were sufficiently terrified from any contradiction. So that how great things soever this last minister performed for the service of that Crown during the minority of the King, they may all, in justice, be imputed to the prudence and providence of cardinal Richelieu, who reduced and disposed the whole nation to an entire subjection and submission to what should be imposed upon them.

Cardinal Mazarin, when he came first to that great ministry, was without any personal animosity against the person of the King or the English nation; and was no otherwise delighted with the distraction and confusion they were both involved in, than as it disabled the whole people from making such a conjunction with the Spaniard as might make the prosecution of that war* (upon which his whole heart was set) the more difficult to him: which he had the more reason to apprehend by the residence of don Alonso de Cardeñas, ambassador from the King of Spain, still at London, making all addresses to the Parliament. When the Queen had been compelled in the last year, upon the advance of the earl of Essex into the west, to transport herself out of Cornwall into France,* she had found there as good a reception as she could expect, and received as many expressions of kindness from the Queen Regent, and as ample promises from the cardinal, as she could wish. So that she promised herself a very good effect from her journey; and did procure from him such a present supply of arms and ammunition, as, though of no great value in itself, she was willing to interpret as a good evidence of the reality of his intentions. But the cardinal did not yet think the King's condition low enough; and rather desired by administering little and ordinary supplies to enable him to continue the struggle, than to see him victorious over his enemies, when he might more remember how slender aid he had received than that he had been assisted, and might make himself arbiter of the peace between the two Crowns. And therefore he was more solicitous to keep a good correspondence with the Parliament, and to profess a neutrality between the King and them, than inclined to give them any jealousy by appearing much concerned for the King.

But after the battle at Naseby was lost, and that the King seemed so totally defeated that he had very little hope of appearing again in the head of an army that might be able to resist the enemy, he [the cardinal] was awakened to new apprehensions, and saw more cause to fear the monstrous power of the Parliament, after they had totally subdued the King, than ever he had the excess of greatness in the Crown: and therefore, besides the frequent incitements he received from the generosity of the Queen Regent, who really desired to apply some substantial relief to the King, he was himself willing to receive any propositions from the Queen of England by which she thought that the King her husband's service might be advanced; and had always the dexterity and artifice, by letting things fall in his discourse in the presence of those who he knew would observe and report what they heard or conceived, to cause that to be proposed to him which he had most mind to do or to engage himself in. And so he had application enough from the covenanting party of Scotland (who from the beginning had depended upon France, by the encouragement and promises of cardinal Richelieu) to know how to direct them to apply themselves to the Queen of England, that they might come recommended by her majesty to him, as a good expedient for the King's service. For they were not now reserved in their complaints of the treatment they received from the Parliament, and of the terrible apprehension they had of being disappointed of all their hopes by the prevalence of the Independent army and of their faction in both Houses; and therefore wished nothing more than a good opportunity to make a firm conjunction with the King; towards which they had all encouragement from the cardinal, if they made their address to the Queen, and her majesty would desire the cardinal to conduct it. And because many things must be promised on the King's behalf to the Scots upon this their engagement, the Crown of France should give credit and engage as well that the Scots should perform all that they should promise, and that the King should make good whatsoever should be undertaken by him, or by the Queen on his behalf.

This was the occasion and ground of sending Monsieur Montreuil into England, as is mentioned before; and he arrived there in January,* with as much credit as the Queen Regent could give him to the Scots, and as the Queen of England could give him to the King; who likewise persuaded his majesty to believe that France was now become really kind to him, and would engage all its power to serve him, and that the cardinal was well assured that the Scots would behave themselves henceforward very honestly; which his majesty was willing to believe, when all other hopes had failed, and all his overtures made by him for a treaty had been rejected. But it was not long before he was undeceived, and discerned that this treaty was not like to produce better fruit than his former overtures had done. For the first information he received from Montreuil after his arrival in England, and after he had conferred with the Scots' commissioners, was, that they peremptorily insisted upon his majesty's condescension and promise for the establishment of the presbyterian government in England as it was in Scotland, without which, he said, there was no hope that they would ever join with his majesty; and therefore the envoy pressed his majesty to give them satisfaction therein, as the advice of the Queen Regent and the cardinal, and likewise of the Queen his wife; which exceedingly troubled the King. And the Scots alleged confidently that the Queen had expressly promised to sir Robert Moray, (a cunning and a dexterous man, who had been employed by them to her majesty,) that his majesty should consent thereunto.* And they produced a writing signed by the Queen, and delivered to sir Robert Moray, wherein there were such expressions concerning religion as nothing pleased the King, and made him look upon that negotiation as rather a conspiracy against the Church between the Roman Catholics and the Presbyterians than an expedient for his restoration or preservation: and he was very much displeased with some persons of near trust about the Queen, to whose misinformation and advice he imputed what her majesty had done in that particular; and thereupon deferred not to let monsieur Montreuil know, that the alteration of the government in the Church was expressly against his conscience, and that he would never consent to it; that what the Queen his wife had seemed to promise proceeded from her not being well informed of the constitution of the government of England, which could not consist with that change that was proposed.

But his majesty offered to give all the assurance imaginable, and hoped that the Queen Regent would engage her royal word on his behalf in that particular, that the maintenance and support of the episcopal government in England should not in any degree shake, or bring the least prejudice to, that government that was then settled in Scotland; and farther he offered, that if the Scots should desire to have the free exercise of their religion, according to their own practice and custom, whilst they should be at any time in England, that he would assign them convenient places to that purpose in London, or any other part of the kingdom where they should desire it. Nor could all the importunity or arguments used by Montreuil prevail with his majesty to enlarge those concessions, or in the least to recede from the positiveness of his resolution; though he informed him of the dissatisfaction both the Scots' commissioners and the Presbyterians in London had in his majesty's resolution, and averseness from gratifying them in that which they always had and always would insist upon; and that the Scots were resolved to have no more to do with his majesty, but were resolved to agree with the Independents, from whom they could have better conditions than from him; and he feared such an agreement was too far advanced already.

Many answers and replies passed between the King and Montreuil in cipher, and with all imaginable secrecy; in which, whatever reproaches were cast upon him afterwards, he always gave the King very clear and impartial information of the temper and of the discourses of those people with whom he was to transact. And though he did upon all occasions with much earnestness advise his majesty to consent to the unreasonable demands of the Scots, which he did believe he would be at last compelled to do, yet it is as certain that he did use all the arguments the talent of his understanding, (which was a very good one,) could suggest to him to persuade the Scots to be contented with what the King had so frankly offered and granted to them; and he did all he could to persuade and convince them that their own preservation, and that of their nation, depended upon the preservation of the King and the support of his regal authority. And it is very memorable, that, in answer to a letter which Montreuil writ to the King, and in which he persuaded his majesty to agree with the Scots upon their own demands, and, amongst other arguments, assured his majesty that the English Presbyterians were fully agreed with the Scots (which his majesty believed they would never do,) the Scots having declared that they would never insist upon the settling any other government than was at that time practised in London; urging many other successes which they had at that time obtained; the King, after some expressions of his adhering to what he had formerly declared, used these words in his letter of the 21st of January to monsieur Montreuil: 'Let them never flatter themselves so with their good successes, without pretending to prophecy I will foretell their ruin except they agree with me, however it shall please God to dispose of me;' which they had great reason to remember after. [*HR*, IX, 161–76]

In the first months of 1646 Charles continued to attempt to draw the Independents into a negotiation, offering religious toleration as an alternative to Presbyterian government, and to seek Catholic help, while Montreuil continued to try to seek a compromise. In March Montreuil went to Oxford bearing an offer from the Scottish commissioners of military assistance. On the basis of this Charles believed he had come to a firm agreement with the Scots. Fatally, however, it was not backed up by the Scottish Parliament.

This was the proceeding of Mons. Montreuil in that whole transaction: and if he were too sanguine upon his first conversation with the officers of the Scots' army and some of the committee, and when he signed that engagement upon the first of April, he made haste to retract that confidence, and was in all his despatches afterwards phlegmatic enough; and after his majesty had put himself into their hands, he did honestly and stoutly charge all the particular persons with the promises and engagements they had given to him, and did all he could to make the cardinal sensible of the indignity that was offered to that Crown in the violation of those promises and engagements; which was the reason of his being commanded to return home as soon as the King came to Newcastle,* lest his too keen resentment might irritate the Scots, and make it appear to the Parliament how far France was engaged in that whole negotiation, which the cardinal had no mind should appear to the world: and there can be no doubt but that the cautions and animadversions which the King received from him, after his engagement, would have diverted him from that enterprise, if his majesty had discerned any other course to take that had been preferable even to the hazard that he saw he must undergo with the Scots. But he was clearly destitute of any other refuge. His hope of drawing out of his few garrisons which remained such a body of horse and foot as might enable him to take the field, though without any fixed design, in the early spring, was dashed by the total rout and defeat the lord Astley underwent; who being upon his march from Worcester towards Oxford, with two thousand horse and foot, the King having appointed to meet him with another body of fifteen hundred horse and foot, letters and orders miscarried and were intercepted, whereby the enemy came to have notice of the resolution, and drew a much greater strength from their several garrisons of Gloucester, Warwick, Coventry, and Evesham, that the lord Astley was no sooner upon his march than they followed him, and the second day, after he had marched all night, and when he thought he had escaped all their quarters, they fell upon his wearied troops, and, though a bold and a stout resistance was made, they were at last totally defeated,* and the lord Astley himself, sir Charles Lucas, who was lieutenant general of the horse, and most of the other officers who were not killed, were taken prisoners, and the few who escaped were so scattered and dispersed that they never came together again, nor did there remain from that minute any possibility for the King to draw any other troops together. Every day brought the news of the loss of some garrison: and as Oxford was already blocked up at a distance by those horse which Fairfax had sent out of the west to that purpose, or to wait upon the King, and follow him close if he should remove out of Oxford, so he had too soon reduced Exeter* and some other garrisons in Devonshire. The governors then, when there was no visible and apparent hope of being relieved, thought that they might deliver up their garrisons before they were pressed with the last extremities, that they might obtain the better conditions; and yet it was observed that better or more honourable conditions were not given to any, than to those who kept the places they were trusted with till they had not one day's victual left; of which we shall observe more hereafter.

By this means Fairfax was within three days of Oxford before the King left it, or fully resolved what to do. He had before sent to eminent commanders of name,* who had blocked up the town at a distance, that if they would pass their words, (how slender a security soever, from such men who had broken so many oaths for the safety of a king,) that they would immediately conduct him to the Parliament, he would have put himself into their hands; for he was yet persuaded to think so well of the city of London, that he would not have been unwilling to have found himself there: but those officers would submit to no such engagements; and great care was taken to have strict guards round about London, that he might not get thither. What should the King do? There was one thing most formidable to him, and which he was resolved to avoid, that was, to be enclosed in Oxford, and so to be given up, or taken, when the town should be surrendered, as a prisoner to the Independents' army; which he was advertised from all hands would treat him very barbarously.

In this perplexity he chose rather to commit himself into the Scots' army; which yet he did not trust so far as to give them notice of his journey by sending for a party of their horse to meet him, as they had proffered; but early in the morning, upon the 27th day of April, he went out of Oxford, attended only by John Ashburnham, and a scholar, (one Hudson,) who understood the by-ways as well as the common, and was indeed a very skilful guide. And in this equipage he left Oxford on a Monday, leaving those of his Council in Oxford who were privy to his going out not informed whether he would go to the Scots' army or get privately into London, and lie there concealed till he might choose that which was best; and it was generally believed that he had not within himself at that time a fixed resolution what he would do; which was the more credited because it was nine days after his leaving Oxford before it was known where the King was; insomuch as Fairfax who came before it the fifth day after his majesty was gone, was sat down, and had made his circumvallation about Oxford, before he knew that the King was in the Scots' army; but the King had wasted that time in several places, whereof some were gentlemen's houses, where he was not unknown though untaken notice of, purposely to be informed of the condition of the marquis of Montrose,* and to find some secure passage that he might find himself with him, which he did exceedingly desire; but in the end went into the Scots' army before Newark,* and sent for Montreuil to come to him.

It was very early in the morning when the King went to the general's lodging, and discovered himself to him; who either was, or seemed to be, exceedingly surprised and confounded at his majesty's presence, and knew not what to say; but presently gave notice of it to the committee, who were no less perplexed. An express was presently sent to the Parliament at Westminster, to inform them of the unexpected news, as a thing they had not the least imagination of. And the Parliament was so disordered with the intelligence, that at first they resolved to command their general to raise the siege before Oxford, and to march with all expedition to Newark; but the Scots' commissioners diverted them from that, by assuring them that all their orders would meet with an absolute obedience in their army. So they made a short despatch to them, in which it was evident that they believed the King had gone to them by invitation, and not out of his own free choice; and implying that they should shortly receive farther direction from them; and in the mean time, that they should carefully watch that his majesty did not dispose himself to go some whither else. The great care in the army was that there might be only respect and good manners shewed towards the King, without any thing of affection or dependence; and therefore the general never asked the word of him, or any orders, nor suffered the officers of the army to resort to him, or to have any discourse with his majesty. Montreuil was ill looked upon, as the man who had brought this inconvenience upon them without their consent; but he was not frighted from owning and declaring what had passed between them, what they had promised, and what they were engaged to do. However, though the King liked not the treatment he received, he was not without apprehension that Fairfax might be forthwith appointed to decline all other enterprises, and to bring himself near the Scots' army, they being too near together already; and therefore he forthwith gave order to the lord Bellasis to surrender Newark, that the Scots might march northward, which they resolved to do; and he giving up that place,* which he could have defended for some months longer from that enemy, upon honourable conditions, that army with great expedition marched towards Newcastle; which the King was glad of, though their behaviour to him was still the same, and great strictness used that he might not confer with any man who was not well known to them, much less receive letters from any.

It was an observation in that time, that the first publishing of extraordinary news was from the pulpit; and by the preacher's text, and his manner of discourse upon it, the auditors might judge, and commonly foresaw, what was like to be next done in the Parliament or Council of State. The first sermon that was preached before the King, after the army rose from Newark to march northwards, was upon the 19th chapter of the 2d book of Samuel, the 41st, 42d, and 43d verses:

41. *And, behold, all the men of Israel came to the king, and said unto the king, Why have our brethren the men of Judah stolen thee away, and have brought the king, and his household, and all David's men with him, over Jordan?*

42. *And all the men of Judah answered the men of Israel, Because the king is near of kin to us: wherefore then be ye angry for this matter? have we eaten at all of the king's cost? or hath he given us any gift?*

43. *And the men of Israel answered the men of Judah, and said, We have ten parts in the king, and we have also more right in David than ye: why then did ye despise us, that our advice should not be first had in bringing back our king? And the words of the men of Judah were fiercer than the words of the men of Israel.*

Upon which words the preacher gave men cause to believe that now they had gotten their king they resolved to keep him, and to adhere to him. But his majesty came no sooner to Newcastle, than both Mons. Montreuil was restrained from having any conference with him, and Mr Ashburnham was advised to shift for himself, or else that he should be delivered up to the Parliament; and both the one and the other were come to Paris when the Queen sent those lords to hasten the Prince's remove from Jersey.* [*HR*, X, 31–6]

Prince Charles had been in Jersey since April. While the King had been negotiating through Montreuil in early 1646, Fairfax had gradually been pushing the remaining royalist forces in the south-west back into Devon and Cornwall. The King sent messages to the Prince's Council with increasing urgency ordering them to take him to France: the Council delayed, arguing that the Prince's departure would lead to a final collapse of royalist resistance in the west, and that if absolutely forced to leave, it would be preferable for him to remain in the King's dominions, in the Scilly Isles, or Jersey, than to go to a foreign power. Not until 2 March 1646 did they decide that the time had come to leave. The Prince, with Hyde and Culpepper, landed in the Scillies two days later, where Hyde began writing the History. *A few weeks later, news of a possible attack on the islands made them move on to the more easily defended Jersey, where they arrived on 17 April. Meanwhile, the Queen, from France, forcefully told them that the Prince*

would be more secure there and claimed that the French would offer mili-
tary support. The Council sent two of its number, Culpepper and Lord
Capel, to persuade her to the contrary. But while they were in Paris,
Montreuil and Ashburnham arrived, apparently with instructions from
the King that the Prince should move to France. When Culpepper and
Capel returned to Jersey in June, the Queen sent Lords Jermyn, Digby,
Wentworth, and Wilmot along with them with a letter to reinforce the case
for the Prince's removal. They arrived on 20 June.

The lords who arrived with this despatch from her majesty had no
imagination that there would have been any question of his highness'
compliance with the Queen's command; and therefore, as soon as they
had kissed the Prince's hand, which was in the afternoon, they desired
that the council might presently be called; and when they came
together, the lords Jermyn, Digby, and Wentworth, being likewise
present and sitting in the council, they desired the Prince that his
mother's letter might be read, and then, since they conceived there
could be no debate upon his highness' yielding obedience to the command of the King and Queen, that they might only consider of the day
when he would begin his journey, and of the order he would observe
in it. The lords of the council represented to the Prince that they were
the only persons that were accountable to the King and to the kingdom
for any resolution his highness should take, and for the consequence
thereof; and that the other lords who were present had no title to
deliver their advice, or to be present at the debate, they being in no
degree responsible for what his highness should resolve to do; and
therefore that the whole matter might be debated, the state of the
King's present condition understood as far as it might be, and the
reasons considered which made it counsellable for his highness to
repair into France, and what might be said against it; and the rather,
because it was very notorious that the King had given no positive
direction in the point, but upon a supposition that the Prince could not
remain secure in Jersey; which was likewise the ground of the Queen's
last command; and which they believed had no foundation of reason,
and that his residence there might be very unquestionably safe. This
begot some warmth and contradiction between persons; insomuch as
the Prince thought it very necessary to suspend the debate till the next
day, to the end that by several and private conferences together
between the lords who came from Paris and those who were in Jersey,
they might convert or confirm each other in the same opinions, at least
that the next debate might be free from passion and unkindness; and

so the council rose, and the several lords betook themselves to use the same arguments, or such as they thought more agreeable to the person, as the lord Digby had before done to his friend, and with the same success.*

The next day, when they were called together, the lord Capel gave an account of all that had passed with the Queen from the time that the lord Culpepper and he came thither; and that the reasons they had carried from the Prince had so far prevailed with the Queen that her majesty resolved to take no final resolution till she received farther advertisement of the King's pleasure; and he did not think that the information she had received from Monsieur Montreuil had weight enough to produce the quick resolution it had done: that he thought it still most absolutely necessary to receive the King's positive command before the Prince should remove out of his majesty's own dominions, there being no shadow of cause to suspect his security there: that he had then offered to the Queen that he would himself make a journey to Newcastle to receive his majesty's commands, and that he now made the same offer to the Prince: and because it did appear that his majesty was very strictly guarded, and that persons did not easily find access to him, and that his own person might be seized upon in his journey thither, or his stay there, or his return back, and so his highness might be disappointed of the information he expected, and remain still in the same uncertainty as to a resolution, he did propose, and consent to, as his opinion, that if he did not return again to Jersey within the space of one month, the Prince should resolve to remove into France, if in the mean time such preparatories were made there which he thought were necessary and were yet defective.

He said, he had been lately at Paris by the Prince's command; and had received many graces from the Queen, who had vouchsafed to impart all her own reasons for the Prince's remove, and the grounds for the confidence she had of the affections of France: but that he did still wonder that, if the Court of France had so great a desire as was pretended that the Prince of Wales should repair thither, in two months' time his highness had been in Jersey they had never sent a gentleman to see him, and to invite him to come thither; nor had these who came now from the Queen brought so much as a pass for him to come into France: that he could not but observe that all that we had hitherto proposed to ourselves from France had proved in no degree answerable to our expectations; as the five thousand foot, which we had expected in the west before the Prince came from thence;* and that we had more reason to be jealous now than ever, since it had been by the advice of France that the King had now put himself into the hands of the Scots; and therefore we ought to be the more watchful in the disposing the person of the Prince by their advice likewise; and concluded, that he could not give his advice or consent that the Prince should repair into France till the King's pleasure might be known, or such other circumstances might be provided in France as had been hitherto neglected.

The lord Digby and the lord Jermyn wondered very much that there should be any doubt of the affections of France, or that it should be believed that the Queen could be deceived, or not well enough informed in that particular: they related many particulars which had passed between the cardinal and them in private conferences, and of the great professions of affection he made to the King; that the ambassador who was now appointed to go thither* was chosen by the Queen herself, and had no other instructions but what she had given him; and that he was not to stay there above a month; at the end of which he was to denounce war against the Parliament if they did not comply with such propositions as he made, and so to return; and then that there should be an army of thirty thousand men immediately transported into England, with the Prince of Wales in the head of them; that that ambassador was already gone from Paris, but that he was not to embark till he should first receive advertisement that the Prince of Wales was landed in France; for that France had no reason to embark themselves so far in the King's quarrel if the Prince of Wales should refuse to venture his person with them, or, it may be, engage against them upon another interest.

They therefore besought the Prince and the lords, that they would consider well, whether he would disappoint his father and himself of so great fruit, as they were even ready to gather, and of which they could not be disappointed, by unseasonable jealousies of the integrity of France, and by delaying to give them satisfaction in the remove of the Prince from Jersey.

These arguments, pressed with all the assurance and confidence imaginable, by persons of that near trust and confidence with the King, and who were not like to be deceived themselves, nor to have any purpose to deceive the Prince, wrought so far with his highness, that he declared himself resolved to comply with the commands of the Queen, and forthwith to remove into France; which being resolved, he wished there might be no more debate upon that point, but that they would all resolve to go with him, and that there might be as great an unity in their counsels as had hitherto always been.

This so positive declaration of the Prince of his own resolution made all farther arguments against it not only useless but indecent; and therefore they replied not to that point; yet every man of the council, (the lord Culpepper only excepted,) besought his highness that he would give them his pardon if they did not farther wait upon him; that they conceived their commission to be now at an end; and that they could not assume any authority by it to themselves if they waited upon him into France, nor expect that their counsels there should be hearkened unto when they were now rejected. And so, after some sharp replies between the lords of different judgments, which made the council break up the sooner, they who resolved not to go into France took their leaves of the Prince, and kissed his hand; his highness then declaring that he would be gone the next day by five of the clock in the morning, though the cross winds, and want of some provisions which were necessary for the journey, detained him there four or five days longer; during which time the dissenting lords every day waited upon him, and were received by him very graciously; his highness well knowing, and expressing to them a confidence in, their affections, and that they would be ready to wait upon him whenever his occasions should be ready for their service. But between them and the other lords there grew by degrees so great a strangeness, that the last day they did not so much as speak to each other; they who came from the Queen taking it very ill that the others had presumed to dissent from what her majesty had so positively commanded. And though they neither loved their persons nor cared for their company, and without doubt, if they had gone into France, would have made them quickly weary of theirs, yet in that conjuncture they believed that the dissent and separation of all those persons who were trusted by the King with the person of the Prince would blast their counsels, and weigh down the single positive determination of the Queen herself.

On the other side, the others did not think that they were treated in that manner that was due to persons so intrusted, and that in truth many ill consequences would result from that sudden departure of the Prince out of the King's dominions, where his residence might have been secure, both in respect of the affairs of England; (where, besides the garrisons of Scilly and Pendennis, which might always be relieved by sea, there remained still within his majesty's obedience Oxford, Worcester, Wallingford, Ludlow, and some other places of less name; which, upon any divisions among themselves that were naturally to be expected, might have turned the scale:) nor did they know what ill consequence it might be to the King that in such a conjuncture the

Prince should be removed, when it might appear more compellable that he should appear in Scotland.

And Mr Ashburnham's opinion, which he had delivered to the lord Capel, wrought very much upon them; for that a man so entirely trusted by the King, and who had seen him as lately as any body, should bring no directions from his majesty to his son, and that he should believe that it was fitter for the Prince to stay in Jersey than to remove into France till his majesty's pleasure was better understood, confirmed them in the judgment they had delivered.

But there was another reason that prevailed with those who had been made privy to it, and which out of duty to the Queen they thought not fit to publish or insist upon; which was the instructions given to Bellièvre, (and which too much manifested the irresolution her majesty had,) not to insist upon what they well knew the King would never depart from; for, though he was required to do all he could to persuade the Presbyterians to join with the King's party, and not to insist upon the destruction of the Church, yet if he found that could not be compassed, the ambassador was to press, as the advice of the King his master, his majesty to part with the Church, and to satisfy the Presbyterians in that point, as the advice of the Queen his wife, and of his own party; which method was afterwards observed and pursued by him, and which those lords perfectly abhorred; and thought not fit ever to concur [in,] or be privy to those counsels which had begun and were to carry on that confusion.

Within a day or two after the Prince's departure from Jersey* the earl of Berkshire left it likewise, and went for England. The lords Capel, Hopton, and the Chancellor remained together in Jersey to expect the King's pleasure, and to attend a conjuncture to appear again in his majesty's service; of all which they found an opportunity to inform his majesty, who very well interpreted all that they had done according to the sincerity of their hearts, yet did believe that if they had likewise waited upon the Prince into France, they might have been able to have prevented, or diverted, those violent pressures which were afterwards made upon him from thence, and which gave him more disquiet than he suffered from all the insolence of his enemies. [*HR*, X, 196–202]

Hyde spent almost two years on Jersey. In this passage, part of the Life, *Clarendon described how he spent his time there, and how he worked on the* History.

The prince having left Jersey about July in the year 1646, the chancellor of the exchequer remained there about two years after; where he presently betook himself to his study; and enjoyed, as he was wont to say, the greatest tranquillity of mind imaginable. Whilst the lords Capel and Hopton stayed there, they lived and kept house together in St Hilary's; which is the chief town of the island: where, having a chaplain of their own, they had prayers every day in the church, at eleven of the clock in the morning; till which hour they enjoyed themselves in their chambers, according as they thought fit; the chancellor betaking himself to the continuance of the History, which he had begun at Scilly, and spending most of his time at that exercise. The other two walked, or rode abroad, or read, as they were disposed; but at the hour of prayers they always met; and then dined together at the lord Hopton's lodging, which was the best house; they being lodged at several houses, with convenience enough. Their table was maintained at their joint expense only for dinners; they never using to sup; but met always upon the sands in the evening to walk, often going to the castle to sir George Carteret;* who treated them with extraordinary kindness and civility, and spent much time with them; and, in truth, the whole island shewed great affection to them, and all the persons of quality invited them to their houses, to very good entertainments; and all other ways expressed great esteem towards them, and appeared very unanimous and resolute to defend the island against any attempt the parliament should make against it. . . .

In early 1647, Capel decided to return to England. Hopton left too, but for France.

And the chancellor being thus left alone, he was with great civility and friendship invited by sir George Carteret to remove from the town, (where he had lived with his friends till then,) and to live with him in the castle Elizabeth; whither he went the next day after the departure of the lord Hopton, and remained there, to his wonderful contentment, in the very cheerful society of sir George Carteret and his lady; in whose house he received all the liberty and entertainment he could have expected in his own family; of which he always retained so just a memory, that there was never any intermission or decay of that friendship he then made: and he remained there till he was sent for again to attend the prince, which will be mentioned in its time.

He built a lodging in the castle, of two or three convenient rooms, to the wall of the church, which sir George Carteret had repaired and beautified; and over the door of his lodging he set up his arms, with this inscription, *Bene vixit, qui bene latuit*:* and he always took pleasure in relating, with what great tranquillity of spirit (though deprived of the joy he took in his wife and children) he spent his time here amongst his books (which he got from Paris) and his papers; between which he seldom spent less than ten hours in the day: and it can hardly be believed how much he read and writ there; insomuch as he did usually compute, that during his whole stay in Jersey, which was some months above two years, he writ [daily] little less than one sheet of large paper with his own hand; most of which are still to be seen amongst his papers.

From Hampton Court, his majesty writ to the chancellor of the exchequer with his own hand; in which he took notice, that he was writing the *History of the late Troubles*; for which he thanked him, saying, that he knew no man could do it so well; and that he would not do it the worse by the helps that he would very speedily send him: (as his majesty shortly after did, in two manuscripts very fairly written, containing all matters of importance that had passed from the time that the prince of Wales went from his majesty into the west, to the very time that his majesty himself went from Oxford to the Scottish army; which were all the passages in the years 1645 and 1646.) He used many gracious expressions in that letter to him; and said, he looked upon him as one of those who had served him with most fidelity, and therefore he might be confident of his kindness; and that he would bring him to him with the first; though, he said, he did not hold him to be infallible, as he might discern by what he had commanded Dr Sheldon, who was then clerk of his closet, to write to him; and at the same time the doctor writ him word, that the king was sorry that he, the chancellor, stayed at Jersey, and did not attend the prince into France; and that if he had been there, he would have been able to have prevented the vexation his majesty had endured at Newcastle by messages from Paris.

The doctor likewise sent him word, that great pains had been taken from Paris to incense the king against him; but that it had so little prevailed, that his majesty had with some sharpness reprehended those who blamed him, and had justified the chancellor. He made haste to answer his majesty's letter, and gave him so much satisfaction, that his majesty said, he was too hard for him. And about the same time the lord Capel came into England; and though he was under security to the parliament for behaving himself peaceably, he was not restrained from seeing the king; and so gave him a very particular information of all that had passed at Jersey; and many other things, of which his majesty had never been informed before; which put it out of any body's power to make any ill impressions in him towards the chancellor. [*Life*, V, 1–7]

13. Cromwell, the Army, and the Independents

While in the custody of the Scottish army Charles continued to negotiate with the Scots and the English. But while he refused to accept the replacement of episcopacy in England there was little prospect of agreement, and his principal aim was to sow discord between the two countries, playing for time while his supporters struggled to find support to mount a further military challenge. Exasperated, the Scots abandoned the King and withdrew from England at the beginning of February 1647, having accepted £400,000 from Parliament for the expenses of their army. The King passed into the hands of the Westminster Parliament, and was lodged under guard at Holdenby or Holmby House, just outside Northampton. Over the next few months Presbyterians—who formed a majority in both Houses of Parliament—and Independents—whose strength lay in the army—struggled over a religious settlement and the control of the military. Presbyterians tried to dispatch the bulk of the army to Ireland, to suppress the Catholic Irish. The rank and file resisted bitterly, choosing 'agitators' to represent their resentment to the officers and through them to Parliament. In April and May 1647 their discontent reached a crisis point, which Cromwell struggled to control. Royalists like Clarendon assumed that he had arranged it as a step towards seizing power.

Clarendon's grasp of events in England at this point was weak, and his account frequently confused in many details.

CROMWELL hitherto carried himself with that rare dissimulation (in which sure he was a very great master,) that he seemed exceedingly incensed against this insolence of the soldiers, was still in the House of Commons when any such addresses were made, and inveighed bitterly against the presumption, and had been the cause of the commitment* of some of the officers. He proposed that the general might be sent down to the army, who, he said, would conjure down this mutinous spirit quickly; and he was so easily believed that he himself was sent once or twice to compose the army;* where after he had stayed two or three days, he would return again to the House, and complain heavily of the great license that was got into the army; that, for his own part, by the artifice of his enemies, and of those who desired that the nation should be again imbrued in blood, he was rendered so odious unto them, that they had a purpose to kill him, if, upon some discovery made to him, he had not escaped out of their hands. And in these and

the like discourses, when he spake of the nation's being to be involved
in new troubles, he would weep bitterly, and appear the most afflicted
man in the world with the sense of the calamities which were like to
ensue. But as many of the wiser sort had long discovered his wicked
intentions, so his hypocrisy could not longer be concealed. The most
active officers and agitators were known to be his own creatures, and
such who neither did nor would do any thing but by his direction. So
that it was resolved by the principal persons of the House of Commons,
that when he came the next day into the House, which he seldom
omitted to do, they would send him to the Tower; presuming that if
they had once severed his person from the army they should easily
reduce it to its former temper and obedience. For they had not the
least jealousy of the general Fairfax, whom they knew to be a perfect
Presbyterian in his judgment, and that Cromwell had the ascendant
over him purely by his dissimulation, and pretence of conscience and
sincerity. And there is no doubt Fairfax did not then, nor long after,
believe that the other had those wicked designs in his heart against the
King, or the least imagination of disobeying the Parliament.

This purpose of seizing upon the person of Cromwell could not be
carried so secretly but that he had notice of it; and the very next morning
after he had so much lamented his desperate misfortune in having lost
all reputation and credit and authority in the army, and that his life
would be in danger if he were with it, when the House expected every
minute his presence, they were informed that he was met out of the town
by the break of day, with one servant only, on the way to the army; where
he had appointed a rendezvous of some regiments of the horse, and from
whence he writ a letter to the House of Commons, that he had the night
before received a letter from some officers of his own regiment, that the
jealousy the troops had conceived of him and of his want of kindness
towards them was much abated, so that they believed, if he would be
quickly present with them, they would all in a short time by his advice
be reclaimed, upon which he had made all the haste he could, and did
find that the soldiers had been abused by misinformation, and that he
hoped to discover the fountain from whence it sprung; and in the mean
time desired that the general, and the other officers in the House, and
such as remained about the town, might be presently sent to their quarters; and that he believed it would be very necessary in order to the
suppression of the late distempers, and for the prevention of the like for
the time to come, that there might be a general rendezvous of the army;
of which the general would best consider when he came down; which
he wished might be hastened. It was now to no purpose to discover what

they had formerly intended, or that they had any jealousy of a person who was out of their reach; and so they expected a better conjuncture; and, in a few days after, the general and the other officers left the town, and went to their quarters.

The same morning that Cromwell left London, cornet Joyce, (who was one of the agitators in the army, a tailor, and a fellow who had two or three years before served in a very inferior employment in Mr Holles's house,) came with a squadron of fifty horse to Holmby,* where the King was, about the break of day; and, without any interruption by the guard of horse or foot which waited there, came with two or three more, and knocked at the King's chamber door, and said he must presently speak with the King. His majesty, surprised with the manner of it, rose out of his bed, and, half dressed, caused the door to be opened, which he knew would otherwise quickly be broken up; they who waited in the chamber being persons of whom he had little knowledge and less confidence. As soon as the door was opened, Joyce and two or three more came into the chamber, with their hats off, and pistols in their hands, and Joyce told the King that he must go with them. His majesty asked, 'Whither?' He answered, 'To the army.' The King asked him 'Where the army was?' He said, 'They would carry him to the place where it was.' His majesty asked, 'By what authority they came?' Joyce answered, 'By *this*;' and shewed them his pistol; and desired his majesty 'that he would cause himself to be dressed, because it was necessary they should make haste.' Neither of the others spake a word; and Joyce, saving the bluntness and positiveness of the few words he spake, behaved not himself rudely. The King said he could not stir before he spake with the committee* to whom he had been delivered, and who were trusted by the Parliament; and so appointed one of those who waited upon him to call them. The committee had been as much surprised with the noise as the King had been, and quickly came to his chamber, and asked Joyce, 'Whether he had any order from the Parliament?' He said, 'No.' 'From the General?' 'No.' 'What authority he came by?' To which he made no other answer than he had made to the King, and held up his pistol. They said, 'They would write to the Parliament to know their pleasure.' Joyce said, 'They might do so, but the King must presently go with them.' Colonel Browne* had sent for some of the troops who were appointed for the King's guard, but they came not; he spake then with the officer who commanded those who were at that time upon the guard, and found that they would make no resistance. And so, after the King had made all the delays he conveniently could, without giving them cause to believe that he was resolved not to have gone, which had been to no purpose, after he had broken his fast, he went into his coach, attended by the few servants who were put about him, and went whither cornet Joyce would conduct him; there being no part of the army known to be within twenty miles of Holmby at that time; and that which administered most cause of apprehension was, that those officers who were of the guard declared that the squadron which was commanded by Joyce consisted not of soldiers of any one regiment, but were men of several troops and several regiments drawn together under him, who was not their proper officer; so that the King did in truth believe that their purpose was to carry him to some place where they might more conveniently murder him. The committee quickly gave notice to the Parliament of what had passed, with all the circumstances; and it was received with all imaginable consternation, nor could any body imagine what the purpose and resolution was.

Nor were they at the more ease, or in any degree pleased, with the account they received from the general* himself; who by his letter informed them, that the soldiers at Holmby had brought the King from thence, and that his majesty lay the next night at colonel Montagu's house,* and would be the next day at Newmarket: that the ground thereof was from some apprehension of some strength gathered to force the King from them; whereupon he had sent colonel Whalley's regiment to meet his majesty. He protested that this remove was without his consent, or the officers about him, or of the body of the army, and without their desire or privity: that he would take care for the security of his majesty's person from danger; and assured the Parliament that the whole army endeavoured peace, and were far from opposing Presbytery or affecting Independency or any purpose to maintain a licentious freedom in religion, or the interest of any particular party, but were resolved to leave the absolute determination of all to the Parliament.

It was upon the third of June that the King was taken from Holmby by cornet Joyce, a full year after he had delivered himself to the Scots at Newark; in all which time the army had been at leisure to contrive all ways to free itself from the servitude of the Parliament, whilst the Presbyterians believed that (in spite of a few factious Independent officers) it was entirely at their devotion, and could never prove disobedient to their commands; and those few wise men who discerned the foul designs of those officers, and by what degrees they stole the hearts and affections of the soldiers, had not credit enough to be believed by their own party. And the joint confidence of the unanimous affection of the city of London to all their purposes, made them despise all opposition; but now, when they saw the King taken out of their hands in this manner, and with these circumstances, they found all their measures broken by which they had formed all their counsels. And as this letter from the general administered too much cause of jealousy of what was to succeed, so a positive information at the same time by many officers, and confirmed by a letter which the Lord Mayor of London had received, that the whole army was upon its march, and would be in London the next day by noon, so distracted them that they appeared beside themselves: however, they presently voted* that the Houses should sit all the next day, being Sunday, and that Mr Marshall should be there to pray for them: that the committee of safety should sit up all that night to consider what was to be done: that the lines of communication should be strongly guarded, and all the train-bands of London should be drawn together upon pain of death. All shops were shut up, and such a general confusion over all the town, and in the faces of all men, as if the army had already entered the town. The Parliament writ a letter to the general, desiring him that no part of the army might come within five and twenty miles of London, and that the King's person might be delivered to the former commissioners who had attended upon his majesty at Holmby; and that colonel Rossiter and his regiment might be appointed for the guard of his person. The general returned for answer, that the army was come to St Alban's before the desire of the Parliament came to his hands, but that, in obedience to their commands, he would advance no farther; and desired that a month's pay might presently be sent for the army. In which they deferred not to gratify them; though as to the re-delivery of the King to the former commissioners, no other answer was returned than that they might rest assured that all care should be taken for his majesty's security.

From that time both Cromwell and Ireton appeared in the council of officers,* which they had never before done, and their expostulations with the Parliament began to be more brisk and contumacious than they had been. The King found himself at Newmarket attended by greater troops and superior officers, so that he was presently freed from any subjection to Mr Joyce, which was no small satisfaction to him; and they who were about him appeared men of better breeding than the former, and paid his majesty all the respect imaginable, and seemed to desire to please him in all things. All restraint was taken off from persons resorting to him, and he saw every day the faces of many who were grateful to him; and he no sooner desired that some of his chaplains might have leave to attend upon him for his devotion but it was yielded to, and they who were named by him (who were Dr Sheldon,

Dr Morley, Dr Sanderson, and Dr Hammond) were presently sent, and gave their attendance, and performed their function at the ordinary hours in their accustomed formalities, all persons who had a mind to it being suffered to be present; to his majesty's infinite satisfaction, who began to believe that the army was not so much his enemy as it was reported to be; and though Fairfax nor Cromwell had not yet waited upon him, the army had sent an address to him,* full of protestation of duty, and besought him that he would be content for some time to reside amongst them, until the affairs of the kingdom were put into such a posture as he might find all things to his own content and security; which they infinitely desired to see as soon as might be, and to that purpose made daily instances to the Parliament. In the mean time he sat still, or removed to such places as were most convenient for the march of the army, being in all places as well provided for and accommodated as he had used to be in any progress; the best gentlemen of the several counties through which he passed daily resorted to him without distinction; he was attended by some of his old trusty servants in the places nearest his person; and that which gave him most encouragement to believe that they meant well, was, that in the army's address to the Parliament* they desired that care might be taken for the settling the King's rights, according to the several professions they had made in their declarations, and that the royal party might be treated with more candour and less rigour. And many good officers who had served his majesty faithfully were civilly received by the officers of the army, and lived quietly in their quarters, which they could not do anywhere else; which raised a great reputation to the army throughout the kingdom, and as much reproach upon the Parliament.

The Parliament at this time had recovered its spirits, when they saw that the army did not march towards them, and not only remained at St Alban's, but was drawn back to a farther distance; which persuaded them that their general was displeased with their former advance: and so [they] proceeded with all passion and vigour against those principal officers who, they knew, contrived all these proceedings. They published declarations* to the kingdom, that they desired to bring the King in honour to his Parliament, which was their business from the beginning, and that he was detained prisoner against his will in the army, and that they had great reason to apprehend the safety of his person. The army, on the other hand, declared that his majesty was neither prisoner nor detained against his will; and appealed to his majesty himself, and to all his friends who had liberty to repair to him, whether he had not more liberty, and was not treated with more respect, since he came into the army than he had been at Holmby, or during the time he remained in those places and with that retinue that the Parliament had appointed. The city seemed very unanimously devoted to the Parliament and incensed against the army; and seemed resolute not only with their train-bands and auxiliary regiments to assist and defend the Parliament, but appointed some of the old officers who had served under the earl of Essex, and had been disbanded under the new model, as Waller, Massey, and others, to list new forces; towards which there was not like to be want of men out of their old forces, and such of the King's as would be glad of the employment. There was nothing they did really fear so much as that the army would make a firm conjunction with the King, and unite with his party, of which there was so much show; and many unskilful men, who wished it, bragged too much; and therefore the Parliament sent a committee to his majesty with an address of another style than they had lately used, with many professions of duty, and declaring that if he was not in all respects treated as he ought to be, and as he desired, it was not their fault, who desired that he might be at full liberty, and do what he would; hoping that the King would have been induced to desire to come to London, and to make complaint of the army's having taken him from Holmby; by which they believed the King's party would be disabused, and withdraw their hopes of any good from the army; and then they thought they should be hard enough for them. [*HR*, X, 88–94]

As attempts continued on both sides to come to an agreement with the King, the army moved towards London, and presented charges on 6 July against eleven Presbyterian members of the House of Commons. Presbyterian members—including the eleven—absented themselves from the House, Parliament disbanded the forces it had been raising, and reversed its attempts to put the City militia under Presbyterian control. That provoked an insurrection in the Presbyterian-dominated City. Riots from 21 to 28 July forced the Independent leadership in both Houses in turn to leave London and take refuge with the army. But on 6 August the army occupied the City. As many Presbyterians ceased to attend Parliament, Independents, once more in the majority, took control.

These kinds of proceedings in all places blasted all the King's hopes, and deprived him of all the rest and quiet he had for some time enjoyed; nor could he devise any remedy. He was weary of depending upon the army, but neither knew how to get from them, nor whither else to resort for help. The officers of those guards which were assigned to attend his person, and who had behaved themselves with good manners and duty towards him, and very civilly towards those of his

party who had used to wait upon his majesty, began now to murmur
at so great resort to him, and to use many who came rudely, and not
suffer them to go into the room where the King was, or, which was
worse, put them out when they were there; and when his majesty
seemed to take notice and be troubled at it, they appeared not to be
concerned, nor answered his majesty with that duty they had used to do.
They affronted the Scots' commissioners* very notably, and would not
suffer them to speak with the King; which caused an expostulation
from the Parliament;* which removed the obstruction for the future,
but procured no satisfaction for the injury they had received, nor
made the same officers more civil towards their persons. Ashburnham
and Berkeley* received many advertisements from some officers, with
whom they had most conversed, and who would have been glad that
the King might have been restored by the army for the preferments
which they expected might fall to their share, that Cromwell and
Ireton resolved never to trust the King, or to do any thing towards his
restoration, and they two steered the whole body; and therefore they
advised that some way might be found to remove his majesty out of
their hands. Major Huntington, one of the best officers they had, and
major to Cromwell's own regiment of horse, upon whom he relied in
any enterprise of importance more than upon any man, had been
employed by him to the King, to say those things from him which had
given the King the most confidence, and were much more than he
had ever said to Ashburnham; and the major did really believe that he
had meant all he said, and the King had a good opinion of the integrity
of the major, upon the testimony he had received from some he knew
had no mind to deceive his majesty; and the man merited the testimony they gave him. He, when he observed Cromwell to grow colder
in his expressions for the King than he had formerly been, expostulated with him, in very sharp terms, for abusing him and making him
the instrument to cozen the King; and though the other endeavoured
to persuade him that all should be well, he informed his majesty of all
he had observed, and told him that Cromwell was a villain, and would
destroy him if he were not prevented; and in a short time after he gave
up his commission, and would serve no longer in the army. Cromwell
himself expostulated with Mr Ashburnham, and complained that the
King could not be trusted, and that he had no affection or confidence
in the army, but was jealous of them and of all the officers: that he
had intrigues in the Parliament, and treaties with the Presbyterians of
the city to raise new troubles; that he had a treaty concluded with
the Scotch commissioners to engage the nation again in blood; and

therefore he would not be answerable if any thing fell out amiss, and contrary to expectation; and that was the reason, besides the old animosity, that had drawn on the affront which the commissioners had complained of. What that treaty was, and what it produced, will be mentioned in a more proper time.

There was at this time a new faction grown up in the army, which were, either by their own denomination or with their own consent, called *Levellers*; who spake insolently and confidently against the King and Parliament and the great officers of the army; professed as great malice against all the lords as against the King, and declared that all degrees of men should be levelled, and an equality should be established, both in titles and estates, throughout the kingdom. Whether the raising this spirit was a piece of Cromwell's ordinary witchcraft, in order to some of his designs, or whether it grew amongst those tares which had been sowed in that confusion, certain it is, it gave him real trouble at last, which must be set down hereafter; but the present use he made of it [was, that,] upon the licentious discourse of that kind which some soldiers upon the guard usually made, the guard upon the King's person was doubled, [and] a restraint put upon the great resort of people who came to see the King; and all pretended to be for his security, and to prevent any violence that might be attempted upon his life, which they seemed to apprehend and detest. In the mean time they neither hindered his majesty from riding abroad to take the air, nor from doing any thing he had a mind to, nor restrained those who waited upon him in his bedchamber, nor his chaplains from performing their functions; though towards all these there was less civility exercised than had been; and the guards which waited nearest were more rude, and made more noise at unseasonable hours than they had been accustomed to do; the captain who commanded them, colonel Whalley, being a man of a rough and brutal temper, who had offered great violence to his nature when he appeared to exercise any civility and good manners. The King every day received little billets or letters, secretly conveyed to him, without any name, which advertised him of wicked designs upon his life, and some of them advised him to make an escape, and repair secretly into the city, where he should be safe; some letters directing him to such an alderman's house; all which his majesty looked upon as artifice to lead him into some strait, from whence he should not easily explicate himself; and yet many who repaired to him brought the same advice from men of unquestionable sincerity, by what reason soever they were swayed.

The King found himself in great perplexity from what he discerned and observed himself, as well as what he heard from others; but what use to make of the one or the other was very hard to resolve: he did really believe that their malice was at the height, and that they did design his murder, but knew not which was a probable way to prevent it. The making an escape, if it were not contrived with wonderful sagacity, would expose him to be assassinated by pretended ignorance, and would be charged upon himself; and if he could avoid their guards, and get beyond them undiscovered, whither should he go, and what place would receive and defend him? The hope of the city seemed not to him to have a foundation of reason; they had been too late subdued to recover courage for such an adventure; and the army now was much more master of it than when they desponded. There is reason to believe that he did resolve to transport himself beyond the seas, which had been no hard matter to have brought to pass; but with whom he consulted for the way of doing it is not to this day discovered, they who were instrumental in his remove pretending to know nothing of the resolution or counsel. But one morning about the beginning of September,* the King having the night before pretended some indisposition, and that he would go to his rest, they who went into his chamber found that he was not there, nor had been in his bed that night. There were two or three letters found upon his table, writ all with his own hand, one to the Parliament, and another to the general; in which he declared the reason of his remove to be, an apprehension that some desperate persons had a purpose to assassinate him; and therefore he had withdrawn himself with a purpose of remaining concealed, until the Parliament had agreed upon such propositions as should be fit for him to consent to; and he would then appear, and willingly consent to any thing that should be for the peace and happiness of the kingdom. There were discovered the treading of horses at a back door of the garden into which his majesty had a passage out of his chamber; and it is true that way he went, having appointed his horse to be there ready at an hour, and sir John Berkeley, Ashburnham, and Legge,* to wait upon him, the two last being of his bed-chamber. Ashburnham seemed only to know what they were to do, the other two having received only orders to attend. When they were free from the apprehension of the guards and the horse quarters, they rode towards the west, and towards that part of Hampshire which led to the New Forest. The King asked Ashburnham where the ship lay; which made the other two conclude that the King resolved to transport himself. After they had made some stay in that part next the sea, and Ashburnham had been some time absent, he returned without any news of the ship; with which the King seemed troubled. Upon this disappointment, the King thought it best, for avoiding all highways, to go to Titchfield, a noble seat of the earl of Southampton, who was not there, but inhabited by the old lady his mother, with a small family, which made the retreat the more convenient. There his majesty alighted, and would speak with the lady, to whom he made no scruple of communicating himself, well knowing her to be a lady of that honour and spirit that she was superior to all kind of temptation. There he refreshed himself, and consulted with his three servants what he should next do, since there was neither ship ready, nor could they presume that they could remain long there undiscovered.

In this debate, the Isle of Wight came to be mentioned (as they say) by Ashburnham, as a place where his majesty might securely repose himself until he thought fit to inform the Parliament where he was. Colonel Hammond was governor there, an officer of the army, and of nearest trust with Cromwell, having by his advice been married to a daughter of John Hampden, whose memory he always adored; yet, by some fatal mistake, this man was thought a person of honour and generosity enough to trust the King's person to, and Ashburnham and Berkeley were sent to him, with orders, first, to be sure that the man would faithfully promise not to deliver his majesty up, though the Parliament or army should require him, but to give him his liberty to shift for himself if he were not able to defend him: and except he would make that promise, they should not let him know where his majesty was, but should return presently to him. With this commission they two crossed the water to the Isle of Wight, the King in the mean time reposing himself at Titchfield. The next day they found Colonel Hammond, who was known to them both, who had conversation with him in the army when the King was well treated there, and their persons had been very civilly treated by most of the officers, who thought themselves qualified sufficiently for Court preferments. They told him that the King was withdrawn from the army; of which he seemed to have had no notice, and to be very much surprised with it. They then said, that the King had so good an opinion of him, knowing him to be a gentleman, and for his relation to Dr Hammond, (whose nephew he was,) that he would trust his person with him, and would from thence write to the Parliament, if he would promise that if his message had not that effect which he hoped it would have, he would leave him to himself to go whither he thought fit, and would not deliver him to the Parliament or army if they should require it. His answer was, that he would pay all the duty and service to his majesty that was in his power; and if he pleased to come thither, he would

receive and entertain him as well as he could; but that he was an inferior officer, and must obey his superiors in whatsoever they thought
fit to command him: with which when he saw they were not satisfied,
he asked where the King was; to which they made no other answer but
that they would acquaint his majesty with his answer, and if he were
satisfied with it they would return to him again. He demanded that
Mr Ashburnham would stay with him and that the other might go to
the King; which Ashburnham refused to do.

After some time spent in debate, in which he made many expressions
of his desire to do any service to his majesty, they were contented that
he should go with them, and Ashburnham said he would conduct him
to the place where the King was; and so, he commanding three or four
servants or soldiers to wait on him, they went together to Titchfield; and,
the other staying below, Ashburnham went up to the King's chamber.
And when he had acquainted him with all that had passed, and that
Hammond was in the house, his majesty brake out in a passionate ex-
clamation, and said, 'Oh, Jack, thou hast undone me!' with which the
other falling into a great passion of weeping, offered to go down and to
kill Hammond; to which his majesty would not consent, and, after some
pausing and deliberation, sent for him up, and endeavoured to persuade
him to make the same promise which had before been proposed: to
which he made the same answer he had done, but with many professions
of doing all the offices he could for his majesty, and seemed to believe
that the army would do well for him. The King believed that there was
now no possible way to get from him, he having the command of the
country, and could call in what help he would; and so he went with him
into the Isle of Wight, and was lodged in Carisbrooke Castle with all
demonstration of respect and duty. [*HR*, X, 125–9]

From Carisbrooke, the King continued to try to divide his enemies, negoti-
ating with the Scots, the army, and Parliament. He sent to Parliament to
request that he come to London to discuss a settlement. Parliament's scepti-
cism about the King's sincerity was expressed in a new and unfavourable set
of propositions, embodied in four bills, to which they required his assent
before further discussions. They were presented to him on 24 December. The
King was required to answer within four days. On 26 December, however,
he signed a secret agreement — the Engagement — with the Scottish com-
missioners, which committed the Scots to lend him military support to
recover his authority in England from the Independents in the army and
Parliament. Although the Engagement remained secret, on 28 December he
rejected the four bills.

Upon the receipt of the King's answer, there appeared a new spirit
and temper in the House of Commons. Hitherto no man had mentioned the King's person without duty and respect, and only lamented
that he was misled by evil and wicked counsellors, who being removed
from him, he might by the advice of his Parliament govern well
enough. But now, upon the refusal to pass these bills, every man's
mouth was opened against him with the utmost sauciness and license,
each man striving to exceed the other in the impudence and bitterness
of his invective. Cromwell declared that the King was a man of great
parts and a great understanding, (faculties they had hitherto endeavoured to have him thought to be without,) but that he was so great
a dissembler, and so false a man, that he was not to be trusted; and
thereupon repeated many particulars, whilst he was in the army, when
his majesty wished that such and such things might be done, which
being done to gratify him, he was displeased, and complained of it: that
whilst he professed with all solemnity that he referred himself wholly
to the Parliament, and depended wholly upon their wisdom and counsel for the settlement and composing the distractions of the kingdom,
he had at the same time secret treaties with the Scots' commissioners
how he might embroil the nation in a new war and destroy the
Parliament. He concluded, that they might no farther trouble themselves with sending messages to him, or farther propositions, but that
they might enter upon those counsels which were necessary towards
the settlement of the kingdom without having further recourse to the
King. Those of his party seconded this good advice, with new
reproaches upon the person of the King, and charging him with such
abominable actions as had been never heard of, and could be only suggested from the malice of their own hearts; whilst men who had any
modesty, and abhorred that way of proceedings, stood amazed and
confounded at the manner and presumption of it, and without courage
to give any notable opposition to their rage. So that, after several days
spent in passionate debates to this purpose, they voted that they would
make no more addresses to the King,* but proceed towards settling
the government, and providing for the peace of the kingdom, in such
a manner as they should judge best for the benefit and liberty of the
subject: and a committee was appointed to prepare a Declaration to
inform and satisfy the people of this their resolution, and the grounds
thereof, and to assure them that they had lawful authority to proceed
in this manner. In the mean time, the King had from the time of his
coming to the Isle of Wight enjoyed the liberty of taking the air, and
refreshing himself throughout the island, and was attended by such

servants as he had appointed or sent for to come thither to him, to the time that he had refused to pass those bills; but from thence he was no more suffered to go out of the castle beyond a little ill garden that belonged to it. And now, after this vote of the House of Commons, that there should be no more addresses made to him, all his servants were removed, and a few new men, utterly unknown to his majesty, were deputed to be about his person to perform all those offices which they believed might be requisite, and of whose fidelity to them they were as well assured as that they were without any reverence or affection for the King.

It is very true, that within few days after the King's withdrawing from Hampton Court, and after it was known that he was in the Isle of Wight, there was a meeting of the general officers of the army at Windsor,* where Cromwell and Ireton were present, to consult what should be now done with the King. For though Cromwell was weary of the Agitators and resolved to break their meetings, and though the Parliament concurred in all he desired, yet his entire confidence was in the officers of the army, who were they who swayed the Parliament, and in the army itself, to bring what he intended to pass. And at this conference, the preliminaries whereof were always fastings and prayers, made at the very council by Cromwell or Ireton, or some other inspired person, as most of the officers were, it was resolved that the King should be prosecuted for his life, as a criminal person: of which his majesty was advertised speedily by Watson, quarter-master-general of the army, who was present, and had pretended from the first coming of the King to the army to have a desire to serve him, and desired to be now thought to retain it; but the resolution was a great secret, of which the Parliament had not the least intimation or jealousy, but was, as it had been, to be cozened by degrees to do what they never intended. Nor was his majesty easily persuaded to give credit to the information; but though he expected, and thought it very probable, that they would murder him, he did not believe that they would attempt it with that formality, or let the people know their intentions. The approach they made towards it was their Declaration that they would make no more addresses to the King,* that by an interregnum they might feel the pulse of the people, and discover how they would submit to another form of government; and yet all writs and process of justice, and all commissions, still issued in the King's name, without his consent or privity; and little other change or alteration, but that what was before done by the King himself, and by his immediate order, was now performed by the Parliament; and instead of Acts of Parliament they made ordinances of the two Houses to serve all their occasions; which found the same obedience from the people.

This Declaration of no more addresses contained a charge against the King of whatsoever had been done amiss from the beginning of his government, or before, not without a direct insinuation as if he had conspired with the Duke of Buckingham against the life of his father; the prejudice he had brought upon the Protestant religion in foreign parts by lending his ships to the King of France, who employed them against Rochelle: they renewed the remembrance and reproach of all those grievances which had been mentioned in their first Remonstrance* of the state of the kingdom, and repeated all the calumnies which had been contained in all their Declarations before and after the war; which had been all so fully answered by his majesty that the world was convinced of their rebellion and treason: they charged him with being the cause of all the blood that had been spilt by his having made a war upon his Parliament and rejected all overtures of peace which had been made to him; and in all these regards they resolved to make no more address to him, but by their own authority to provide for the peace and welfare of the kingdom.

This Declaration found much opposition in the House of Commons, in respect of the particular reproaches they had now cast upon the person of the King, which they had heretofore in their own published Declarations to the people charged upon the evil counsellors and persons about him; and some persons had been sentenced and condemned for those very crimes which they now accused his majesty of. But there was much more exception to their conclusion from those premises, that therefore they would address themselves no more to him; and John Maynard, a member of the House, and a lawyer of great eminence, who had too much complied and concurred with their irregular and unjust proceedings, after he had with great vehemence opposed and contradicted the most odious parts of their Declaration, told them plainly, that by this resolution of making no more addresses to the King they did as far as in them lay dissolve the Parliament; and that from the time of that determination he knew not with what security, in point of law, they could meet together, or any man join with them in their counsels: that it was of the essence of Parliaments that they should upon all occasions repair to the King; and that his majesty's refusal at any time to receive their petitions, or to admit their addresses, had been always held the highest breach of their privilege, because it tended to their dissolution without dissolving them; and therefore if they should now on their parts determine that they would receive no more messages from him, (which was likewise a part of their Declaration), nor make any more address to him, they did, upon the matter, declare that they were no longer a Parliament: and then, how could the people look upon them as such? This argumentation being boldly pressed by a man of that learning and authority, who had very seldom not been believed, made a great impression upon all men who had not prostituted themselves to Cromwell and his party. But the other side meant not to maintain their resolution by discourses, well knowing where their strength lay, and so still called for the question; which was carried by a plurality of voices, as they foresaw it would; very many persons who abhorred the determination not having courage enough to provoke the powerful men by owning their dissent; others satisfying themselves with the resolution to withdraw themselves, and to bear no farther part in the counsels; which Maynard himself did, and came no more to the House in very many months, nor till there seemed to be such an alteration in the minds of men, that there would be a reversal of that monstrous determination; and many others did the same.

When this Declaration was thus passed in the Commons, and by them sent to the House of Peers for their concurrence, the manner or the matter was not thought of that importance as to need much debate, but with as little formality as was possible it had the concurrence of that House;* and was immediately printed and published, and new orders sent to the Isle of Wight for the more strict looking to and guarding the King, that he might not escape.

The publishing this Declaration wrought very different effects in the minds of the people from what they expected it would produce; and it appeared to be so publicly detested, that many who had served the Parliament in several unwarrantable employments and commissions, from the beginning of the war, in the city and in the country, withdrew themselves from the service, and much inveighed against the Parliament for declining all the principles upon which they had engaged them. Many private persons took upon them to publish answers to that odious Declaration,* that, the King himself being under so strict a restraint that he could make no answer, the people might not be poisoned with the belief of it. And the several answers of this kind wrought very much upon the people, who opened their mouths very loud against the Parliament and the army; and the clamour was increased by the increase of taxes and impositions, which were raised by new ordinances of Parliament upon the kingdom; and though they were so entirely possessed of the whole kingdom and the forces and garrisons thereof that they had no enemy to fear or apprehend, yet they disbanded no part of their army; and notwithstanding they raised incredible sums of money, upon the sale of the Church and the Crown lands,* for which they found purchasers enough among their own party in the city, army, and country, and upon composition with delinquents,* and the sale of their lands who refused or could not be admitted to compound, (which few refused to do who could be admitted, in regard that their estates were all under sequestration, and the rents thereof paid to the Parliament, so that till they compounded they had nothing to support themselves, whereby they were driven into extreme want and necessities, and were compelled to make their compositions, at how unreasonable rates soever, that they might thereby be enabled to sell some part that they might preserve the rest, and their houses from being pulled down or let fall down, and their woods from being wasted or spoiled; but notwithstanding all these vast receipts, which they ever pretended should ease the people of their burden, and should suffice to pay the army,) their expenses at sea and land, and their debts, were so great that they raised the public taxes; and, besides all customs and excise, they levied a monthly contribution of a hundred and fifty thousand pounds by a land tax throughout the kingdom; which was more than had been ever done before, and being at a time when they had no enemy who contended with them, was an evidence that it would have no end, and that the army was still to be kept up, to make good the resolution they had taken to have no more to do with the King; and that made the resolution generally the more odious. And all this grew the more insupportable, by reason that, upon the publishing this last monstrous Declaration, most of those persons of condition, who, as hath been said before, had been seduced to do them service throughout the kingdom, decline to appear longer in so detestable an employment; and now a more inferior sort of the common people succeeded in those employments, who thereby exercised so great insolence over those who were in quality above them, and who always had a power over them, that was very grievous; and for this, let the circumstances be what they would, no redress could ever be obtained, all distinction of quality being renounced. And they who were not above the condition of ordinary inferior constables six or seven years before, were now the justices of peace, sequestrators, and commissioners; who executed the commands of the Parliament in all the counties of the kingdom with such rigour and tyranny as was natural for such persons to use over and towards those upon whom they had formerly looked at such a distance. But let their sufferings be never so great, and the murmur and discontent never so general, there was no shadow of hope by which they might discern any possible relief; so that they who had struggled as long as they were able submitted patiently to the yoke, with the more satisfaction in that they saw many of those who had been the principal contrivers of all the mischiefs, to satisfy their own ambition and that they might govern over others, reduced now to almost as ill a condition as themselves, at least to as little power and authority and security; whilst the whole government of the nation remained, upon the matter, wholly in their hands who in the beginning of the Parliament were scarce ever heard of, or their names known but in the places where they inhabited. [*HR*, X, 146–51]

Royalists were deeply struck by how Cromwell came to power without, at any time, seeming to have sought it. Clarendon, like others, found it difficult to take at face value the religious enthusiasm of Independents, thinking it a mask for political ambition. He contrasted their success with the failure of Presbyterian political strategies.

It was a wonderful difference, throughout their whole proceedings, between the heads of those who were thought to sway the Presbyterian councils and those who governed the Independents, though they were equally masters of dissimulation, and had equally malice and wickedness in their intentions, though not of the same kind, and were equally unrestrained by any scruples or motions of conscience; the Independents always doing that which, how ill and unjustifiable soever, contributed still to the end they aimed at, and to the conclusion they meant to bring to pass; whereas the Presbyterians, for the most part, did always somewhat that reasonably must destroy their own end, and cross that which they first and principally designed. And there were two reasons that might naturally produce this unsuccess in the latter, at least hindered the even progress and current which favoured the other. First, their councils were most distracted and divided, being made up of many men whose humours and natures must be observed and complied with, and whose concurrence was necessary to the carrying on, though their inclinations did not concur in, the same designs; whereas the other party was entirely led and governed by two or three, to whom they resigned implicitly the conduct of their interest; who advanced when they saw it seasonable, and stood still, or retired, or even declined the way they best liked, when they saw any inconvenient jealousy awaked by the progress they had made.

In the second place, the Presbyterians, (by whom I mean the Scots,) formed all their counsels by the inclinations and affections of the people; and first considered how they might corrupt, and seduce, and dispose, them to second their purposes, and how far they might depend upon their concurrence and assistance, before they resolved to make any attempt; and this made them in such a degree submit to their senseless and wretched clergy, whose infectious breath corrupted and governed the people, and whose authority was prevalent upon their own wives and in their domestic affairs; and yet they never communicated to them more than the outside of their designs. Whereas, on the other side, Cromwell, and the few others with whom he consulted, first considered what was absolutely necessary to their main and determined end, and then, whether it were right or wrong, to make all other means subservient to it; to cozen and deceive men, as long as they could induce them to contribute to what they desired, upon motives how foreign soever, and when they would keep company with them no longer, or farther serve their purposes, to compel them by force to submit to what they should not be able to oppose. And so the one resolved only to do what they believed the people would like and approve; and the other, that the people should like and approve what they had resolved. And this difference in the measures they took was the true cause of the so different success in all they undertook. Machiavelli was in the right, though he got an ill name by it with those who take what he says from the report of other men, or do not enough consider themselves what he says, and his method in speaking: he was as great an enemy to tyranny and injustice in any government as any man then was or now is, and says, that a man were better be a dog than to be subject to those passions and appetites which possess all unjust and ambitious and tyrannical persons; but he confesses, that they who are so transported, and have entertained such wicked designs as are void of all conscience, must not think to prosecute them by the rules of conscience, which was laid aside or subdued before they entered upon them; they must make no scruple of doing all those impious things which are necessary to compass and support the impiety to which they have devoted themselves; and therefore he commends Caesar Borgia* for not being startled with breach of faith, perjuries, and murders, for the removal of those men who he was sure would cross and enervate the whole enterprise he had resolved and addicted himself to, and blames those usurpers who had made themselves tyrants, for hoping to support a government by justice which they had assumed unjustly, and which, having wickedly attempted, they manifestly lost by not being wicked enough. The common old adage, that he who hath drawn his sword against his prince ought to throw away the scabbard, never to think of sheathing it again, hath never been received in a neighbour climate, but hath been looked upon, in the frolic humour of that nation, as a gaiety that manifests a noble spirit, and may conduce to many advantages, and hath been controlled by some wonderful successes in this age, in those parts which used not to be so favourable to such attempts: yet without doubt the rule will still hold good; and they who enter upon unwarrantable enterprises must pursue many unwarrantable ways to preserve themselves from the penalty of the first guilt.

Cromwell, though the greatest dissembler living, always made his hypocrisy of singular use and benefit to him, and never did any thing, how ungracious or imprudent soever it seemed to be, but what was necessary to the design; even his roughness and unpolishedness, which in the beginning of the Parliament he affected, contrary to the smoothness and complacency which his cousin and bosom friend Mr Hampden practised towards all men, was necessary; and his first public declaration in the beginning of the war to his troop when it was first mustered, that he would not deceive or cozen them by the perplexed and involved expressions in his commission, to fight for 'King and Parliament,' and therefore told them, that if the King chanced to be in the body of the enemy that he was to charge, he would as soon discharge his pistol upon him as at any other private person, and if their conscience would not permit them to do the like, he advised them not to list themselves in his troop or under his command, which was generally looked upon as imprudent and malicious, and might by the professions the Parliament then made have proved dangerous to him, yet served his turn, and severed [from others], and united, all the furious and incensed men against the government, whether ecclesiastical or civil, to look upon him as a man for their turn, and upon whom they might depend, as one who would go through his work that he undertook. And his strict and unsociable humour in not keeping company with the other officers of the army in their jollities and excesses, to which most of the superior officers under the earl of Essex were inclined, and by which he often made himself ridiculous or contemptible, drew all those of the like sour or reserved natures to his society and conversation, and gave him opportunity to form their understandings, inclinations, and resolutions, to his own model. And by this he grew to have a wonderful interest in the common soldiers, out of which, as his authority increased, he made all his officers, well instructed how to live in the same manner with their soldiers, that they might be able to apply them to their own purposes. Whilst he looked upon the Presbyterian humour as the best incentive to rebellion, no man more a Presbyterian; he sung all psalms with them to their tunes, and loved the longest sermons as much as they; but when he discovered that they would prescribe some limits and bounds to their rebellion, that it was not well breathed, and would expire as soon as some few particulars were granted to them in religion which he cared not for, and then that the government must run still in the same channel, it concerned him to make it believed that the State had been more delinquent than the Church, and that the people suffered more by the civil than by the ecclesiastical power; and therefore that the change of one would give them little ease, if there were not as great an alteration in the other, and if the whole government in both were not reformed and altered; which though it made him generally odious, and irreconciled many of his old friends to him, yet it made those who remained more cordial and firm to him, and he could better compute his own strength and upon whom he might depend. And this discovery made him contrive the [new] model [of the army]; which was the most unpopular act, and disobliged all those who first contrived the rebellion, and who were the very soul of it; and yet if he had not brought that to pass, and changed a general who, though not very sharpsighted, would never be governed, nor applied to any thing he did not like, for another who had no eyes,* and so would be willing to be led, all his designs must have come to nothing, and he remained a private colonel of horse, not considerable enough to be in any figure upon an advantageous composition.

After all the successes of his new model, he saw his army was balanced by that of the Scots, who took themselves to have equal merit with the other, and was thought to have contributed no less towards the suppression of the King than that under Fairfax had done, and who, after all the victories, and reduction of the King to that lowness, desired still a composition, and to submit again to the subjection of the King; nor was it yet time for him to own or communicate his resolution to the contrary, lest even many of those who wished the extirpation of monarchy might be startled at the difficulty of the enterprise, and with the power that was like to oppose them. And therefore he was first to incense the people against the Scots' nation, as being a mercenary aid entertained at a vast charge to the kingdom, that was only to be paid their wages and to be dismissed, without having the honour to judge with them upon what conditions the King should be received and restored; the accomplishing whereof ought to be the peculiar glory of the Parliament without a rival, and that the King might owe the benefit wholly to them. And this was as popular an argument as he could embark himself in, the whole kingdom in general having a great detestation of the Scots; and they who most desired the King's restoration wished that he might have as little obligation to them as was possible, and that they might have as little credit afterwards with him. And with this universal applause, he compelled the Scots to depart the kingdom, with that circumstance as must ever afterwards render them odious and infamous. There seemed nothing more dangerous and destructive to the power and interest of the army, in so general a discontent throughout the kingdom, than a division, and mutiny within itself; that the common soldiers should erect an authority distinct from their officers, and by which they would choose to govern against their superior commanders, at least without them, and to fancy that they had an interest of their own severed from that of the army, and for the preservation whereof they were to trust none but themselves; which had been never heard of before in any army, and was looked upon as a presage of the ruin of the whole, and of those who had adhered to them; and yet, if he had not raised this seditious spirit in the army, he could not have prevented the disbanding some part of the army and sending another part of it into Ireland, before the Scots left Newcastle; nor have been able to have taken the King from Holmby into the hands of the army after the Scots were gone. And after all his hypocrisy towards the King and his party, by which he prevented many inconveniences which might have befallen him, he could never have been rid of him again so unreproachfully as by his changing his own countenance, and giving other cause to the King to suspect the safety of his person, and thereupon to make his escape from the army, by which he quickly became a prisoner, and so was deprived of any resort, from whence many mischiefs might have proceeded to have disturbed his counsels. And how constantly he pursued this method in his subsequent actions will be observed in its place. [*HR*, X, 168–71]

14. The Second Civil War and the Trial of the King

Following the return to Scotland of the Scottish commissioners in February 1648, the Scottish Parliament—though deeply divided—agreed to accept the Engagement and support the King against the English Parliament and army. In April it set out an ultimatum to them, and began to raise soldiers. In South Wales, disbanded soldiers who had not received their full arrears of pay revolted. In England itself, royalists were working to turn a resurgence of sympathy for the King and widespread discontent about the behaviour of the army into an armed rising. Excitement grew in the royalist camp: as the Prince of Wales, now in France, anticipated a call to England to join the Scots or lead the rebellion, Hyde, after nearly two years in Jersey, hastened to join him.

THE lord Capel, who was in the most secret part of all these intrigues in England, being entirely trusted by those who would not trust any of the Presbyterians nor communicate their purposes to them, had written to the Chancellor who remained still in Jersey, the hopes he had of a good conjuncture, and his own resolution to embark himself in the attempt as soon as it should be ripe; and had signified the King's command to him, that as soon as he [the Chancellor] should be required to wait upon the Prince he should without delay obey the summons: and the King had likewise writ to the Queen very positively, that when it should be necessary for the Prince to remove out of France, the Chancellor should have notice of it, and be required to give his attendance upon the person of his royal highness in the condition he had formerly done. And about the beginning of May, in the year 1648, the lord Capel, who had always corresponded with him, and informed him of the state of affairs, and all that concerned himself, writ to him that all things were now so ripe that he believed the Prince would not find it fit to remain longer in France; and thereupon conjured him that he would be ready, if he should be sent for, as he was confident he would, to attend upon his highness; which, he said, all the King's friends expected he should do, and which he was resolved to do, as soon as he [the Prince] should be out of France, though he should receive no order or invitation so to do.

About the middle of May the Queen, according to his majesty's command, sent to the Chancellor to Jersey, commanding that he would wait upon the Prince in the Louvre at Paris, upon a day that was past before the letter came to his hands. But he no sooner received the summons, than he betook himself to the journey, and to transport himself into Normandy: where, after he was landed, he made what haste he could to Caen, supposing he should there find Secretary Nicholas, who had given him notice that he had received the same command. When he came to Caen, he found the Secretary's lady there, but himself was gone to Rouen, to the lord Cottington, and intended to stay there till the other should arrive, and to consult together there upon their farther journey. The old earl of Bristol, who had lived likewise at Caen, was gone with the Secretary to Rouen, having likewise received the same summons with the other to attend the Prince at the Louvre. The Chancellor hastened to Rouen, where he found the lord Cottington, who held still the office and precedence of Lord High Treasurer of England, the earl of Bristol, and Secretary Nicholas, who were all his very good friends, and very glad of his arrival. They had received advertisement the day before that the Prince, with all his small train, was passed by towards Calais; and direction was sent that the Chancellor, whom they supposed to be on the way, should stay at Rouen till they should receive new orders from Calais, where his royal highness would take new measures what he was to do. So they stayed together at Rouen, where there were at the same time very many English of quality in their own condition, who were driven out of England as well as they for their fidelity to the King, and had brought somewhat with them for their support abroad till they might upon some good change return to their own country. In the mean time they lived very decently together in that city, where they were well esteemed. The way between Rouen and Calais was so dangerous, without a very strong convoy, that no day passed without robberies and murders, so that they were glad of their order not to stir from thence till they should receive a very particular direction from the Prince; and within few days they received advice that the Prince had, as soon as he came to Calais, put himself on board a ship that he found there, and was bound for Holland, from whence they were to hear from him how they should dispose of themselves. Whereupon they all resolved to remove from Rouen to Dieppe, from whence they might embark themselves for Holland if they saw cause; and the ways by land, in regard that both the French and the Spanish armies were in the field, were very dangerous.

The Prince's remove from Paris on such a sudden proceeded from an accident in England that was very extraordinary, and looked like a call from Heaven. The Parliament had prepared, according to custom, a good fleet of ten or a dozen ships for the summer guard, and appointed Rainborowe* (who had been bred at sea, and was the son of an eminent commander at sea lately dead, but he himself, from the time of the new model, had been an officer of foot in the army, and was a colonel of special note and account, and of Cromwell's chief confidents) to be admiral thereof; which offended the earl of Warwick much, and disposed him to that concurrence with his brother. And captain Batten* was as much unsatisfied, who had acted so great a part in the first alienating the fleet and the affections of the seamen from the King, and had ever been their vice-admiral afterwards, and the person upon whom they principally relied at sea, and Rainborowe, as long as he remained in the navy, had been under his command. And both the earl and he well knew that this man was now made admiral of this fleet because they, being Presbyterians, should have no credit or influence upon it; which made them solicitous enough that the seamen should not be well pleased with the alteration, and they looked upon Rainborowe as a man that had forsaken them, and preferred the land before the sea service. The seamen are a nation by themselves, a humorous and fantastic people; fierce, and rude, and resolute, in whatsoever they resolve or are inclined to, but unsteady and inconstant in pursuing it, and jealous of those to-morrow by whom they are governed this day. These men, observing the general discontent of the people, and that, however the Parliament was obeyed by the power of the army, both army and Parliament were grown very odious to them, and hearing so much discourse of an army from Scotland ready to enter into the kingdom, they concluded that the King would be restored; and then remembering that the revolt of the fleet* was the preamble to the loss of his majesty's authority every where else, and the cause of all his misfortunes, they imagined it would be a glorious thing to them if they could lead the way to his majesty's restoration by their declaring for him. And this was an agitation among the common seamen, without communicating it to any officer of the quality of master of a ship. This inclination was much improved in them by a general disposition in Kent to an insurrection for the King, and by some gentlemen's coming on board the ships, according to the custom of that country, who fomented the good disposition in the seamen by all the ways they could.

At this very time there appeared general throughout Kent the same indigested affection to the King, and inclination to serve him, as was among the seamen, and was conducted with much less order and caution, neither the one or the other having been designed by those who did take care of the King's affairs, and who did design those insurrections which happened in other parts of the kingdom. They knew nothing, that is, contributed nothing to the distemper amongst the seamen, though they were not without some hope that, upon other revolutions, somewhat might likewise fall out at sea to the advantage of the King's affairs. They had an expectation from Kent, where they knew the people were generally well affected, and depended upon two or three gentlemen of that country who had been officers in the King's army, and resolved to bring in some troops of horse when the occasion should be ripe; but it was resolved that the Scots' army should be entered the kingdom, by which the Parliament army would be upon their march towards them, before they would have any appearance of force in the parts near London; and then they believed that both country and city would rise together. And so those gentlemen of Kent who were privy to any design lay privately in London, to avoid all cabals in their country; so that what fell out there was by mere chance and accident, that could neither be foreseen or prevented.

There happened to be at some jovial meeting in Kent about that time one Mr L'Estrange,* a younger brother of a good family in Norfolk, who had been always of the King's party, and for attempting somewhat in his own country for his majesty's service had been taken prisoner by the Parliament, and by a court of war condemned to die, but being kept in prison till the end of the war, was then set at liberty, as one in whom there was no more danger. But he retained his old affections, and more remembered the cruel usage he had received than that they had not proceeded as cruelly with him as they might have done. He had a great friendship with a young gentleman, Mr Hales,* who lived in Kent, and was married to a lady of a noble birth and fortune, he being heir to the greatest fortune of that country, but was to expect the inheritance from the favour of an old severe grandfather, who for the present kept the young couple from running into any excess, the mother of the lady being of as sour and strict a nature as the grandfather, and both of them so much of the Parliament party that they were not willing that any part of their estates should he hazarded for the King. At the house of this Mr Hales, Mr L'Estrange was, when, by the communication which that country always hath with the ships which lie in the Downs, the report first did arise that the fleet would presently declare for the King, and those seamen who came on shore talked as if the city of London would join with them. This drew many gentlemen of the country, who wished well, to visit the ships, and they returned more confirmed of the truth of what they had heard. Good-fellowship was a vice generally spread over that country, and this young great heir, who had been always bred amongst his neighbours, affected that which they were best pleased with, and so his house was a rendezvous for those who delighted in that exercise, and who every day brought him the news of the good inclinations in the fleet for the King; and all men's mouths were full of the general hatred the whole kingdom had against the Parliament as well as the army. Mr L'Estrange was a man of a good wit, and a fancy very luxuriant, and of an enterprising nature, and observed, by the good company that came to the house, that the affections of all that large and populous country were for the King. He began to tell Mr Hales, that though his grandfather did in his heart wish the King well, yet his carriage had been such in his conjunction with the Parliament that he [Hales] had more need of the King's favour than of his grandfather's to be heir to that great estate; and that certainly nothing could be more acceptable to his grandfather, or more glorious to him, than to be the instrument of both; and therefore advised him to put himself into the head of his own country, which would be willing to be led by him; that when the Scots were entered into the northern parts, and all the kingdom should be in arms, he might, with the body of his countrymen, march towards London; which would induce both the city and the Parliament to join with him, whereby he should have the honour to restore the King.

The company that frequented the house thought the discourse very reasonable, and saw that the issue must be very honourable: the young lady of the house was full of zeal for the King, and was willing her husband should be the instrument of his delivery: and the young gentleman himself had not been enough conversant in affairs of the world as to apprehend the danger or hazard in the attempt, and so referred himself and the whole business to be governed and conducted by Mr L'Estrange, whom they all believed by his discourse to be an able soldier. He writes some letters to particular gentlemen, who he was informed would receive them willingly, and signed warrants to the constables of hundreds with his own name, which had been never heard of in the country, requiring in his majesty's name all persons to appear, at a time and place appointed, to advise together, and to lay hold on such opportunities as should be offered for relieving the King and delivering him out of prison. There was an incredible appearance of the country at the place appointed,* where Mr L'Estrange appeared with Mr Hales, and those persons who had been used to their company. Mr L'Estrange spake to them in a style very much his own, and being not very clear to be understood the more prevailed over them. He spake like a man in authority, inveighed against the tyranny of the army, which subdued the Parliament, of their barbarous imprisonment of the King, and of a conspiracy they had to murder him; that the affections of that noble country were well known to his majesty, and that he had therefore appointed the fleet that was in the Downs to join with them; and that he doubted not but they would together be too strong for his enemies, who were like to have enough to do to defend themselves in many other places; and that his majesty was willing that they should have a gentleman of their own country, well known to them, to be their general; and named Mr Hales, who was present. There was not one man who so much asked for any letter or commission, or other authority from the King; but very frankly and unanimously declared that they would be all ready to join, and march as their general Hales should direct; and so another day and place was appointed for another appearance, and listing and forming their regiments; and in the mean time Mr L'Estrange set out such declarations and engagements as he thought most like to prevail with the people, and required that they should be read in all churches; which was done accordingly. And the next appearance was greater than the former, and with the same courage, many coming armed both horse and foot, and shewing a marvellous alacrity to the engagement. Their general then gave out his commissions for several regiments, and a new day was appointed for their rendezvous, when all should come armed, and keep together in a body, until it should be fit to march to London.

It was known that the fleet was gone out of the Downs, but it was as well known that it had absolutely renounced the service of the Parliament, and rejected all their officers. And it was easy to persuade the people that they were gone upon some important enterprise, and would speedily return; and it was insinuated, that it was gone to the Isle of Wight to release the King, who would return with it into Kent; which made them hasten their preparations.

When the King made the earl of Northumberland admiral,* he declared, and it was inserted in his commission, that he should enjoy that office during the minority of the duke of York; and the duke having made his escape at this time,* when there was this commotion amongst the seamen, it was no sooner known that his highness was in Holland, but the seamen talked aloud that they would go to their admiral; and the gentlemen of Kent stirring them up and inflaming them to that resolution, and the seamen again pressing the gentlemen to hasten their rising in arms, that they might assist and second each other, they both declared themselves sooner than they ought to have done, and before they were prepared for an enterprise of that importance.

The Parliament was well informed of the distemper amongst the seamen, and had therefore forborn putting the half of the provisions aboard the ships, which, for the greatest part, lay ready in the Downs, wanting only half the victual they were to have for the summer service. But those officers which were on board, finding they had no authority, and that the seamen mocked and laughed at them, sent every day to inform the Parliament what mutinous humour the whole fleet was in. Whereupon they sent Rainborowe and some other officers thither, presuming that the presence of the admiral would quickly quiet all. And he being a man of a rough imperious nature, as soon as he came on board his ship, began to make a strict inquiry into the former disorders and mutinous behaviour, upon which all the men of his ship retired into their old fortress of *One and All*,* and presently laid hold on him, and put him, and such other officers of the ship whom they liked not, into the boat, and sent them on shore. Which was no sooner known to the rest of the ships, but they followed their example, and used their officers in the same manner.* And after they had for some days been feasted and caressed by the people of Kent, some of the gentlemen putting themselves on board to join with them and in order to assist them towards providing such necessaries as were wanting, they went out of the Downs, and stood for Holland, that they might find their admiral, and let fall their anchors before the Brill. What was done by the gentlemen of Kent on shore, and the success thereof, will be related hereafter.

This so very seasonable revolt of the fleet, in a conjuncture when so many advantages were expected, was looked upon as a sure omen of the deliverance of the King. And upon the report that the ships were before Calais, as if they had expected somebody there, which was true for some time, it was thought fit that the Prince (who had hitherto thought of nothing but being sent for by the Scots, and how to find himself with them) should make all possible haste to Calais. And this was the cause of that his sudden motion, which was yet retarded for want of money and all other things necessary for his journey. The cardinal* shewed no manner of favouring all these appearances of advantage to the King; he gave less countenance to Scotland than he had ever done when it was in rebellion against the King; and, notwithstanding all his promises* with reference to Ireland, the marquis of Ormond remained still at Paris, without obtaining arms or money in any proportion, both which he had promised so liberally, and was, after all importunities, compelled to transport himself into Ireland (where he was so importunately called for) without any manner of supplies which were expected. And now, when the remove of the Prince was so behoofful, he [the cardinal] utterly refused to furnish him with any money; all which discountenances were shortly after remembered to Cromwell as high merit. [*HR*, XI, 22–31]

The revolts in Wales and in Kent had been unplanned and were premature. With the Scots not yet ready to march, the army was able to confront them with relative ease. As Cromwell moved against the rising in Wales, Fairfax, who had intended to march north towards the Scots and their royalist allies, remained in the south-east to oppose the Kentish rebels, although Clarendon attributed the change of plan to Fairfax's Presbyterian leanings.

Fairfax with the numerous part of the army remained in and about London, to suppress the insurrection in Kent, and to watch any other which should fall out in the city or thereabouts; of which they had more apprehension than of all the power of Scotland. And so when the Parliament was advertised by their troops which were first sent that they were too weak to advance farther, and heard that the earl of Norwich was declared general of the Kentish troops, and was marching in the head of them to Blackheath, Fairfax drew all his army together and his cannon, and marched over London Bridge to meet the men of Kent at Blackheath, and to stop their march to London. The earl was now advanced too far, and Fairfax advanced too fast, to put the former counsel* in practice, by breaking down the bridges and keeping the passes; and they who had opposed that counsel, and were so forward to advance, thought they were now too far. The countrymen were weary of being all night in the field, though it was the warmest season of the year, the month of July,* and many withdrew themselves every day; so that they who remained had no reason to believe themselves equal to the power that marched towards them, and yet there were more left than could hope to preserve themselves by flying and by concealment. And therefore the earl, upon conference with those who remained, and were resolved to run the utmost hazard, resolved to pass themselves and their horses, by such boats as they had ready about Greenwich and down the river, over into Essex, where they knew they had many friends, and where Fairfax and his army could not visit them in some days. And so they made a shift to transport themselves* to the number of near two thousand men, horse and foot; whereof many were officers and soldiers who had served the King, and young gentlemen grown up into those families, who had been too young to appear before.

They found many persons in Essex ready to join with them, who came sooner together than they intended upon the alarum of Kent, and who had purposed to have passed over into Kent, to have joined with and assisted those who had so frankly appeared for the King, if they had not been prevented by their unexpected coming to them. There was the brave lord Capel, sir William Compton, sir Charles Lucas, sir George Lisle, sir Bernard Gascoigne, all excellent officers, with whom colonel Farr, who had served the Parliament, and was a known creature and confidant of the earl of Warwick, and had at that time the command of Languard Point, a fort of importance upon the sea, joined with them, and many other gentlemen and officers of name, who had drawn together many soldiers; so that when they were joined together, with those who came from Kent, they made a body of above three thousand horse and foot, with officers enough to have formed and commanded a very good army.

They knew well Fairfax would quickly visit them, and therefore they chose to post themselves in Colchester, a great and populous town, which though unfortified, they cast up such works before the avenues that they did not much fear to be forced by an assault; and resolved to expect the conjunction with other of their friends, and were most confident that the Scots' army, which they heard was upon its march, would be with them before they could be in distress.

They had scarce put themselves and the town, which was not glad of their company, into any order, before Fairfax came upon them; who made no stay in Kent after he heard what was become of the earl of Norwich and his friends, but left two or three troops of horse to settle that county, with the assistance of their committees,* who had been driven from thence, and, returning now victorious, knew well enough how to deal with those who had revolted from them. When he came first before Colchester, and saw it without any fortification, he thought presently to have entered the town with his army; but he found so rude resistance, that, by the advice of Ireton, who was left by Cromwell to watch the general as well as the army, he resolved to encompass it with his army, and, without hazarding the loss of men, to block them up till famine should reduce them; and disposed his army accordingly, which quickly stopped up all passages by which either men or provisions should get into the town, though by many brave sallies from within their quarters were often beaten up, and many valiant men were lost on all sides. [*HR*, XI, 59–62]

The siege of Colchester continued to tie down Fairfax in Essex as news arrived that the Scottish army, under the Duke of Hamilton, had begun its march south, aiming to rendezvous with English royalists, commanded by

Sir Marmaduke Langdale. Cromwell had ended resistance in South Wales on 4 July; having done so, he set off north to join with the units of the army already there under John Lambert, to oppose the Scottish invasion.

It was near the middle of July when the duke entered into England with his army, and then he came to Carlisle, and immediately took that government from sir Philip Musgrave, and drew out all the English garrison, and put Scots in their place. And after some few days' stay there, the English and Scots' forces met at a rendezvous, in the way to Penrith in Cumberland, where Lambert then quartered: and if they had continued their march, (as they ought to have done,) it is very probable they had broken that body of Lambert's. But the duke would quarter that night two miles short; and Lambert in the same night marched from thence in great disorder and confusion to the edge of Yorkshire. The duke rested many days, that all his forces might come up, which came slowly up out of Scotland. As soon as they were come up, he marched to Kendal, where he rested again a full fortnight; the reason whereof nobody could imagine; except it were that those forces which were up in several parts of the kingdom for the King might undergo some defeat, that they might not so unite as to control or obstruct the Presbyterian design. For after that army was entered into England, and moved, as hath been said, by such very slow marches, and so negligently, and with so little apprehension of an enemy, that it was quartered at so huge a distance that the head-quarter was very often twenty miles distant from some part of the army (the duke himself performing no part of the office of a general, but taking his ease, and being wholly governed by David Leslie, the lieutenant general of the army, and two or three other officers), sir Marmaduke Langdale marched with his body of English, consisting of near four thousand foot and seven or eight hundred horse, always a day before the army; by which they intended to have timely advertisement of the enemy's motion, and for which they made no other provision, and likewise meant that he should bear the first brunt of them, desiring to weaken him by all the ways they could.

They had not marched many days, it being now near the middle of August, when sir Marmaduke Langdale advertised the duke, by an express, that he had received unquestionable intelligence that Cromwell was within two or three days' march, and resolved to engage his army as soon as possibly he could, and that he would not be diverted from it by the people's gathering together at any distance from him in what posture soever; and therefore desired his grace that he would keep his army close together, for that they could not be far asunder with any security; and [declared] that he himself would rest, and wait the advance of the enemy, and then retire back as he should find it necessary.

The duke, notwithstanding this advertisement, reformed not the order of his march in any degree, but was persuaded that the enemy could not be so near; and that if Cromwell was advanced to such a distance, it was only with such a party as he would not presume to engage with their whole army. And in this confidence he marched as he had done before. Sir Marmaduke sent him every day advice that confirmed the former, and that his horse had encountered some of the enemy, and that their whole body was at hand; but that it was true it was not a body equal in number to their army, yet all that Cromwell expected was to join [battle] with him. All this gained not credit, till sir Marmaduke himself, making his retreat with very sharp skirmishes, in which many men fell on both sides, was pursued into the head quarters of the duke; whither he likewise brought with him some prisoners, who averred, that the whole body of the army was within five or six miles, and marched as fast as they were able.

The duke was confounded with the intelligence, and, at his wits' end, knew not what to do: the army was not together; and that part that was about him was without any order, and made no show of any purpose to fight. In this amazement, the duke stayed himself with some officers at Preston, and caused his foot to be drawn over a bridge, that they might march towards Wigan, a pretty town in Lancashire, where he should, as he thought, find some regiments, and where they might make some stand till the rest should come up. In the mean time sir Marmaduke Langdale returned to his troops, the duke having promised to send him some troops to assist, and that some foot should be sent to keep a lane that would flank his men upon his retreat. Sir Marmaduke retired before the enemy, and drew up his troops into the closes near Preston. The enemy followed him close, and pressed him very hard; notwithstanding which he maintained the dispute for above six hours* with great courage, and with very great loss to the enemy in officers and common soldiers; insomuch as they seemed to retire, at least to make a stand. And in all this time the Scots sent him no assistance, but concluded that it was not Cromwell's whole army that assaulted him, but only some party, which he would himself be well enough able to disengage himself from. And sir Marmaduke Langdale told me often afterwards, that he verily believed that if one thousand foot had then been sent to him he should have gained the day; and Cromwell himself acknowledged that he never saw foot fight so desperately as those did.

The Scots continued their march over the bridge, without taking any care to secure the lane which he had recommended to them; by which Cromwell's horse came upon his flank, whilst he was equally pressed in the van. So that his excellent body of foot being broken, sir Marmaduke and such of his horse as kept together were driven into the town, where the duke remained yet with some officers; all which retreated over a ford to the foot, who were in equal disorder. For as soon as the English forces were broken, the Scots were presently beaten from the bridge, and forced to a very disorderly march. However, the duke had still his own army entire; with which he continued to march two or three days, till he came to Uttoxeter; and in that time many of the Scottish noblemen forsook him, and rendered themselves prisoners to the gentlemen of the country; and Cromwell's troops pressed so hard upon the rear, that they killed, and took as many prisoners as they pleased, without hazarding one man of their own. [The duke] was scarce got into Uttoxeter, when his troops, which made no resistance, were beaten in upon him, and so close pursued by Cromwell's horse that himself and all the principal officers (some few excepted, who, by lying concealed, or by the benefit of the swiftness of their horse[s], made their escape) were taken prisoners:* the duke himself neither behaving himself like a general nor a gentleman of courage, which he was not before thought to want, but making all submissions and all the excuses, when he was brought to Cromwell, that a poor-spirited man could do.

Thus his whole army was routed and defeated; more killed out of contempt than that they deserved it by any opposition; the rest taken prisoners, all their cannon and baggage taken, and their colours; only some of their horse, which had been quartered most backward, made haste to carry news to their country of the ill success of their arms. They who did not take the way for Scotland, were for the most part taken by the activity of the country or the horse that pursued them; whereof sir Marmaduke Langdale, after he had made his way with some of his officers and soldiers, who stood with him till they found it safest to disperse themselves, had the fortune to be discovered, and was so taken prisoner, and sent to the castle of Nottingham. And all this great victory was got by Cromwell with an army not amounting to a third part of the Scots in number, if they had been all together; and which was not diminished half a hundred men in obtaining this victory, after the English forces had been defeated. [*HR*, XI, 72–7]

The hopes of royalists that they would be able to coordinate the risings in England with the Scottish invasion were disappearing long before the defeat

*of the Scots. The original royalist scheme—before the Kentish rising had
complicated matters—had been a rising close to London, synchronized with
the invasion. It was planned by Lord Holland.*

When the earl of Norwich and the lord Capel with the Kentish and
Essex troops were enclosed in Colchester, their friends could not reasonably hope that the Scotch army, which had so long deferred their
march into England contrary to their promise, would, though they
were now come in, march fast enough to relieve Colchester before they
should be reduced by famine. The earl of Holland thought it necessary, since many who were in Colchester had engaged themselves upon
his promises and authority, now to begin his enterprise; to which the
youth and warmth of the duke of Buckingham,* who was general of
the horse, the lord Francis Villiers his brother, and divers other young
noblemen, spurred him on. And he might have the better opinion of
his interest and party, in that his purpose of rising, and putting himself
into arms for the relief of Colchester, was so far from being a secret
that it was the common discourse of the town; a great appearance every
morning at his lodging of those officers who were known to have
served the King; his commissions shewed in many hands; and no question being more commonly asked than, 'When doth my lord Holland
go out?' and the answer, 'Such and such a day.' And the hour he did
take horse, when he was accompanied by an hundred horse from his
house, was publicly talked of two or three days before.

His first rendezvous was Kingston upon Thames;* where he stayed
two nights and one whole day, expecting a great resort to him, not
only of officers, but of common men, who had promised, and listed
themselves under several officers; and he imputed the security he had
enjoyed so long, notwithstanding his purpose was so generally known,
to the apprehension both the Parliament and the army had of the
affections of the city to join with him; and he did believe that he should
not only remain secure at Kingston as long as he should think fit to stay
there, but that some entire regiments of the city would march out with
him for the relief of Colchester.

During the short stay he made at Kingston, some officers and
soldiers, both of horse and foot, came thither; and many persons of
honour and quality, in their coaches, came to visit him and his company from London, and returned thither again, to provide what was
still wanting, and resolved to be with him soon enough. The principal
officer the earl relied upon (though he had better) was Dalbier,*
a Dutchman of name and reputation, and good experience in war; who

had served the Parliament as commissary general of the horse under the earl of Essex, and, having been left out in the new model, was amongst those discontented officers who looked for an opportunity to be revenged on the army, which they despised for their ill breeding and much preaching. And thus Dalbier was glad to depend upon the earl of Holland, who thought himself likewise happy in such an officer. The keeping good guards, and sending out parties towards the Kentish parts, where it was known some troops remained since the last commotion there, was committed to his care. But he discharged it so ill, or his orders were so ill observed, that the second or third morning after their coming thither, some troops of horse under the command of colonel Rich (eminent for praying but of no fame for fighting) fell into the town, before those within had notice to be ready to receive them; the earl and most of the rest making too much haste out of the town, and never offering to charge those troops. And in this confusion the lord Francis Villiers, (a youth of rare beauty and comeliness of person,) not being upon his horse so soon as the rest, or endeavouring to make some resistance, was unfortunately killed, with one or two more of little note. Most of the foot made a shift to conceal themselves, and some officers, until they found means to retire to their close mansions in London. The earl with near a hundred horse (the rest wisely taking the way to London, where they were never inquired after) wandered without purpose or design, and was, two or three days after, beset in an inn at St Neots in Huntingtonshire by those few horse who pursued him, where the earl delivered himself prisoner* to the officer without resistance; yet at the same time Dalbier and Kenelm Digby, the eldest son of sir Kenelm, were killed upon the place; whether out of former grudges, or that they offered to defend themselves, was not known. The duke of Buckingham had severed himself before from them, and happily found a way into London, where he concealed himself till he had an opportunity to secure himself by being transported into Holland, where the Prince was, who received him with great grace and kindness. The earl of Holland remained prisoner in the place where he was taken, until by order from the Parliament he was sent to Windsor Castle, where, notwithstanding that he was Constable of it, he was kept prisoner with great strictness.

The total defeat of the Scots' army within very few days succeeds this; and when those noble persons within Colchester were advertised of both, they knew well that there was no possibility of relief, nor could they expect it longer, being pressed with want of all kind of victual, and having eaten near all their horses; so that they sent to Fairfax, to treat about the delivery of the town upon reasonable conditions; but he refused to treat, or to give any conditions, if they would not render to mercy all the officers and gentlemen; the common soldiers they were contented to dismiss. They spent a day or two in deliberation; proposed the making a brisk sally, and thereby to shift for themselves, as many as could; but they had too few horses, and the few that were left uneaten were too weak for that enterprise. Then, that they would open a port, and every man die with their arms in their hands; but that way they could only be sure of being killed, without hurting their adversaries, who had ways enough securely to assault them. Whereupon they were in the end obliged to deliver themselves up* prisoners at mercy; and were thereupon, all the officers and gentlemen, led into the public hall of the town, where they were locked up, and a strong guard set upon them. They were required presently to send a list of all their names to the general, which they presently did; and, within a short time after, a guard was sent to bring sir Charles Lucas and sir George Lisle and sir Bernard Gascoigne to the general, who being sat with his council of war, they were carried in, and in a very short discourse told, that after so long and so obstinate a defence, until they found it necessary to deliver themselves up to mercy, it was necessary, for the example of others, and that the peace of the kingdom might be no more disturbed in that manner, that some military justice should be executed; and therefore that council had determined that they three should be presently shot to death, for which they were advised to prepare themselves; and without considering or hearing what they had a mind to say for themselves, they were led into a yard that was contiguous, where they found three files of musketeers, ready for their despatch.

Sir Bernard Gascoigne (who was a gentleman of Florence who had served the King in the war, and afterwards remained in London till the unhappy adventure of Colchester, and then accompanied his friends thither) had only English enough to make himself understood that he desired a pen and ink and paper, that he might write a letter to his prince, the Great Duke, that his highness might know in what manner he lost his life, to the end his heirs might possess his estate. The officer that attended the execution thought fit to acquaint the general and council, without which he durst not allow him pen and ink, which he thought he might reasonably demand. When they were informed of it, they thought it a matter worthy some consideration; they had chosen him out of the list for his quality, conceiving him to be an English gentleman, and preferred him for being a knight, that they might sacrifice three of that rank.

This delay brought the news of this bloody resolution to the prisoners in the town, who were infinitely afflicted with it; and the lord Capel prevailed with an officer, or soldier, of their guard, to carry a letter, signed by the chief persons and officers, and in the name of the rest, for not losing time, to the general; in which they took notice of that judgment, and desired him either to forbear the execution of it, or that they might all, who were equally guilty with those three, undergo the same sentence with them. The letter was delivered, but had no other effect than the sending to the officer to despatch his order, reserving the Italian to the last. Sir Charles Lucas was their first work, who fell dead; upon which George Lisle ran to him, embraced and kissed him, and then stood up, and looked those who were to execute him in the face; and thinking they stood at too great a distance, spake to them to come nearer; to which one of them said, 'I'll warrant you, sir, we'll hit you:' to which he answered smiling, 'Friends, I have been nearer you when you have missed me.' And thereupon they all fired upon him, and did their work home, so that he fell down dead of many wounds without speaking word. Sir Bernard Gascoigne had his doublet off, and expected the next salvo; but the officer told him he had order to carry him back to his friends, which at that time was very indifferent to him. The council had considered, that if they should in this manner have taken the life of a foreigner, who seemed to be a person of quality, their friends or children who should visit Italy might pay dear for many generations; and therefore they commanded the officer, when the other two should be dead, to carry him back again to the other prisoners.

The two who were thus murdered were men of great name and esteem in the war; the one being held as good a commander of horse, and the other of foot, as the nation had; but of very different tempers and humours. Lucas was the younger brother to the lord Lucas, and his heir both to the honour and estate, and had a present fortune of his own. He had been bred in the Low Countries, and always amongst the horse, so that he had little conversation in that Court, where great civility was practised and learned. He was very brave in his person, and in a day of battle a gallant man to look upon and follow; but at all other times and places, of a nature not to be lived with, an ill understanding, a rough and a proud nature, which made him during the time of their being in Colchester more intolerable than the siege, or any fortune that threatened them; yet they all desired to accompany him in his death. Lisle was a gentleman who had had the same education with the other, and at the same time an officer of foot; had all the courage of the other, and led his men to a battle with such an alacrity that no man was ever better followed, his soldiers never forsaking him; and the *tertia** which he commanded never left any thing undone which he led them upon. But then, to this fierceness of courage, he had the softest and most gentle nature imaginable; loved all, and beloved of all, and without a capacity to have an enemy.

The manner of taking the lives of these worthy men was new and without example, and concluded by most men to be very barbarous, and was generally imputed to Ireton, who swayed the general, and was upon all occasions of an unmerciful and bloody nature. As soon as this bloody sacrifice was ended, Fairfax, with his chief officers, went to the town-house to visit the prisoners; and the general (who was an ill orator in the most plausible occasion) applied with his civility to the earl of Norwich and the lord Capel; and, seeming in some degree to excuse the having done that which he said military justice did require, he told them that all the lives of the rest were safe; and that they should be well treated, and disposed of as the Parliament should direct. The lord Capel had not so soon digested this so late barbarous proceeding, as to receive the visit of those who caused it with such a return as his condition might have prompted him, but said that they should do well to finish their work, and execute the same rigour to the rest; upon which there were two or three such sharp and bitter replies between him and Ireton, that cost him his life in few months after. When the general had given notice to the Parliament of his proceedings, he received order to send the earl of Norwich and the lord Capel to Windsor castle, where they had the society of the earl of Holland to lament each other's misfortunes; and after some time they were all sent to the Tower. [*HR*, XI, 102–9]

The capture of Colchester brought an end to the Second Civil War, although it took Cromwell until November to secure submission of all of the North, and to arrange a settlement of Scotland with the Marquess of Argyll, whose faction had opposed the Engagement and Hamilton's expedition into England. In the aftermath of the fighting, Parliament — against the will of Independents in the House of Commons and the army — made another attempt to come to terms with the King. He and its commissioners held talks at Newport, in the Isle of Wight, in September and October. As before, they failed to produce agreement, and Charles was suspected of spinning them out in hope of effecting his escape. The army, pushed forward by Cromwell's radical ally and son-in-law Henry Ireton, demanded the trial of the King. The House of Commons, still much more moderate, equivocated. On 6

December soldiers led by Colonel Thomas Pride surrounded the House. In 'Pride's Purge', they removed those members most in favour of an agreement with the King. That evening, Cromwell returned from the North. There followed intense discussion within the Army and the remaining members of Parliament about how to proceed. On 23 December the Commons set up a committee to consider the charges that might be made against the King, and the procedure of the court, but only when a last attempt to come to terms with him had failed did the doubters — including Cromwell — agree to go ahead with the trial.

When the committee had prepared such a charge, which they called an 'Impeachment of High Treason against Charles Stewart, King of England,' digested into several articles, which contained all those calumnies they had formerly digested into that declaration of *No more addresses* to be made to him, with some additional reproaches, it was read in the House; and after it was approved there, they sent it to the House of Peers for their concurrence.* That House had very little to do from the time that Cromwell returned from Scotland, and were few in number, and used to adjourn for two or three days together for want of business; so that it was believed that they who had done so many mad things, rather than they would dissent from the House of Commons, would likewise concur with them in this, rather than sever from them when they were so triumphant. But, contrary to this expectation, when this impeachment was brought up to the Peers, it was so ill received that there was not one person who concurred with them; which, considering the men, and what most of them had done, might seem very strange. And when they had with some warmth rejected it,* they adjourned for a week, presuming they should thereby at least give some interruption to that career which the House of Commons was upon, and in that time some expedient might be found to reconcile the proceedings in both Houses. But they were as much deceived in this; the House of Commons was very well pleased with it, and thought they had given them ease which they could not so well have contrived for themselves. So they proceeded in their own method; and when the day came to which the Lords had adjourned their House, they found their doors all locked, and fastened with padlocks, that there should be no more entrance for them; nor did any of them ever after sit in that House as Peers, till Cromwell, long after, endeavoured in vain to have erected a House of Peers of his own creation;* in which some of them then very willingly took their places.

The charge and accusation upon which they resolved to proceed against the King being thus settled and agreed upon, they began to consider in what manner and form to proceed, that there might be some appearance of justice. Nothing could be found in the common or statute law which could direct or warrant them; nor could the precedent of deposing Richard the Second* (the sole precedent of that kind) be applied to their purpose; for, how foul soever the circumstances precedent had been, he had made a resignation of his royalty before the Lords in Parliament; so that his deposition proceeded from himself, and with his own consent, and so would not agree in any particular with the case in question. So that they must make a new form to warrant their proceedings. And a new form they did erect, which was never before heard of. They constituted and erected a court that should be called *The High Court of Justice*, which should consist of so many judges, who should have authority to try the King, whether he were guilty of what he was accused of or no; and in order thereunto, to examine such witnesses as should be produced: the number of the judges to be eight and forty, whereof the major part might proceed.

They could not have found such a number yet amongst themselves, after so many barbarities and impieties, upon whom they might depend in this last tragical expedition. And therefore they laid this for a ground, that if they should make only their own members to be judges in this case, they might appear in the eyes of the people to be too much parties, as having from the beginning maintained a war, though defensive, against the King, and so not so fit to be the only judges who were in the fault: on the other hand, if they should name none of themselves, it might be interpreted that they looked upon it as too dangerous a province to engage themselves in, and therefore they had put it off to others; which would discourage others from undertaking it. And therefore they resolved that the judges should be nominated promiscuously, as well of members of the House as of such other good and godly men in the kingdom as they should think fit to nominate. Whosoever would not be one himself when named, (as there were yet many amongst them, who, out of conscience or of fear, utterly protested against it,) should take upon him to name another man; which he could not but think was equally unlawful: so that few took upon them to nominate others who would reject the province themselves.

All the chief officers of the army were named, and accepted the office; and such aldermen and citizens of London as had been most violent against peace, and some few country gentlemen whose zeal had been taken notice of for the cause, and who were like to take such a preferment as a testimony of the Parliament's confidence in them, and would thereupon embrace it. When such a number of men were nominated as were thought in all respects to be equal to the work, they were to make choice of a speaker, or prolocutor, who should be called Lord President of that high court, who must manage and govern all the proceedings there, ask the witnesses all proper questions, and answer what the prisoner should propose. And to that office one Bradshaw [was chosen,] a lawyer of Gray's Inn, not much known in Westminster Hall, though of good practice in his chamber,* and much employed by the factious and discontented persons. He was a gentleman of an ancient family in Cheshire and Lancashire, but of a fortune of his own making. He was not without parts, and of great insolence and ambition. When he was first nominated, he seemed much surprised, and very resolute to refuse it; which he did in such a manner, and so much enlarging upon his own want of ability to undergo so important a charge, that it was very evident that he had expected to be put to that apology. And when he was pressed with more importunity than could have been used by chance, he required time to consider of it, and he would then give his final answer; which he did the next day;* and with great humility accepted the office, which he administered with all the pride, impudence, and superciliousness imaginable. He was presently invested with great state, and many officers and a guard assigned for the security of his person, and the dean's house at Westminster given to him for ever for his residence and habitation; a good sum of money, about five thousand pounds, was appointed to be presently paid to him, to put himself in such an equipage and way of living as the dignity of the office which he held would require. And now, the Lord President of the High Court of Justice seemed to be the greatest magistrate in England. And though it was not thought seasonable to make any such declaration, yet some of those whose opinions grew quickly into ordinances, upon several occasions declared, that they believed that office was not to be looked upon as necessary *pro hac vice*,* for continuance, and he who executed it deserved to have an ample and a liberal estate conferred upon him for ever: which sudden mutation and exaltation of fortune could not but make a great impression upon a vulgar spirit, accustomed to no excesses, and acquainted only with a very moderate fortune. All this being done, they made choice of some lawyers (eminent for nothing but their obscurity, and that they were men scarce known or heard of in the profession) to perform the offices of Attorney General and Solicitor General for the State, to prosecute the prisoner at his trial, and to manage the evidence against him. Other officers of all kinds were appointed to attend and perform the several officers of their new court; which was ordered to be erected in

Westminster Hall, for which such architects were appointed as were thought fit to give direction therein.

The King was now sent for from Hurst castle,* and when he came out of the boat which transported him from thence he was received by colonel Harrison with a strong party of horse; by whom he was to be conducted to Windsor castle. Harrison was the son of a butcher near Nantwich in Cheshire, and had been bred up in the place of a clerk under a lawyer of good account in those parts; which kind of education introduces men into the language and practice of business, and, if it be not resisted by the great ingenuity of the person, imbues young men with more pride than any other kind of breeding, and disposes them to be pragmatical and insolent, though they have the skill to conceal it from their masters, except they find them (as they are too often) inclined to cherish it. When the rebellion first began, this man quitted his master, (who as he had relation to the King's service, so he discharged his duty faithfully,) and put himself into the Parliament army; where, having first obtained the office of a cornet, he got up by diligence and sobriety to the state of a captain, without any signal notice taken of him, till the new model of the army, when Cromwell, who possibly had knowledge of him before, found him of a spirit and disposition fit for his service, much given to prayer and to preaching, and otherwise of an understanding capable to be trusted in any business, to which his clerkship contributed very much: and then he was preferred very fast; so that by the time the King was brought to the army he had been a colonel of horse, and looked upon as inferior to few after Cromwell and Ireton in the council of the officers and in the government of the Agitators; and there were few men with whom Cromwell more communicated, or upon whom he more depended for the conduct of any thing committed to him. He received the King with outward respect; kept himself bare,* but attended him with great strictness and was not to be approached by any address of the King; answering questions in short and few words, and when importuned, with rudeness. He manifested an apprehension that the King had some thought of making an escape, and did all things in order to prevent it. Being to lodge at Windsor, and so to pass by Bagshot, the King expressed a desire to see his little park at Bagshot and to dine at the lodge there, a place where he had used to take much pleasure; and did not dissemble the knowing that the lord Newburgh, who had lately married the lady Aubigny, lived there; and said, he would send a servant to let that lady know that he would dine with her, that she might provide a dinner for him. Harrison well knew the affection of that lord and lady, and was very unwilling he should make any stay there; but finding the King so fixed upon it that he would not be otherwise removed from it than by not suffering him to go thither, he chose to consent, and that his majesty should send a servant; which he did the night before he intended to dine there.

Both lord and lady were of known duty and affection to the King; the lady, after her husband the lord Aubigny had been killed at Edgehill, having so far incensed the Parliament that she had endured a long imprisonment, under a suspicion or evidence that she had been privy to that design which had been discovered by Mr Waller,* upon which Tomkins and Challoner had been put to death, and had likewise [herself] been put to death if she had not made her escape to Oxford. After the war was ended, she had, with the King's approbation, married the lord Newburgh; who having the same affections, they had from the time of the King's being at Hampton Court concerted with his majesty upon such and such ways, that in the strictest restraint he was under they found a way to write to and to hear from him. And most of the letters which passed between the King and the Queen passed through their hands; who had likewise a cipher with the King, by which they gave him notice of any thing they judged of importance for him to know. They had given him notice that he would be sent for from the Isle of Wight, and advised him to find some way that he might dine at the lodge at Bagshot; and that he should take occasion, if he could, to lame the horse he rode upon, or to find such fault with his going, that he might take another horse out of the lord Newburgh's stables to continue the rest of his journey upon. That lord much delighted in horses, and had at that time one in his stables the most notorious for fleetness that was in England; and the purpose was, to mount the King upon that horse, that, when he found a fit opportunity, he might upon the sudden set spurs to his horse; and if he could get out of the company that encompassed him, he might possibly, by the swiftness of the horse and his skill in the most obscure ways of that forest, convey himself to another place in their view; and so, three or four good horses were laid in several places. And this was the reason that the King had so earnestly insisted upon dining at Bagshot; which being in his way, and his custom in his journey being always to dine, they could not deny him that liberty.

Before the King came thither Harrison had sent some horse with an officer to search the house, and all about the park, that he might be sure that no company lurked which might make some attempt. And the King all the morning found fault with the going of his horse, and said he would change it, and procure a better. When he came to the lodge, he found his dinner ready, but was quickly informed that the horse so much depended upon was the day before, by the blow of another horse, so lamed, that he could not be of use to the purpose he was designed for. And though that lord had other good horses which in such an exigent might be made use of, yet the King had observed so great difficulty to be in the attempt all his journey, when he was encompassed always in the middle of a hundred horse, the officers all exceedingly well horsed, and every man, officer and soldier, having a pistol ready spanned in one hand, that he resolved not to pursue that design. And Harrison had already told him that he had provided a better horse for him; and it was believed he would never have permitted him to have made use of one of the lord Newburgh's. So that, after having spent three or four hours there with very much satisfaction to himself, though he was not suffered to be in any room without the company of six or seven soldiers, who suffered little to be spoken except it was so loud that they could hear it too, he took a sad farewell of them, appearing to have little hope ever to see them again. The lord Newburgh rode some miles in the forest to wait upon the King, till he was required by Harrison to return. His majesty lodged that night* at his castle of Windsor, and was soon after carried to St James's. In this journey, Harrison observing that the King had always an apprehension that there was a purpose to murder him, and had once let fall some words of the odiousness and wickedness of such an assassination and murder, which could never be safe to the persons who undertook it, he told him plainly that he needed not to entertain any such imagination or apprehension; that the Parliament had too much honour and justice to cherish so foul an intention; and assured him that whatever the Parliament resolved to do would be very public, and in a way of justice, to which the world should be witness, and would never endure a thought of secret violence: which his majesty could not persuade himself to believe, nor did imagine that they durst ever produce him in the sight of the people under any form whatsoever of a public trial. . . .

When he was first brought to Westminster Hall, which was upon the 20th of January, before their High Court of Justice, he looked upon them, and sat down, without any manifestation of trouble, never stirring his hat; all the impudent judges sitting covered, and fixing their eyes upon him, without the least show of respect. The odious libel, which they called a 'charge and impeachment,' was then read by the clerk, which contained, That he had been admitted King of England, and trusted with a limited power, to govern according to law; and by his oath and office was obliged to use the power committed to him for the good and benefit of the people: but that he had, out of a wicked design to erect to himself an unlimited and tyrannical power, and to overthrow the rights and liberties of the people, traitorously levied war against the present Parliament and the people therein represented. And then it mentioned his first appearing at York with a guard, then his being at Beverley, then his setting up his standard at Nottingham, the day of the month and the year in which the battle had been at Edgehill, and all the other several battles which had been fought in his presence; in which, it said, he had caused and procured many thousands of the freeborn people of the nation to be slain: that after all his forces had been defeated, and himself become a prisoner, he had in that very year caused many insurrections to be made in England, and given a commission to the Prince his son to raise a new war against the Parliament, whereby many who were in their service, and trusted by them, had revolted, broken their trust, and betook themselves to the service of the Prince against the Parliament and the people: that he had been the author and contriver of the unnatural, cruel, and bloody war, and was therein guilty of all the treasons, murders, rapines, burnings, spoils, desolations, damage, and mischief to the nation, and which had been committed in the said war, or been occasioned thereby; and that he was therefore impeached for the said treasons and crimes, on the behalf of the people of England, as a tyrant, traitor, and murderer, and a public implacable enemy to the commonwealth of England; and prayed that he might be put to answer to all the particulars, to the end that such an examination, trial, and judgment might be had thereupon as should be agreeable to justice.

Which being read, their president Bradshaw, after he had insolently reprehended the King for not having stirred his hat, or shewed more respect to that high tribunal, told him, that the Parliament of England had appointed that court to try him for the several treasons and misdemeanours which he had committed against the kingdom during the evil administration of his government, that upon the examination thereof justice might be done. And after a great sauciness and impudence of talk, he asked the King what answer he made to that impeachment.

The King, without any alteration in his countenance by all that insolent provocation, told them, he would first know of them by what authority they presumed by force to bring him before them, and who gave them power to judge of his actions, for which he was accountable to none but God; though they had been always such as he need not be ashamed to own them before all the world. He told them, that he was their King, and they his subjects, who owed him duty and obedience; that no Parliament had authority to call him before them; but that they were not the Parliament, nor had any authority from the Parliament to sit in that manner: that of all the persons who sat there, and took upon them to judge him, except those persons who being officers of the army he could not but know whilst he was forced to be amongst them, there were only two faces which he had ever seen before, or whose names were known to him. And after urging their duty that was due to him, and his superiority over them, by such lively reasons and arguments as were not capable of any answer, he concluded, that he would not so much betray himself and his royal dignity as to answer any thing they objected against him, which were to acknowledge their authority; though he believed that every one of themselves, as well as the spectators, did in their own consciences absolve him from all the material things which were objected against him.

Bradshaw advised him in a very arrogant manner not to deceive himself with an opinion that any thing he had said would do him any good; that the Parliament knew their own authority, and would not suffer it to be called in question and debated; therefore wished him to think better of it against he should be next brought thither, and that he would answer directly to his charge; otherwise he could not be so ignorant as not to know what judgment the law pronounced against those who stood mute, and obstinately refused to plead. And so the guard carried his majesty back to St James's; where they treated him as before.

There was an accident happened that first day which may be fit to be remembered. When all those who were commissioners had taken their places, and the King was brought in, the first ceremony was to read their commission, which was the ordinance of Parliament for the trial; and then the judges were all called, every man answering to his name as he was called; and the president being first called and making answer, the next who was called, being the general, lord Fairfax, and no answer being made, the officer called him the second time, when there was a voice heard that said, 'he had more wit than to be there;' which put the court into some disorder, and somebody asking who it was, there was no other answer but a little murmuring. But presently, when the impeachment was read, and that expression used of 'all the good people of England,' the same voice in a louder tone answered, 'No, nor the hundredth part of them!' upon which, one of the officers bade the soldiers give fire into that box whence those presumptuous words were uttered. But it was quickly discerned that it was the general's wife, the lady Fairfax, who had uttered both those sharp sayings; who was presently persuaded or forced to leave the place, to prevent any new disorder. She was of a very noble extraction, one of the daughters and heirs of Horace lord Vere of Tilbury; who, having been bred in Holland, had not that reverence for the Church of England as she ought to have had, and so had unhappily concurred in her husband's entering into rebellion, never imagining what misery it would bring upon the kingdom; and now abhorred the work in hand as much as any body could do, and did all she could to hinder her husband from acting any part in it. Nor did he ever sit in that bloody court, though out of the stupidity of his soul he was throughout overwitted by Cromwell, and made a property to bring that to pass which could very hardly have been otherwise effected.

As there was in many persons present at that woeful spectacle a real duty and compassion for the King, so there was in others so barbarous and brutal a behaviour towards him that they called him *Tyrant* and *Murderer*; and one spit in his face, which his majesty without expressing any trouble wiped off with his handkerchief. . . .

The several unheard of insolences which this excellent prince was forced to submit to at the other times he was brought before that odious judicatory, his majestic behaviour under so much insolence, and resolute insisting upon his own dignity, and defending it by manifest authorities in the law as well as by the clearest deductions from reason, the pronouncing that horrible sentence* upon the most innocent person in the world, the execution of that sentence* by the most execrable murder that ever was committed since that of our blessed Saviour, and the circumstances thereof; the application and interposition that was used by some noble persons to prevent that woeful murder, and the hypocrisy with which that interposition was deluded; the saint-like behaviour of that blessed martyr, and his Christian courage and patience at his death; are all particulars so well known, and have been so much enlarged upon in a treatise peculiarly applied to that purpose, that the farther mentioning it in this place would but afflict and grieve the reader, and make the relation itself odious; and therefore no more shall be said here of that lamentable tragedy, so much to the dishonour of the nation and the religion professed by it.

But it will not be unnecessary to add the short character of his person, that posterity may know the inestimable loss which the nation then underwent, in being deprived of a prince whose example would have had a greater influence upon the manners and piety of the nation than the most strict laws can have. To speak first of his private qualifications as a man, before the mention of his princely and royal virtues; he was, if ever any, the most worthy of the title of an honest man; so great a lover of justice, that no temptation could dispose him to a wrongful action, except it were so disguised to him that he believed it to be just. He had a tenderness and compassion of nature, which restrained him from ever doing a hard-hearted thing; and therefore he was so apt to grant pardon to malefactors, that his judges represented to him the damage and insecurity to the public that flowed from such his indulgence; and then he restrained himself from pardoning either murders or highway robberies, and quickly discerned the fruits of his severity by a wonderful reformation of those enormities. He was very punctual and regular in his devotions; so that he was never known to enter upon his recreations or sports, though never so early in the morning, before he had been at public prayers; so that on hunting-days his chaplains were bound to a very early attendance. And he was like-wise very strict in observing the hours of his private cabinet devotions; and was so severe an exactor of gravity and reverence in all mention of religion, that he could never endure any light or profane word in reli-gion, with what sharpness of wit soever it was covered: and though he was well pleased and delighted with reading verses made upon any occasion, no man durst bring before him any thing that was profane or unclean; that kind of wit had never any countenance then. He was so great an example of conjugal affection, that they who did not imitate him in that particular did not brag of their liberty: and he did not only permit but direct his bishops to prosecute those scandalous vices in the ecclesiastical courts, against persons of eminence and near relation to his service.

His kingly virtues had some mixture and allay that hindered them from shining in full lustre, and from producing those fruits they should have been attended with. He was not in his nature bountiful, though he gave very much: which appeared more after the duke of Buckingham's death, after which those showers fell very rarely; and he paused too long in giving, which made those to whom he gave less sensible of the benefit. He kept state to the full, which made his Court very orderly; no man presuming to be seen in a place where he had no pretence to be. He saw and observed men long before he received any about his person, and did not love strangers, nor very confident men. He was a patient hearer of causes, which he frequently accustomed himself to, at the Council board; and judged very well, and was dexterous in the mediating part: so that he often put an end to causes by persuasion, which the stubbornness of men's humours made dilatory in courts of justice.

He was very fearless in his person, but not enterprising; and had an excellent understanding, but was not confident enough of it; which made him oftentimes change his own opinion for a worse, and follow the advice of a man that did not judge so well as himself. And this made him more irresolute than the conjuncture of his affairs would admit. If he had been of a rougher and more imperious nature, he would have found more respect and duty; and his not applying some severe cures to approaching evils proceeded from the lenity of his nature and the tenderness of his conscience, which in all cases of blood made him choose the softer way, and not hearken to severe counsels, how reasonably soever urged. This only restrained him from pursuing his advantage in the first Scots' expedition, when, humanly speaking, he might have reduced that nation to the most slavish obedience that could have been wished. But no man can say he had then many who advised him to it, but the contrary, by a wonderful indisposition all his Council had to fighting or any other fatigue. He was always an immoderate lover of the Scottish nation, having not only been born there, but educated by that people, and besieged by them always, having few English about him until he was king; and the major number of his servants being still of those, who he thought could never fail him; and then no man had such an ascendant over him, by the lowest and humblest insinuations, as duke Hamilton had.

As he excelled in all other virtues, so in temperance he was so strict, that he abhorred all debauchery to that degree, that, at a great festival solemnity, where he once was, when very many of the nobility of the English and Scots were entertained, [being] told by one who withdrew from thence, what vast draughts of wine they drank, and that there was one earl who had drank most of the rest down and was not himself moved or altered, the King said that he deserved to be hanged; and that earl coming shortly into the room where his majesty was, in some gaiety, to show how unhurt he was from that battle, the King sent one to bid him withdraw from his majesty's presence; nor did he in some days after appear before the King.

There were so many miraculous circumstances contributed to his ruin, that men might well think that heaven and earth conspired it, and that the stars designed it. Though he was, from the first declension of his power, so much betrayed by his own servants, that there were very few who remained faithful to him, yet that treachery proceeded not from any treasonable purpose to do him any harm, but from particular and personal animosities against other men. And afterwards, the terror all men were under of the Parliament, and the guilt they were conscious of themselves, made them watch all opportunities to make themselves gracious to those who could do them good; and so they became spies upon their master, and from one piece of knavery were hardened and confirmed to undertake another, till at last they had no hope of preservation but by the destruction of their master. And after all this, when a man might reasonably believe that less than a universal defection of three nations could not have reduced a great King to so ugly a fate, it is most certain that in that very hour when he was thus wickedly murdered in the sight of the sun, he had as great a share in the hearts and affections of his subjects in general, was as much beloved, esteemed, and longed for by the people in general of the three nations, as any of his predecessors had ever been. To conclude: he was the worthiest gentleman, the best master, the best friend, the best husband, the best father, and the best Christian that the age in which he lived had produced. And if he was not the best King, if he was without some parts and qualities which have made some kings great and happy, no other prince was ever unhappy who was possessed of half his virtues and endowments, and so much without any kind of vice. [*HR*, XI, 217–43]

15. Scotland and Spain: 1649–1651

During the King's trial, Prince Charles was at The Hague in the Netherlands. He had been there since the return of his fleet from its attempts to support the royalists at Colchester, as the guest of the Prince of Orange, his brother-in-law. The news of the King's execution—making him King Charles II—reached his court on 4 February. The Scottish factions, that of the Marquess of Argyll, and that of the Duke of Hamilton and the supporters of the Engagement, now led by Hamilton's brother, the Earl of Lanark, and the Earl of Lauderdale, were united in their outrage. Hamilton himself was executed by the new English republic on 9 March (along with two of the other leaders of the Second Civil War, Holland and Capel). Lanark succeeded as the 2nd Duke. The new King was proclaimed in Edinburgh, and he was invited to come to Scotland—if he agreed to accept the Covenant, and Presbyterian church government. Both Scottish factions were equally afraid of an agreement between the King and the Marquess of Montrose who had given them so much trouble in 1645.

WHILST these tragedies were acting in England, and ordinances formed, as hath been said, to make it penal in the highest degree for any man to assume the title, or to acknowledge any man to be king,* the King himself remained in a very disconsolate condition at the Hague. Though he knew the desperate state his father was long in, yet the barbarous stroke so surprised him, that he was in all the confusion imaginable, and all about him were almost bereft of their understanding. The truth is, it can hardly be conceived with what a consternation this terrible news was received by all the common people of that country. There was a woman at the Hague, of the middling rank, who, being with child, with the horror of the mention of it fell into travail and in it died. There could not be more evidence of a general detestation, than there was amongst all men of what quality soever. Within two or three days, which they gave to the King's recollection, the States presented themselves in a body to his majesty, to condole with him for the murder of his father, in terms of great sorrow and condolence, save that there was not bitterness enough against the rebels and murderers. The States of Holland, apart, performed the same civility towards his majesty; and the body of the clergy, in a very good Latin oration, delivered by the chief preacher of the Hague, lamented the misfortune in terms of as much asperity, and detestation of the actors as unworthy the name of Christians, as could be expressed.

The desperateness of the King's condition could not excuse his sinking under the burden of his grief; but those who were about him besought him to resume so much courage as was necessary for his present state. He thereupon caused those of his father's Council who had attended him to be sworn of his Privy Council, adding only Mr Long his secretary, who before was not of the Council. All which was done before he heard from the Queen his mother; who, notwithstanding the great agony she was in, which without doubt was as great a passion of sorrow as she was able to sustain, wrote to the King that he could not do better than to repair into France as soon as was possible, and in the mean time desired him not to swear any persons to be of his Council till she could speak with him; whether it was that she did not think those persons to be enough at her devotion, or that she would have them to receive that honour upon her recommendation.

The King himself had no mind to go into France, where he thought he had not been treated with excess of courtesy; and he resolved to perform all filial respect towards the Queen his mother, without such a condescension and resignation of himself as she expected; and to avoid all *éclaircissements* upon that subject, he heartily desired that any other course might be found more counsellable than that he should go into France. He himself lived with and upon the Prince of Orange, who supplied him with all things necessary for his own person, for his mourning, and the like: but towards any other support for himself and his family, he had not enough to maintain them one day, and there were very few of them who could maintain themselves in the most private way. And it was visible enough that they should not be long able to reside in the Hague, where there was at that very time an agent for the Parliament, Strickland, who had been there some years, but pretended at that time to reside there with his wife, who was a Dutch woman, and without any public character, though he was still under the same credentials. And their advertisements from London assured them that the Parliament had nominated one who was presently to be sent as their ambassador or envoy to the States, to give them an account of their affairs, and to invite them to enter into an alliance with them. So that it was time to think of some other retreat for the King; and none appeared then so reasonable in their view as Ireland; from whence they heard that prince Rupert was arrived safely at Kinsale with the fleet;* that the lord Inchiquin had made a cessation with the Irish* before the Lord Lieutenant came thither, and the Irish had deserted the Pope's nuncio, who was driven away, and had embarked himself for France; that the marquis of Ormond was received by the lord Inchiquin with all the obedience imaginable, by which he became entirely possessed of the whole province of Munster; and that the confederate Catholics had invited him to Kilkenny, where he had made a full peace with them; so that they were preparing an army to march under his command against Dublin. This news made them hope that every day would improve it so much, that it would be fit for the King to transport his own person thither in the spring.

In this conjuncture there arrived a gentleman,* one sir Joseph Douglas, with a letter from the Privy Council of Scotland, by which they sent him word that they had proclaimed him King of Scotland, and sent him the proclamation, and wished that he would prepare himself to repair into that his kingdom, in order to which they would speedily send another invitation to him. And that invitation arrived at the same time with some commissioners deputed by the Council, and three or four preachers sent from the commissioners of the Kirk. The proclamation indeed declared, that, for as much as the late King was, contrary to the dissent and protestation of that kingdom, removed by a violent death, by the Lord's blessing there was left unto them a right-eous heir and lawful successor, Charles, who was become their true and lawful King; but upon condition of his good behaviour, and strict observation of the Covenant, and his entertaining no other persons about him but such as were godly men and faithful to that obligation. A proclamation so strangely worded, that, though it called him their King, manifested enough to him that he was to be subject to their deter-minations in all the parts of his government. And the commissioners, both laity and clergy, spake no other language; and, saving that they bowed their bodies and made low reverences, they appeared more like ambassadors from a free state to an equal ally than like subjects sent to their own sovereign. At the same time, though not in the same ship, arrived likewise from Scotland the earl of Lanark and earl of Lauderdale; the former not knowing till he came into Holland that he was duke Hamilton by the slaughter of his elder brother. But they two were so far from having any authority from their country, that they were fled from thence as proscribed persons and malefactors. The earl of Lauderdale, after his departure from the Hague in that discontent that is mentioned before,* bent his course for Scotland, but before he came thither he was informed that the state of all things had been reversed, and the Engagement declared unlawful, and to what penalties himself was liable if he should be taken. Whereupon, without suffering his ship to go into any port, he found means to send on shore to some friends, and so to concert all things, that, without being discovered if himself did go on shore, the earl of Lanark and himself, and some other persons liable to danger if they were found, put themselves on board the same ship, and arrived in Holland about that time when the other messengers from the State and from the Kirk came from Scotland, and when the news came of the execution of duke Hamilton.*

Whereupon the new duke kept his chamber for some days, without so much as waiting upon the King; who sent a gracious message to him to condole for the loss of his brother; and all the lords, and other persons of quality about the King, made their visits to him with all civility. This duke was not inferior in wisdom and parts of understanding to the wisest man of that nation, and was very much esteemed by those who did not like the complying and insinuating nature of his brother. He was a man of great honour, courage, and sincerity in his nature, and, which was a rare virtue in the men of that time, was still the same man he pretended to be, and had very much to say in his own defence for the errors he had run into; which he acknowledged always with great ingenuity, and abhorred the whole proceedings of his countrymen, and at this time brought a heart and affection clearer, and less clogged with scruples and reservations, for the King's service than any other of them did. [*HR*, XII, 1–5]

In late February and March, the King's Council argued over the merits of a Scots or an Irish alliance. Hyde — deeply hostile to Presbyterianism, and becoming close to Ormond — was the strongest advocate of the Irish mission, and also encouraged the Marquess of Montrose in his plans to mount a new insurrection in Scotland. Hyde's failure to persuade the King's Council to agree a Declaration effectively ruling out a Scottish Presbyterian alliance may have persuaded him to agree to accompany an old associate, Lord Cottington, on a mission to seek financial support from Spain. They arrived in Madrid at the end of November 1649. But given Spain's own continuing war with France, and the wariness of the Spanish about provoking a dispute with the apparently settled English republic, their embassy was unlikely to be successful. The Spanish government made no arrangements for their accommodation. Hyde and Cottington were frequently moved to protest about the quality of their reception.

The Court well knew of their arrival, but took no notice of it. The lord Cottington therefore sent to don Lewis,* to desire that he might have a private audience of him *incognito*; which he presently consented to, and appointed the next morning to meet in the King's garden; which was at such a distance from the Court that it was not in the view of it; and there they met at the hour. Don Lewis was a man of little ceremony, and used no flourishes in his discourses, which made most men believe that he said all things from his heart; and he seemed to speak so cordially, that the lord Cottington, who was not easy to be imposed upon, did think that they should have a house very speedily, and that he had a good inclination to favour them in what they came about. He spake with more commotion than was natural to him in the business of the murder of the King; excused all the omissions towards the ambassadors, which should be all repaired out of hand, after the few days which yet remained to be spent in *fiestas* for the Queen;* during which time, he said, no officers would obey any orders which diverted them from the sight of the triumphs; and wished that the ambassadors would see the masquerade that afternoon, and the *toros* the day following.

The lord Cottington returned home very well satisfied; and he had not been half an hour in the house, when a gentleman came from don Lewis to invite the ambassadors to see those exercises which are mentioned before, and sent them word that there should be places provided for them. The Chancellor went that afternoon to the place assigned, where he saw the masquerade and the running the course. That of the masquerade is an exercise they learned from the Moors, performed by squadrons of horse seeming to charge each other with great fierceness, with bucklers* in their left hands, and a kind of cane in their right, which, when they come within little more than a horse-length, they throw with all the strength they can, and against them they defend themselves with very broad bucklers; and as soon as they have thrown their darts, they wheel about in a full gallop, till they can turn to receive the like assault from those whom they had charged; and so several squadrons of twenty or five and twenty horse run round and charge each other. It hath at first the appearance of a martial exercise; the horses are very beautiful, and well adorned; the men richly clad, and must be good horsemen, otherwise they could not obey the quick motion and turns of their horses; all the rest is too childish: the darts are nothing else but plain bulrushes of the biggest growth. After this they run the course; which is like our running at the ring;* save that two run still together, and the swifter hath the prize, a post dividing them at the end. From the start they run their horses full speed about fifty paces, and the judges are at that post to determine who is first at the end. There the King and don Lewis ran several courses, in all which don Lewis was too good a courtier to win any prize, though he always lost it by very little. The appearance of the people was very great, and the ladies in all the windows made a very rich show; otherwise the show itself had nothing wonderful. Here there happened to be some sudden sharp words between the admirante of Castile, a haughty young man, and the marquis de Leche, the eldest son of don Lewis de Haro; the which being taken notice of, they were both dismissed the squadrons wherein they were, and committed to their chambers.

The next day, and so for two or three days together, both the ambassadors had a box prepared for them to see the *toros*; which is a spectacle very wonderful. Here the place was very noble, being the market-place, a very large square, built with handsome brick houses, which had all balconies, which were adorned with tapestry and very beautiful ladies. Scaffolds were built round the first story, the lower rooms being shops, and for ordinary use; and in the division of those scaffolds all the magistrates and officers of the town knew their places. The pavement of the place was all covered with gravel, which in summer time was upon those occasions watered by carts charged with hogsheads of water. As soon as the King comes, some officers clear the whole ground from the common people, so that there is no man seen upon the plain but two or three *alguazils*, magistrates, with their small white wands. Then one of the four gates which lead into the streets is opened, at which the *torreadors* enter, all persons of quality richly clad, and upon the best horses in Spain, every one attended by eight or ten more lackeys, all clinkant* with gold and silver lace, who carry the spears which their masters are to use against the bulls; and with this entry many of the common people break in, for which sometimes they pay very dear. The persons on horseback have all cloaks folded up upon their left shoulder, the least disorder of which, much more the letting it fall, is a very great disgrace; and in that grave order they march to the place where the King sits, and after they have made the reverences, they place themselves at a good distance from one another, and expect the bull. The bulls are brought in the night before from the mountains by people used to that work, who drive them into the town when nobody is in the streets, into a pen made for them, which hath a door that opens into that large space; the key whereof is sent to the King, which the King, when he sees everything ready, throws to an alguazil, who carries it to the officer that keeps the door, and he causes it to be opened, when a single bull is ready to come out. When the bull enters, the common people, who sit over the door or near it, strike him, or throw short darts with sharp points of steel, to provoke him to rage. He commonly runs with all his fury against the first man he sees on horseback, who watches him so carefully, and avoids him so dexterously, that when the spectators believe him to be even between the horns of the bull, he avoids by the quick turn of his horse, and with his lance strikes the bull upon a vein that runs through his poll, with which in a moment he falls down dead. But this fatal stroke can never be struck but when the bull comes so near upon the turn of the horse that his horn even touches the rider's leg, and so is at such a distance that he can shorten his lance, and use the full strength of his arm in the blow. And they who are the most skilful in the exercise do frequently kill the beast with such an exact stroke insomuch as in a day two or three fall in that manner: but if they miss the vein, it only gives a wound that the more enrages him. Sometimes the bull runs with so much fierceness, (for if he scapes the first man, he runs upon the rest as they are in his way,) that he gores the horse with his horns that his guts come out, and he falls before the rider can get from his back. Sometimes by the strength of his neck he raises horse and man from the ground, and throws both down, and then the greatest danger is another gore upon the ground. In any of these disgraces, or any other by which the rider comes to be dismounted, he is obliged in honour to take his revenge upon the bull by his sword, and upon his head, towards which the standers by assist him by running after the bull and hocking* him, by which he falls upon his hinder legs; but before that execution can be done, a good bull hath his revenge upon many poor fellows. Sometimes he is so unruly that nobody dares to attack him, and then the King calls for the mastiffs, whereof two are let out at a time, and if they cannot master him, but are themselves killed, as frequently they are, the King then, as the last refuge, calls for the English mastiffs; of which they seldom turn out above one at a time; and he rarely misses taking the bull and holding him by the nose till the men run in; and after they have hocked him, they quickly kill him. In one of those days there were no fewer than sixteen horses, as good as any in Spain, the worst of which would that very morning have yielded three hundred pistoles, killed, and four or five men, besides many more of both hurt: and some men remained perpetually maimed: for after the horsemen have done as much as they can, they withdraw themselves, and then some accustomed nimble fellows, to whom money is thrown when they perform their feats with skill, stand to receive the bull, whereof the worst are reserved till the last: and it is a wonderful thing to see with what steadiness those fellows will stand a full career of the bull, and by a little quick motion upon one foot avoid him, and lay a hand upon his horn, as if he guided him from him; but then the next standers by, who have not the same activity, commonly pay for it; and there is no day without much mischief. It is a very barbarous exercise and triumph, in which so many men's lives are lost, and always ventured; but so rooted in the affections of that nation, that it is not in the King's power, they say, to suppress it, though, if he disliked it enough, he might forbear to be present at it. There are three festival days in the year, whereof midsummer is one, on which the people hold it to be their right to be treated with these spectacles, not only in great cities, where they are never disappointed, but in very ordinary towns, where there are places provided for it. Besides those ordinary annual days, upon any extraordinary accidents of joy, as at this time for the arrival of the Queen, upon the birth of the King's children, or any signal victory, these triumphs are repeated, which no ecclesiastical censures or authority can suppress or discountenance. For Pope Pius the Fifth, in the time of Philip the Second, and very probably with his approbation, if not upon his desire, published a bull against the *toros* in Spain, which is still in force, in which he declared, that nobody should be capable of Christian burial who lost his life at those spectacles, and that every clergyman who should be present at them stood excommunicated *ipso facto*; and yet there is always one of the largest galleries assigned to the office of the Inquisition and the chief of the clergy, which is always filled besides that many religious men in their habits get other places; only the Jesuits, out of their submission to the supreme authority of the Pope, are never present there, but on those days do always appoint some such solemn exercise to be performed that obliges their whole body to be together. [*HR*, XII, 88–90]

While Hyde and Cottington were frustrated by the polite, but unhelpful, response from the Spanish, all prospect of the King landing in Ireland had been ruled out by Cromwell's determined and bitterly fought campaign there from August 1649 to May 1650. To Hyde's dismay, at the beginning of May Charles agreed to the terms offered by the Scots including a promise to accept the Covenant. In June he arrived in Scotland. His hostility to Presbyterianism, and the Scots' suspicion of his motives, and of his supporters, made the alliance an exceptionally uncomfortable one. Expecting a second invasion, the English Parliament recalled Cromwell from Ireland to take command of the army, and at the end of June, made a declaration of war. By the end of July, Cromwell was in Scotland; in September he routed the Scots at the battle of Dunbar.

The defeat finally put an end to any hopes of Spanish support. Hyde and Cottington received notice to leave Spain in December, although Cottington decided to stay on privately. The defeat did enable Charles to overcome the political hold of the Marquess of Argyll and to place himself in a commanding

position over the Scottish factions. Retreating beyond the Forth he recruited
a new army. At the end of July 1651, threatened by Cromwell's advance into
Perthshire, he led it into England, with Cromwell following close on his heels.
There was no general rising of royalists in support of the King, as he had
hoped; shortly after his exhausted army arrived at Worcester, on 22 August,
its only English troops, a small force from Lancashire led by the Earl of
Derby, were crushed at Wigan.

When the news of this defeat came to Worcester, as it did even almost
as soon as the King came thither, it exceedingly afflicted his majesty, and
abated much of the hope he had of a general rising of the people on his
behalf. His army was very little increased by the access of any English;
and though he had passed near the habitation of many persons of honour
and quality, whose affections and loyalty had been notorious, not a man
of them repaired to him. The sense of their former sufferings remained,
and the smart was not over; nor did his stay in Worcester for so many
days add any resort to his Court. The gentlemen of the country whom
his coming thither had redeemed from imprisonment remained still
with him, and were useful to him; they who were in their houses in the
country, though as well affected, remained there, and came not to him;
and though letters from London had given him cause to believe that
many prepared to come to him, which for some days they might easily
have done, none appeared, except only some common men who had
formerly served the last King, who repaired again to Worcester.

There were some other accidents and observations which administered matter of mortification to the King. The duke of Buckingham had
a mind very restless, and thought he had not credit enough with the
King if it were not made manifest that he had more than any body else:
and therefore, as soon as the King had entered England, though he had
reason to believe that his majesty had not been abundantly satisfied with
his behaviour in Scotland, he came to him, and told him, the business
was now to reduce England to his obedience, and therefore he ought to
do all things gracious and popular in the eyes of the nation; and nothing
could be less so to it than that the army should be under the command
of a Scotch general: that David Leslie was only lieutenant general, and
it had been unreasonable whilst he remained in Scotland to have put
any other to have commanded over him; but that it would be as unreasonable, now they were in England, and had hope to increase the army
by the access of the English, upon whom his principal dependence must
be, to expect that they would be willing to serve under him; that it
would not consist with the honour of any peer of England to receive his

orders, and he believed that very few of that rank would repair to his majesty till they were secure from that apprehension; and used much more discourse to that purpose. The King was so much surprised with it that he could not imagine what he meant, and what the end of it would be, and asked him who it was that he thought fit his majesty should give that command to; when, to his astonishment, the duke told him he hoped his majesty would confer it upon him; at which he was so amazed, that he found an occasion to break off the discourse by calling upon somebody who was near to come to him, and, by asking many questions, declined the former argument. But the duke would not be so put off, but the next day, in the march, renewed his importunity, and told the King that he was confident what he had proposed to him was so evidently for his service that David Leslie himself would willingly consent to it. The King, angry at his prosecuting it in that manner, told him he could hardly believe that he was in earnest, or that he could in truth believe that he could be fit for such a charge; which he seemed to wonder at, and asked wherein his unfitness lay. To which the King replied, that he was too young; and he as readily alleged, that Harry the Fourth of France* commanded an army and won a battle when he was younger than he. So that in the end he [the King] was compelled to tell him that he would have no generalissimo but himself; upon which the duke was so discontented, that he came no more to the council, scarce spoke to the King, neglected every body else and himself, insomuch as for many days he never put on clean linen nor conversed with any body; nor did he recover this ill humour whilst the army stayed at Worcester.

There was another worse accident fell out soon after the King's coming thither. Major general Massey, who thought himself now in his own territory, and that all between Worcester and Gloucester would be quickly his own conquest, knowing every step both of the land and the river, went out with a party to secure a pass which the enemy might make over the river; which he did very well; but would then make a farther inroad into the country, and possess a house which was of small importance, and in which there were men to defend it; where he received a very dangerous wound with ray-shot, that tore his arm and hand in such manner that he was in great torment, and could not stir out of his bed in a time when his activity and industry was most wanted. And by this means the pass which he secured was either totally neglected or not enough taken care for.

There was no good understanding between the officers of the army. David Leslie appeared dispirited and confounded, and gave and revoked his orders, and sometimes contradicted them. He did not love Middleton,* and was very jealous that all the officers loved him too well; who was indeed an excellent officer, and kept up the spirits of the rest, who had no esteem of Leslie. In this very unhappy distemper was the Court and the army in a season when they were ready to be swallowed by the malice and multitude of the enemy, and when nothing could preserve them but the most sincere unity in their prayers to God, in which they were miserably divided, and a joint concurrence in their counsels and endeavours.

The King had been about [twelve] days in Worcester, when Cromwell was known to be within less than half a day's march, with an addition of very many regiments of horse and foot to those which he had brought with him from Scotland; and many other regiments were drawing towards him of the militia of the several counties, under the command of the principal gentlemen of the country: so that he was already very much superior, if not double in number, to the army the King had with him. However, if those rules had been observed, those works cast up, and that order in quartering their men, as were resolved upon when the King came thither, there must have been a good defence made, and the advantages of the ground, the river, and the city, would have preserved them from being presently overrun. But, alas! the army was in amazement and confusion. Cromwell, without troubling himself with the formality of a siege, marched directly on as to a prey, and possessed the hill and all other places of advantages with very little opposition. It was upon the third of September when the King, having been upon his horse most part of the night and taken a full view of the enemy, and every body being upon the post they should be, and the enemy making such a stand that it was concluded he meant to make no attempt that night, and, if he should, he would be repelled with ease, his majesty, a little before noon, retired to his lodging to eat and refresh himself; where he had not been near an hour when the alarum came that both armies were engaged, and though his majesty's horse was ready at the door, and he presently mounted, before, or as soon as, he came out of the city, he met the whole body of his horse running in so great fear that he could not stop them, though he used all the means he could, and called to many officers by their names, and hardly preserved himself, by letting them pass by, from being overthrown and overrun by them.

Cromwell had used none of the delay nor circumspection which was imagined, but directed the troops to fall on in all places at once, and had caused a strong party to go over the river at that pass which

Massey had formerly secured, which was a good distance from the town, and being not at all guarded, they were never known to be on that side the river till they were even ready to charge the King's troops. On that part where Middleton was, and with whom duke Hamilton charged, there was a very brave resistance; and they charged the enemy so vigorously that they beat the body that charged them back; but they were quickly overpowered, and many gentlemen being killed, and Middleton hurt, and duke Hamilton's leg broke short off with a shot, the rest were forced to retire and shift for themselves. In no other part there was resistance made; but such a general consternation possessed the whole army, that the rest of the horse fled, and all the foot threw down their arms before they were charged. When the King came back into the town, he found a good body of horse which had been persuaded to make a stand, though much the major part passed through upon the spur without making any pause. The King desired those who stayed that they would follow him, that they might look upon the enemy, who, he believed, did not pursue them. But when his majesty had gone a little way, he found most of the horse were gone the other way, and that he had none but a few servants of his own about him. Then he sent to have the gates of the town shut, that none might get in one way nor out the other: but all was confusion; there were few to command, and none to obey: so that the King stayed till very many of the enemy's horse were entered the town, and then he was persuaded to withdraw himself.

Duke Hamilton fell into the enemy's hands, and the next day* died of his wounds, and thereby prevented the being made a spectacle, as his brother had been; which the pride and animosity of his enemies would no doubt have done, having the same pretence, by his being a peer of England as the other was. He was in all respects to be much preferred before the other, a much wiser, though it may be a less cunning, man: for he did not affect dissimulation, which was the other's masterpiece. He had unquestionable courage, in which the other did not abound. He was in truth a very accomplished person, of an excellent judgment, and clear and ready expressions: and though he had been driven into some unwarrantable actions, he made it very evident he had not been led by any inclinations of his own, and passionately and heartily ran to all opportunities of redeeming it: and in the article of his death he expressed a marvellous cheerfulness that he had the honour to lose his life in the King's service, and thereby to wipe out the memory of his former transgressions, which he always professed was odious to himself.

As the victory cost the enemy no blood, so after it there was not much cruelty used to the prisoners who were then taken. [But] very many of those who ran away were every day knocked in the head by the country people, and used with their barbarity. Towards the King's menial servants, (whereof most were taken) there was nothing of severity; but within few days they were all discharged and set at liberty.

Though the King could not get a body of horse to fight, he could have too many to fly with him; and he had not been two hours from Worcester, when he found about him near, if not above, four thousand of his horse. There was David Leslie with all his own equipage, as if he had not fled upon the sudden; so that good order and regularity and obedience might yet have made a hopeful retreat even into Scotland itself. But there was paleness in every man's looks, and jealousies and confusion in their faces, and nothing could worse befall the King than a safe return into Scotland; which yet he could not reasonably promise to himself in that company. But when the night covered them, he found means to withdraw himself with one or two of his own servants, whom he likewise discharged when it began to be light; and after he had made them cut off his hair, he betook himself alone into an adjacent wood, and relied only upon Him for deliverance who alone could and did miraculously deliver him. . . .

It is great pity that there was never a journal made of that miraculous deliverance, in which there might be seen so many visible impressions of the immediate hand of God. When the darkness of the night was over, after the King had cast himself into that wood, he discerned another man, who had gotten upon an oak, who was in that wood, near the place where the King had rested himself, and had slept soundly. The man upon the tree had first seen the King, and knew him, and came down from the tree to him, and was known to the King, being a gentleman of the neighbour county of Staffordshire, who had served his late majesty during the war, and had now been one of the few who resorted to the King after his coming to Worcester. His name was Carelesse,* who had had a command of foot, above the degree of a captain, under the lord Loughborough. He persuaded the King, since it could not be safe for him to go out of the wood, and that as soon as it should be fully light the wood itself would probably be visited by those of the country, who would be searching to find those whom they might make prisoners, that he would get up into that tree where he had been, where the boughs were so thick with leaves, that a man would not be discovered there without a narrower inquiry than people usually make in places which they do not suspect. The King thought it good counsel, and with the other's help climbed into the tree, and then helped his companion to ascend after him; where they sat all that day, and securely saw many who came purposely into the wood to look after them, and heard all their discourse, how they would use the King himself if they could take him. This wood was either in or upon the borders of Staffordshire; and though there was a highway near one side of it, where the King had entered into it, yet it was large, and all other sides of it opened amongst enclosures, and it pleased God that Carelesse was not unacquainted with the neighbour villages. And it was part of the King's good fortune that this gentleman was a Roman Catholic, and thereby was acquainted with those of that profession of all degrees: and it must never be denied that those of that faith, that is, some of them, had a very great share in his majesty's preservation.

The day being spent in the tree, it was not in the King's power to forget that he had lived two days with eating very little, and two nights with as little sleep; so that when the night came he was willing to make some provision for both: so that he resolved, with the advice and assistance of his companion, to leave his blessed tree; and so when the night was dark they walked through the wood into those enclosures which were farthest from any highway, and making a shift to get over hedges and ditches, and after walking at least eight or nine miles, which were the more grievous to the King by the weight of his boots, (for he could not put them off, when he cut off his hair, for want of shoes,) before morning they came to a poor cottage, the owner whereof, being a Catholic, was known to Carelesse. He was called up, and as soon as he knew one of them he easily concluded in what condition they both were, and presently carried them into a little barn full of hay, which was a better lodging than he had for himself. But when they were there, and had conferred with their host of the news and temper of the country, it was resolved that the danger would be the greater if they stayed together; and therefore that Carelesse should presently be gone, and should within two days send an honest man to the King to guide him to some other place of security; and in the mean time his majesty should stay upon the hay-mow. The poor man had nothing for him to eat, but promised him good buttermilk the next morning; and so he was once more left alone, his companion, how weary soever, departing from him before day; the poor man of the house knowing no more than that he was a friend of the captain's, and one of those who had escaped from Worcester. The King slept very well in his lodging, till the time that his host brought him a piece of bread and a great pot of buttermilk, which he thought the best food he had ever eaten. The poor man spoke very intelligently to him of the country, and of the people who were well and ill affected to the King, and of the great fear and terror that possessed the hearts of those who were best affected. He told him that he himself lived by his daily labour, and that what he had brought him was the fare he and his wife had; and that he feared if he should endeavour to procure better it might draw suspicion upon him, and people might be apt to think he had somebody with him that was not of his own family; however, if he would have him get some meat he would do it, but if he could bear this hard diet, he should have enough of the milk, and some of the butter that was made with it. The King was satisfied with his reason, and would not run the hazard for a change of diet; desired only the man that he might have his company as often and as much as he could give it him; there being the same reason against the poor man's discontinuing his labour as the alteration of his fare.

After he had rested upon this hay-mow and fed upon this diet two days and two nights, in the evening before the third night another fellow, a little above the condition of his host, came to the house, sent from Carelesse, to conduct the King to another house more out of any road near which any part of the army was like to march. It was above twelve miles that he was to go, and was to use the same caution he had done the first night, not to go in any common road; which his guide knew well how to avoid. Here he new dressed himself, changing clothes with his landlord, and putting on those which he usually wore: he had a great mind to have kept his own shirt, but he considered that men are not sooner discovered by any mark in disguises than by having fine linen in ill clothes; and so he parted with his shirt too, and took the same his poor host had then on. Though he had foreseen that he must leave his boots, and his landlord had taken the best care he could to provide an old pair of shoes, yet they were not easy to him when he first put them on, and in a short time after grew very grievous to him. In this equipage he set out from his first lodging in the beginning of the night, under the conduct of his comrade, who guided him the nearest way, crossing over hedges and ditches, that they might be in least danger of meeting passengers. This was so grievous a march, and he was so tired, that he was even ready to despair, and to prefer being taken, and suffered to rest, before purchasing his safety at that price. His shoes had after the walking a few miles hurt him so much that he had thrown them away, and walked the rest of the way in his ill stockings, which were quickly worn out; and his feet, with the thorns in getting over hedges, and with the stones in other places, were so hurt and wounded, that he many times cast himself upon the ground, with a desperate and obstinate resolution to rest there till the morning, that he might shift with less torment, what hazard soever he run. But his stout guide still prevailed with him to make a new attempt, sometimes promising that the way should be better, and sometimes assuring him that he had but little further to go: and, in this distress and perplexity, before the morning they arrived at the house designed, which though it was better than that which he had left, his lodging was still in the barn, upon straw instead of hay, a place being made as easy in it as the expectation of a guest could dispose it. Here he had such meat and porridge as such people use to have, with which, but especially with the butter and the cheese, he thought himself well feasted; and took the best care he could to be supplied with other, little better, shoes and stockings: and after his feet were enough recovered that he could go, he was conducted from thence to another poor house, within such a distance as put him not to much trouble: for having not yet in his thought which way, or by what means, to make his escape, all that was designed was only by shifting from one house to another to avoid discovery; and being now in that quarter which was more inhabited by the Roman Catholics than most other parts in England, he was led from one to another of that persuasion, and concealed with great fidelity. But he then observed that he was never carried to any gentleman's house, though that country was full of them, but only to poor houses of poor men, which only yielded him rest, with very unpleasant sustenance; whether there was more danger in those better houses, in regard of the resort and the many servants, or whether the owners of great estates were the owners likewise of more fears and apprehensions.

Within few days, a very honest and discreet person, one Mr Huddlestone a Benedictine monk, who attended the service of the Catholics in those parts, came to him, sent by Carelesse, and was a very great assistance and comfort to him. And when the places to which he carried him were at too great a distance to walk, he provided him a horse, and more proper habit than the rags he wore. This man told him that the lord Wilmot lay concealed likewise in a friend's house of his; which his majesty was very glad of, and wished him to contrive some means how they might speak together; which the other easily did, and within a night or two brought them into one place. Wilmot told the King that he had by very good fortune fallen into the house of an honest gentleman, one Mr Lane, a person of an excellent reputation for his fidelity to the King, but of so universal and general a good name, that, though he had a son who had been a colonel in the King's service during the late war, and was then upon his way with men to Worcester the very day of the defeat, men of all affections in the country and of all opinions paid the old man a very great respect: that he had been very civilly treated there, and that the old gentleman had used some diligence to find out where the King was, that he might get him to his house, where he was sure he could conceal him till he might contrive a full deliverance. He told him he had withdrawn from that house, and put himself amongst the Catholics, in hope that he might discover where his majesty was, and having now happily found him, advised him to repair to that house, which stood not near any other house.

The King inquired of the monk of the reputation of this gentleman, who told him that he was a gentleman of a fair estate, exceedingly beloved, and the oldest justice of peace of that county of Stafford; and though he was a very zealous Protestant, yet he lived with so much civility and candour towards the Catholics, that they would all trust him as much as they would do any of their own profession, and that he could not think of any place of so good repose and security for his majesty to repair to. The King, who by this time had as good a mind to eat well as to sleep, liked the proposition, yet thought not fit to surprise the gentleman, but sent Wilmot thither again, to assure himself that he might be received there, and was willing that he should know what guest he received; which hitherto was so much concealed, that none of the houses where he had yet been knew, or seemed to suspect, more than that he was one of the King's party that fled from Worcester. The monk carried him to a house at a reasonable distance, where he was to expect an account from the lord Wilmot, who returned very punctually, with as much assurance of welcome as he could wish. And so they two went together to Mr Lane's house, where the King found he was welcome, and conveniently accommodated in such places as in a large house had been provided to conceal the persons of malignants, or to preserve goods of value from being plundered; where he lodged and eat very well, and began to hope that he was in present safety. Wilmot returned under the care of the monk, and expected summons when any farther motion should be thought to be necessary.

In this station the King remained in quiet and blessed security many days, receiving every day information of the general consternation the kingdom was in, out of the apprehension that his person might fall into the hands of his enemies, and of the great diligence they used in inquiry for him. He saw the proclamation* that was issued out and printed, in which a thousand pounds were promised to any man who would deliver and discover the person of Charles Stewart, and the penalty of high treason declared against those who presumed to harbour or conceal him: by which he saw how much he was beholding to all those who were faithful to him. It was now time to consider how he might find himself near the sea, from whence he might find some means to transport himself: and he was now near the middle of the kingdom, saving that it was a little more northward, where he was utterly unacquainted with all the ports and with that coast. In the west he was best acquainted, and that coast was most proper to transport him into France; to which he was most inclined. Upon this matter he communicated with those of the family to whom he was known, that is, with the old gentleman the father, a very grave and venerable person, the colonel his eldest son, a very plain man in his discourse and behaviour, but of a fearless courage and an integrity superior to any temptation, and a daughter of the house, of a very good wit and discretion, and very fit to bear any part in such a trust. It was a benefit, as well as an inconvenience, in those unhappy times, that the affections of all men were almost as well known as their faces, by the discovery they had made of themselves, in those sad seasons, in many trials and persecutions: so that men knew not only the minds of their next neighbours, and those who inhabited near them, but, upon conference with their friends, could choose fit houses, at any distance, to repose themselves in securely, from one end of the kingdom to another, without trusting the hospitality of a common inn: and men were very rarely deceived in their confidence upon such occasions but [that] the persons with whom they were at any time could conduct them to another house of the same affection.

Mr Lane had a niece, or very near kinswoman, who was married to a gentleman, one Mr Norton, a person of eight or nine hundred pounds *per annum*, who lived within four or five miles of Bristol, which was at least four or five days' journey from the place where the King then was, but a place most to be wished for the King to be in, because he did not only know all that country very well, but knew many persons very well to whom in an extraordinary case he durst make himself known. It was hereupon resolved that Mrs Lane should visit this cousin, who was known to be of good affections, and that she should ride behind the King, who was fitted with clothes and boots for such a service, and that a servant of her father's, in his livery, should wait upon her. A good house was easily pitched upon for the first night's lodging, where Wilmot had notice given him to meet. And in this equipage the King begun his journey; the colonel keeping him company at a distance, with a hawk upon his fist, and two or three spaniels; which, where there were any fields at hand, warranted him to ride out of the way, keeping his company still in his eye, and not seeming to be of it. And in this manner they came to their first night's lodging: and they need not now to contrive to come to their journey's end about the close of the evening, for it was now in the month of October* far advanced, that the long journeys they made could not be despatched sooner. Here the lord Wilmot found them; and their journeys being then adjusted, he was instructed where he should be every night: and so they were seldom seen together in the journey, and rarely lodged in the same house at night. And in this manner the colonel hawked two or three days, till he had brought them within less than a day's journey of Mr Norton's house, and then he gave his hawk to the lord Wilmot, who continued the journey in the same exercise.

There was great care taken when they came to any house that the King might presently be carried into some chamber, Mrs Lane declaring that he was a neighbour's son, whom his father had lent her to ride before her in hope that he would the sooner recover from a quartan ague, with which he had been miserably afflicted, and [was] not yet free. And by this artifice she caused a good bed to be still provided for him, and the best meat to be sent; which she often carried herself, to hinder others from doing it. There was no resting in any place till they came to Mr Norton's,* nor any thing extraordinary that happened in the way, save that they met many people every day in the way who were very well known to the King; and the day that they went to Mr Norton's they were necessarily to ride quite through the city of Bristol, a place and people the King had been so well acquainted with, that he could not but send his eyes abroad to view the great alterations which had been made there after his departure from thence: and when he rode near the place where the great fort had stood, he could not forbear putting his horse out of the way, and rode, with his mistress behind him, round about it.

They came to Mr Norton's house sooner than usual, and it being on a holyday, they saw many people about a bowling-green that was before the door; and the first man the King saw was a chaplain of his own, who was allied to the gentleman of the house, and was sitting upon the rails to see how the bowlers played. So that William, by which name the King went, walked with his horse into the stable, until his mistress could provide for his retreat. Mrs Lane was very welcome to her cousin, and was presently conducted to her chamber, where she no sooner was than she lamented the condition of a good youth who came with her, and whom she had borrowed of his father to ride before her, who was very sick, being newly recovered of an ague; and desired her cousin that a chamber might be provided for him, and a good fire made: for that he would go early to bed, and was not fit to be below stairs. A pretty little chamber was presently made ready, and a fire prepared, and a boy sent into the stable to call William, and to shew him his chamber; who was very glad to be there, freed from so much company as was below. Mrs Lane was put to find some excuse for making a visit at that time of the year, and so many days' journey from her father, and where she had never been before, though the mistress of the house and she had been bred together, and friends as well as kindred. So she pretended that she was, after a little rest, to go into Dorsetshire to another friend.

When it was supper-time, there being broth brought to the table, Mrs Lane filled a little dish, and desired the butler, who waited at the table, to carry that dish of porridge to William, and to tell him that he should have some meat sent to him presently. The butler carried the porridge into the chamber, with a napkin and spoon and bread, and spake kindly to the young man, who was willing to be eating. And the butler looking narrowly upon him fell upon his knees, and with tears told him he was glad to see his majesty. The King was infinitely surprised, yet recollected himself enough to laugh at the man, and to ask him what he meant. The man had been falconer to Tom Jermyn, and made it appear that he knew well enough to whom he spake, repeating some particulars which the King had not forgot. Whereupon the King conjured him not to speak of what he knew, so much as to his master, though he believed him a very honest man. The fellow promised, and faithfully kept his word; and the King was the better waited upon during the time of his abode there.

Dr Gorges, the King's chaplain, being a gentleman of a good family near that place, and allied to Mr Norton, supped with them; and, being a man of a cheerful conversation, asked Mrs Lane many questions concerning William, of whom he saw she was so careful by sending up meat to him; how long his ague had been gone, and whether he had purged since it left him, and the like: to which she gave such answers as occurred. The doctor, from the final prevalence of the Parliament, had, as many others of that function had done, declined his profession, and pretended to study physic. As soon as supper was done, out of good nature, and without telling any body, he went to see William. The King saw him coming into the chamber, and withdrew to the inside of the bed, that he might be farthest from the candle; and the doctor came and sat down by him, felt his pulse, and asked him many questions, which he answered in as few words as was possible, and expressing great inclination to go to his bed; to which the doctor left him, and went to Mrs Lane, and told her that he had been with William, and that he would do well; and advised her what she should do if his ague returned. And the next morning the doctor went away, so that the King saw him no more, of which he was right glad. The next day the lord Wilmot came to the house with his hawk to see Mrs Lane, and so conferred with William; who was to consider what he was to do. They thought it necessary to rest some days, till they were informed what port lay most convenient for them, and what person lived nearest to it upon whose fidelity they might rely: and the King gave him directions to inquire after some persons, and some other particulars, of which when he should be fully instructed he should return again to him. In the mean time he lodged at a house not far from Mr Norton's, to which he had been recommended.

After some days' stay here, and communication between the King and the lord Wilmot by letters, the King came to know that colonel Francis Wyndham lived within little more than a day's journey of the place where he was, of which he was very glad; for, besides the inclination he had to his elder brother, whose wife had been his nurse, this gentleman had behaved himself very well during the war, and had been governor of Dunster Castle, where the King had lodged when he was in the west. After the end of the war, and when all other places were surrendered in that county, he likewise surrendered that, upon fair conditions, and made his peace, and afterwards married a wife with a competent fortune, and lived quietly with her, without any suspicion of having lessened his affection towards the King.

The King sent Wilmot to him, and acquainted him where he was, and that he would gladly speak with him. It was not hard for him to choose a good place where to meet, and there, upon the day appointed, after the King had taken his leave of Mrs Lane, who remained with her cousin Norton, the King and the lord Wilmot met the colonel, and in the way encountered in a town through which they passed Mr Kirton, a servant of the King's, who well knew the lord Wilmot, who had no other disguise than the hawk, but took no notice of him, nor suspected the King to be there; yet that day made the King more wary of having him in his company upon the way. At the place of meeting they rested only one night, and then the King went to the colonel's house, where he rested many days, whilst colonel Wyndham projected at what place the King might embark, and how they might procure a vessel to be ready there; which was not easy to find, there being so great caution in all the ports, and so great a fear possessing those who were honest, that it was hard to procure any vessel that was outward bound to take in any passenger.

There was a gentleman, one Mr Ellesdon, who lived near Lyme* in Dorsetshire, and who was well known to colonel Wyndham, having been a captain in the King's army, and was still looked upon as a very honest man. With him the colonel consulted how they might get a vessel to be ready to take in a couple of gentlemen, friends of his, who were in danger to be arrested, and transport them into France. Though no man would ask who the persons were, yet every man suspected who they were; at least they concluded that it was some of Worcester party. Lyme was generally as malicious and disaffected a town to the King's interest as any town in England could be, yet there was in it a master of a bark of whose honesty this captain was very confident. This man was lately returned from France, and had unladen his vessel, when Ellesdon asked him when he would make another voyage, and he answered as soon as he could get loading for his ship. The other asked, whether he would undertake to carry over a couple of gentlemen, and land them in France, if he might be as well paid for his voyage as he used to be when he was freighted by the merchants; in conclusion, he told him he should receive fifty pounds for his fare. The large recompense had that effect that the man undertook it, though he said he must make his provision very secretly; for that he might be well suspected for going to sea again without being freighted after he was so newly returned. Colonel Wyndham, being advertised of this, came together with the lord Wilmot to the captain's house, from whence the lord and the captain rode to a house near Lyme, where the master of the bark met them; and the lord Wilmot being satisfied with the discourse of the man, and his wariness and foreseeing suspicions which would arise, it was resolved that on such a night, which upon consideration of the tides was agreed upon, the man should draw out his vessel from the pier, and being at sea should come to such a point about a mile from the town, where his ship should remain upon the beach when the water was gone; which would take it off again about the break of day the next morning. There was very near that point, even in the view of it, a small inn, kept by a man who was reputed honest, to which the cavaliers of the country often resorted; and London road passed that way, so that it was seldom without resort. Into that inn the two gentlemen were to come in the beginning of the night, that they might put themselves on board. And all things being thus concerted, and good earnest given to the master, the lord Wilmot and the colonel returned to the colonel's house, above a day's journey from the place, the captain undertaking every day to look that the master should provide, and if any thing fell out contrary to expectation, to give the colonel notice at such a place, where they intended the King should be the day before he was to embark.

The King, being satisfied with these preparations, came at the time appointed to that house* where he was to hear that all went as it ought to do; of which he received assurance from the captain, who found that the man had honestly put his provisions on board, and had his company ready, which were but four men, and that the vessel should be drawn out that night: so that it was fit for the two persons to come to the aforesaid inn; and the captain conducted them within sight of it, and then went to his own house, not distant a mile from it; the colonel remaining still at the house where they had lodged the night before, till he might hear the news of their being embarked.

They found many passengers in the inn; and so were to be contented with an ordinary chamber, which they did not intend to sleep long in, but as soon as there appeared any light, Wilmot went out to discover the bark, of which there was no appearance. In a word, the sun rose, and nothing like a ship in view. They sent to the captain, who was as much amazed, and he sent to the town; and his servant could not find the master of the bark, which was still in the pier. They suspected the captain, and the captain suspected the master. However, it being past ten of the clock, they concluded it was not fit for them to stay longer there, and so they mounted their horses again to return to the house where they had left the colonel, who they knew resolved to stay there till he were assured that they were gone.

The truth of the disappointment was this. The man meant honestly, and had made all things ready for his departure; and the night he was to go out with his vessel he had stayed in his own house, and slept two or three hours; and the time of the tide being come, that it was necessary to be on board, he took out of a cupboard some linen and other things which he used to carry with him to sea. His wife had observed that he had been for some days fuller of thoughts than he used to be, and that he had been speaking with seamen who used to go with him, and that some of them had carried provisions on board the bark; of which she had asked her husband the reason; who had told her that he was promised freight speedily, and therefore he would make all things ready. She was sure that there was yet no lading in the ship, and therefore, when she saw her husband take all those materials with him, which was

a sure sign that he meant to go to sea, and it being late in night, she
shut the door, and swore he should not go out of the house. He told
her he must go, and was engaged to go to sea that night; for which he
should be well paid. His wife told him she was sure he was doing somewhat that would undo him, and she was resolved he should not go out
of his house; and if he should persist in it, she would call the neighbours, and carry him before the mayor to be examined, that the truth
might be found out. The poor man, thus mastered by the passion and
violence of his wife, was forced to yield to her, that there might be no
farther noise; and so went into his bed.

And it was very happy that the King's jealousy hastened him from
that inn. It was the solemn fast day, which was observed in those times
principally to inflame the people against the King and all those who
were loyal to him; and there was a chapel in that village and over against
that inn, where a weaver, who had been a soldier, used to preach, and
utter all the villainy imaginable, against the order of government: and
he was then in the chapel preaching to his congregation when the King
went from thence, and telling the people that Charles Stewart was
lurking somewhere in that country, and that they would merit from
God Almighty if they could find him out. The passengers who had
lodged in the inn that night had, as soon as they were up, sent for
a smith to visit their horses, it being a hard frost. The smith, when he
had done what he was sent for, according to the custom of that people,
examined the feet of the other two horses, to find more work. When he
had observed them, he told the host of the house that one of those
horses had travelled far, and that he was sure that his four shoes had
been made in four several counties; which, whether his skill was able
to discover or no, was very true. The smith going to the sermon told
this story to some of his neighbours, and so it came to the ears of the
preacher when his sermon was done. And immediately he sent for an
officer, and searched the inn, and inquired for those horses; and being
informed that they were gone, he caused horses to be sent to follow
them, and to make inquiry after the two men who rode those horses,
and positively declared that one of them was Charles Stewart.

When they came again to the colonel, they presently concluded that
they were to make no longer stay in those parts, nor any more to
endeavour to find a ship upon that coast; and so, without farther delay,
they rode back to the colonel's house, where they arrived in the night.
Then they resolved to make their next attempt more southward, in
Hampshire and Sussex, where colonel Wyndham had no interest. And
they must pass through all Wiltshire before they came thither, which

would require many days' journey: and they were first to consider what honest houses there were in or near the way, where they might securely repose; and it was thought very dangerous for the King to ride through any great town, as Salisbury or Winchester, which might probably lie in their way.

There was between that and Salisbury a very honest gentleman, colonel Robert Phelips, a younger brother of a very good family, which had always been very loyal, and he had served the King during the war. The King was resolved to trust him; and so sent the lord Wilmot to a place from whence he might send to Mr Phelips to come to him, and when he had spoken with him, Mr Phelips should come to the King, and Wilmot was to stay in such a place as they two should agree. Mr Phelips accordingly came to the colonel's house, which he could do without suspicion, they being nearly allied. The ways were very full of soldiers, which were sent now from the army to their quarters; and many regiments of horse and foot were assigned for the west, of which Desborough* was major general. These marches were like to last for many days, and it would not be fit for the King to stay so long in that place. Thereupon he resorted to his old security of taking a woman behind him, a kinswoman of colonel Wyndham, whom he carried in that manner to a place not far from Salisbury, to which colonel Phelips conducted him. And in this journey he passed through the middle of a regiment of horse, and presently after met Desborough walking down a hill with three or four men with him, who had lodged in Salisbury the night before; all that road being full of soldiers.

The next day, upon the plains, Dr Henchman, one of the prebends of Salisbury, met the King, the lord Wilmot and colonel Phelips then leaving him to go to the sea-coast to find a vessel, the doctor conducting the King to a place called Heale, three miles from Salisbury, belonging then to sergeant Hyde,* who was afterwards Chief Justice of the King's Bench, and then in the possession of the widow of his elder brother, a house that stood alone, from neighbours and from any highway; where coming in late in the evening, he supped with some gentlemen who accidentally were in the house, which could not well be avoided. But the next morning he went early from thence, as if he had continued his journey; and the widow, being trusted with the knowledge of her guest, sent her servants out of the way, and at an hour appointed received him again, and accommodated him in a little room, which had been made since the beginning of the troubles (the seat always belonging to a malignant family) for the concealment of delinquents.

And here he lay concealed, without the knowledge of some gentle-men who lived in the house and of others who daily resorted thither, for many days, the widow herself only attending him with such things as were necessary, and bringing him such letters as the doctor received from the lord Wilmot and colonel Phelips. A vessel being at last provided upon the coast of Sussex, and notice thereof sent to Dr Henchman, he sent to the King to meet him at Stonehenge, upon the plains, three miles from Heale, whither the widow took care to direct him; and being there met, he attended him to the place, where colonel Phelips received him: who the next day delivered him to the lord Wilmot, who went with him to a house in Sussex, recommended by colonel Gunter, a gentleman of that country, who had served the King in the war; who met him there, and had provided a little bark at Brightemsted,* a small fisher-town, where he went early on board, and by God's blessing arrived safely in Normandy.

The earl of Southampton, who was then at his house at Titchfield in Hampshire, [and] had been advertised of the King's being in the west and of his missing his passage at Lyme, sent a trusty gentleman to those faithful persons in the country who he thought were most like to be employed for his escape if he came into those parts, to let them know that he had a ship ready, and if the King came to him he should be safe; which advertisement came to the King the night before he embarked, and when his vessel was ready. But his majesty ever acknowledged the obligation with great kindness, he being the only person of that condition who had the courage to solicit such a danger, though all men heartily wished his deliverance. It was about the end of November* that the King landed in Normandy, in a small creek; from whence he got to Rouen, and then gave notice to the Queen of his arrival, and freed his subjects in all places from their dismal apprehensions.

Though this wonderful deliverance and preservation of the person of the King was an argument of general joy and comfort to all his good subjects, and a new seed of hope for future blessings, yet his present condition was very deplorable. France was not at all pleased with his being come thither, nor did quickly take notice of his being there. The Queen his mother was very glad of his escape, but in no degree able to contribute towards his support, they who had interest with her finding that all she had, or could get, too little for their own unlimited expense. Besides, the distraction that Court had been lately in,* and was not yet free from the effects of it, made her pension to be paid with less punctuality than it had used to be; so that she was forced to be in debt both to her servants and for the very provisions of her house; nor had the King one shilling towards the support of himself and his family.

As soon as his majesty came to Paris, and knew that the Chancellor [of the Exchequer] was at Antwerp,* he commanded Seymour, who was of his bedchamber, to send to him to repair thither: which whilst he was providing to do, Mr Long, the King's secretary, who was at Amsterdam, and had been removed from his attendance in Scotland by the marquis of Argyll, writ to him, that he had received a letter from the King, by which he was required to let all his majesty's servants who were in those parts know, that it was his pleasure that none of them should repair to him to Paris until they should receive farther order, since his majesty could not yet resolve how long he should stay there: of which, Mr Long said, he thought it his duty to give him notice, with this, that the lord Culpepper and himself, who had resolved to have made haste thither, had in obedience to this command laid aside that purpose. The Chancellor concluded that this inhibition concerned not him, since he had received a command from the King to wait upon him. Besides, he had still the character of ambassador upon him, which he could not lay down till he had kissed his majesty's hand. So he pursued his former purpose, and came to Paris in the Christmas,* and found that the command to Mr Long had been procured by the Queen with an eye principally upon the Chancellor, who some there had no mind should be with the King; though, when there was no remedy, the Queen received him graciously. But the King was very well pleased with his being come, and for the first four or five days he spent many hours with him in private, and informed him of very many particulars of the barbarous treatment he had received in Scotland, and the reason of his march into England, the confusion at Worcester, and all the circumstances of his happy escape and deliverance; many parts whereof are comprehended within this relation, and are exactly true.* For, besides all those particulars which the King himself was pleased to communicate unto him, so soon after the transaction of them, and when they had made so lively an impression in his memory, and of which the Chancellor at that time kept a very punctual memorial, he had at the same time the daily conversation of the lord Wilmot, who informed him of all he could remember: and sometimes the King and he recollected many particulars in their discourse together, in which the King's memory was much better than the other's. And after the King's blessed return into England, he had frequent conferences with many of those who had acted several parts towards the escape; whereof many were of his nearest alliance, and others his most intimate friends; towards whom his majesty always made many gracious expressions of his acknowledgment. So that there is nothing in this short relation the verity whereof can justly be suspected, though, as is said before, it is great pity that there could be no diary made, indeed no exact account of every hour's adventures from the coming out of Worcester, in that dismal confusion, to the hour of his embarkation at Brighthemsted; in which there was such a concurrence of good nature, charity, and generosity, in persons of the meanest, and lowest extraction and condition, who did not know the value of the precious jewel that was in their custody, yet all knew him to be escaped from such an action as would make the discovery and delivery of him to those who governed over and amongst them of great benefit and present advantage to them; and in those who did know him, of courage, loyalty, and activity; that we may reasonably look upon the whole as the inspiration and conduct of God Almighty, as a manifestation of his power and glory, and for the conviction of that whole nation, which had sinned so grievously; and if it hath not wrought that effect in both, it hath rendered both the more unexcusable.

As the greatest brunt of the danger was diverted by those poor people in his night-marches on foot, with so much pain and torment that he often thought that he paid too dear a price for his life, before he fell into the hands of persons of better quality and places of more conveniency, so he owed very much to the diligence and fidelity of some ecclesiastical persons of the Romish persuasion, especially to those of the order of St Benedict; which was the reason that he expressed more favours after his restoration to that order than to any other, and granted them some extraordinary privilege about the service of the Queen, not concealing the reason why he did so; and which ought to have satisfied all men that his majesty's indulgence towards all of that profession, by restraining the severity and rigour of the laws which had been formerly made against them, had its rise from a fountain of princely justice and gratitude, as of royal bounty and clemency. [*HR*, XIII, 94–109]

16. The Nadir of Royalism and the Death of Cromwell

The failure of the Scottish expedition, and the now seemingly impregnable position of the English republic, left few avenues open for the recovery of the kingdom. Despite royalist hopes, the political crises in England — Cromwell's dispute with the Rump Parliament, his dismissal of it in April 1653, the quarrels in Barebones's Parliament, and his assumption of the title and role of Lord Protector in December 1653 — turned out to be barren of opportunities to exploit.

The royal court settled itself unhappily and uncomfortably in Paris, reluctantly hosted by the French under the patronage of Charles I's French Queen Henrietta Maria, as it searched for financial or military support from other countries. In fact, such support became ever less likely as the republic's navy established a formidable reputation through its victories over the Dutch in the Anglo-Dutch war of 1652–4. By the end of 1653 France was in negotiations with Cromwell for an alliance. It was expected that a condition of any such treaty would be the expulsion of Charles II. In anticipation, in early 1654 he resolved to move to Germany, whose princes had agreed to provide a financial contribution.

Hyde had become established as one of the King's senior advisers, in practice the King's principal secretary as well as chancellor. This was despite the settled hostility of the Queen and her allies, including the former Attorney General and now Lord Keeper Sir Edward Herbert.

SHORTLY after the prince was gone,* the King began to think of a day for his own departure, and to make a list of his servants which he intended should wait upon him. He foresaw that the only end of his journey was to find some place where he might securely attend such a conjuncture as God Almighty should give him, that might invite him to new activity, his present business being to be quiet; and therefore he was wont to say, that he would provide the best he could for it by having only such about him as could be quiet. He could not forget the vexation the Lord Keeper had always given him, and how impossible it was for him to live easily with any body, and so, in the making the list of those who were to go with him, he left his name out; which he [the Keeper] could not be long without knowing, and thereupon he came to the King, and asked him whether he did not intend that he should wait upon him. His majesty told him, 'No,' for that he resolved to make no use of his Great Seal; and therefore that he should stay at Paris, and not put himself to the trouble of such a journey which he himself intended to make without the ease and benefit of a coach: which in truth he did, putting his coach-horses into a waggon, wherein his bed and clothes were carried, nor was he owner of a coach in some years after. The Keeper expostulated with him in vain upon the dishonour that it would be to him to be left behind; and the next day brought his Great Seal, and delivered it to him, and desired that he would sign a paper, in which his majesty acknowledged that he had received again his Great Seal from him; which the King very willingly signed; and he immediately removed his lodging, and left the Court, and never after saw his majesty; which did not at all please the Queen, who was as much troubled that he was to stay where she was as that he did not go with the King.

The Queen prevailed with the King, at parting, in a particular in which he had fortified himself to deny her, which was, that he would leave the duke of Gloucester* with her; which she importuned him so much, that, without very much disobliging her, he could not resist. She desired him to consider in what condition he had been bred, without learning either exercise or language, or having ever seen a Court or good company; and being now in a place, and he at an age, that might be instructed in all these, to carry him away from all these advantages, to live in Germany, would be interpreted by all the world not only to be want of kindness towards his brother but want of all manner of respect to her. The reasonableness of this discourse, together with the King's utter disability to support him in the condition that was fit for him, would easily have prevailed, if it had not been the fear that the purpose was to pervert him in his religion; which when the Queen had assured the King was not in her thought, and that she would not permit any such attempt to be made, his majesty consented to it.

And now the day being appointed for his majesty to begin his journey, the King desired that the Chancellor [of the Exchequer] might likewise part in the Queen's good grace, at least without her notable disfavour, which had been so severe towards him that he had for some months not presumed to be in her presence: so that though he was very desirous to kiss her majesty's hand, he knew not how to make any advance towards it. But the day before the King was to be gone, the lord Percy, who was directed by his majesty to speak in the affair, and who in truth had kindness for the Chancellor, and knew the prejudice against him to be very unjust, brought him word that the Queen was content to see him, and that he would accompany him to her in the afternoon.

And accordingly at the hour appointed by her majesty they found her alone in her private gallery; and the lord Percy withdrawing to the other end of the room, the Chancellor told her majesty, that now she had vouchsafed to admit him into her presence, he hoped she would let him know the ground of the displeasure she had conceived against him; that so, having vindicated himself from any fault towards her majesty, he might leave her with a confidence in his duty, and receive her commands with an assurance that they should be punctually obeyed by him. The Queen, with a louder voice and more emotion than she was accustomed to, told him, that she had been contented to see him, and to give him leave to kiss her hand, to comply with the King's desires, who had importuned her to it; otherwise, that he lived in that manner towards her, that he had no reason to expect to be welcome to her: that she need not assign any particular miscarriage of his, since his disrespect towards her was notorious to all men; and that all men took notice that he never came where she was, though he lodged under her roof, (for the house was hers,) and that she thought she had not seen him in six months before, which she looked upon as so high affront that only her respect towards the King prevailed with her to endure it.

When her majesty made a pause, the Chancellor said that her majesty had only mentioned his punishment, and nothing of his fault: that how great soever his infirmities were, in defect of understanding or in good manners, he had yet never been in Bedlam, which he had deserved to be if he had affected to publish to the world that he was in the Queen's disfavour, by avoiding to be seen by her: that he had no kind of apprehension that they who thought worst of him would ever believe him to be such a fool as to provoke the wife of his dead master, the greatness of whose affections to her was well known to him, and the mother of the King, who subsisted by her favour; and all this in France, where himself was a banished person, and she at home, where she might oblige or disoblige him at her pleasure. So that he was well assured that nobody would think him guilty of so much folly and madness as not to use all the endeavours he possibly could to obtain her grace and protection: that it was very true he had been long without the presumption of being in her majesty's presence, after he had undergone many sharp instances of her displeasure, and after he had observed some alteration and aversion in her majesty's looks and countenance upon his coming into the room where she was and during the time he stayed there; which others likewise observed so much, that they withdrew from holding any conversation with him in those places out of fear to offend her majesty: that he had often desired, by several persons, to

know the cause of her majesty's displeasure, and that he might be
admitted to clear himself from any unworthy suggestions which had
been made before her majesty, but could never obtain that honour; and
therefore he had conceived that he was obliged, in good manners, to
remove so unacceptable an object from the eyes of her majesty by not
coming into her presence, which all who knew him could not but know
to be the greatest mortification that could be inflicted upon him; and
therefore he most humbly besought her majesty at this audience, which
might be the last he should receive of her, she would dismiss him with
the knowledge of what he had done amiss, that he might be able to make
his innocence and integrity appear, which he knew had been blasted by
the malice of some persons, and thereby misunderstood and misinterpreted by her majesty. But all this prevailed not with her majesty, who,
after she had, with her former passion, objected his credit with the
King, and his endeavours to lessen that credit which she ought to have,
concluded, that she should be glad to see reason to change her opinion;
and so, carelessly extended her hand towards him, which he kissing, her
majesty departed to her chamber. [*HR*, XIV, 91–4]

The King's melancholy departure from Paris at the end of June 1654
marked a further decline in his fortunes, despite a sense of relief at leaving
behind the faction-ridden atmosphere of the Queen's court at Saint-Germain.
During the summer, the King spent time with his sister, the Princess Royal,
at Aachen and elsewhere. At the end of September, his court finally settled
at Cologne.

Cologne is a city most pleasantly situated upon the banks of the Rhine;
of a large extent, and fair and substantial buildings; and encompassed
with a broad and excellent wall, upon which are fair walks of great
elms, where two coaches may go on breast, and for the beauty of it is
not inferior to the walls of Antwerp, but rather superior, because [this]
goes round the town. The government is under the senate and consuls,
of whom there was one then consul who was descended from father to
son of a patrician Roman family, that had continued from the time
the colony was first planted there. It had never been otherwise subject
to the bishop than in some points which refer to his ecclesiastical jurisdiction, which they sometimes endeavouring to enlarge, the magistrates always oppose; which gives the subject of the discourse of
jealousies and contests between their prince and them, which are
neither so frequent nor of that moment as they are reported to be. The
Elector never resides there,* but keeps his court at the castle of Bonn,
near four miles from thence. And that Elector, who was of the House

of Bavaria, and a melancholic and peevish man, had not then been in the city in very many years. The number of churches and religious houses is incredible, insomuch as it was then averred that the religious persons and churchmen made up a full moiety of the inhabitants of the town; and their interest and authority so far prevailed, that some few years before the King came thither they expelled all those of the Protestant religion, contrary to the advice of the wisest of the magistrates, who confess that the trade of the town was much decayed thereby, and the poverty thereof much increased. And it is very possible that the vast number and unskilful zeal of the ecclesiastical and religious persons may at some time expose that noble city to the surprise of some powerful prince, who will quickly deprive them of their long enjoyed privileges. And there was in that very time of the King's stay there a design by the French to have surprised it, Schomberg* lying many days in wait there to have performed that service, which was very hardly prevented. The people are so much more civil than they were reported to be, that they seem to be the most conversable, and to understand the laws of society and conversation better than any other people of Germany. To the King they were so devoted, that when they understood that he was not so fixed to the resolution of residing at Aachen but that he might be diverted from it, they very handsomely made tender to him of any accommodation that city could yield him, and of all the affection and duty they could pay him; which his majesty most willingly accepted; and, giving order for the payment of the rent for the house he had taken at Aachen, which he had not at all used, and other disbursements which the master of the house had made to make it the more convenient for his majesty, and likewise sending very gracious letters to the magistrates of that town for the civility they had expressed towards him, he sent for that part of his family which remained there, to attend him at Cologne, where he declared he would spend that winter. [*HR*, XIV, 111]

In the autumn of 1654, the King and the Princess visited the Duke of Newburgh, at Düsseldorf, before the Princess returned home to The Hague. Soon afterwards, a new headache presented itself to the king.

Within a short time after his majesty's return to Cologne, he received news* that exceedingly afflicted him, and the more, that he knew not what remedy to apply to the mischief which he saw would befall him. From Paris, he heard that the Queen had put away the tutor he had left to attend his brother the duke of Gloucester, who remained at Paris upon her majesty's desire that he might learn his exercises.

The Queen had conferred with him upon the desperateness of his condition, in respect of the King his brother's fortune, and the little hope that appeared that his majesty could ever be restored, at least if he did not himself become Roman Catholic, whereby the Pope and other princes of that religion might be united in his quarrel, which they would never undertake upon any other obligation: that it was therefore fit that the duke, who had nothing to support him, nor could expect any thing from the King, should be instructed in the Catholic religion; that so, becoming a good Catholic, he might be capable of those advantages which her majesty should be able to procure for him: that the Queen of France would hereupon confer abbeys and benefices upon him, to such a value as would maintain him in that splendour as was suitable to his birth; that in a little time the Pope would make him a cardinal, by which he might be able to do the King his brother much service, and contribute to his recovery; whereas without this he must be exposed to great necessity and misery, for that she was able no longer to give him maintenance. She found the duke more obstinate than she expected from his age; he was so well instructed in his religion, that he disputed against the change; urged the precepts he had received from the King his father, and his dying in the faith he had prescribed to him; put her majesty in mind of the promise she had made to the King his brother at parting; and acknowledged that he had obliged himself to his majesty that he would never change his religion; and therefore besought her majesty that she would not farther press him, at least till he should inform the King of it. The Queen well enough knew the King's mind, and thought it more excusable to proceed in that affair without imparting it to him; and therefore took upon her the authority of a mother, and removed his tutor from him, and committed the duke to the care of the abbot Montagu* her almoner, who having the pleasant abbey at Pontoise entertained his highness there, sequestered from all resort of such persons who might confirm him in his averseness from being converted.

As soon as the King received this advertisement, which both the duke and his tutor made haste to transmit to him, he was exceedingly perplexed. On the one hand, he knew the reproaches which would be cast upon him by his enemies, who took all the pains they could to persuade the world that he himself had changed his religion; and though his exercise of it was so public wherever he was that strangers resorted to it, and so could bear witness of it, yet their impudence was such in their positive averment, that they persuaded many in England, and especially of those of the Reformed religion abroad, that his majesty was in truth a Papist; and his leaving his brother behind him in France, where it was evident the Queen would endeavour to pervert him, would be an argument that he did not desire to prevent it. On the other side, he knew well the little credit he had in France, and how far they would be from assisting him in a contest of such a nature with his mother. However, that the world might see plainly that he did all that was in his power, he sent the marquis of Ormond with all possible expedition into France, who he very well knew would steadily execute his commands. He writ a letter of complaint to the Queen* of her having proceeded in that manner in a matter of so near importance to him, and conjured her to discontinue the prosecution of it, and to suffer his brother the duke of Gloucester to repair with the marquis of Ormond to his presence. He commanded the duke not to consent to any propositions which should be made to him for the change of his religion, and that he should follow the advice of the marquis of Ormond and accompany him to Cologne. And he directed the marquis of Ormond to let Mr Montagu, and whosoever of the English who should join with him, know, that they should expect such a resentment from his majesty, if they did not comply with his commands, as should be suitable to his honour and to the affront they put upon him.

The marquis behaved himself with so much wisdom and resolution, that though the Queen was enough offended with him, and with the expostulation the King made with her, and imputed all the King's sharpness and resolution to the counsel he received from the marquis and the Chancellor, yet she thought not fit to extend her power in detaining the duke both against the King's and his own will; and the duke, upon receipt of the King's letter, declared that he would obey his majesty; and the abbot found that he must enter into an absolute defiance with the King if he persisted in advising the Queen not to comply with his directions: so that after two or three days deliberation, the Queen, expressing very much displeasure at the King's proceeding, and that she should be wholly divested of the power and authority of a mother, told the marquis that the duke might dispose of himself as he pleased, and that she would not concern herself farther, nor see him any more. And thereupon the duke put himself into the hands of the marquis, who immediately removed him from Pontoise to the house of an English lord who lived then in Paris; where he remained for some days, until the marquis could borrow money (which was no easy matter) to defray the journey to the King, and then they quickly left Paris, and shortly after came to the King, who was infinitely delighted with the marquis his negotiation and success, and kept his brother always with him till the time that he returned into England, the Queen remaining as much unsatisfied. [*HR*, XIV, 117–19]

Royalists in England had been entirely unsuccessful in their attempts to mount any serious challenge to Cromwell's rule: the army was too powerful, Cromwell's intelligence network too effective, and they too amateurish. To the frustration of many of them, the leaders of the 'Sealed Knot', the group commissioned by the King to lead royalist plotting in England, erred well on the side of caution. But at the beginning of 1655, following conflict between the Protector and his Parliament over control of the army and religious toleration, messages from England calling for action became more insistent.

The rest and quiet that the King proposed to himself in this necessitated retreat was disturbed by the impatience and activity of his friends in England, who, notwithstanding all his majesty's commands and injunctions not to enter upon any sudden and rash insurrections, which could only contribute to their own ruin without the least benefit or advantage to his service, were so pricked and stung by the insolence of their enemies and the uneasiness of their own condition and fortune, that they could not rest. They sent expresses every day to Cologne for commissions and instructions, and made an erroneous judgment of their own strength and power, and concluded that all who hated the present government would concur with them to overthrow it, at least would act no part in the defence of it. They assured the King that they had made sufficient provision of arms and ammunition, and had so many persons engaged to appear upon any day that should be assigned that they only desired that his majesty would appoint that day; and that they were so united, that even the discovery before the day, and the clapping up many persons in prison, (which they expected) should not break the design. The King knew well enough that they would be deceived, and that though the persons who sent those expresses were very honest men, and had served well in the war, and were ready to engage again, yet they were not equal to so great a work. Yet it was not fit to discountenance or dishearten them; for as many of his party were too restless and too active, so there were more of them remiss and lazy, and even abandoned to despair. And the truth is, the unequal temper of those who wished very well, and the jealousy, at least the want of confidence in each other, made the King's part exceeding difficult. Very many who held correspondence with his majesty, and those he assigned to that office, would not trust each other; every body chose their own knot with whom they would converse, and would not communicate

with any body else; for which they had too just excuses from the discoveries which were [made] every day by want of wit as much as want
of honesty; and so men were cast into prison, and kept there, upon
general jealousies. But this reservation, since they could not all resolve
to be quiet, proved very grievous to the King; for he could not convert
and restrain those who were too forward by the counsel of those who
stood in a better light and could discern better what was to be done,
because they could not be brought together to confer; and they who
appeared to be less desperate were by the others reproached with being
less affectionate, and to want loyalty as much as courage: and so they
who were undone upon one and the same account, were oppressed and
torn in pieces by one and the same enemy and could never hope for
recovery but by one and the same remedy, grew to reproach and revile
one another, and contracted a greater animosity between themselves
than against the common adversary. Nor could the King reconcile this
distemper, nor preserve himself from being invaded by it.

Though the messengers who were sent were addressed to the King
himself and to the Chancellor and were so carefully concealed that no
notice was taken or advertisement sent by the many spies who were
suborned to give intelligence of any one express that was sent to
Cologne, yet they had commonly some friend or acquaintance in the
Court with whom they conferred; and ever returned worst satisfied
with those who made objections against what they proposed, or
seemed to doubt that they would not be able to perform what they so
confidently promised; and it was thought a very reasonable conviction
of a man who liked not the most extravagant undertaking, if he were
not ready to propose a better: so that his majesty thought fit often to
seem to think better of many things promised than in truth he did.
The messengers which were sent this winter to Cologne, (who, I say
still, were honest men, and sent from those who were such,) proposed
to the King, (which they had formerly done), that, when they were in
arms, and had provided a place where his majesty might land safely, he
would then be with them, that there might be no dispute upon command: and in the spring they sent to him that the day was appointed,
the 18th of April, when the rising would be general, and many places
seized upon, and some declare for the King, which were in the hands
of the army: for they still pretended, and did believe, that a part of
the army would declare against Cromwell at least, though not for the
King: that Kent was united to a man; Dover Castle would be possessed, and the whole county in arms upon that day; and therefore that
his majesty would vouchsafe to be in some place concealed upon the

sea-coast, which it was very easy for him to be, on that day; from whence, upon all being made good that was undertaken, and full notice given to his majesty that it was so, he might then, and not before, transport himself to that part which he thought to be in the best posture to receive him, and might give such other directions to the rest as he found necessary. And even all these particulars were communicated in confidence by the messengers to their friends who were near the King, and who again thought it but reasonable to raise the spirits of their friends by letting them know in how happy a condition the King's affairs were in England, and that his friends were in so good a posture throughout the kingdom, that they feared not that any discovery might be made to Cromwell, being ready to own and justify their counsels with their swords: so that it quickly became more than whispered throughout the Court that the King was only expected to be nearer England, how disguised soever, that he might quickly put himself into the head of the army that would be ready to receive him, whereby all emulations about command might be prevented, or immediately taken away; and if his majesty should now neglect this opportunity, it might easily be concluded, that either he was betrayed, or that his counsels were conducted by men of very shallow capacities and understanding.

How weakly and improbably soever these preparations were adjusted, the day was positively appointed, and was so near at the time when his majesty had notice of it that it was not possible for him to send orders to contradict it; and he foresaw that if any thing should be attempted without success, it would be imputed to his not being at a distance to countenance it. On the other hand, it was neither difficult nor hazardous to his majesty to remove that reproach, and to be in a place from whence he might advance if there were cause, or retire to Cologne if there were nothing to do; and all this with so little noise, that his absence should scarce be taken notice of. Hereupon the messenger returned with the King's approbation of the day, and direction that as soon as the day should be past an express should be directed to Flushing, and at the sign of the *City of Rouen*, (a known harbour* in that town,) to enquire for an Englishman, (whose name was given him,) who should be able to inform him whither he should repair to speak with the King.

Before the messenger's departure, or the King's resolution was taken, the earl of Rochester, who was always jealous that somebody would be general before him, upon the first news of the general disposition and resolution to be in arms, desired the King that he would permit him to go over in disguise, to the end that, finding the way to London, which was very easy, he might, upon advising with the principal persons engaged, of whom there was none who had not been commanded by him, or was [not] inferior to him in command, assist them in their enterprise, and make the best of that force which they could bring together: and if he found that in truth they were not competently provided to sustain the first shock, he might by his advice and authority compose them to expect a better conjuncture, and in the mean time to give over all inconsiderate attempts; and there would be little danger in his withdrawing back again to his majesty.

And in this errand he left Cologne, under pretence of pursuing his business with the German princes upon the donative of the Diet,* in which he used to make many journeys; and nobody suspected that he was gone upon any other design. But when he came into Flanders, he was not at all reserved; but in the hours of good fellowship, which was a great part of the day and night, communicated his purpose to any body he did believe would keep him company and run the same hazard with him; and finding sir Joseph Wagstaff, who had served the King in the last war very honestly, and was then watching at the sea-coast to take the first opportunity to transport himself as soon as he should hear of the general insurrection, (which all letters to all places mentioned as a matter resolved on,) Rochester frankly declared what he was going about; and so they hired a bark at Dunkirk,* and without any misadventure found themselves in safety together at London: but many of those who should have been in arms were seized upon, and secured in several prisons.

The messenger being despatched, the King at the time appointed, and that he might be sure to be near at the day, left Cologne* very early in the morning, attended only by the marquis of Ormond and one groom to look to their horses: nor was it known to any body but to the Chancellor and the Secretary (Nicholas,) whither the King was gone, they making such relations to inquisitive people as they thought fit. The day before the King went, sir John Mennes and John Nicholas, eldest son to the Secretary, were sent into Zealand, to stay there till they should receive farther orders; the former of them being the person designed to be at the sign of the *Rouen* in Flushing, and the other to be near to prepare any thing for the King's hand that should be found necessary, and to keep the ciphers; both of them persons of undoubted fidelity.

There was a gentleman who lived in Middleburg and of one of the best families and best fortune there, who had married an English lady, who had been brought up in the court of the Queen of Bohemia, and was the daughter of a gentleman of a very noble family, who had been long an officer in Holland. The King had made this Dutchman a baronet; and some who were nearly acquainted with him were confident that his majesty might secretly repose himself in his house, without any notice taken of him, as long as it would be necessary for him to be concealed. And his majesty being first assured of this, made his journey directly thither in the manner mentioned before; and being received as he expected in that house, he gave present notice to Sir John Mennes and Mr Nicholas, that they might know whither to resort to his majesty upon any occasion. And upon his first arrival there, he received intelligence that the messenger who had been despatched from Cologne met with cross winds and accidents in his return, which had been his misfortune likewise in his journey thither, so that he came not so soon to London as was expected; whereupon some conceived that the King did not approve the day, and therefore excused themselves from appearing at the time; others were well content with the excuse, having discerned, with the approach of the day, that they had embarked themselves in a design of more difficulty than was at first apprehended; and some were actually seized upon and imprisoned, by which they were incapable of performing their promise. Though this disappointment confirmed the King in his former belief that nothing solid could result from such a general combination, yet he thought it fit, now he was in a post where he might securely rest, to expect what the earl of Rochester's presence, of whose being in London he was advertised, might produce. And by this time the Chancellor, according to order, was come to Breda; from whence he every day might hear from and send to the King.

There cannot be a greater manifestation of the universal prejudice and aversion in the whole kingdom towards Cromwell and his government, than that there could be so many designs and conspiracies against him, which were communicated to so many men, and that such signal and notorious persons could resort to London and remain there, without any such information or discovery as might enable him to cause them to be apprehended; there being nobody intent and zealous to make any such discoveries but such whose trade it was, for great wages, to give him those informations; and they seldom care whether what they inform be true or no. The earl of Rochester consulted with great freedom in London with the King's friends, and found that the persons imprisoned were only taken upon general suspicion, and as being known to be of that party, not upon any particular discovery of what they designed or intended to do, and that the same spirit still possessed those who were at liberty. The design in Kent appeared not reasonable, at least not to begin upon; but he was persuaded (and he was very credulous) that in the north there was a foundation of strong hope, and a party ready to appear powerful enough to possess themselves of York, nor had the army many troops in those parts. In the west likewise there seemed to be a strong combination, in which many gentlemen were engaged, and their agents were then in London, and were exceedingly importunate to have a day assigned, and desired no more than that sir Joseph Wagstaff might be authorized to be in the head of them, who had been well known to them; and he was as ready to engage with them. The earl of Rochester liked the countenance of the north better, and sent Marmaduke Darcy, a gallant gentleman, and nobly allied in those parts, to prepare the party there; appointed a day and place for the rendezvous, and promised to be himself there; and was contented that sir Joseph Wagstaff should go into the west, who, upon conference with those of that country, likewise appointed their rendezvous upon a fixed day,* to be within two miles of Salisbury. And it was an argument that they had no mean opinion of their strength, that they appointed to appear that very day when the judges were to keep their assizes in that city, and where the sheriff and principal gentlemen of the county were obliged to give their attendance. And of both these resolutions the earl of Rochester, who knew where the King was, took care to advertise his majesty, who from hence had his former faint hopes renewed; and in a short time after they were so improved, that he thought of nothing more than how he might with the greatest secrecy transport himself into England; for which he did expect a sudden occasion.

Sir Joseph Wagstaff had been formerly major general of the foot in the King's western army, a man generally beloved; and though he was rather for execution than counsel, a stout man, who looked not far before him, yet he had a great companionableness in his nature, which exceedingly prevailed with those who in the intermission of fighting loved to spend their time in jollity and mirth. He, as soon as the day was appointed, left London, and went to some of his friends' houses in the country, near the place, that he might assist the preparations as much as was possible. Those of Hampshire were not so punctual at their own rendezvous as to be present at that near Salisbury at the hour; however, Wagstaff and they of Wiltshire appeared to expectation. Penruddock, a gentleman of a fair fortune and great zeal and forwardness in the service, Hugh Grove, and other persons of condition, were there, with a body of near two hundred horse well armed, which they presumed would every day be improved upon the access of those who had engaged themselves in the western association, especially if the fame of their being up, and effecting any thing, should come to their ears. They accounted that they were already strong enough to visit Salisbury in all its present lustre, knowing that they had many friends there, and reckoning that all who were not against them were for them, and that they should there increase their numbers both in foot and horse, with which the town then abounded: nor did their computation and conjecture fail them. They entered the city about five of the clock in the morning:* they appointed some officers, of which they had plenty, to cause all the stables to be locked up, that all the horses might be at their devotion; others to break open the gaols, that all there might attend their benefactors. They kept a good body of horse upon the market-place, to encounter all opposition; and gave order to apprehend the judges and the sheriff, who were yet in their beds, and to bring them into the market-place with their several commissions, resolving or not caring to seize upon the persons of any others.

All this was done with so little noise or disorder as if the town had been all of one mind. And they who were within doors, except they were commanded to come out, stayed still there, being more desirous to hear than to see what was done; very many being well pleased, and not willing that others should discern it in their countenance. When the judges were brought out in their own robes, and humbly produced their commissions, and the sheriff likewise, Wagstaff resolved, after he had caused the King to be proclaimed, to cause them all three to be hanged, who were half dead already, having well considered, with the policy which men in such actions are naturally possessed with, how he himself should be used if he were under their hands, and therefore choosing to be beforehand with them. But having not thought fit to deliberate this beforehand with his friends, whereby their scrupulous consciences might have been confirmed, many of the country gentlemen were so startled with this proposition that they protested against it; and poor Penruddock was so passionate to preserve their lives, as if works of this nature could be done by halves, that the major general durst not persist in it, but was prevailed with to dismiss the judges, and, having taken their commissions from them, to oblige them upon another occasion to remember to whom they owed their lives, resolving still to hang the sheriff, who positively, though humbly and with many tears, refused to proclaim the King; which being otherwise done, they likewise prevailed with him rather to keep the sheriff alive, and to carry him with them to redeem an honester man out of the hands of their enemies. This was an ill omen to their future agreement and submission to the commands of their general; nor was the tender-heartedness so general but that very many of the gentlemen were much scandalized at it, both as it was a contradiction to their commander in chief, and as it would have been a seasonable act of severity to have cemented those to perseverance who were engaged in it, and kept them from entertaining any hopes but in the sharpness of their swords.

The noise of this action was very great both in and out of the kingdom, whither it was quickly sent. And without doubt it was a bold enterprise, and might have produced wonderful effects, if it had been prosecuted with the same resolution, or the same rashness, it was entered into. All that was reasonable in the general contrivance of insurrection and commotion over the whole kingdom was founded upon a supposition of the division and faction in the army, which was known to be so great that Cromwell durst not draw the whole army to a general rendezvous, out of apprehension that when they should once meet together he should no longer be master of them. And thence it was concluded, that, if there were in any one place such a body brought together as might oblige Cromwell to make the army, or a considerable part of it, to march, there would at least be no disposition in them to fight to strengthen that authority which they abhorred. And many did at that time believe that if they had remained with that party at Salisbury for some days, which they might well have done without any disturbance, that their numbers would have much increased, and their friends farther west must have been prepared to receive them, when their retreat had been necessary by a stronger part of the army's marching against them. Cromwell himself was amazed; he knew well the distemper of the kingdom and in his army, and now when he saw such a body gathered together without any noise, that durst in the middle of the kingdom enter into the chief city of it, when his judges and all the power of that county was in it, and take them prisoners, and proclaim the King in a time of full peace, and when no man durst so much as name him but with a reproach, he could not imagine that such an enterprise could be undertaken without a universal conspiracy, in which his own army could not be innocent; and therefore knew not how to trust them together. But all this apprehension vanished, when it was known that within four or five hours after they had performed this exploit they left the town with very small increase or addition to their numbers.

The truth is, they did nothing resolutely after their first action, and were in such disorder and discontent between themselves, that without staying for their friends out of Hampshire, (who were, to the number of two or three hundred horse, upon their way, and would have been at Salisbury that night,) upon pretence that they were expected in Dorsetshire, they left the town, and took the sheriff with them, about two of the clock in the afternoon; but were so weary of their day's labour, and their watching the night before, that they grew less in love with what they were about, and differed again amongst themselves about the sheriff, whom many desired should be presently released; and that party carried it in hope of receiving good offices afterwards from him. And in this manner they continued on their march westward. They from Hampshire and other places, who were behind them, being angry for their leaving Salisbury, would not follow, but scattered themselves; and they who were before them, and heard in what disorder they had left Wiltshire, likewise dispersed. So that after they had continued their journey into Devonshire, without meeting any who would join with them, horse and man were so tired for want of meat and sleep that one single troop of horse, inferior in number, and commanded by an officer of no credit in the war, being in those parts by chance, followed them at a distance, till they were so spent that he rather entreated than compelled them to deliver themselves.* Some, and amongst those Wagstaff, quitted their horses, and found shelter in some honest houses, where they were concealed till opportunity served to transport them into the parts beyond the seas, where they arrived safely. But Mr Penruddock, Mr Grove, and most of the rest, were taken prisoners, upon promise given by the officer that their lives should be saved; which they quickly found he had no authority to make good, for Cromwell no sooner heard of his cheap victory, than he sent judges away with a new commission of oyer and terminer,* and order to proceed with the utmost severity against the offenders. But Rolle, his chief justice,* who had so luckily scaped at Salisbury, had not recovered the fright, and would no more look those men in the face who had dealt so kindly with him, but expressly refused to be employed in the service, raising some scruples in point of law whether the men could be legally condemned; upon which Cromwell shortly after turned him out of his office, having found others who executed his commands. Penruddock and Grove lost their heads at Exeter, and others were hanged there, who, having recovered the faintness they were in when they rendered, died with great courage and resolution, professing their duty and loyalty to the King. Many were sent to Salisbury, and tried and executed there, in the place where they had so lately triumphed; and some who were condemned, where there were fathers and sons and brothers, that the butchery might appear with some remorse, were reprieved, and sold, and sent slaves to the Barbadoes; where their treatment was such that few of them ever returned into their own country. And thus this little fire, which probably might have kindled and inflamed all the kingdom, was for the present extinguished in the west, and Cromwell secured without the help of his army; which he saw, by the countenance it then shewed when they thought he would have use of them, it was high time to reform; and in that he resolved to use no longer delay.

The design of the north, which was thought to be much better prepared and provided for, made less noise, and expired most peaceably. The earl of Rochester, who saw danger at a distance with great courage, [but] looked upon it less resolutely when it was nearer, made his journey from London, with a friend or two, into Yorkshire at the time appointed,* and found such an appearance of gentlemen upon the place as might very well have deserved his patience. It appeared that there had been some mistake in the notice that had been given, and they who did appear undertook for many who were absent that if he would appoint another short day for the rendezvous he should be well attended. Marmaduke Darcy had spent his time very well amongst them, and found them well disposed, and there could be no danger in staying the time proposed, many of them having houses where he might be well concealed; and the country generally wished well to the King, and to those who concerned themselves in his affairs. But he took many exceptions; complained as if they had deceived him; and asked many questions, which were rather reasonable than seasonable, and which would have furnished reasons against entering upon the design, which were not to be urged now when they were to execute, and when indeed they had gone too far to retire. He had not yet heard of the success at Salisbury, yet did not think the force which the gentlemen were confident they could draw together, before they could meet with any opposition, sufficient to enter upon an action that was like to be dangerous in the end, and so he resolved to stay no longer; the gentlemen being as much troubled that he had come at all, they parted with little good will to each other, the earl returning through byroads to London, which was the securest place, from whence he gave the King notice of the hopelessness of affairs. If he had not been a man very fortunate in disguises, he could never have escaped so many perambulations; for as he was the least wary in making his journeys in safe hours, so he departed very unwillingly from all places where there was good eating and drinking, and entered into conferences with any strangers he met or joined with. . . .

As soon as the King received advertisement of the ill successes in England, and that all their hopes were for the present blasted there, he left Zealand, and, returning by Breda, stayed in a dorp* near the town till the Chancellor attended him, and then returned with all speed to Cologne; where his little Court was quickly gathered together again, and better disposed to sit still and expect God's own time. His majesty was exceedingly afflicted for the loss of so many honest gentlemen in England, who had engaged themselves so desperately, not only without but expressly against his majesty's judgment: and he was the more troubled, because he was from several of his friends from thence advertised that all his counsels were discovered,* and that Cromwell had perfect intelligence of whatsoever he resolved to do, and of all he said himself, so that it would not be safe for any body to correspond with him, or to meddle in his affairs and concernments: that his coming into Zealand, and his continuance there, was known to Cromwell, with all the particulars of his motion; that many persons of condition were seized upon and imprisoned for having a design to possess themselves of some towns and places of strength, which intelligence could not be given but from Cologne; implying that the miscarriage in all the late designs proceeded wholly from the treason of some persons near his majesty. He did not at all wonder that Cromwell and his instruments took great pains to make it generally to be believed that they knew all that was resolved or thought of at Cologne; but that any men who were really devoted to his service, and who had kindness and esteem for all those who were trusted by his majesty, should be wrought upon to believe those reports, very much disturbed him. [*HR*, XIV, 123–37]

Despite continued efforts to secure alliances with foreign powers or promote conspiracies in England, the period immediately after the suppression of Penruddock's rising was the lowest point in royalist fortunes, as Clarendon's retrospective survey made clear.

The King remained at Cologne above two years, contending with the rigour of his fortune with great temper and magnanimity, whilst all the princes of Europe seemed to contend amongst themselves who should most eminently forget and neglect him, and whilst Cromwell exercised all imaginable tyranny over those nations who had not been sensible enough of the blessings they enjoyed under his majesty's [father's] peaceable and mild government; so that he might have enjoyed some of that comfort and pleasure which Velleius Paterculus says that Marius and Carthage had when his banishment reduced him to end his life in the ruins of that city, as he did; *cum Marius aspiciens Carthaginem, illa intuens Marium, alter alteri possent esse solatio*;* whilst he refreshed himself with the memory of his greatness when he overthrew that great and famous city, and she, again, delighted to behold her destroyer expelled from his country, which he had served so eminently, and forced, forsaken of all men, to end his life and to be buried in her ashes. If the King's nature could have been delighted with such reflections, he might have had argument abundant, in seeing Scotland, which first threw off wantonly its own peace and plenty, and infected the other two kingdoms with its rebellion, now reduced and governed by a rod of iron,* vanquished and subdued by those to whom they had taught the science of rebellion, and with whom they had joined, by specious pretences and vows and horrible perjuries, to subdue and destroy their own natural prince, and dissolve the government they had been subject to since they were a people; in seeing the pride and insolence of that nation, which had used to practise such ill manners towards their kings, suppressed, contemned, and subdued by those who had been instructed by them how to use their arms, and exposed to slavery under the discipline and castigation of men who were not born gentlemen, but bred up in the trades and professions of the common people. These men governed in their houses, and prescribed new laws to them to live by, which they had never been accustomed to, and which they were compelled to obey, upon penalty of their lives and estates; whilst their adored idol, Presbytery, (which had pulled off the crown from the head of the King,) was trod under foot, laughed at and contemned; and their preachers, who threatened their princes with their rude thunder of excommunication, disputed with, scoffed at, and controlled by, artificers, and corrected by the strokes and blows of a corporal; and all this subjection supported at their own charge, and their fierce governors paid by them out of their own estates.

He beheld Ireland, that began its rebellion with inhuman massacres and butcheries of their peaceable and innocent neighbours, after the other of Scotland was suppressed, or so compounded that the blessing of peace had again covered the three nations, if this sottish people had not, without any provocation, but of their own folly and barbarity, with that bloody prologue engaged again the three kingdoms in a raging and devouring war; so that though Scotland blew the first trumpet, it was Ireland that drew the first blood; and if they had not at that time rebelled, and in that manner, it is very probable all the miseries which afterwards befell the King and his dominions had been prevented. These unhappy people, when they saw that they could not make war, but were beaten as often as encountered, would not yet make peace; or if they did, they no sooner made it than broke it, with all the circumstances of treachery and perjury that can make any foul action the most odious. And after they had again, for their last preservation, returned to their obedience to the King, and put themselves again under his protection, they quickly repented of their loyalty, offered themselves to the sovereignty of a foreign prince; and when they had seen their natural King murdered by his rebels for want of that assistance which they might have given him, and chose rather to depend on the clemency of the usurper, and so drove from them the governor and government of their King: [I say,] his majesty saw now these miserable people grovelling at the feet of their proud conquerors, reduced to the highest desolation, and even to the point of extirpation. The blood they had wantonly and savagely spilt in the beginning of the rebellion, they now saw plentifully revenged in streams of their own blood from one end of the kingdom to the other; whilst those persons who first contrived the rebellion, and could never be reached by the King, and they who caused every peace to be broken which had been made with his majesty, with all the possible affronts to his royal dignity and authority, after they had endeavoured by all the treacherous offices against the royal power to reconcile themselves to their new masters, were every day taken and infamously put to death by their authority who usurped the government; who sold, as hath been said before, above one hundred thousand of them to the service of foreign princes, under whom they perished for want of bread, and without regard; so that there is not an account in history of any nation, the Jews only excepted, that hath ever been reduced to a more complete misery and contempt than the Irish were in the view of his majesty at this time. And it was the more extraordinary, in that it was without the pity of any, all the world looking upon them as deserving the fate they underwent.

England, that seemed to glory in the conquest of those two kingdoms, and to reign peaceably over them, yielded a prospect, too, full of variety. Though the King's heart was even broken with the daily information he received of the ruin and destruction that his faithful and loyal party underwent and the butchery that was frequently acted upon them, and the extreme tyranny the usurper exercised over the whole nation was grievous to him, yet he could not be equally afflicted to see those who had been the first authors of the public calamity to be now so much sharers in it, that they were no more masters of their estates than they were whom they had first caused to be spoiled, and that themselves were brought and exposed upon those scaffolds which they had caused to be erected for others; that no part of the new government was in any of their hands which had pulled down the old; and that after monarchy had been made so odious to the people, the whole wealth of the nation was become at the disposal of one man; and that those lords without whose monstrous assistance the sceptre could never have been wrested out of the hands of the King were now numbered and marshalled with the dregs of the people: in a word, that Cromwell was not so jealous of any as of those who had raised him, and contrived and proposed nothing more to himself than to suppress those, or to drive them out of the kingdom, who had been the principal means to suppress the royal authority, and to drive the royal family and all that adhered to it into banishment.

This prospect the King had of the three kingdoms which had revolted from him during his residence at Cologne; and with those manifestations of God's vengeance upon those ingrateful nations, of which he had a most tender and compassionate feeling, he was not without some glimmering light to discern an approach of that recompense which the divine justice usually assigns to those who patiently attend his vindication. [*HR*, XV, 1–4]

However, one new avenue shortly opened to the royalists. Cromwell's attacks on Spanish possessions in the West Indies in April 1655 and his agreement of a treaty with France in October 1655 created the possibility of an alliance with France's enemy Spain. In April 1656 the Spanish agreed to provide the King with troops, ships, and supplies to support an uprising in England, and the royal court left Cologne for the Spanish territories in the Netherlands, under attack from the French. Many courtiers who had fought in the Civil Wars, including James, Duke of York, joined the Spanish army.

Cromwell's increasingly regal rule in England, formalized (though without the title of King) through the articles of the Humble Petition and Advice in June 1657, provoked growing discontent from all quarters — including the levellers, with whom Hyde was in touch in 1656. Hyde and other royalists struggled to construct an insurrection and to persuade the Spanish that it had some prospect of success. Hopes of a rising were raised at the end of 1657, but dashed in early 1658, and it was concluded that another attempt would be inadvisable before the winter. As the Spanish refused to allow the King to join their army, he spent the summer in recreation at Hochstraten, close to the border with the Dutch Republic. He was there in September when startling news arrived from England.

Whilst the King spent his time in this manner, about the middle of September, the duke of York, who remained still with the troops at

Nieuwpoort to defend that place, as don Juan and the rest remained about Furnes and Bruges, sent an express to the King to let him know that the letters from England, and some passengers, reported confidently that Cromwell was dead; which, there having been no news of his sickness, was not at first easy to be believed. But every day brought confirmation of it; so that his majesty thought fit to give over his country life, and returned again to Brussels, that he might be ready to make use of any advantage which in that conjuncture, upon so wonderful an alteration, he might reasonably expect.

It had been observed in England, that though from the dissolution of the last Parliament all things seemed to succeed at home and abroad to his wish, and his power and greatness to be better established than ever it had been, yet Cromwell never had the same serenity of mind he had been used to, after he had refused the crown, but was out of countenance, and chagrin, as if he were conscious of not having been true to himself, and much more apprehensive of danger to his person than he had used to be; insomuch as he was not so easy of access, nor so much seen abroad, and seemed to be in some disorder when his eyes found any stranger in the room, upon whom they were still fixed. When he intended to go to Hampton Court, which was his principal delight and diversion, it was never known till he was in the coach which way he would go; and was still hemmed in by his guards before and behind; and the coach in which he went was always thronged as full as it could be with his servants, who were armed; and he never returned the same way he went; and rarely lodged two nights together in one chamber, but had many furnished and prepared, to which his own key conveyed him, and those he would have with him, when he had a mind to go to bed: which made his fears the more taken notice of and public, because he had never been accustomed to those precautions.

It is very true he knew of many combinations to assassinate him, by those who he knew wished the King no good. And when he had discovered the design of Sindercombe,* who was a very stout man, and one who had been much in his favour, and who had twice or thrice by wonderful and unexpected accidents been disappointed in the minute he made sure to kill him, and [had] caused him to be apprehended, his behaviour was so resolute in his examination and trial as if he thought he should still be able to do it; and it was manifest that he had many more associates, who were undiscovered, and as resolute as himself; and though he got him condemned to die, the fellow's carriage and words were such, as if he knew well how to avoid the judgment; which made Cromwell believe that a party in the army would attempt his rescue; whereupon he gave strict charge that he should be carefully looked to in the Tower, and three or four of the guard always with him day and night. And at the day for his execution, those troops he was most confident of were upon the Tower-hill, where the gallows were erected. But when the guard called him to arise in the morning, they found him dead in his bed; which gave trouble exceedingly to Cromwell; for besides that he hoped at his death, that, to avoid the utmost rigour of it, he would have confessed many of his confederates, he now found himself under the reproach of having caused him to be poisoned, as not daring to bring him to public justice. Nor could he suppress that scandal, though it did appear, upon examination, that the night before, when he [Sindercombe] was going to bed in the presence of his guard, his sister came to take her leave of him; and whilst they spake together at the bedside, he rubbed his nose with his hand, of which they then took no notice; and she going away, he put off his clothes, and leaped into his bed with some snuffling in his nose, and said, this was the last bed he should ever go into; and seemed to turn to sleep, and never in the whole night made the least noise or motion, save that he sneezed once. When the physicians and surgeons opened his head, they found he had snuffed up through his nostrils some very well prepared poison, that in an instant curdled all the blood in that region, which presently suffocated him. The man was drawn by a horse to the gallows where he should have hanged, and buried under it, with a stake driven through him, as is usual in the case of self-murderers: yet this accident perplexed Cromwell very much; and though he was without the particular discovery which he expected, he made a general discovery by it that he was more odious in his army than he believed he had been.

He seemed to be much afflicted at the death of his friend the earl of Warwick,* with whom he had a fast friendship, though neither their humours or their natures were like. And the heir of that house, who had married his youngest daughter, died about the same time;* so that all his relation to, or confidence in, that family was at an end, the other branches of it abhorring his alliance. His domestic delights were lessened every day; and he plainly discovered that his son Falconbridge* his heart was set upon an interest destructive to his, and grew to hate him perfectly. But that which broke his peace was the death of his daughter Claypole,* who had been always his greatest joy, and who had in her sickness, which was of a nature the physicians knew not how to deal with, had several conferences with him which exceedingly perplexed him. And though nobody was near enough to hear the particulars, yet her often mentioning, in the pains she endured, the blood her father had spilt, made people conclude that she had presented his worst actions to his consideration. And though he never made the least show of remorse for any of those actions, it is very certain that either what she said or her death affected him wonderfully.

Whatever it was, about the middle of August he was seized on by a common tertian ague, from which he believed a little ease and divertisement at Hampton Court would have freed him. But the fits grew stronger, and his spirits much abated; so that he returned again to Whitehall; when his physicians began to think him in danger, though the preachers, who prayed always about him, and told God Almighty what great things he had done for him, and how much more need he had still of his service, declared, as from God, that he should recover; and he himself did not think he should die, till even the time that his spirits failed him; and then declared to them that he did appoint his son to succeed him, his eldest son Richard; and so expired upon the third day of September, (a day he thought always very propitious to him, and on which he had triumphed for several victories,*) 1658; a day very memorable for the greatest storm of wind that had ever been known, for some hours before and after his death, which overthrew trees, houses, and made great wrecks at sea, and was so universal, that there were terrible effects of it both in France and Flanders, where all people trembled at it; besides the wrecks all along the coast, many boats having been cast away in the very rivers; and within few days, after, that circumstance of his death that accompanied that storm was known.

He was one of those men *quos vituperare ne inimici quidem possunt nisi ut simul laudent*;* for he could never have done half that mischief without great parts of courage and industry and judgment. And he must have had a wonderful understanding in the natures and humours of men, and as great a dexterity in the applying them, who from a private and obscure birth, (though of a good family,) without interest of estate, alliance or friendships, could raise himself to such a height, and compound and knead such opposite and contradictory tempers, humours, and interests, into a consistence that contributed to his designs and to their own destruction; whilst himself grew insensibly powerful enough to cut off those by whom he had climbed, in the instant that they projected to demolish their own building. What Velleius Paterculus said of Cinna may very justly be said of him, *Ausum eum quae nemo auderet bonus; perfecisse quae a nullo nisi fortissimo perfici possent*.* Without doubt, no man with more wickedness ever attempted any thing, or brought to pass what he desired more wickedly, more in the face and contempt of religion and moral honesty; yet wickedness as great as his could never have accomplished those trophies without the assistance of a great spirit, an admirable circumspection and sagacity, and a most magnanimous resolution.

When he appeared first in the Parliament, he seemed to have a person in no degree gracious, no ornament of discourse, none of those talents which use to reconcile the affections of the standers by: yet as he grew into place and authority, his parts seemed to be renewed, as if he had concealed faculties till he had occasion to use them; and when he was to act the part of a great man, he did it without any indecency through the want of custom.

After he was confirmed and invested Protector by *The humble Petition and Advice*,* he consulted with very few upon any action of importance, nor communicated any enterprise he resolved upon with more than those who were to have principal parts in the execution of it; nor to them sooner than was absolutely necessary. What he once resolved, in which he was not rash, he would not be dissuaded from, nor endure any contradiction of his power and authority, but extorted obedience from them who were not willing to yield it.

When he had laid some very extraordinary tax upon the city, one Cony, an eminent fanatic, and one who had heretofore served him very notably, positively refused to pay his part,* and loudly dissuaded others from submitting to it, as an imposition notoriously against the law and the propriety of the subject, which all honest men were bound to defend. Cromwell sent for him, and cajoled him with the memory of the old kindness and friendship that had been between them, and that of all men he did not expect this opposition from him, in a matter that was so necessary for the good of the commonwealth. But it was always his fortune to meet with the most rude and obstinate behaviour from those who had formerly been absolutely governed by him, and they commonly put him in mind of some expressions and saying of his own in cases of the like nature; so this man remembered him how great an enemy he had expressed himself to such grievances, and declared that all who submitted to them and paid illegal taxes were more to blame, and greater enemies to their country, than they who imposed them, and that the tyranny of princes could never be grievous but by the tameness and stupidity of the people. When Cromwell saw that he could not convert him, he told him that he had a will as stubborn as his, and he would try which of them two should be master; and thereupon, with some terms of reproach and contempt, he committed the man to prison; whose courage was nothing abated by it; but as soon as the term came, he brought his *habeas corpus* in the King's Bench, which they then called the Upper Bench. Maynard, who was of counsel with the prisoner, demanded his liberty with great confidence, both upon the illegality of the commitment, and the illegality of the imposition, as being laid without any lawful authority. The judges could not maintain or defend either, but enough declared what their sentence would be; and therefore the Protector's Attorney required a farther day to answer what had been urged. Before that day, Maynard was committed to the Tower,* for presuming to question or make doubt of his authority; and the judges were sent for, and severely reprehended for suffering that license; and when they with all humility mentioned the law and *Magna Charta*, Cromwell told them, their *magna farta* should not control his actions, which he knew were for the safety of the commonwealth. He asked them who made them judges; whether they had any authority to sit there but what he gave them; and that if his authority were at an end, they knew well enough what would become of themselves; and therefore advised them to be more tender of that which could only preserve them; and so dismissed them with caution, that they should not suffer the lawyers to prate what it would not become them to hear.

Thus he subdued a spirit that had been often troublesome to the most sovereign power, and made Westminster Hall as obedient and subservient to his commands as any of the rest of his quarters. In all other matters which did not concern the life of his jurisdiction, he seemed to have great reverence for the law, and rarely interposed between party and party. And as he proceeded with this kind of indignation and haughtiness with those who were refractory and dared to contend with his greatness, so towards those who complied with his good pleasure, and courted his protection, he used a wonderful civility, generosity, and bounty.

To reduce three nations, which perfectly hated him, to an entire obedience to all his dictates; to awe and govern those nations by an army that was indevoted to him and wished his ruin; was an instance of a very prodigious address. But his greatness at home was but a shadow of the glory he had abroad. It was hard to discover which feared him most, France, Spain, or the Low Countries, where his friendship was current at the value he put upon it. And as they did all sacrifice their honour and their interest to his pleasure, so there is nothing he could have demanded that either of them would have denied him. To manifest which, there need only two instances. The first is, when those of the Valley of Lucerne had unwarily rebelled against the duke of Savoy, which gave occasion to the Pope and the neighbour princes of Italy to call and solicit for their extirpation, which their prince positively resolved upon, Cromwell sent his agent* to the duke of Savoy, (a prince with whom he had no correspondence or commerce,) and so engaged the cardinal,* and even terrified the Pope himself, without so much as doing any grace to the English Catholics, (nothing being more usual than his saying that his ships in the Mediterranean should visit Civitavecchia, and that the sound of his cannon should be heard in Rome,) that the duke of Savoy thought it necessary to restore all that he had taken from them, and did renew all those privileges they had formerly enjoyed and newly forfeited.

The other instance of his authority was yet greater, and more incredible. In the city of Nîmes, which is one of the fairest in the province of Languedoc, and where those of the [reformed] Religion do most abound, there was a great faction at that season when the consuls (who are the chief magistrates) were to be chosen.* Those of the Religion had the confidence to set up one of themselves for that magistracy; which they of the Roman religion resolved to oppose with all their power. The dissension between them made so much noise, that the intendant of the province, who is the supreme minister in all civil affairs throughout the whole province, went thither to prevent any disorder that might happen. When the day of the election came, those of the Religion possessed themselves with many armed men of the town-house, where the election was to be made. The magistrates sent to know what their meaning was; to which they answered, they were there to give their voices for the choice of the new consuls, and to be sure that the election should be fairly made. The bishop of the city, the intendant of the province, with all the officers of the church, and the present magistrates of the town, went together in their robes to be present at the election, without any suspicion that there would be any force used. When they came near the gate of the town-house, which was shut, and they supposed would be opened when they came, they within poured out a volley of musket-shot upon them, by which the dean of the church and two or three of the magistrates of the town were killed upon the place, and very many others wounded, whereof some died shortly after. In this confusion, the magistrates put themselves into as good a posture to defend themselves as they could, without any purpose of offending the other, till they should be better provided; in order to which they sent an express to the Court with a plain relation of the whole matter of fact, and that there appeared to be no manner of combination with those of the Religion in other places of the province, but that it was an insolence in those of the place, upon their presumption of their great numbers, which were little inferior to those of the Catholics. The Court was glad of the occasion, and resolved that this provocation, in which other places were not involved, and which nobody could excuse, should warrant all kind of severity in that city, even to the pulling down their temples, and expelling many of them for ever out of the city; which, with the execution and forfeiture of many of the principal persons, would be a general mortification to all of the Religion in France, with whom they were heartily offended. And a part of the army was forthwith ordered to march towards Nîmes, to see this executed with the utmost rigour.

Those of the Religion in the town were quickly sensible into what condition they had brought themselves, and sent with all possible submission to the magistrates to excuse themselves, and to impute what had been done to the rashness of particular men, who had no order for what they did. The magistrates answered, that they were glad they were sensible of their miscarriage; but they could say nothing upon the subject till the King's pleasure should be known, to whom they had sent a full relation of all that had passed. The other very well knew what the King's pleasure would be, and forthwith sent an express, one Moulins, a Scotchman, who had lived many years in that place and in Montpelier, to Cromwell, to desire his protection and interposition. The express made so much haste, and found so good a reception the first hour he came, that Cromwell, after he had received the whole account, bade him refresh himself after so long a journey, and he would take such care of his business, that by the time he came to Paris he should find it despatched; and that night sent away another messenger to his ambassador Lockhart,* who by the time Moulins came thither had so far prevailed with the cardinal, that orders were sent to stop the troops which were upon their march towards Nîmes; and within few days after, Moulins returned with a full pardon and amnesty from the King, under the Great Seal of France, so fully confirmed with all circumstances, that there was never farther mention made of it, but all things passed as if there had never been any such thing. So that nobody can wonder that his memory remains still in those parts, and with those people, in great veneration.*

He would never suffer himself to be denied any thing he ever asked of the cardinal, alleging that the people would not be otherwise satisfied; which he [the cardinal] bore very heavily, and complained of to those with whom he would be free. One day he visited madam de Turenne* and when he took his leave of her, she, according to her custom, besought him to continue gracious to the churches. Whereupon the cardinal told her that he knew not how to behave himself; if he advised the King to punish and suppress their insolence, Cromwell threatened them to join with the Spaniard; and if he shewed any favour to them, at Rome they accounted him an heretic.

He was not a man of blood, and totally declined Machiavelli's method, which prescribes upon any alteration of a government, as a thing absolutely necessary, to cut off all the heads of those, and extirpate their families, who are friends to the old [one.] And it was confidently reported, that in the council of officers it was more than once proposed that there might be a general massacre of all the royal party, as the only expedient to secure the government, but Cromwell would never consent to it; it may be, out of too much contempt of his enemies. In a word, as he had all the wickednesses against which damnation is denounced and for which hell-fire is prepared, so he had some virtues which have caused the memory of some men in all ages to be celebrated; and he will be looked upon by posterity as a brave bad man. [*HR*, XV, 142–56]

17. Restoration

The hopes raised among royalists by the death of Cromwell were soon disappointed as power was transferred quietly to his son Richard. But cracks in the fabric of the new regime were quickly apparent. The new Protector's ability to hold the army in check as his father had done was always in doubt, and the republican opponents of the Protectorate dominated the proceedings of the Parliament he summoned to resolve his financial problems. In June 1659 the army deposed Richard in a bloodless coup, and recalled the Rump, the Parliament which had executed the King, and which his father had dismissed in April 1653.

The Rump's own relationship with the army had never been an easy one, though, and the revival of an explicitly republican government made a new attempt to construct an alliance between royalists and Presbyterians a distinct possibility. Determined to overcome the caution of the Sealed Knot, new men offered to replace it as coordinators of royalist conspiracies. At the same time, one explanation for the Sealed Knot's caution was discovered.

THERE was in this conjuncture a very unhappy accident, which did do much harm, and might have done much more. From the death of Oliver, they who were in the secretest part of affairs discerned evidently that their new Protector would never be able to bear the burden, and so thought how they might do such service to the King that might merit from him. One who had a part in the office of secrecy,* sent an express to the King, to inform him of many particulars of moment, and to give him some advices, what his majesty was to do which was reasonable and prudent to be done. He sent him word what persons might be induced to serve him, and what way he was to take to induce them to it, and what other persons would never do it, what professions soever they might make. He made offer of his service to his majesty, and constantly to advertise him of whatsoever was necessary for him to know; and as an instance of his fidelity and his usefulness, he advertised his majesty of a person* who was much trusted by him and constantly betrayed him, that he received a large pension from Cromwell, and that he constantly gave Thurloe intelligence of all that he knew, but that it was with so great circumspection that he was never seen in his presence: that in his contract he had promised to make such discoveries as should prevent any danger to the State, but that he would never endanger any man's life, nor be produced to give in evidence against any; and that this very person had discovered the marquis of Ormond's being in London* the last year to Cromwell, but could not be induced to discover where his lodging was; only undertook his journey should be ineffectual, and that he should quickly return; and then they might take him if they could, to which he would not contribute; to conclude, his majesty was desired to trust this man no more, and to give his friends notice of it for their caution and indemnity.

The King, and they who were most trusted by him in his secret transactions, believed not this information, but concluded that it was contrived to amuse him, and to distract all his affairs by a jealousy of those who were intrusted in the conduct of them. The gentleman accused had from the beginning to the end of the war given testimony of his duty and allegiance, and was universally thought to be superior to all temptation of infidelity. He was a gentleman, was very well bred, and of very good parts, a courage eminently known, and a very good officer, and in truth of so general a good reputation, that if the King had professed to have any doubt of his honesty his friends would have thought he had received ill infusions without any ground; and he had given a very late testimony of his sincerity by concealing the marquis of Ormond, who had communicated more with him than with any man in England during his being there. On the other side, all the other information and advice that was sent was very important, and could have no end but his majesty's service; and the offices which the gentleman offered to perform for the future were of that consequence that they could not be overvalued. This intelligence could not be sent with a hope of getting money; for the present condition of him who sent it was so good that he expected no reward till the King should be enabled to give it; and he who was sent in the errand was likewise a gentleman who did not look for the charges of his journey: and how could it have been known that that person had been trusted by the marquis of Ormond if he had not discovered it himself?

In this perplexity, his majesty would not depart from his confidence in that gentleman [accused]. As to all other particulars he confessed himself much satisfied in the information he had received, acknowledged the great service, and made all those promises which were necessary in such a case; only frankly declared, that nothing could convince him of the infidelity of that gentleman, or make him withdraw his trust from him, but the evidence of his handwriting, which was well known. This messenger no sooner returned to London but another was despatched,* with all that manifestation of the truth of what had been before informed, that there remained no more room to doubt.

A great number of his letters were sent, whereof the character was well known; and the intelligence communicated was of such things as were known to very few besides that person himself.

One thing was observed throughout the whole, that he never communicated any thing in which there was a necessity to name any man who was of the King's party and had been always so reputed: but what was undertaken by any of the Presbyterian party, or by any who had been against the King, was poured out to the life. Amongst those, he gave information of Massey's design upon Gloucester,* and of his being concealed in some place near the same. If at any time he named any who had been of the King's party, it was only of them who were satisfied with what they had done, how little soever, and resolved to adventure no more. Whereupon very many were imprisoned in several places, and great noise of want of secrecy or treachery in the King's councils; which reproach fell upon those who were about the person of the King.

It was a new perplexity to the King that he knew not by what means to communicate this treason to his friends, lest the discovery of it might likewise come to light; which must ruin a person of merit, and disappoint his majesty of that service which must be of that huge moment. In this conjuncture Mr Mordaunt came to Brussels,* and informed his majesty of all those particulars relating to the posture his friends were in which are mentioned before; and amongst the other orders he desired, one was, that somewhat might be sent to that knot of men whereof the accused person was one, who he said were looked upon as principally trusted by his majesty, and were all men of honour, but so wary and incredulous, that others were much discouraged by their coldness; and therefore wished that they might be quickened, and required to concur with the most forward. Hereupon the King asked him what he thought of such a one, naming the person. Mr Mordaunt answered, it was of him they complained principally; who, they thought, was the cause of all the wariness in the rest, who looked upon him not only as an excellent officer but as a prudent and discreet man, and therefore, for the most part, all debates were referred to him; and he was so much given to objections, and to raising difficulties, and making things unpracticable, that most men had an unwillingness to make any proposition to him. The King asked him whether he had any suspicion of his want of honesty. The other answered, that he was so far from any such suspicion, that, though he did not take him to be his friend, by reason of the many disputes and contradictions frequently between them, he would put his life into his hand to-morrow.

It was not thought reasonable that Mr Mordaunt should return into England with a confidence in this man, and therefore his majesty freely told all he knew but the way by which he knew it, or that he had his very letters in his own hand, which would quickly have discovered how he came by them; and charged him no farther to communicate with that person, and to give his friends such caution as might not give a greater disturbance to his affairs by raising new factions amongst them, or provoke him to do more mischief, which was in his power to do. But for all this there was another expedient found; for by the time Mr Mordaunt returned to London, the person who gave the King the advertisement, out of his own wisdom, and knowledge of the ill consequence of that trust, caused papers to be posted up in several places, by which all persons were warned not to look upon such a man (who was named) as faithful to the King, but as one who betrayed all that he was trusted with; which in the general had some effect, though many worthy men still continued their intimacy with him, and communicated with him all they knew to be resolved.

It was towards the end of June that Mr Mordaunt left Brussels, with a resolution that there should be a general rendezvous throughout England of all who would declare for the King, upon a day named,* about the middle of July, there being commissions in every county directed to six or seven known men, with authority to them to choose one to command in chief in that county, till they should make a conjunction with other forces who had a superior commission from the King. And those commissioners had in their hands plenty of commissions under the King's hand, for regiments and governments, to distribute to such as they judged fit to receive them; which was the best model (how liable soever to exception) that in so distracted a state of affairs could be devised.

The King, as is said, resolved at the day appointed to be at Calais; which resolution was kept with so great secrecy at Brussels, that, towards the time, his majesty had left the town before it was suspected, and when he was gone, it was as little known whither he was gone; there being as much care taken to have it concealed from being known in France as in England. Therefore, as the King went out in the morning, so the duke of York went out in the afternoon, another way, his highness his motion being without any suspicion or notice, by reason of his command in the army. The King went attended by the marquis of Ormond, the earl of Bristol, (who was the guide, being well acquainted with the frontiers on both sides,) and two or three servants, all *incognito* and as companions; and they found their way to Calais, where they stayed. The duke of York, with four or five of his own menial servants, and the lord Langdale, who desired to attend his highness, went to Boulogne; where he remained with equal privacy; and [they] corresponded with each other.

The affairs in England had no prosperous aspect; every post brought news of many persons of honour and quality committed to several prisons throughout the kingdom before the day appointed; which did not terrify the rest. The day itself was accompanied with very unusual weather at that season of the year, being the middle of July. The night before had an excessive rain, which continued all the next day, with so terrible a cold high wind that the winter had seldom so great a storm: so that the persons who over England were drawing to their appointed rendezvous were infinitely dismayed, and met with many cross accidents; some mistook the place, and went some whither else, others went where they should be and were weary of expecting those who should have been there.

In the beginning of the night, when Massey was going for Gloucester, a troop of the army beset the house where he was, and took him prisoner; and putting him before one of the troopers well guarded, they made haste to carry him to a place where he might be secure. But that tempestuous night had so much of good fortune in it, that, in the darkest part of it, the troop marching down a very steep hill with woods on both sides, he, either by his activity or the connivance of the soldier who was upon the same horse with him, found means that, in the steepest of the descent, they both fell from the horse, and he disentangled himself from the embraces of the other, and, being strong and nimble, got into the woods, and so escaped out of their hands, though his design was broken.

Of all the enterprises for the seizing upon strong places only one succeeded, which was that undertaken by sir George Booth; all the rest failed. The lord Willoughby of Parham, and sir Horace Townsend, and most of their friends, were apprehended before the day, and made prisoners, most of them upon general suspicions, as men able to do hurt. Only sir George Booth, being a person of the best quality and fortune of that county of those who had never been of the King's party, came into Chester, with such persons as he thought fit to take with him, the night before: so that though the tempestuousness of the night and the next morning had the same effect as in other places to break or disorder the rendezvous, that was appointed within four or five miles of that city, yet being himself there with a good troop of horse that he brought with him, and finding others, though not in the number he

looked for, he retired with those he had into Chester, where his party
was strong enough: and sir Thomas Myddleton, having kept his
rendezvous, came thither to him, and brought strength enough with
him to keep those parts at their devotion, and to suppress all who had
inclination to oppose them.

Then they published their Declaration, rather against those who
called themselves the Parliament and usurped the government by the
power of the army, than owning directly the King's interests; and
desiring well affected men of all conditions, especially the city of
London, to join with them, in order to the calling a free Parliament,
for settling the government of the nation in Church and State, to the
determinations whereof they would willingly submit, and lay down
their arms; with those expressions which they knew would be most
acceptable to the Presbyterians, but giving all countenance and reception, and all imaginable assurance, to the King's party, who had all
direction from the King to concur and to unite themselves to them.

What disappointments soever there were in other places, the fame
of this action of these two gentlemen raised the spirits of all men. And
they who were at liberty renewed their former designs; and they who
could not promise themselves places of refuge prepared themselves to
march to Chester, if sir George Booth did not draw nearer with his
army; which in truth he meant to have done, if the appointments
which had been made had been observed. But when he heard that all
other places failed, and of the multitude of persons imprisoned, upon
whose assistance he most depended, he was in great apprehension that
he had begun the work too soon; and though his numbers increased
every day, he thought it best to keep the post he was in, till he knew
what was like to be done elsewhere.

This fire was kindled in a place which the Parliament least suspected,
and therefore they were the more alarumed at the news of it, and knew
it would spread far if it were not quickly quenched; and they had now
too soon use of their army, in which they had not confidence. There
were many officers whom they had much rather trust than Lambert,
but there was none they thought could do their business so well; so they
made choice of him to march with such troops as he liked, and with the
greatest expedition, to suppress this new rebellion, which they saw had
many friends. They had formerly sent for two regiments out of Ireland,
which they knew more devoted to the republican interest, and those
they appointed Lambert to join with. He undertook the charge very
willingly, being desirous to renew his credit with the soldiers, who
had loved to be under his command, because, though he was strict in

discipline, he provided well for them, and was himself brave upon any action. He cared to take nothing with him that might hinder his march, which he resolved should be very swift, to prevent the increase of the enemy in numbers. And he did make incredible haste; so that sir George Booth found he was [with]in less than a day's march before he thought he could have been half the way. Sir George himself had not been acquainted with the war, and the officers who were with him were not of one mind or humour; yet all were desirous to fight, (the natural infirmity of the nation, which could never endure the view of an enemy without engaging in a battle,) and instead of retiring into the town, which they might have defended against a much greater army than Lambert had with him longer than he could stay before it, they marched to meet him, and were after a short encounter routed by him,* and totally broken, so that the next day the gates of Chester were opened to him; sir George Booth himself making his flight in a disguise, but was taken upon the way, and sent prisoner to the Tower.

Lambert prosecuted the advantage he had got, and marched into North Wales, whither sir Thomas Myddleton was retired with his troops to a strong castle of his own;* and he thought neither the man nor the place were to be behind him. But it was to no purpose for one man to oppose a whole kingdom, where all other persons appeared subdued. And therefore, after a day or two making show of resistance, he made such conditions as he could obtain, and suffered his goodly house for the strength of the situation to be pulled down.

And this success put an end to all endeavours of force in England; and the army had nothing to do but to take all persons prisoners whose looks they did not like, so that all prisons in England were filled; whilst the Parliament, exalted with their conquest, consulted what persons they would execute, and how they should confiscate the rest; by means thereof they made no doubt they should destroy all seeds of future insurrections on the behalf of the King, most of the nobility being at present in custody. And they resolved, if other evidence was wanting, that their suspicion should be their conviction. [*HR*, XVI, 28–43]

Nevertheless, the Rump was far from secured by the suppression of Booth's uprising. The army quickly became dissatisfied with its attention to military concerns, and the Rump became worried by the behaviour of Lambert, and his undisguised courtship of the rank and file. A confrontation ended on 13 October with the second dismissal of the Rump by armed force and the assumption of power by the army's Council of Officers, ruling through a Committee of Safety which included civilians.

Entirely unexpectedly, the commander of the English army which had garrisoned Scotland since 1651, Lieutenant General Monck, declared his opposition to the coup. For the first time since the creation of the New Model Army, its leaders were fundamentally at odds. On 28 October the Committee of Safety took a decision to send Lambert north against Monck, taking all the troops that could be spared.

General Monck was a gentleman of a very good extraction, of a very ancient family in Devonshire, always very loyally affected. Being a younger brother he entered early into the life and condition of a soldier, upon that stage where all Europe then acted, between the Spaniard and the Dutch; and had the reputation of a very good foot-officer in the lord Vere's regiment in Holland, at the time when he assigned it to the command of colonel Goring.* When the first troubles began in Scotland, Monck, with many other officers of the nation, left the Dutch service, and betook themselves to the service of the King. And in the beginning of the Irish rebellion he was sent thither, with the command of the lord of Leicester's own regiment of foot, (who was then Lieutenant of Ireland,) and continued in that service with singular reputation of courage and conduct. When the war brake out in England between the King and the Parliament, he fell under some discountenance upon a suspicion of some inclination to the Parliament; which proceeded only from his want of bitterness in his discourses against them, rather than from any inclinations towards them; as appeared by his behaviour at Nantwich,* where he was taken prisoner, and remained in the Tower till the end of the war. For though his behaviour had been such in Ireland, when the transportation of the regiments from thence to serve the King in England* was in debate, that it was evident enough that he had no mind his regiment should be sent in that expedition, and his answers to the lord Ormond were so rough and doubtful, (having had no other education but Dutch and Devonshire,) that he thought not fit to trust him, but gave the command of the regiment to Harry Warren, the lieutenant colonel of it, an excellent officer, generally known, and exceedingly beloved where he was known; those regiments were sent to Chester; but there were others at the same time sent to Bristol, and with them Monck was sent prisoner, and from Bristol to the King at Oxford, where, being known to many persons of quality, and his eldest brother being at the same time most zealous in the King's service in the west and most useful, his professions were so sincere, (being throughout his whole life never suspected of dissimulation,) that all men thought him very worthy of all trust; and the King was willing to send him into the west, where all men had a great opinion of his ability to command. But he desired that he might serve with his old friends and companions; and so, with the King's leave, made all possible haste towards Chester, where he arrived the very day before the defeat at Nantwich; and though his lieutenant colonel was very desirous to give up the command again to him, and to receive his orders, he would by no means at that time take it, but chose to serve as a volunteer in the first rank, with a pike in his hand, and was the next day taken prisoner with the rest, and with most of the other officers sent to Hull, and shortly after from thence to the Tower of London.

He was no sooner there, than the lord Lisle, who had great kindness for him, and good interest in the Parliament, persuaded him, with much importunity, to take a commission in that service, and offered him a command superior to what he had ever had before; which he positively and disdainfully refused to accept, though the straits he suffered in prison were very great, and he thought himself not kindly dealt with, that there was neither care for his exchange nor money sent for his support. But there was all possible endeavour used for the first, by offering several officers of the same quality for his exchange; which was always refused; there having been an ordinance made that no officer who had been transported out of Ireland should ever be exchanged; so that most of them, remained still in prison with him in the Tower, and the rest in other prisons; who all underwent the same hardnesses by the extreme necessity of the King's condition, which could not provide money enough for their supply; yet all was done towards it that was possible.

When the war was at an end, and the King a prisoner, Cromwell prevailed with him, [Monck,] for his liberty and money, which he loved heartily, to engage himself again in the war of Ireland. And from that time he continued very firm to him [Cromwell,] who was liberal and bountiful to him, and took him into his entire confidence; and after he had put the command of Scotland into his hands,* he feared nothing from those quarters; nor was there any man in either of the armies upon whose fidelity to him he more depended. And those of his western friends who thought best of him thought it to no purpose to make any attempt upon him whilst he [Cromwell] lived. But as soon as Cromwell was dead, he was generally looked upon as a man more inclined to the King than any other in any authority, if he might discover it without too much loss or hazard. His elder brother had been entirely devoted to the King's service, and all his relations were of the same faith. He had no fumes of religion which turned his head, nor any credit with, or dependence upon, any who were swayed by those trances; only he was cursed, after a long familiarity, to marry a woman of the lowest extraction,* the least wit, and less beauty, who, taking no care for any other part of herself, had deposited her soul with some Presbyterian ministers, who disposed her to that interest. She was a woman *nihil muliebre praeter corpus gerens*,* so utterly unacquainted with all persons of quality of either sex, that there was no possible approach to him by her.

He had a younger brother, a divine,* who had a parsonage in Devonshire, and had through all the ill times carried himself with signal integrity, and, being a gentleman of a good family, was in great reputation with all those who constantly adhered to the King. Sir Hugh Pollard and sir John Grenville, who had both friendship for the general and old acquaintance and all confidence in his brother, advised with him, whether, since Cromwell was now gone, and in all reason it might be expected that his death would be attended with a general revolution, by which the King's interest would be again disputed, he did not believe that the general might be wrought upon, in a fit conjuncture, to serve the King, in which he would be sure to meet with a universal concurrence from the whole Scotch nation. The honest person thought the overture so reasonable, and wished so heartily it might be embraced, that he offered himself to make a journey to him [his brother] into Scotland, upon pretence of a visit, (there having been always a brotherly affection performed between them,) and directly to propose it to him. Pollard and Grenville informed the King of this design, and believed well themselves of what they wished so much, and desired his majesty's approbation and instruction. The King had reason to approve it, and sent such directions as he thought most proper for such a negotiation. And so his brother began his journey towards Edinburgh, where the general received him well.* But after he had stayed some time there; and found an opportunity to tell him on what errand he came, he found him to be so far from the temper of a brother, that, after infinite reproaches for his daring to endeavour to corrupt him, he required him to leave that kingdom, using many oaths to him that if he ever returned to him with the same proposition he would cause him to be hanged; with which the poor man was so terrified, that he was glad when he was gone, and never had the courage after to undertake the like employment.

And at that time there is no question the general had not the least thought or purpose ever to contribute to the King's restoration, the hope whereof he believed to be desperate; and the disposition that did grow in him afterwards did arise from those accidents which fell out, and even obliged him to undertake that which proved so much to his profit and glory. And yet from this very time, his brother being known and his journey taken notice of, it was generally believed in Scotland, that he had a purpose to serve the King; which his majesty took no pains to disclaim, either there or in England.

Upon the several sudden changes in England, and the army's possessing itself of the entire government, he [Monck] saw he should quickly be overrun and destroyed by Lambert's greatness, of which he had always great emulation, if he did not provide for his own security. And therefore when he heard of his march towards the north, he used all inventions to get time, by entering into treaties,* and in hope that there would appear some other party that would own and avow the Parliament interest, as he had done; nor had he then more in his imagination than his own profit and greatness under the establishment of its government.

When he heard of Lambert's being past York, and his making haste to Newcastle,* and had purged out of his army all those whose affections and fidelity were suspected by him, he called the States of Scotland* together, which he had subdued to all imaginable tameness, though he had exercised no other tyranny over them than was absolutely necessary to reduce the pride and stubbornness of that people to an entire submission to the yoke. In all his other carriage towards them but what was in order to that end, he was friendly and companionable enough; and as he was feared by the nobility and hated by the clergy, so he was not unloved by the common people, who received more justice and less oppression from him than they had been accustomed to under their own lords. When the Convention appeared before him, he told them that he had received a call from heaven and earth to march with his army into England for the better settlement of the government there; and though he did not intend his absence should be long, yet he foresaw that there might be some disturbance of the peace which they enjoyed, and therefore he expected and desired that in any such occasion they would be ready to join with the forces he left behind in their own defence. In the second place, which was indeed all he cared for, he very earnestly pressed them that they would raise him a present sum of money for supplying the necessities of the army, without which it could not march into England.

From the time that he had settled his government in that kingdom, he had shewed more kindness to, and used more familiarity with, such persons who were most notorious for affection to the King, as finding them a more direct and punctual people than the rest; and when these men resorted to him upon this Convention, though they could draw nothing from him of promise or intimation to any such purpose, yet he was very well content that they should believe that he carried with him very good inclinations to the King; of which imagination of theirs he received very great advantage; for they gave him a twelvemonth's tax over the kingdom, which complied with his wish, and enabled him to draw his army together. And after he had assigned those whom he thought fit to leave behind him, under the command of major general Morgan, he marched with the rest to Berwick, where a good part of his horse and foot expected him, having put an end to his treaty at London, and committed and cashiered colonel Wilkes, one of his commissioners he had sent thither, upon his return to Scotland, for having consented to something prejudicial to him, and expressly contrary to his instructions. However, he desired to gain farther time, and consented to another treaty to be held at Newcastle, which, though he knew [it] would be governed by Lambert, was like not to be without some benefit to him, because it would keep up the opinion in the Committee of Safety that he was inclined to accommodation of peace. [*HR*, XVI, 96–103]

As Monck played for time, other opponents of the army's coup appeared. The garrison of Portsmouth revolted in support of the Rump, the Channel fleet defected, and other units around London started to turn mutinous. There were riots in London and the City demanded not just the restoration of the Rump, but a new, free Parliament. On 26 December the army leadership gave in and readmitted the Rump to the House of Commons. Monck finally began his march from Scotland on 2 January 1660, while Lambert's army melted away.

The principal persons of all counties through which he marched flocked to him in a body with addresses to the same purpose. The city of London sent a letter to him by their sword-bearer, to offer their service; and all concluded for a free Parliament, legally chosen by the free votes of the people. He received all with much civility and few words; took all occasions publicly to declare that nothing should shake his fidelity to the present Parliament, yet privately assured those who he thought necessary should hope well, that he would procure a free Parliament; so that every body promised himself that which he most wished.

The Parliament was far from being confident that he was above temptation; the manner of his march, with such a body contrary to their desires, his receiving so many addresses from the people, and his treating malignants so civilly, startled them much; though his professions of fidelity to the Parliament, and referring all determinations to their wisdoms, had a good aspect, yet they feared that he might observe too much how generally odious they were grown to the people, which might lessen his reverence towards them. To prevent this as much as might be, and to give some check to that license of addresses and resort of malignants, they sent two of their members of most credit (Scott and Robinson,) under pretence of giving their thanks to him for the service he had done, to continue and be present with him, and to discountenance and reprehend any boldness that should appear in any delinquents. But this served but to draw more affronts upon them; for those gentlemen who were civilly used by the general would not bear any disrespect from those, of whose persons they had all contempt, and for the authority of those who sent them had no kind of reverence. As soon as the city knew of the deputing these two members, they likewise sent four of their principal citizens to perform the same compliments, and to confirm him in his inclinations to a free Parliament, as the remedy all men desired.

He continued his march with very few halts till he came to St Albans. There he stopped for some days, and sent to the Parliament that he had some apprehension that those regiments and troops of the army who had formerly deserted them, though for the present they were returned to their obedience, would not live peaceably with his men, and therefore desired that all the soldiers who were then quartered in the Strand, Westminster, or other suburbs of the city, might be presently removed, and sent to more distant quarters, that there might be room for his army. This message was unexpected, and exceedingly perplexed them, and made them see their fate would still be to be under the force and awe of an army. However, they found it necessary to comply, and sent their orders to all soldiers to depart, which with the reason and ground of their resolution, was so disdainfully received, that a mutiny did arise amongst the soldiers, and the regiment that was quartered in Somerset House expressly refused to obey those orders; so that there was like to be new uproars. But their officers who would have been glad to inflame them upon such an occasion were under restraint; and so at last all was composed, and officers and soldiers removed to the quarters which were assigned them, with animosity enough against those who were to succeed them in their old [ones.] And about the middle of February* general Monck with his army marched through the city into the Strand and Westminster, where it was quartered; his own lodgings being provided for him in Whitehall.

He was shortly after conducted to the Parliament, which had before, when they saw there was no remedy, conferred the office and power of general of all the forces in the three kingdoms upon him, as absolutely as ever they had given it to Cromwell. There he had a chair appointed for him to sit in; and the Speaker made a speech to him, in which he extolled the great service he had done to the Parliament, and therein to the kingdom, which was in danger to have lost all the liberty they had gotten with so vast an expense of blood and treasure, and to have been made slaves again, if he had not magnanimously declared himself in their defence; the reputation whereof was enough to blast all their enemies' designs, and to reduce all to their obedience. He told him his memory should flourish to all ages, and the Parliament (whose thanks he presented to him) would take all occasions to manifest their kindness and gratitude for the service he had done.

The general was not a man of eloquence, or of any volubility of speech; he assured them of his constant fidelity, which should never be shaken, and that he would live and die in their service; and then informed them of the several addresses which he had received in his march, and of the observation he made of the general temper of the people, and their impatient desire of a free Parliament, which he mentioned with more than his natural warmth, as a thing they would expect to be satisfied in; (which they observed and disliked;) yet concluded, that having done his duty in this representation, and thereby complied with his promise which he had made to those who had made the addresses, he entirely left the consideration and determination of the whole to their wisdoms; which gave them some ease, and hope that he would be faithful, though inwardly they heartily wished that he was again in Scotland, and that they had been left to contend with the malignity of their old army; and they longed for some occasion that he might manifest his fidelity and resignation to them, or give them just occasion to suspect and question it.

The late confusions and interruptions of all public receipts had wholly emptied those coffers out of which the army and all other expenses were to be supplied. And though the Parliament had, upon their coming together again, renewed their ordinances for all collections and payments, yet money came in very slowly; and the people generally had so little reverence for their legislators, that they gave very slow obedience to their directions: so that they found it necessary for their present supply, till they might by degrees make themselves more universally obeyed, to raise a present great sum of money upon the city; which could not be done but by the advice and with the consent of the Common Council; that is, it could not be levied and collected orderly and peaceably without their distribution.

The Common Council* was constituted of such persons who were weary of the Parliament, and would in no degree submit to or comply with any of their commands. They did not only utterly refuse to consent to this new imposition, but in the debate of it excepted against the authority, and, upon the matter, declared that they would never submit to any imposition that was not granted by a free and lawful Parliament. And it was generally believed that they had assumed this courage upon some confidence they had in the general; and the apprehension of this made the Parliament to be in the greater perplexity and distraction. This would immediately put an end to their empire; and they resolved therefore upon this occasion to make a full experiment of their own power and of their general's obedience.

The Parliament, having received a full information from those aldermen, and others, whose interest was bound up with theirs, of all that had passed at the Common Council, and of the seditious discourses and expressions made by several of the citizens, referred it to the consideration of the Council of State what was fit to be done towards the rebellious city, and to reduce them to that submission which they ought to pay to the Parliament. The Privy Council* deliberated the matter, and returned their advice to the Parliament, that some part of the army might be sent into the city, and remain there, to preserve the peace thereof and of the commonwealth, and to reduce it to the obedience of the Parliament. And in order thereunto, and for their better humiliation, they thought it convenient that the posts and chains should be removed from and out of the several streets of the city, and that the portcullises and gates of the city should be taken down and broken. Over and above this, they named ten persons, who had been the principal conductors in the Common Council, all citizens of great reputations; and advised that they might be apprehended and committed to prison, and that thereupon a new Common Council might be elected, that would be more at their devotion.

This round advice was embraced by the Parliament; and they had now a fit occasion to make experiment of the courage and fidelity of their general, and commanded him to march into the city with his whole army, and to execute all those particulars which they thought so necessary to their service; and he as readily executed their commands;* led his army into the town, neglected the entreaties and prayers of all who applied to him, (whereof there were many who believed he meant better towards them,) caused as many as he could of those who were

proscribed to be apprehended, and sent them to the Tower, and, with
all the circumstances of contempt, pulled down and brake the gates
and portcullises, to the confusion and consternation of the whole city;
and having thus exposed it to the scorn and laughter of all who hated
it, which was the whole kingdom, he returned himself to Whitehall,
and his army to their former quarters; and by this last act of outrage
convinced those who expected somewhat from him how vain their
hopes were, and how incapable he was of embracing any opportunity
to do a noble action, and confirmed his masters that they could not be
too confident of his obedience to their most extravagant injunctions.
And without doubt, if they had cultivated this tame resignation of his
with any temper and discretion, by preparing his consent and approbation to their proceedings, they would have found a full condescension from him, at least no opposition to their counsels. But they were
so infatuated with pride and insolence, that they could not discern the
ways to their own preservation.

Whilst he was executing this their tyranny upon the city, they were
contriving how to lessen his power and authority, and resolved to join
others with him in the command of the army; and upon that very day
they received a petition, which they had fomented, presented to the
Parliament by a man notorious in those times, and who hath been
formerly mentioned, Praise God Barebones,* in the head of a crowd of
sectaries. The petition began with all the imaginable bitterness and
reproaches upon the memory of the late King, and against the person
of the present King and all the nobility, clergy, and gentry of the kingdom which adhered to him; the utter extirpation of all which it pressed
with great acrimony. It took notice of many discourses of calling a new
Parliament, at least of admitting those members to sit in the present
Parliament who had been excluded in the year 1648; either of which,
they [the petitioners] said, would prove the inevitable destruction of all
the godly in the land; and therefore they besought them with all earnestness, that no person whatsoever might be admitted to the exercise
of any office or function in the State or in the Church, no not so much
as to teach a school, who did not first take the oath of abjuration of
the King and of all his family, and that he would never submit to the
government of any one single person whatsoever; and that whosoever
should presume so much as to propose or mention the restoration of
the King, in Parliament or in any other place, should be adjudged
guilty of, and condemned for, high treason.

This petition was received with great approbation by the House,
their affection much applauded, and the thanks of the Parliament very

solemnly returned by the Speaker; all which information the general received at Whitehall when he returned out of the city, and was presently attended by his chief officers, who, with open mouths, inveighed against the proceedings of the Parliament, their manifest ingratitude to him and the indignity offered to him, in their giving such countenance to a rabble of infamous varlets, who desired to set the whole kingdom in a flame, to comply with their fantastic and mad enthusiasms; and that they [the Parliament] would never have admitted such an infamous address with approbation except they had first resolved upon his ruin and destruction, which he was assuredly to look for if he did not prevent it by his wisdom and sagacity; and thereupon told him of the underhand endeavours which were used to work upon the affections of the soldiers.

The general had been prepared, by the conferences of Scott and Robinson* in the march, to expect that as soon as he came to the Parliament he must take the oath of abjuration of the King and his family; and therefore they advised him to offer the taking it himself, before it should be proposed to him, as a matter that would confirm all men in an entire confidence in him; and he discovered not the least aversion from it. And when he came to the Parliament, they forebore that day to mention it, being a day dedicated only to caress him and to give him thanks, in which it could not be seasonable to mingle any thing of distrust. But they meant roundly to have pressed him to it, if this opportunity, which they looked upon as a better earnest of his fidelity, had not fallen out; and without doubt he had not yet taken any such resolution as would have made him pause in the giving them that satisfaction. But being now awakened by this alarum from his officers, and the temper they were in, and his phlegm a little curdled, he began to think himself in danger, and that this body of men that was called the Parliament had not reputation enough to preserve themselves and those who adhered to them. He had observed throughout the kingdom, as he marched, how opprobrious they were in the estimation of all men, who gave them no other term or appellation but the *rump*, as the fag end of a carcass long since expired. All that night was spent in consultation with his officers; nor did he then form any other design than so to unite his army to him that they might not leave him in any resolution he should think fit to take.

In the morning,* the very next morning after he had broken the gates and the hearts of the city, he called his army again together, and marched with it into London, taking up his own quarters at an alderman's house, where he dined. At the same time he left Whitehall he sent a letter to the Parliament, in which he roundly took notice of their unreasonable, unjust, and unpolitic proceedings; of their abetting and countenancing wicked and unchristian tenents in reference to religion, and such as would root out the practice of any religion; of their under-hand corresponding with those very persons whom they had declared to be enemies, and who had been principally instrumental in all the affronts and indignities they had undergone, in and after their dissolu-tion. And thereupon he advised them in such terms as they could not but understand for the most peremptory command, that within such a time, (a time prescribed in his letter,) they would issue out writs for a new Parliament, that so their own sitting might be determined; which was the only expedient that could return peace and happiness to the kingdom, and which both the army and kingdom expected at their hands. This letter was no sooner delivered to the House than it was printed, and carefully published and dispersed throughout the city, to the end that they who had been so lately and so wofully disappointed might see how throughly he was embarked, and so entertain no new jealousies of him.

After he had dined, and disposed his army in such manner and order as he thought fit, he sent to the Lord Mayor and aldermen to meet him at the Guildhall; where, after many excuses for the work of yesterday, they plighted their troth each to other in such a manner, for their perfect union and adhering to each other for the future, that, as soon as they came from thence, the Lord Mayor attended the general to his lodging, and all the bells of the city proclaimed and testified to the town and kingdom that the army and the city were of one mind. And as soon as the evening came, there was a continued light by bon-fires throughout the city and suburbs, with such a universal exclam-ation of joy as had never been known and cannot be expressed, with such ridiculous expressions of scorn and contempt of the Parliament as testified the no regard, or rather the notable detestation, they had of it; there being scarce a bonfire at which they did not roast rumps, and pieces of flesh they made like them, which they said was for the cele-bration of the funeral of the Parliament. There can be no invention of fancy, wit, or ribaldry, that was not that night exercised to defame the Parliament and to magnify the general.

In such a huddle and mixture of loose people of all conditions, and such a transport of affections, it could not be otherwise but that some men would drink the King's health; which was taken no notice of; nor did one person of condition once presume to mention him. All this, how much soever it amazed and distracted the Parliament, did not so dishearten them but that they continued still to sit, and proceeded in all things with their usual confidence. They were not willing to despair of recovering their general again to them; and to that purpose they sent a committee to treat with him, and to make all such proffers to him as they conceived were most like to comply with his ambition or to satisfy his insatiable avarice. The entertainment he gave this committee was the engaging them in a conference with another committee of the excluded members, to the end that he might be satisfied by hearing both, how one could have right to sit there as a Parliament and the other be excluded: and when he had heard them all, he made no scruple to declare, that in justice the secluded members ought to be admitted, but that matter was now over by his having required the calling another Parliament and the dissolution of this.

After he had put the city into the posture they desired, and found no danger threatened him from any place, he returned again to his quarter in Whitehall, and disposed his army to those posts which he judged most convenient. He then sent for the members of the Parliament to come to him, and many others who had been excluded, and lamented the sad condition the kingdom was in, which he principally imputed to the disunion and divisions which had arisen in Parliament between those who were faithful to the commonwealth; that he had had many conferences with them together, and was satisfied by those gentlemen who had been excluded of their integrity; and therefore he had desired this conference between them, that he might communicate his own thoughts to them; in doing whereof, that he might not be mistaken in his delivery or misapprehended in his expressions, as he had lately been, he had put what he had a mind to say in writing; which he commanded his secretary to read to them. The writing imported, that the settlement of the nation lay now in their hands, and that he was assured they would become makers-up of its woeful breaches, in pursuit whereof they would be sure of all his service, and [he] should think all his pains well spent; that he would impose nothing upon them, but took leave to put them in mind, that the old foundations upon which the government had heretofore stood were so totally broken down and demolished, that in the eye of human reason they could never be re-edified and restored but in the ruin of the nation; that the interest of the city of London would be best preserved by the government of a commonwealth, which was the only means to make that city to be the bank for the whole trade of Christendom; that he thought a moderate, not a rigid, Presbyterian government would be most acceptable, and the best way of settlement

in the affairs of the Church; that their care would be necessary to settle
the conduct of the army, and to provide maintenance for the forces by
sea and land; and concluded with a desire that they would put a period
to the present Parliament, and give order for the calling another that
might make a perfect settlement, to which all men might submit.

There was no dissimulation in this, that he might cover and conceal
his good intentions for the King; for without doubt he had not to this
hour entertained any purpose or thought to serve him, but was really
of the opinion he expressed in his paper, that it was a work impossible;
and desired nothing but that he might see a commonwealth established, in such a model as Holland was, where he had been bred, and
that himself might enjoy the authority and place which the Prince of
Orange possessed in that government.* He had not from his marching
out of Scotland to this time had any conversation with any one person
who had served the King, or indeed had he acquaintance with any
such; nor had he hitherto, or long after did he, set one of the King's
friends at liberty, though all the prisons were full of them; but, on the
contrary, they were every day committed, and it was guilt enough to
be suspected but to wish for the King's restoration.

As soon as the conference above mentioned was ended with the
members of the Parliament, they who had been excluded from the year
1648 repaired to the House and without any interruption, which they
had hitherto found, took their places;* and, being superior in number
to the rest, they first repealed and abolished all the orders by which
they had been excluded; then they provided for him who had so well
provided for them, by renewing and enlarging the general's commission, and revoking all other commissions which had been granted to
any to meddle with, or assign quarters to, any part of the forces. They
who had sat before had put the whole militia of the kingdom into the
hands of sectaries, persons of no degree or quality, and notorious only
for some new tenent in religion, and for some barbarity exercised upon
the King's party. All these commissions were revoked, and the militia
put under the government of the nobility and principal gentry
throughout the kingdom; yet with this care and exception, that no
person should be capable of being trusted in that province who did not
first declare under his hand, that he did confess and acknowledge that
the war raised by the two Houses of Parliament against the late King
was just and lawful, until such time as force and violence was used
upon the Parliament in the year 1648.

In the last place, they raised an assessment of one hundred thousand
pounds by the month, for the payment of the army and defraying the

public expenses for six months, to which the whole kingdom willingly submitted; and the city of London, upon the credit and security of that Act, advanced as much ready money as they were desired. And having thus far redressed what was past, and provided as well as they could for the future, they issued out writs to call a Parliament, to meet upon the 25th day of April next ensuing, (being April 1660,) and then, on the 16th day of March, after they had appointed a Council of State, consisting of many sober and honest gentlemen, who had never wished the King ill, they dissolved that present Parliament, against all the importunities used by the sectaries, who in multitudes flocked together, and made addresses in the name of the city of London, that they would not dissolve themselves, and to the unspeakable joy of all the rest of the kingdom, who, notwithstanding their very different affections, expectations, and designs, were unanimous in their weariness and detestation of the Long Parliament.

When the King, who had rather an imagination than an expectation that the march of general Monck to London with his army might produce some alteration that might be useful to him, heard now of his entire submission to the Parliament, and of his entering the city and disarming it, the commitment of the principal citizens, and breaking their gates and portcullises, all the little remainder of his hopes was extinguished, and he had nothing left before his eyes but a perpetual exile, attended with all those discomforts of which he had too long experienced, and which he must now expect would be improved with the worst circumstances of neglect, which use to wait upon that condition. And a greater consternation and dejection of mind cannot be imagined than at that time covered the whole Court of the King. But God would not suffer the King long to be wrapped up in that melancholic cloud. As the general's second march into the city was the very next day after his first, and dispelled the mists and fogs which the other had raised, so the very evening of that day which had brought the news of the first in the morning, brought likewise an account to his majesty of the second, with all the circumstances of bells and bonfires and burning of rumps, and such other additions as might reasonably be true, and which a willing relator would not omit.

When it began to be dark, the lord marquis of Ormond brought a young man with him to the Chancellor's lodging at Brussels, which was under the King's bedchamber, and to which his majesty every day vouchsafed to come for the despatch of any business. The marquis said no more but that that man had formerly been an officer under him, and he believed he was an honest man; besides, that he brought a line or

two of credit from a person they would both believe; but that his discourse was so strange and extravagant that he knew not what to think
of it; however, he would call the King to judge of it; and so went
out of the room, leaving the man there, and immediately returned with
the King.

The man's name was Bayly, who had lived most in Ireland, and had
served there as a foot-officer under the marquis. He looked as if he had
drank much, or slept little. His relation was, that in the afternoon of
such a day he was with sir John Stephens in Lambeth House, used
then as a prison for many of the King's friends; where, whilst they
were in conference together, news was brought into the house by several persons that the general was marched with his whole army into the
city, it being the very next day after he had been there and broke down
their gates and pulled down their posts, and that he had a conference
with the mayor and aldermen, which was no sooner ended but that all
the city bells rang out; and he heard the bells very plain at Lambeth;
and that he stayed there so late till they saw the bonfires burning and
flaming in the city: upon which sir John Stephens had desired him that
he would immediately cross the river, and go into London, and inquire
what the matter was, and if he found any thing extraordinary in it, that
he would take post, and make all possible haste to Brussels, that the
King might be informed of it; and so gave him a short note in writing
to the marquis of Ormond, that he might believe all that that messenger would inform him: that thereupon he went over the river, walked
through Cheapside, saw the bonfires and the King's health drank in
several places, heard all that the general had done, and brought a copy
of the letter which the general had sent to the Parliament at the time
when he returned with his army into the city; and then told many
things which were, he said, publicly spoken concerning sending for the
King: and then he took post for Dover, and hired a bark that brought
him to Ostend.

The time was so short from the hour he left London that the expedition of his journey was incredible; nor could any man undertake to
come from thence in so short a time upon the most important affair and
for the greatest reward. It was evident, by many pauses and hesitations
in his discourse and some repetitions, that the man was not composed,
and at best wanted sleep; yet his relation could not be a mere fiction and
imagination. Sir John Stephens was a man well known to his majesty
and the other two, and had been sent over lately by the King with
some advice to his friends; and it was well known that he had been
apprehended at his landing, and was sent prisoner to Lambeth House.

And though he had not mentioned in his note any particulars, yet he had given him credit, and nothing but the man's own devotion to the King could reasonably tempt him to undertake so hazardous and chargeable a journey. Then the general's letter to the Parliament was of the highest moment, and not like to be feigned; and, upon the whole matter, the King thought he had argument to raise his own spirits, and that he should do but justly in communicating his intelligence to his dispirited family and servants; who, upon the news thereof, were proportionably revived to the despair they had swallowed, and, according to the temper of men who had lain under long disconsolation, thought all their sufferings over, and laid in a stock of unreasonable presumption that no success could procure satisfaction for.

But the King, who thanked God for this new dawning of hope, and was much refreshed with this unexpected alteration, was yet restrained from any confidence that this would produce any such revolution as would be sufficient to do his work, towards which he saw cause enough to despair of assistance from any foreign power. The most that he could collect from the general's letter, besides the suppressing the present tyranny of the Parliament, was, that the secluded members would be again admitted, and, it may be, able to govern that council; which administered no solid ground of comfort or confidence. Few of those excluded members had been true members of Parliament, but elected into their places after the end of the war who had been expelled for adhering to the King, and so had no title of sitting there but what the counterfeit great seal had given them, without and against the King's authority. These men, with others who had been lawfully chosen, were willing and desirous that the concessions made by the late King at the Isle of Wight* might be accepted; which in truth did, with the preservation of the name and life of the King, as much establish a republican government as was settled after his murder; and because they would insist upon that, they were, with those circumstances of force and violence which are formerly mentioned, excluded from the House; without which that horrid villainy could never have been committed.

Now what could the King reasonably expect from these men's re-admission into the government, but that they would resume their old conclusions, and press him to consent to his father's concessions, and which his late majesty yielded unto with much less cheerfulness than he walked to the scaffold, and upon the promise of many powerful men then in the Parliament that he should not be obliged to accomplish that agreement? These revolvings wrought much upon his majesty, though he thought it necessary to appear pleased with what was done, and to expect much greater things from it; which yet he knew not how to contribute to, till he should receive a farther account from London of the revolutions.

Indeed, when all he heard before was confirmed by several expresses, who passed with much freedom, and were every day sent by his friends, who had recovered their courage to the full, and discerned that these excluded members were principally admitted to prepare for the calling a new Parliament, and to be sure to make the dissolution of this unquestionable and certain, his majesty recovered all his hopes again; which were every day confirmed by the addresses of many men who had never before applied themselves to him; and many sent to him for his majesty's approbation and leave to serve and sit in the next Parliament. And from the time that the Parliament was dissolved, the Council of State behaved themselves very civilly towards his majesty's friends, and released many of them out of prison: and Annesley, the president of the Council, was very well contented that the King should receive particular information of his devotion, and of his resolution to do him service; which he manifested in many particulars of importance, and had the courage to receive a letter from his majesty, and returned a dutiful answer: all which had a very good aspect, and seemed to promise much good. Yet the King knew not what to think of the general's paper, which he had delivered at his conference with the members;* for which he could have no temptation but his violent affection to a commonwealth. None of his [majesty's] friends could find any means of address to him [Monck]; yet they did believe, and were much the better for believing it, that the King had some secret correspondence with him; and some of them sent to the King, of what importance it would be that he gave them some credit, or means of access, to the general, by which they might receive his order and direction in such things as occurred on the sudden, and that they might be sure to do nothing that might cross any purpose of his. To which the King returned no other answer but that they should have patience, and make no attempt whatsoever, and that in due time they should receive all advertisements necessary; it being not thought fit to disclaim the having intelligence with or hopes of the general, since it was very evident, that the opinion that he did design to serve the King, or that he would be at last obliged to do it whether he designed to do it or no, did really as much contribute to the advancement of his [majesty's] service as if he had dedicated himself to it. And the assurance that other men had that he had no such intention hindered those obstructions, jealousies, and interruptions, which very probably might have lessened his credit with his own army, or united all the rest of the forces against him. [*HR*, XVI, 118–43]

During late March and early April, as elections were held for the Convention Parliament, Monck finally accepted a channel of communication with the royal court, through his Devon neighbours and relatives William Morrice and Sir John Grenville. He dictated to them what he felt were the minimum requirements for a Restoration—principally the satisfaction of the material concerns of the army, rather than formal limitations on the King's power. The Declaration of Breda, drafted by Hyde and directed by Charles to both Houses of the new Parliament, embodied those terms. When Parliament met on 25 April, the demand for the King's immediate return outweighed any interest in setting constitutional conditions. Following the presentation of the King's Declaration, both Houses voted, on 1 May, for a return to royal government.

Persons now came to Breda, not, as heretofore to Cologne and to Brussels, under disguises and in fear to be discovered, but with bare faces, and the pride and vanity to be taken notice of, to present their duty to the King; some being employed to procure pardons for those who thought themselves in danger, and to stand in need of them; others brought good presents in English gold to the King, that their names, and the names of their friends who sent them, might be remembered amongst the first of those who made the first demonstrations of their affections that way to his majesty, by supplying his necessities; which had been discontinued for many years, to a degree that cannot be believed, and ought not to be remembered. And by these supplies his majesty was enabled, besides the payment of his other debts, not only to pay all his servants the arrears of their board-wages, but to give them all some testimony of his bounty, to raise their spirits after so many years of patient waiting for deliverance: and all this before the delivery of the King's letter by the general to the Parliament.

The King had not been many days in Breda before the States General sent deputies of their own body to congratulate his majesty's arrival in their dominions, and to acknowledge the great honour he had vouchsafed to do them. And shortly after, other deputies came from the States of Holland, beseeching his majesty that he would grace that province with his kingly presence at the Hague, where preparations should be made for his reception, in such a manner as should testify the great joy of their hearts for the blessings which the divine Providence was pouring upon his head. And his majesty accepting their invitation, they returned in order to make his journey thither, and his entertainment there, equal to their professions.

In the mean time Breda swarmed with English, a multitude repairing thither from all other places as well as London, with presents, and protestations how much they had longed and prayed for this blessed change, and magnifying their sufferings under the late tyrannical government, when many of them had been zealous ministers and promoters of it. The magistrates of the town took all imaginable care to express their devotion to the King, by using all civilities towards, and taking care for the accommodation of, the multitude of his subjects who resorted thither to express their duty to him. So that no man would have imagined, by the treatment he now received, that he had been so lately forbid to come into that place;* which indeed had not proceeded from the disaffection of the inhabitants of that good town, who had always passion for his prosperity, and even then publicly detested the rudeness of their superiors, whom they were bound to obey.

All things being in readiness, and the States having sent their yachts and other vessels for the accommodation of his majesty and his train, as near to Breda as the river would permit, the King, with his royal sister and brothers, left that place upon Friday the fourteenth day of May, and within an hour embarked themselves on board the yachts, which carried them to Rotterdam; Dort,* and the other places near which they passed, making all those expressions of joy, by the conflux of the people to the banks of the river and all other ways, which the situation of those places would suffer. At Rotterdam they entered into their coaches; from whence to the Hague (at least five English miles) they seemed to pass through one continued street, by the wonderful and orderly appearance of the people on both sides, with such acclamations of joy as if themselves were now restored to peace and security.

The entrance into the Hague, and the reception there, and the conducting his majesty to the house provided for his reception, was very magnificent, and in all respects answerable to the pomp, wealth, and greatness of that State. And the treatment of his majesty, and all who had relation to his service, at the State's charge, during the time of his abode there, which continued many days, was incredibly splendid and noble; and the universal joy so visible and real, that it could only be exceeded by that of his own subjects. The States General in a body, and the States of Holland in a body, performed their compliments with all solemnity; and then the several persons, according to their faculties, made their professions; and a set number of them was appointed always to wait in the Court, to receive his majesty's commands. All the ambassadors and public ministers of kings, princes, and states, repaired to his majesty, and professed the joy of their masters on his majesty's behalf: so that a man would have thought that this revolution had been brought to pass by the general combination and activity of Christendom, that appeared now to take so much pleasure in it.

The King had been very few days at the Hague when he heard that the English fleet was in sight of Scheveling and shortly after, an officer from admiral Montagu was sent to the King, to present his duty to him, and to the duke of York, their high admiral, to receive his orders. As soon as Montagu came on board the fleet in the Downs, and found those officers more frank in declaring their duty to the King, and resolution to serve him, than he expected, that he might not seem to be sent by the Parliament to his majesty but to be carried by his own affection and duty, without expecting any command from them, the wind coming fair, he set up his sails, and stood for the coast of Holland, leaving only two or three of the lesser ships to receive their orders, and to bring over those persons who, he knew, were designed to wait upon his majesty; which expedition was never forgiven him by some men, who took all occasions afterwards to revenge themselves upon him.

The duke of York went the next day on board the fleet, to take possession of his command;* where he was received by all the officers and seamen with all possible duty and submission, and with those exclamations which are peculiar to that people, and in which they excel. After he had spent the day there, in receiving information of the state of the fleet, and a catalogue of the names of the several ships, his highness returned with it that night to the King, that his majesty might make alterations, and new christen those ships which too much preserved the memory of their late governors and of the republic.

Shortly after, the committee of Lords [and Commons] arrived at the Hague, where the States took care for their decent accommodation. And the next day they desired admission to his majesty, who immediately received them very graciously. From the House of Peers were deputed six of their body, and, according to custom, twelve from the Commons. The peers were, the earls of Oxford, Warwick, and Middlesex; the lords, the viscount Hereford, the lord Berkeley of Berkeley Castle, and the lord Brooke. From the Commons were sent, the lord Fairfax, the lord Bruce, the lord Falkland, the lord Castleton, the lord Herbert, the lord Mandeville, Denzil Holles, sir Horatio Townsend, sir Anthony Ashley Cooper, sir George Booth, sir John Holland, and sir Henry Cholmeley. These persons presented the humble invitation and supplication of the Parliament, that his majesty would be pleased to return, and take the government of the kingdom into his hands, where he should find all possible affection, duty, and obedience from all his

subjects; and lest his return, so much longed for, might be retarded by
the want of money to discharge those debts which he could not but
have contracted, they presented from the Parliament the sum of fifty
thousand pounds to his majesty; having likewise order to pay the sum
of ten thousand pounds to the duke of York and five thousand to the
duke of Gloucester; which was a very good supply to their several
necessities. And the King treated all the committee very graciously
together, and every one of them severally and particularly very obli-
gingly. So that some of them, who were conscious to themselves of
their former demerit, were very glad to find that they were not to fear
any bitterness from so princely and so generous a nature.

The city of London had too great a hand in driving the King from
thence not to appear equally zealous for his return thither. And therefore they did at the same time send fourteen of their most substantial
citizens to assure his majesty of their fidelity and most cheerful submission, and that they placed all their felicity and hope of future prosperity in the assurance of his majesty's grace and protection, for the
meriting whereof their lives and fortunes should be always at his majesty's disposal; and they presented to him from the city the sum of ten
thousand pounds. The King told them he had always had a particular
affection for the city of London, the place of his birth, and was very
glad that they had now so good a part in his restoration, of which he
was informed, and how much he was beholding to every one of them;
for which he thanked them very graciously, and knighted them all; an
honour no man in the city had received in near twenty years, and with
which they were much delighted.

It will hardly be believed that this money presented to the King by
the Parliament and the city, and charged by bills of exchange upon the
richest merchants in Amsterdam, who had vast estates, could not be
received in many days, though some of the principal citizens of
London who came to the King went themselves to solicit it, and had
credit enough themselves for much greater sums if they had brought
over no bills of exchange. But this was not the first time (and of which
somewhat hath been said before) that it was evident to the King, that
it is not easy in that most opulent city, with the help of all the rich
towns adjacent and upon the greatest credit, to draw together a great
sum of ready money; the custom of that country, which flourishes so
much in trade, being to make their payments in paper by assignations,
and having very rarely occasion for a great sum in any one particular
place. And so at this time his majesty was compelled, that he might not
defer the voyage he so impatiently longed to make, to take bills of

exchange from Amsterdam upon their correspondents in London, for above thirty thousand pounds of the money that was assigned; all which was paid in London as soon as demanded.

With these committees from the Parliament and from the city there came a company of clergymen, to the number of eight or ten, who would not be looked upon as chaplains to the rest, but, being the popular preachers of the city, (Reynolds, Calamy, Case, Manton, and others,) were the most eminent of the Presbyterians, and desired to be thought to represent that party. They desired to be admitted all together to have a formal audience from his majesty, where they were tedious enough in presenting their duties, and magnifying the affections of themselves and their friends, who, they said, had always, according to the obligation of their Covenant, wished his majesty very well, and had lately, upon the opportunity that God had put into their hands, informed the people of their duty; which they presumed his majesty had heard had proved effectual, and been of great use to him. They thanked God for his constancy to the Protestant religion, and professed that they were no enemies to moderate episcopacy, only desired that such things might not be pressed upon them in God's worship which in their judgment who used them were acknowledged to be matters indifferent, and by others were held unlawful.

The King spake very kindly to them, and said he had heard of their good behaviour towards him, and that he had no purpose to impose hard conditions upon them with reference to their conscience; they well knew that he had referred the settling all differences of that nature to the wisdom of the Parliament, which best knew what indulgence and toleration was necessary for the peace and quiet of the kingdom. But his majesty could not be so rid of them; but they desired several private audiences of him, which he never denied; wherein they told him, that the Book of Common Prayer had been long discontinued in England, and the people having been disused to it, and many of them having never heard it in their lives, it would be much wondered at, if his majesty should, at his first landing in the kingdom, revive the use of it in his own chapel, whither all persons would resort; and therefore they besought him that he would not use it so entirely and formally, and have some parts only of it read, with mixture of other good prayers which his chaplains might use.

The King told them with some warmth, that, whilst he gave them liberty, he would not have his own taken from him; that he had always used that form of service, which he thought the best in the world, and would not discontinue it, in places where it was more disliked than he

hoped it was by them; that when he came into England, he would not
much inquire how it was used in other churches, though he doubted
not he should find it used in many, but he was sure he would have no
other used in his own chapel. Then they besought him with more
importunity, that the use of the surplice might be discontinued by his
chaplains, because the sight of it would give great offence and scandal
to the people. They found the King as inexorable in that point as in the
other; and [he] told them plainly, that he would not be restrained himself when he gave others so much liberty; that it had been always held
a decent habit in the Church, constantly practised in England till these
late ill times; that it had been still retained by him; and though he was
bound for the present to tolerate much disorder and undecency in the
exercise of God's worship, he would never in the least degree discountenance the good old order of the Church in which he had been bred
by his own practice. Though they were very much unsatisfied with
him, whom they thought to have found more flexible, yet they ceased
further troubling him, in hope and presumption that they should find
their importunity in England more effectual.

After eight or ten days spent at the Hague in triumphs and festivals,
which could not have been more splendid if all the monarchs of
Europe had met there, and which were concluded with several rich
presents made to his majesty, the King took his leave of the States with
all the professions of amity their civilities deserved, and embarked
himself* on the *Prince*, which had before been called the *Protector*, but
had been new christened the day before, as many other had been, in
the presence and by the order of his royal highness the admiral. And
upon the 24th day of May the fleet set sail, and, in one continued
thunder of the cannon, arrived so early on the 26th near Dover that his
majesty disembarked, and being received by the general at the brink of
the sea, he presently took coach, and came that night to Canterbury,
where he stayed the next day, being Sunday, and went to his devotions
to the cathedral, which was very much dilapidated and out of repair;
yet the people seemed glad to hear the Common Prayer again. Thither
came very many of the nobility and other persons of quality to present
themselves to the King; and there his majesty assembled his Council
and swore the general of the Council, and Mr Morrice, whom he there
knighted, and gave him the signet, and swore him Secretary of State.
That day he gave the Garter* to the general, and likewise to the marquis of Hertford and the earl of Southampton, (who had been elected
many years before,) and sent it likewise by Garter herald and king-at-
arms to admiral Montagu, who remained in the Downs.

On Monday he went to Rochester, and the next day, being the 29th of May and his birthday, he entered London, all the ways from Dover thither being so full of people and exclamations as if the whole kingdom had been gathered. About or above Greenwich the Lord Mayor and aldermen met him, with all those protestations of joy which can hardly be imagined; and the concourse so great that the King rode in a crowd from the bridge to Temple Bar. All the companies of the city stood in order on both sides, giving loud thanks for his majesty's presence. And he no sooner came to Whitehall but the two Houses of Parliament solemnly cast themselves at his feet, with all the vows of affection and fidelity to the world's end. In a word, the joy was so unexpressible and so universal, that his majesty said smilingly to some about him, that he doubted it had been his own fault that he had been absent so long, for he saw nobody that did not protest he had ever wished for his return.

In this wonderful manner, and with this miraculous expedition, did God put an end in one month (for it was the first of May that the King's letter was delivered to the Parliament, and his majesty was at Whitehall upon the 29th of the same month) to a rebellion that had raged near twenty years, and been carried on with all the horrid circumstances of parricide, murder, and devastation, that fire and the sword, in the hands of the wickedest men in the world, could be ministers of, almost to the desolation of two kingdoms, and the exceeding defacing and deforming the third. Yet did the merciful hand of God in one month bind up all these wounds, and even made the scars as undiscernible as in respect of their deepness was possible. And if there wanted more glorious monuments of this deliverance, posterity would know the time of it by the death of the two great favourites of the two Crowns, cardinal Mazarin and don Lewis de Haro, who both died within three or four months,* with the wonder, if not the agony, of this undreamed of prosperity, and as if they had taken it ill that God Almighty would bring such a work to pass in Europe without their concurrence and against all their machinations. [*HR*, XVI, 232–47]

CLARENDON
BEFORE THE CIVIL WAR

Extracts from *The Life*

18. Law and Polite Learning: The Education of a Lawyer

The first part of Clarendon's Life, *covering his early years up until his entry into the King's service, was written at Montpelier, between 23 July 1668 (the date given at the beginning of this part of the manuscript) and 27 March 1669 (the date given at the end). Hyde's father Henry Hyde was one of four sons, two of whom rose to senior legal office: Laurence, who became Attorney General to James I's Queen, and Nicholas, who became Lord Chief Justice of the King's Bench in 1627. Though legally trained, Henry Hyde never practised. He travelled abroad, then lived on a small but sufficient estate at Dinton, in Wiltshire, 'with great cheerfulness and content'. Edward Hyde was his third son, the youngest to survive childhood, and was originally destined for the Church.*

EDWARD HYDE, being the third son of his father, was born at Dinton upon the eighteenth day of February in the year 1608,* being the fifth year of king James; and was always bred in his father's house under the care of a schoolmaster, to whom his father had given the vicarage of that parish, who, having been always a schoolmaster, (though but of very indifferent parts,) had bred many good scholars, and this person of whom we now speak, principally by the care and conversation of his father, (who was an excellent scholar, and took pleasure in conferring with him, and contributed much more to his education than the school did,) was thought fit to be sent to the university soon after he was thirteen years of age; and being a younger son of a younger brother, was to expect a small patrimony from his father, but to make his own fortune by his own industry; and in order to that, was sent by his father to Oxford at that time, being about Magdalen election time, in expectation that he should have been chosen demy of Magdalen college,* the election being to be at that time, for which he was recommended by a special letter from King James to Dr Langton then president of that college; but upon pretence that the letter came too late, though the election was not then begun, he was not chosen, and so remained in Magdalen hall (where he was before admitted) under the tuition of Mr John Oliver, a fellow of that college, who had been junior of the act* a month before, and a scholar of eminency, who was his tutor.

The year following, the president of the college having received reprehension from the lord Conway then secretary of state, for giving no more respect to the king's letter, he was chosen the next election in the first place, but that whole year passed without any avoidance of a demy's place, which was never known before in any man's memory, and that year king James died, and shortly after, Henry his elder brother, and thereupon his father having now no other son, changed his former inclination, and resolved to send his son Edward to the inns of court: he was then entered in the Middle Temple by his uncle Nicholas Hyde, who was then treasurer of that society, and afterwards lord chief justice of the king's bench; but by reason of the great plague then at London in the first year of king Charles, and the parliament being then adjourned to Oxford, whither the plague was likewise then brought by sir James Hussy, one of the masters of the chancery, who died in New college the first night after his arrival at Oxford, and shortly after Dr Chaloner, principal of Alban hall, who had supped that night with sir James Hussy, he did not go to the Middle Temple till the Michaelmas term after the term at Reading, but remained partly at his father's house, and partly at the university, where he took the degree of bachelor of arts, and then left it, rather with the opinion of a young man of parts and pregnancy of wit, than that he had improved it much by industry, the discipline of that time being not so strict as it hath been since, and as it ought to be; and the custom of drinking being too much introduced and practised, his elder brother having been too much corrupted in that kind, and so having at his first coming given him some liberty, at least some example towards that license, insomuch as he was often heard to say, 'that it was a very good fortune to him that his father so soon removed him from the university,' though he always reserved a high esteem of it.

Before the beginning of Michaelmas term (which was in the year 1625) the city being then clear from the plague, he went from Marlborough after the quarter sessions with his uncle Nicholas Hyde, who was afterwards chief justice, to London, and arrived there about ten of the clock in the morning, the eve of the term, and dined that day in the Middle Temple hall, being then between sixteen and seventeen years of age. In the evening he went to prayers to the Temple church, and was there seized upon by a fit of an ague very violently, which proved a quartan, and brought him in a short time so weak, that his friends much feared a consumption, so that his uncle thought fit shortly after Alhollandtide* to send him into the country to Purton in North Wiltshire, whither his father had removed himself from Dinton; choosing rather to live upon his own land, the which he had purchased many years before, and to rent Dinton, which was but a lease for lives, to a tenant. He came home to his father's house very weak, his ague continuing so violently upon him (though it sometimes changed its course from a quartan to a tertian, and then to a quotidian, and on new year's day he had two hot fits and two cold fits) until Whitsunday following, that all men thought him to be in a consumption; it then left him, and he grew quickly strong again. In this time of his sickness his uncle was made chief justice: it was Michaelmas following before he returned to the Middle Temple, having by his want of health lost a full year of study; and when he returned, it was without great application to the study of the law for some years, it being then a time when the town was full of soldiers, the king having then a war both with Spain and France, and the business of the Isle of Rhé* shortly followed; and he had gotten into the acquaintance of many of those officers, which took up too much of his time for one year: but as the war was quickly ended, so he had the good fortune quickly to make a full retreat from that company, and from any conversation with any of them, and without any hurt or prejudice from their conversation; insomuch as he used often to say, 'that since it pleased God to preserve him whilst he did keep that company, (in which he wonderfully escaped from being involved in many inconveniences,) and to withdraw him so soon from it, he was not sorry that he had some experience in the conversation of such men, and of the license of those times,' which was very exorbitant: yet when he did indulge himself that liberty, it was without any signal debauchery, and not without some hours every day, at least every night, spent amongst his books; yet he would not deny that more than to be able to answer his uncle, who almost every night put a case to him in law, he could not bring himself to an industrious pursuit of the law study, but rather loved polite learning and history, in which, especially in the Roman, he had been always conversant.

In the year 1628 his father gave him leave to ride the circuit* in the summer with his uncle the chief justice, who then rode the Norfolk circuit; and indeed desired it, both that he might see those counties, and especially that he might be out of London in that season when the small pox raged very furiously, and many persons, some whereof were very familiar with him, died of that disease in the Middle Temple itself. It was about the middle of July when that circuit began, and Cambridge was the first place the judges begun at; Mr Justice Harvey (one of the judges of the common pleas) was in commission with the chief justice: they both came into Cambridge on the Saturday night, and the next day Mr Edward Hyde fell sick, which was imputed only to his journey the day before in very hot weather; but he continued so ill the day or two following, that it was apprehended that he might have the small pox; whereupon he was removed out of Trinity college, where the judges were lodged, and where he had a chamber, to the Sun inn, over against the college gate, the judges being to go out of town the next day; but before they went, the small pox appeared; whereupon his uncle put him under the care of Mr Crane an eminent apothecary, who had been bred up under Dr Butler, and was in much greater practice than any physician in the university; and left with him Laurence St Loe one of his servants, who was likewise his nephew, to assist and comfort him. It pleased God to preserve him from that devouring disease, which was spread all over him very furiously, and had so far prevailed over him, that for some hours both his friends and physician consulted of nothing but of the place and manner of his burial; but as I said, by God's goodness he escaped that sickness, and within few days more than a month after his first indisposition he passed in moderate journeys to his father's house at Purton, where he arrived a day or two before Bartholomew day. [*Life*, I, 7–10]

Clarendon remembered the day, because it was on St Bartholomew's day 1628 that the Duke of Buckingham had been assassinated by one John Felton, and he had heard the news when reading to his father about the Roman Catholic martyr of the same name. Not long afterwards, in 1631, the death of his uncle and patron, the Lord Chief Justice, endangered his steady advancement in his legal career.

The loss of so beneficial an encouragement and support in that profession did not at all discourage his nephew in his purpose; rather added new resolution to him; and to call home all straggling and wandering appetites, which naturally produce irresolution and inconstancy in the mind, with his father's consent and approbation he married a young lady* very fair and beautiful, the daughter of sir George Ayliffe, a gentleman of a good name and fortune in the county of Wilts, where his own expectations lay, and by her mother (a St John) nearly allied to many noble families in England. He enjoyed this comfort and composure of mind a very short time, for within less than six months after he was married, being upon the way from London towards his father's house, she fell sick at Reading, and being removed to a friend's house near that town, the small pox discovered themselves, and (she being with child) forced her to miscarry; and she died within two days. He bore her loss with so great passion and confusion of spirit, that it shook all the frame of his resolutions, and nothing but his entire duty and reverence to his father kept him from giving over all thoughts of books, and transporting himself beyond the seas to enjoy his own melancholy; nor could any persuasion or importunity from his friends prevail with him in some years to think of another marriage. There was an ill accident in the court befell a lady* of a family nearly allied to his wife, whose memory was very dear to him, and there always continued a firm friendship in him to all her alliance, which likewise ever manifested an equal affection to him; amongst those was William viscount Grandison, a young man of extraordinary hope, between whom and the other there was an entire confidence. The injury was of that nature, that the young lord thought of nothing but repairing it his own way; but those imaginations were quickly at an end, by the king's rigorous and just proceeding against the persons offending, in committing them both to the Tower, and declaring that 'since he was satisfied that there was a promise of marriage in the case, the gentleman should make good his promise by marrying the lady; or be kept in prison, and for ever banished from all pretence or relation to the court,' where he had a very great credit and interest. This declaration by the king made the nearest friends of the lady pursue the design of this reparation more solicitously, in which they had all access to the king, who continued still in his declared judgment in the matter. In this pursuit Mr Hyde's passionate affection to the family embarked him, and they were all as willing to be guided by his conduct; the business was to be followed by frequent instances at court, and conferences with those who had most power and opportunity to confirm the king in the sense he had entertained; and those conferences were wholly managed by him, who thereby had all admission to the persons of alliance to the lady, and so concerned in the dishonour, which was a great body of lords and ladies of principal relations in court, with whom in a short time he was of great credit and esteem; of which the marquis of Hamilton was one, who having married an excellent lady, cousin-german to the injured person, seemed the most concerned and most zealous for her vindication, and who had at that time the most credit of any man about the court, and who upon that occasion entered into a familiarity with him, and made as great professions of kindness to him as could pass to a person at that distance from him, which continued till the end and conclusion of that affair, when the marquis believed that Mr Hyde had discovered some what of sincerity in him in that prosecution, which he pretended so much to assert.

The mention of this particular little story, in itself of no seeming consequence, is not inserted here only as it made some alterations, and accidentally introduced him into another way of conversation than he had formerly been accustomed to, and which in truth by the acquaintance by the friends and enemies he then made, had an influence upon the whole course of his life afterwards; but that it made such impressions upon the whole court, by dividing the lords and ladies both in their wishes and appearances, that much of that faction grew out of it, which survived the memory of the original; and from this occasion (to shew us from how small springs great rivers may arise) the women, who till then had not appeared concerned in public affairs, began to have some part in all business; and having shewn themselves warm upon this amour, as their passions or affections carried them, and thereby entered into new affections, and formed new interests; the activity in their spirits remained still vigorous when the object which first inspired it was vanished and put in oblivion. Nor were the very ministers of state vacant upon this occasion; they who for their own sakes, or, as they pretended, for the king's dignity, and honour of the court, desired the ruin of the gentleman, pressed the magnitude of the crime, in bringing so great a scandal upon the king's family, which would hinder persons of honour from sending their children to the court; and that there could be no reparation without the marriage, which they therefore only insisted upon, because they believed he would prefer banishment before it; others who had friendship for him and believed that he had an interest in the court, which might accommodate himself and them if this breach were closed any way, therefore if the king's severity could not be prevailed upon, wished it concluded by the marriage; which neither himself nor they upon whom he most depended would ever be brought to consent to; so that all the jealousies and animosities in the court or state came to play their own prizes in the widening or accommodating this contention. In the conclusion, on a sudden, contrary to the expectation of any man of either party, the gentleman was immediately sent out of the kingdom, under the formality of a temporary and short banishment, and the lady commended to her friends, to be taken care of till her delivery; and from that time never word more spoken of the business, nor shall their names ever come upon the stage by any record of mine. It was only observed, that at this time there was a great change in the friendships of the court, and in those of the marquis of Hamilton, who came now into the queen's confidence, towards whom he had always been in great jealousy; and another lady more appeared in view, who had for the most part before continued behind the curtain; and who in few years after came to a very unhappy and untimely end.

Now after a widowhood of near three years, Mr Hyde was inclined again to marry, which he knew would be the most grateful thing to his father (for whom he had always an infinite reverence) he could do: and though he needed no other motive to it, he would often say, that though he was now called to the bar, and entered into the profession of the law, he was not so confident of himself that he should not start aside if his father should die, who was then near seventy years of age, having long entertained thoughts of travels, but that he thought it necessary to lay some obligation upon himself, which would suppress and restrain all those appetites; and thereupon resolved to marry, and so, being about the age of twenty-four years; in the year of our Lord 1632, he married the daughter of sir Thomas Aylesbury,* baronet, master of requests to the king; by whom he had many children of both sexes, with whom he lived very comfortably in the most uncomfortable times, and very joyfully in those times when matter of joy was administered, for the space of five or six and thirty years; what befell him after her death will be recounted in its place. From the time of his marriage he laid aside all other thoughts but of his profession, to the which he betook himself very seriously; but in the very entrance into it he met with a great mortification: some months after he was married, he went with his wife to wait upon his father and mother at his house at Purton, to make them sharers in that satisfaction which they had so long desired to see, and in which they took great delight.

His father had long suffered under an indisposition (even before the time his son could remember) which gave him rather frequent pains than sickness; and gave him cause to be terrified with the expectation of the stone, without being exercised with the present sense of it; but from the time he was sixty years of age it increased very much, and four or five years before his death, with circumstances scarce heard of before, and the causes whereof are not yet understood by any physician: he was very often, both in the day and the night, forced to make water, seldom in any quantity, because he could not retain it long enough; and in the close of that work, without any sharp pain in those parts, he was still and constantly seized on by so sharp a pain in the left arm for half a quarter of an hour, or near so much, that the torment made him as pale (whereas he was otherwise of a very sanguine complexion) as if he were dead; and he used to say, 'that he had passed the pangs of death, and he should die in one of those fits.' As soon as it was over, which was quickly, he was the cheerfullest man living; eat well such things as he could fancy, walked, slept, digested, conversed with such a promptness and vivacity upon all arguments (for he was *omnifariam doctus**) as hath been seldom known in a man of his age: but he had the image of death so constantly before him in those continual torments, that for many years before his death he always parted with his son as to see him no more; and at parting still shewed him his will, discoursing very particularly and very cheerfully of all things he would have performed after his death.

He had for some time before resolved to leave the country, and to spend the remainder of his time in Salisbury, where he had caused a house to be provided for him, both for the neighbourhood of the cathedral church, where he could perform his devotions every day, and for the conversation of many of his family who lived there, and not far from it; and especially that he might be buried there, where many of his family and friends lay; and he obliged his son to accompany him thither before his return to London; and he came to Salisbury on the Friday before Michaelmas day in the year 1632, and lodged in his own house that night. The next day he was so wholly taken up in receiving visits from his many friends, being a person wonderfully reverenced in those parts, that he walked very little out of his house. The next morning, being Sunday, he rose very early, and went to two or three churches; and when he returned, which was by eight of the clock, he told his wife and his son, 'that he had been to look out a place to be buried in, but found none against which he had not some exception, the cathedral only excepted: where he had made a choice of a place near a kinsman of his own name, and had shewed it to the sexton, whom he had sent for to that purpose; and wished them to see him buried there;' and this with as much composedness of mind as if it had made no impression of mind; then went to the cathedral to sermon, and spent the whole day in as cheerful conversation with his friends, (saving only the frequent interruptions his infirmity gave him once in two or three hours, sometimes more, sometimes less,) as the man in the most confirmed health could do. Monday was Michaelmas day, when in the morning he went to visit his brother sir Laurence Hyde, who was then making a journey in the service of the king, and from him went to the church to a sermon, where he found himself a little pressed as he used to be, and therefore thought fit to make what haste he could to his house, and was no sooner come thither into a lower room, than having made water, and the pain in his arm seizing upon him, he fell down dead, without the least motion of any limb. The suddenness of it made it apprehended to be an apoplexy; but there being nothing like convulsions, or the least distortion or alteration in the visage, it is not like to be from that cause; nor could the physicians make any reasonable guess from whence that mortal blow proceeded. He wanted about six weeks of attaining the age of seventy, and was the greatest instance of the felicity of a country life that was seen in that age; having enjoyed a competent, and to him a plentiful fortune, a very great reputation of piety and virtue, and his death being attended with universal lamentation. It cannot be expressed with what agony his son bore this loss, having, as he was used to say, 'not only lost the best father, but the best friend and the best companion he ever had or could have;' and he was never so well pleased, as when he had fit occasions given him to mention his father, whom he did in truth believe to be the wisest man he had ever known; and he was often heard to say, in the time when his condition was at highest, 'that though God Almighty had been very propitious to him, in raising him to great honours and preferments, he did not value any honour he had so much as the being the son of such a father and mother, for whose sakes principally he thought God had conferred those blessings upon him.' [*Life*, I, 13–17]

The death of his father marked, in Clarendon's memory, a very clear break
with the past, the beginning of a phase in which he applied himself with
more seriousness to his career (he was called to the bar in November 1633),
and became known to Archbishop Laud. Yet, while working hard, he
scorned the ordinary drudgery and connections of a legal career, and mixed
with London's literary and intellectual elite.

Whilst he was only a student of the law, and stood at gaze, and irresolute what course of life to take, his chief acquaintance were Ben Jonson, John Selden, Charles Cotton, John Vaughan, sir Kenelm Digby, Thomas May, and Thomas Carew, and some others of eminent faculties in their several ways. Ben Jonson's name can never be forgotten, having by his very good learning, and the severity of his nature and manners, very much reformed the stage; and indeed the English poetry itself. His natural advantages were, judgment to order and govern fancy, rather than excess of fancy, his productions being slow and upon deliberation, yet then abounding with great wit and fancy, and will live accordingly; and surely as he did exceedingly exalt the English language in eloquence, propriety, and masculine expressions, so he was the best judge of, and fittest to prescribe rules to poetry and poets, of any man, who had lived with, or before him, or since: if Mr Cowley* had not made a flight beyond all men, with that modesty yet, to ascribe much of this to the example and learning of Ben Jonson. His conversation was very good, and with the men of most note; and he had for many years an extraordinary kindness for Mr Hyde, till he found he betook himself to business, which he believed ought never to be preferred before his company. He lived to be very old, and till the palsy made a deep impression upon his body and his mind.

Mr Selden was a person whom no character can flatter, or transmit in any expressions equal to his merit and virtue. He was of so stupendous learning in all kinds and in all languages, (as may appear in his excellent and transcendent writings,) that a man would have thought he had been entirely conversant amongst books, and had never spent an hour but in reading and writing; yet his humanity, courtesy, and affability was such, that he would have been thought to have been bred in the best courts, but that his good nature, charity, and delight in doing good, and in communicating all he knew, exceeded that breeding. His style in all his writings seems harsh and sometimes obscure; which is not wholly to be imputed to the abstruse subjects of which he commonly treated, out of the paths trod by other men; but to a little undervaluing the beauty of a style, and too much propensity to the language of antiquity: but in his conversation he was the most clear discourser, and had the best faculty of making hard things easy, and presenting them to the understanding, of any man that hath been known. Mr Hyde was wont to say, that he valued himself upon nothing more than upon having had Mr Selden's acquaintance from the time he was very young; and held it with great delight as long as they were suffered to continue together in London; and he was very much troubled always when he heard him blamed, censured, and reproached, for staying in London, and in the parliament, after they were in rebellion, and in the worst times, which his age obliged him to do; and how wicked soever the actions were which were every day done, he was confident he had not given his consent to them; but would have hindered them if he could with his own safety, to which he was always enough indulgent. If he had some infirmities with other men, they were weighed down with wonderful and prodigious abilities and excellencies in the other scale.

Charles Cotton was a gentleman born to a competent fortune, and so qualified in his person and education, that for many years he continued the greatest ornament of the town, in the esteem of those who had been best bred. His natural parts were very great, his wit flowing in all the parts of conversation; the superstructure of learning not raised to a considerable height; but having passed some years in Cambridge, and then in France, and conversing always with learned men, his expressions were ever proper and significant, and gave great lustre to his discourse upon any argument; so that he was thought by those who were not intimate with him, to have been much better acquainted with books than he was. He had all those qualities which in youth raise men to the reputation of being fine gentlemen; such a pleasantness and gaiety of humour, such a sweetness and gentleness of nature, and such a civility and delightfulness in conversation, that no man in the court, or out of it, appeared a more accomplished person; all these extraordinary qualifications being supported by as extraordinary a clearness of courage and fearlessness of spirit, of which he gave too often manifestation. Some unhappy suits in law, and waste of his fortune in those suits, made some impression upon his mind; which being improved by domestic afflictions, and those indulgences to himself which naturally attend those afflictions, rendered his age less reverenced than his youth had been; and gave his best friends cause to have wished that he had not lived so long.

John Vaughan was then a student of the law in the Inner Temple, but at that time indulged more to the politer learning; and was in truth a man of great parts of nature, and very well adorned by arts and books, and so much cherished by Mr Selden, that he grew to be of entire trust and friendship with him, and to that owed the best part of his reputation: for he was of so magisterial and supercilious a humour, so proud and insolent a behaviour, that all Mr Selden's instructions, and authority, and example, could not file off that roughness of his nature, so as to make him very grateful. He looked most into those parts of the law which disposed him to least reverence to the crown, and most to popular authority; yet without inclination to any change in government; and therefore, before the beginning of the civil war, and when he clearly discerned the approaches to it in parliament, (of which he was a member,) he withdrew himself into the fastnesses of his own country, North Wales, where he enjoyed a secure, and as near an innocent life, as the iniquity that time would permit; and when the king returned, he appeared under the character of a man who had preserved his loyalty entire, and was esteemed accordingly by all that party.

His friend Mr Hyde, who was then become lord high chancellor of England, renewed his old kindness and friendship towards him, and was desirous to gratify him all the ways he could, and earnestly pressed him to put on his gown again, and take upon him the office of a judge; but he excused himself upon his long discontinuance, (having not worn his gown, and wholly discontinued the profession from the year 1640, full twenty years,) and upon his age, and expressly refused to receive any promotion; but continued all the professions of respect and gratitude imaginable to the chancellor, till it was in his power to manifest the contrary, to his prejudice, which he did with circumstances very uncommendable.

Sir Kenelm Digby was a person very eminent and notorious throughout the whole course of his life, from his cradle to his grave; of an ancient family and noble extraction; and inherited a fair and plentiful fortune, notwithstanding the attainder of his father. He was a man of a very extraordinary person and presence, which drew the eyes of all men upon him, which were more fixed by a wonderful graceful behaviour, a flowing courtesy and civility, and such a volubility of language, as surprised and delighted; and though in another man it might have appeared to have somewhat of affectation, it was marvellous graceful in him, and seemed natural to his size, and mould of his person, to the gravity of his motion, and the tune of his voice and delivery. He had a fair reputation in arms, of which he gave an early testimony in his youth, in some encounters in Spain and Italy, and afterwards in an action in the Mediterranean sea, where he had the command of a squadron of ships of war, set out at his own charge under the king's commission; with which, upon an injury received, or apprehended from the Venetians, he encountered their whole fleet, killed many of their men, and sunk one of their galleasses; which in that drowsy and unactive time was looked upon with a general estimation, though the crown disavowed it. In a word, he had all the advantages that nature, and art, and an excellent education could give him; which, with a great confidence and presentness of mind, buoyed him up against all those prejudices and disadvantages, (which the attainder and execution of his father, for a crime of the highest nature; his own marriage with a lady, though of an extraordinary beauty, of as extraordinary a fame; his changing and rechanging his religion; and some personal vices and licenses in his life,) which would have suppressed and sunk any other man, but never clouded or eclipsed him, from appearing in the best places, and the best company, and with the best estimation and satisfaction.

Thomas May was the eldest son of his father, a knight, and born to a fortune, if his father had not spent it; so that he had only an annuity left him, not proportionable to a liberal education: yet since his fortune could not raise his mind, he brought his mind down to his fortune, by a great modesty and humility in his nature, which was not affected, but very well became an imperfection in his speech, which was a great mortification to him, and kept him from entering upon any discourse but in the company of his very friends. His parts of nature and art were very good, as appears by his translation of Lucan, (none of the easiest work of that kind,) and more by his supplement to Lucan, which being entirely his own, for the learning, the wit, and the language, may be well looked upon as one of the best dramatic poems in the English language. He writ some other commendable pieces, of the reign of some of our kings. He was cherished by many persons of honour, and very acceptable in all places; yet, (to shew that pride and envy have their influences upon the narrowest minds, and which have the greatest semblance of humility,) though he had received much countenance, and a very considerable donative from the king, upon his majesty's refusing to give him a small pension, which he had designed and promised to another very ingenious person, whose qualities he thought inferior to his own, he fell from his duty, and all his former friends, and prostituted himself to the vile office of celebrating the infamous acts of those who were in rebellion against the king; which he did so meanly, that he seemed to all men to have lost his wits when he left his honesty; and so shortly after died miserable and neglected, and deserves to be forgotten.

Thomas Carew was a younger brother of a good family, and of excellent parts, and had spent many years of his youth in France and Italy; and returning from travel, followed the court; which the modesty of that time disposed men to do some time, before they pretended to be of it; and he was very much esteemed by the most eminent persons in the court, and well looked upon by the king himself, some years before he could obtain to be sewer to the king;* and when the king conferred that honour upon him, it was not without the regret even of the whole Scotch nation, which united themselves in recommending another gentleman to the place: of so great value were those relations held in that age, when majesty was beheld with the reverence it ought to be. He was a person of a pleasant and facetious wit, and made many poems, (especially in the amorous way,) which for the sharpness of the fancy, and the elegancy of the language in which that fancy was spread, were at least equal, if not superior to any of that time; but his glory was, that after fifty years of his life, spent with less severity or exactness than it ought to have been, he died with the greatest remorse for that license, and with the greatest manifestation of Christianity that his best friends could desire. [*Life*, I, 26–33]

19. Great Tew

Despite his wide acquaintance in the literary circles of 1630s London, his closest friendship was with Lucius Cary, Viscount Falkland.

AMONG these persons Mr Hyde's usual time of conversation was spent, till he grew more retired to his more serious studies, and never discontinued his acquaintance with any of them, though he spent less time in their company; only upon Mr Selden he looked with so much affection and reverence, that he always thought himself best when he was with him: but he had then another conjunction and communication that he took so much delight in, that he embraced it in the time of his greatest business and practice, and would suffer no other pretence or obligation to withdraw him from that familiarity and friendship; and took frequent occasions to mention their names with great pleasure; being often heard to say, 'that if he had any thing good in him, in his humour, or in his manners, he owed it to the example, and the information he had received in, and from that company, with most of whom he had an entire friendship.' And they were in truth, in their several qualifications, men of more than ordinary eminence, before they attained the great preferments many of them lived to enjoy. The persons were, sir Lucius Cary, eldest son to the lord viscount Falkland, lord deputy of Ireland; sir Francis Wenman of Oxfordshire; Sidney Godolphin of Godolphin in Cornwall; Edmund Waller of Beaconsfield; Dr Gilbert Sheldon; Dr George Morley; Dr John Earle; Mr John Hales of Eton; and Mr William Chillingworth.

With sir Lucius Cary he had a most entire friendship without reserve, from his age of twenty years to the hour of his death, near twenty years after:* upon which there will be occasion to enlarge when we come to speak of that time and often before, and therefore we shall say no more of him in this place, than to shew his condition and qualifications, which were the first ingredients into that friendship, which was afterwards cultivated and improved by a constant conversation and familiarity, and by many accidents which contributed thereto. He had the advantage of a noble extraction, and of being born his father's eldest son, when there was a greater fortune in prospect to be inherited, (besides what he might reasonably expect by his mother,) than came afterwards to his possession. His education was equal to his birth, at least in the care, if not in the climate; for his father being deputy of

Ireland, before he was of age fit to be sent abroad, his breeding was in the court, and in the university of Dublin; but under the care, vigilance, and direction of such governors and tutors, that he learned all those exercises and languages, better than most men do in more celebrated places; insomuch as when he came into England, which was when he was about the age of eighteen years, he was not only master of the Latin tongue, and had read all the poets, and other of the best authors with notable judgment for that age, but he understood, and spake, and wrote French, as if he had spent many years in France.

He had another advantage, which was a great ornament to the rest, that was, a good, a plentiful estate, of which he had the early possession. His mother was the sole daughter and heir of the lord chief baron Tanfield, who having given a fair portion with his daughter in marriage, had kept himself free to dispose of his land, and his other estate, in such manner as he should think fit; and he settled it in such manner upon his grandson sir Lucius Cary, without taking notice of his father, or mother, that upon his grandmother's death, which fell out about the time that he was nineteen years of age, all the land, with two very excellent houses* excellently well furnished, (worth above 2000*l.* per annum,) in a most pleasant country, and the two most pleasant places in that country, with a very plentiful personal estate, fell into his hands and possession, and to his entire disposal.

With these advantages, he had one great disadvantage (which in the first entrance into the world is attended with too much prejudice) in his person and presence, which was in no degree attractive or promising. His stature was low, and smaller than most men; his motion not graceful; and his aspect so far from inviting, that it had somewhat in it of simplicity; and his voice the worst of the three, and so untuned, that instead of reconciling, it offended the ear, so that nobody would have expected music from that tongue; and sure no man was less beholden to nature for its recommendation into the world: but then no man sooner or more disappointed this general and customary prejudice; that little person and small stature was quickly found to contain a great heart, a courage so keen, and a nature so fearless, that no composition of the strongest limbs, and most harmonious and proportioned presence and strength, ever more disposed any man to the greatest enterprise; it being his greatest weakness to be too solicitous for such adventures: and that untuned tongue and voice easily discovered itself to be supplied and governed by a mind and understanding so excellent, that the wit and weight of all he said carried another kind of lustre and admiration in it, and even another kind of acceptation from the persons present, than any ornament of delivery could reasonably promise itself, or is usually attended with; and his disposition and nature was so gentle and obliging, so much delighted in courtesy, kindness, and generosity, that all mankind could not but admire and love him.

In a short time after he had possession of the estate his grandfather had left him, and before he was of age, he committed a fault against his father, in marrying a young lady,* whom he passionately loved, without any considerable portion, which exceedingly offended him; and disappointed all his reasonable hopes and expectation of redeeming and repairing his own broken fortune, and desperate hopes in court, by some advantageous marriage of his son; about which he had then some probable treaty. Sir Lucius Cary was very conscious to himself of his offence and transgression, and the consequence of it, which though he could not repent, having married a lady of a most extraordinary wit and judgment, and of the most signal virtue and exemplary life, that the age produced, and who brought him many hopeful children, in which he took great delight; yet he confessed it, with the most sincere and dutiful applications to his father for his pardon that could be made; and in order to the prejudice he had brought upon his fortune, by bringing no portion to him, he offered to repair it, by resigning his whole estate to his disposal, and to rely wholly upon his kindness for his own maintenance and support; and to that purpose, he had caused conveyances to be drawn by counsel, which he brought ready engrossed to his father, and was willing to seal and execute them, that they might be valid: but his father's passion and indignation so far transported him, (though he was a gentleman of excellent parts,) that he refused any reconciliation, and rejected all the offers that were made him of the estate; so that his son remained still in the possession of his estate against his will; for which he found great reason afterwards to rejoice: but he was for the present so much afflicted with his father's displeasure, that he transported himself and his wife into Holland, resolving to buy some military command, and to spend the remainder of his life in that profession: but being disappointed in the treaty he expected, and finding no opportunity to accommodate himself with such a command, he returned again into England; resolving to retire to a country life, and to his books; that since he was not like to improve himself in arms, he might advance in letters.

In this resolution he was so severe, (as he was always naturally very intent upon what he was inclined to,) that he declared, he would not see London in many years, which was the place he loved of all the world;

and that in his studies, he would first apply himself to the Greek, and pursue it without intermission, till he should attain to the full understanding of that tongue: and it is hardly to be credited, what industry he used, and what success attended that industry: for though his father's death, by an unhappy accident, made his repair to London absolutely necessary in fewer years than he had proposed for his absence, yet he had first made himself master of the Greek tongue, (in the Latin he was very well versed before,) and had read not only all the Greek historians, but Homer likewise, and such of the poets as were worthy to be perused.

Though his father's death brought no other convenience to him, but a title to redeem an estate, mortgaged for as much as it was worth, and for which he was compelled to sell a finer seat of his own; yet it imposed a burden upon him, of the title of a viscount, and an increase of expense, in which he was not in his nature too provident or restrained; having naturally such a generosity and bounty in him, that he seemed to have his estate in trust for all worthy persons who stood in want of supplies and encouragement, as Ben Jonson, and many others of that time, whose fortunes required, and whose spirits made them superior to, ordinary obligations; which yet they were contented to receive from him, because his bounties were so generously distributed, and so much without vanity and ostentation, that, except from those few persons from whom he sometimes received the characters of fit objects for his benefits, or whom he entrusted, for the more secret deriving them to them, he did all he could, that the persons themselves who received them should not know from what fountain they flowed; and when that could not be concealed, he sustained any acknowledgment from the persons obliged with so much trouble and bashfulness, that they might well perceive, that he was even ashamed of the little he had given, and to receive so large a recompense for it.

As soon as he had finished all those transactions, which the death of his father had made necessary to be done, he retired again to his country life, and to his severe course of study, which was very delightful to him, as soon as he was engaged in it: but he was wont to say, that he never found reluctancy in any thing he resolved to do, but in his quitting London, and departing from the conversation of those he enjoyed there; which was in some degree preserved and continued by frequent letters, and often visits, which were made by his friends from thence, whilst he continued wedded to the country; and which were so grateful to him, that during their stay with him, he looked upon no book, except their very conversation made an appeal to some book; and truly his whole conversation was one continued *convivium philosophicum*, or *convivium theologicum*, enlivened and refreshed with all the facetiousness of wit, and good humour, and pleasantness of discourse, which made the gravity of the argument itself (whatever it was) very delectable. His house where he usually resided, (Tew, or Burford, in Oxfordshire), being within ten or twelve miles of the university, looked like the university itself, by the company that was always found there. There were Dr Sheldon, Dr Morley, Dr Hammond, Dr Earle, Mr Chillingworth, and indeed all men of eminent parts and faculties in Oxford, besides those who resorted thither from London; who all found their lodgings there, as ready as in the colleges; nor did the lord of the house know of their coming or going, nor who were in his house, till he came to dinner, or supper, where all still met; otherwise, there was no troublesome ceremony or constraint, to forbid men to come to the house, or to make them weary of staying there; so that many came thither to study in a better air, finding all the books they could desire in his library, and all the persons together, whose company they could wish, and not find in any other society. Here Mr Chillingworth wrote, and formed, and modelled, his excellent book* against the learned Jesuit Mr Knott, after frequent debates upon the most important particulars; in many of which, he suffered himself to be overruled by the judgment of his friends, though in others he still adhered to his own fancy, which was sceptical enough, even in the highest points.

In this happy and delightful conversation and restraint, he remained in the country many years; and until he had made so prodigious a progress in learning, that there were very few classic authors in the Greek or Latin tongue that he had not read with great exactness. He had read all the Greek and Latin fathers; all the most allowed and authentic ecclesiastical writers; and all the councils, with wonderful care and observation; for in religion he thought too careful and too curious an inquiry could not be made, amongst those, whose purity was not questioned, and whose authority was constantly and confidently urged, by men who were furthest from being of one mind amongst themselves: and for the mutual support of their several opinions, in which they most contradicted each other; and in all those controversies, he had so dispassioned a consideration, such a candour in his nature, and so profound a charity in his conscience, that in those points, in which he was in his own judgment most clear, he never thought the worse, or in any degree declined the familiarity, of those who were of another mind; which, without question, is an excellent temper for the propagation and advancement of Christianity. With these great advantages of industry, he had a memory retentive of all that he had ever read, and an understanding and judgment to apply it seasonably and appositely, with the most dexterity and address, and the least pedantry and affectation, that ever man, who knew so much, was possessed with, of what quality soever. It is not a trivial evidence of his learning, his wit, and his candour, that may be found in that discourse of his, against the infallibility of the church of Rome, published since his death,* and from a copy under his own hand, though not prepared and digested by him for the press, and to which he would have given some castigations.

But all his parts, abilities, and faculties, by art and industry, were not to be valued, or mentioned, in comparison of his most accomplished mind and manners: his gentleness and affability was so transcendent and obliging, that it drew reverence, and some kind of compliance, from the roughest, and most unpolished, and stubborn constitutions; and made them of another temper in debate, in his presence, than they were in other places. He was in his nature so severe a lover of justice, and so precise a lover of truth, that he was superior to all possible temptations for the violation of either; indeed so rigid an exacter of perfection, in all those things which seemed but to border upon either of them, and by the common practice of men were not thought to border upon either, that many who knew him very well, and loved and admired his virtue, (as all who did know him must love and admire it,) did believe that he was of a temper and composition fitter to live in *republica Platonis*, than in *faece Romuli*:* but this rigidness was only exercised towards himself; towards his friends' infirmities no man was more indulgent. In his conversation, which was the most cheerful and pleasant that can be imagined, though he was young, (for all I have yet spoken of him doth not exceed his age of twenty-five or twenty-six years: what progress he made afterwards will be mentioned in its proper season in this discourse,) and of great gaiety in his humour, with a flowing delightfulness of language, he had so chaste a tongue and ear, that there was never known a profane or loose word to fall from him, nor in truth in his company; the integrity and cleanliness of the wit of that time not exercising itself in that license before persons for whom they had any esteem.

Sir Francis Wenman would not look upon himself under any other character than that of a country gentleman, though no man of his quality in England was more esteemed in court. He was of a noble extraction, and of an ancient family in Oxfordshire, where he was possessed of a competent estate; but his reputation of wisdom and integrity gave him an interest and credit in that country much above his fortune; and no man had more esteem in it or power over it. He was a neighbour to the lord Falkland, and in so entire friendship and confidence with him, that he had great authority in the society of all his friends and acquaintance. He was a man of great sharpness of understanding, and of a piercing judgment; no man better understood the affections and temper of the kingdom, or indeed the nature of the nation, or discerned further the consequence of counsels, and with what success they were like to be attended. He was a very good Latin scholar, but his ratiocination was above his learning; and the sharpness of his wit incomparable. He was equal to the greatest trust and employment, if he had been ambitious of it, or solicitous for it; but his want of health produced a kind of laziness of mind, which disinclined him to business, and he died a little before the general troubles of the kingdom, which he foresaw with wonderful reluctancy, and when many wise men were weary of living so long.

Sidney Godolphin was a younger brother of Godolphin, out by the provision left by his father, and by the death of a younger brother, liberally supplied for a very good education, and for a cheerful subsistence, in any course of life he proposed to himself. There was never so great a mind and spirit contained in so little room; so large an understanding and so unrestrained a fancy in so very small a body; so that the lord Falkland used to say merrily, that he thought it was a great ingredient into his friendship for Mr Godolphin, that he was pleased to be found in his company, where he was the properer man; and it may be, the very remarkableness of his little person made the sharpness of his wit, and the composed quickness of his judgment and understanding, the more notorious and notable. He had spent some years in France, and in the Low Countries; and accompanied the earl of Leicester in his ambassage into Denmark, before he resolved to be quiet, and attend some promotion in the court; where his excellent disposition and manners, and extraordinary qualifications, made him very acceptable. Though every body loved his company very well, yet he loved very much to be alone, being in his constitution inclined somewhat to melancholy, and to retirement amongst his books; and was so far from being active, that he was contented to be reproached by his friends with laziness; and was of so nice and tender a composition, that a little rain or wind would disorder him, and divert him from any short journey he had most willingly proposed to himself; insomuch as, when he rid abroad with those in whose company he most delighted, if the wind chanced to be in his face, he would (after a little pleasant murmuring) suddenly turn his horse, and go home. Yet the civil war no sooner began, (the first approaches towards which he discovered as soon as any man, by the proceedings in parliament, where he was a member, and opposed with great indignation,) than he put himself into the first troops which were raised in the west for the king; and bore the uneasiness and fatigue of winter marches with an exemplar courage and alacrity; until by too brave a pursuit of the enemy, into an obscure village in Devonshire, he was shot with a musket; with which (without saying any word more, than, Oh God! I am hurt) he fell dead from his horse; to the excessive grief of his friends, who were all that knew him; and the irreparable damage of the public.

Edmund Waller was born to a very fair estate, by the parsimony or frugality of a wise father and mother; and he thought it so commendable an advantage, that he resolved to improve it with his utmost care, upon which in his nature he was too much intent; and in order to that, he was so much reserved and retired, that he was scarce ever heard of, till by his address and dexterity he had gotten a very rich wife in the city, against all the recommendation, and countenance, and authority of the court, which was thoroughly engaged on the behalf of Mr Crofts; and which used to be successful, in that age, against any opposition. He had the good fortune to have an alliance and friendship with Dr Morley, who had assisted and instructed him in the reading many good books, to which his natural parts and promptitude inclined him; especially the poets: and at the age when other men used to give over writing verses, (for he was near thirty years of age when he first engaged himself in that exercise, at least that he was known to do so,) he surprised the town with two or three pieces of that kind; as if a tenth muse had been newly born, to cherish drooping poetry. The doctor at that time brought him into that company which was most celebrated for good conversation; where he was received, and esteemed, with great applause and respect. He was a very pleasant discourser, in earnest and in jest, and therefore very grateful to all kind of company, where he was not the less esteemed for being very rich.

He had been even nursed in parliaments, where he sat when he was in his infancy; and so when they were resumed again, (after a long intermission and interdiction,) he appeared in those assemblies with great advantage, having a graceful way of speaking; and by thinking much upon several arguments, (which his temper and complexion, that had much of melancholic, inclined him to,) he seemed often to speak upon the sudden, when the occasion had only administered the opportunity of saying what he had thoroughly considered, which gave a great lustre to all he said; which yet was rather of delight than weight. There needs no more be said to extol the excellence and power of his wit, and pleasantness of his conversation, than that it was of magnitude enough to cover a world of very great faults; that is, so to cover them, that they were not taken notice of to his reproach; viz. a narrowness in his nature to the lowest degree; an abjectness, and want of courage to support him in any virtuous undertaking; an insinuation and servile flattery to the height the vainest and most imperious nature could be contented with; that it preserved and won his life from those who were most resolved to take it, and in an occasion in which he ought to have been ambitious to have lost it; and then preserved him again, from the reproach and contempt that was due to him for so preserving it, and for vindicating it at such a price; that it had power to reconcile him to those whom he had most offended and provoked; and continued to his age with that rare felicity, that his company was acceptable, where his spirit was odious; and he was at least pitied, where he was most detested.

Of Doctor Sheldon, there needs no more be said in this place, (there being frequent occasions to mention him hereafter in the prosecution of this discourse,) than that his learning, and gravity, and prudence, had in that time raised him to such a reputation, when he was chaplain in the house to the lord keeper Coventry, (who exceedingly esteemed him, and used his service not only in all matters relating to the church, but in many other businesses of importance, and in which that great and good lord was nearly concerned,) and when he was afterwards warden of All Souls' college in Oxford, that he then was looked upon as very equal to any preferment the church could [yield] or hath since yielded unto him; and sir Francis Wenman would often say, when the doctor resorted to the conversation at the lord Falkland's house, as he frequently did, that 'Dr Sheldon was born and bred to be archbishop of Canterbury.'

Doctor Morley (of whom more must likewise be said in its place) was a gentleman of very eminent parts in all polite learning; of great wit, and readiness, and subtilty in disputation; and of remarkable temper and prudence in conversation, which rendered him most grateful in all the best company. He was then chaplain in the house, and to the family, of the lord and lady Carnarvon, which needed a wise and a wary director.* From some academic contests he had been engaged in, during his living in Christ Church in Oxford, where he was always of the first eminency, he had, by the natural faction and animosity of those disputes, fallen under the reproach of holding some opinions which were not then grateful to those churchmen who had the greatest power in ecclesiastical promotions; and some sharp answers and replies he used to make in accidental discourses, and which in truth were made for mirth and pleasantness' sake, (as he was of the highest facetiousness,) were reported, and spread abroad to his prejudice: as being once asked by a grave country gentleman, (who was desirous to be instructed what their tenets and opinions were,) 'what the Arminians* held,' he pleasantly answered, that *they held all the best bishoprics and deaneries in England*; which was quickly reported abroad, as Mr Morley's definition of the Arminian tenets.

Such and the like harmless and jocular sayings, upon many accidental occasions, had wrought upon the archbishop of Canterbury, Laud, (who lived to change his mind, and to have a just esteem of him,) to entertain some prejudice towards him; and the respect which was paid him by many eminent persons, as John Hampden, Arthur Goodwin,* and others, who were not thought friends to the prosperity the church was in, made others apprehend that he was not enough zealous for it. But that disaffection and virulency (which few men had then owned and discovered) no sooner appeared, in those and other men, but Dr Morley made haste as publicly to oppose them, both in private and in public; which had the more effect to the benefit of the church, by his being a person above all possible reproach, and known and valued by more persons of honour than most of the clergy were, and being not only without the envy of any preferment, but under the advantage of a discountenanced person. And as he was afterwards the late king's chaplain, and much regarded by him, and as long about him as any of his chaplains were permitted to attend him; so presently after his murder he left the kingdom, and remained in banishment till his majesty's happy return.

Doctor Earle was at that time chaplain in the house to the earl of Pembroke, lord chamberlain of his majesty's household, and had a lodging in the court under that relation. He was a person very notable for his elegance in the Greek and Latin tongues; and being fellow of Merton college in Oxford, and having been proctor of the university, and some very witty and sharp discourses being published in print without his consent, though known to be his, he grew suddenly into a very general esteem with all men; being a man of great piety and devotion; a most eloquent and powerful preacher; and of a conversation so pleasant and delightful, so very innocent and so very facetious, that no man's company was more desired and more loved. No man was more negligent in his dress, and habit, and mien; no man more wary and cultivated in his behaviour and discourse; insomuch as he had the greater advantage when he was known, by promising so little before he was known. He was an excellent poet, both in Latin, Greek, and English, as appears by many pieces yet abroad; though he suppressed many more himself, especially of English, incomparably good, out of an austerity to those sallies of his youth. He was very dear to the lord Falkland, with whom he spent as much time as he could make his own; and as that lord would impute the speedy progress he made in the Greek tongue, to the information and assistance he had from Mr Earle, so Mr Earle would frequently profess, that he had got more useful learning by his conversation at Tew, (the lord Falkland's house,) than he had at Oxford. In the first settling of the prince's family, he was made one of his chaplains; and attended on him when he was forced to leave the kingdom, and therefore we shall often have occasion to mention him hereafter. He was amongst the few excellent men who never had nor ever could have an enemy, but such a one who was an enemy to all learning and virtue, and therefore would never make himself known.

Mr John Hales had been Greek professor in the university of Oxford; and had borne all the labour of that excellent edition and impression of St Chrysostom's Works, set out by sir Harry Saville; who was then warden of Merton college, when the other was fellow of that house. He was chaplain in the house with sir Dudley Carleton, ambassador at the Hague in Holland, at the time when the synod of Dort* was held, and so had liberty to be present at the consultations in that assembly; and hath left the best memorial behind him, of the ignorance, and passion, and animosity, and injustice of that convention; of which he often made very pleasant relations; though at that time it received too much countenance from England. Being a person of the greatest eminency for learning, and other abilities, from which he might have promised himself any preferment in the church, he withdrew himself from all pursuits of that kind into a private fellowship in the college of Eton, where his friend sir Harry Saville was provost; where he lived amongst his books, and the most separated from the world of any man then living: though he was not in the least degree inclined to melancholy, but, on the contrary, of a very open and pleasant conversation; and therefore was very well pleased with the resort of his friends to him, who were such as he had chosen, and in whose company he delighted, and for whose sake he would sometimes, once in a year, resort to London, only to enjoy their cheerful conversation.

He would never take any cure of souls; and was so great a contemner of money, that he was wont to say, that his fellowship, and the bursar's place, (which, for the good of the college, he held many years,) was worth him fifty pounds a year more than he could spend; and yet, besides his being very charitable to all poor people, even to liberality, he had made a greater and better collection of books, than were to be found in any other private library that I have seen; as he had sure read more, and carried more about him in his excellent memory, than any man I ever knew, my lord Falkland only excepted, who I think sided him. He had, whether from his natural temper and constitution, or from his long retirement from all crowds, or from his profound judgment and discerning spirit, contracted some opinions which were not received, nor by him published, except in private discourses; and then rather upon occasion of dispute, than of positive opinion: and he would often say, his opinions he was sure did him no harm, but he was far from being confident that they might not do others harm who entertained them, and might entertain other results from them than he did; and therefore he was very reserved in communicating what he thought himself in those points, in which he differed from what was received.

Nothing troubled him more than the brawls which were grown from religion; and he therefore exceedingly detested the tyranny of the church of Rome; more for their imposing uncharitably upon the consciences of other men, than for the errors in their own opinions: and would often say, that he would renounce the religion of the church of England tomorrow, if it obliged him to believe that any other Christians should be damned; and that nobody would conclude another man to be damned, who did not wish him so. No man more strict and severe to himself; to other men so charitable as to their opinions, that he thought that other men were more in fault for their carriage towards them, than the men themselves were who erred; and he thought that pride and passion, more than conscience, were the cause of all separation from each other's communion; and he frequently said, that that only kept the world from agreeing upon such a liturgy, as might bring them into one communion; all doctrinal points, upon which men differed in their opinions, being to have no place in any liturgy. Upon an occasional discourse with a friend, of the frequent and uncharitable reproaches of heretic and schismatic, too lightly thrown at each other, amongst men who differ in their judgment, he writ a little discourse of schism, contained in less than two sheets of paper; which being transmitted from friend to friend in writing, was at last, without any malice, brought to the view of the archbishop of Canterbury, Dr Laud, who was a very rigid surveyor of all things which never so little bordered upon schism; and thought the church could not be too vigilant against, and jealous of, such incursions.

He sent for Mr Hales, whom, when they had both lived in the university of Oxford, he had known well; and told him, that he had in truth believed him to be long since dead; and chid him very kindly for having never come to him, having been of his old acquaintance: then asked him, whether he had lately written a short discourse of schism, and whether he was of that opinion which that discourse implied. He told him that he had, for the satisfaction of a private friend, (who was not of his mind) a year or two before, writ such a small tract, without any imagination that it would be communicated; and that he believed it did not contain any thing that was not agreeable to the judgment of the primitive fathers: upon which, the archbishop debated with him upon some expressions of Irenaeus and the most ancient fathers; and concluded with saying, that the time was very apt to set new doctrines on foot, of which the wits of the age were too susceptible and that there could not be too much care taken to preserve the peace and unity of the church; and from thence asked him to his condition, and whether he wanted anything: and the other answering, that he had enough and wanted or desired no addition, so dismissed him with great courtesy; and shortly after sent for him again, when there was a prebendary of Windsor fallen, and told him, the king had given him the preferment, because it lay so convenient to his fellowship of Eton; which (though indeed the most convenient preferment that could be thought of for him) the archbishop could not without great difficulty persuade him to accept, and he did accept it rather to please himself; because he really believed he had enough before. He was one of the least men in the kingdom; and one of the greatest scholars in Europe.

Mr Chillingworth was of a stature little superior to Mr Hales, (and it was an age in which there were many great and wonderful men of that size,) and a man of so great a subtilty of understanding, and so rare a temper in debate, that, as it was impossible to provoke him into any passion, so it was very difficult to keep a man's self from being a little discomposed by his sharpness and quickness of argument, and instances, in which he had a rare facility, and a great advantage over all the men I ever knew. He had spent all his younger time in disputation, and had arrived to so great a mastery, as he was inferior to no man in those skirmishes: but he had, with his notable perfection in this exercise, contracted such an irresolution and habit of doubting, that by degrees he grew confident of nothing, and a sceptic, at least, in the greatest mysteries of faith.

This made him, from first wavering in religion, and indulging to scruples, to reconcile himself too soon and too easily to the church of Rome; and carrying still his own inquisitiveness about him, without any resignation to their authority, (which is the only temper can make that church sure of its proselytes,) having made a journey to St Omer's,* purely to perfect his conversion by the conversation of those who had the greatest name, he found as little satisfaction there; and returned with as much haste from them; with a belief, that an entire exemption from error was neither inherent in nor necessary to any church: which occasioned that war, which was carried on by the Jesuits with so great asperity and reproaches against him, and in which he defended himself by such an admirable eloquence of language, and clear and incomparable power of reason, that he not only made them appear unequal adversaries, but carried the war into their own quarters; and made the pope's infallibility to be as much shaken, and declined by their own doctors, (and as great an acrimony amongst themselves upon that subject,) and to be at least as much doubted, as in the schools of the reformed or protestant; and forced them since to defend and maintain those unhappy controversies in religion, with arms and weapons of another nature than were used or known in the church of Rome when Bellarmine died;* and which probably will in time undermine the very foundation that supports it.

Such a levity, and propensity to change, is commonly attended with great infirmities in, and no less reproach and prejudice to the person; but the sincerity of his heart was so conspicuous, and without the least temptation of any corrupt end; and the innocence and candour of his nature so evident, and without any perverseness; that all who knew him clearly discerned, that all those restless motions and fluctuations proceeded only from the warmth and jealousy of his own thoughts, in a too nice inquisition for truth. Neither the books of the adversary, nor any of their persons, though he was acquainted with the best of both, had ever made great impression upon him; all his doubts grew out of himself, when he assisted his scruples with all the strength of his own reason, and was then too hard for himself; but finding as little quiet and repose in those victories, he quickly recovered, by a new appeal to his own judgment; so that he was, in truth, upon the matter, in all his sallies and retreats, his own convert; though he was not so totally divested of all thoughts of this world, but that when he was ready for it, he admitted some great and considerable churchmen to be sharers with him in his public conversion.

Whilst he was in perplexity, or rather some passionate disinclination to the religion he had been educated in, he had the misfortune to have much acquaintance with one Mr Lewgar, a minister of that church; a man of a competency of learning in those points most controverted with the Romanists, but of no acute parts of wit or judgment; and wrought so far upon him, by weakening and enervating those arguments, by which he found he was governed, (as he had all the logic, and all the rhetoric, that was necessary to persuade very powerfully men of the greatest talents,) that the poor man, not able to live long in doubt, too hastily deserted his own church, and betook himself to the Roman: nor could all the arguments and reasons of Mr Chillingworth make him pause in the expedition he was using, or reduce him from that church after he had given himself to it; but he had always a great animosity against him, for having (as he said) unkindly betrayed him, and carried him into another religion, and there left him. So unfit are some constitutions to be troubled with doubts after they are once fixed.

He did really believe all war to be unlawful; and did not think that the parliament (whose proceedings he perfectly abhorred) did in truth intend to involve the nation in a civil war, till after the battle of Edgehill; and then he thought any expedient or stratagem that was like to put a speedy end to it, to be the most commendable: and so having too mathematically conceived an engine, that should move so lightly as to be a breastwork in all encounters and assaults in the field, he carried it, to make the experiment, into that part of his majesty's army, which was only in that winter season in the field, under the command of the lord Hopton, in Hampshire, upon the borders of Sussex; where he was shut up in the castle of Arundel; which was forced, after a short, sharp siege, to yield for want of victual; and poor Mr Chillingworth with it, falling into the rebels' hands; and being most barbarously treated by them, especially by that clergy which followed them; and being broken with sickness, contracted by the ill accommodation, and want of meat and fire during the siege, which was in a terrible season of frost and snow, he died shortly after in prison. He was a man of excellent parts and of a cheerful disposition; void of all kind of vice, and endued with many notable virtues; of a very public heart, and an indefatigable desire to do good; his only unhappiness proceeded from his sleeping too little, and thinking too much; which sometimes threw him into violent fevers.

This was Mr Hyde's company and conversation, to which he dedicated his vacant times, and all that time which he could make vacant, from the business of his profession; which he indulged with no more passion than was necessary to keep up the reputation of a man that had no purpose to be idle; which indeed he perfectly abhorred: and he took always occasion to celebrate the time he had spent in that conversation with great satisfaction and delight. Nor was he less fortunate in the acquaintance and friendships which he made with the persons in his profession; who were all eminent men, or of the most hopeful parts; who being all much superior to him in age and experience, and entirely devoted to their profession, were yet well pleased with the gaiety of his humour, and inoffensive and winning behaviour; and this good inclination of theirs was improved by the interest they saw he had in persons of the best quality, to whom he was very acceptable, and his condition of living, which was with more splendour than young lawyers were accustomed to.

Those persons were, Mr Lane, who was then attorney to the prince of Wales, and afterwards lord chief baron of the exchequer, and lastly, upon the death of the lord Littleton, was made keeper of the great seal, who died in banishment, and of whom we shall say more hereafter; Mr Geoffrey Palmer, afterwards attorney general, who will likewise have another part in this story; Mr John Maynard; and Bulstrode Whitelocke; all men of eminent parts, and great learning out of their professions; and in their professions, of signal reputation: and though the two last did afterwards bow their knees to Baal,* and so swerved from their allegiance, it was with less rancour and malice than other men: they never led, but followed; and were rather carried away with the torrent, than swam with the stream; and failed through those infirmities which less than a general defection and a prosperous rebellion could never have discovered. With these, and very few other persons of other societies, and of more than ordinary parts in the profession, he conversed. In business and in practice, with the rest of the profession, he had at most a formal acquaintance, and little familiarity; very seldom using, when his practice was at highest, so much as to eat in the hall,* without which no man ever got the reputation of a good student: but he ever gave his time of eating to his friends; and was wont pleasantly to say, 'that he repaired himself with very good company at dinner, for the ill company he had kept in the morning;' and made himself amends for the time he lost with his friends, by declining suppers, and with a part of that time which was allowed for sleep: but he grew every day more intent on business and more engaged in practice, so that he could not assign so much time as he had used to do to his beloved conversation.

The countenance he received from the archbishop of Canterbury, who took all occasion to mention him as a person he had kindness for; the favour of the lord Coventry, manifested as often as he came before him; the reception he found with the lord privy seal, the earl of Manchester, who had raised the court of requests to as much business as the chancery itself was possessed of, and where he was looked upon as a favourite; the familiarity used towards him by the earl of Pembroke, who was lord chamberlain of the king's house, and a greater man in the country than the court; by the earl of Holland, and many other lords and ladies, and other persons of interest in the court, made him looked upon by the judges in Westminster hall with much condescension; and they, who before he put on his gown looked upon him as one who designed some other course of life, (for though he had been always very punctual in the performance of all those public exercises the profession obliged him to, both before and after he was called to the bar; yet in all other respects he lived as if he thought himself above that course of life,) now when they no sooner saw him put on his gown, but that he was suddenly in practice, and taken notice of particularly in all courts of justice with unusual countenance, thought he would make what progress he desired in that profession.

As he had those many friends in court, so he was not less acceptable to many great persons in the country, who least regarded the court, and were least esteemed by it; and he had that rare felicity, that even they who did not love many of those upon whom he most depended were yet very well pleased with him and with his company. The earl of Hertford and the earl of Essex, whose interests and friendships were then the same, and who were looked upon with reverence by all who had not reverence for the court; and even by all in the court who were not satisfied there, (which was, and always will be, a great people,) were very kind to him, and ready to trust him in any thing that was most secret: and though he could not dispose the archbishop or the earl of Essex* to any correspondence or good intelligence with each other, which he exceedingly laboured to do, and found an equal aversion in both towards each other; yet he succeeded to his wish in bringing the archbishop and the earl of Hertford to a very good acquaintance and inclination to each other; which they both often acknowledged kindly to him, and with which the earl of Essex was as much unsatisfied. . . .

Under this universal acquaintance and general acceptation, Mr Hyde led for many years as cheerful and pleasant a life as any man did enjoy, as long as the kingdom took any pleasure in itself. His practice grew every day as much as he wished, and would have been much more, if he had wished it; by which, he not only supported his expense, greater much than men of his rank and pretences used to make, but increased his estate by some convenient purchases of land adjoining to his other; and he grew so much in love with business and practice, that he gave up his whole heart to it; resolving, by a course of severe study, to recover the time he had lost upon less profitable learning; and to intend nothing else, but to reap all those benefits to which that profession could carry him, and to the pursuing whereof he had so many and so unusual encouragements; and towards which it was not the least, that God had blessed him with an excellent wife, who perfectly resigned herself to him; and who then had brought him, before any troubles in the kingdom, three sons and a daughter, which he then and ever looked upon as his greatest blessing and consolation.

Because we shall have little cause hereafter to mention any other particulars in the calm part of his life, whilst he followed the study and practice of the law, it will not in this place appear a very impertinent digression to say, that he was in that very time when fortune seemed to smile and to intend well towards him, and often afterwards, throughout the whole course of his life, wont to say, that 'when he reflected upon himself and his past actions, even from the time of his first coming to the Middle Temple, he had so much more cause to be terrified upon the reflection, than the man had who viewed Rochester bridge in the morning that it was broken, and which he had galloped over in the night; that he had passed over more precipices than the other had done, for many nights and days, and some years together; from which nothing but the immediate hand of God could have preserved him.' For though it is very true, the persons before mentioned were the only men, in whose company, in those seasons of his life, he took delight; yet he frequently found himself in the conversation of worse, and indeed of all manner of men; and it being in the time when the war was entered into against the two crowns, and the expeditions made to, and unprosperous returns from Cadiz and the Isle of Rhé,* the town was full of soldiers, and of young gentlemen who intended to be soldiers, or as like them as they could; great license used of all kinds, in clothes, in diet, in gaming; and all kinds of expenses equally carried on, by men who had fortunes of their own to support it, and by others, who, having nothing of their own, cared not what they spent, whilst they could find credit: so that there was never an age, in which, in so short a time, so many young gentlemen, who had not experience in the world, or some good tutelar angel to protect them, were insensibly and suddenly overwhelmed in that sea of wine, and women, and quarrels, and gaming, which almost overspread the whole kingdom, and the nobility and gentry thereof. And when he had, by God's immediate blessing, disentangled himself from these labyrinths, (his nature and inclination disposing him rather to pass through those dissolute quarters, than to make any stay in them,) and was enough composed against any extravagant excursions; he was still conversant with a rank of men (how worthy soever) above his quality, and engaged in an expense above his fortune, if the extraordinary accidents of his life had not supplied him for those excesses; so that it brought no prejudice upon him, except in the censure of severe men, who thought him a person of more license than in truth he was, and who, in a short time, were very fully reconciled to him.

He had without doubt great infirmities; which by a providential mercy were seasonably restrained from growing into vices, at least into any that were habitual. He had ambition enough to keep him from being satisfied with his own condition, and to raise his spirit to great designs of raising himself, but not to transport him to endeavour it by any crooked and indirect means. He was never suspected to flatter the greatest man, or in the least degree to dissemble his own opinions or thoughts, how ingrateful soever it often proved; and even an affected defect in, and contempt of, those two useful qualities, cost him dear afterwards. He indulged his palate very much, and took even some delight in eating and drinking well, but without any approach to luxury; and, in truth, rather discoursed like an epicure than was one, having spent much time in the eating hours with the earl of Dorset, the lord Conway, and the lord Lumley, men who excelled in gratifying their appetites. He had a fancy sharp and luxuriant; but so carefully cultivated and strictly guarded, that he never was heard to speak a loose or a profane word; which he imputed to the chastity of the persons where his conversation usually was, where that rank sort of wit was religiously detested: and a little discountenance would quickly root those unsavoury weeds out of all discourses, where persons of honour are present.

He was in his nature inclined to pride and passion, and to a humour between wrangling and disputing very troublesome, which good company in a short time so much reformed and mastered, that no man was more affable and courteous to all kind of persons; and they who knew the great infirmity of his whole family, which abounded in passion, used to say, he had much extinguished the unruliness of that fire. That which supported and rendered him generally acceptable was his generosity, (for he had too much a contempt for money,) and the opinion men had of the goodness and justice of his nature, which was transcendent in him, in a wonderful tenderness and delight in obliging. His integrity was ever without blemish, and believed to be above temptation. He was firm and unshakable in his friendships; and, though he had great candour towards others in the differences of religion, he was zealously and deliberately fixed in the principles both of the doctrine and discipline of the church: yet he used to say to his nearest friends, in that time, when he expected another kind of calm for the remainder of his life, 'though he had some glimmering light of, and inclination to, virtue in his nature, that the whole progress of his life had been full of desperate hazards; and that only the merciful hand of God Almighty had prevented his being both an unfortunate and a vicious man:' and he still said, that 'God had vouchsafed that signal goodness to him, for he piety and exemplar virtue of his father and mother;' whose memory he had always in singular veneration: and he was pleased with what his nearest ally and bosom friend, sergeant Hyde,* (who was afterwards chief justice of the king's bench,) used at that time to say of him, that his cousin had passed his time very luckily, and with notable success, and was like to be very happy in the world; but he would never advise any of his friends to walk in the same paths, or to tread in his steps. [*Life*, I, 34–73]

EXPLANATORY NOTES

1. THE MISGOVERNMENT OF CAROLINE ENGLAND

5 *his majesty that now is*: i.e. Charles I.

Isle of Rhé: an attempt in 1627 to support the rebellion of French Huguenots at La Rochelle.

a general peace was shortly concluded: peace with France was agreed in April 1629; with Spain in December 1630.

6 *Parliaments were summoned, and again dissolved*: Charles I's first Parliament met on 18 June 1625, and was dissolved on 12 August; the second Parliament met on 6 February 1626, and was dissolved on 15 June.

no more assemblies of that nature expected: Charles's third Parliament met on 17 March 1628; was prorogued on 26 June; met again on 20 January 1629; adjourned on 2 March to pre-empt an order to adjourn by the King, and was dissolved on 10 March. A 'Proclamation for suppressing of false rumours touching Parliaments' was issued on 27 March.

Remonstrance or votes of the last day: the Remonstrance, attacking the King's favourite the Duke of Buckingham, was presented to the King by the House of Commons on 17 June 1628; a second Remonstrance, against the King's interpretation of the Petition of Right, was in preparation when the King prorogued Parliament on 26 June. The votes on the last day Parliament met, 2 March 1629, were against innovations in religion and the collection of customs duties without parliamentary authority.

7 *never before heard of in Parliament*: a subsidy was a tax of a set value in the pound levied on both lands and goods. Clarendon refers to the heavy wartime taxation imposed by Parliament on the regions within its power at the time of writing (1646).

were exacted throughout the whole kingdom: the Forced Loan, for which the first commission was issued in October 1626.

Petition of Right: the Petition of Right was given royal assent in June 1628 at the end of the first session of Charles I's third Parliament. It said that no one could be forced to provide money without common consent through Act of Parliament.

charges and accusations: the Duke of Buckingham was attacked in the House of Commons shortly before its dissolution in August 1625; in May 1626 the House presented formal impeachment charges against him. Immediately before the dissolution in 1629 Sir John Eliot proposed to impeach Weston.

murder of the first: at Portsmouth, on 23 August 1628, by John Felton.

9 *bishop of Lincoln, then Lord Keeper, sir H. Marten, and sir H. Spiller*: John Williams, Bishop of Lincoln, was Lord Keeper from 1621 to 1625; Hyde

may refer to allegations about his conduct of Chancery business in 1621–2. Sir Henry Marten was Judge of the High Court of Admiralty, and Hyde may refer to his difficulties over the capture of a French ship during 1626. Henry Spiller, a clerk in the Exchequer, was prosecuted by the Commons in 1610 for his protection of Catholic recusants.

this present Parliament: i.e. the Long Parliament of November 1640, still in being in 1646.

10 *tonnage and poundage*: i.e. customs duties. The King's right to collect tonnage and poundage without explicit parliamentary authorization had been one of the issues that provoked the dissolution of March 1629.

the Board: the Council Board, i.e. the Privy Council. Hyde also refers to the 'Council-Table'.

law of knighthood: the obsolete right of the King to summon all who had an estate worth 40 shillings or more to receive knighthood was revived in 1630. Those who refused were fined.

11 *sale of the old lands, and . . . new pensions*: a large amount of the royal estate was sold in 1626–30; pensions were regular payments made by the Crown to favoured courtiers.

old laws of the forest: an initiative to exercise neglected royal rights in ancient forests and to extend them beyond their currently generally accepted boundaries, and to fine individuals for encroachments.

Ship-Money: raised from 1634 initially on coastal corporate towns, and from 1635 on all counties and corporations.

publicly argued before all the judges of England: John Hampden's prosecution for failure to pay ship money was argued in November and December 1637 before the judges of all three benches, sitting in Exchequer chamber. Judgement was given in early 1638. Five out of the judges found for Hampden.

Star-chamber: the Star Chamber was the Privy Council sitting as a judicial body.

Thucydides said of the Athenians: *History of the Peloponnesian War*, I, 53. The quotation is from the translation by Thomas Hobbes.

12 *observation long ago by Thucydides*: *History of the Peloponnesian War*, I, 77, paraphrased from the Hobbes translation.

14 *my lord Finch's speech*: Sir John Finch, the Lord Chief Justice of the Common Pleas, had been Speaker of the House of Commons in 1629. He was largely responsible for the majority opinion in the judgement on the ship money case, and his remarks in his own speech on the conduct and powers of Parliament were particularly resented.

distresses: seizure of goods or belongings in order to pay a debt legally due.

15 *ad informandam conscientiam*: to inform the mind.

16 *from the dissolution . . . to the beginning of this Parliament*: i.e. from 1629 to November 1640.

16 *bona si sua norint*: 'o fortunatos nimium, sua si bona norint', Virgil, *Georgics*, II, 248 (how happy, if he did but know it).

mingling with a stranger nation: i.e. the union of the Crowns of England and Scotland on James's accession.

the noise of treason: the Gunpowder Plot of 1605.

the absence of the Prince in Spain: the journey of James I's son Prince Charles (later Charles I) to Spain in 1623, in company with the Duke of Buckingham, to secure his marriage to King Philip IV of Spain's daughter, the Infanta.

17 *those two books of the late lord archbishop of Canterbury . . . and of Mr Chillingworth*: William Laud's *A Relation of the Conference betweene William Laud . . . and Mr. Fisher the Jesuit* (1639) and William Chillingworth's *The Religion of Protestants a Safe Way to Salvation* (1638), both moderate defences of the Church of England against Roman Catholic polemic.

18 *that which Pericles was proud of upon his deathbed*: Plutarch, *Life of Pericles*, 38. Pericles says that his greatest title to fame was that 'no Athenian ever put on mourning because of me'.

which Nerva was deified for uniting: Tacitus, *Life of Agricola*, I, 3: 'Nerva Caesar res olim dissociabilis miscuerit, principatum ac libertatem' ('Nerva Caesar brought together things once dissociated, sovereignty and freedom').

in ordine ad spiritualia: i.e. for spiritual purposes.

20 *the death of Abbot, archbishop of Canterbury*: 4 August 1633.

death of Dr Bancroft: 2 November 1610.

conference at Hampton Court: a disputation between conformist and puritan clergy held before the King in January 1604, on whether any changes to the articles of religion and the liturgy of the Church of England were required.

21 *kindled at Geneva*: i.e. under the influence of continental Protestantism, especially Calvinism, particularly due to the residence there of English Protestant exiles during the reign of Queen Mary, 1553–8.

bishop Andrewes, bishop Overall: the anti-Calvinists Lancelot Andrewes (1555–1626), Bishop of Chichester (1605–9), Ely (1609–18), and Winchester (1618–26), and John Overall (1561–1619), Bishop of Coventry and Lichfield (1614–18) and Norwich (1618–19).

24 *Arminius*: Jacob Hermans or Jacobus Arminius (1560–1609), anti-Calvinist theologian, professor of theology at Leiden, 1603–9, promoter of the Arminian Remonstrance of 1610 which led to the controversy determined by the Synod of Dort, an assembly of the Dutch reformed Church at Dordrecht in 1618–19 with some invited foreign delegates. It concluded by confirming the Calvinistic theology of the Dutch Church, resulting in the deprivation of large numbers of Arminian clergy.

25 *High Commission court*: a court established under the royal prerogative and the 1559 Act of Supremacy with wide jurisdiction in spiritual matters.

rebuilding and repairing St Paul's Church: the restoration and embellishing of Old St Paul's Cathedral, instigated in 1631.

a divine, a common lawyer, and a doctor of physic: Henry Burton, William Prynne, and John Bastwick, all proceeded against in Star Chamber in 1637 for seditious libel. See also p. 69.

27 *He published a discourse and treatise*: *The Holy Table Name and Thing* (1637).

2. THE SCOTTISH COVENANT AND THE SHORT PARLIAMENT

29 *the Sunday before*: 16 July 1637.

The proclamation had appointed it to be read the Easter before: the Scottish Privy Council issued a Proclamation in December 1637 requiring each parish to buy copies of the book before Easter and ordering that it should be used, without specifying a date for it to come into effect.

30 *the Sunday morning appointed for the work*: 23 July 1637.

32 *erected several Tables*: i.e. assemblies. In fact, the Tables emerged later, in 1638.

called a General Assembly: one of the demands of the Covenant was that there should be no change to the government of the Church without a free Assembly and Parliament. The General Assembly did not meet until November 1638, formally summoned by the Privy Council in September.

subscribing a Covenant: the National Covenant, first signed at Greyfriars kirk on 28 February 1638.

33 *they obliged themselves to pursue the extirpation of bishops*: the original Covenant did not make this commitment; but the General Assembly on 8 December 1638 agreed to abolish episcopacy, and this was embodied in a gloss on the Covenant called the Glasgow Declaration.

34 *Proclamations and Declarations at large*: proclamation of 27 February 1639; the *Large Declaration concerning the late Tumults in Scotland* containing a detailed account of proceedings in Scotland appeared later in the year.

35 *lay leiger*: acted as a resident ambassador.

36 *burned by the common hangman*: 'Some Conditions of His Majesties Treaty with His Subjects of Scotland before the English Nobility.' The proclamation condemning the pamphlet was issued on 11 August 1639.

death of the lord Aston: Walter Aston, Baron Aston of Forfar, d. 13 August 1639.

37 *the Prince*: Charles, Prince of Wales (later Charles II).

secretary Coke: Sir John Coke (1563–1644), principal Secretary of State from 1625; left office on 31 January 1640.

38 *Isle of Rhé*: see above, note to p. 5.

40 *Mr Pym . . . brake the ice*: 17 April 1640.

40 *Mr Grimston*: Harbottle Grimston (1603–85); the speakers on 17 April were Francis Rous (1580–1659) and Pym, with Pym speaking second. Grimston spoke the following day, when Hyde himself spoke.

41 *Peard, a bold lawyer*: Peard is recorded speaking on ship money a few days later, on 23 April, when he was interrupted by the Solicitor General, Sir Edward Herbert, protesting about the word 'abomination'.

42 *did give their advice to this purpose at a conference*: the King attended the House of Lords on 24 April; the conference took place on 25 April.

43 *the next day it was resumed*: the first day was Saturday, 2 May 1640. The detail given here is not all included in the written message. The debate was resumed on Monday, 4 May.

46 *fourth or fifth of May*: 5 May.

48 *lord Conway*: Edward Conway, 2nd Viscount Conway (1594–1655), commander of the horse under Northumberland.

that infamous, irreparable rout at Newburn: 28 August 1640

3. THE OPENING OF THE LONG PARLIAMENT

50 *very first day they met together*: this conflates speeches of 7 and 11 November 1640; in the latter Pym formally moved the impeachment of Strafford.

51 *sir John Clotworthy*: later 2nd Viscount Massareene (d. 1665), elected for Maldon, Essex, possibly through the influence of Robert Rich, Earl of Warwick; he had been elected for Bossiney, Cornwall, in the Short Parliament, possibly through the influence of the Earl of Bedford.

53 *they voted unanimously*: 11 November 1640.

54 *so they declared*: 9 November 1640.

charged them in one of his Declarations: the *Declaration concerning the proceedings of this present Parliament* (12 August 1642).

55 *sent up an accusation against the lord archbishop of Canterbury*: 18 December 1640.

56 *the same night withdrew himself*: 6 December 1640.

57 *His commitment at York the year before*: in preparation for his first war against the Scots in 1639 Charles had summoned the English nobility to assist him, and required them in April to swear an oath to fight in the King's cause 'to the utmost hazard of their lives and fortunes'.

58 *exhibition*: an allowance.

59 *Warwick, Brooke, Wharton, Paget, Howard*: Robert Greville, 2nd Baron Brooke (1607–43); Philip Wharton, 4th Baron Wharton (1613–96); William Paget, 6th Baron Paget (1609–78); Edward Howard, 1st Baron Howard of Escrick (d. 1675). For Warwick see Biographical Register.

60 *practice in Westminster Hall*: the courts of King's Bench and Common Pleas were held in Westminster Hall, part of the Palace of Westminster. The court of Exchequer was in an adjoining building.

a design of sedition: in 1629, for the circulation of a paper written by Sir Robert Dudley in 1614 called 'a proposition to bridle the impertinency of Parliaments'.

62 *disobligation from the lord Strafford by his being created baron of Raby*: Sir Henry Vane senior was offended when Strafford took the title of Baron of Raby as well as Earl of Strafford when he was elevated to the peerage in January 1640. Raby was Vane's estate in Durham.

63 *long imprisonment and sharp prosecution afterwards*: Holles was one of those responsible for the demonstration in the House of Commons in 1629 preventing the Speaker from adjourning the House. He (with others) was imprisoned for six months and fined.

Sir Gilbert Gerard, the lord Digby, Strode, Haselrig: Sir Gilbert Gerard (1587–1670), MP for Middlesex; for Digby, Haselrig, and Strode see Biographical Register.

Hotham, Cholmeley and Stapleton: Sir Hugh Cholmeley (1600–57), MP for Beverley, former friend of Strafford, and eventually a royalist; Sir Philip Stapleton (1603–47), MP for Boroughbridge; for Hotham see Biographical Register.

et adversus omnes alios hostile odium: 'and all others they hate as enemies' (Tacitus, *Histories*, V, 5).

64 *laid aside his gown and practice*: i.e. ceased to practise as a barrister.

illegality of the court of York: the Council of the North, a court with civil and criminal jurisdiction based at York, and a key instrument in enforcing royal control in the North. The committee to investigate it was appointed on 23 December 1640. The Council in the Marches of Wales had a similar, though more extensive, jurisdiction in Wales and the English counties bordering it.

the marshal's court: i.e. the Court of Chivalry, which, though of medieval origin, had been reformed and re-established in the 1630s, and was used to prosecute 'scandalous words', i.e. libel. Hyde had led the protests against it in the Long Parliament.

65 *sitting covered*: i.e. wearing his hat, a privilege allowed him as a member of the House of Lords.

4. STRAFFORD

66 *two great persons*: i.e. Strafford and Laud.

was licensed to take care of himself: according to Clarendon Hamilton had secured the King's permission to work closely with his parliamentary opponents by convincing him that he was seeking to broker a settlement.

in one day: 19 February 1641.

67 *postulatum*: a postulate, something taken as a basis for the discussion.

69 *Mr White*: John White (1590–1645), MP for Southwark.

Prynne . . . John Bastwick . . . and Henry Burton: see above, p. 25 and note.

70 *closet-keeper*: domestic assistant to the clerk of the closet, a post in the royal household. The latter was in holy orders, and acted as a chaplain in attendance on the King.

pestilent and seditious libel . . . vented: Newes from Ipswich, discovering certaine late detestable practises of some domineering lordly prelates (1636).

ore tenus: a form of procedure in the court of Star Chamber in which proceedings were conducted without written statements.

71 *petitions were presented*: 7 November 1640.

72 *and so they were brought*: 28 November 1640.

73 *a declaration*: presented on 23 January 1641.

a petition: presented on 11 December 1640.

74 *the new Canons*: regulations for the Church drawn up by Convocation in May 1640; condemned by the House of Commons on 9 December.

Mr Marshall: Stephen Marshall (1594/5–1655), vicar of Finchingfield, Essex, and an influential figure among the London clergy.

75 *and thereupon related*: i.e. Digby related. Digby was one of the committee appointed to manage the prosecution of Strafford.

near 200 in the House: the bill passed the Commons on 21 April 1641. The vote was 59 against; 204 for.

brought to the bar: 29 April 1641.

76 *Common Council*: an elected assembly representing the wards of the City of London.

bishop Morton, bishop Hall: Thomas Morton (1564–1659), Bishop of Durham 1632–59; Joseph Hall (1574–1656), Bishop of Exeter 1627–41, of Norwich 1641–56.

77 *a short bill that was brought in*: 30 March 1641.

79 *about six months after*: after the first bill was rejected by the Lords, a second one was introduced in October 1641.

day when the conference had been: 26 April 1641.

Piccadilly: a gaming house established on the south side of Piccadilly in the 1630s.

81 *praemunire*: meaning here the offence of introducing a foreign power into the country (Strafford was accused of planning to bring Irish troops to overpower the English Parliament).

82 *died shortly after*: 9 May 1641.

83 *immediately went to the House*: 1 May 1641.

the late Protestation: a commitment to defend the reformed Protestant religion, the power and privileges of Parliament, and the rights and liberties of the subject, agreed in the House of Commons on 3 May 1641, and taken by its members; agreed by the Lords and taken by them the following day.

84 *it passed that House*: 8 May 1641.

the archbishop of York: John Williams (still bishop of Lincoln at this point); see Biographical Register.

85 *a great person*: Mountjoy Blount, 1st Earl of Newport (*c*.1597–1666), formally appointed constable of the Tower on 6 May.

87 *the epitaph which Plutarch records*: Plutarch, *Life of Sulla*, 38.

5. THE GRAND REMONSTRANCE AND THE MAKING OF A ROYALIST PARTY

91 *the night before it was to be executed*: 22 October 1641.

sir John Clotworthy: see above, p. 51: and note.

earl of Leicester: Robert Sidney, 2nd Earl of Leicester (1595–1677), appointed Lord Lieutenant in June, but only recently returned to England from an embassy in France. The information arrived on 31 October 1641.

being covered: see above, p. 65 and note.

92 *conusance*: i.e. cognizance: outside their remit.

94 *the next morning*: 22 November 1641.

95 *with some asseveration*: i.e. emphatically.

96 *Hotham, Cholmeley, and Stapleton*: see above, p. 63 and note.

court of York: see above, p. 64 and note.

98 *they obtained an order*: 15 December 1641.

102 *he brought in a very short bill*: the bill was presented on 21 December 1641.

deputy lieutenants: the militia was based on each community providing men when required for the purpose of national defence. Each county's militia was commanded by a Lord Lieutenant, usually a local aristocrat, who commissioned deputy lieutenants, local gentlemen, as its principal officers.

than it had six months before: the first bill to exclude bishops from civil jurisdiction had been rejected by the House of Lords in June 1641. A second bill had been introduced into the Commons and passed in October.

the infamous Burton: i.e. Henry Burton: see above, p. 25 and note.

103 *guards that attended upon the Houses*: Parliament had voted to set a guard during the King's absence in Scotland in October. When the King returned he dismissed it.

his majesty answered: 27 November 1641.

104 *train-bands*: the county militia.

Quis custodiet ipsos custodes?: 'who will guard the guardians?'

106 *archbishop of York*: John Williams; see Biographical Register.

107 *Court of Aldermen and at the Common Council*: the Court of Aldermen was the executive council of London; for Common Council see above, p. 76 and note.

Newgate: the City of London's prison.

captain Venn: John Venn (1586–1650), MP for London, later a regicide.

110 *they were both invested in those offices*: at the beginning of January 1642.

112 *published and printed*: His Majesties Declaration, To all his Loving Subjects published with the advice of His Pririe Councell (1641).

presented by Mr Percy: see above, p. 89. The interview related here must have taken place on New Year's Eve 1641 or New Year's Day 1642.

113 *him who had served him so ill*: Oliver St John.

6. THE FIVE MEMBERS

114 *sharp reprehension himself had met with*: Digby had been imprisoned in 1634 for fighting a duel within the precincts of Whitehall Palace.

115 *called him by writ to the House of Peers*: 9 June 1641.

116 *a day when the two Houses sat*: 3 January 1642.

ensuing articles: the articles themselves are omitted here.

117 *his nephew, the Prince Elector*: Charles Louis, Prince Elector Palatine of the Rhine, in London to secure support in the recovery of his former territories in Germany from the Empire.

118 *To your tents, O Israel*: 1 Kings 12: 16: a call to rebellion, as in Jeroboam's rising against King Rehoboam.

120 *no sooner passed the House of Peers*: 5 February 1642.

121 *those of greatest trust*: Sir John Culpepper and perhaps Falkland.

122 *the other for pressing*: i.e. to enable troops to be raised to suppress the Irish rebellion.

boutefeus: people who raise discontent; agitators.

123 *under his new governor*: Hertford had been appointed governor to the Prince in August 1641 as a concession to the moderate parliamentary reformers.

124 *resolved to send to his majesty*: 24 February 1642.

125 *Greenwich*: the old royal palace at Greenwich.

dine with Porter: Endymion Porter (1587–1649), one of the King's most trusted household servants.

126 *Theobalds*: Theobalds House in Hertfordshire.

127 *and the next morning*: 28 February 1642.

common-halls: an assembly consisting of all of the members of London's livery companies (bodies representing particular trades or crafts), used, among other things, for the election of the City's sheriffs. See also above, pp. 76, 107, and notes.

128 *an answer from Huntingdon*: 15 March 1642.

130 *so they had used sir Ralph Hopton*: 4 March 1642.

a tax upon the committee: i.e. an accusation against them.

131 *the heart of the King*: Proverbs 25: 3.

132 *incogitancy*: thoughtlessness.

ordinance . . . for the execution of the militia: the Militia Ordinance, passed in March 1642, asserting Parliament's control over the Militia. Parliament referred to its legislative acts not approved by the King as ordinances.

134 *which the Crown had a little before made use of*: see above, p. 12.

135 *Salus populi suprema lex*: 'the safety of the people is the supreme law.'

that of the Psalmist is yet inverted: Psalm 57: 6: 'They have digged a pit before me; they are fallen into the midst thereof themselves.'

7. EDGEHILL

136 *the tables kept by his officers of state*: i.e. free meals for employees of the royal household.

prince and duke of York: Charles I's eldest sons, Prince Charles (later Charles II) and James (later James II).

by that ship: the *Providence* which arrived from Holland in early July bringing arms and munitions purchased by the Queen.

141 *campania*: flat open ground.

lashty: slackness.

twenty-fifth day of August: in fact, 22 August 1642.

145 *they have made her many widows in the midst thereof*: Ezekiel 22: 25.

146 *that Athenian nun in Plutarch*: Theano: Plutarch, *Life of Alcibiades*, 22.

sir Arthur Aston: (1590/3–1649). There seems little doubt that Aston, one of the ablest of the royalist officers, was a Catholic, despite Clarendon's uncertainty.

147 *upon the propositions for plate and horses*: i.e. the Ordinance of both Houses of July 1642, for bringing in plate, money, and horses.

success at Worcester: a skirmish at Powick Bridge, outside Worcester, on 23 September.

lord chief justice Heath: (1575–1649) made Lord Chief Justice in October 1643, in succession to Sir John Bramston (1577–1654).

commission of oyer and terminer: a commission authorizing a judge to hold courts for particular offences, such as treasons, felonies, etc.

148 *under prince Maurice and prince Harry*: the sons of William the Silent, Prince of Orange: Prince Maurice of Nassau and Prince Frederick Henry of Nassau, under whom Lindsey had served in the wars against Spain in the Netherlands in 1624–6.

149 *earl of Bedford*: William Russell, 5th Earl, later 1st Duke of Bedford (1616–1700); see Biographical Register.

Kimbolton, St John's, Wharton, Robartes, Rochford, and Feilding: Oliver St John, 5th Baron St John of Bletso (1603–42); Philip Wharton, 4th Baron Wharton (1613–96); John Robartes, 2nd Baron Robartes (1606–85); John Carey, Viscount Rochford (1628–66), son of the 1st Earl of Dover. For Feilding, see Biographical Register under Basil Feilding, later 2nd Earl of Denbigh (*c*.1608–1675), son of the 1st Earl, William Feilding (*c*.1587–1643). For Kimbolton, see Biographical Register.

152 *carabine*: a type of firearm between a musket and a pistol.

153 *battle of Lewes*: the victory of Simon de Montfort over Henry III and his son Prince Edward (later Edward I) in May 1264.

8. THE DEATH OF FALKLAND

159 *letter of his own to the queen*: the letter is dated 23 January 1643.

160 *master of the wards*: the head of the Court of Wards and Liveries, a government department which administered revenues deriving from feudal rights of the Crown. Wardship, the chief of them, was abolished by an ordinance of Parliament in 1646.

161 *Sir Charles Caesar. . . died*: 6 December 1642; Dr Duck was the civil lawyer Arthur Duck (1580–1648). The Master of the Rolls was a senior office in Chancery.

162 *lord Wenman, Mr Pierrepoint, Mr Whitelocke*: Clarendon names only a handful of a larger number of commissioners. Thomas, Viscount Wenman (1596–1665), was MP for Oxfordshire. For Whitelocke and Pierrepoint, see Biographical Register.

iniquum petere ut aequum feras: to seek something excessive in order to obtain something acceptable.

163 *a cessation*: i.e. a ceasefire.

166 *the commission the parliament would have given him*: Northumberland laid down his command of the navy when the King revoked his commission on 28 June 1642. Parliament commissioned the Earl of Warwick to replace him.

167 *to leave Oxford the next day*: resolutions voted on 3 April 1643.

168 *that great favourite*: the Duke of Buckingham.

169 *landed in the north*: 22 February 1643, at Bridlington.

174 *Erat illi consilium ad facinus aptum . . . deerat*: Cicero, *Oratio in Catilinam*, III. The quotation refers to Catiline, not Cinna.

175 *ordinance of pressing*: the 'Ordinance for the speedy Raising and Impresting of men, for the Defence of the Kingdom', August 1643.

associated counties: Parliament had created two command structures covering several counties at the end of December 1642: the Eastern

Association and the Midland Association. Thomas Grey, Lord Grey of Groby, was commander of the Midland Association.

176 *leaguer*: camp.

179 *in battalia*: in order of battle.

the Artillery Garden: an area in Spitalfields, London, used for militia training.

180 *rampire*: rampart.

181 *Roundway hill*: i.e. the battle earlier in the year at Roundway Down, when Waller attributed his defeat to Essex's failure to support him.

fixed a garrison again at Reading: Reading had fallen to a siege by Essex in April.

182 *Turpe mori, post te, solo non posse dolore*: 'my shame if, after your death, I cannot die of grief alone': Lucan, *The Civil War*, IX, 108.

183 *his house*: Great Tew Manor, Oxfordshire.

corrupted his two younger brothers . . . and perverted his sisters: Falkland's mother converted to Catholicism in 1625; after his father's death Falkland looked after his younger brothers, but they were kidnapped in 1636 at her instigation so that they could be brought up as Catholics, as her younger daughters already were.

185 *haud semper errat fama, aliquando et elegit*: 'common fame does not always err; sometimes it makes the right choice.' Tacitus, *Agricola*, 9.

186 *ad amussim*: to the letter.

in republica Platonis, non in faece Romuli: 'in the republic of Plato, not in the sewers of Romulus.' Cicero, *Letters to Atticus*, II, 1.

187 *in tanto viro injuria virtutum fuerit*: 'in such a man would be to do injustice to his virtues.' Tacitus, *Agricola*, 9.

the first bill to take away the votes of bishops: see above, pp. 78–9.

189 *et in luctu bellum inter remedia erat*: 'in his grief, he found war a remedy.' Tacitus, *Agricola*, 29.

adversus malos injucundus: 'severe against evil-doers.' Tacitus, *Agricola*, 22.

190 *ingeminate the word Peace, Peace*: i.e. repeat the word. See Jeremiah 6: 14, 8: 11.

leaguer: see above, note to p. 176.

9. MARSTON MOOR

192 *The general*: i.e. Patrick Ruthven, Earl of Forth.

that which Plutarch says of soothsaying: Plutarch, *Life of Gaius Marius*, 42.

193 *In the multitude of counsellors there is safety*: Proverbs, 11: 14.

195 *per saltum*: at a leap.

196 *there was no more spirit in her*: 2 Chronicles 9: 4.

199 *conferred upon the marquis of Hertford*: the position of Groom of the Stole, Holland's before the Civil War.

rendered himself to the Parliament at London: he gave himself up at Uxbridge; his surrender was reported to the House of Lords on 6 November 1643.

200 *Livy, (lib. 24)*: Livy, *History of Rome*, XXIV, 45.

in medio ardore belli tanquam in pace libera: ibid. 'as freely in the middle of war as in peacetime.'

si abire a Romanis liceat, redire ad eos non liceat: ibid. 'if it was allowed to leave the Romans, but not to return to them.'

201 *tum consultandum, utrum defectio prior plus merita sit poenae an hic reditus veniae*: 'then it is to be considered whether his original defection may be weighed more than his return here.'

Vel ad decimam usque generationem a proselytis cave: 'beware of proselytes [i.e. converts] for ten generations.'

202 *died . . . of . . . morbus pediculosus*: on 8 December 1643. Morbus pediculosus was a disease connected with an infestation of lice; however, he died of an abscess, perhaps a bowel cancer.

Arminius: see above, p. 24 and note.

204 *the last summer*: in 1643. The reference is to Book VII, 143 of the *History*.

are committed to their rest: in the Henry VII Chapel in Westminster Abbey.

205 *to Prince Maurice*: Rupert's brother Maurice had been besieging Lyme Regis since mid-March 1644. Rupert's visit to Oxford took place on 25 April.

207 *one of them*: i.e. Digby.

208 *the conjunction with the Scottish commissioners in one council*: the Committee of both Kingdoms, established on 16 February 1644.

209 *the relief of Latham, and the reduction of Bolton*: 28 May 1644.

to prevent the reproaches and mutinies which distracted them: 2 July 1644.

211 *the marquis of Montrose had kindled already a fire*: Montrose had marched into south-western Scotland with a small army on 14 April 1644 as the leader of a Scottish royalist movement, but was quickly forced to retreat again.

10. THE DEFEAT OF ESSEX AND
THE RISE OF CROMWELL

218 *his young daughter*: Henrietta, later Henriette-Anne, Duchess of Orléans (1644–70).

Lady Dalkeith: Anne Villiers (1610–54), a relation of Hyde's first wife.

219 *as he had begun at Buckingham*: during the King's stay there in June 1644.

220 *arrested him in the King's name of high treason*: 12 August 1644.

226 *View Hall*: in fact Hall, now Hall Farm; Hyde misread his source.

227 *The night*: 31 August 1644.

230 *the battle of York*: i.e. Marston Moor.

233 *Cromwell accused the Earl of Manchester*: in the House of Commons, 25 November 1644.

239 *this debate ended in appointing a committee*: Clarendon probably confuses the debate on 19 December (after the day of fasting on 18 December), when it was agreed to send the self-denying ordinance up to the Lords, with debates earlier in the passage of the ordinance.

11. THE FAILURE OF PEACE AND THE END OF THE WAR: UXBRIDGE AND NASEBY

240 *met at Uxbridge*: on 29 January 1645.

241 *otherwise than that by the Parliament's ordinance . . . the Book of Common Prayer was not permitted to be read*: the 'Ordinance for taking away the Book of Common Prayer, and for establishing and putting in execution of the Directory for the publique worship of God', January 1645. The Directory was the form of worship prepared by the Assembly of Divines (the Westminster Assembly) which had been established in June 1643.

242 *one Love*: Christopher Love (1618–51). The sermon, *England's Distemper Having Division and Error as its Cause*, was preached on 30 January 1645. Love was executed in 1651 for his involvement in a Scottish-inspired plot to restore the King.

243 *Mr Henderson*: Alexander Henderson (c.1583–1646), the most important of the clerical leaders of the Covenanting movement; a member of the Westminster Assembly.

244 *defended his knighthood*: the House of Commons had originally intended to ignore any titles (including Hyde's knighthood) which had been conferred by the King since 1642.

249 *Lane, Gardiner, Bridgeman, and Palmer*: Sir Richard Lane (1584–1652), the King's Chief Baron of the Exchequer and later Lord Keeper of the Privy Seal; Sir Orlando Bridgeman (1609–74), Lord Chief Justice after the Restoration; Sir Thomas Gardiner (1591–1652), the King's Solicitor General and later Attorney General; for Geoffrey Palmer, see Biographical Register.

Prideaux: Edmund Prideaux (1601–59), Solicitor General to Parliament from 1648, and Attorney General 1649–59.

250 *by declaring the cessation void*: the ceasefire agreed by the King's Lord Lieutenant, the Marquess of Ormond, with the Irish confederates in September 1643.

252 *the repulse he had formerly received at Oxford*: see above, pp. 165–7.

Wilton . . . or Hatfield: the principal houses of Pembroke and Salisbury in Wiltshire and Hertfordshire respectively.

253 *Crew*: John Crew, later 1st Baron Crew (1597/8–1679), MP for Brackley.

256 *they parted a little before the break of day*: 23 February 1645.

   The loss of Shrewsbury: 22 February.

   after recovered again: part of Weymouth had been taken by Sir Lewis
   Dyves for the royalists earlier in the month. The royalists were expelled
   by 28 February.

262 *Carnwath*: Robert Dalyell, 1st Earl of Carnwath (d. 1654).

12. THE KING'S SURRENDER AND
THE ROYALIST DIASPORA

266 *Winchester . . . rendered upon easy conditions*: Winchester surrendered
   before Basing was taken: Basing House was stormed on 14 October 1645;
   Winchester surrendered on 5 October.

   had formerly sent for a treaty of peace: Charles had sent a first message to
   Parliament on 5 December 1645, proposing a new treaty, to which he
   received no answer. On the 15th he sent another message, to which the
   two Houses responded on the 23rd. On the 26th and 29th he made further proposals. Parliament was highly suspicious that he aimed to
   exacerbate the splits between Presbyterians and Independents at
   Westminster.

267 *and at last offered*: 23 March 1646.

   they published an ordinance: 31 March 1646.

268 *to find their content and satisfaction in advancing the King's interest*: an
   attempt at negotiating with the Independents in the army had been begun
   through Sir William Vavasour in late October 1645, although its exposure
   in December had led to Vavasour's expulsion from England.

269 *sent an envoy, one Montreuil, to London*: Cardinal Mazarin, chief minister
   to the Queen Regent (Louis XIII's queen, Anne of Austria, ruling in the
   minority of her son Louis XIV), had sent Montreuil to London in July
   1645.

270 *Isle of Rhé*: see above, p. 5 and note.

   when she had unadvisedly withdrawn herself from thence: i.e. Henrietta
   Maria and Louis XIII's mother, Henri IV's queen, Marie de Médicis,
   who left France following the failure of her attempt to remove Richelieu
   in 1630. She did not return before her death in 1642.

   when she carried the princess royal into Holland: in February 1642: see
   above, p. 123.

   putting Casal into the hands of France: in the war over the succession to the
   duchy of Mantua (Piedmont), in 1628–31, when Louis XIII supported
   the French claimant against rivals supported by the Hapsburg emperor.
   Mazarin, an envoy of the Pope charged with making peace, was instrumental in securing a settlement satisfactory to France in 1630–1, which

ended the occupation of Casale by Hapsburg troops. Mazarin was not made a cardinal until 1641.

271 *fomenting another rebellion*: the revolt in 1632 of Gaston, Duke of Orléans (Louis XIII's brother, referred to as 'Monsieur'), against the influence of Richelieu, backed by the Queen Mother, for which the Duke of Montmorency was executed.

that war: of France and Spain, formally declared in May 1635, and not ended until the Treaty of the Pyrennees in 1659.

to transport herself out of Cornwall into France: see above, p. 219.

272 *arrived there in January*: Montreuil had arrived in the summer of 1645; he met the King in Oxford on 3–5 January 1646.

273 *that his majesty should consent thereunto*: Moray visited the Queen in October 1645, with a paper prepared by the Scottish commissioners. He returned to England in December with her reluctant assent to the proposals.

275 *as soon as the King came to Newcastle*: see below, p. 277–8.

they were at last totally defeated: 21 March 1646 at Stow-on-the-Wold.

Exeter: surrendered 13 April 1646.

276 *sent to eminent commanders of name*: by a letter from the Earl of Southampton to Cols. Rainborowe and Fleetwood, read in the House of Commons on 27 April 1646.

277 *condition of the marquis of Montrose*: Montrose was still in Scotland after his defeat at Philiphaugh in September, attempting to find further support to renew his attacks on the Covenanters.

went into the Scots' army before Newark: 5 May 1646.

he giving up that place: 6 May 1646.

278 *to hasten the Prince's remove from Jersey*: see below, p. 279.

280 *had before done to his friend, and with the same success*: i.e. to Hyde, without success.

before the Prince came from thence: probably referring to the Queen's hopes of troops from France in November 1645.

281 *the ambassador who was now appointed to go thither*: Pomponne de Bellièvre, appointed French ambassador to England in June, arrived there in July 1646. His instructions from Mazarin were said (inaccurately) to have been drawn up on the basis of the 'Queen's memorandum', a draft by Digby.

283 *the Prince's departure from Jersey*: 26 June 1646.

284 *sir George Carteret*: (1610?–1680), lieutenant governor of Jersey.

Bene vixit, qui bene latuit: 'he has lived well, who has led a quiet life' (a common phrase, adapted from Ovid, *Tristia*, III, 4, l. 25: 'bene qui latuit bene uixit').

13. CROMWELL, THE ARMY, AND THE INDEPENDENTS

286 *commitment*: i.e. arrest.

was sent once or twice to compose the army: Cromwell, with other military officers, was sent by the Commons on 30 April 1647 to hold discussions with the officers. They reported back on 21 May.

288 *came with a squadron of fifty horse to Holmby*: Joyce arrived on 3 June 1647 with about 500 horse. They took the King away on the following morning.

the committee: the commissioners appointed by Parliament in January 1647 to receive the person of the King from the Scots, and in April to present peace proposals.

Colonel Browne: Major-General Richard Browne (1602–69), an army officer and Presbyterian MP. Browne was one of the commissioners appointed in January 1647 and was present at Holmby during Joyce's visit, although the commander of the garrison there was Colonel Richard Graves.

289 *from the general*: i.e. Fairfax; his letter was read in the House of Commons on 7 June.

colonel Montagu's house: Hinchingbrooke House, near Huntingdon.

290 *they presently voted*: on 7 June.

the council of officers: i.e. the Council of the Army, a new body, proposed in the *Solemn Engagement of the Army*, agreed by the soldiers on 5 June.

291 *had sent an address to him*: on 21 April; there may have been a later address.

the army's address to the Parliament: probably the *Remonstrance* of the army of 23 June.

They published declarations: the ordinance of 31 July, which was agreed only after the withdrawal of the Independent members from the House (see below, p. 292).

293 *the Scots' commissioners*: the Earl of Lauderdale, one of the four commissioners whom the Scots had sent to England in April 1647, originally to encourage Charles to accept the Presbyterian-backed peace proposals, was now trying to promote a scheme for a Scottish invasion of England.

expostulation from the Parliament: i.e. from the Scottish Parliament.

Ashburnham and Berkeley: John Ashburnham and Sir John Berkeley, who arrived back in England separately in July, Berkeley with a mission to facilitate negotiations between the King and the army.

295 *about the beginning of September*: in fact, 11 November.

Legge: William Legge: see Biographical Register.

298 *they voted that they would make no more addresses to the King*: 3 January 1648.

299 *meeting of the general officers of the army at Windsor*: 22 December 1647.

 Declaration that they would make no more addresses to the King: the Declaration of the House of Commons of 11 February 1648, which confirmed and explained the January vote.

300 *in their first Remonstrance*: the Grand Remonstrance of 1641: see above, p. 93.

301 *it had the concurrence of that House*: in fact the Lords did not consider or approve the Declaration.

 to publish answers to that odious Declaration: including Hyde himself, whose *An Answer to a Pamphlet, entitled a Declaration of the Commons of England in Parliament assembled* appeared early in the year, with a fuller version in July.

302 *sale of the Church and Crown lands*: sales of bishops' lands were authorized under an ordinance of November 1646; of Crown lands under an Act of July 1649.

 composition with delinquents: Parliament had sequestrated (i.e. confiscated) the revenues from the estates of delinquents (i.e. its enemies) from the beginning of the war. Surrendered royalists were allowed to compound— to pay a fine—in order to recover control of their own lands.

304 *he commends Caesar Borgia*: *The Prince*, chapter 7.

306 *changed a general who . . . would never be governed . . . for another who had no eyes*: i.e. removed Manchester in favour of Fairfax: see above, p. 239.

14. THE SECOND CIVIL WAR AND
THE TRIAL OF THE KING

310 *Rainborowe*: Thomas Rainborowe (d. 1648): successful military and naval commander; MP from 1647 for Droitwich; prominent in the Putney debates of 1647; killed later in 1648 in a royalist attempt to capture him at Pontefract Castle.

 Batten: William Batten (1600/1–1667): vice admiral and treasurer of the navy since 1642; commander at sea after 1645.

 the revolt of the fleet: in July 1642.

311 *L'Estrange*: Roger L'Estrange (1616–1704), later a journalist, and after the Restoration official press censor.

 Mr Hales: Edward Hales (1626–83 or 1684), later 2nd Baronet, who succeeded his grandfather, the 1st Baronet, in 1654. He had married, by 1645, Anne, the daughter and co-heir of the 2nd Baron Wootton of Marley.

312 *There was an incredible appearance of the country at the place appointed*: at Rochester on 22 May 1648.

313 *When the King made the Earl of Northumberland admiral*: in April 1638.

 the duke having made his escape at this time: in April 1648, from St James's Palace in London.

314 *One and All*: the practice in mutinies of concealing the identities of any ringleaders, through round robins and other devices.

used their officers in the same manner: 27 May 1648.

The cardinal: Mazarin.

all his promises: i.e. Mazarin's.

315 *former counsel*: Clarendon explains that it had initially been proposed to march to Rochester, and hold eastern Kent; however, this plan had been abandoned in favour of an advance to Blackheath.

the month of July: in fact it was June.

they made a shift to transport themselves: 4 June 1648.

316 *their committees*: the county committees, created by Parliament for various government functions in each county, including the raising of taxes. Their activities were among the grievances that helped to provoke the Second Civil War.

318 *maintained the dispute for above six hours*: 17 August 1648.

319 *were taken prisoners*: 25 August 1648.

320 *the duke of Buckingham*: the 2nd Duke of Buckingham (1628–87): see the Biographical Register.

Kingston upon Thames: 4/5 July 1648.

Dalbier: John Dalbier.

321 *the earl delivered himself prisoner*: 10 July 1648.

322 *obliged to deliver themselves up*: the articles of capitulation were agreed on 27 August 1648, and the town surrendered the following day.

324 *tertia*: a division of infantry.

325 *they sent it to the House of Peers for their concurrence*: on 1 January 1649.

when they had . . . rejected it: 2 January 1649.

House of Peers of his own creation: the 'Other House', a second Chamber established under the 1657 Humble Petition and Advice in 1658.

326 *precedent of deposing Richard the Second*: in 1399, when Henry Bolingbroke was said to have secured an agreement to resign the kingship from Richard II before he was formally deposed by Parliament.

327 *not much known in Westminster Hall, though of good practice in his chamber*: i.e. who did not do much pleading in court, but provided advice to his clients.

which he did the next day: Bradshaw was appointed on 10 January 1649.

pro hac vice: for this time only.

328 *Hurst castle*: the King had been moved from Carisbrooke to Hurst Castle on the Solent on 1 December 1648. He was brought away on 19 December.

kept himself bare: i.e. removed his hat.

329 *that design which had been discovered by Mr Waller*: Waller's Plot, for which Edmund Waller, an MP and friend of Hyde's, had been arrested on 31 May 1643.

330 *that night*: 23 December 1648.

333 *the pronouncing that horrible sentence*: sentence of death, given on 27 January 1649.

the execution of that sentence: on 30 January, outside the Banqueting House, Whitehall.

15. SCOTLAND AND SPAIN: 1649–1651

337 *or to acknowledge any man to be king*: the House of Commons in January had made it treason to proclaim the new King; in March its Act abolishing the kingly office made it treason to set anyone up as King.

338 *at Kinsale with the fleet*: the ships that had mutinied from Parliament in 1648 (see above, p. 314)had been placed under the command of Prince Rupert, following the failure of their attempt to support the royalists in Colchester.

cessation with the Irish: after the collapse of his 1646 treaty with the Confederate Irish rebels as a result of the influence of the papal nuncio, Rinuccini, the royalist Lord Lieutenant, the Marquess of Ormond, had left the country in July 1647. Murrough O'Brien, Earl of Inchiquin (1614–74), Parliament's commander against the Confederate Irish in Munster, had in April 1648 declared that he would support the King against Parliament, and in May agreed a truce with the Irish despite Rinuccini's opposition. Ormond returned to Ireland in September 1648, and himself came to terms with the Confederates at Kilkenny on 17 January 1649. Rinuccini left a month later.

339 *there arrived a gentleman*: Douglas arrived at Rotterdam on 20 February 1649.

that discontent that is mentioned before: Lauderdale had been pressing the then Prince Charles to accept the Scottish Parliament's terms and join Hamilton's army before the news of the defeat at Preston had arrived in September 1648, and had clashed with Hyde over the issue.

340 *and when the news came of the execution of duke Hamilton*: in early March 1649.

don Lewis: Luis de Haro, Marquis of Carpio (1598–1661), principal minister of King Philip IV of spain.

341 *fiestas for the Queen*: Mariana of Austria, Philip IV's second wife, whom he married in 1649.

bucklers: small round shields.

running at the ring: a form of tilting, in which the rider spears a ring at speed.

342 *clinkant*: glittering.

343 *hocking*: cutting the tendons of the leg.

346 *Harry the Fourth of France*: Henri IV (1553–1610), Charles II's grandfather.

347 *Middleton*: Major-General John Middleton (1608–74).

348 *the next day*: in fact on 12 September 1651.

349 *Carelesse*: William Carelesse, or Carlos (d. 1689). He changed his name in 1658 on entering Spanish military service.

353 *proclamation*: 10 September 1651.

355 *in the month of October*: 10–12 September.

   Mr Norton's: Abbots Leigh, Somerset.

358 *Lyme*: Lyme Regis.

359 *came . . . to that house*: 22 September 1651.

361 *Desborough*: John Disbrowe (1608–80).

   sergeant Hyde: Hyde's cousin (the son of Laurence Hyde) Sir Robert Hyde (1595/6–1665), appointed Lord Chief Justice of the Common Pleas (not King's Bench) in 1660.

362 *Brightemsted*: Brightelmstone, now Brighton.

   about the end of November: 16 October 1651.

   the distraction that Court had lately been in: the Fronde, a series of rebellions and factional struggles in France, continued from 1649 to 1653. Mazarin's decision to go into voluntary exile in February 1651 did result in a brief lull; but the troubles were renewed with the Prince of Condé's open revolt in September, and Mazarin's return in December.

363 *was at Antwerp*: Hyde had migrated to Antwerp on his return from Spain in July 1651, where he was formally regarded as the King's ambassador.

   in the Christmas: Hyde was at Paris by 30 December 1651.

   and are exactly true: Hyde's account of the King's escape is in fact contradicted by many of the other accounts.

16. THE NADIR OF ROYALISM AND THE DEATH OF CROMWELL

365 *after the prince was gone*: Prince Rupert left Paris for Germany early in June 1654.

366 *duke of Gloucester*: Prince Henry, Duke of Gloucester: see Biographical Register.

368 *The Elector never resides there*: the Electoral state of Cologne was held by the city's Archbishop; the City itself was, as Clarendon states, largely outside his control, however. The current Elector was Maximilian Heinrich.

369 *Schomberg*: (1615–90), a German in French military service during the 1650s.

   he received news: in letters dated 6 and 8 November 1654.

370 *abbot Montagu*: Walter Montagu (1604/5–1677), brother of the 2nd Earl of Manchester, converted to Catholicism in 1635, and devoted servant of Queen Henrietta Maria.

371 *He writ a letter of complaint to the Queen*: 10 November 1654.

374 *harbour*: i.e. an inn.

375 *the donative of the Diet*: the pension which had been granted to Charles II in autumn 1653 by the imperial diet (parliament) at Regensburg. Although it was relatively generous, payment was erratic, and Rochester was sent on a number of missions to secure it.

hired a bark at Dunkirk: arrived in England 19 February 1655.

left Cologne: 14 February 1655.

377 *rendezvous upon a fixed day*: 8 March 1655.

378 *about five of the clock in the morning*: 12 March 1655.

380 *rather entreated than compelled them to deliver themselves*: 14 March 1655.

new commission of oyer and terminer: see above, p. 147 and note.

Rolle, his chief justice: Henry Rolle (1589/90–1656), appointed Chief Justice in 1648.

381 *at the time appointed*: 8 March.

382 *dorp*: a village.

all his counsels were discovered: the penetration of Charles II's court by the intelligence network run by the secretary to the Council of State, John Thurloe, was only discovered later. Thurloe's principal agents there at this time were Sir John Henderson and Henry Manning, the latter a friend of Rochester's. For Thurloe's relationship with Sir Richard Willys, see below, pp. 394–6.

383 *cum Marius aspiciens Carthaginem . . . solatio*: Velleius Paterculus, *The Roman History*, II, 19, 4: 'Marius, looking on Carthage, and Carthage looking on Marius, could offer consolation the one to the other.'

Scotland . . . now reduced and governed by a rod of iron: after the defeat of the Scottish army at the battle of Worcester and the reduction of other Scottish forces in the course of 1651, Scotland was incorporated into England in 1652. Part of the English army remained quartered there, latterly under General Monck, for the rest of the Interregnum.

386 *Sindercombe*: parliamentarian soldier, leveller, and associate of the leveller Edward Sexby; mastermind of a series of schemes to assassinate Cromwell in 1656 and 1657: captured and tried on 9 February 1657, committed suicide in the Tower, 13 February.

387 *death of his friend the earl of Warwick*: 19 April 1658.

the heir of that house . . . died about the same time: Warwick's grandson and heir Robert Rich had married Cromwell's daughter Frances on 14 November 1657. He died on 16 February 1658.

387 *his son Falconbridge*: Thomas Belasyse, 2nd Viscount (later 1st Earl) Fauconberg (1627/8–1700), married Mary Cromwell as his second wife in November 1657, though he was widely considered to be a royalist.

death of his daughter Claypole: Elizabeth Claypole, Cromwell's second daughter, died on 6 August 1658.

388 *several victories*: Dunbar, on 3 September 1650; and Worcester, on 3 September 1651.

quos vituperare ne inimici quidem possunt nisi ut simul laudent: Pliny, *Letters*, III, 12: 'whom not even their enemies can criticize without at the same time praising.'

Ausum eum quae nemo auderet bonus; perfecisse quae a nullo nisi fortissimo perfici possent: Velleius Paterculus, II, 24: 'he dared things that no good citizen would have dared to do, and achieved things only the most remarkable man could have done.'

389 *humble Petition and Advice*: installed on 26 June 1657.

positively refused to pay his part: November 1654.

390 *Maynard was committed to the Tower*: Sir John Maynard, in May 1655, with the two other counsel in the case. The case led to the resignation of the Lord Chief Justice, Henry Rolle.

391 *sent his agent*: Samuel Morland, in May 1655.

the cardinal: Mazarin.

when the consuls . . . were to be chosen: in January 1658.

392 *Lockhart*: William Lockhart (1621–75), ambassador to France, 1656–8.

his memory remains still in those parts . . . in great veneration: Clarendon may have gained some of the detail of this story in his exile after 1668: Montpelier is less than 40 km from Nîmes.

madam de Turenne: the Huguenot wife of the French Marshal Turenne (Henri de La Tour d'Auvergne, vicomte de Turenne).

17. RESTORATION

394 *One who had a part in the office of secrecy*: Samuel Morland.

he advertised his majesty of a person: probably between April and July 1659. The person concerned was Sir Richard Willys.

395 *the marquis of Ormond's being in London*: in early February 1658.

another was despatched: in July 1659.

396 *Massey's design upon Gloucester*: see below, p. 398.

Mr Mordaunt came to Brussels: in late June 1659.

397 *upon a day named*: 1 August 1659.

400 *were after a short encounter routed by him*: 19 August 1659.

to a strong castle of his own: Chirk Castle in Denbighshire. Myddleton, a former senior parliamentary officer, had joined Booth at Chester. He surrendered on 24 August.

401 *assigned it to the command of colonel Goring*: in 1634.

behaviour at Nantwich: in January 1644.

from thence to serve the King in England: i.e. after Ormond's cessation with the Irish rebels in September 1643: Monck's refusal to provide an un-equivocal commitment to the royal cause resulted in Ormond sending him in custody to Bristol.

402 *after he had put the command of Scotland into his hands*: April 1654.

403 *a woman of the lowest extraction*: Anne Clarges, the daughter of a farrier.

nihil muliebre praeter corpus gerens: Velleius Paterculus, *Hist. Rom.*, II, 74: 'she had nothing of womanhood save her sex.'

a younger brother, a divine: Nicholas Monck (*c.*1610–1661), later Bishop of Hereford.

where the general received him well: August 1659.

404 *by entering into treaties*: Monck sent commissioners to London following a Council of War on 3 November, who signed a treaty in London on 15 November, which was rejected by Monck when news of it arrived in Scotland on 22 November.

making haste to Newcastle: Lambert reached Newcastle by 23 November.

States of Scotland: a meeting of representatives of shires and burghs on 15 November.

406 *about the middle of February*: 3 February 1660.

408 *Common Council*: for Common Council, see above, p. 76 and note. Their refusal to pay taxes occurred on 8 February.

Privy Council: i.e. Council of State.

he as readily executed their commands: 9/10 February 1660.

409 *Praise God Barebones*: Praisegod Barbone or Barbon (1598–1678/9), whose name became attached to the Barebones Parliament of 1653. His petition was presented on 9 February.

410 *Scott and Robinson*: see above, p. 406.

In the morning: 11 February 1660.

413 *authority and place which the Prince of Orange possessed in that government*: the stadholdership, a sort of hereditary chief executive role, where the legislative power was held by elected representatives in the States General.

took their places: 21 February 1660.

416 *concessions made . . . at the Isle of Wight*: in the Treaty of Newport, in October 1648, and including conceding control of the militia for twenty years, and the offer of a severely limited episcopacy.

417 *which he had delivered at his conference with the members*: see above, pp. 412–13 and note.

419 *so lately forbid to come into that place*: one of the terms of the April 1654 treaty ending the Anglo-Dutch War of 1652–4 was that the enemies of the English republic were to be excluded from the Netherlands.

419 *Dort*: Dordrecht.

420 *to take possession of his command*: James continued to hold the position of Lord High Admiral.

423 *embarked himself*: 22 May 1660. The ship was the *Royal Charles*, previously known as the *Naseby*.

gave the Garter: i.e. conferred the Order of the Garter on.

424 *died within three or four months*: Mazarin died in March 1661; Luis de Haro in November 1661.

18. LAW AND POLITE LEARNING: THE EDUCATION OF A LAWYER

427 *eighteenth day of February in the year 1608*: i.e. 1609, following the common practice in England of counting the years from the feast of the Annunciation, 25 March.

demy of Magdalen college: a form of scholarship used at Magdalen.

the act: an annual event where candidates for degrees were examined through disputations.

428 *Alhollandtide*: All Hallows', or All Saints' day, 1 November.

429 *Isle of Rhé*: see above, p. 5, and note.

ride the circuit: i.e. attend the assizes, where royal justices were each summer dispatched to groups of counties to hear criminal and civil cases.

430 *he married a young lady*: Anne Ayliffe, on 4 February 1632.

431 *an ill accident in the court befell a lady*: the affair of Henry Jermyn and Viscount Grandison's sister Eleanor Villiers, which led to Jermyn's expulsion from the court in May 1633 when he refused to marry his pregnant lover. Grandison and Eleanor Villiers were the children of Sir Edward Villiers (Buckingham's half-brother) and Barbara St John, sister of Anne Ayliffe's mother, Anna St John.

433 *the daughter of sir Thomas Aylesbury*: Frances, in fact on 10 July 1634.

434 *omnifarium doctus*: learned in everything.

435 *Mr Cowley*: Abraham Cowley (1618–67).

439 *sewer to the king*: a servant who waited on the king at meals.

19. GREAT TEW

440 *near twenty years after*: as Falkland was killed in 1643, and Clarendon born in 1609, Falkland in 1609 or 1610, this is an example of Clarendon's frequently vague approach to dates.

441 *two very excellent houses*: at Great Tew and Burford, in Oxfordshire.

442 *marrying a young lady*: Lettice Morrison, in 1630.

444 *his excellent book*: *The Religion of Protestants* (1638), an answer to the Jesuit Edward Knott's *Mercy and Truth* (1634).

445 *published since his death*: Of the infallibility of the Church of Rome (1645).

in republica Platonis, than in faece Romuli: see above, p. 186 and note.

448 *needed a wise and a wary director*: Caernarvon came from a strongly Catholic family, although it is his wild-living reputation to which Clarendon probably refers.

449 *Armininians*: see above, p. 24 and note.

Arthur Goodwin: (d. 1643). A leading member of the Long Parliament, and associate of John Hampden.

450 *synod of Dort*: see above, note to p. 24.

453 *St Omer's*: the College of Saint-Omer, now in Artois, France, which operated as a college for the education of English Catholics. In fact, Chillingworth went to the other college in northern France, at Douai.

when Bellarmine died: Cardinal Bellarmine (1542–1621), Catholic theologian and controversialist.

455 *bow their knees to Baal*: i.e. submit to the usurped powers: Romans 11: 14.

to eat in the hall: to take dinners with other lawyers in the Inns of Court.

456 *the archbishop or the earl of Essex*: see above, p. 58.

457 *the Isle of Rhé*: see above, p. 5 and note.

459 *sergeant Hyde*: see above, p. 361 and note.

BIOGRAPHICAL REGISTER

The Biographical Register provides very brief details of individuals mentioned more than once in the text, or of particular significance. Page numbers are shown in bold.

ABBOT, GEORGE (1562–1633), evangelical and strongly anti-Catholic Archbishop of Canterbury 1611–33, out of favour following the accession of Charles I in 1625: **20**.

ANNESLEY, ARTHUR (1614–86), Irish politician who sat for Dublin in Richard Cromwell's Parliament in 1659, and was president of the Council of State in early 1660. Created 1st Earl of Anglesey in 1660: **417**.

ASHBURNHAM, JOHN (1602/3–71), a groom of the bedchamber from 1628, and a member of Parliament in November 1640. Attended on the King during his journey from Oxford to the Scottish army in 1646. Following attendance on the Queen in Paris, returned to the King at Hampton Court in 1647, and was involved in his failed escape attempt: **276, 278, 279, 283, 293–7**

ASTLEY, JACOB (1579–1652), created 1st Baron Astley in 1644, soldier with military experience on the continent appointed to senior positions in the armies raised in 1639 and 1640 to fight the Scots, and in the army raised in 1642. He was made governor of Oxford, a member of the Council of War, and from 1643 commander of the foot: **180, 205, 207, 261, 262, 265, 275**.

ASTON, SIR ARTHUR (between 1590 and 1593–1649), soldier with military experience in northern Europe appointed to senior positions in the army raised for the second war against the Scots in 1640. A Roman Catholic. Killed at the storming of Drogheda by Cromwell in 1649: **146, 150, 153**.

AUBIGNY, KATHERINE STEWART, Lady Aubigny (d. 1650), wife of Lord George Stewart, killed at the battle of Edgehill; involved in 1643 in a plot to raise royalist forces within London, parallel to the Waller Plot, for which she was imprisoned. Married in 1648 James Livingston, Viscount Newburgh, and with him entertained Charles I on his way to his trial in December that year: **328–30**.

AYLESBURY, SIR THOMAS (1579/80–1658), secretary to the Duke of Buckingham as Lord High Admiral, Surveyor General, and Master of the Mint. Hyde married his daughter Frances in 1634: **433**.

BALFOUR, SIR WILLIAM (d. 1660), soldier with military experience in the Netherlands in the 1620s, appointed lieutenant of the Tower of London in 1630, but became associated with the parliamentary reformers in 1640/41. Forced out of the lieutenancy by the King in December 1641; appointed lieutenant general of horse in the parliamentary army in 1642, but did not serve after February 1645: **149, 150, 153, 157–8, 227, 228**.

BANCROFT, RICHARD (bap. 1544, d. 1610), Archbishop of Canterbury 1604–10 insistent on conformity to the articles and ceremonies of the Church of England: **20**.

BEDFORD, EARL OF, *see* Russell, Francis, 4th Earl, and Russell, William, 5th Earl and 1st Duke

BERKELEY, SIR JOHN, BARON BERKELEY OF STRATTON (bap. 1607, d. 1678), associate of Lord Holland and Henry Jermyn; MP in the Short Parliament, involved in the Army Plot of May 1641, later one of the commanders of the King's armies in the west. Commissioned by the Queen to negotiate between the King and army in 1647, and involved in the King's escape from Hampton Court. Returned to Paris, and was made governor of the Duke of York, later succeeding Byron as master of his household, and said to have converted to Roman Catholicism; created Baron Berkeley of Stratton in 1658: **260, 293, 296–7**.

BOOTH, SIR GEORGE (1622–84), parliamentary colonel in Cheshire, elected MP in 1646, secluded in Pride's Purge, leader of the August 1659 uprising in Cheshire. Created Lord Delamer in 1661: **398–400**.

BRADSHAW, JOHN (bap. 1602, d. 1659), lawyer prominent in business on behalf of Parliament in the 1640s, particularly in the trials of royalists, appointed in January 1649 Lord President of the high court of justice to try Charles I. Subsequently made Lord President of the Council of State: **327**.

BRISTOL, EARL OF, *see* Digby, George, 2nd Earl, and Digby, John, 1st Earl

BROOKE, LORD, *see* Greville, Robert,

BUCKINGHAM, DUKE OF, *see* Villiers, George

BUTLER, JAMES, MARQUESS OF ORMOND (1610–88), Anglo-Irish nobleman, ally of the Earl of Strafford when Lord Deputy of Ireland, fought against the Irish rebels, and made Lord Lieutenant of Ireland in January 1644. Made peace on the King's orders in 1646, but this was repudiated by the Irish leaders, and Ormond abandoned Ireland, following an agreement with the English Parliament in 1647. Attempted to strike an agreement with the Irish in 1648/9, but failed to achieve it. In exile in the Interregnum a close ally of Hyde's: undertook a mission to English royalists in 1658. After the Restoration made a duke and in 1662 again appointed Lord Lieutenant: **48, 314–15, 371–2, 375, 395, 397, 401, 414, 415.**

BYRON, SIR JOHN, 1ST BARON BYRON (1598/9–1652), soldier, appointed lieutenant of the Tower of London in December 1641 as the King's replacement for Sir William Balfour. Fought at Edgehill and elsewhere, and created Baron Byron in October 1643. After the end of the war lived at the Queen's court in Paris, and after involvement in the Second Civil War became attached to the household of the Duke of York: **150, 331–2**.

BYRON, SIR NICHOLAS (bap. 1596, d. 1648), soldier, relative of Sir John Byron, fought in the Netherlands in the 1630s, and in the war against the Scots in 1639: **149**.

CAPEL, ARTHUR, 1ST BARON CAPEL OF HADHAM (bap. 1632, d. 1683), wealthy MP for Hertfordshire in 1640, whose growing disillusion with the parliamentary leadership caught the attention of the King, who made him Baron Capel in August 1641. Unsuccessful soldier; one of the royalist commissioners at the Uxbridge Treaty; appointed to the Prince of Wales's council and went with him and Hyde to the Scillies and Jersey, remaining there after the departure of the Prince to France. Left for England in 1647, and one of the leaders of the 1648 risings, for which he was executed in March 1649: **257, 279, 280–1, 283, 284, 285, 308, 316, 320, 323, 324, 337.**

CAREW, THOMAS (1594/5–1640), poet, educated at Merton College, Oxford, and the Middle Temple; associated with the Villiers family; one of the circle around Falkland in the 1630s. Appointed to a minor court position in 1630: **435, 439.**

CARY, LUCIUS, 2ND VISCOUNT FALKLAND (1609/10–1643), son of the Lord Deputy of Ireland. Cary received an inheritance before the death of his father from his mother's father, the lawyer Sir Lawrence Tanfield, including estates at Great Tew and Burford in Oxfordshire. Married against his father's will in 1630, provoking a row which led him to seek military service in the Netherlands, but he returned in 1632, and inherited his father's Irish viscountcy in 1633. Cultivated a literary and philosophical circle at his house at Great Tew. An MP in the Short and Long Parliaments, he, with Hyde, was initially associated with the attacks on the misgovernment of the 1630s, but became distant from the parliamentary reformers over episcopacy and presbyterianism. At the beginning of 1642 he became a privy counsellor and Secretary of State; at the end of May he joined the King's camp at York. His death at the battle of Newbury in 1643 prompted a famous eulogy from Hyde: **53, 78–9, 94–5, 108–11, 114, 125, 126, 127, 128, 129, 148, 161, 164, 182–90, 440–45, 446, 450, 451.**

CAVENDISH, WILLIAM, EARL, MARQUESS, AND DUKE OF NEWCASTLE (bap. 1593, d. 1676), made governor to the Prince of Wales in 1638, though forced to resign in 1641 when suspected of involvement in Army Plot. At the beginning of the war he was made commander of royalist forces in the northern counties. Created marquess in 1643; but left for France after his defeat at Marston Moor: **37, 170, 174, 204, 209–16.**

CECIL, WILLIAM, 2ND EARL OF SALISBURY (1591–1668), of uncertain views during the Civil War, but plumped for the Commonwealth, serving as an MP in the Rump Parliament and a member of its Council of State: **252.**

CHILLINGWORTH, WILLIAM (1602–44), theologian, a close associate of William Laud, converted to Roman Catholicism in 1629, and although he returned to the Church of England around 1632, his allegiance remained equivocal. One of the central figures in the circle around Falkland at Great Tew in the 1630s, where he wrote his great work *The Religion of Protestants* (1638). Served in the royalist army, but captured at the surrender of Arundel Castle in 1643, and died in 1644: **17, 444, 452–4.**

CLIFFORD, HENRY, 5TH EARL OF CUMBERLAND (1592–1643), prominent in the defence of the North during the wars against the Scots, and appointed the King's commander in Yorkshire in July 1642, though he negotiated a truce with Lord Fairfax later in the year, and largely ceded his commands to others: **140, 214**.

COMPTON, SIR WILLIAM (1625–63), royalist governor of Banbury in the first Civil War, major general under Norwich in the second, and one of the principal royalist conspirators of the Sealed Knot in the 1650s: **316**.

COTTINGTON, FRANCIS, 1ST BARON COTTINGTON (1579?–1652), Chancellor of the Exchequer from 1629 and Master of the Court of Wards in 1635; a major ally of the Earl of Strafford in the 1630s. He resigned his offices during the attacks on Strafford, but joined the King at Oxford during the war. Later in exile in France. Took Hyde with him on the embassy to Spain in 1649, and after it was ended remained in the country until his death: **108, 309, 340–4.**

COTTON, CHARLES (d. 1658), literary figure, member of the Falkland circle in the 1630s. Father of the poet Charles Cotton (1630–87): **435, 436–7**.

COVENTRY, THOMAS, 1ST BARON COVENTRY (1578–1640), an associate of the 1st Duke of Buckingham, Lord Keeper 1625–40: **456**.

CREW, JOHN, 1ST BARON CREW (1597/8–1679), MP in the Long Parliament, one of the parliamentary commissioners at Uxbridge in 1645; one of the secluded members at Pride's Purge; created Baron Crew in 1661: **253**

CROMWELL, OLIVER (1599–1658), MP for Cambridge in the Short and Long Parliaments, where he was associated with the radicals among the parliamentary leadership; made his name commanding parliamentary forces in East Anglia; appointed lieutenant general of the army commanded by the Earl of Manchester in 1644, and exempted from the self-denying ordinance; formally appointed commander in chief in 1650. Made Lord Protector in 1653: **65, 94–5, 210, 232–4, 238–5, 254, 260, 262, 263, 266, 269, 286–8, 290–1, 293, 294, 296, 298, 299, 303–7, 315, 316–19, 325, 344–5, 347, 372, 373, 374, 379, 3801, 382, 385, 402.**

CULPEPPER, SIR JOHN, 1ST BARON CULPEPPER (bap. 1600, d. 1660), MP in the Short and Long Parliaments, associated with the parliamentary reformers in 1640–1, but like Hyde and Falkland defended episcopacy and opposed the Grand Remonstrance. Appointed with Falkland to the Privy Council at the beginning of 1642, made Chancellor of the Exchequer, and in May joined the King at York; made Master of the Rolls in early 1643, and Baron in October 1644. One of the King's commissioners at Uxbridge, and a member of the Prince of Wales's council, with which he moved to Jersey in 1646, and then went with the Prince to France. Hyde and he fell out over whether concessions could be made to the Presbyterians on episcopacy, although they continued to work closely together: **108–11, 114, 125, 126, 127, 129, 161, 205, 207, 218, 230–2, 257, 278–8, 363**.

CUMBERLAND, EARL OF, *see* Clifford, Henry

DENBIGH, EARL OF, *see* Feilding, Basil

DEVEREUX, ROBERT, 3RD EARL OF ESSEX (1591–1646), soldier and politician, serving in the Rhineland and Low Countries in the 1620s, and one of the opponents in Parliament of the 1st Duke of Buckingham. Humiliated by his appointment to subordinate posts in the army against the Scots in 1639, and his replacement in 1640 as lieutenant general by Strafford. Leading member of the parliamentary reform movement, appointed to the Privy Council in 1641. Became captain general of the parliamentary forces in July 1642: 35, 36, 58, 66, 76, 80–1, 117, 127, 129, 136, 146–8, 155, 156, 157–8, 170, 173–81, 192, 204, 207, 208, 218–29, 232–3, 235, 239, 249, 251, 253, 254, 263, 456.

DIGBY, GEORGE, 2ND EARL OF BRISTOL (1653) (1612–77), married to daughter of Francis, Earl of Bedford, and associated with the parliamentary reform movement in the Parliaments of 1640, but moved towards support for the King with his father, opposed Strafford's attainder, and became one of the King's principal advisers, blamed for the attempt to arrest the five members. Made Secretary of State in succession to Falkland. Served in the French army 1648–53, inherited the earldom of Bristol in 1653; his conversion to Roman Catholicism in 1659 disqualified him from high political office and estranged him from Clarendon, whom he attempted to destroy in a bungled impeachment attempt in 1663: 63, 74, 111, 114–16, 120, 178, 205, 207, 218, 230, 279, 280, 281, 282, 397.

DIGBY, JOHN, 1ST EARL OF BRISTOL (1580–1653), ambassador to Spain in the Early 1620s who clashed with the 1st Duke of Buckingham and lost the favour of Charles I over the Spanish marriage negotiations in 1623–4. He eventually returned to favour in 1641 as he tried to broker a deal to save the life of Strafford, but was regarded by Parliament as one of the King's most hardline councillors: 66, 114, 309.

DIGBY, SIR KENELM (1603–65), philosopher son of a gunpowder plotter friend of Ben Jonson, married to the celebrated beauty Venetia Stanley. Brought up a Roman Catholic, converted to the Church of England, but returned to Catholicism in the 1630s: 321, 435, 438

DORSET, EARL OF, *see* Sackville, Edward

EARLE, JOHN (1601–65), divine, friend of Hyde and Falkland, tutor to the Prince of Wales from 1641, and chaplain to Charles II in exile; made Bishop of Worcester in 1662, of Salisbury in 1663: 444, 449–50.

ESSEX, EARL OF, *see* Devereux, Robert

FAIRFAX, FERDINANDO, 2ND LORD FAIRFAX (1584–1648), soldier and politician, MP in November 1640, and leading figure among Yorkshire gentry; in December 1642 made general of the parliamentary forces in the northern counties. Resigned his commission under the self-denying ordinance: 174, 204, 210, 254.

FAIRFAX, SIR THOMAS, 3RD LORD FAIRFAX (1612–71), soldier, fought in the war against the Scots; made second in command of the parliamentary forces in the North, after his father. In early 1645 made commander in chief of the New Model Army. Resigned his commission in 1650: 174, 239, 260, 263, 265, 266, 275, 276, 277, 278, 289–90, 315–16, 321–4, 332–3, 420.

FALKLAND, VISCOUNT, *see* Cary, Lucius

FEILDING, BASIL, 2ND EARL OF DENBIGH (1608–75), diplomat and friend of Hyde in the 1630s whose equivocal commitment to the parliamentary cause in the Civil War turned into support for the army and independents in 1647 and 1648. Nominated to, but did not sit in the court that tried King Charles I: **149, 252–3**.

FIENNES, NATHANIEL (1607/8–1669), politician, son of Viscount Saye and Sele, MP in Short and Long Parliaments, close to John Pym; appointed governor of Bristol in May 1643, which he surrendered to the King. Supporter of the army against Presbyterians in 1647, but secluded at Pride's Purge. Later close to Cromwell: **61, 77, 88, 159**.

FIENNES, WILLIAM, 1ST VISCOUNT SAYE AND SELE (1582–1662), politician, supporter of religious radicals, and opponent of Laud in the 1630s. Leading opposition figure in the November 1640 Parliament, appointed to the Council in February 1641. Leading independent politician during the war; but his continued support for negotiations with the King left him without influence after 1648: **56, 77, 82–3, 151**

FINCH, JOHN, BARON FINCH (1584–1660), appointed Chief Justice of the Court of Common Pleas in 1634, took the lead in the ship money case against Hampden in 1637, made Lord Keeper in January 1640. Impeached in December, and fled to the Netherlands: **55**.

GASCOIGNE, SIR BERNARD (1614–87), Florentine soldier of fortune, who fought in the First Civil War, and joined the royalist forces in the second war in 1648. Eventually released, and became naturalized after the Restoration: **316, 322–4**.

GERARD, CHARLES, 1ST EARL OF MACCLESFIELD (*c.*1618–94), Lancashire gentleman who commanded a royalist brigade at Edgehill; made lieutenant general in South Wales in 1644, created Lord Gerard of Brandon in 1645, and Earl of Macclesfield after the Restoration: **264, 265**.

GLEMHAM, SIR THOMAS (1595–1649), soldier, served in the King's army against the Scots, in 1642 appointed governor of York and second-in-command to the Earl of Cumberland; appointed governor of Oxford in 1645 and surrendered it in 1646: **140, 211**.

GODOLPHIN, SIDNEY (1610–43), poet, and one of Falkland's circle in the 1630s; friend of Hobbes; MP in 1640, killed in a fight with parliamentary forces in Devon: **446–7**.

GORING, GEORGE, BARON GORING (1608–57), soldier, son of George Goring, later Earl of Norwich, served in the Netherlands in the 1630s; appointed governor of Portsmouth in 1639; fought in the King's army against the Scots; leader of Army Plot in 1641, when he saved himself by betraying its details. In 1642 declared for the King in Portsmouth, but was forced to surrender it. Appointed general of horse in July 1644, and in 1645 led royal forces in the south-west, though in constant conflict with the Prince of Wales's council. Defeated by the New Model Army in late 1645, he retired to the continent and served in the Spanish army: **137–8, 209, 219, 221, 224, 226–8, 230–1, 260, 265, 401**.

GORING, GEORGE, 1ST EARL OF NORWICH (1585–1663), diplomat, official in the household of Queen Henrietta Maria; became involved in royal administration after 1639, and spent much of the war on the continent, raising money and in negotiations with the French. In England in 1648, he was drawn into the Second Civil War: though condemned to death for his involvement he was eventually released: **315–16, 320, 324.**

GRAHAM, JAMES, 1ST MARQUESS OF MONTROSE (1612–50), military commander on behalf of the Scottish Covenanters, opposed Argyll, whom he attempted to overthrow. Led royalist risings in Scotland in 1644–5 and 1649–50; captured and executed after the failure of the last: **211, 257, 265, 277, 337, 340.**

GRANDISON, WILLIAM VILLIERS, VISCOUNT, *see* Villiers, William

GRENVILLE, JOHN, 1ST EARL OF BATH (1628–1701), son of a distinguished royalist commander, an important royalist conspirator in the 1650s; a relation of General Monck, with whom he negotiated on behalf of the King in 1659 and 1660: **403, 418.**

GREVILLE, ROBERT, 2ND BARON BROOKE (1607–43), political and religious radical, married to the daughter of the 4th Earl of Bedford; made commander of the West Midland Association at the end of 1642; killed at the siege of Lichfield: **77, 151.**

GURNEY, SIR RICHARD (bap. 1578, d. 1647), elected Lord Mayor of London in 1641; in 1642 arranged for royal commission of array to be proclaimed in the City, and imprisoned in the Tower of London: **107, 127.**

HALES, JOHN (1584–1656), professor of Greek at Oxford, and fellow of Eton, one of the associates of Falkland, advocate of reason in religion: **450–2.**

HAMILTON, JAMES, 3RD MARQUESS AND 1ST DUKE OF HAMILTON (1606–49), Scottish favourite of Charles I; appointed royal commissioner in Scotland in April 1638, and general of the King's forces there in April 1639; his advocacy of a negotiated peace led to his resignation as commissioner in July. His closeness to the King's opponents in the English Parliament and his alliance with the Covenanter leader Argyll raised suspicion of Hamilton's motives, and when his alliance with Argyll fell apart in 1643 he was imprisoned by the King. Following the parliamentary victory he became leader of the party supporting the 1647 Engagement with the King, and the commander of the army that invaded England in 1648 to support it. Captured, he was executed in 1649: **31, 35–7, 66, 129, 316, 335, 337, 340, 431.**

HAMILTON, WILLIAM, EARL OF LANARK, 2ND DUKE OF HAMILTON (1616–51), brother of the 1st Duke; appointed Secretary of State for Scotland, March 1639. With his brother closely involved in the 1647 Engagement; after his brother's defeat, fled to the Netherlands, and then returned to Scotland with Charles II in 1650. Died from wounds received at the battle of Worcester: **337, 339–40, 348.**

HAMMOND, HENRY (1605–60), chaplain to Charles I, theologian and devotional writer, uncle of Robert Hammond: **291, 296, 444.**

HAMMOND, ROBERT (1620/21–1654), soldier, appointed governor of the Isle of Wight in August 1647; had custody of the King after he came to Hampshire in his flight from Hampton Court in November. Nephew of Henry Hammond: **296–7**.

HAMPDEN, JOHN (1595–1643), politician, whose refusal to pay ship money resulted in its acceptance by the judges in 1638. Close to Lord Saye and Sele, John Pym, and other leaders of the parliamentary reform movement in 1640. Died of wounds received at Chalgrove in 1643: **11, 41, 44, 45, 59, 77, 79, 88, 95, 116, 155, 170–4, 203, 296, 305, 449**.

HARO, DON LUIS DE MARQUIS OF CARPIO (1598–1661), principal minister of King Philip IV of Spain: **340–2, 424**.

HASELRIG, SIR ARTHUR (1601–61), MP in 1640, close associate of Pym and other parliamentary reformers; leader of the war party after Pym's death; did not support the regicide, but sat in the Rump Parliament. Opponent of its dissolution and of Cromwell; leader of attempt to recreate republican government in 1659: **63, 88, 116, 119**.

HENRY, PRINCE, DUKE OF GLOUCESTER (1640–60), third surviving son of Charles I and Henrietta Maria; in parliamentary custody until released in 1652: **366, 369–72, 421**.

HERBERT, SIR EDWARD (*c.*1591–1657), appointed Solicitor General in 1640, and Attorney General in January 1641, in which role he presented the articles of impeachment against the five members. Was reappointed Attorney General by Charles II in 1649, but became close to James, Duke of York; appointed Lord Keeper in 1653, but an ill-conceived attack on Hyde led to his loss of favour: **41, 46, 116, 365–6**.

HERBERT, PHILIP, 4TH EARL OF PEMBROKE (1584–1650), became Lord Chamberlain in 1626, Earl in 1630. Alienated from the court, he supported the attainder of Strafford and was dismissed as Chamberlain in July 1641; sat in the House of Lords throughout the war, though refused to take part in the trial of the King: **248, 251, 252, 254, 449, 456**.

HERTFORD, EARL AND MARQUESS OF, *see* Seymour, William

HOLLAND, EARL OF, *see* Rich, Henry

HOLLES, DENZIL, 1ST BARON HOLLES (1598–1680), MP, veteran of the parliamentary battles of the late 1620s, and one of the five members whom Charles I tried to arrest in 1642. Presbyterian and advocate of abolition of episcopacy and alliance with the Scots. Promoted peace negotiations during the 1640s, and chief opponent of the army and Independents in 1647: **63, 77, 116, 253, 420**.

HOPTON, RALPH, BARON HOPTON (bap. 1596, d. 1652), MP in the Short and Long Parliaments; joined the King at the beginning of the Civil War; leading royalist commander in the west, made Baron Hopton in 1643, followed the Prince of Wales into exile after defeat in 1646: **130, 174, 205, 207, 220, 257, 283, 284, 454**.

HOTHAM, SIR JOHN (1585–1645), MP in Long Parliament, made governor of Hull by Parliament in January 1642, and refused admission to the King.

Executed by Parliament in 1645 on evidence that he was preparing to change sides: **52, 63, 96, 97, 140**.

HYDE, SIR NICHOLAS (*c.*1572–1631), Hyde's uncle, appointed Lord Chief Justice of the King's Bench in 1627: **427, 428, 429, 430**.

IRETON, HENRY (bap. 1611, d. 1651), soldier and intellectual leader of the army, whose long association with Oliver Cromwell began in 1643: married Cromwell's daughter; became MP in 1645. Appointed deputy to Cromwell in the Irish campaign in 1650–1: **269, 290, 293, 299, 316, 324**.

JAMES, PRINCE, DUKE OF YORK (1633–1701), second son of Charles I and Henrietta Maria; in parliamentary custody until his escape in 1648. King James II 1685–8: **153, 313, 385, 397–8, 420, 421**.

JERMYN, HENRY, EARL OF ST ALBANS (bap. 1605, d. 1684), favourite of Queen Henrietta Maria, involved in the Army Plot in 1641, enemy of Hyde's, whose disgrace he attempted to secure in 1654. Created Earl of St Albans in 1659: **178, 279, 281**.

JONSON, BEN (1572–1637), poet and playwright: **435–6, 443**.

KIMBOLTON, LORD, *see* Montagu, Edward

LAMBERT, JOHN (1619–84), soldier and army leader in confrontation with Parliament in 1647, Cromwell's second in command in the Scottish campaign in 1650–2. Powerful figure within the Protectorate regime until 1657; his attempts to resist the Restoration were unavailing: **317, 399–400, 401, 404, 405**

LANARK, EARL OF, *see* Hamilton, William, 2nd Duke of Hamilton

LANE, JANE (d. 1689), daughter of Thomas Lane of Bentley Hall, near Wolverhampton, and Anne Bagot; played a major role in the escape of Charles II: **354–7**.

LANGDALE, SIR MARMADUKE (bap. 1598, d. 1661), royalist soldier, who saw service on the continent, and played a major part in the royalist war effort in the North. Joined Hamilton's forces in 1648 and defeated with them at the battle of Preston. Convert to Roman Catholicism: **261, 262, 317–19, 398**.

LAUD, WILLIAM (1573–1645), Bishop of St David's 1621–6, Bishop of Bath and Wells 1626–8, Bishop of London 1628–33, Archbishop of Canterbury 1633–45. Impeached by Parliament in February 1641, tried in 1644, and executed in 1645: **20–8, 29, 55, 76, 246–7, 435, 449, 452, 456**.

LAUDERDALE, EARL OF, *see* Maitland, John.

LEGGE, WILLIAM (1607/8–1670), served with Dutch and Swedish armies on the continent and with the King's forces in the wars against the Scots. Protégé of Prince Rupert; governor of Oxford in 1645, but dismissed and imprisoned when Rupert was dismissed that year: **195**.

LENTHALL, WILLIAM (1591–1662), Speaker of the House of Commons throughout the Long Parliament: **117**.

LESLIE, ALEXANDER, EARL OF LEVEN (*c.*1580–1661), soldier, saw service in the Netherlands and in the Swedish army. Joined Scottish Covenanters in 1638 and commanded their army throughout the war, and during the campaigns of 1650–1, though he remained in Scotland rather than accompany Charles II in the invasion of England: **34, 209**.

LESLIE, DAVID, 1ST LORD NEWARK (1601–82), soldier, saw service with Alexander Leslie in the Swedish army; appointed major general in Scottish army in 1643, commander of the Scottish army invading England in 1651: **317, 345, 349**.

LEVEN, EARL OF, *see* Leslie, Alexander

LINDSEY, ROBERT, 1ST EARL OF LINDSEY (1582–1642), soldier, saw military and naval service in the Netherlands and against Spain and France in the 1620s, vice admiral of the fleet which went to the Île de Rhé in 1627. Appointed lieutenant general of the King's army in August 1642, and died of his wounds after the battle of Edgehill: **136, 148, 153, 156, 157–8**.

LISLE, SIR GEORGE (d. 1648), royalist officer, fought at Naseby and elsewhere: one of the leaders of the rebellion in Kent in 1648; shot following the surrender of Colchester: **316, 322–4**.

LITTLETON, EDWARD, BARON LITTLETON (1589–1645), Solicitor General 1634, argued the ship money case for the Crown; appointed Chief Justice of the Common Pleas in 1640, and Lord Keeper in 1641. Decamped to York in 1642 after he expressed equivocal views on the militia ordinance and indicated his doubts about the arrest of the five members: **55, 91**.

LIVINGSTON, JAMES, 1ST EARL OF NEWBURGH (1621/2–70), second husband of Katherine Stewart, Lady Aubigny, and royalist officer, who fought at Worcester: **328–30**.

LONG, ROBERT (*c.*1602–73), Surveyor General to Queen Henrietta Maria, appointed secretary to the Prince of Wales in 1645: **338, 363**.

LUCAS, SIR CHARLES (1612/13–1648), royalist officer, fought at Marston Moor, joined the Earl of Norwich in the Second Civil War; shot following the surrender of Colchester: **275, 316, 322–4**.

MAITLAND, JOHN, EARL AND DUKE OF LAUDERDALE (1616–82), one of the main figures in maintaining the alliance of the Scottish Covenanters with the English Parliament in the early 1640s, and involved in the talks at Uxbridge. Kept a close relationship with the English Presbyterians and negotiated the Engagement with the King in 1648: **245–6, 337, 339**.

MANCHESTER EARLE OF, *see* Montagu, Edward.

MARTEN, HENRY (1601/2–1680), radical MP in the Parliaments of 1640, early proponent of the deposition of Charles I, and regicide in 1649: **89**.

MARY, PRINCESS ROYAL (1631–60), eldest daughter of Charles I and Henrietta Maria, married to Prince William of Orange in 1641: **368, 369**.

MASSEY, SIR EDWARD (1604/9–1674), parliamentarian officer, appointed governor of Gloucester in 1643. Presbyterian MP from 1646, one of the eleven members impeached in 1647, secluded at Pride's Purge; took part in the Worcester campaign in 1651 and in the rising in 1659: **174, 175, 292, 346, 348, 398**.

MAY, THOMAS (*c.*1596–1650), poet and historian; translator of Lucan's *Pharsalia* (1626/7) and author of a continuation of it, published in 1630.

Supported and wrote on behalf of Parliament, including *The History of the Parliament of England* (1647). Possibly the only historian apart from Churchill to receive a state funeral: **435, 438–9.**

MAYNARD, SIR JOHN (1604–90), lawyer, MP in the Long Parliament, **300–1, 390, 455.**

MAZARIN, JULES (1602–61), chief minister to Louis XIII, Louis XIV and the Queen Regent in France: **270–2, 275, 281, 314–15, 391, 392–3, 424.**

MONCK, GEORGE (1608–70), soldier, served on the expedition to La Rochelle in 1627, in the campaigns against the Scots in 1639 and 1640, then in Ireland against the rebellion in the early 1640s, and again, on behalf of Parliament, in 1647–9, and with Cromwell in the Scottish campaigns in 1650–1, where he became lieutenant general of the ordnance. Served at sea in the war against the Dutch in 1652–4 before being made commander in chief of the forces in Scotland. His return with his army south in 1659–60 paved the way for the Restoration: **401–18, 423.**

MONTAGU, EDWARD, 1ST EARL OF SANDWICH (1625–72), officer in parliamentary army, MP after 1645, secluded in Pride's Purge; supporter of Cromwell, and appointed general at sea in 1656. Reappointed general at sea with Monck in March 1660: **420, 423.**

MONTAGU, EDWARD, LORD KIMBOLTON (1626), LORD MANDEVILLE (1626), 2ND EARL OF MANCHESTER (1642) (1602–71), one of the principal parliamentary reformers in 1640–2, the one peer whom Charles attempted to impeach with the five MPs in January 1642. In 1643 appointed major general of the Eastern Association, and commanded the victorious army at Marston Moor. In November 1644 Cromwell demanded his removal from command because of his failure to prosecute the war vigorously enough, and he was forced to resign his commission as a result of the self-denying ordinance. Retired from public life after the establishment of the republic, but returned as Speaker of the House of Lords in 1660: **57, 64, 66, 116, 119, 149, 204, 232–4, 239, 254.**

MORAY, SIR ROBERT (1608/9–73), soldier, saw service in the French army in the 1640s; involved in late 1640s in negotiations between Charles I and the Scottish Presbyterians: **272.**

MORDAUNT, JOHN, 1ST VISCOUNT MORDAUNT (1626–75), royalist conspirator, whose offer to coordinate royalist plans in 1659 challenged the existing Sealed Knot network: **396–7.**

MORLAND, SIR SAMUEL (1625–95), diplomat, served Cromwell as ambassador to the Duke of Savoy: **391, 394–5.**

MORLEY, GEORGE (1598?–1684), friend of Falkland in the 1630s; member of royalist delegation at the Uxbridge Treaty, acted as Hyde's chaplain in Antwerp in the 1650s. Bishop of Worcester, 1660–2, and Winchester, 1662–84: **291, 444, 447, 448–9.**

NEWBURGH, LORD, *see* Livingston, James

NEWCASTLE, EARL, MARQUESS, AND DUKE OF, *see* Cavendish, William

RUPERT, PRINCE, COUNT PALATINE OF THE RHINE (1619–82), son of
Frederick V, Elector Palatine, and nephew of Charles I, exiled from
Bohemia, gained military experience in the Netherlands in the late 1630s;
came to England in 1642 with his brother Maurice, and made commander
of the horse; highly successful cavalry commander, made captain general of
all royal forces in November 1644, but dismissed after the surrender of
Bristol in 1645, and left for France in 1646. Took command of the fleet that
defected to the royalists in 1648–53: **147, 148, 149, 152, 153, 170, 176, 178,
180, 192, 204, 205, 209–16, 219, 221, 230, 260–4, 265, 338.**

RUSSELL, FRANCIS, 4TH EARL OF BEDFORD (bap. 1587, d. 1641), leading
figure in parliamentary reform movement, appointed to the Privy Council
in February 1641. His death later in the year was blamed for the failure to
achieve a settlement: **56, 61, 66, 76, 79–80, 82, 109, 203.**

RUSSELL, WILLIAM, 5TH EARL AND 1ST DUKE OF BEDFORD (1616–1700),
son of the 4th Earl, appointed after his father's death commander of parliament's forces in the west; fought at Edgehill, but soon after defected to the
King. Returned to parliamentary allegiance in December 1643. Played little
further part in the war or public life until the Restoration: **149, 150, 199.**

RUTHVEN, PATRICK, EARL OF FORTH AND EARL OF BRENTFORD (d. 1651),
soldier, who served in Swedish army; appointed marshal general of the royal
army in 1642, and Lord General after the death of Lindsey after Edgehill.
Created Earl of Forth in 1642, and Earl of Brentford in 1644; replaced as
Lord General by Rupert in November 1644: **159, 192, 205, 218, 230.**

SACKVILLE, EDWARD, 4TH EARL OF DORSET (1590–1652), loyal supporter of
the King, but advocate of accommodation in the war, involved in prelimin-
ary negotiations for the Treaty of Uxbridge in 1645: **104, 458.**

ST JOHN, OLIVER (*c.*1598–1673), lawyer with connections to the Earls of
Bedford, John Hampden, and Oliver Cromwell; came to prominence by
serving as counsel for Hampden in the ship money case; at the beginning of
the Long Parliament worked closely with other parliamentary reformers;
appointed Solicitor General in January 1641 as part of a scheme to conciliate
the King's opponents. Moved towards independency during the Civil War,
and became one of the principal parliamentary leaders: **47, 60, 75, 101–2,
113, 203, 249.**

SALISBURY, EARL OF, *see* Cecil, William

SAVILLE, THOMAS, BARON SAVILLE, 1ST EARL OF SUSSEX (1590–1657/9),
opponent of Strafford, one of the peers closely in contact with the Covenanters
in 1640; moved towards the King, whom he joined at York, but remained
equivocal in allegiance and despite creation as Earl of Sussex in 1644 imprisoned in 1645 for his contacts with the other side: **66, 87.**

SELDEN, JOHN (1584–1654), lawyer and scholar, leading opponent of the
court in the Parliaments of the late 1620s and in the Long Parliament.
Mentor of Hyde: **435, 436, 437, 440.**

SEYMOUR, WILLIAM, 2ND EARL AND 1ST MARQUESS OF HERTFORD AND
2ND DUKE OF SOMERSET (1587–1660), married to sister of the 3rd Earl of

Essex, to whom he was close. Appointed to the Privy Council in February 1641, and appointed governor of the Prince of Wales in August. Fought for the King in the south-west, but held no command after his rows with Prince Rupert in 1644: **66, 80–1, 123, 138, 174, 199, 222, 423, 456**.

SHELDON, GILBERT (1598–1677), royalist divine; warden of All Souls College, and Oxford Vice Chancellor, participant in Falkland's circle at Great Tew. Took part in the Uxbridge negotiations; Bishop of London 1660–3, and Archbishop of Canterbury 1663–77: **285, 290, 444, 448**.

SOUTHAMPTON, EARL OF, *see* Wriothesley, Thomas, 4th Earl

STEWART, JOHN, 1ST EARL OF TRAQUAIR (*c.*1599–1659), appointed Lord High Treasurer for Scotland in 1636, and served as the King's commissioner in 1639: **29–30, 35**.

STEWART, DR RICHARD (1595–1651), chaplain to the King from 1633; one of the commissioners at the Uxbridge Treaty in 1645; in exile with Charles II: **243**.

STRAFFORD, *see* Wentworth, Thomas

STRODE, WILLIAM (bap. 1594, d. 1645), opponent of the court in the Parliaments of the 1620s and in the Short and Long Parliaments, regarded as one of the most radical of the reformers, one of the five impeached by the King in 1642: **63, 97, 116, 119**.

STUART, JAMES, 1ST DUKE OF RICHMOND (1612–55), created Duke of Richmond and appointed Lord Steward of the King's Household in 1641; involved in setting up the negotiations at Uxbridge, and attended Charles I during his trial and execution: **124, 241, 244, 245**.

TRAQUAIR, EARL OF, *see* Stewart, John

VANE, SIR HENRY (1589–1655), diplomat who attracted the favour of the Marquess of Hamilton and Queen Henrietta Maria, appointed Secretary of State in 1640; his part in the impeachment of Strafford led to his dismissal from court and office in December: **37, 46, 249**.

VANE, SIR HENRY THE YOUNGER (bap. 1613, d. 1662), son of Sir Henry Vane; friend of John Pym and opponent of Laudian church reforms who emerged as one of the principal opponents of the court in the Long Parliament in 1640; played a crucial role in proceedings against Strafford and subsequently a key figure in the war party, negotiating the entry of the Scots into war. Avoided involvement in the King's trial, but a leading light during the Commonwealth. Executed after the Restoration: **61, 75, 77, 234–5, 237–8, 269**.

VAUGHAN, JOHN (1603–74), lawyer, intellectual heir of John Selden. Played a leading part among the parliamentary opponents of the government in the 1660s and in the impeachment of Clarendon in 1667: **435, 437–8**.

VERNEY, SIR EDMUND (1590–1642), soldier, appointed Knight Marshal in 1625; killed at Edgehill: **142, 150, 153**.

VILLIERS, GEORGE, 1ST DUKE OF BUCKINGHAM (1592–1628), favourite of James I and Charles I; companion of Prince Charles (Charles I) in his mission to Spain in 1623; assassinated in 1628: **7, 168, 300, 334**.

Travel Writing 1700–1830

Women's Writing 1778–1838

WILLIAM BECKFORD	Vathek
JAMES BOSWELL	Life of Johnson
FRANCES BURNEY	Camilla
	Cecilia
	Evelina
	The Wanderer
LORD CHESTERFIELD	Lord Chesterfield's Letters
JOHN CLELAND	Memoirs of a Woman of Pleasure
DANIEL DEFOE	A Journal of the Plague Year
	Moll Flanders
	Robinson Crusoe
	Roxana
HENRY FIELDING	Jonathan Wild
	Joseph Andrews and Shamela
	Tom Jones
WILLIAM GODWIN	Caleb Williams
OLIVER GOLDSMITH	The Vicar of Wakefield
MARY HAYS	Memoirs of Emma Courtney
ELIZABETH INCHBALD	A Simple Story
SAMUEL JOHNSON	The History of Rasselas
	The Major Works
CHARLOTTE LENNOX	The Female Quixote
MATTHEW LEWIS	Journal of a West India Proprietor
	The Monk
HENRY MACKENZIE	The Man of Feeling

ÉMILE ZOLA

**L'Assommoir
The Attack on the Mill
La Bête humaine
La Débâcle
Germinal
The Kill
The Ladies' Paradise
The Masterpiece
Nana
Pot Luck
Thérèse Raquin**